MW01625889

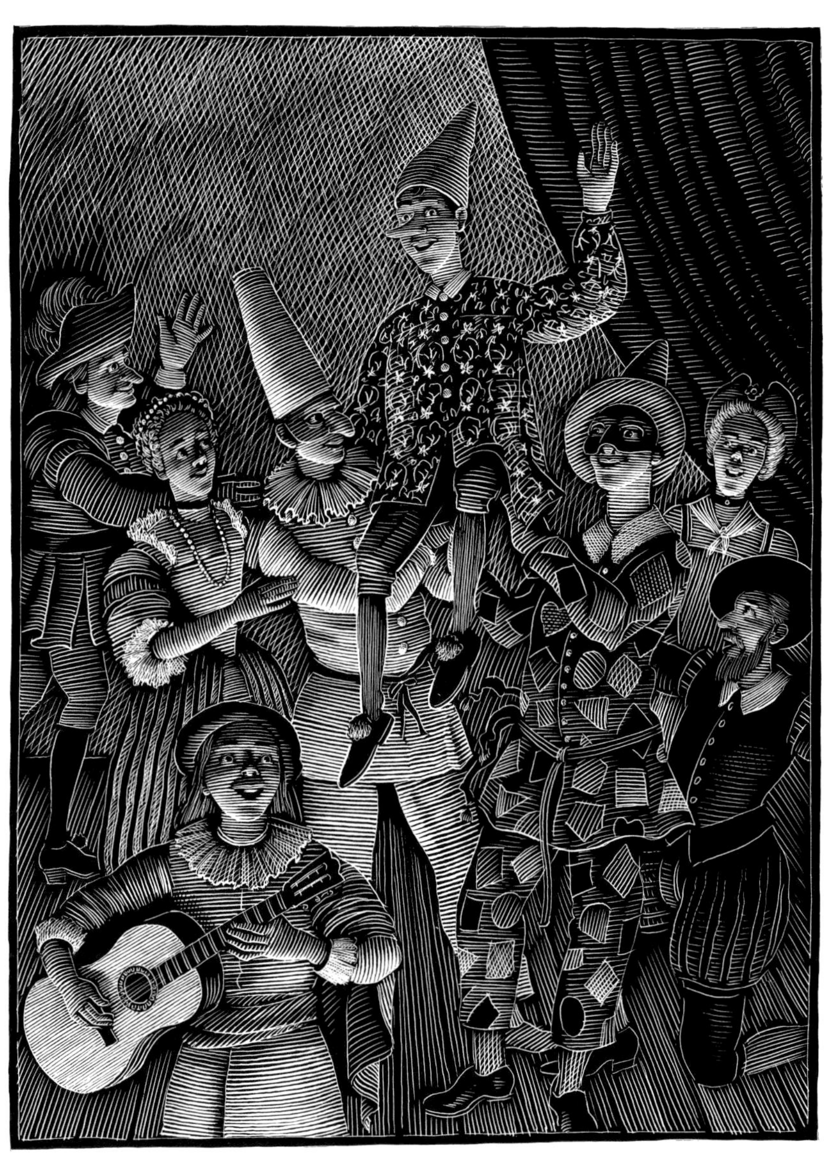

The puppet show, from the Sterling Classics edition of *Pinocchio*.

Light Revealed

SCRATCHBOARD ENGRAVINGS BY SCOTT MCKOWEN

FIREFLY BOOKS

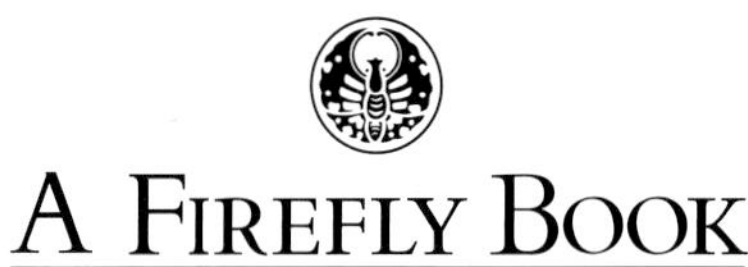

Published by Firefly Books Ltd. 2022

First printing

Library of Congress Control Number: 2019904146

Library and Archives Canada Cataloguing in Publication
Title: Light revealed / scratchboard engravings by Scott McKowen.
Names: McKowen, Scott, author, artist.
Description: Includes index.
Identifiers: Canadiana 20190099550 | ISBN 9780228101994 (hardcover)
Subjects: LCSH: McKowen, Scott. | LCSH: Scratchboard drawing.
Classification: LCC NC143.M42 A2 2022 | DDC 741.971—dc23

Published in the United States by
Firefly Books (U.S.) Inc.
P.O. Box 1338, Ellicott Station
Buffalo, New York 14205

Published in Canada by
Firefly Books Ltd.
50 Staples Avenue, Unit 1
Richmond Hill, Ontario L4B 0A7

Book designed by Scott McKowen.

Printed in China

IMAGE CREDITS

Page 8: *The Poster Man* by John Orlando Parry licensed from Bridgeman Images.

Page 22: photo © University of Leicester.

Page 40: photo of Benedict Campbell as King Lear © David Cooper.

Page 48: Holbein portraits from the Royal Collection, Windsor Castle.

Page 50: three cartoons by W. Heath Robinson licensed from Mary Evans Picture Library.

Page 52: Goya drawing from the Staatliche Museen zu Berlin, Kupferstichkabinett.

Page 66 (top): phrenological head photo licensed from Bridgeman Images.

Page 84: *Pavlova taking a Bow* by Laura Knight licensed from Bridgeman Images.

Page 102: *Caroline, or Change* (top) illustration © Paul Davis.

Page 104: photo © Christina Poddubiuk.

Page 116: photo courtesy of Public Delivery, a non-profit arts organization in Seoul, South Korea.

Page 130: photo of Julie Martell as Mary Poppins © David Cooper.

Page 138: photo of the *Museum of the Moon*, © Scott Wishart, reproduced courtesy of Stratford Summer Music.

Page 144: installation photos of *Forty Part Motet* courtesy of Janet Cardiff.

Page 202: three caricatures by Richard Dighton licensed from Bridgeman Images.

Page 220: Bust of Queen Nefertiti licensed from Alamy Ltd.

Page 231: photo of Scott's drawing table © Ann Baggley.

Canada

We acknowledge the financial support of the Government of Canada.

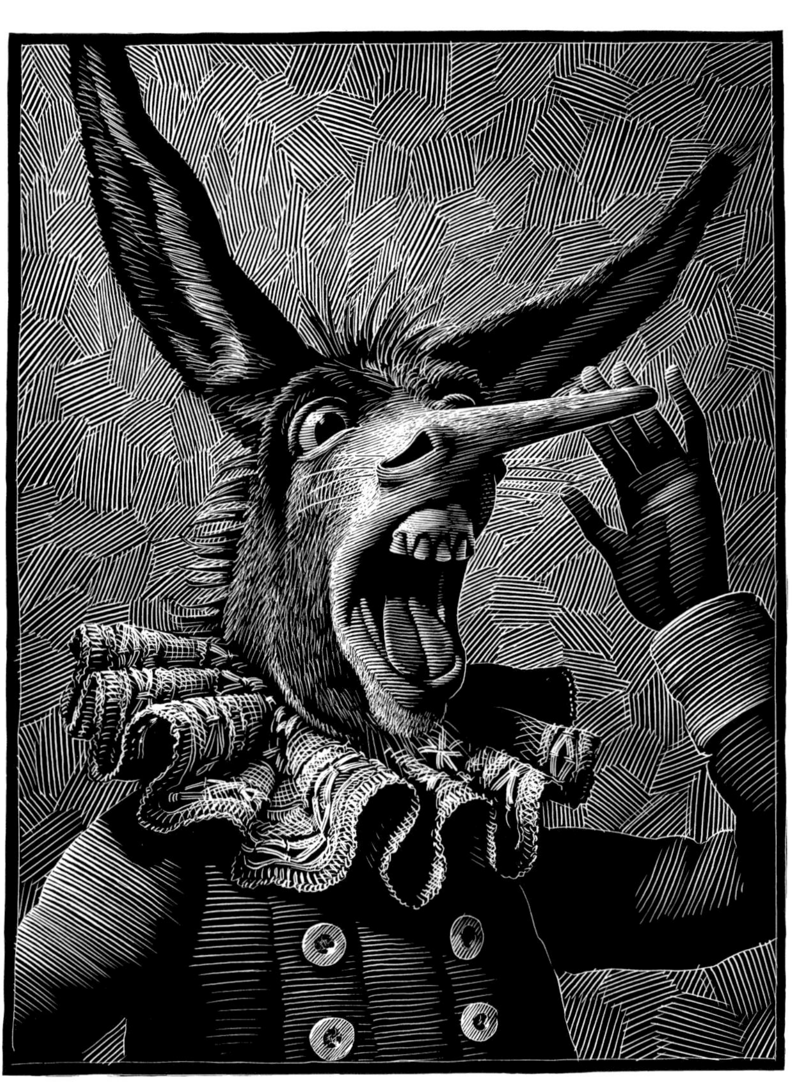

Pinocchio turning into a donkey, from the Sterling Classics edition of *Pinocchio*.

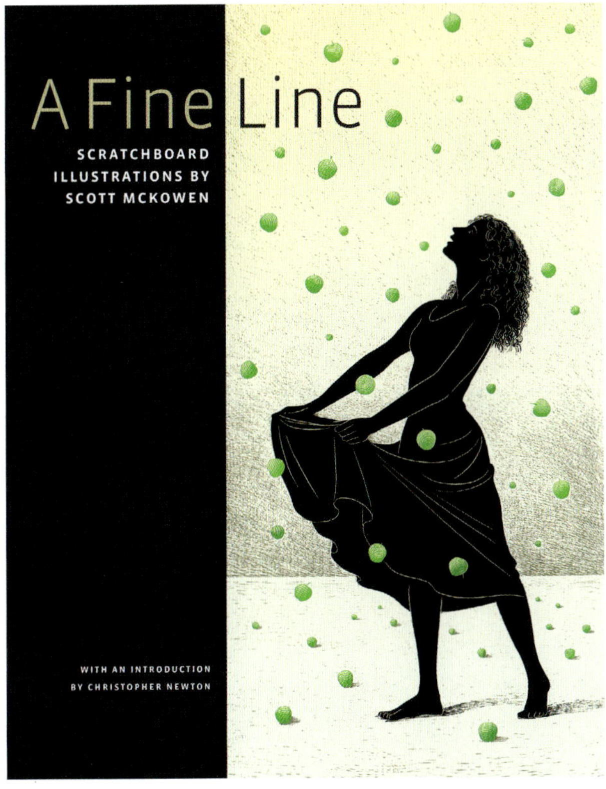

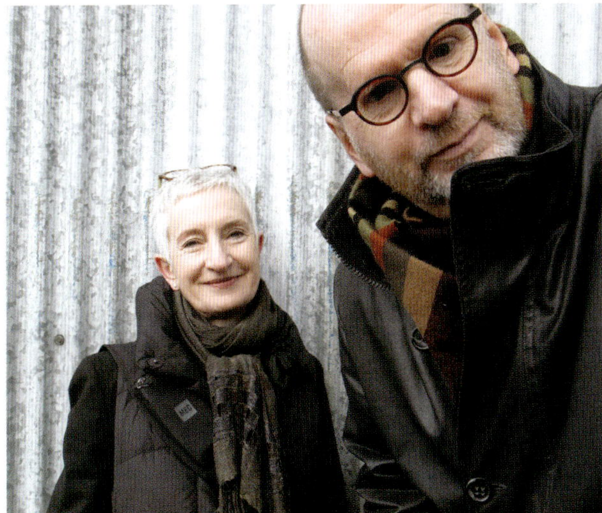

Firefly Books published *A Fine Line: Scratchboard Illustrations by Scott McKowen* in 2009. I was thrilled and honoured to share this record of my (then) 20-year career using this medium. I included commentary about each illustration assignment and its solution. Christopher Newton wrote a brilliant introduction; Milton Glaser and Neil Gaiman generously contributed quotations for the jacket. The book was well-reviewed both in Canada and in the U.S., but all good things come to an end and it went out of print after five years. Nobody ever expected it to be a bestseller. You can still find copies on eBay or Advanced Book Exchange, but the world has moved on.

Second chances don't come along very often but early in 2018, at the end of an email conversation on another topic, Lionel Koffler at Firefly expressed an interest in publishing an updated second edition of the book. An interesting range of illustration assignments had kept me very busy over the ensuing decade, so I knew that this new volume would be even richer than the first edition.

I have been careful about duplication of content — readers who have the first edition in their library need a reason to buy the new book. A few old favourites are still here to provide a comprehensive overview for readers who never saw the old book. There's a lot more Shakespeare after seven seasons of work for The Shakespeare Theatre of New Jersey and three for Groundling Theatre Company in Toronto.

Communication Arts invited me to sit on the jury for their prestigious Illustration Annual in 2012. It was an inspiration and a reminder of the extraordinarily high standards of imagination and skill set by my colleagues in this profession. At my age, I'm constantly aware that there are younger, cooler-than-me artists out there doing great work. If I have a competitive advantage, it's at the concept stage. Christina Poddubiuk's name appears frequently throughout this book because the great concepts behind my best illustrations are often hers. My wife and creative partner juggles her own thriving career as a theatre costume and set designer, runs the business affairs of our studio and still finds time to brainstorm poster ideas with me. Anyone who has seen Christina's costume sketches knows she's a superb draughtsman — she often looks over my shoulder and gently points out when I need to look more closely at eyes lining up or the shape of a nose. I can't begin to adequately acknowledge her intelligence, her instincts for what makes a great poster and her patience with me. This book is as much hers as it is mine.

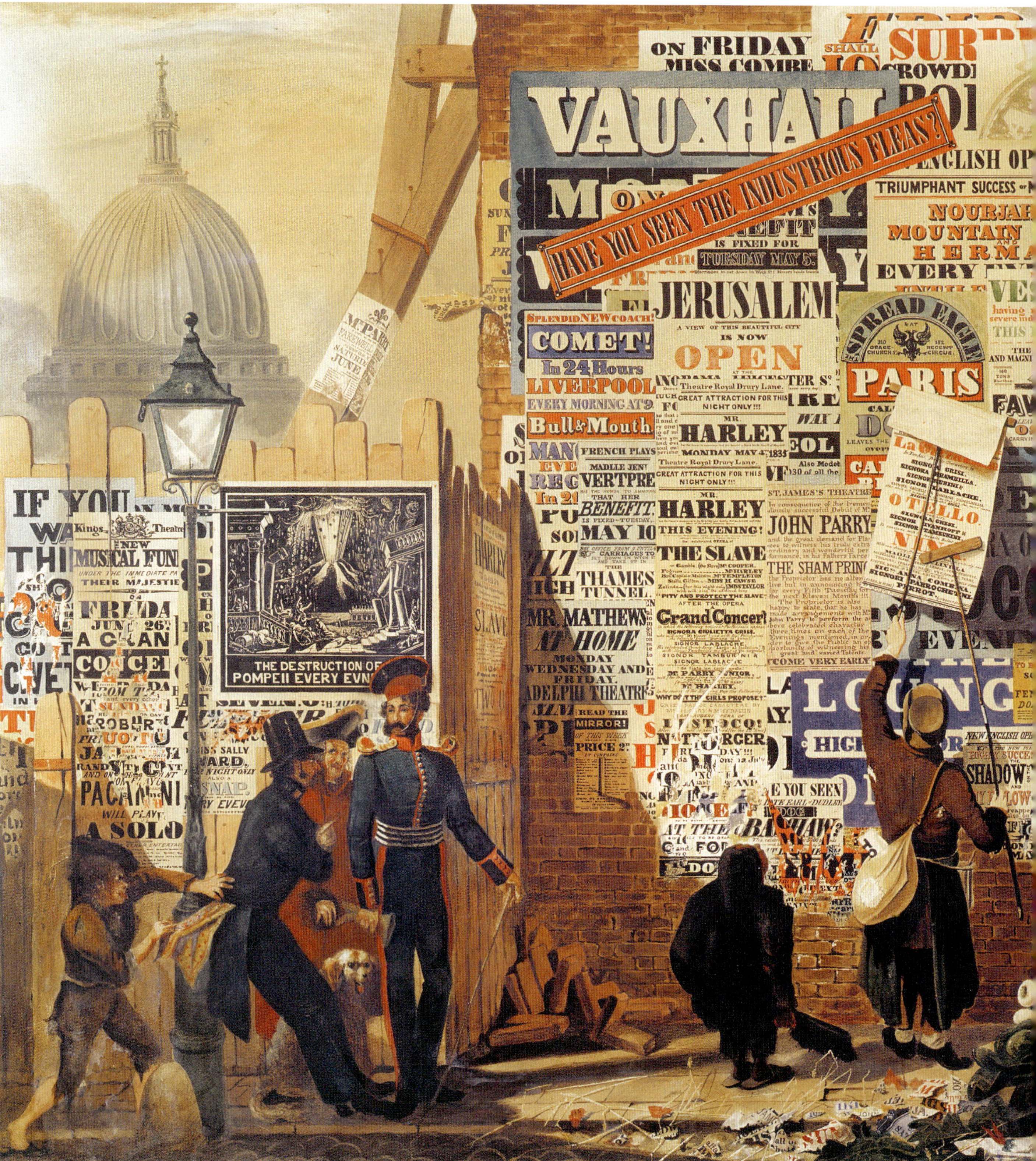

The Poster Man, 1835, by John Orlando Parry.

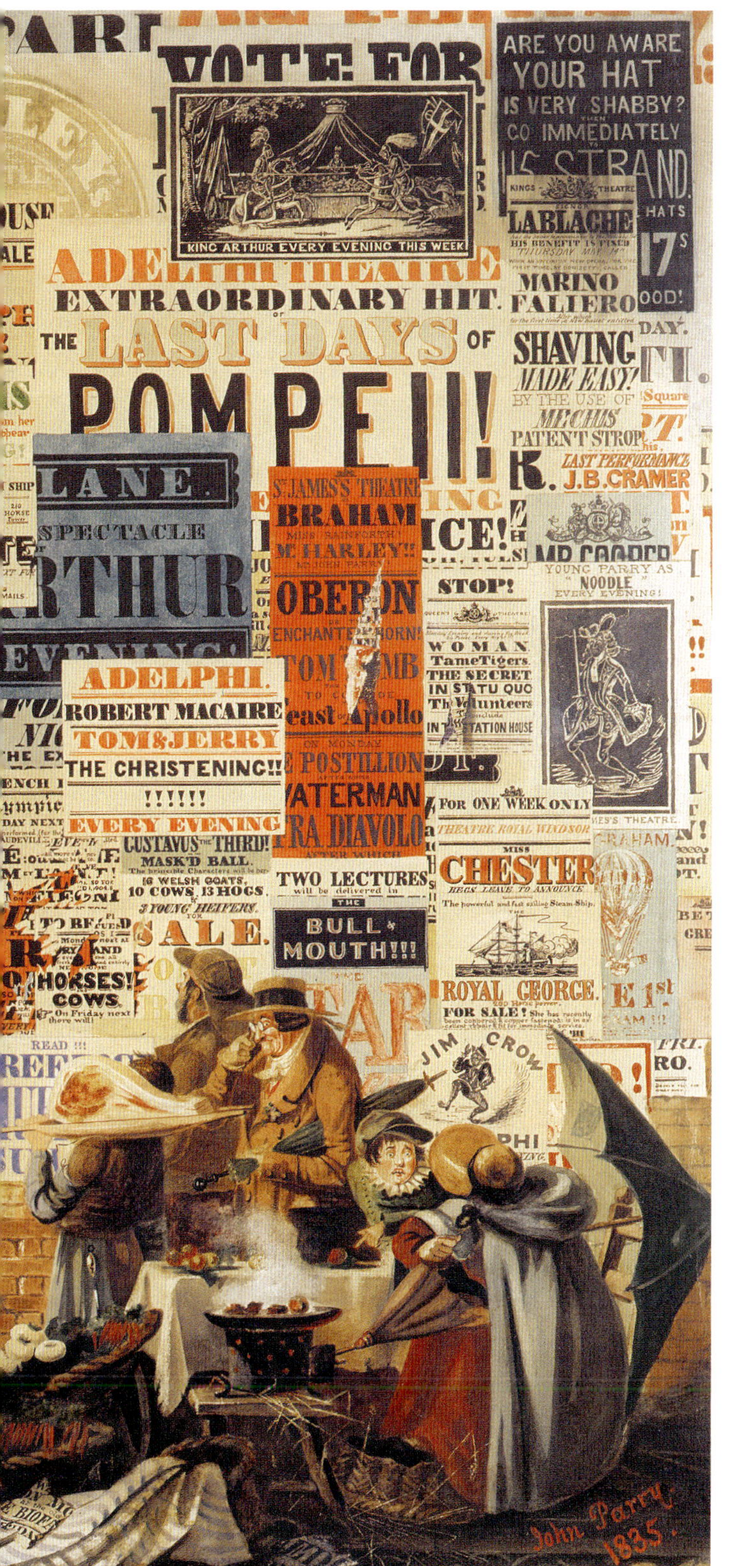

The stage! The theatrical profession. There's genteel comedy in your walk and manner, juvenile tragedy in your eye, and touch and go farce in your laugh. You'll do as well as if you had thought of nothing else but the lamps, from your birth downwards. You can be useful to us in a hundred ways: think what capital bills a man of your education could write for the shop windows… Why you could write us a piece to bring out the whole strength of the company, whenever we wanted one. We'll have a new show-piece out directly, new and splendid scenery — you must manage to introduce a real pump and two washing tubs… I bought 'em cheap, at a sale the other day and they'll come in admirably. That's the London plan… Most of the theatres keep an author on purpose. It'll look very well in the bills in separate lines – Real Pump! Splendid Tubs! Great Attraction! You don't happen to be anything of an artist, do you? If you had been, we might have had a large wooden woodcut of the last scene for the posters, showing the whole depth of the stage with the pump and tubs in the middle!

When Charles Dickens wrote *The Life and Adventures of Nicholas Nickleby*, in 1839, he knew all too well the fine line that existed between the theatre and the poster, and while Dickens satirizes the commercial necessity of advertising and generating appeal for performance, there is a sense here too of the theatre's vitality and interdependence on the marketplace which has always informed poster art and given it context for discussion.

There is indeed a fine line in the magnificent and captivating scratchboard illustration and poster art of Scott McKowen.

The working title for this book was *Reading Between the Lines* — apt for this collection of images, as all the work created by Scott is inspired from, at its source, a reading of lines of text for a play or a story. Reading in this context does not only suggest a comprehension of the words — their apparent sense in the lines of dialogue or stage directions — but rather the accumulated meaning and intention of the lines that reveal the drama underneath and the moments of a life lived between them. All plays are words written to be spoken aloud. At best, a script is a roadmap for a performance. A play text is not easy to read, for the experience is, in a way, incomplete. A play is only a work of literature by chance and/or necessity. The lines in a play are devised to be spoken in an imagined moment of time, enacted by characters, interpreted by actors, conceived and brought to cohesion or collision by directors, visually made manifest by designers, realized by a team of technicians and craftspeople, under the organization, guidance and creativity of stage managers, producers and coaches, then, ultimately, only coming to life with an audience who listens and sees.

Theatre comes from the Greek word *theatrum*, meaning "a place for seeing." And since its earliest history, the poster to announce the play has been our first encounter with the text; our first invitation to a way of seeing the drama. For many of us, it is the beginning of our journey into the vast spaces that exist between the lines. After the play is over, it becomes a reminder or keepsake of our witnessing and a continued image to reflect upon our experience.

There are so many images in Scott's work that do this for me. In particular, his visual reading of the plays of Shakespeare give very familiar lines a fresh perspective and opportunity for reconsideration.

Poster art is a fine line between the promise of the drama and the encountering of it. It often crosses the lines of commerce (when used in advertising) and artfulness (when it takes on a talisman-like property, capturing the moment when you saw a play that forever changed the way you saw or understood the world around you). It is the bastard child of the private and public experience, the commodification of an artwork and its ultimate expression. It is high and low. It embodies an age-old dialogue in the theatre between success and significance.

I remember many years ago a theatre publicist telling me that Scott's poster art was problematic as a publicity tool because as soon as you put up one of Scott's posters, they were quickly taken down; stolen, to be hung as frame ready artworks in someone's home. The problem, he said, was the poster not only made you want to see the play, but more powerfully wanted you to own the poster. This was true for me — as for years, Scott's posters for the Grand Theatre in London hung in my studio, all stolen from callboards and theatre lobbies and the once-famous theatre poster-papered walls of the downstairs hallway to the washrooms of the Epicure Café on Queen Street in Toronto. At the same time, poster art's commercial use never gives it the high art status or recognition of its compositional complexity and expressive power. One is more likely to recognize the work in this book from a newspaper or theatre-bill than an art gallery catalogue, and consequently a collection of these images together is a welcome chance to look at Scott McKowen's body of work and consider these images on their own terms.

Much has been written about the advent of the theatre poster in the 19th century, and certainly the work of Scott McKowen references this influence. His engraving style and long association with the Shaw Festival and the plays of Bernard Shaw can attribute this, but the relationship of the poster to Western theatre dates back as far as the Middle Ages. In many of the Mystery Cycle plays, performances were announced by processions of the performers themselves, sometimes accompanied by "vexillators" — people carrying banners, which depicted the play in images and text. For those who could read, brief, handwritten details of the performance were handed out and stuck to posts in the town, giving rise to the word "poster."

During the English renaissance of the 16th and 17th centuries, we know the poster played a vital role in the performance of plays. Ben Jonson's 1614 Jacobean city comedy, *Bartholomew Fair*, opens with two characters who are the makers of "bills" to attract the audience to the performance.

The most effective way of attracting a crowd was by a large and colourful banner and the sound of the drum and trumpet. There is always an aspect of trumpets and drums to poster art. A recruitment to gather. A call to summon our interest in a persuasive and compelling way.

It is a whimsical coincidence, and in no small part an important contributing factor to the power of Scott's illustration that his chosen medium is scratchboard engraving. Defined by strong graphic lines and cross-hatching, it is a medium that is both figurative and representational, as it always reminds the viewer of its construction and organization of line and shadow. It is a bold and muscular visual style that evokes the history of woodcuts and steel engraving, and yet in Scott's rendering it is entirely modern in subject and sensibility and therefore somehow timeless. Scott describes the medium like this: "Scratchboard is a white clay surface, fused to a piece of Masonite and then coated with a thin layer of black ink. White lines are 'scratched' into the all-black surface using an X-ACTO knife. When you pick up a black pen and draw on white paper, you build up layers of hatching to render shadow areas. Scratchboard is exactly the opposite — you're drawing the highlights."

This process of "drawing the highlights" expresses the very nature of reading a theatre text and interpretation. Somehow to express shadow, you must define where the light hits and refracts. Conversely, light is always defined by the shadow that surrounds it or threatens to engulf its subject into darkness. There is reading required of images too, and in these works there is as much subtext as story in the lines of shadow and light.

What makes you want to see a play? What draws us into the theatre and turns a consideration into a commitment? As I pore over the poster artwork of Scott McKowen, I am struck by his ability to capture the essence of a play — to distill the lines into a compelling image. His work holds not only an interpretation or (god forbid) an explanation of the text — but rather, evokes the mystery, the ongoing question prompted by the play. The images in his work create a dialogue with the theatre text which inspired it and a discussion begins. His art endows new work with the authority of tradition and classical text with a quality of innovation.

The lines of a theatre text are written for collaboration and in order to give them dimension, the artist and audience must read between the lines in a search for nuance, context, paradox and intention. The actor speaks in the theatre to alter the world or circumstance around them. All language is a form of

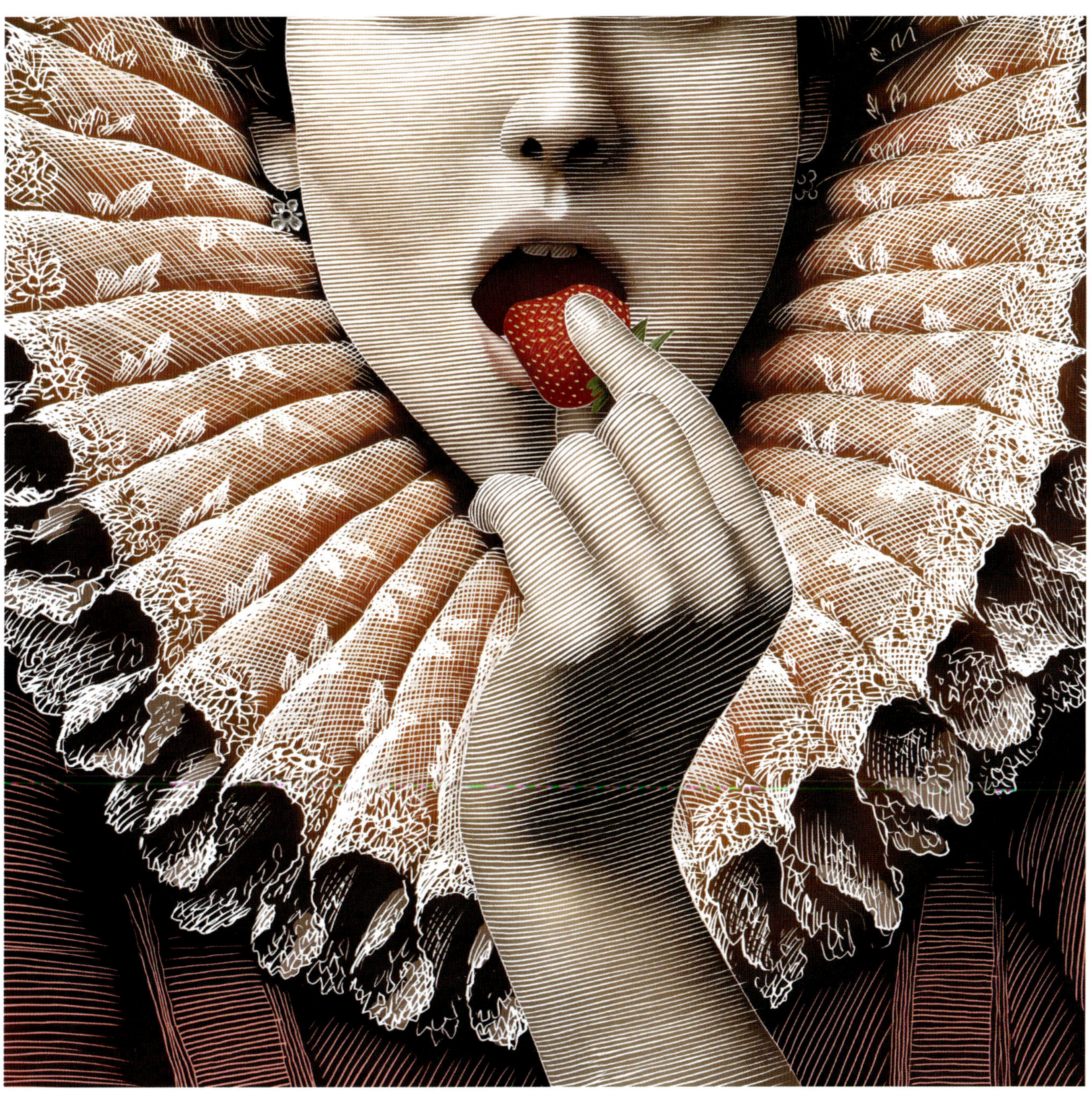

Poster illustration for Shakespeare's *Othello* portraying Desdemona instead of the title character. The central symbol in the play is the strawberry handkerchief — Othello's first gift and token of his love. It's the symbol of Desdemona's fidelity and chastity. And it's the handkerchief that makes him crazy when Cassio shows up with it — it becomes, in Othello's mind, proof of his wife's betrayal.

disagreement; its will is to bring about change. Every theatre artist must read the lines for sense and context, but read between them for impact and feeling. Make no mistake, Scott McKowen is a theatre artist. A theatre artist who makes posters and illustrates books. His creative and life partner, theatre designer Christina Poddubiuk, also speaks to this practice of collaboration and collective theatre-making. Together, Scott and Christina operate Punch & Judy Inc., the design studio out of which these images are conceived and workshopped, devised and created. The combined influence and knowledge shared from historical artforms and craftsmanship to contemporary technologies and innovations forge a rich resource and meeting place of ideas in theatre, dance, opera and music.

Scott McKowen is intently aware of finding the right image to entice people to performance — but also in an elusive way — to express the work of art itself.

How many of us have a play or a movie or a novel, that defines for us an embodiment of a philosophy? And a poster or an image to go along with it? How often have I heard someone define an approach to their understanding the world through an author and the encounter with their text? What is a poster? An advertisement or an artistic expression? It is a container for information; a title, an author, a theatre company, sometimes a cast list, a sponsor, a telephone number to call for tickets? Or is it something else?

Today's theatre relies upon previews, reviews and arts

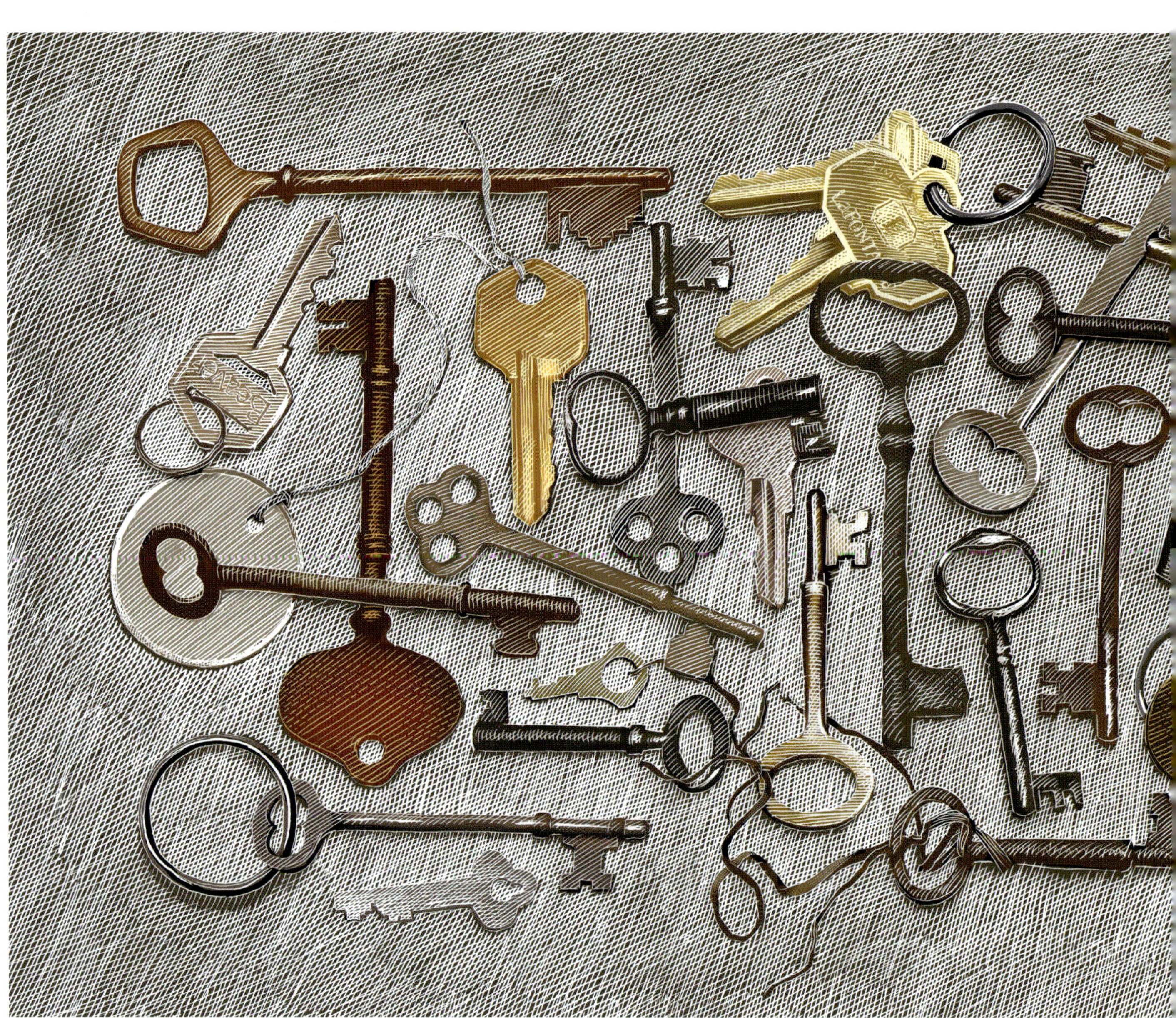

A book cover concept that was approved at pencil sketch stage, then vetoed by the publisher after final art had been completed (and paid for). A great example of how scratchboard renders metallic surfaces, and also of how the approval process and protocol can sometimes go off the rails.

features in all forms of print and predominantly in the always expanding and independent world of social media. The theatre blogosphere of the 21st century has all the vernacular and chaotic disorder of a papered Victorian alleyway or street: a cacophony of competing events and entertainments, political, social and cultural assemblies vying for audience, attention and authentic and necessary representation. In a modern world, how do images contain multiple meanings and entry points for a single story and speak to all the complexities of audience and artforms?

Part of reading between lines demands new ways of seeing very old forms. As the theatre explores questions of authorship, interpretation and critique within the context of emergent technologies and disciplinary restructuring, as theatre makers and audiences contend with the intersection between the arts and politics, as we analyze and the shifting public interest in arts and culture and dissect the impact of Truth and Reconciliation on cultural production in Canada, there are new avenues and needs for images that speak to and describe the theatre we make and the stories we are telling. I look back on the work of Scott McKowen and how he sees and reads between the lines, and look forward to his careful and measured gaze as we attempt to read the days ahead. These lines on a page can be read as lines of connection and understanding to something new.

PETER HINTON

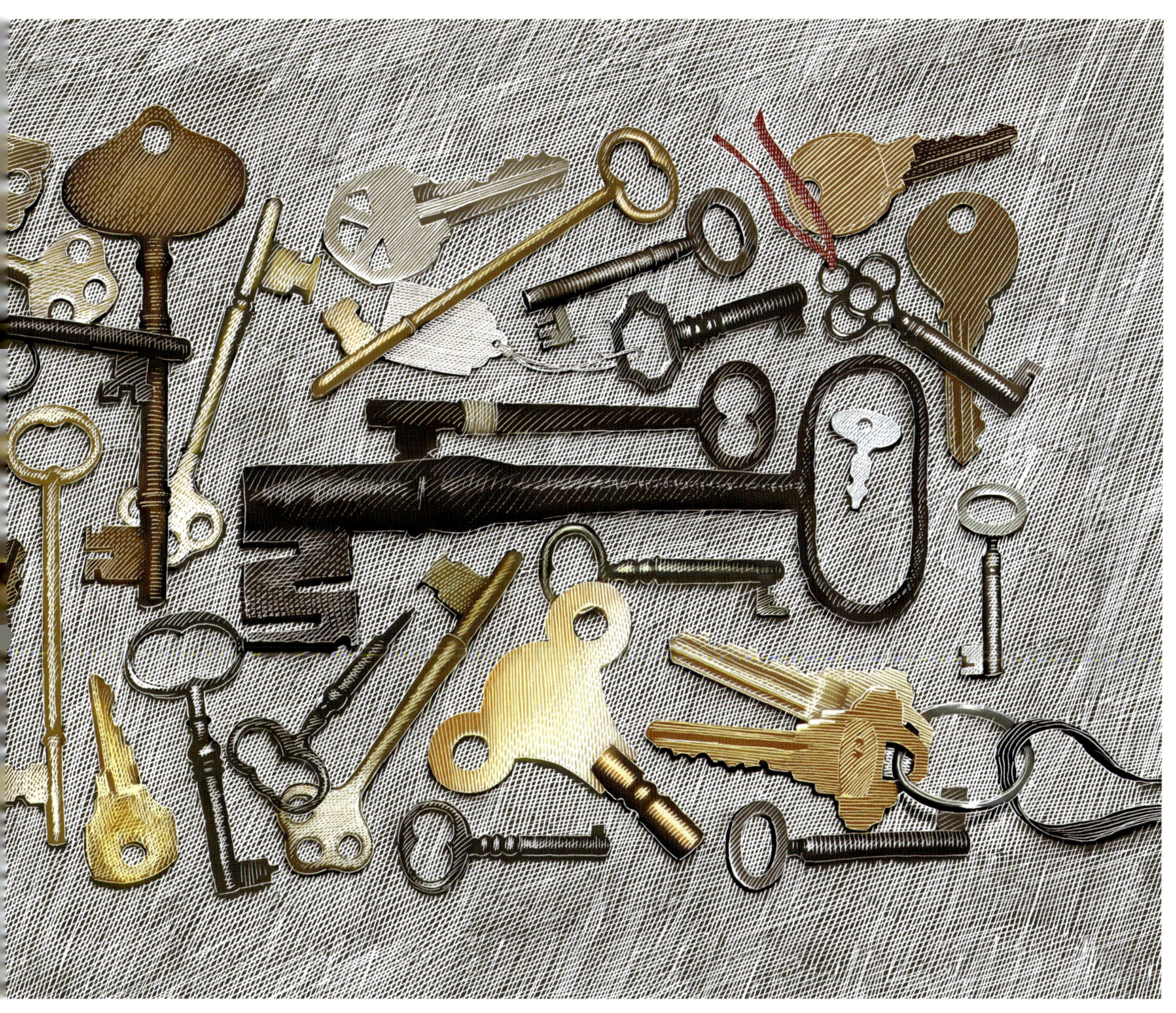

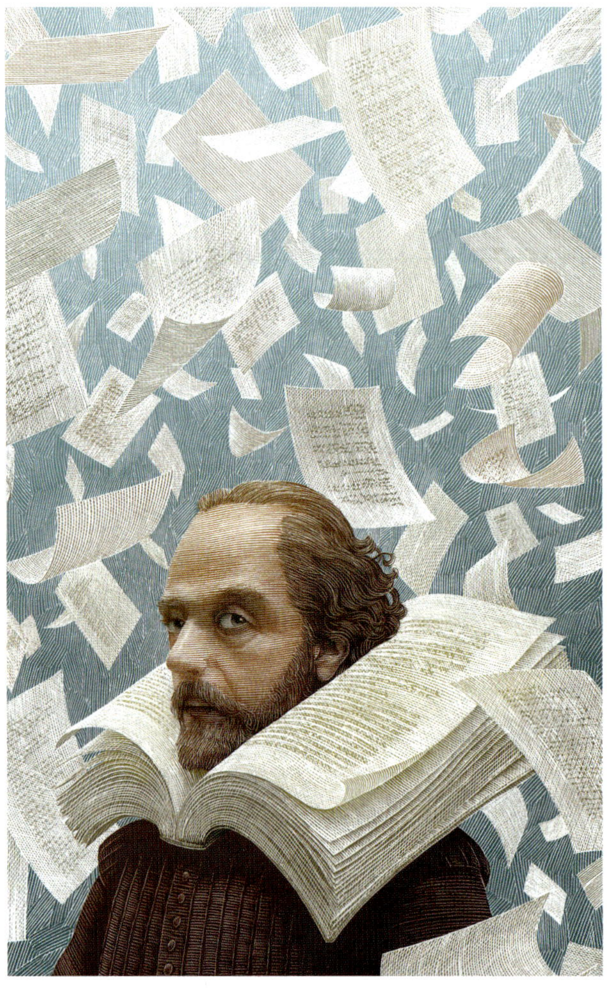

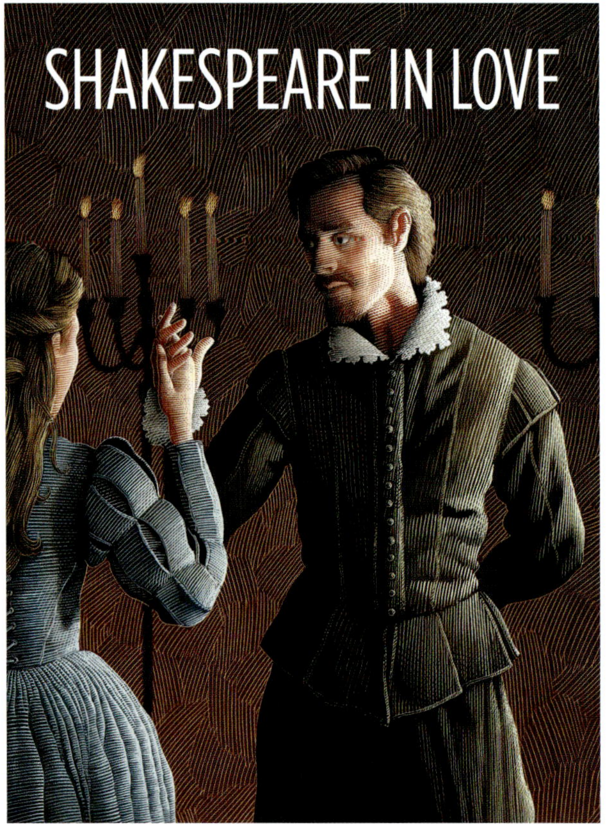

I started a happy working relationship with The Shakespeare Theatre of New Jersey in 2013. I had to come up with a poster that season for *As You Like It*. The play's themes of Man learning from Nature led to an unexpected "chaos theory" concept — a young Will Shakespeare contemplating a butterfly on the tip of his finger. The insect's life cycle from caterpillar to chrysalis to butterfly mirrors the Seven Ages of Man speech.

A rough pencil sketch was approved, and I started casting about for a model. I wanted someone younger and more appealing than the face we're familiar with from the historical portraits. I thought of the genius casting of Joseph Fiennes in *Shakespeare in Love*, but knew we could not work with Hollywood stars on our non-profit theatre budget.

Christina was designing sets and costumes for a production of *Romeo and Juliet* at the Denver Center Theatre Company and suggested that Matthew Simpson, the actor playing Tybalt, would be fabulous — and he already had the perfect costume! I visited Denver to see the show, approached Simpson and learned that he had already been cast in the upcoming Shakespeare New Jersey season. Sometimes everything falls serendipitously into place.

The Shakespeare Theatre of New Jersey's 2015 season poster makes reference to Bill Cain's play *Equivocation*, in which Shakespeare is a main character. In the play, King James I commissions the Bard to dramatize the events surrounding the infamous Gunpowder Plot — a failed attempt to assassinate the king in 1605. This image was suggested by a highly theatrical scene in the play in which a blizzard of paper falls from above the stage, as the fictional Shakespeare is wrestling with his conscience about writing a play as political propaganda. I stole the idea of the book as a ruff — from myself. I had used this idea for a portrait of Shakespeare's Spanish contemporary Miguel de Cervantes, reproduced on page 219.

Speaking of *Shakespeare in Love*, The Shakespeare Theatre of New Jersey produced the stage play adaptation of the film in 2017. I suggested a double portrait of Will and Viola de Lesseps (but we only see her from behind) in an Elizabethan dance pose — essentially the "and palm to palm is holy palmer's kiss" moment in *Romeo and Juliet*. Jon Barker, the actor cast in the title role for this production, posed for the illustration, and it became another in our series of cover portraits of the Bard.

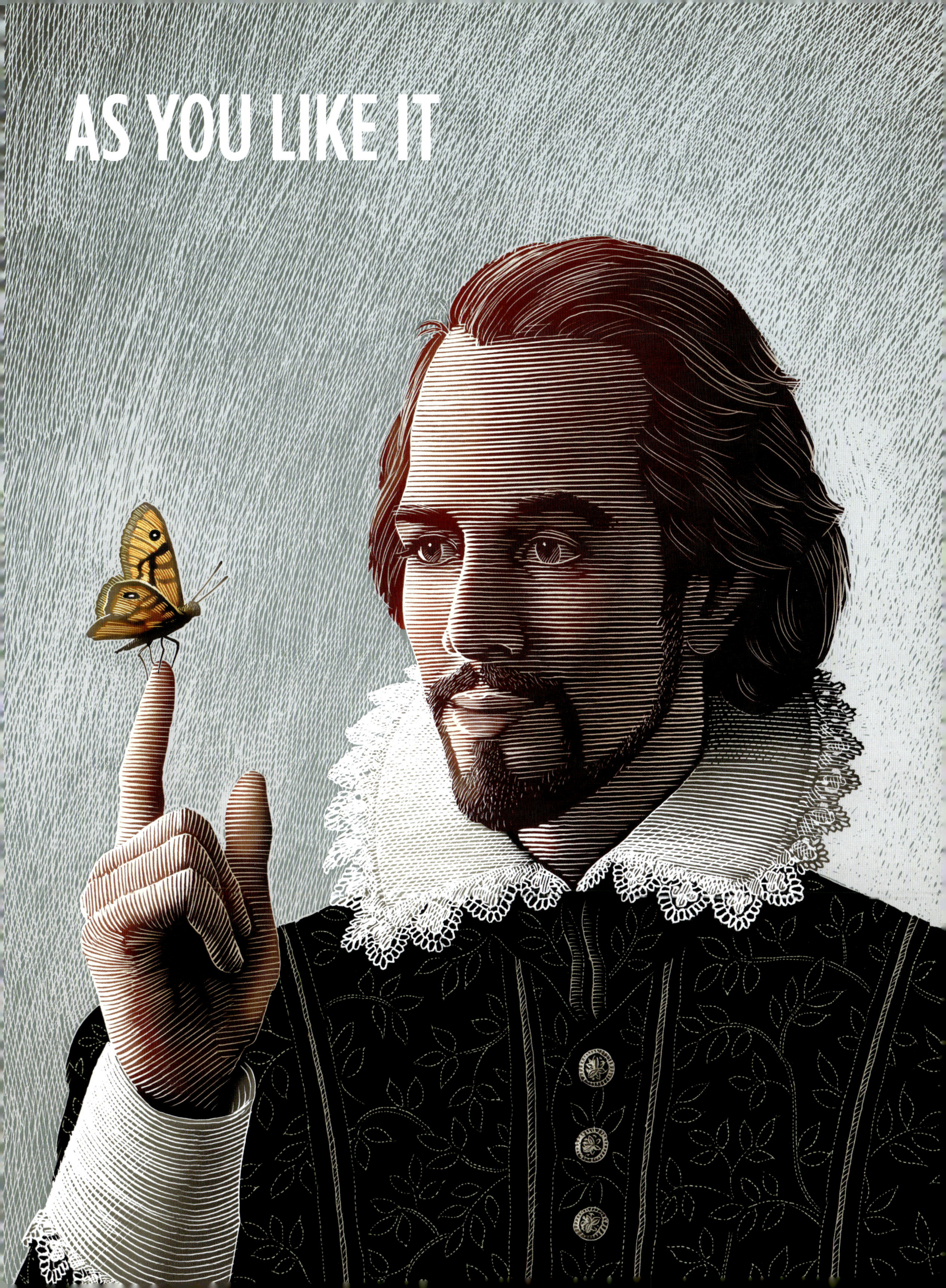
AS YOU LIKE IT

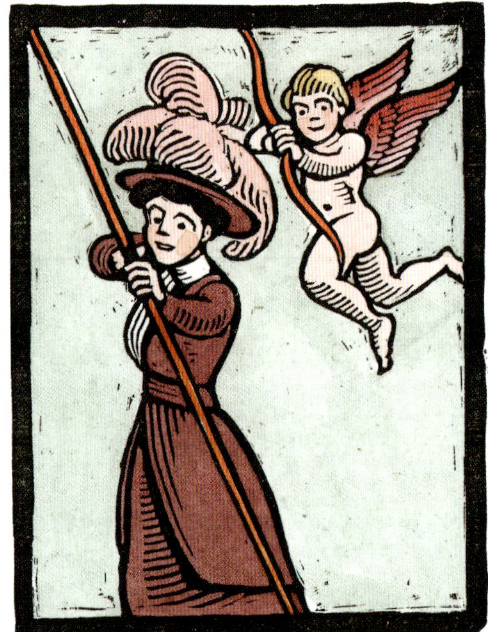

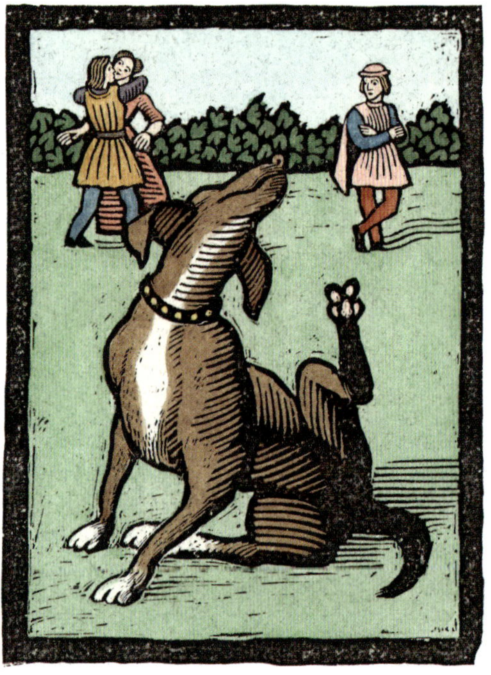

Scholars seem to agree that *The Comedy of Errors* is one of Shakespeare's earliest plays. Its principal source is *Menaechmi* by Plautus; several Latin editions were available in England in the 16th century. The comedy in the Roman play comes from the confusion caused by a set of twins, both named Menaechmus. Shakespeare ups the game, and the possibilities of mistaken identity, in his play by creating two sets of twins, accidentally separated at birth.

Antipholus, a merchant from Syracuse, and his servant Dromio arrive in Ephesus not knowing that their long-lost identical twins live parallel lives there. Comic mayhem ensues between masters and servants, husbands and wives, a sister-in-law, a courtesan, a goldsmith and a conjurer who thinks the cause of the chaos is demonic possession and attempts an exorcism. The Abbess at the local priory sorts everything out and families are happily reunited.

My poster for a 2010 production by The Acting Company in New York is one of my favourite examples of Christina Poddubiuk's remarkable ability to distill a play down to a visual metaphor that tells the whole story. A school of Syracuse fish is swimming in one direction and a school of Ephesus fish in the opposite direction; two pairs of lost "outsiders" — each moving in the wrong direction — represent the two very confused sets of twins.

The Comedy of Errors has been turned into an opera, a musical (several times — *The Boys from Syracuse* by Richard Rodgers and Lorenz Hart on Broadway in 1938 and *Oh, Brother!* off-Broadway in 1981; and also in 1981 by Trevor Nunn and Guy Woolfenden at the Royal Shakespeare Company) and film adaptations such as *Big Business* with Bette Midler and Lily Tomlin.

I created posters for the Stratford Festival's 1992 season using scratchboard to mimic the look of the bold, primitive woodcuts used in early 19th-century chapbooks and "penny dreadfuls." I'm not including a lot of old work in this book but the concepts for two early Shakespeare comedies seem worth a revisit here. In *Love's Labour's Lost*, the youthful King of Navarre and his three scholarly companions have vowed to forsake the company of women. The visual pun on Cupid was suggested by the hunting scene in which the Princess of France and her three ladies-in-waiting shoot a deer with bows and arrows. *The Two Gentlemen of Verona* deals with themes of friendship and infidelity and the foolish behaviour of people in love. Launce, the servant of Proteus, shares several very funny scenes with his dog, Crab. I put the main characters in the background and focussed on the dog, "the most scene-stealing non-speaking role in the canon."

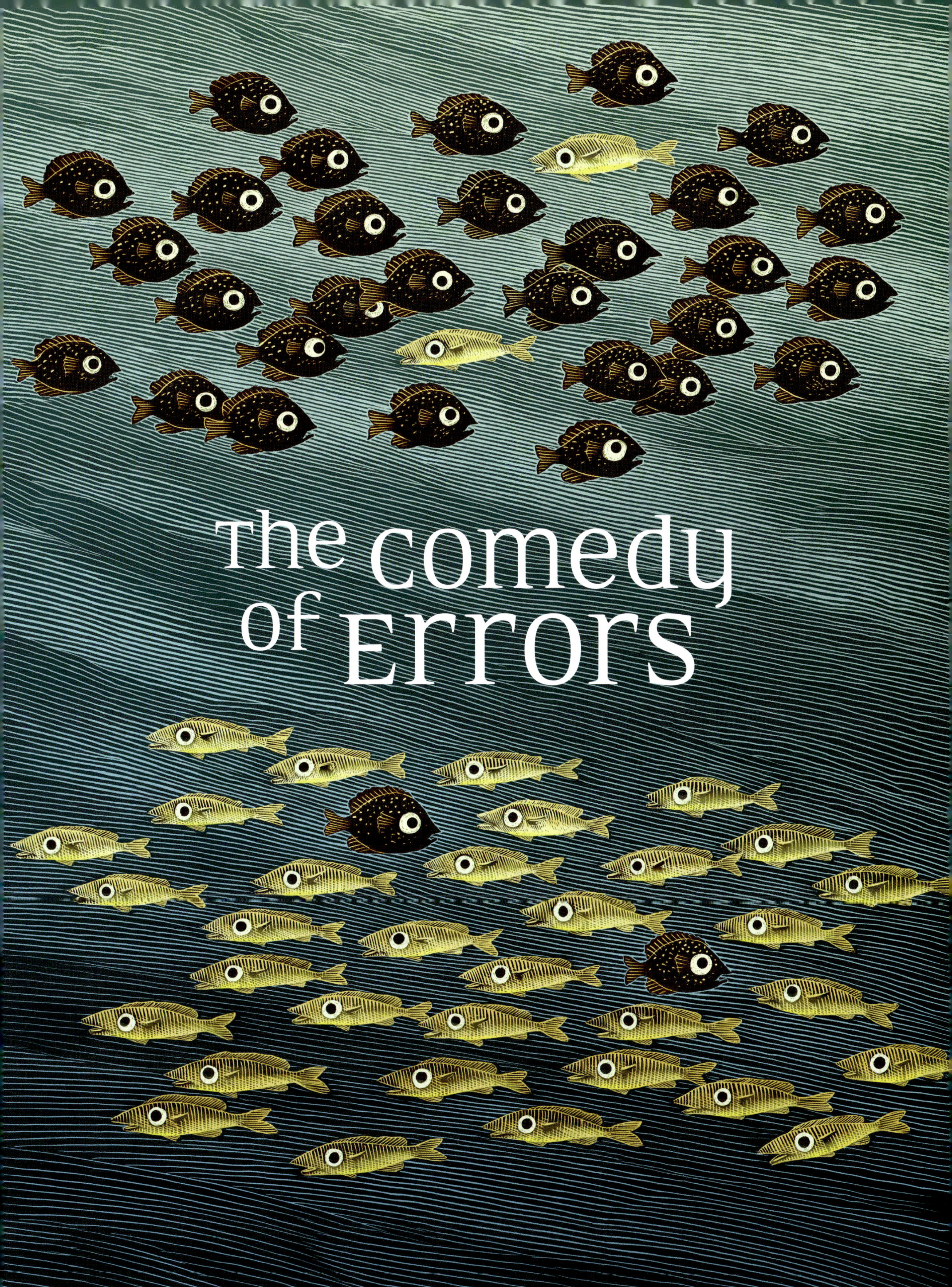
The comedy of Errors

The Shakespeare Theatre of New Jersey programmed *Coriolanus* in 2016 — certainly an interesting choice for a tumultuous election year, as much of the action in the play revolves around a campaign for high office. Coriolanus is an aristocrat and a decorated military hero, but he is openly contemptuous of the common citizens whose votes he needs to get elected. I thought of a political propaganda poster — a *trompe l'oeil* street collage of overlapping layers of ephemera. During election campaigns, you see a candidate's face everywhere; then when the polls close (or maybe when allegiances shift), that face is gone — ripped, rained on and plastered over. The military uniform is based on a photo of Mussolini, to reflect the period of this production.

I wrestled with ideas for the same theatre's 2018 poster for *Titus Andronicus*, the unbelievably violent and bloody revenge play with terrifying scenes of rape, mutilation and cannibalism. I had sketched a lion attacking a horse, based on an ancient statue in the Capitoline Museums. Nobody was completely happy with the concept so we shifted into nightmare territory with a *chimera* — a monster from classical mythology composed of a lion's head, a goat's body and a serpent's tail. This seemed to mirror the unnatural world of the play.

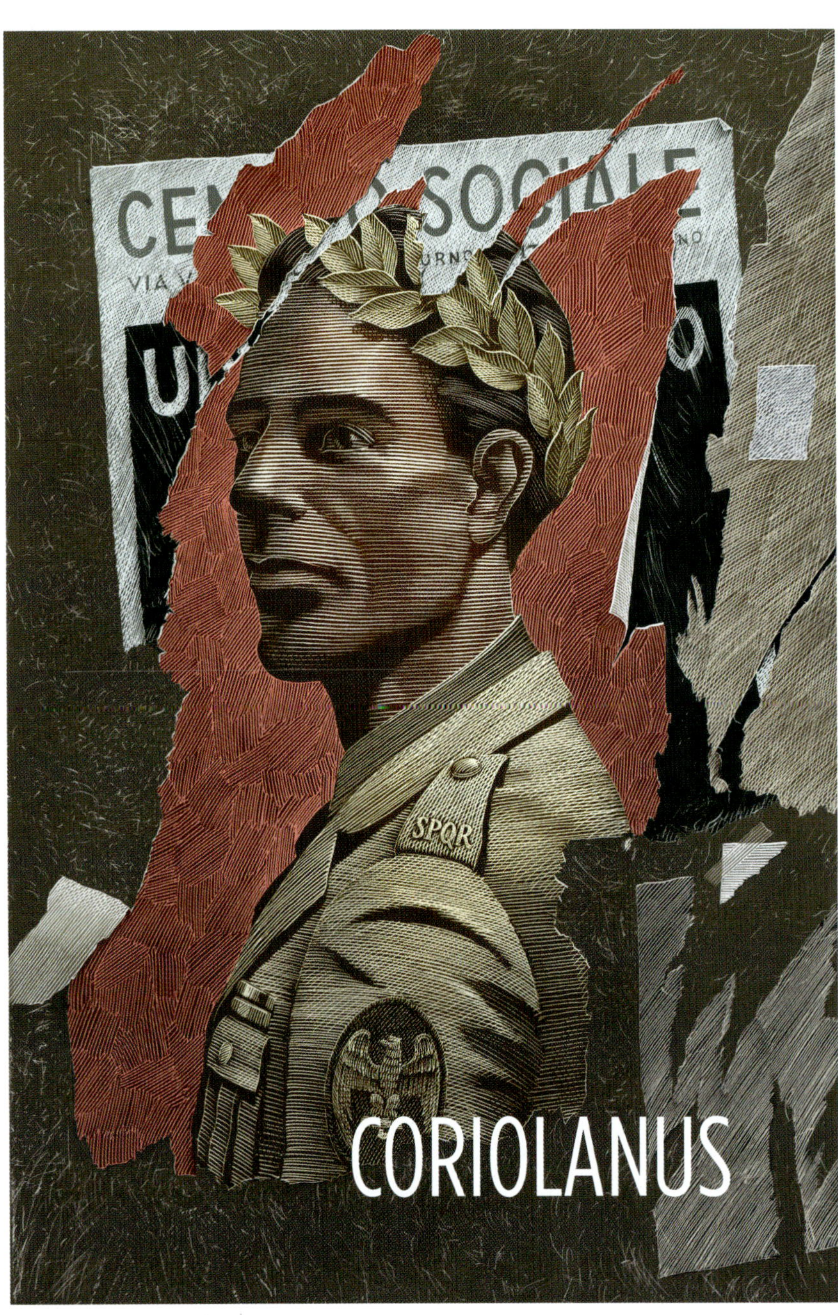

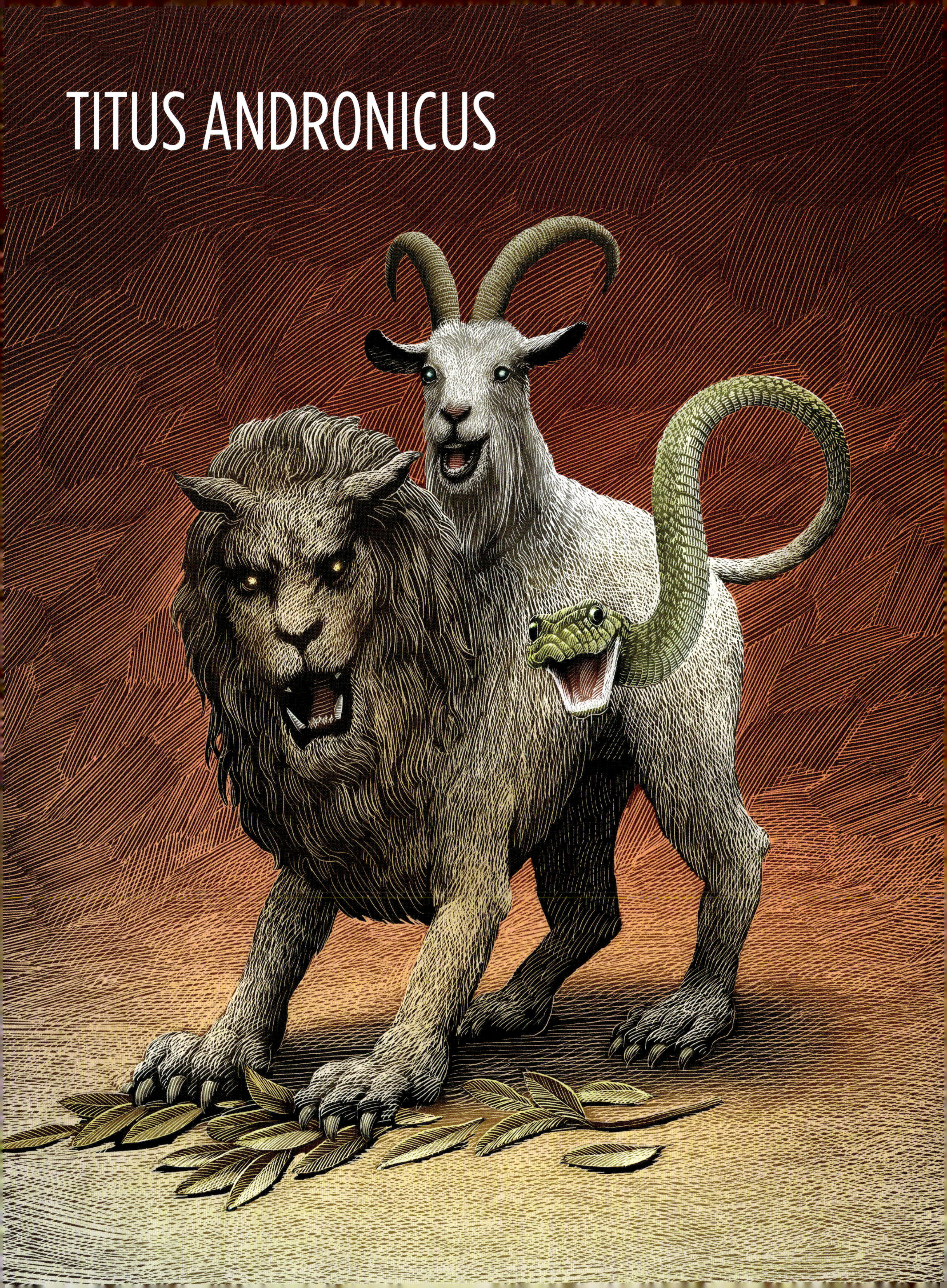
TITUS ANDRONICUS

Repercussion Theatre has produced Shakespeare in Montreal's city parks for over 25 years — but their 2014 production of *Harry the King: The Famous Victories of Henry V* was the first time the company had tackled the history plays. Paul Hopkins' adaptation of *Henry IV* Parts One and Two and *Henry V* traces the journey of Prince Hal from rebellious youth to mature and beloved monarch. This high-octane show was calculated to appeal to younger audiences — perhaps some of them could identify with Prince Harry. The *Montreal Gazette* review of the production described the actors playing Hal and Hotspur as "dashing" and "seductive," adding "these guys are hot talent."

Henry V opens with a prologue inviting the audience to use their imagination to conjure the vivid scenes about to be played out: "Think when we talk of horses, that you see them printing their proud hoofs i' the receiving earth." The poster illustration was my attempt to conjure the adrenaline of the battlefield.

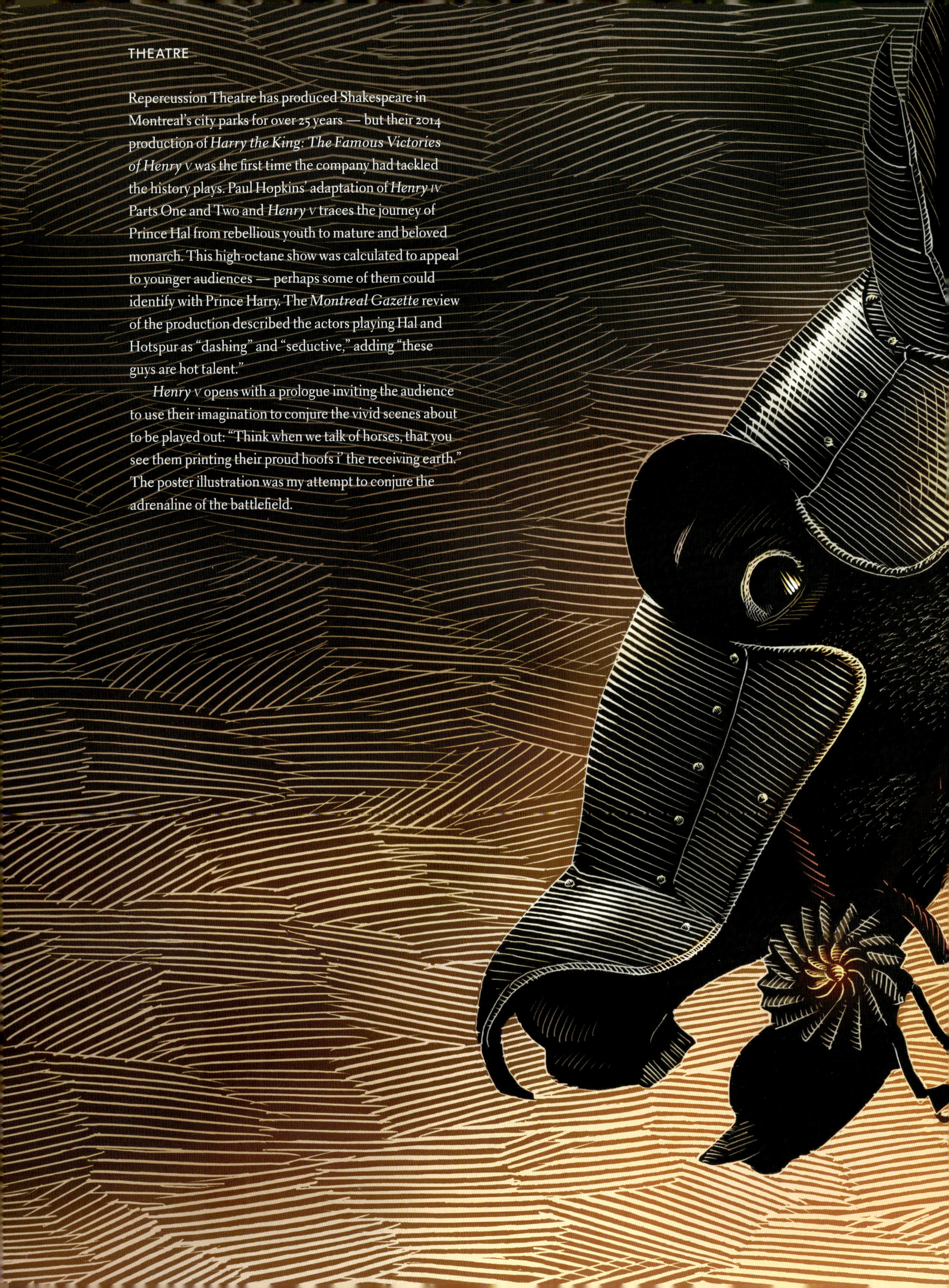

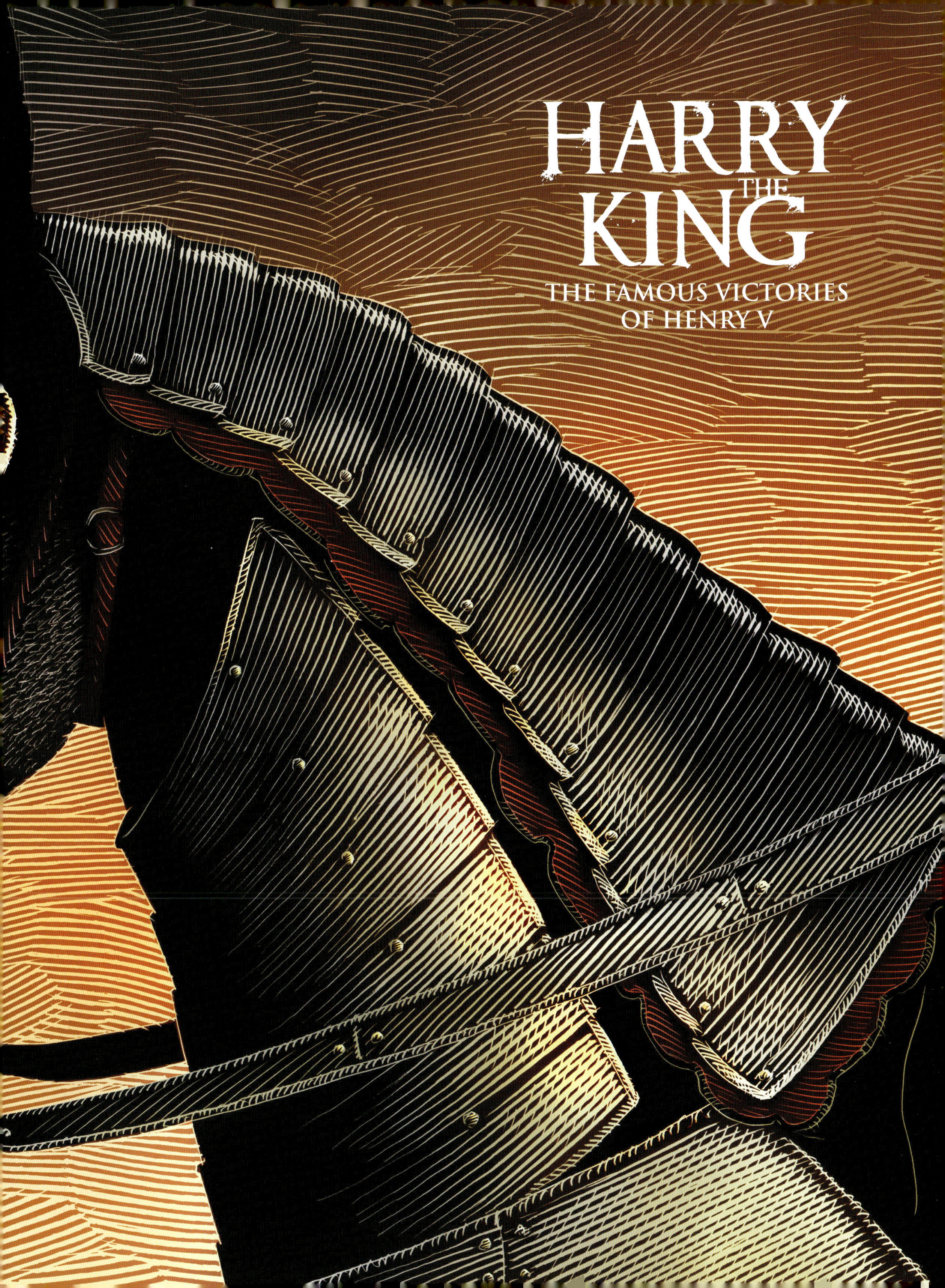
HARRY
THE
KING
THE FAMOUS VICTORIES
OF HENRY V

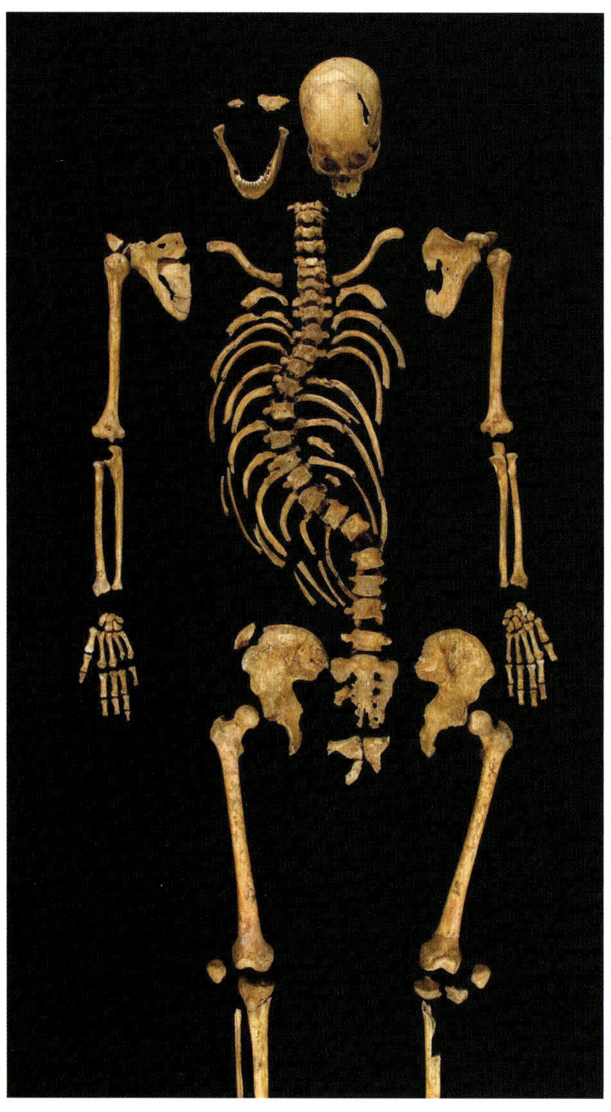

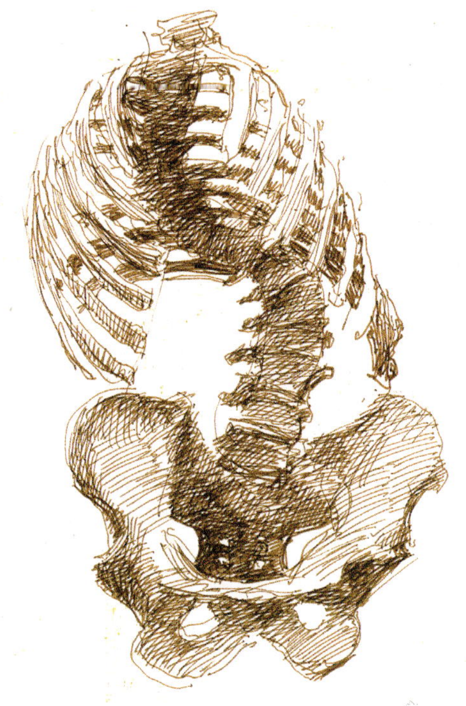

Richard III is famously described as a "bottled spider" and a "poisonous bunch-backed toad" in Shakespeare's play. The character is traditionally played as a hunchback, but the real nature of his physical deformity has always been open to speculation — until 2012 when his skeletal remains were discovered under a parking lot in Leicester, England. Confirmation was made by archaeologists at the University of Leicester after extensive testing including carbon dating and DNA matches with two living descendants of the king's sister, Anne of York.

Richard was killed fighting the forces of Henry Tudor at the Battle of Bosworth in 1485, ending the Wars of the Roses. Shakespeare wrote *Richard III* around 1593. It's easy to see how, a century after the fact, a great poet and playwright might exaggerate physical deformity into moral depravity and evil intent for dramatic effect. Whenever Richard III's name comes up today it's Shakespeare's character that always comes to mind.

But the discovery of the king's skeleton in 2012 showed Shakespeare was wrong. Here was proof that Richard had scoliosis — a sideways curvature of the spine that may have caused his right shoulder to look higher than his left. But he did not have kyphosis, which causes the curved back that we associate with a hunchback (more than 50 degrees of curvature). The Hunterian Museum in London has a skeleton with kyphoscoliosis (a combination of both) — I had made a sketch of it on a visit there 10 years ago so I had a sense of this comparison.

That drawing, along with the photographs of Richard's deconstructed skeleton made before it was reburied in Leicester Cathedral, inspired this gleefully macabre poster for The Shakespeare Theatre of New Jersey in 2016. I think there's a distinctly arachnidian feel to that twisted spine and ribcage.

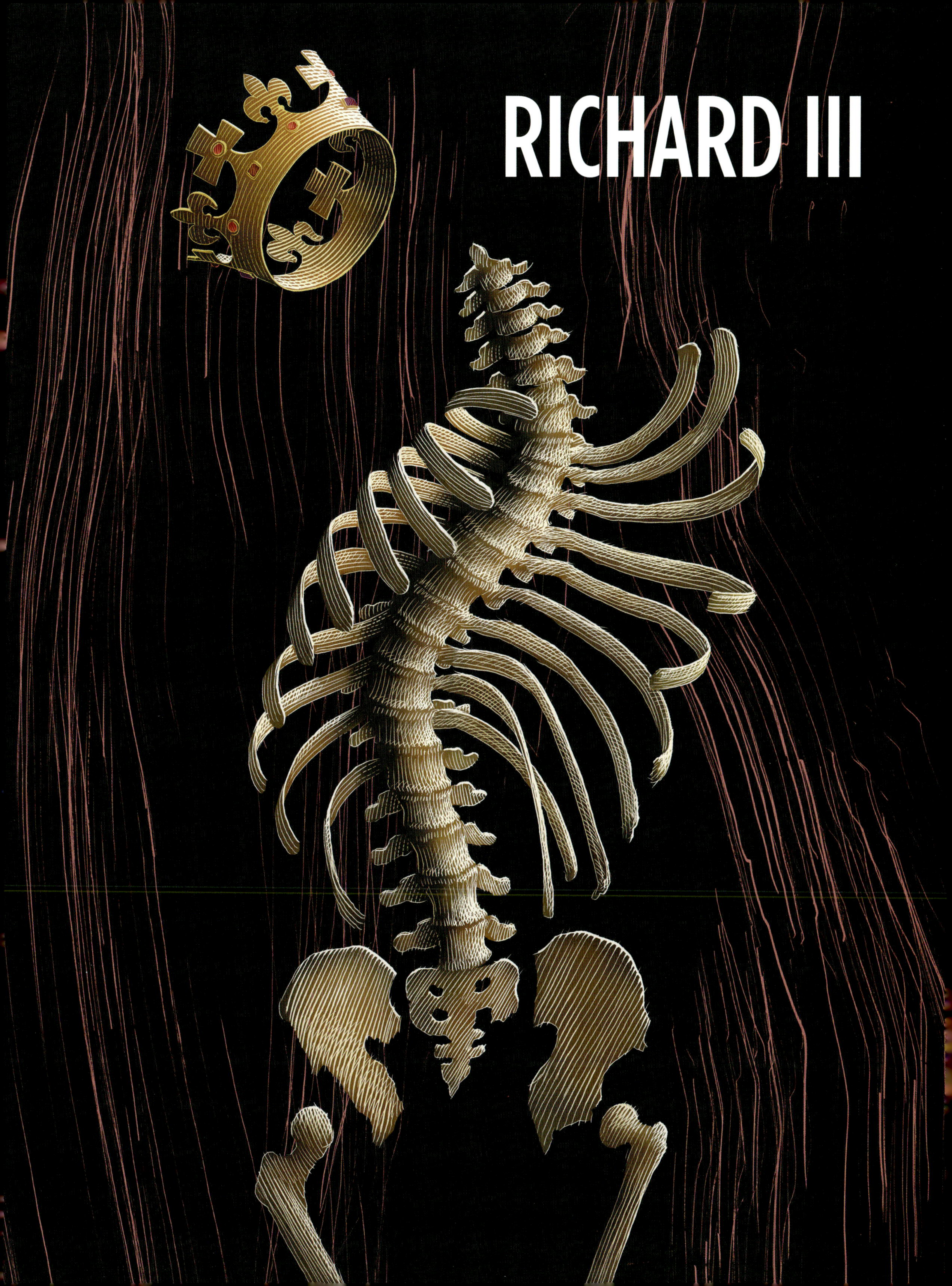
RICHARD III

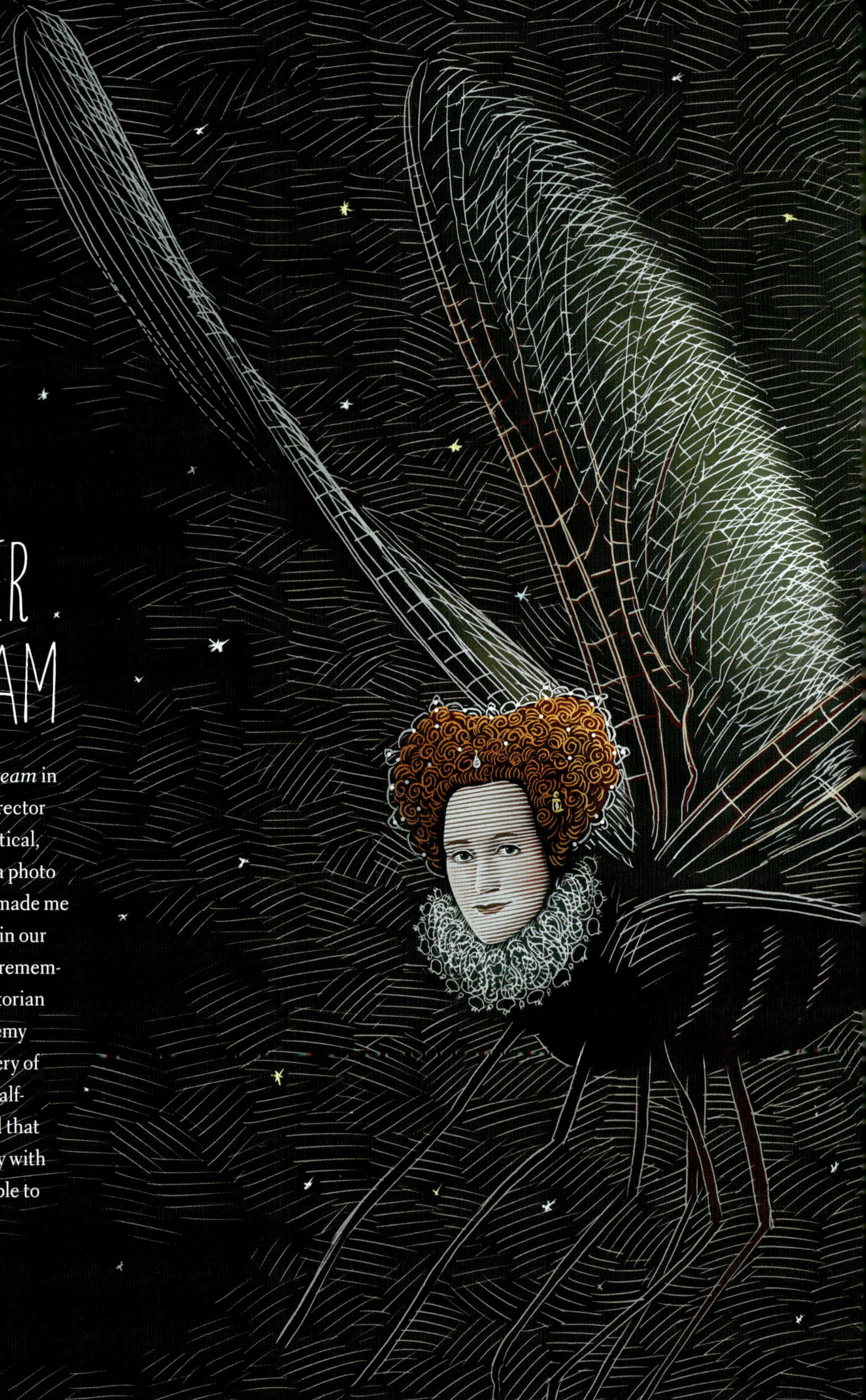

A MIDSUMMER NIGHT'S DREAM

Repercussion Theatre presented *Dream* in Montreal's city parks in 2013. The director asked for something disarming, mystical, intriguing and cob-webby. She sent a photo of light bulbs strung in trees, which made me think of fireflies. We often see them in our backyard on warm summer nights. I remembered a wonderful exhibition of Victorian fairy painting, from the Royal Academy in London, that visited the Art Gallery of Ontario in 1998 — full of fairies as half-human, half-butterfly creatures. And that led to this strange, glowing dragonfly with a human face. I don't think it's possible to get too surreal for this play.

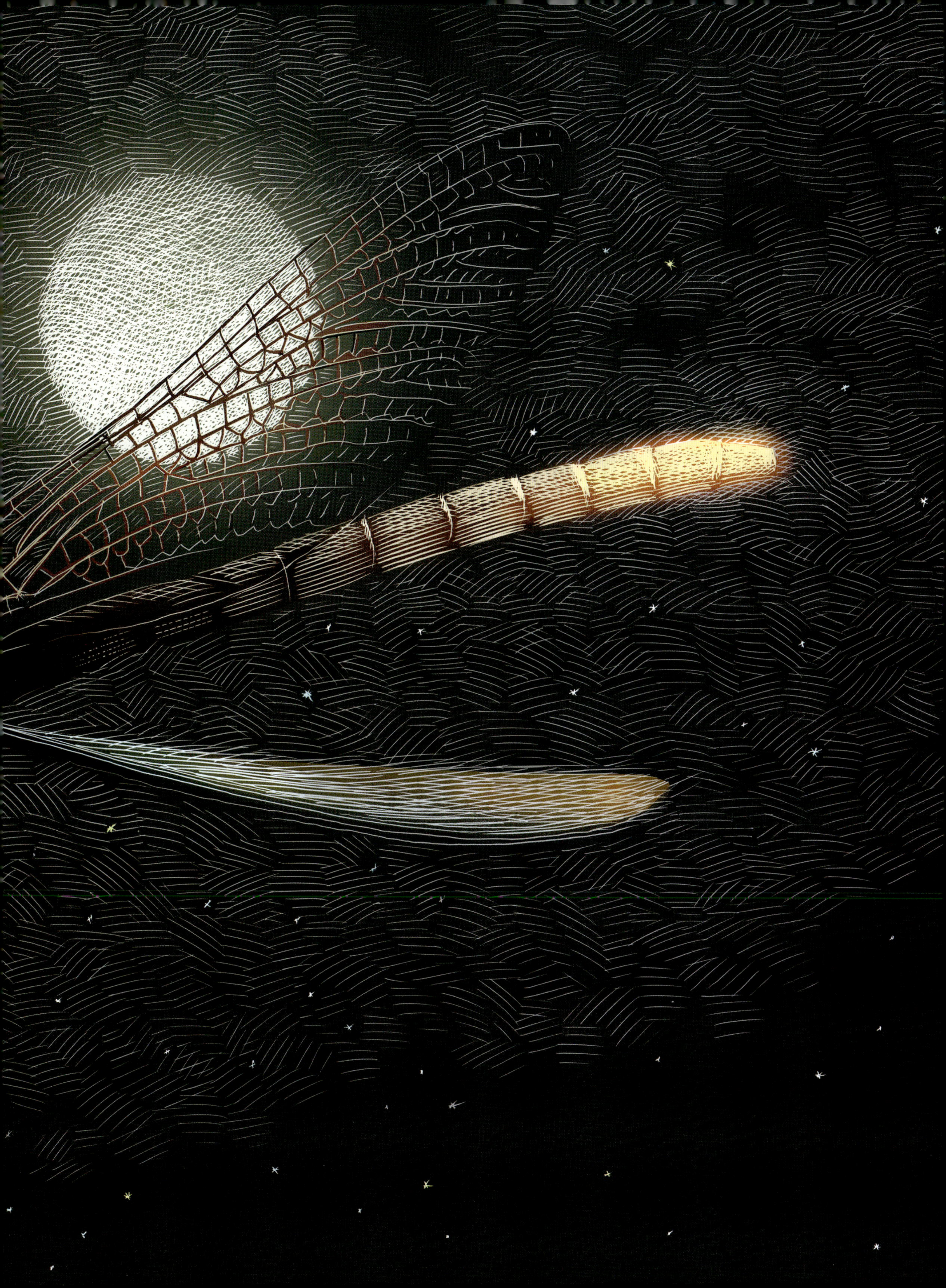

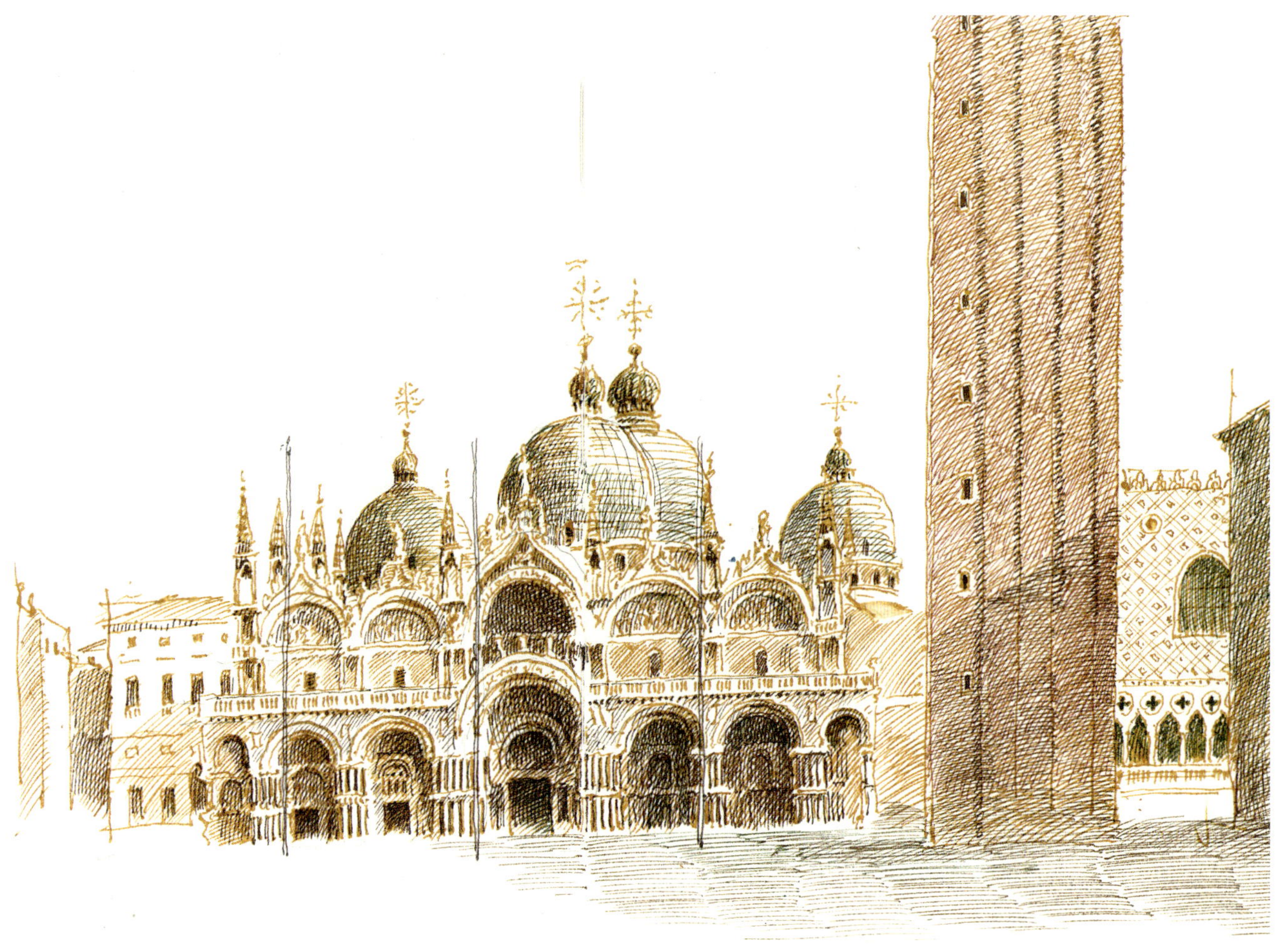

Sketchbook page from one of Scott's trips to Venice.

I have seen many productions of *The Merchant of Venice* — Christina designed the Stratford Festival's 1984 production directed by Mark Lamos with John Neville as Shylock, Domini Blythe as Portia and Seana McKenna as Jessica — and I have visited this spooky and fascinating city several times. But my first opportunity to think about a poster only came in 2017, for a production at The Shakespeare Theatre of New Jersey. I started with some sketches of Shylock but Artistic Director Bonnie Monte felt that he is not the centre of the play. She asked for an image about wealth and power. Christina pushed that idea a half-step farther, suggesting the words splendour and loss.

The poster is a split-screen image. San Giorgio Maggiore is sparkling on the horizon. Beneath that, on the bottom of the sea, is a wreck of coins and caskets — Antonio's ships are thought to have been lost at sea. This is also a reference to Shylock's loss when his daughter elopes with a Christian and steals from him ("My ducats…").

It's night — I wanted a reference to Lorenzo and Jessica's scene at Belmont in Act v, Scene i, which begins "How sweet the moonlight sleeps upon this bank!" This is the speech that inspired Ralph Vaughan Williams' beautiful *Serenade to Music*, composed in 1938. I noticed only recently how well splendour and loss are reflected in this famous text — in the middle of extolling the glory of the music of the spheres, Lorenzo brings us back to earth with "But whilst this muddy vesture of decay doth grossly close it in, we cannot hear it."

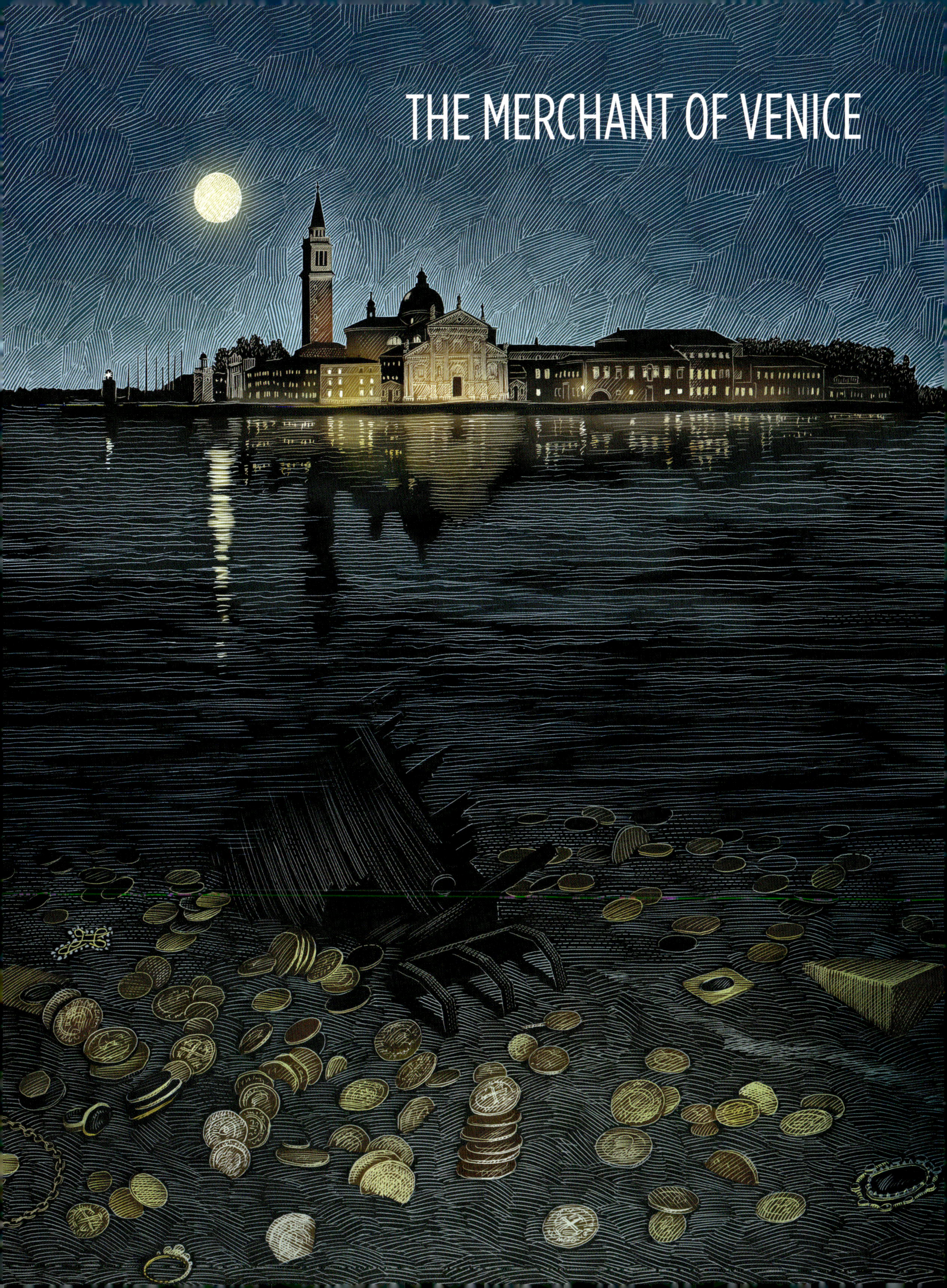
THE MERCHANT OF VENICE

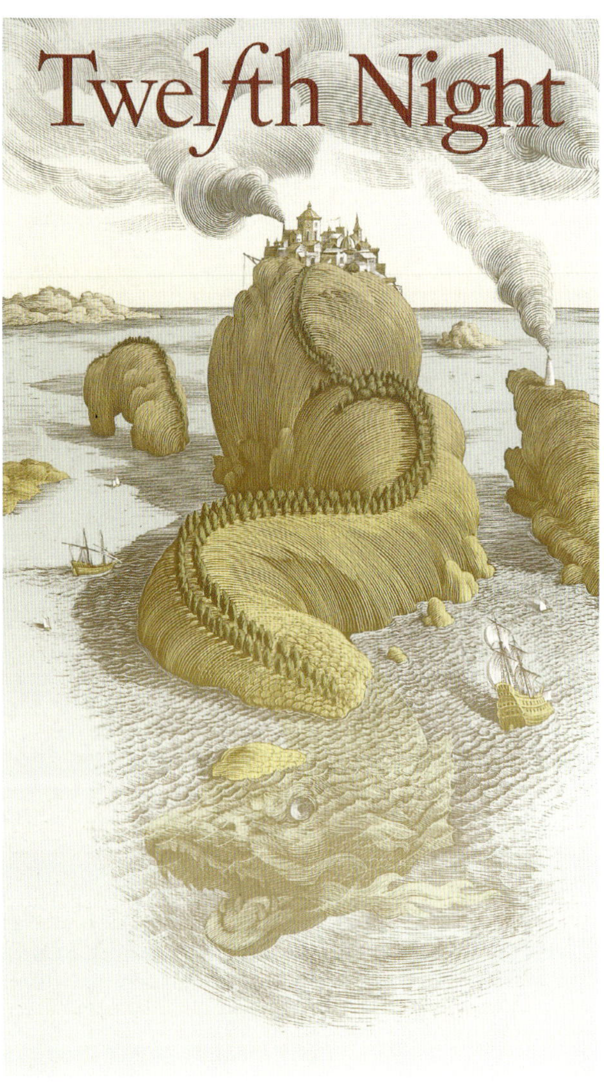

Shakespeare's *Twelfth Night* is often played as youthful comedy, but the best productions I have seen allow the bittersweet side of the story to emerge. For The Acting Company's 1993 production, Director Bartlett Sher asked for an image that would be playful and inviting — but at the same time mysterious and a little scary. As the play begins, Viola is shipwrecked on the coast of Illyria and believes her twin brother, Sebastian, has drowned. Mr. Sher had decided on a 17th-century setting for his production, so I used the engravings of Jacques Callot (1592–1635) as inspiration — in particular his fabulously dramatic seascapes.

The organic shapes of Callot's islands led to the idea of the sea monster. They made me think of those blurry photographs purporting to show the Loch Ness Monster, its body snaking in and out of the water. The idea of stepping onto what you think is dry land — but proves to be something else when seen from a different perspective — seemed to fit Mr. Sher's vision. This poster won a silver medal in the Society of Illustrators 1995 Annual Exhibition in New York — the first time I had entered that prestigious competition.

The play came up again in 2009. The Pearl Theatre Company wanted an image that would suggest "passion run amok" through the play's lovelorn characters. The brochure copy observed, "they love the people they can't have and ignore the people they can." Who says Shakespeare isn't modern?

I needed a fresh approach, and Christina's perspective as a costume designer came to my rescue. Two identical Elizabethan doublets on wardrobe stands represent the twins — one male, the other a bit smaller to fit a woman. And these inanimate objects have an irresistible attraction to each other — they lean towards each other and their sleeves intertwine, as if there were arms inside.

The costume details are borrowed from a famous portrait miniature in the Victoria and Albert Museum — Richard Sackville, 3rd Earl of Dorset, painted by Isaac Oliver in 1616.

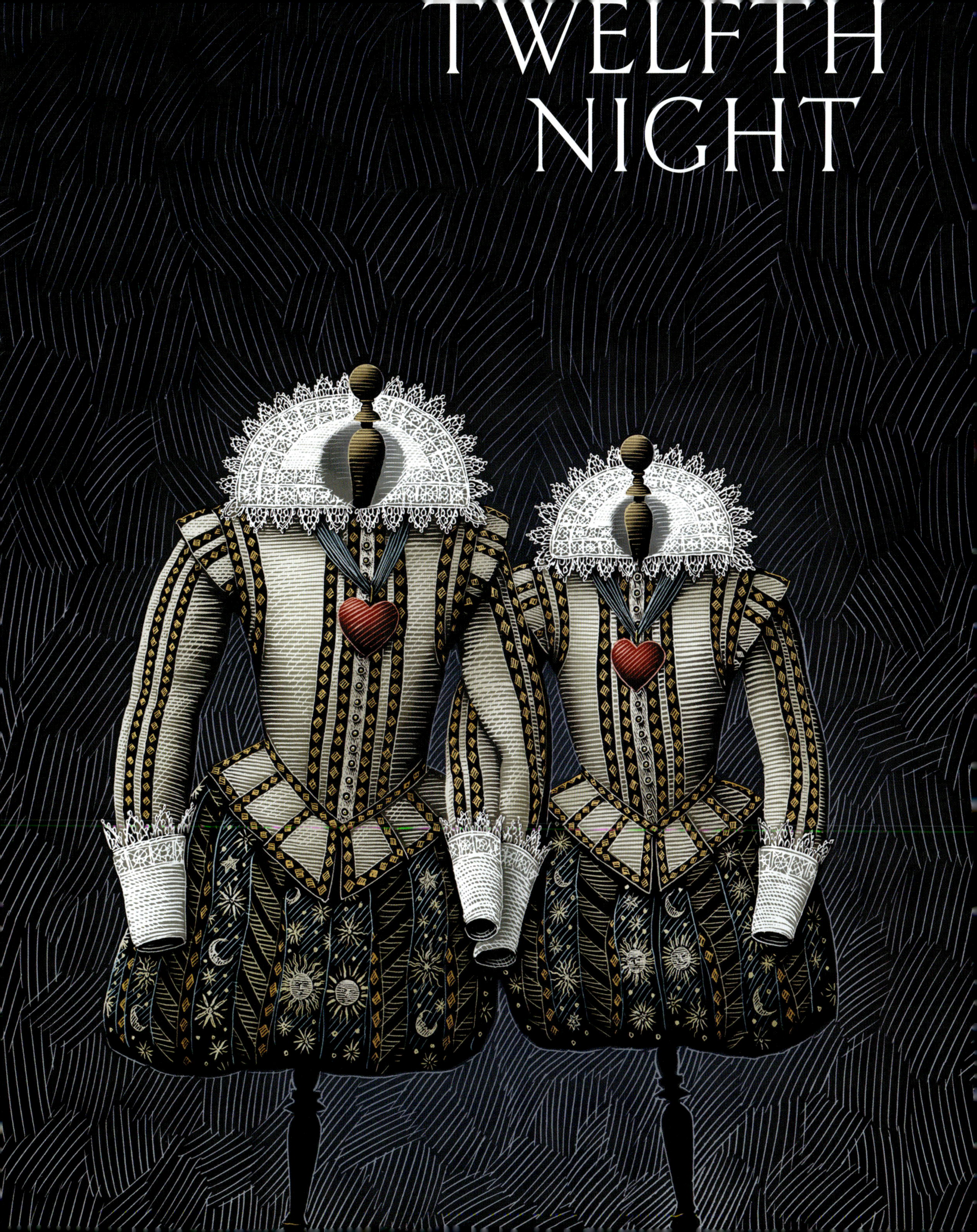
TWELFTH
NIGHT

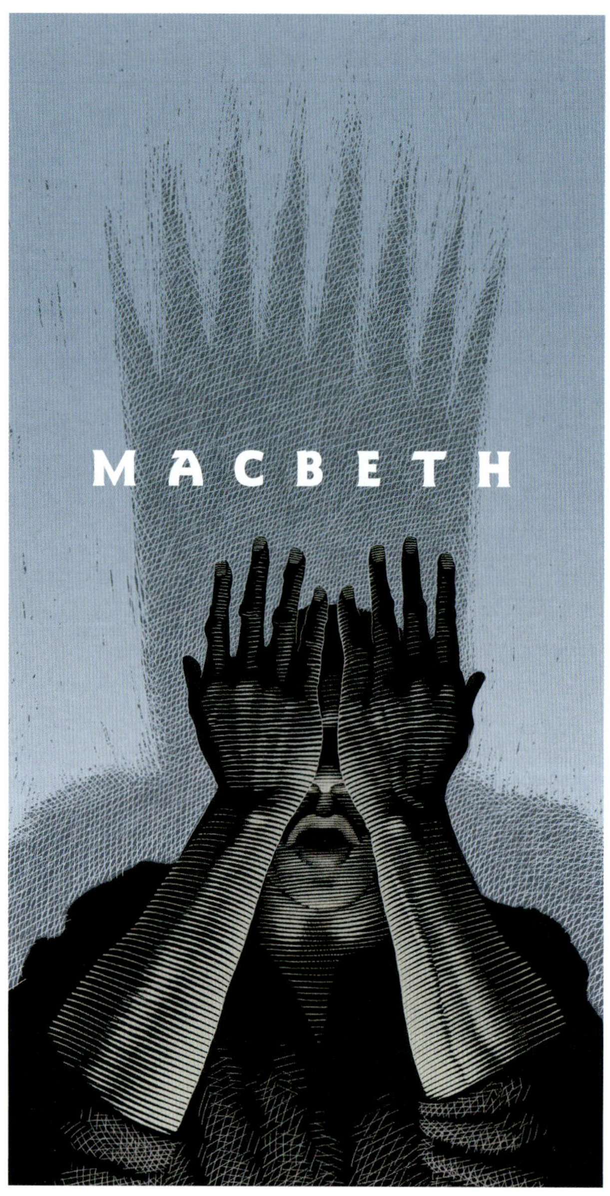

Shakespeare's *Julius Caesar* is shockingly violent — one reason that it still resonates after more than four centuries. Brutus and Cassius express concern that they don't want to be seen as "butchers," but in his famous funeral oration Marc Antony points out the contrast between their words and their actions. Many posters for the play use the noble visage of the title character, familiar through ancient statuary. For The Acting Company's 2010 poster, Christina suggested taking the portrait idea a surreal step further. The scratchboard lines render the cool, classical elegance of marble, but the focal point is a visceral wound in his neck and chest. The blood makes for a chilling, dramatic contrast with the marble — but as the saying goes, you can't get blood from a stone.

"The Scottish Play" was written to please the Scottish King James, who had succeeded to the English throne when Elizabeth died in 1603. James considered himself an expert on the occult and had even written a book called *Daemonologie*.

Isaac Asimov points out in his *Guide to Shakespeare* that the witches in the play are not Shakespeare's invention — they were already associated with the early Scottish king Macbeth in the source material for the story. Asimov contends that their name, "the weird sisters," shows that they are more than mere witches. The word "weird" comes from the Anglo-Saxon word "wyrd," meaning "fate." So the weird sisters are actually the Norns — in Nordic mythology the three sisters representing past, present and future, who were the goddesses of destiny.

In their first encounter in Act I, the First Witch hails Macbeth as Thane of Glamis (the past). The Second hails him as Thane of Cawdor (the present — Macbeth has just been given this second title by King Duncan — although he does not yet know it). The Third Witch speaks of what is to come: "All hail, Macbeth, that shalt be King hereafter!"

And this is a self-fulfilling prophecy. Once the idea of kingship is planted, dark thoughts start reverberating inside Macbeth's head. His frightening line in Act III — "O, full of scorpions is my mind, dear wife!" — inspired this poster image. Macbeth's gesture of horror — hands covering his eyes — conveys the nightmares unfolding in his mind. The light source from below makes the scene appropriately eerie (a more familiar meaning of weird) and creates the crown-like shadow of his fingers above his head. This suggests that the apparitions conjured by the witches are a figment of Macbeth's imagination.

The title role in this production at Great Lakes Theater Festival in 2000 was played by Derrick Lee Weeden, and Director James Bundy requested an African-American face on the poster. My brother-in-law Tom Loveless in Lansing, Michigan, modelled for the illustration.

JULIUS CAESAR

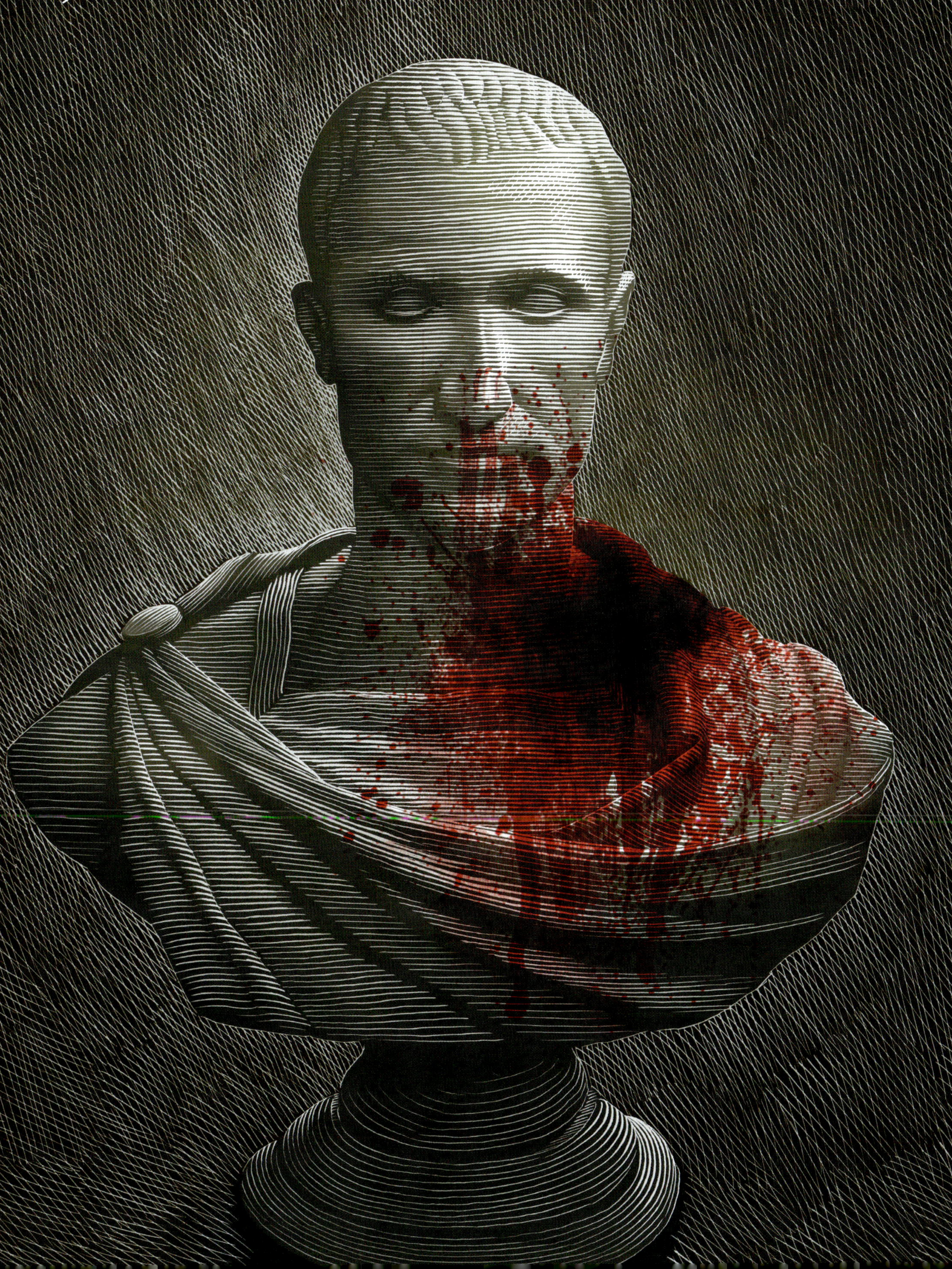

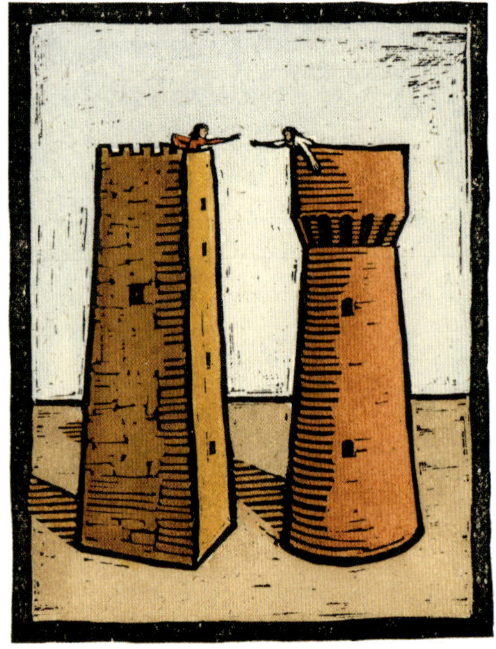

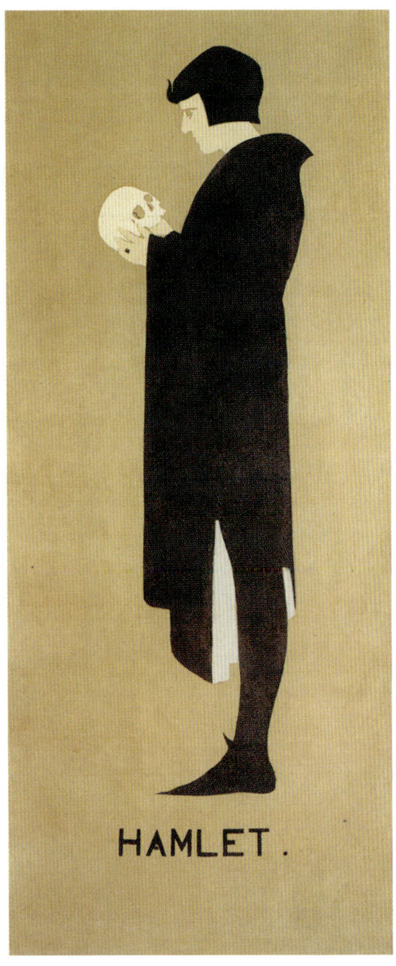

1894 poster for Edward Gordon Craig as Hamlet, by J. & W. Beggarstaff — the pseudonym of William Nicholson and James Pryde.

David Davalos' witty play is a modern spin on *Hamlet* and assumes a basic familiarity with Shakespeare — not unlike Tom Stoppard's *Rosencrantz and Guildernstern Are Dead. Wittenberg* is a sort of prequel — Hamlet is a senior at Wittenberg University and can't make up his mind about declaring a major. He studies theology with Martin Luther and philosophy with Doctor Faustus, and he's the star of the varsity tennis team!

In one scene, Faustus devises a word association game — he will say a word and asks Hamlet to reply with the first thought that come into his head. The exchange sounds like this: "... Frailty/Woman... Queen/Denmark... Prison/ Freedom..." — the words are fired back and forth like a tennis ball over the net. Then in Act II there's a scene with an actual tennis game between Hamlet and Laertes.

Wittenberg was on The Shakespeare Theatre of New Jersey's 2014 playbill. (It was my second poster image for the play — the first was for The Pearl Theatre Company in New York.) A skull seemed a prerequisite; but a skull wearing a mortarboard with a tennis ball stuck in the eye socket added just the right note of sophormoric humour and irreverent Pop Art sensibility.

I had sketched in a block of 16th-century text in the background — theatre is all about words, and I love including them as part of an illustration. Much debate went into the choice of text. I had initially thought about using a page from a Gutenberg Bible (the Doctor Faustus side of Hamlet's education is represented by the skull and mortarboard; I thought that biblical text might reinforce Martin Luther's curriculum, for balance).

In the end we went back to *Hamlet*. We considered the scene were Claudius persuades Hamlet not to return to Wittenberg. We tried "The play's the thing wherein I'll catch the conscience of the king." We settled on Hamlet's "There are more things in heaven and earth, Horatio, Than are dreamt of in your philosophy" — perhaps as close as the play comes to black comedy.

For *Romeo and Juliet* in the Stratford Festival's 1992 season series of "chapbook" illustrations, a pair of medieval towers symbolizes the "two households, both alike in dignity" that separate the young lovers. Their plans and dreams almost work out — but remain, tragically, just out of reach. Christina and I visited Umbria in September, 1991, treating our holiday as a retreat to brainstorm ideas for this series of illustrations. I recall sitting in an ancient stone palazzo one evening, listening to a wonderful concert of Monteverdi madrigals, when this concept materialized in my head.

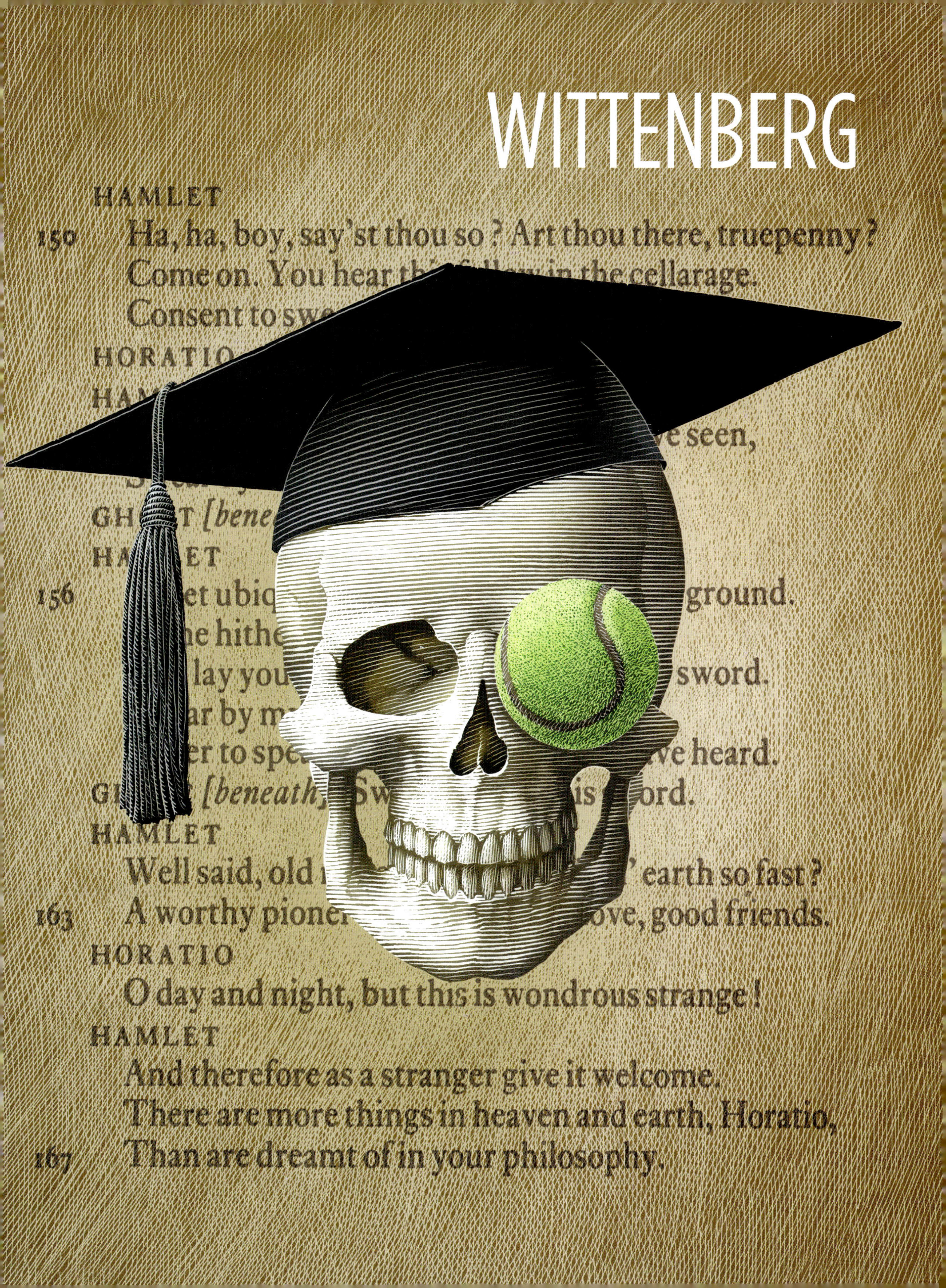

WITTENBERG

HAMLET

150 Ha, ha, boy, say'st thou so? Art thou there, truepenny?
Come on. You hear th fellow in the cellarage.
Consent to swe

HORATIO

HAM

ve seen,

GH T [bene

HA ET

156 et ubiq ground.
e hithe
lay you sword.
ar by m
er to spe ve heard.

G [beneath] Sw is ord.

HAMLET

Well said, old ' earth so fast?
163 A worthy pioner ove, good friends.

HORATIO

O day and night, but this is wondrous strange!

HAMLET

And therefore as a stranger give it welcome.
There are more things in heaven and earth, Horatio,
167 Than are dreamt of in your philosophy.

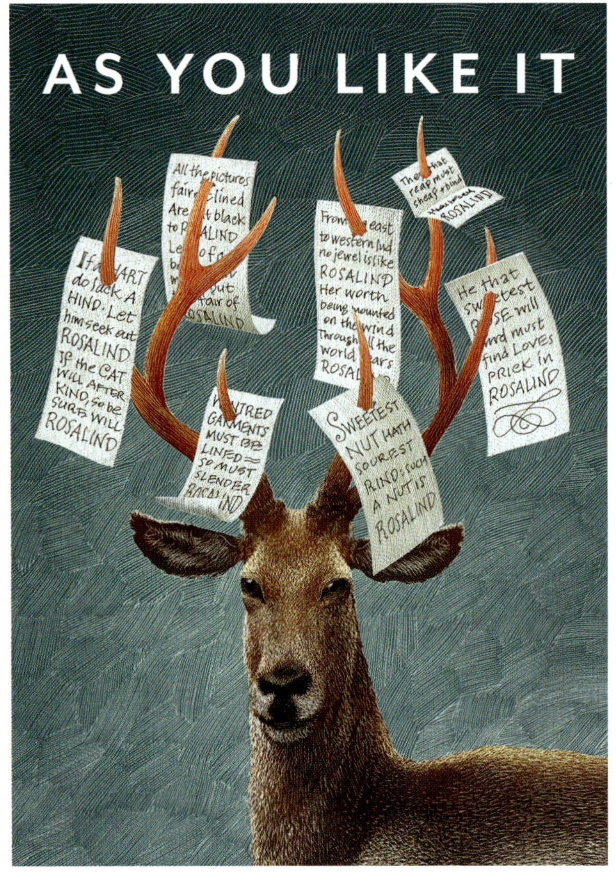

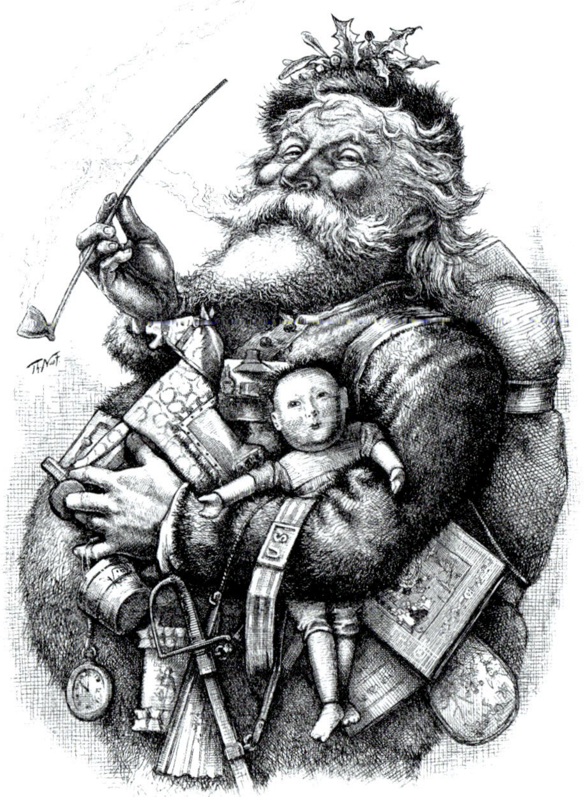

The Merry Wives of Windsor features one of Shakespeare's iconic characters, Sir John Falstaff, the fat knight first introduced in *King Henry IV Part One* and *Part Two*. Here, Falstaff fancies himself a Casanova, pursuing Mistress Ford and Mistress Page — two married women — simultaneously. The two title characters are (more or less) happily married and have zero romantic interest in Falstaff. When they receive his identical, unwanted love letters, they join forces to teach him a lesson through a series of comic revenge schemes.

The play has no particular connection to the holiday season, but The Shakespeare Theatre of New Jersey programmed it in December 2015, and the poster assignment came with a request to give the image a Christmas theme.

There is already a fat knight associated with the holiday season — Santa Claus. So my Falstaff is an adaption of Thomas Nast's famous engraving, published in *Harper's Weekly* in 1881, which helped establish our traditional image of Saint Nicholas. The jovial twinkle in his eye makes me think of Dickens' Ghost of Christmas Present. I replaced the toys, backpack and clay pipe with "a cup of sack" and the love letters. The final scene of the play takes place at midnight in Windsor Forest where Falstaff has been tricked into dressing as Herne the Hunter, a character from folklore portrayed with antlers on his head — so that was the final touch to connect the image to the play.

Studying Nast's engraving carefully, I was surprised (when you take the toys away) that the figure is not very carefully observed — his left arm is too small and the right hand holding the pipe is in a completely impossible place anatomically. So I worked with a model to recreate the pose. Nast's coat looks a little threadbare and scratchy so I borrowed a 17th-century doublet (size 52) from the Stratford Festival costume warehouse. But Nast's expression is perfect, and I followed the prototype as faithfully as I could so that our Falstaff would look familiar — like an old friend.

Deer populate a number of Shakespeare's comedies. They are mentioned half a dozen times in the text of *As You Like It*, including Jacques' lament for a wounded deer in the Forest of Arden. Deer antlers look a lot like tree branches, which led to this surreal connection with the love-sick Orlando's poems to Rosalind, with which he litters the forest, for a 2019 poster for Shakespeare New Jersey.

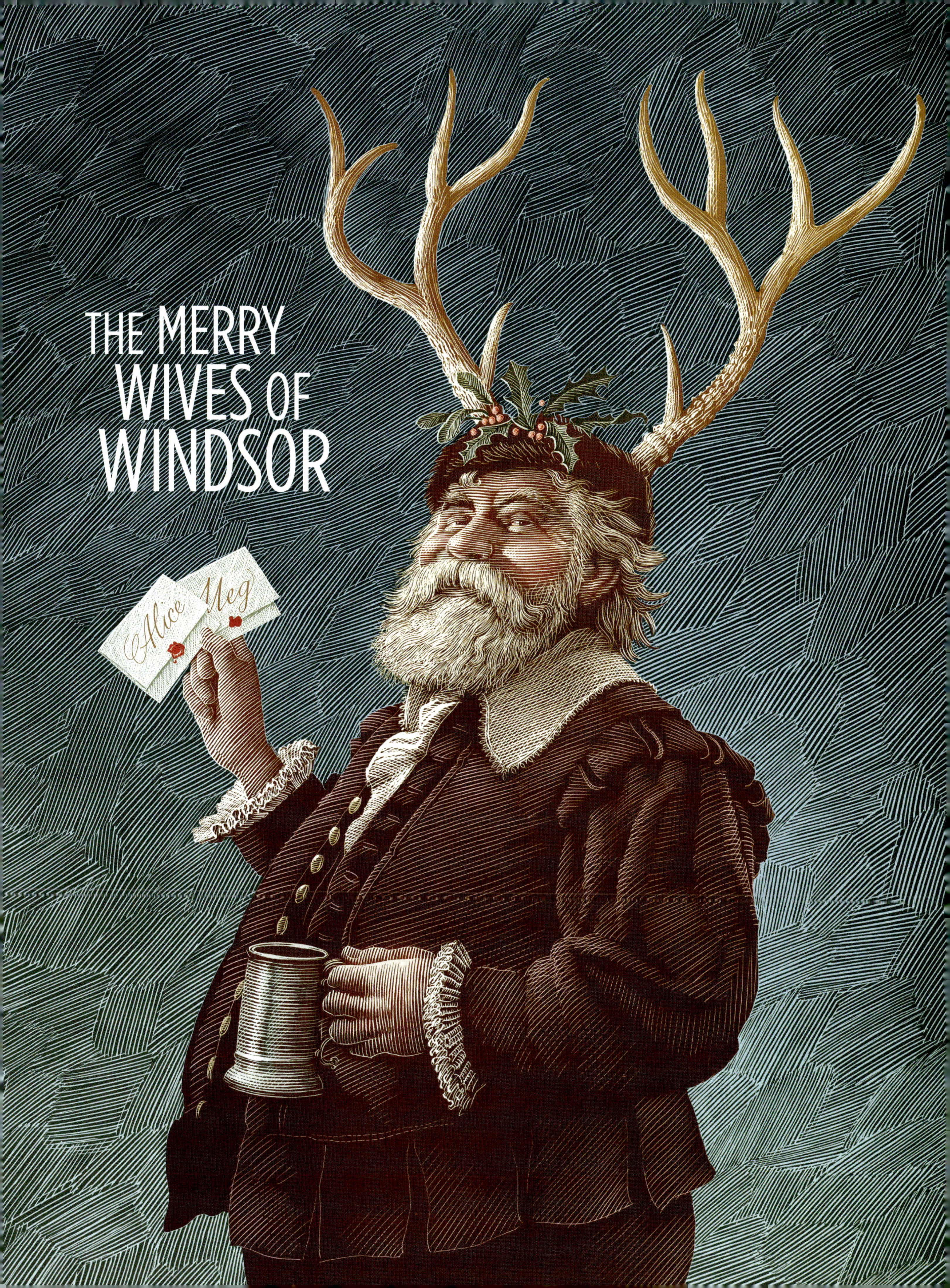
THE MERRY
WIVES OF
WINDSOR
Alice
Meg

Groundling Theatre Company's inaugural production in 2016 was *The Winter's Tale*, directed by Graham Abbey with a superlative cast led by Tom McCamus, Michelle Giroux, Lucy Peacock and Brent Carver.

Like *Pericles* and *Cymbeline*, *The Winter's Tale* is a story of the turning wheel of fortune. Leontes, King of Sicily, inexplicably believes that his pregnant wife Hermione has been unfaithful with his best friend Polixenes, King of Bavaria. His jealous rage leads to the loss of everything important in his life — his wife, his newborn daughter, his young son, his loyal friends and courtiers. Sixteen years later, the remorseful Leontes is overwhelmed when (almost) everything lost is restored to him. In the extraordinary final scene of reconciliation and forgiveness, Paulina tells Leontes, "It is required you do awake your faith," as she reveals a statue of the queen that magically comes back to life.

That statue scene is a tall order for any director to stage. In this production it was one of those brilliant, heartstopping moments that you can't believe you've just had the good fortune to witness. The show won the Dora Award for best production of the year, and Robert Cushman, theatre critic for the *National Post*, who has seen a lot more Shakespeare than I, called it "the best Shakespeare I've seen in Toronto."

I used the statue as my poster image — Michelle Giroux, who played Hermione in the production, posed in my studio for the illustration, and I coloured the engraving lines to look like marble. Thorny, blackened branches grow up around the her, gradually turning green with tiny leaves and finally bursting into blossom — something dead coming back to life.

The illustration was juried into New York Society of Illustrators 2016 Annual Exhibition, and then — wonderful surprise! — it was chosen as the front cover image for the catalogue of the show, *Illustrators 58*.

I revisited the play in 2018 for The Shakespeare Theatre of New Jersey. Bonnie Monte scheduled it as the "winter" production in December and requested an image with a seasonal feel. The bear and the baby scene in Act III is almost impossible to stage but has interesting possibilities for illustration. The play certainly has fairy-tale aspects (Leontes is a bear in human form); the hourglass signifies the passage of time.

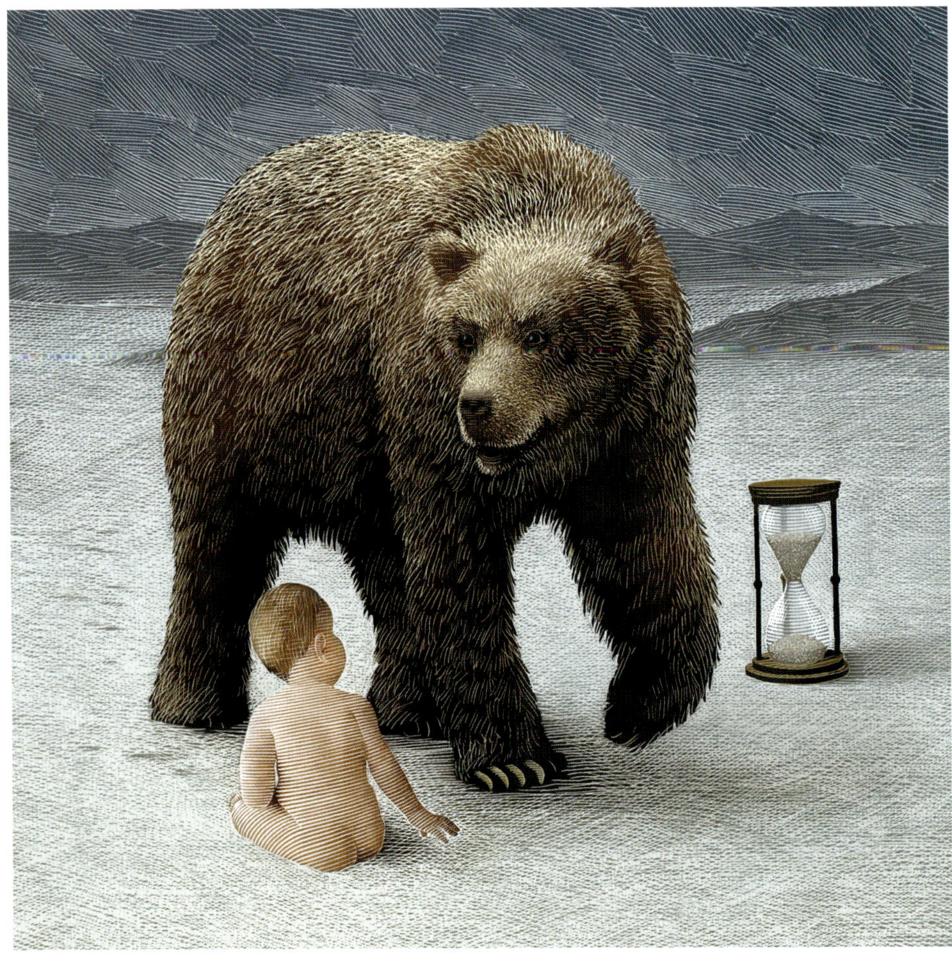

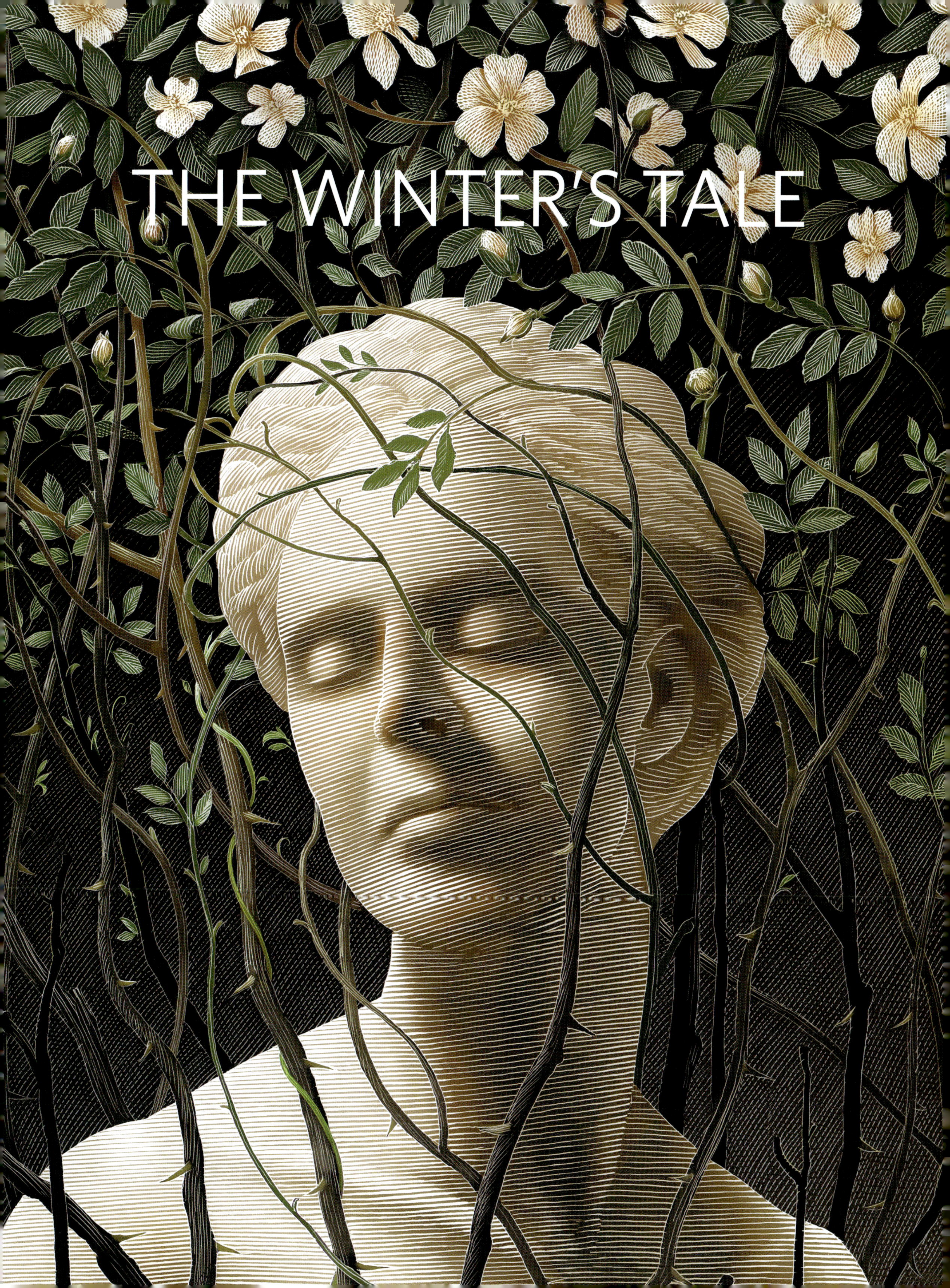
THE WINTER'S TALE

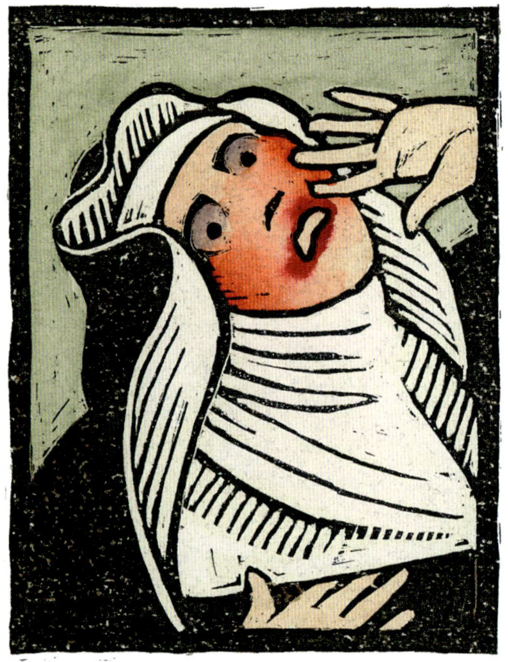

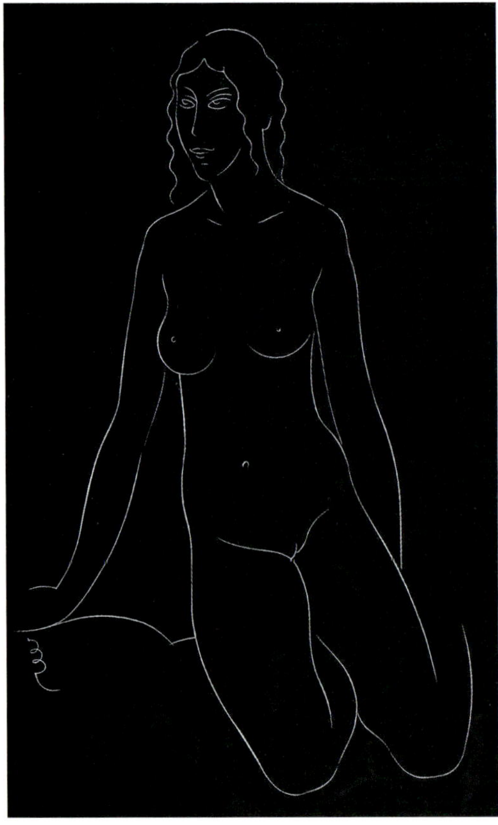

A wood engraving from Eric Gill's *25 Nudes*, printed by Hague & Gill Ltd., High Wycombe, 1938.

Measure for Measure is classified as one of Shakespeare's comedies, but it's a painful story of sexual harassment and abuse that rivals the Harvey Weinstein scandal. In 2017, Groundling Theatre Company in Toronto produced this "problem play" that anticipates the #MeToo campaign by 400 years.

Angelo holds power as the head of state in Vienna, although the office is delegated to him only temporarily. He is something of a puritan — he establishes moralistic vice laws and arrests a young man named Claudio for getting his girlfriend pregnant. To make an example of him, Angelo sentences him to death for fornication. Claudio's sister Isabella, about to become a nun, pleads with Angelo for mercy. Angelo is aroused by Isabella and proposes that if she will have sex with him, he will free Claudio. Isabella is horrified — she loves her brother more than anything in the world, but she has devoted herself to purity. When Isabella protests that she will denounce his lascivious proposition in public, Angelo points out that, given his reputation and position, nobody will believe her.

The premise for the image is that the play is about women's control over their own bodies and their own sexuality. The image is strong, positive and powerful — it says "respect" and "ownership" and "protective" and "value." Graham Abbey, the director, literally gasped when I first showed the concept sketch — exactly the reaction I was hoping for because that's the same response the play should provoke.

Christina came up with this concept, and it's one of her best. She also suggested that a simple, sensual line drawing would be more successful than a fully rendered figure because it would be more abstract. I took inspiration from the sensual woodcuts of British artist Eric Gill (1882–1940), imitating the elegant line quality of his woodcuts in scratchboard. I have a first edition copy of Gill's *25 Nudes*, published in 1938, which I bought on eBay — only to discover from an inscription on the title page that this copy was pre-owned by the American painter Robert Motherwell (signed and dated London, 1939). Wonderful inspiration. (Gill created highly imaginative woodcut illustrations for many of Shakespeare's plays; some of his erotic ones appear in an edition of *All the Love Poems of Shakespeare*.)

I illustrated the season brochure for the Stratford Festival's 1992 season using scratchboard to mimic the look of bold, primitive woodcuts used in early 19th-century chapbooks and "penny dreadfuls." I'm not including a lot of old work here but *Measure* was on the playbill and I still like this concept. Lipstick and heavy makeup smeared on a face associated with chastity seemed a powerful metaphor for the play's themes of sexual immorality.

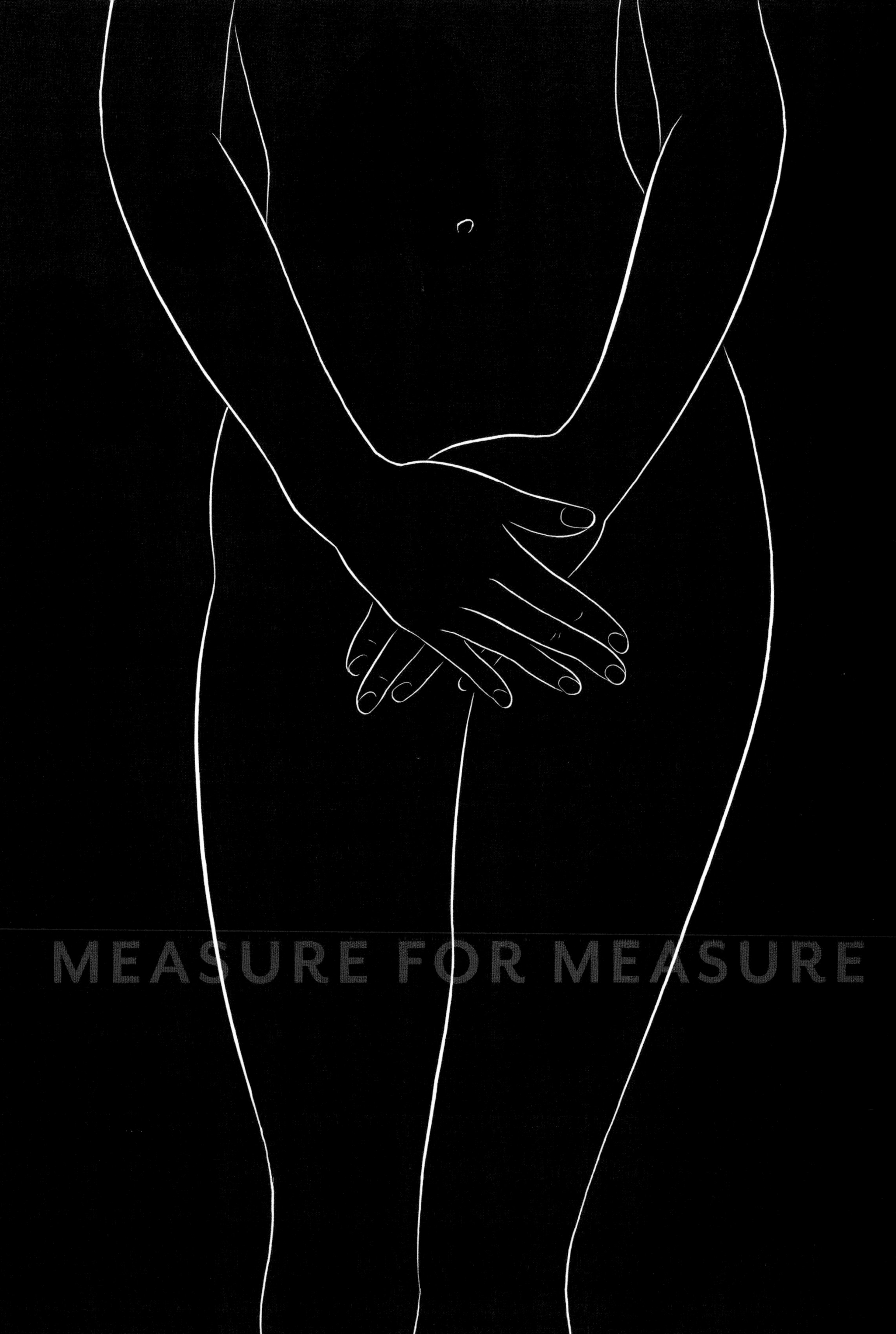

MEASURE FOR MEASURE

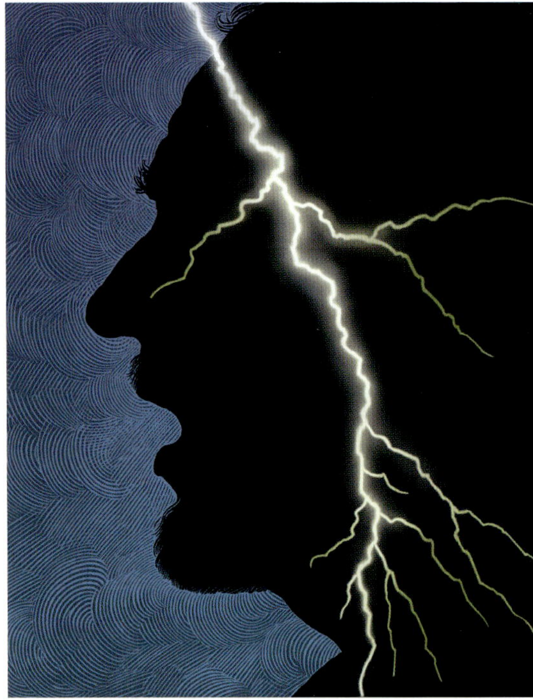

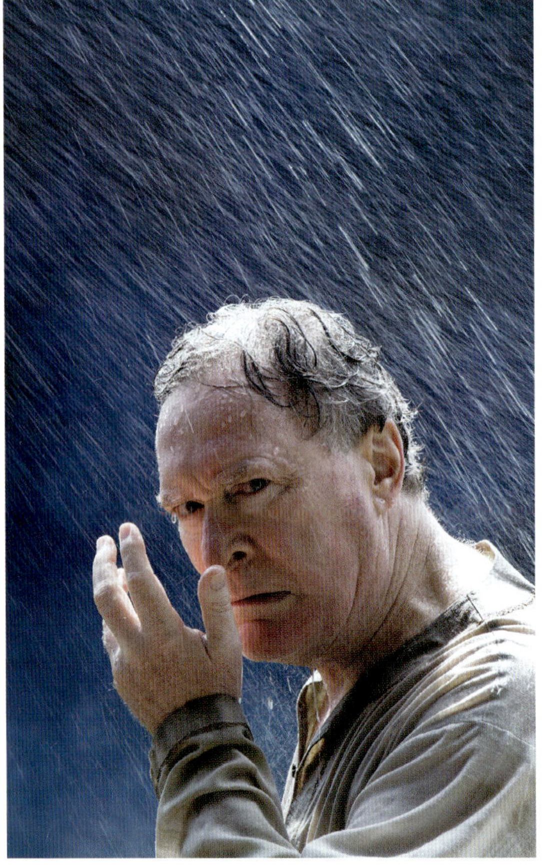

I was thrilled to be included (with 14 posters!) in *Presenting Shakespeare: 1100 Posters from Around the World*, a wonderful book by Mirko Ilić and Steven Heller, published in 2015. The book is organized by play — the *King Lear* chapter, for example, features 60 posters so the reader can compare how different artists have approached this iconic masterpiece. There's a huge variety of styles, but I noticed that almost all the posters in the *Lear* chapter are variations on a portrait of an old man with a beard (and sometimes a crown). My posters for Denver Center Theatre Company in 2007 and Theatre Calgary in 2015, a David Cooper photo of Benedict Campbell in a rainstorm, both included in *Presenting Shakespeare*, answer to this description.

So I was particularly pleased to break that mould with a poster for Groundling Theatre Company's 2018 production of *Lear* in Toronto, featuring Seana McKenna in the title role. Seana had played a number of male characters at Stratford — Richard III and Jacques, and she was about to take on Julius Caesar. But changing the story of *King Lear* from a paternal relationship with royal daughters to a maternal one is a more fundamental shift, and it was essential that the poster image convey that dynamic.

Graham Abbey talked about all the tropes of the play — gaining wisdom (too late) through the loss of everything else. He observed in a director's note in the house programme that Lear's outraged "I gave you all" takes on a new and deeper meaning when spoken by a mother to a child.

Christina nailed the concept in a tiny thumbnail sketch one evening over dinner. An overhead "eye of the storm" view of Seana, naked, curled womb-like into a fetal position, looking at us with a mad glint in her eye. Wind and leaves and flowers swirling around her. Graham liked the concept; more importantly, Seana liked the concept and posed for the illustration in my studio.

I was happy with the drawing but even with flying leaves it didn't quite have the sense of swirling wind I was hoping for — it felt a little static. So I used some coarse sandpaper to make rough concentric scratches on a fresh piece of board, and layered these over the illustration, in cyan, which amped up the energy level.

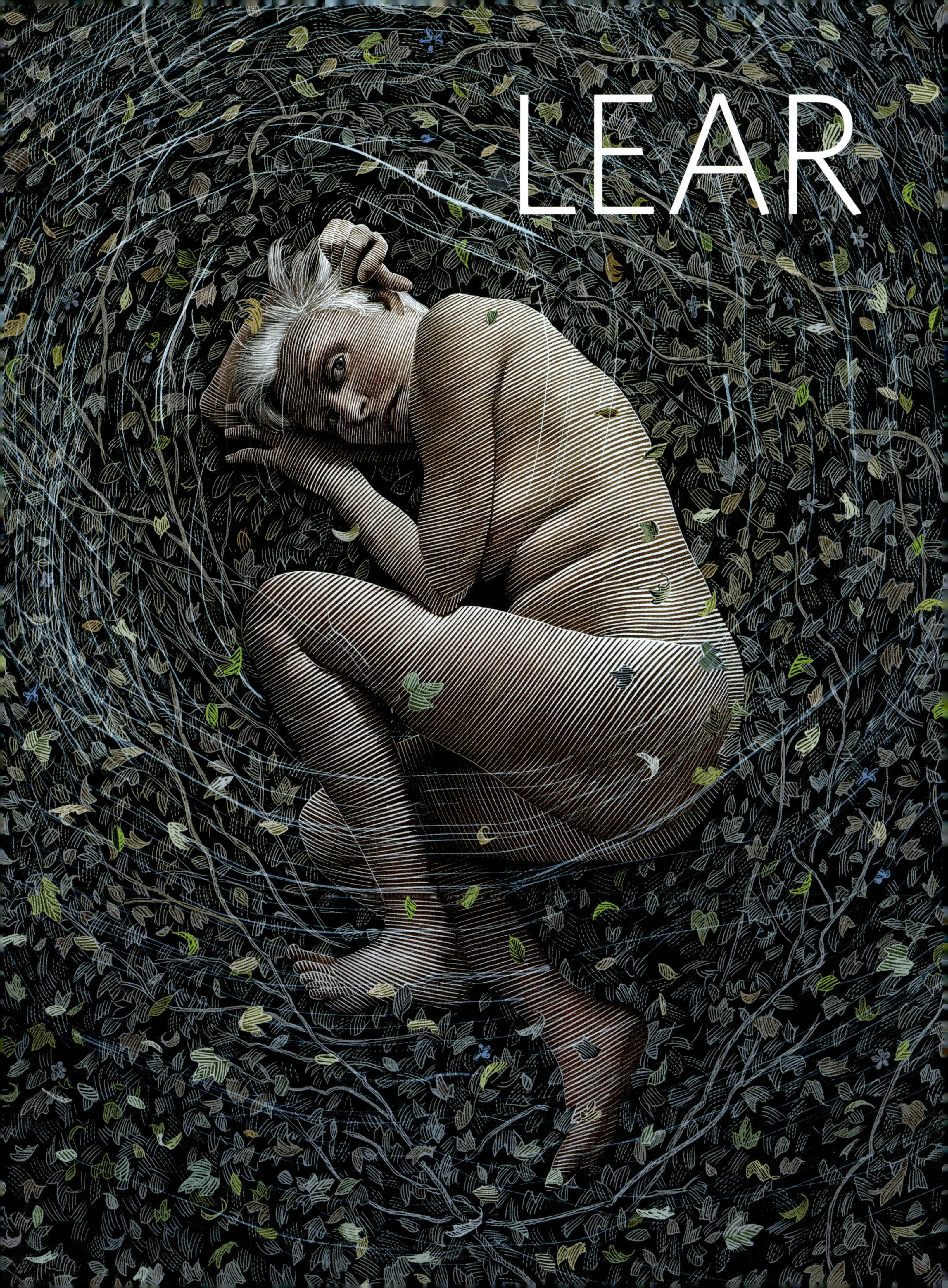
LEAR

Pericles, Prince of Tyre holds a special place in the canon for me. Stratford's production in 1974 starring Nicholas Pennell and Martha Henry was a seminal experience — it was the first time a Shakespeare play really came alive for me. It's a vivid adventure story opening with the title character solving a deadly riddle to win the hand of a beautiful princess (like Calàf in *Turandot*), only to discover that evil and danger are hidden in the solution. He flees for his life, beginning an epic tour of the ancient Mediterranean world. He meets the true love of his life; they produce a baby daughter, named Marina because she is born on a ship at sea. Then the wheel of fortune turns and Pericles loses wife and daughter through the perils of tempests, shipwrecks and the jealousy of false friends. Everything lost, he wanders, grieving, for many years.

A decade later, through a series of extraordinary coincidences, Pericles and Marina meet as strangers, each offering their story of loss as a kind of therapy for the other — and slowly piece together that they are father and daughter. I remember watching this scene in that 1974 Stratford production through floods of tears. I have gone out of my way to see other productions over the years, hoping that they will be as moving. (They rarely are.) One that came very close was Scott Wentworth's superb production at Stratford in 2015 with Evan Buliung and Deborah Hay, reimagined as if it was a Dickens novel and set in the Victorian period.

My poster, for a 2013 production at The Shakespeare Theatre of New Jersey, shows Pericles' ship caught in a storm at sea. The goddess Diana (identified by her crescent moon) is creating the tempest — but at the same time holding the ship in a protective embrace.

The inspiration for this concept came from an ancient stone carving on the side of a church in Rome. We were brainstorming for this project while on holiday, and Christina noticed this cryptic image on the exterior wall of a church. Piecing together the Latin, I realized that this is a "flood plaque" marking the high water level when the Tiber overflowed its banks in 1557. I marvel how the planets align sometimes — a picture of a hand, a ship and the sea, created half a century before *Pericles* was written, provided the perfect elements for our poster.

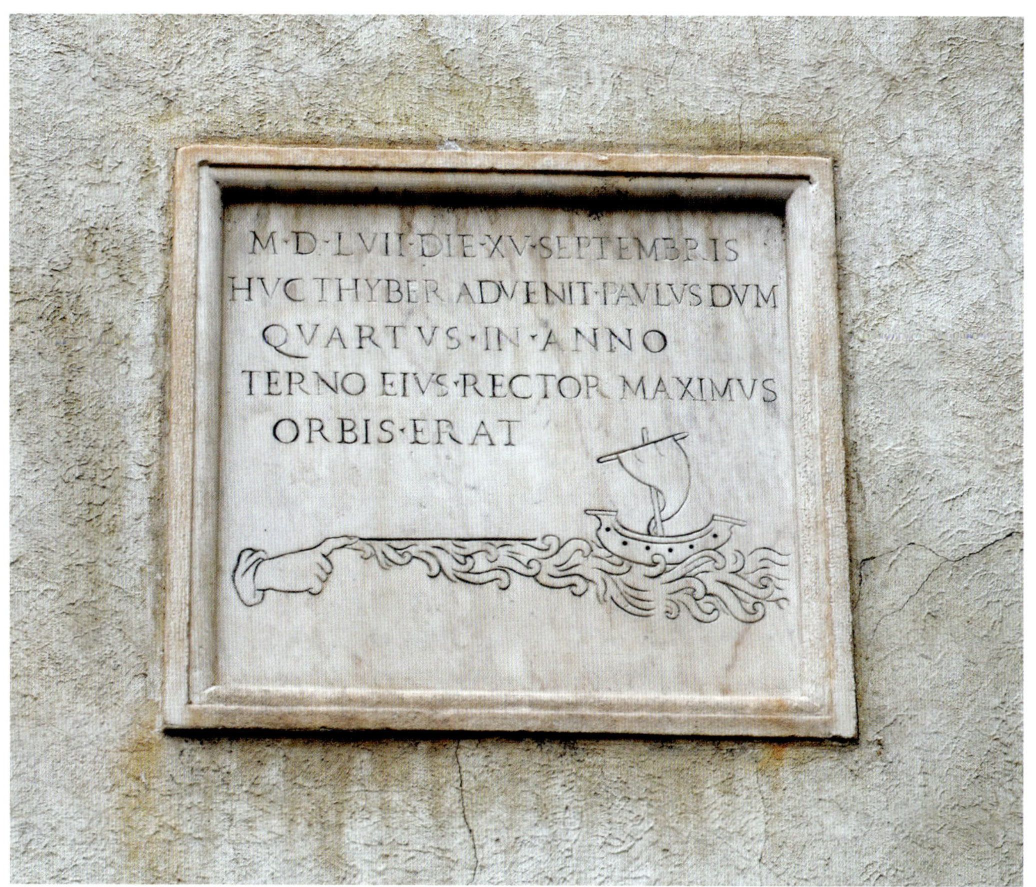

Flood plaque, dated 1557, on the facade of the Basilica Santa Maria Sopra Minerva in Rome. Minerva was the Roman goddess of wisdom, equivalent to Athena in the Greek pantheon. Bernini's famous *Elephant and Obelisk* statue stands in the piazza in front of this church.

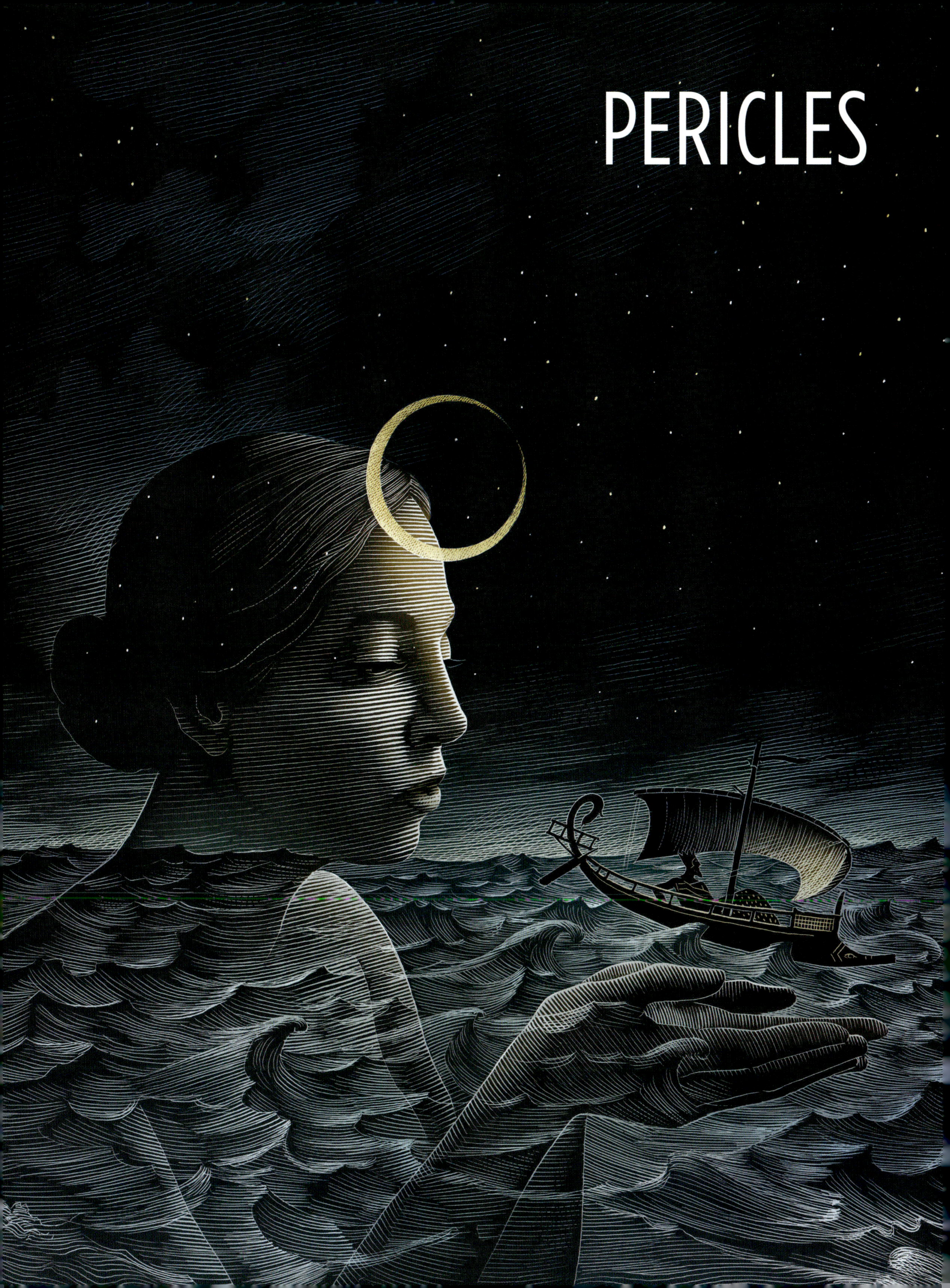
PERICLES

The shipwreck scene that opens *The Tempest* is impossible to adequately stage — but it's great fun to represent in a poster illustration.

Prospero uses his powerful magic to raise the storm that gives the play its name, in order to take revenge on enemies from his past. Twelve years earlier, Prospero was the Duke of Milan. His brother Antonio engineered a *coup d'état*, forcing Prospero to flee with his three-year-old daughter, Miranda. They ended up on a desert island where Miranda grew up ignorant of her father's history. But now Antonio is travelling on a ship near the island, and Prospero plans to settle old scores.

The storm scene is vivid and terrifying — Antonio, his travelling companions and all the sailors are certain that the ship is sinking and they are about to drown. In the audience, we think so too because our perspective is from on board the ship. But then our point of view shifts and we realize that Shakespeare has anticipated virtual reality by four centuries. The wreck is a highly convincing illusion — the ship and everyone on board are all safe.

When the assignment came along for a 2014 production of *The Tempest* at The Shakespeare Theatre of New Jersey, I did my own conjuring of this scene. Most of my pencil sketches were underwater visions, anticipating Ariel's "Full Fathom Five thy father lies" speech.

Prospero's Books, Peter Greenaway's complex 1991 film adaptation of the play starring John Gielgud as Prospero (and a very young Mark Rylance as Ferdinand), gave me the idea for the sinking ship. Greenaway's toy ship model was seen in a swimming pool with naked mermaids cavorting around it. I tried for a more realistic rendering of an early 17th-century vessel (the play was written around 1610–11). The sinking ship is wrapped in a delicate, glowing net, drawn on a separate piece of scratchboard and layered over the main image using the powerful magic that I have at my own fingertips — that of Photoshop — to suggest Prospero's powerful charm.

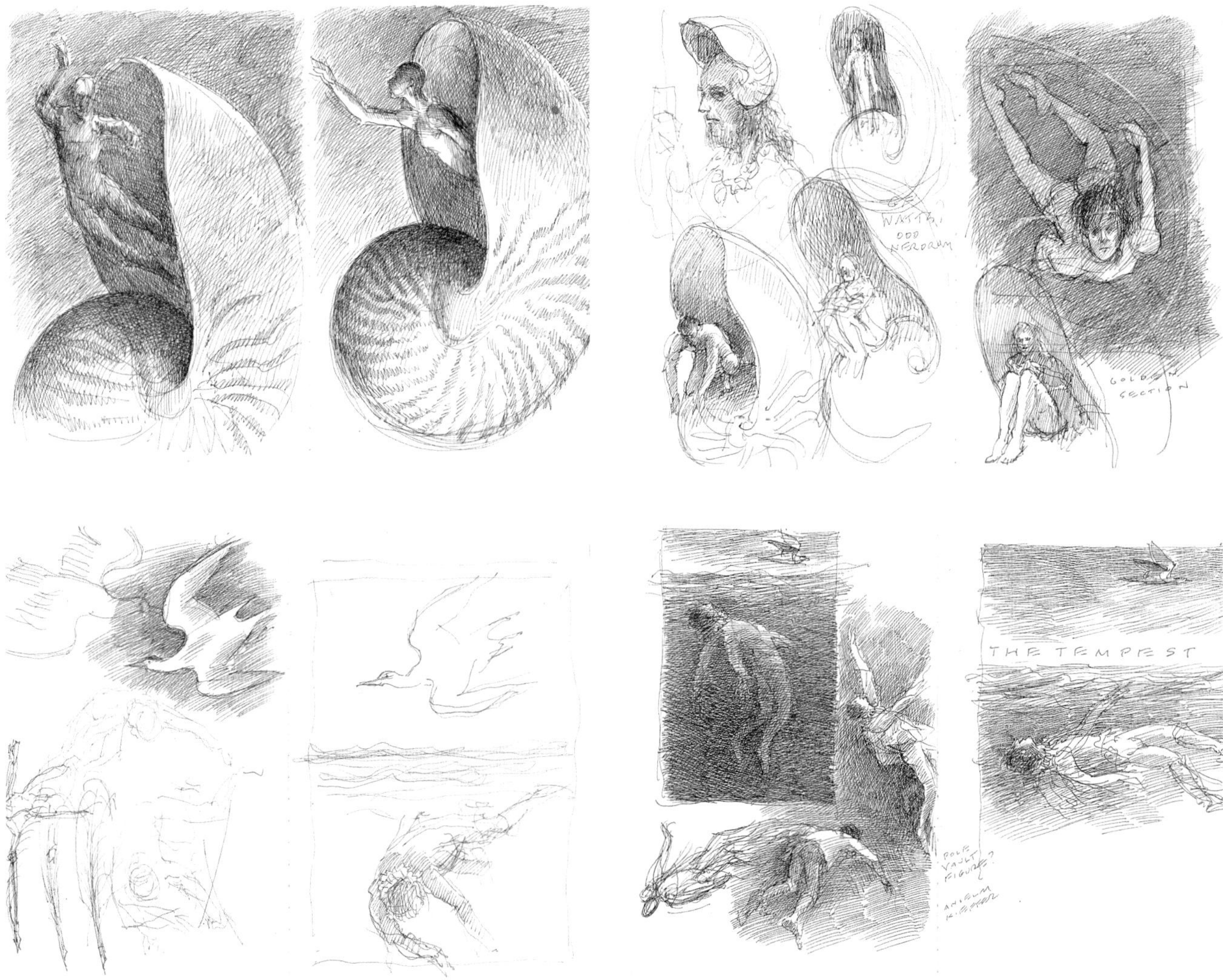

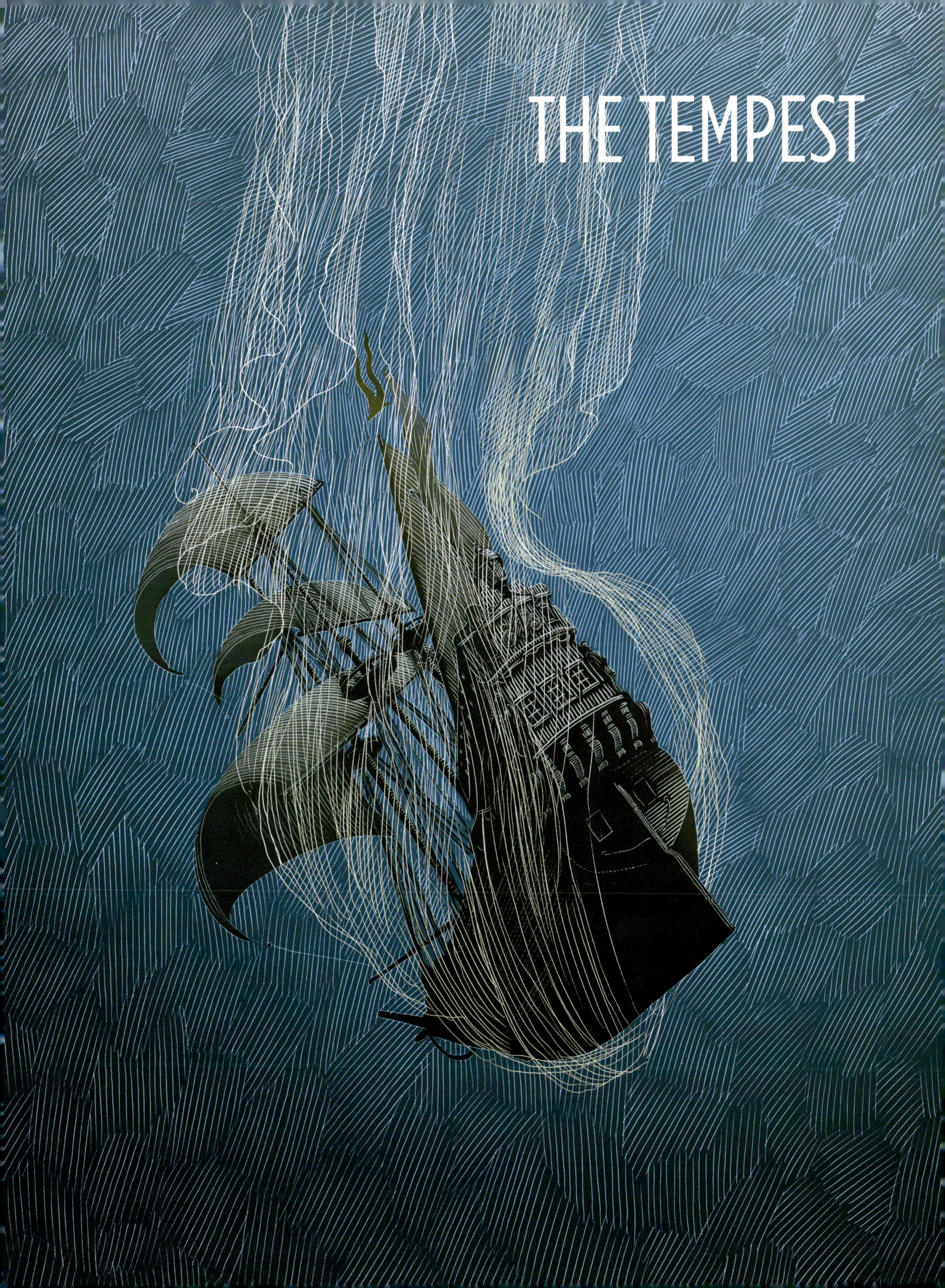
THE TEMPEST

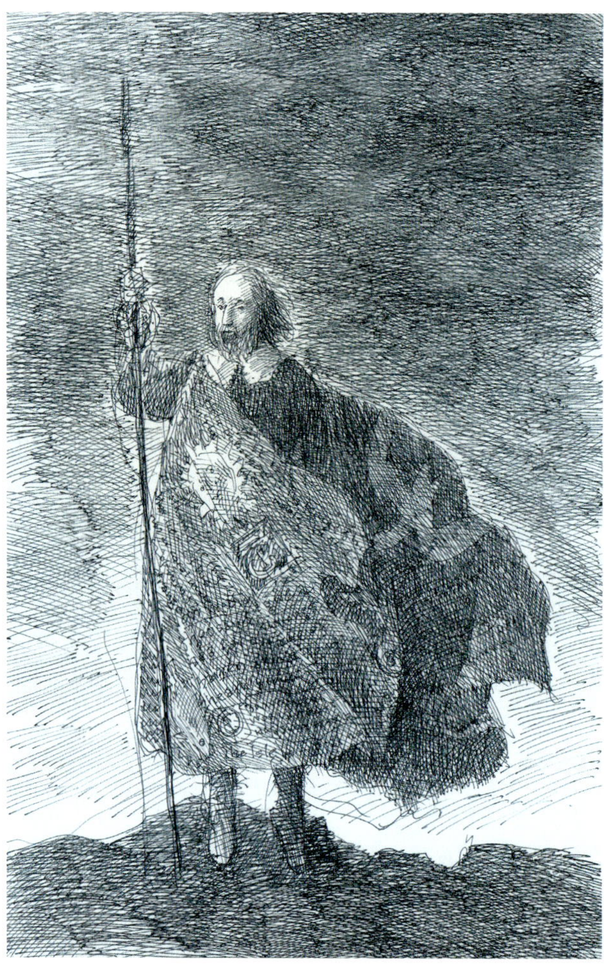

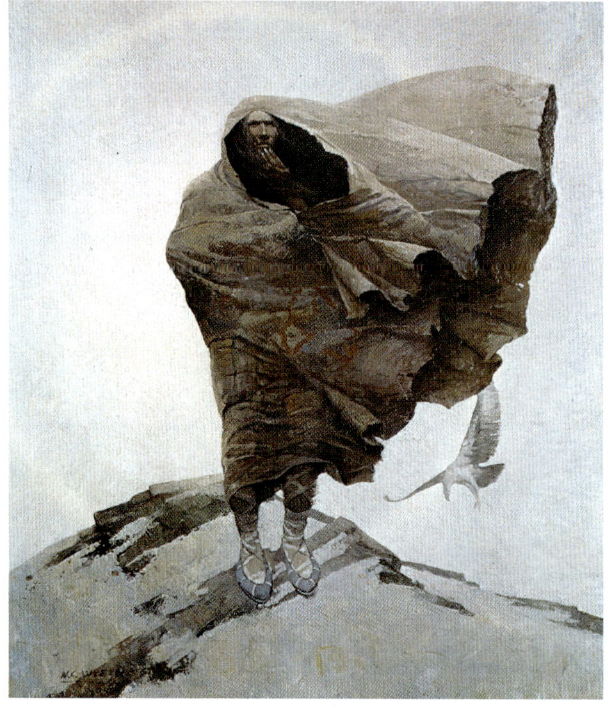

Scott's concept sketch for Prospero; *Winter* by N.C. Wyeth, illustration from "The Moods" by George T. Marsh, published in *Scribner's Magazine*, 1909.

The Tempest is one of Shakeseare's final plays, and Prospero's epilogue is often thought of as the playwright's farewell to the theatre. One of my 2014 pencil sketch concepts showed an elderly William Shakespeare as Prospero, wrapped in his magic robe which is covered in text and images from the play — sun, birds, fish, a dolphin, a seahorse, a nautilus shell.

Bonnie Monte, the director for this production at The Shakespeare Theatre of New Jersey, happened to be visiting our studio in Stratford and I was able to present my pencil sketches for the whole season in person. I can tell a lot more about a client's response when we are sitting together in the same room than I can from email correspondence. Bonnie loved this sketch, but was torn because she couldn't resist the sinking ship concept — so her decision was to proceed with both! The ship would become the image for *The Tempest*, and Shakespeare/Prospero would be the season poster and the brochure cover. This followed up our youthful Shakespeare with the butterfly in 2013, establishing a formal series of cover portraits of the house playwright.

This illustration is a little homage to N.C. Wyeth (1882–1945), one of my great heroes from the golden age of American illustration. Wyeth dressed a number of his characters in wind-blown cloaks that create a wonderful sense of drama — Captain Bill Bones or the unforgettable Blind Pew in *Treasure Island*, or the solitary First Nations figure in *Winter* from "The Moods." Howard Pyle's *Flying Dutchman* on the storm-tossed deck of his ship comes immediately to mind in this same genre.

I liked the sense of a storm passing through — the wind replacing black clouds with a hint of blue sky to signal forgiveness and reconciliation at the end of the play. This illustration struck a chord with Lionel Koffler who nominated it for the front cover of this book — the clearing sky seemed to resonate with the title. I agreed, with the proviso that it's certainly not my farewell to the theatre.

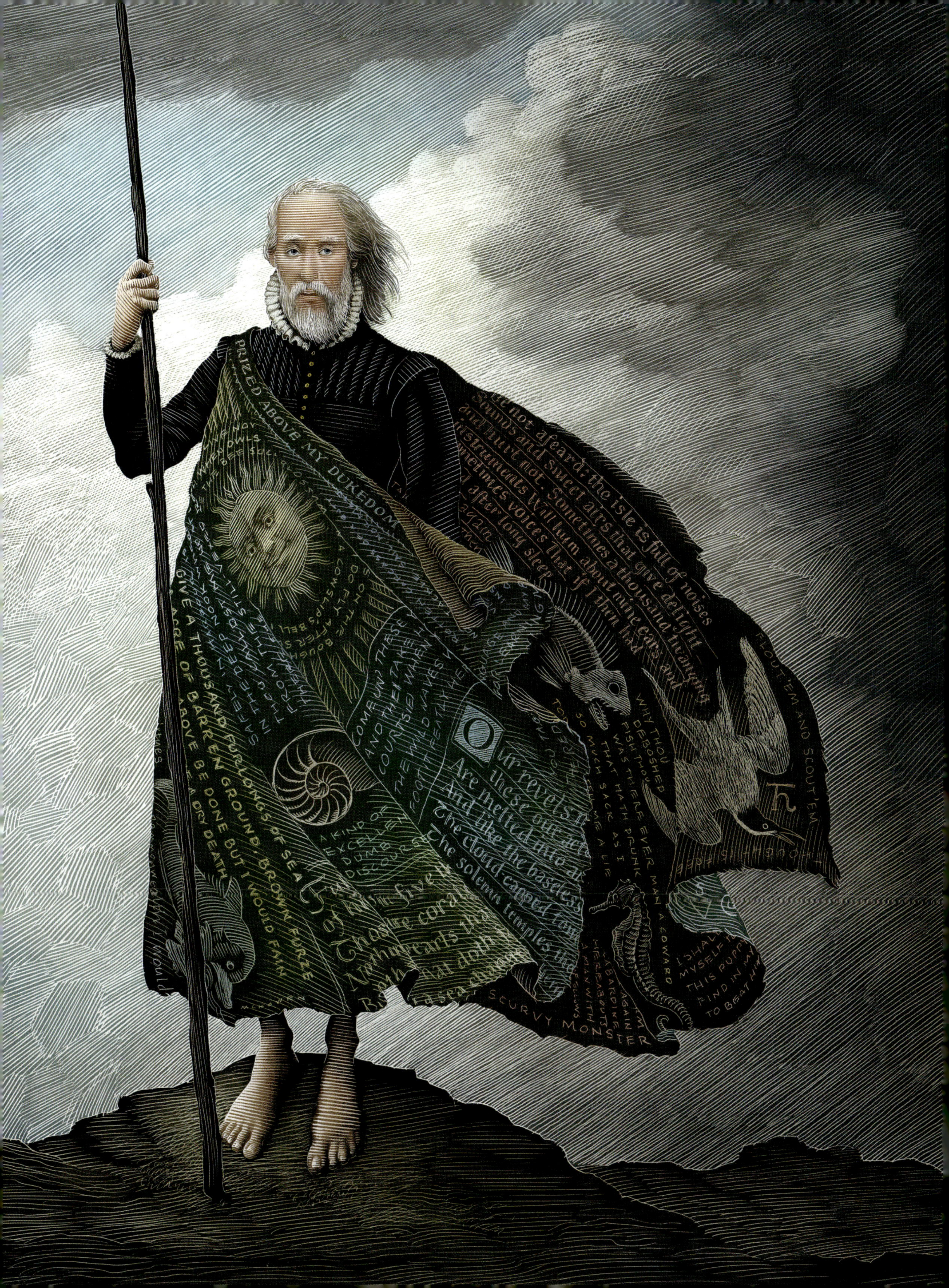

PRIZED ABOVE MY DUKEDOM
Be not afeard: the isle is full of noises
Sounds and sweet airs that give delight and hurt not. Sometimes a thousand twangling
instruments will hum about mine ears, and
sometimes voices that if I then had
after long sleep
GIVE A THOUSAND FURLONGS OF SEA
ACRE OF BARREN GROUND BROWN FURZE
ABOVE BE DONE BUT I WOULD FAIN
A DRY DEATH
Our revels
Are melted into
And like the baseless
The cloud capped tow
The solemn temples
SCURVY MONSTER
FLOUT 'EM AND SCOUT 'EM

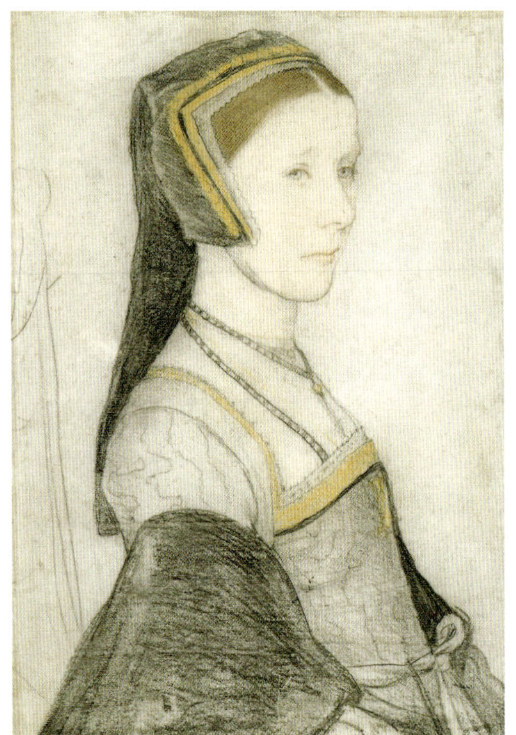

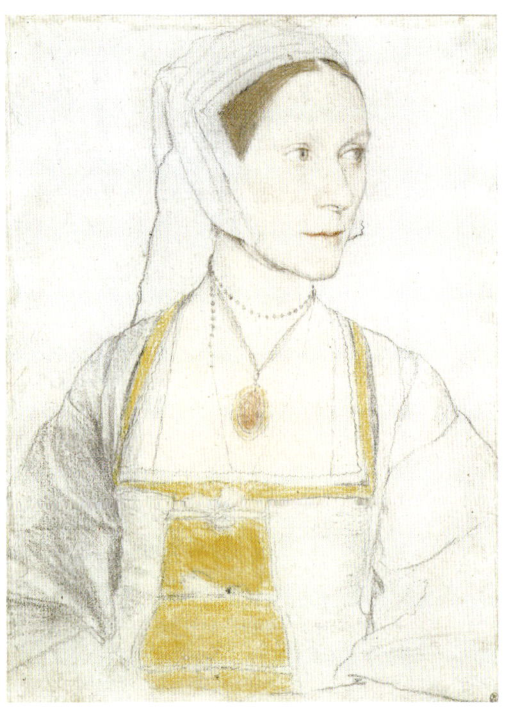

Hans Holbein's 1527 portraits of Anne Cresacre, ward of Sir Thomas More, and More's youngest daughter, Cecily Heron.

Shakespeare wrote *Henry VIII* in collaboration with John Fletcher in 1613 — two years after *The Tempest*. It's a pageant of tumultuous events at the Tudor court as the king becomes increasingly anxious to produce a legitimate male heir. Powerful princes of Church and State rise and fall depending on how well and for how long they are able to please His Majesty. Similar trajectories were in store for his six wives, but the play ends before those heads start to roll. I saw a wonderful production at the RSC in 1983 starring Richard Griffiths, Gemma Jones and John Thaw (which boasted a brilliant poster illustration by Ralph Steadman).

I have always visualized the world of the Tudors through the clear and confident drawings of the German artist Hans Holbein the Younger (*c*.1497–1543). Holbein had painted portraits of the great scholar Desiderius Erasmus in Rotterdam in 1523, which led to an invitation to work for Erasmus' friend Sir Thomas More in England, who would soon become Henry VIII's Lord Chancellor. Holbein created portraits of More's family and humanist circle in 1526–28, but then in 1532 found himself caught up in the events depicted in Shakespeare's play. Henry VIII was preparing to divorce Catherine of Aragon and marry Anne Boleyn, in defiance of the pope. Thomas More opposed Henry's actions, which led to his arrest and execution. Holbein evidently had to choose sides, and he found favour and patronage with Thomas Cromwell (a principal character in the play) and the family of Anne Boleyn. By 1536 Holbein was employed as the King's Painter, and he created his most famous image — King Henry VIII in a heroic pose, hand on hip and feet apart.

The play's final scene recreates the christening of Henry and Anne Boleyn's baby daughter, the future Queen Elizabeth. My poster concept for The Shakespeare Theatre of New Jersey's 2014 production inverted expectations — instead of the larger-than-life title character, I proposed a father/daughter portrait dominated by a huge infant Elizabeth wearing a portrait miniature of her father around her neck.

I based my baby Elizabeth on a Holbein portrait of her half-brother Edward VI (son of Henry VIII and Jane Seymour) — hoping that the wrong sex might be compensated for by family resemblance.

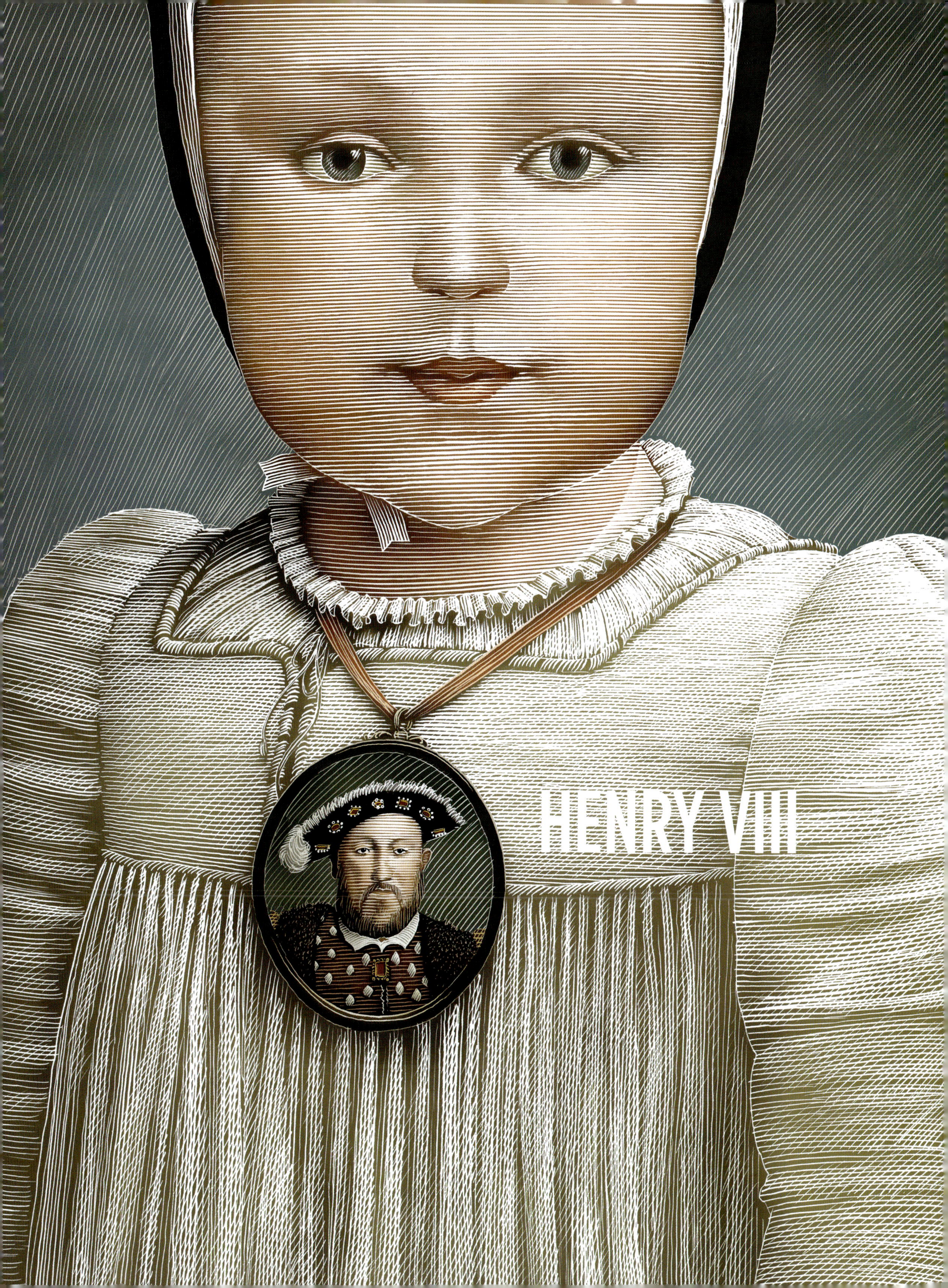
HENRY VIII

Ben Jonson's 1610 farce *The Alchemist* is a pungent satire on greed and gullibility. A trio of con artists — Face, Subtle and a prostitute named Dol Common — pretend to have supernatural knowledge and offer to help their "clients" to financial or social success. Subtle is a charlatan and assumes the role of alchemist, a purveyor of the Philosopher's Stone, the magical substance whose touch turns dross into gold. Their operation is successful but when customers start overlapping, the trio starts improvising to keep their stories straight. It's like watching a juggler adding more and more flying objects until you're holding your breath, waiting for everything to come crashing down.

This poster assignment came along in 2014 for a production at The Shakespeare Theatre of New Jersey. My concept was inspired by the implausible contraptions of W. Heath Robinson (1872–1944), the unsung hero of British eccentricity. Robinson's delightful drawings feature ridiculously complicated machines for achieving simple objectives. Bonnie Monte's production included modern references in the staging, which seemed like licence enough to embrace the anachronism of using Robinson. I devised a 17th-century steampunk figure wearing goggles and rubber gloves, cobbled together out of glass beakers and bits of hardware from a mad scientist's chemistry lab.

Bonnie agreed that Robinson was a perfect reference point — but when she saw my first pencil sketches she was concerned that they were too whimsical for the play. There's an innocent charm to Robinson's work that doesn't reflect Jonson's dark world of scheming con artists. I added a trio of nasty looking rats scurrying along the floor and a range of alchemical symbols, equations and formulas scrawled on the wall, like graffiti. And I added a subtle layer of texture to make the wall feel dirty and gritty. These adjustments darkened the tone sufficiently, and it became one of the favourite images from that season. It was included in that year's New York Society of Illustrators Annual Exhibition.

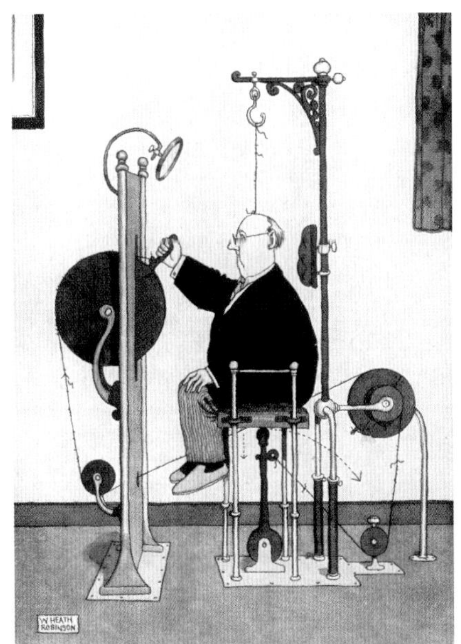

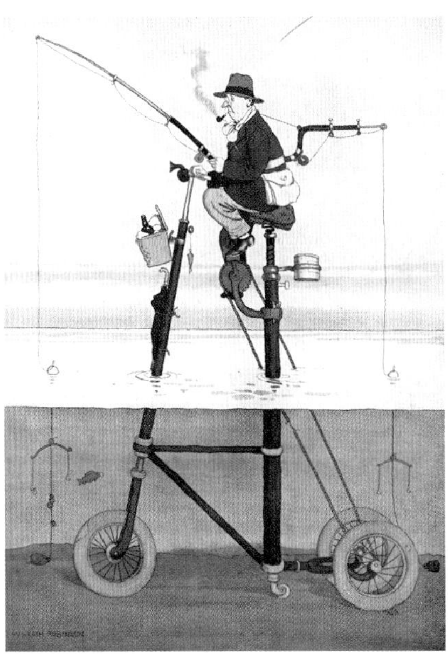
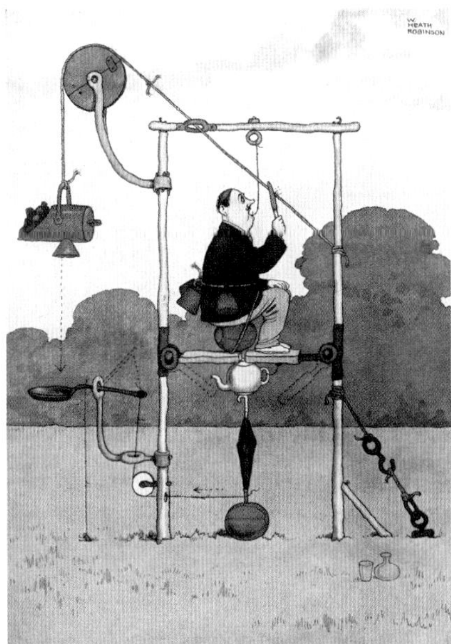

Three drawings by W. Heath Robinson, published in *The Bystander* in 1927: "A simple device for removing a wart from the top of the head;" "The Whitebait Cycle, for anglers frustrated by the exorbitant cost of hiring boats at the seaside" and "Another well-thought-out experiment in self-dentistry."

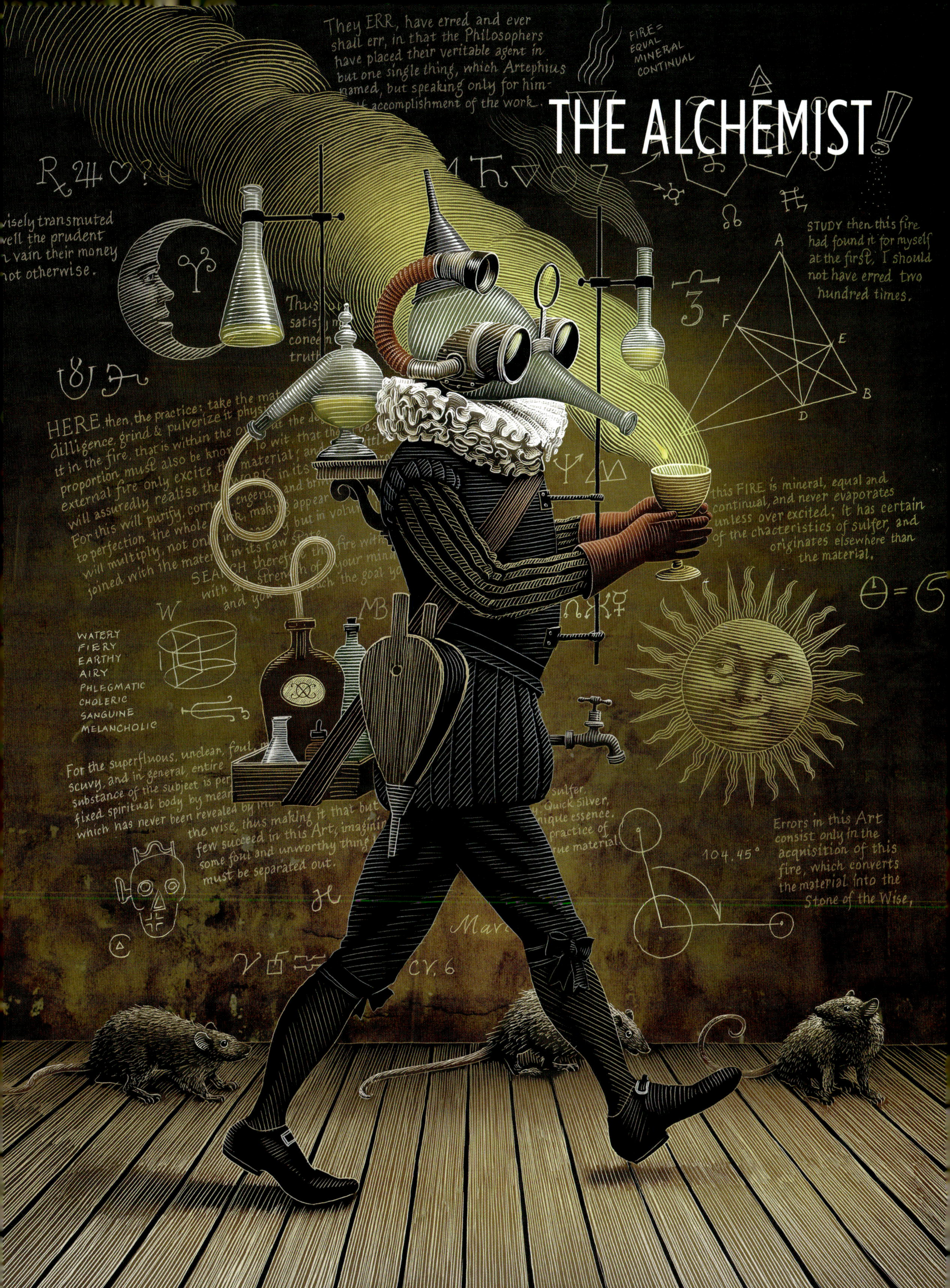

THE ALCHEMIST!
They ERR, have erred and ever shall err, in that the Philosophers have placed their veritable agent in but one single thing, which Artephius named, but speaking only for him-
FIRE = EQUAL MINERAL CONTINUAL
STUDY then this fire had found it for myself at the first, I should not have erred two hundred times.
this FIRE is mineral, equal and continual, and never evaporates unless over excited; it has certain of the chacteristics of sulfer, and originates elsewhere than the material.
WATERY
FIERY
EARTHY
AIRY
PHLEGMATIC
CHOLERIC
SANGUINE
MELANCHOLIC
Errors in this Art consist only in the acquisition of this fire, which converts the material into the Stone of the Wise,
104.45°
CV. 6

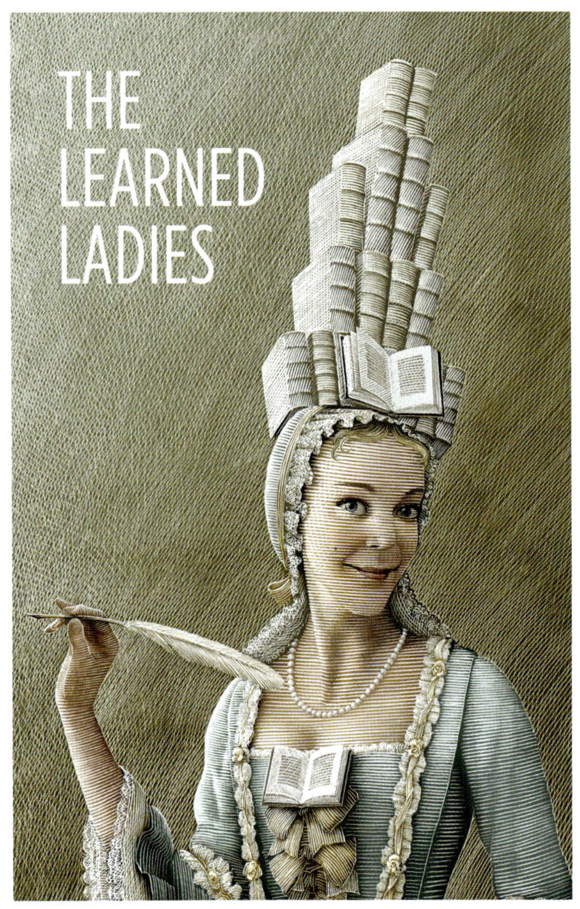

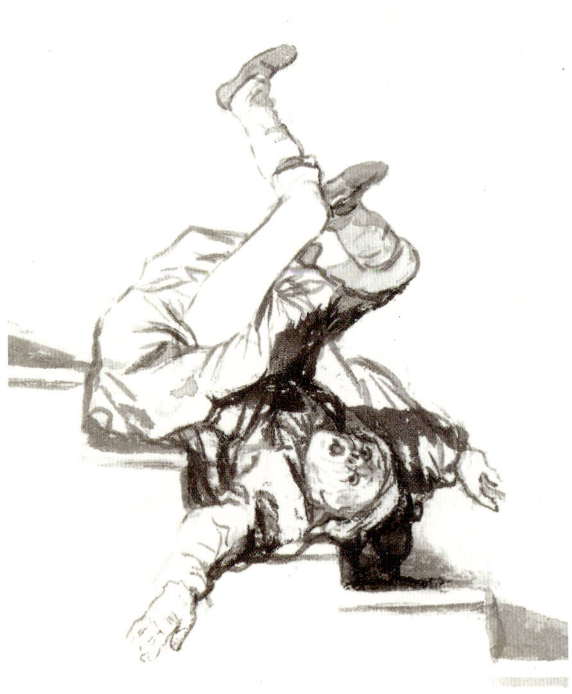

¿Valentias? Quenta con los años, c.1815–1820, by Francisco Goya.

I know Molière's plays reasonably well, so I was surprised in 2017 when The Shakespeare Theatre of New Jersey programmed one that I had never heard of — *The Bungler*. It's about a love-struck young man named Lélie and his crafty valet Mascarille — we get overtones of Don Giovanni and Leporello, or Count Almaviva and Figaro in *The Barber of Seville*. It's *Jeeves and Wooster* set in the 17th century.

Lélie is enamoured of a lovely young lady but of course he has a rival, and there are any number of impediments to his happiness — so he enlists Mascarille to figure out a way to win the girl. Mascarille is clever and diligent and invents a series of excellent schemes — but as each one plays out, at the critical moment, Lélie enters and gives the game away — he blurts out exactly the wrong thing (with Mascarille frantically gesturing at him to shut up) — and each plan goes up in flames.

Everything comes eventually to a happy resolution, but the humour comes from this good-natured dimwit constantly screwing things up. So I was looking for a visual metaphor for "putting one's foot in it." A pratfall of some kind? And the solution came as a gift from Francisco Goya — I remembered a little drawing of a woman falling head over heels down a staircase. It's from one of the great Spanish master's sketchbooks — the drawing is entitled "Showing off? Remember your age." Timeless and pertinent advice from an old master.

I set up the pose with a model to change the costume details from 18th-century Spain to 17th-century France. Actor Mike Nadajewski has a wonderful physical sense of comic movement on stage, and I knew he would be perfect for this illustration. I built the "staircase" out of sofa cushions in my studio so that nobody would get hurt.

Shakespeare New Jersey presented Molière's *The Learned Ladies* in 2014 — it's a delicious satire on academic pretension, education of women and *préciosité*. Christina suggested a witty concept, drawn from costume history. A *fontange* is the tall headdress, made with pleated layers of starched lace and ribbon, popular with aristocratic ladies in the late 17th century. The higher your *fontange*, the more fashionable you were. (It must have required some engineering to keep these attached and in place!) Christina's idea was to make fun of the intellectual posturing of Molière's characters with a fantasy *fontange* made of books. Deborah Hay was the model for my illustration.

The New York Times loved the production, and Christina and I took the train from Penn Station 40 minutes west to Madison, New Jersey, that summer to catch a performance. We had a great time and noticed that the costume designer for the show had borrowed the book *fontange* from the poster and adapted it for a number of the costumes on stage.

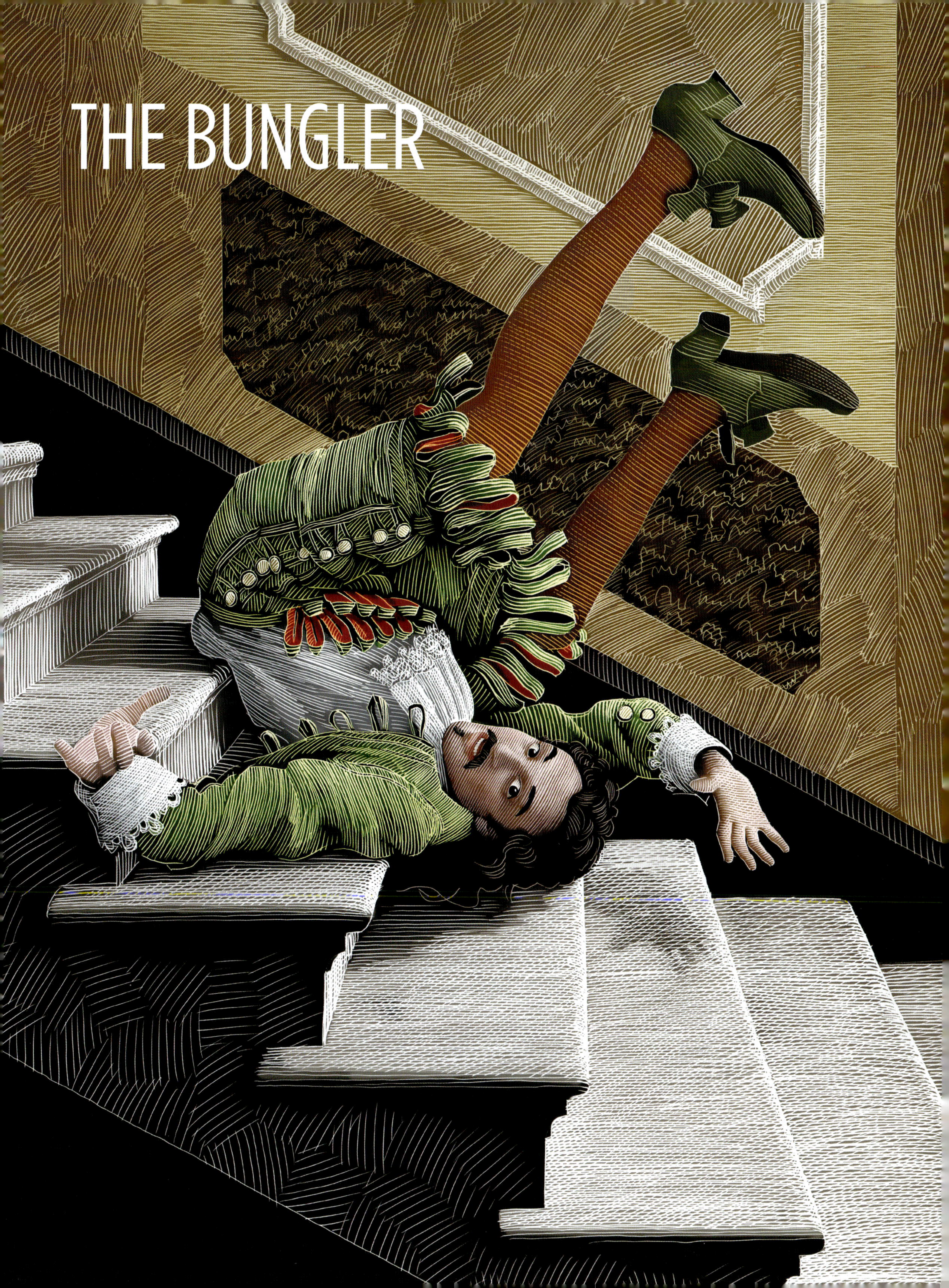
THE BUNGLER

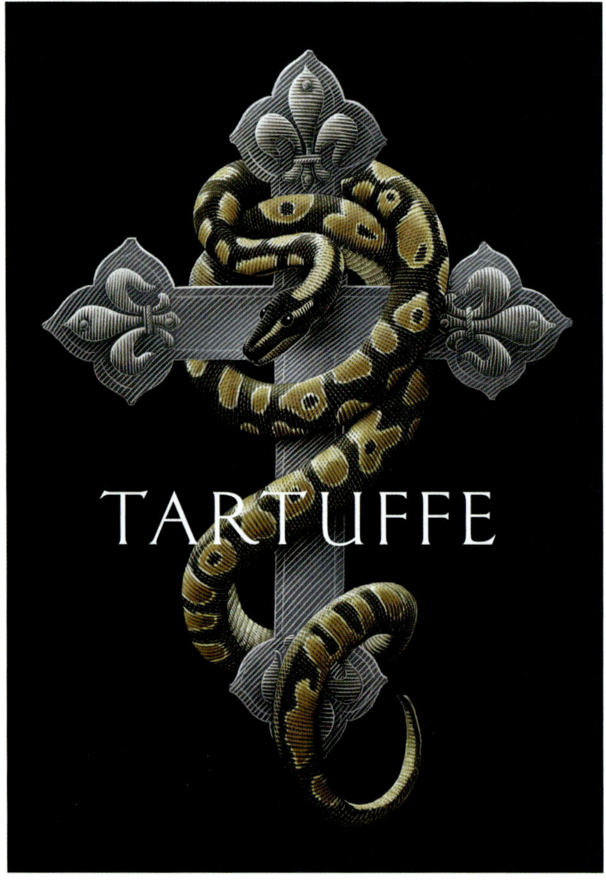

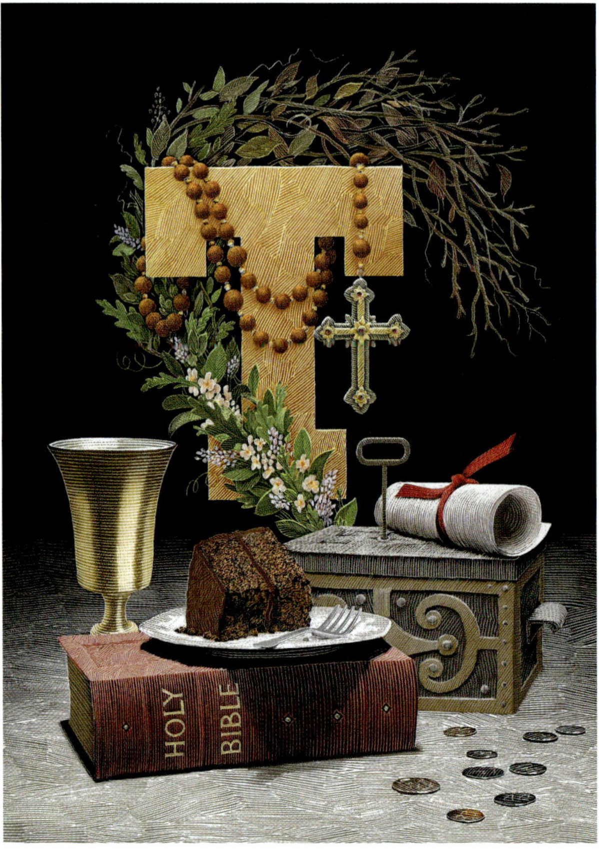

I have at least six different *Tartuffe* posters in my portfolio over the years — for Yale Repertory Theatre, The Acting Company, and most recently The Shakespeare Theatre of New Jersey. The corset poster for the Roundabout Theatre and the snake for The Pearl Theatre Company were included in the first edition of *A Fine Line* and they are still favourites — both strike a balance between the comedy and the sharp satire in the play.

Joe Dowling, director of the Roundabout's 2002 production, felt that the poster image should lean towards the darker complexities of the play. The production was set "in period" (Molière wrote the play in 1664) and starred Brian Bedford as Orgon and Henry Goodman as Tartuffe. I began with sketches showing Orgon being duped by Tartuffe in various ways; then, attempting to work in the religious plot, I gave Tartuffe little devil horns. None of these ideas were working, and Dowling suggested that we go for something more sensual. That led to the corset.

Orgon's wife Elmire is the target of Tartuffe's lust — in order to prove to her husband that Tartuffe is an imposter and a villain, she pretends to submit to Tartuffe's sexual advances (on the dining room table with Orgon concealed, hilariously, underneath). The shape of the corset and its calligraphic laces convey the 17th-century setting; its graphic treatment, like a hot pink Pop Art icon, gives the poster a contemporary feel.

My poster for The Pearl in 2009 emphasized the potency of Molière's religious satire. When it premiered, the play was well received by the public and even by King Louis XIV — but the Archbishop of Paris threatened to excommunicate anyone who watched, performed in or even read the play. One priest even argued that Jean-Baptiste Poquelin should be burned at the stake for having written it. In Christian symbolism, the snake is a reference to Satan, the Tempter, enemy of God and the agent of the Fall. Wrapped around a crucifix, this seemed a perfect metaphor for the title character's hypocrisy.

Bonnie Monte had a very specific vision for a poster to represent her 2018 production at Shakespeare New Jersey — a title initial borrowed from the signage on the facade of Trump Tower and a half-eaten slice of chocolate cake resting on a Bible. I'm still not quite sure of the rationale for these objects, but the engraving lines helped me render them as if they were a 17th-century still life.

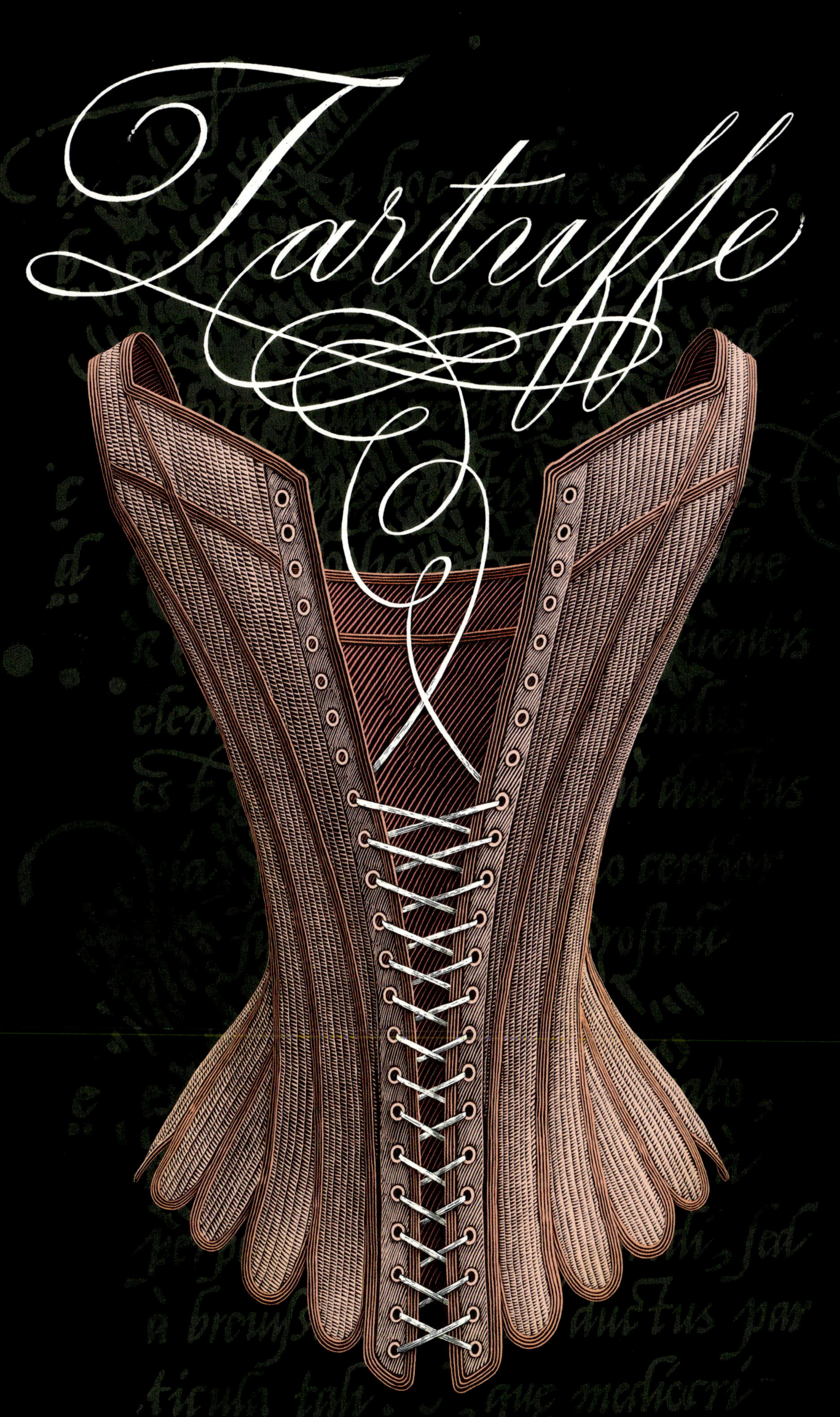
Tartuffe

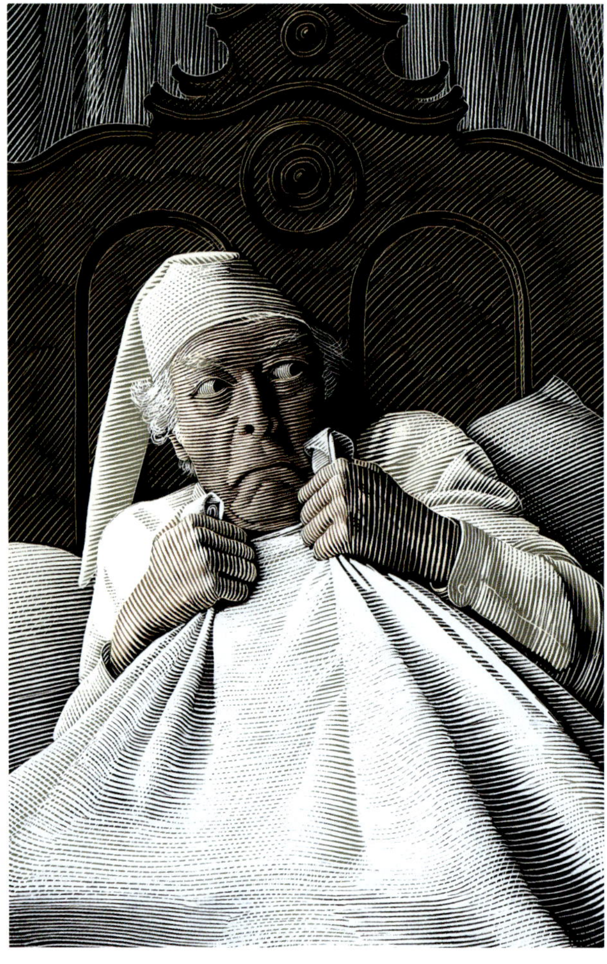

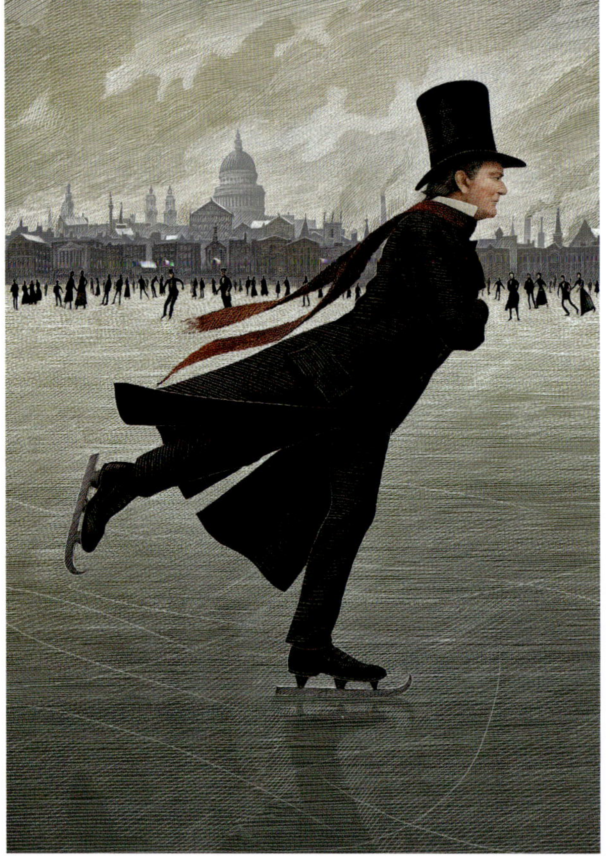

It's faintly ironic that so many theatre companies rely on Charles Dickens' *A Christmas Carol* for a lucrative holiday season at the box office.

Notwithstanding its happy ending, *Carol* is one of the greatest ghost stories of all time. For a 1999 production at Great Lakes Theater Festival in Cleveland, I felt the poster image should be something spooky. Instead of depicting the spirits, I focussed on Ebenezer's reaction to the spirits. I needed a model who could convey fright — but with a sense of fun, like the amusement park ride you're too terrified to get on, and then can't wait to go on again. Bernard Behrens was a brilliant character actor at the Shaw Festival for many seasons — his fabulously expressive face was perfect for Scrooge.

Dennis Garnhum's production at the Grand Theatre in London, Ontario, in 2017 included a "Frost Fair" scene on the Thames with the entire cast on ice skates (roller blades create a very convincing illusion on stage). Benedict Campbell starred in this production, so the concept for the poster was a portrait of Scrooge on skates. Ice skating in the Victorian period calls to mind *The Reverend Robert Walker Skating on Duddingston Loch* painted by the Scottish artist Henry Raeburn in the 1790s. Dickens first published his novella in 1843, so I had to change some Georgian costume details into High Victorian. I moved the scene from northern Scotland to the centre of London, using early photographs as reference for the warehouses along the Thames Embankment. Scrooge is a practical man — if his office was on one side of the river and home was on the other, I imagined that he might well have laced on his skates to get back and forth to work. The designer of this production adapted my London cityscape from the poster to surround the set on stage — life imitating art!

Rod Beattie, an actor at the Stratford Festival for many seasons, performs *A Christmas Carol* as a *tour de force* one-man show. He has the entire book memorized, and uses his remarkable, nuanced vocal range to define the characters. I've heard him recite the text, and it's mesmerizing. I turned Rod into Jacob Marley as Scrooge encounters him in the door knocker — here's Dickens' extraordinary description:

> "And then let any man explain to me, if he can, how it happened that Scrooge, having his key in the lock of the door, saw in the knocker, without its undergoing any intermediate process of change — not a knocker, but Marley's face. Marley's face. It was not in impenetrable shadow as the other objects in the yard were, but had a dismal light about it, like a bad lobster in a dark cellar. It was not angry or ferocious, but looked at Scrooge as Marley used to look: with ghostly spectacles turned up on its ghostly forehead."

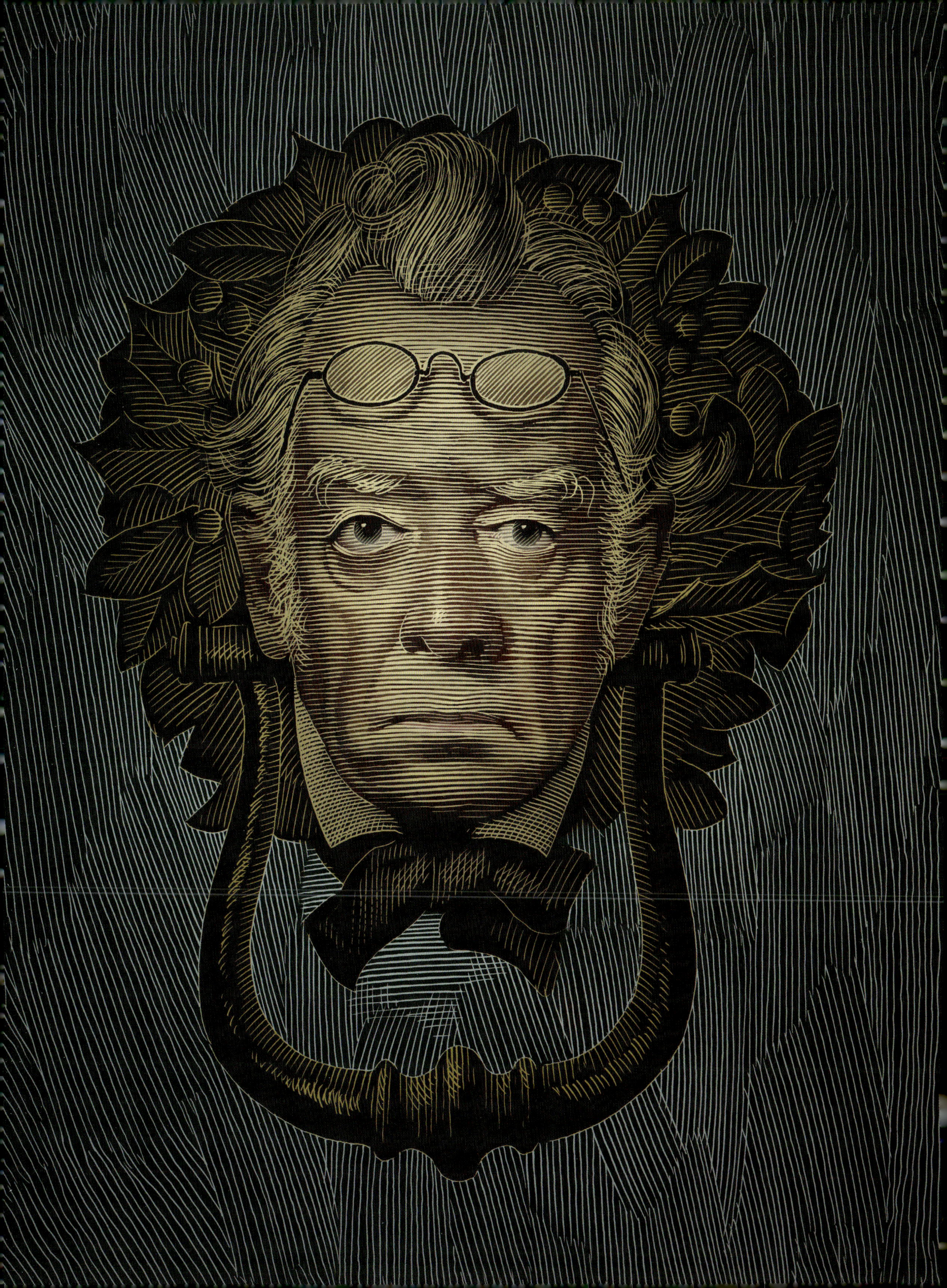

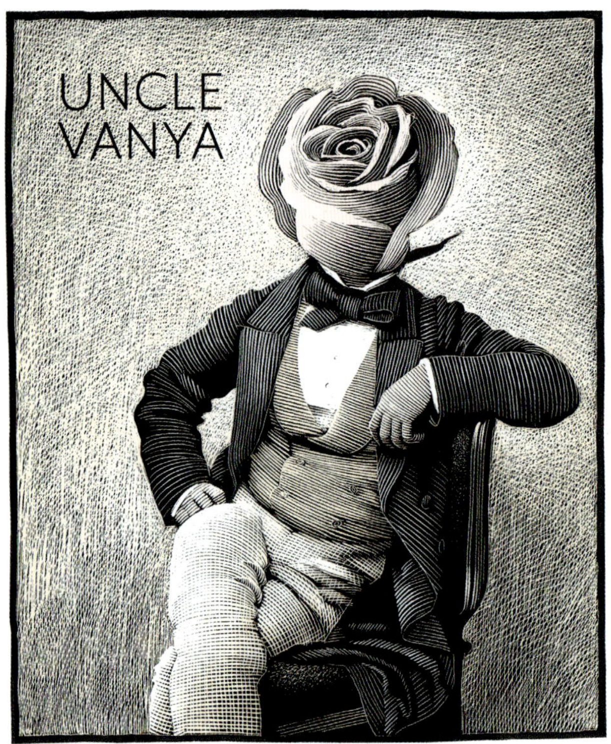

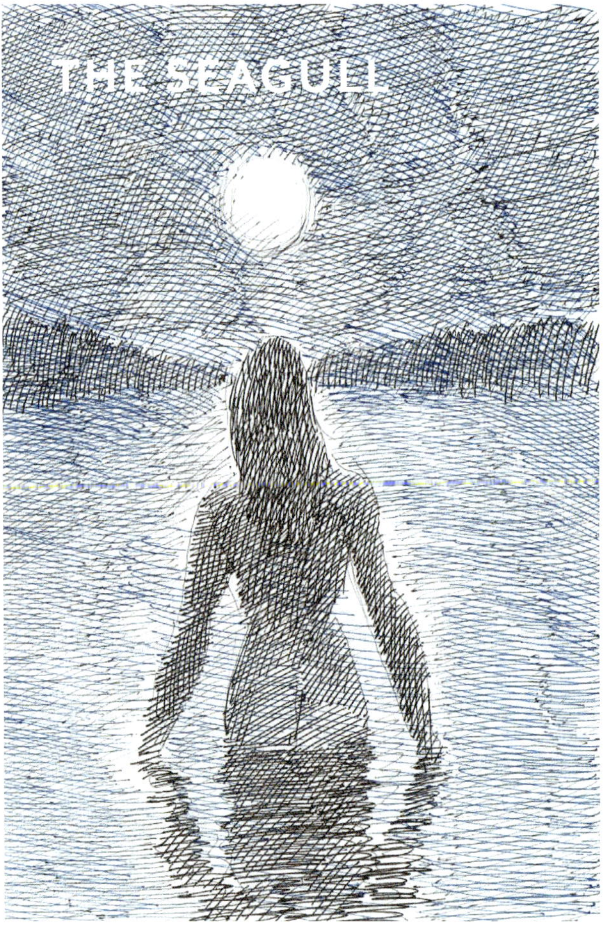

My favourite scene in *Uncle Vanya* comes in Act III: Vanya is hopelessly in love with Yelena and has cut a bouquet of roses for her in the garden. Holding the flowers, he walks in on Yelena and Doctor Astrov, interrupting their unexpected moment of spontaneous passion. It's simultaneously very funny and horribly embarrassing — a perfect Chekhov moment.

I have tackled *Uncle Vanya* several times, but my favourite is still a poster for Daniel Sullivan's 1996 production at Seattle Repertory Theatre. It's a simple, seated portrait of the title character — but his head is a giant rose, a symbol of his dreams and romantic infatuations. The scratchboard engraving lines give the poster a 19th-century flavour, while the surreal twist makes the poster a firmly contemporary graphic.

Director Scott Elliott told me that his 1997 Broadway production of Chekhov's *Three Sisters* for the Roundabout Theatre would be "set in 1900 in an extravagant black box." He would be emphasizing darkness and claustrophobia, and he wanted the poster to reflect this minimalist approach. "The more stark the better." The sketch that everyone responded to was the simplest — a woman in the dark, holding up a candle. It was not meant to illustrate a specific scene (although it feels a bit like Act III, after the 3AM fire) — or even a particular character, but to conjure up a sense of these girls stuck in this provincial backwater, trying to figure out where they belong, where they want to be. Scratchboard is wonderful for rendering lighting effects — I was after the mystery and stillness of a Georges de La Tour painting, adapted into 19th-century engraving lines.

I did not make it to New York to see the production, and I'm still sorry I missed it. The starry cast included Billy Crudup, Calista Flockhart, Paul Giamatti, Amy Irving, Eric Stoltz, David Strathairn, Lili Taylor and Jeanne Tripplehorn.

The Stratford Festival asked me to art direct poster images for their 2019 season. Christina remarked, "Well, that's the job you moved here for 38 years ago." For many years, Stratford had relied on costume portraits of their star actors, photographed against seamless paper backdrops in a studio. I took the assignment as an opportunity to try to tell more of a story about each play. Artistic Director Antoni Cimolino talked about *The Seagull*'s modern sensibility, which comes from the young characters — Konstantin and Nina, struggling to find their voices as creative artists and bashing their poor, doomed heads against the walls. But Antoni was still thinking that the brochure image should feature the senior company members playing Arkadina and Trigorin. I proposed a sketch of Nina, rising from the lake (or the Avon River here in Stratford) in the moonlight, and everyone loved it — but then the play dropped out of the season. Maybe it will come back in a future season so we can take this concept sketch to a finished image.

THREE SISTERS

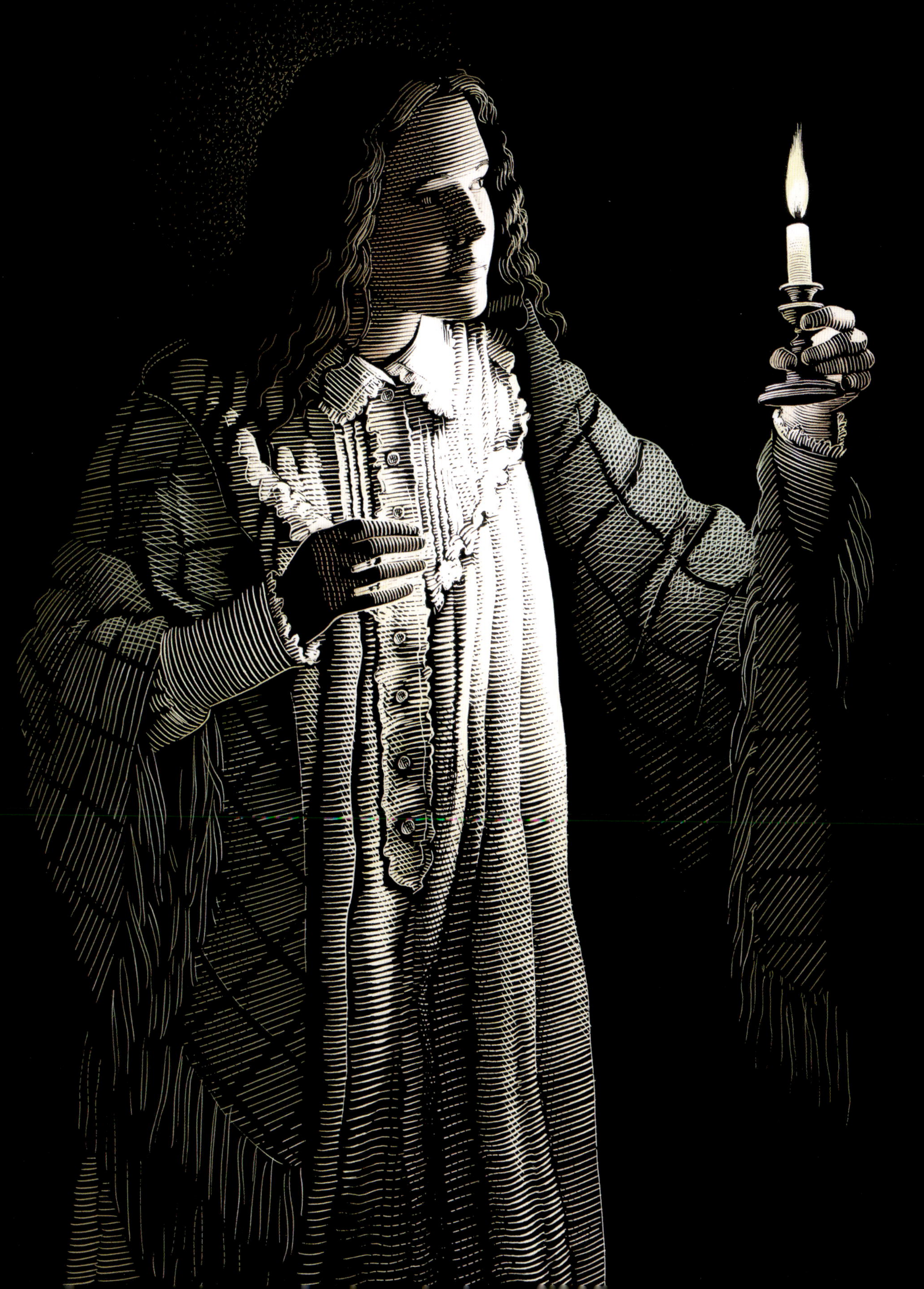

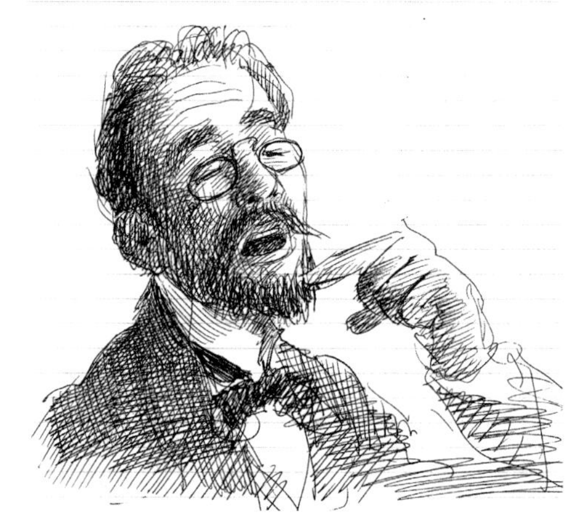

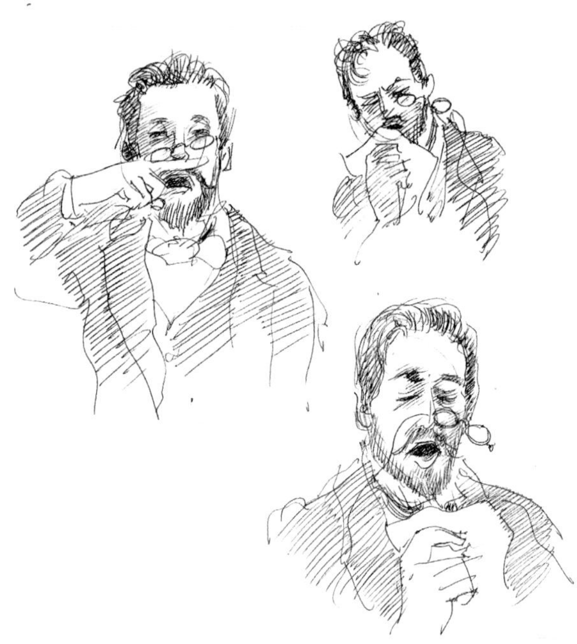

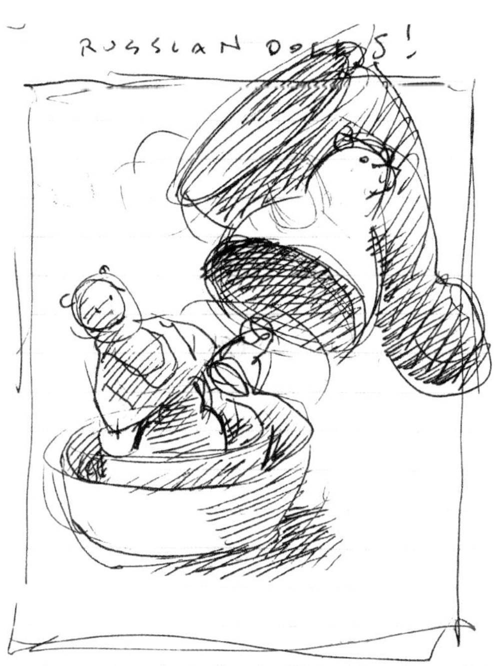

Anton Chekhov wrote the four plays that established his reputation as one of history's great playwrights in the last few years of his life. *The Seagull, Uncle Vanya, Three Sisters* and *The Cherry Orchard* have had a profound influence on how plays have been written, acted and produced in the past hundred years because of their emphasis on subtext — what characters are thinking but not necessarily saying.

But Chekhov had first made his name as a comic writer, decades earlier, in the 1880s with a series of popular one-act "vaudevilles" including *The Bear, The Sneeze* and *The Proposal.* The Shaw Festival presented two of these in a riotous double-bill entitled *Love Among the Russians* in 2006. In 2010, The Pearl Theatre Company in New York presented an evening of these short comedies, newly adapted by Michael Frayn, under the package title *The Sneeze* and I was asked to come up with a poster.

My initial thought was a literal interpretation of the title. Chekhov is the common denominator here so I thought it would be fun to do a portrait of him in that uncomfortable, involuntary moment just before a huge sneeze. I sent sketches to the client and the verdict was: go back to the drawing board.

As she so often does, Christina rescued me with a concept far more appropriate for the project because it was so much more fun. Russian nesting dolls — they're tiny, witty and full of surprises, just like the plays. Their proper name is *matryoshka,* literally "little matron." They are a tourist cliché nowadays but the first Russian nested doll set was carved in 1890 from a design by folk crafts painter Sergey Malyutin — early enough that Chekhov himself might well have smiled at the novelty and surprise of one figure inside another, inside another.

I sketched a series of dolls in an orderly progression from smallest to largest, but that felt too static and they quickly turned into an explosion of dolls in mid-air. I was able to borrow a set of nesting dolls from a friend in Stratford who had brought them back from a trip to Russia and used them to set up and light this composition. The largest one is Anton Chekhov himself; the other figures are a range of character types from his one-act plays. There's a bear, both because of the individual play title and the Russian national symbol.

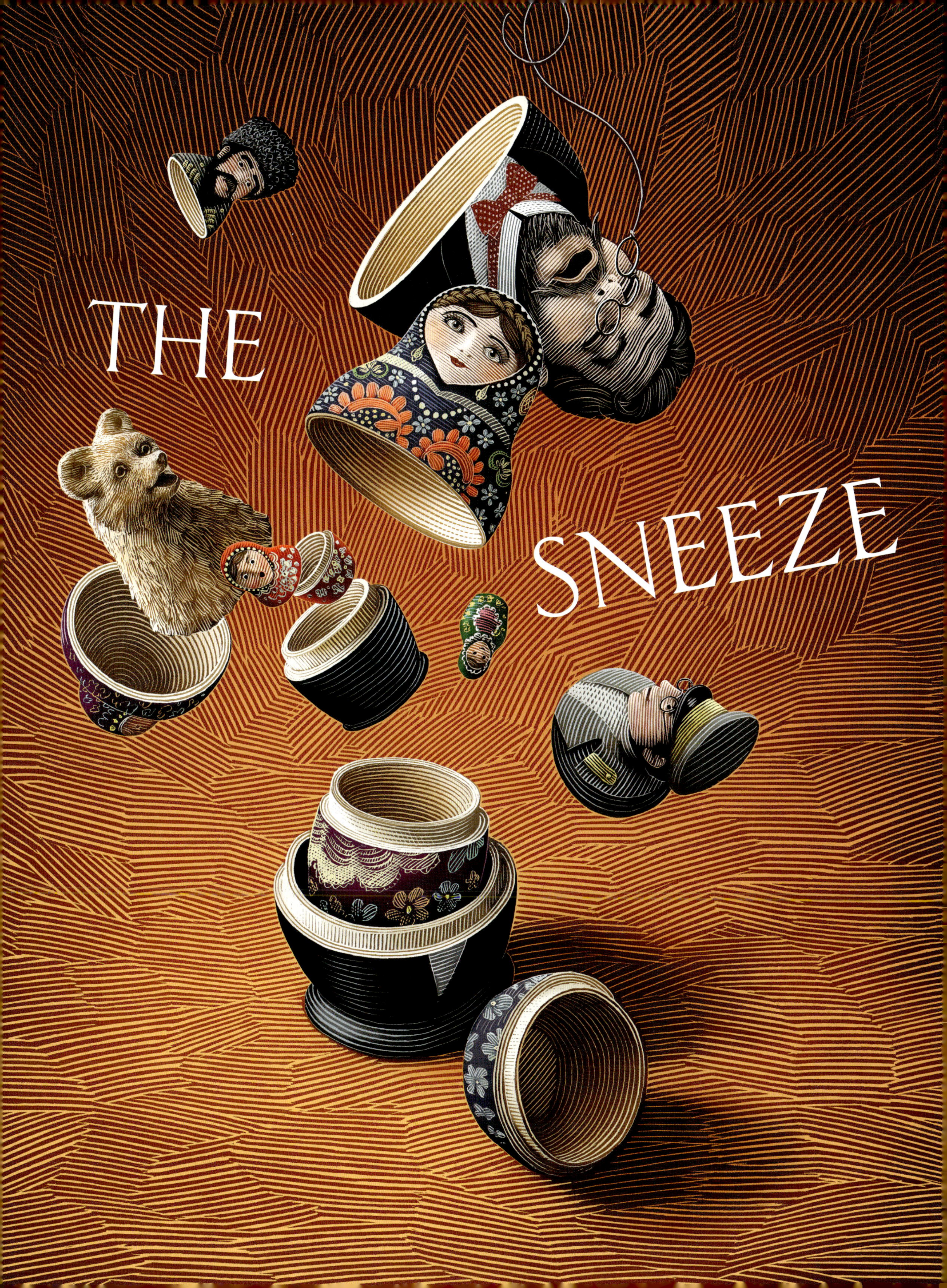
THE
SNEEZE

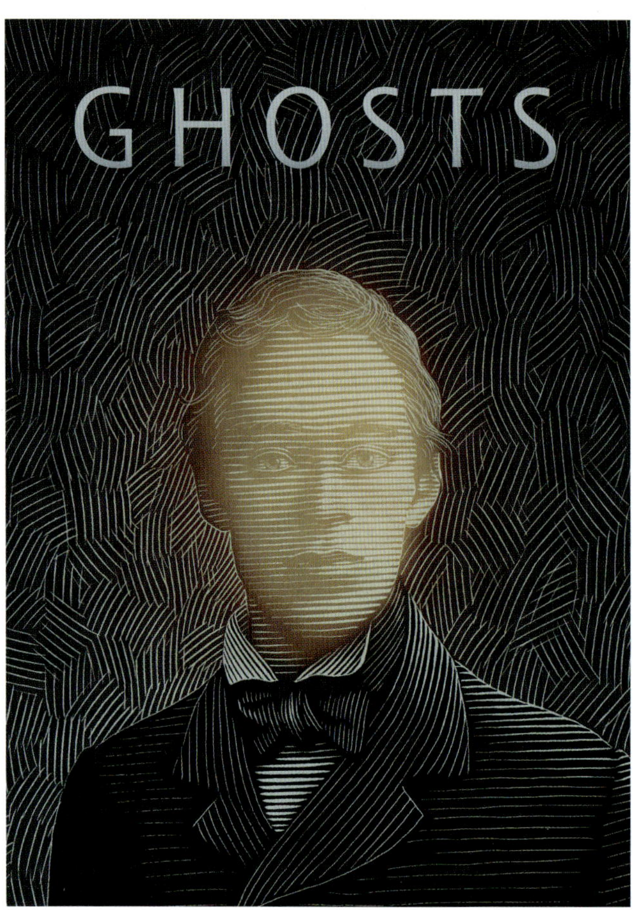

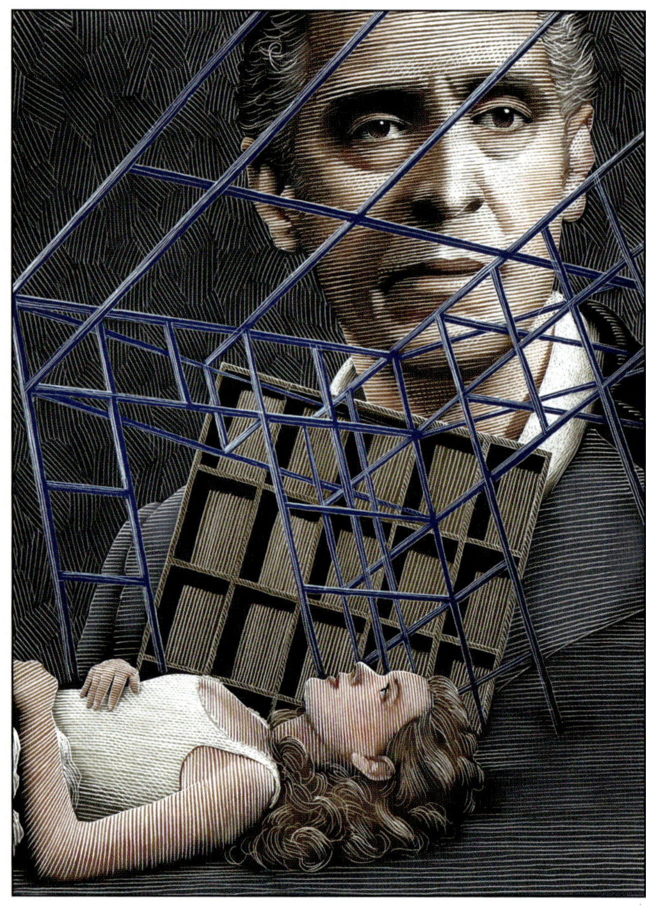

I worked for The Pearl Theatre Company in New York, one of the very few repertory companies in the U.S., for five seasons; unfortunately the company no longer exists. Henrik Ibsen's *Rosmersholm* was on the playbill in 2010. The *New York Times* review of this production mentioned that this was one of Freud's favourite plays — with so much desire and silent guilt roiling under its surface, he used the play to illustrate his psychoanalytic theories. Johannes Rosmer and his young housekeeper Rebecca West share a passionate faith in a bright, progressive future. They also share a passion for each other. But all their idealism is shot down as dark family secrets are uncovered.

The director used the phrase "gazing into an existential abyss" in a preliminary phone chat about the play, which I couldn't get out of my head. We learn that Rosmer's wife drowned herself in the millpond before the action of the play starts. Rebecca West commits suicide in the same manner in the final scene. The illustration could be either of them facing their moment of truth.

Ibsen wrote *Ghosts* in 1881. Like *A Doll's House*, it was deliberately sensational — a powerful and frank treatment of "taboo" subjects including venereal disease, incest, infidelity and euthanasia. Osvald, the young protagonist, is dying of congenital syphilis. He tells his mother that, according to his doctor, the disease manifests itself initially as "a sort of softening of the brain." I wanted my poster image for The Pearl's 2008 production to suggest a rotting away from the inside — Osvald as a ghost. I engraved the portrait in scratchboard; then, using Photoshop filters, I experimented with ways of fading the engraving lines over his face — as if his vitality is fading away.

Chris Curry, an art director at *The New Yorker*, called me in 2013 to illustrate a review (by Hilton Als) of a new production of *The Master Builder* at Brooklyn Academy of Music, starring John Turturro as the architect Halvard Solness and Wrenn Schmidt as the seductive Hilde Wangel. Poster illustrations are always created before a production exists — sometimes before casting is in place. For a review, the magazine could easily use production photography, but commissioning original illustration is part of their perspective on the cultural life of New York. It's part of what makes them *The New Yorker*.

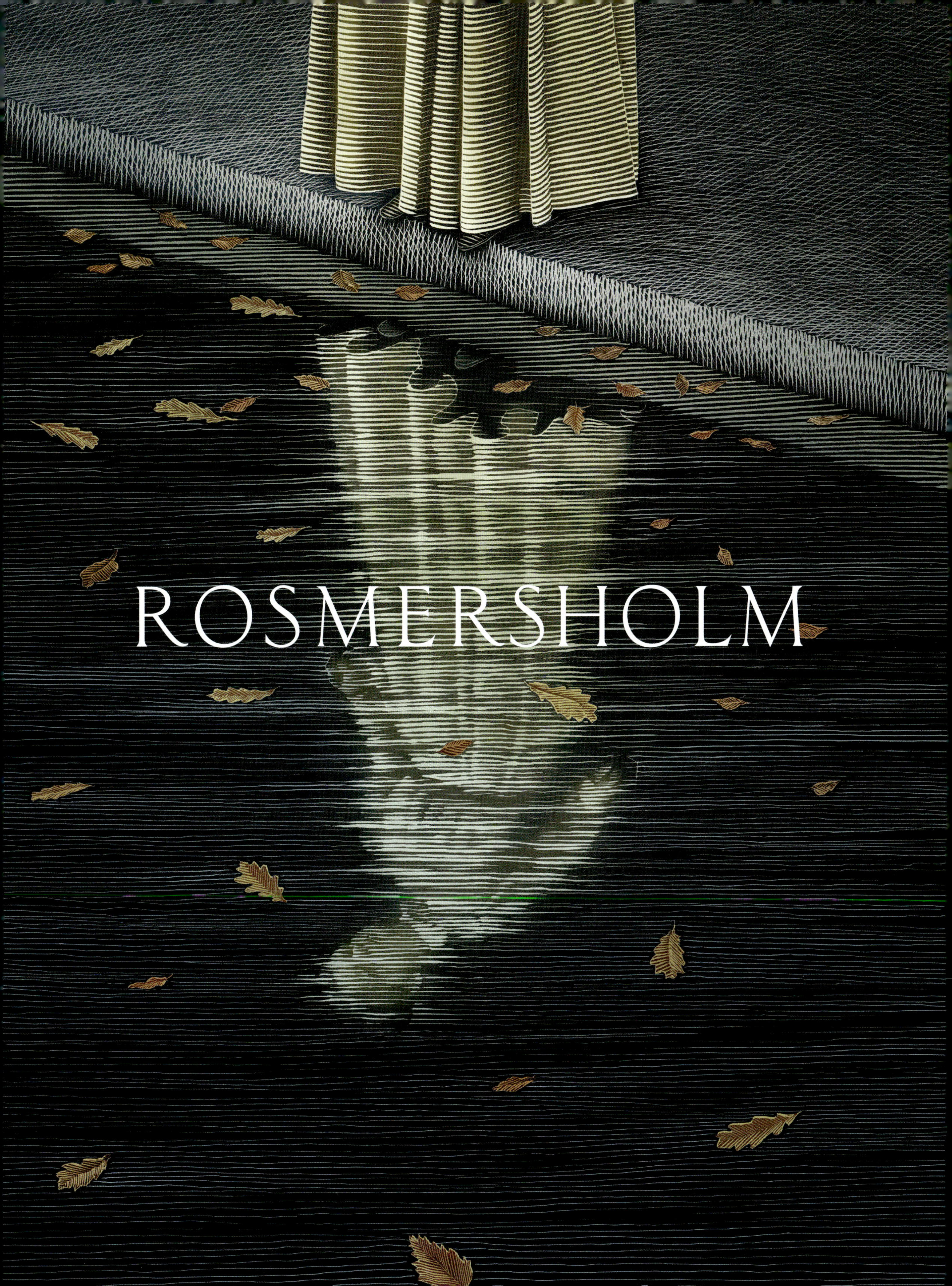
ROSMERSHOLM

"She's from Brazil — where the nuts come from." The high comedy of *Charley's Aunt* is established in this famous line from the text, often quoted in the brochure copy describing Brandon Thomas' old (1892) chestnut. The character being referred to is Donna Lucia d'Alvadorez from Brazil, visiting her nephew, an undergrad at Oxford. But she doesn't arrive when she said she would, so someone has to impersonate her — it's Oscar Wilde crossed with *Fawlty Towers*.

Charley's Oxford roommate Lord Fancourt Babberly impersonates Donna Lucia (until the real one shows up). He enters in full drag costume, but I thought the moment he's about to climb into the dress would be fun as an illustration. I loved the idea of the hoop skirt "cage" — underwear worn over his trousers. One of my favourite *toilette* paintings is *Nana* by Edouard Manet — I borrowed the famous pose and composition, changing the boudoir setting to an undergraduate dorm room (a lot of champagne is consumed throughout the play). George Krissa was the perfect model for Lord Fancourt.

Lynn Nottage based her 2003 play *Intimate Apparel* on the life of her great-grandmother. Esther is a talented black seamstress who makes beautiful undergarments for clients ranging from wealthy white patrons to black prostitutes. According to *The New York Times*, the play is "a rich, vivid portrait of turn-of-the-last-century New York; a feminist lament of intelligent, talented women defined and controlled by men; and a soft-focus glimpse into the beating hearts behind the archives of African-American life a century ago." Daniel Sullivan directed the New York premiere in 2004 for the Roundabout Theatre Company. A small sewing shop in Stratford let me borrow this fabulous (working) machine; my friend Alia Hussey stood in for an up-and-coming young actress named Viola Davis, as Esther.

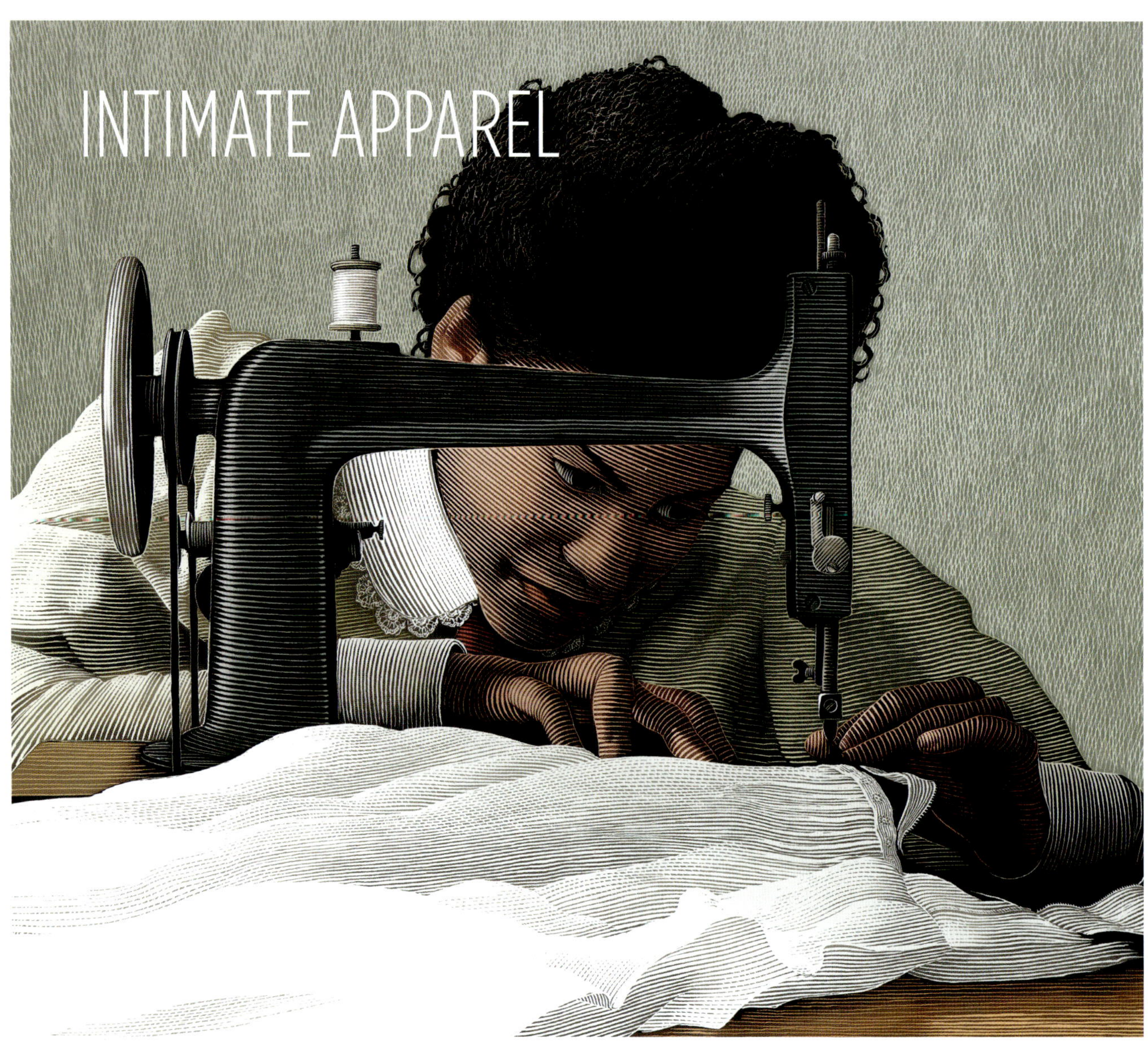

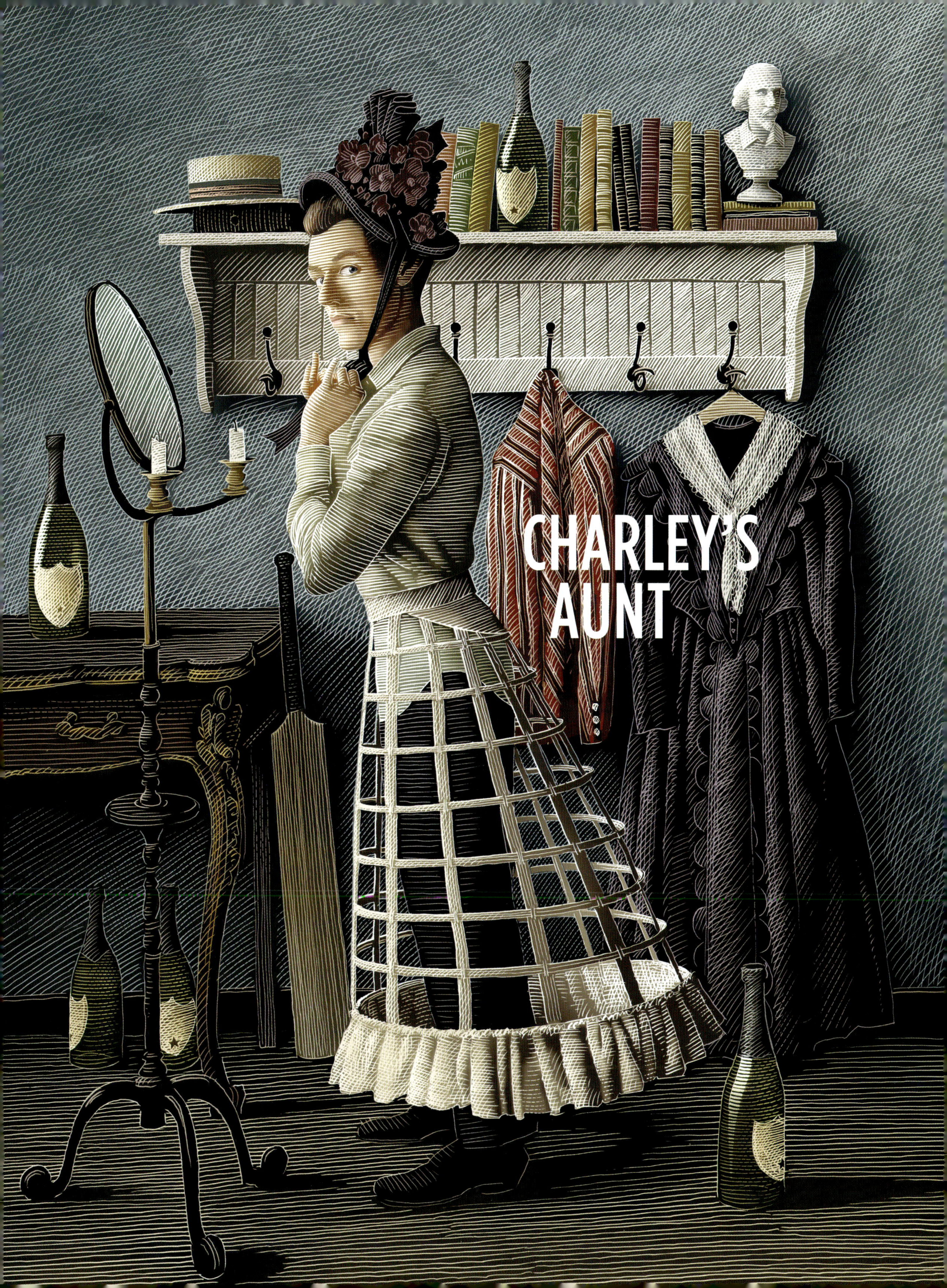
CHARLEY'S
AUNT

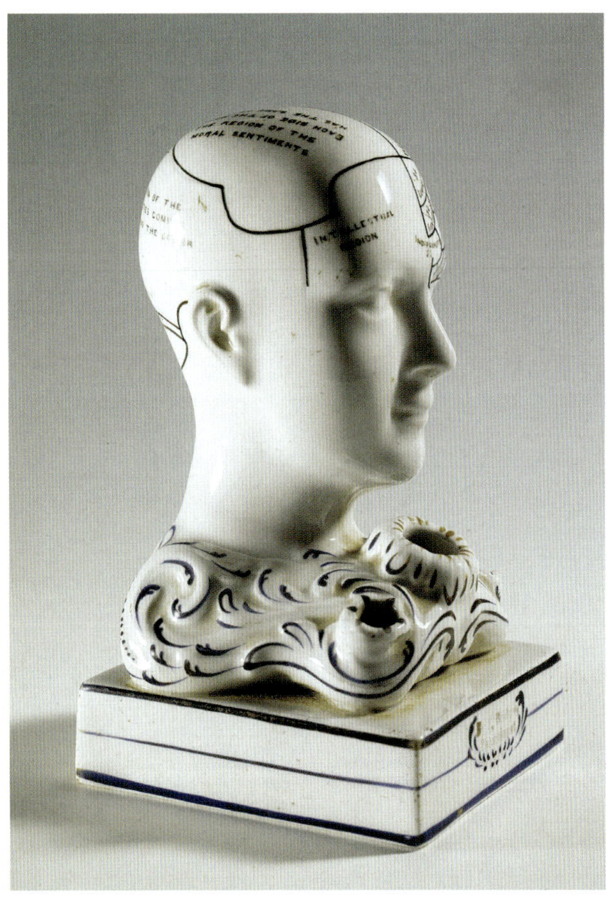

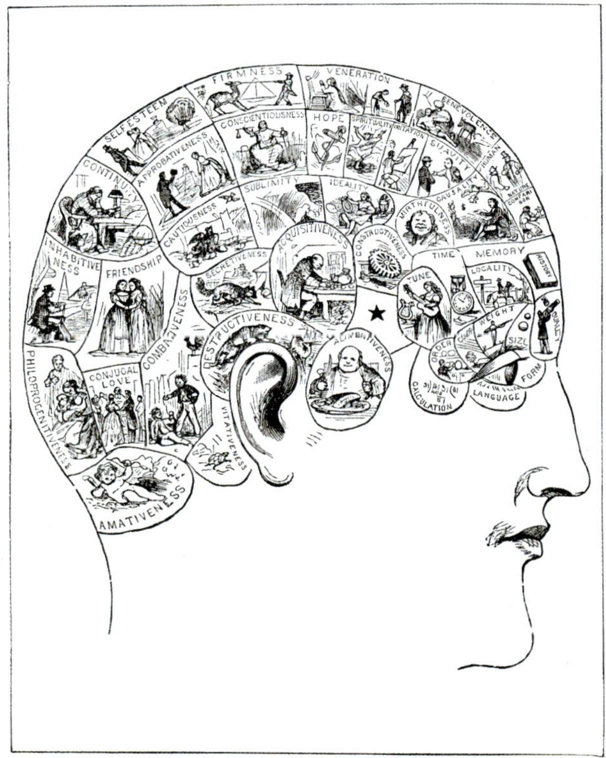

The Shakespeare Theatre of New Jersey presented the world premiere of Cathy Tempelsman's *A Most Dangerous Woman* in 2013. Set mostly in the 1850s, the play introduces the writer Mary Ann Evans, a smart woman in her 30s, self-described as "plucky." She's a book editor in London, working in the man's world of British literature. But she also writes her own fiction and is emboldened to publish her work under the professional pseudonym George Eliot. Female authors were published under their own names in the Victorian era, but their work was generally stereotyped as lighthearted romance. Eliot used a male pen name to ensure that her work would be taken seriously — and she became one of the great authors of the 19th century.

The play is biographical. Eliot's private life was unconventional and scandalized the hypocritical society of her day. Her passions in real life were often reflected in the world of her fiction — characters from Eliot's novels appear throughout the play in brief vignettes, underscoring emotional moments in her life and the social prejudices of her times. A character from *Daniel Deronda* remarks, "You may try, but you can never imagine what it is to have a man's force of genius in you, and yet to suffer the slavery of being a girl."

Eliot was a proponent of phrenology — the idea that a person's character and mental capacity is indicated by the shape of their skull — and the play includes a scene in which Eliot is examined by a phrenologist. This pseudoscience was hugely popular during in Victorian era. It attracted devotees such as Edgar Allan Poe, Honoré de Balzac, President James Garfield, Charlotte and Emily Brontë and Otto von Bismark. Queen Victoria employed a phrenologist to examine her children. Mark Twain visited a phrenologist in London in 1872 or '73 — under a pseudonym — and was surprised to be told that he had a cavity where there should have been a bump, which indicated that he lacked a sense of humour.

The idea that different areas of brain have specific functions was based in real science, but phrenology extrapolated this far beyond empirical knowledge. I love the illustrated diagrams from the period (both two- and three-dimensional) charting the localized "modules" of the brain that govern specific functions. These gave me the idea of a phrenological portrait of George Eliot with the areas of her brain devoted to her famous novels.

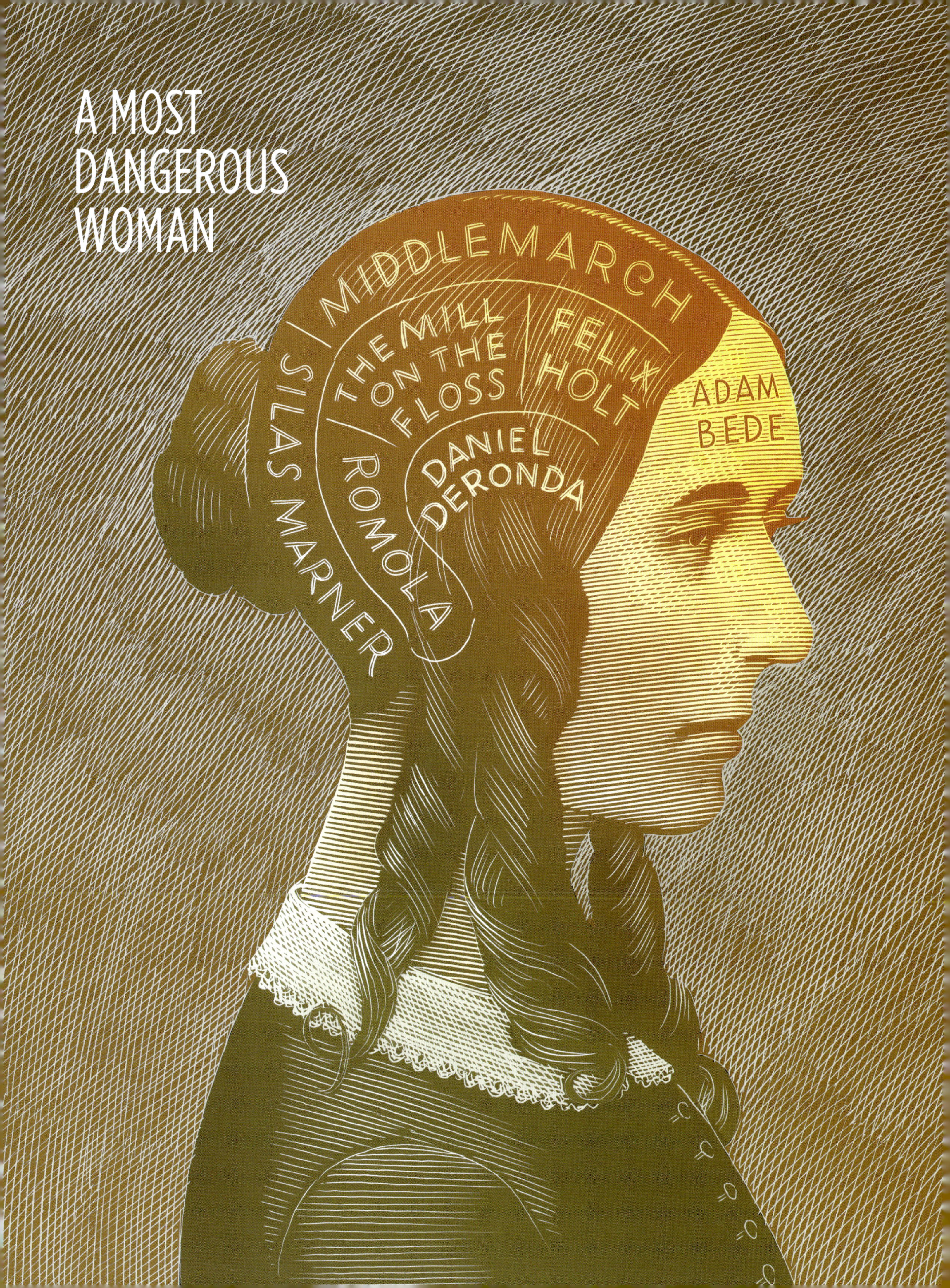
A MOST DANGEROUS WOMAN
MIDDLEMARCH
THE MILL ON THE FLOSS
FELIX HOLT
ADAM BEDE
SILAS MARNER
ROMOLA
DANIEL DERONDA

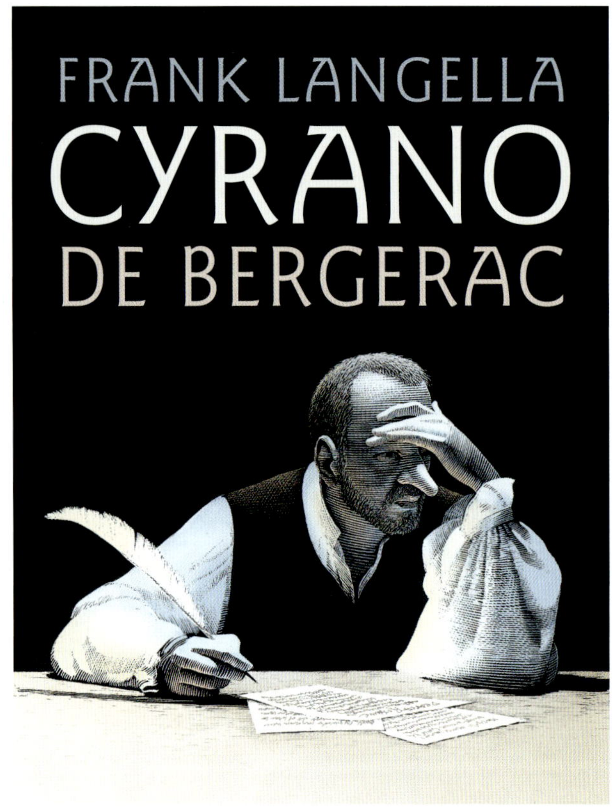

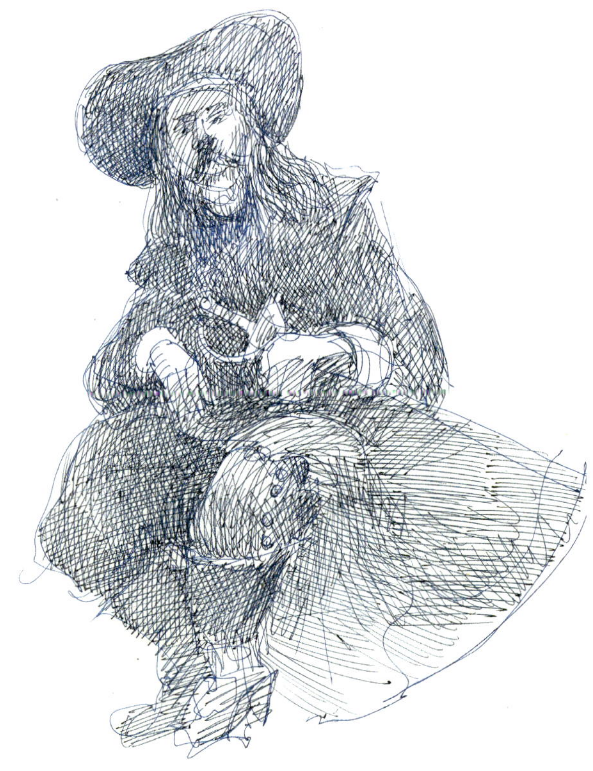

Scott often brings a sketchbook to dress rehearsals and draws, as inconspicuously as possible, in darkened auditoriums; this is Tom Rooney as Cyrano, in Act V, during a dress rehearsal for the Shaw Festival's 2019 production.

Edmond Rostand's great masterpiece *Cyrano de Bergerac* premiered in Paris in 1897. Cyrano is the greatest swordsman in France. He has the noble soul of a poet — this play, more than any other I can think of, reminds us that the pen is mightier than the sword. And he has an impossibly large nose. Cyrano is in love with Roxane but is too deeply, painfully shy to tell her so. Roxane has noticed Christian, a handsome new cadet in Cyrano's regiment; Christian has fallen for Roxane at first sight — but he is too painfully tongue-tied to have any chance with her. Cyrano proposes to supply the words that Christian will use to win Roxane — which works brilliantly for four of the play's five acts.

I have seen many fine productions — the Shaw Festival's legendary 1982–83 staging with Heath Lamberts and Marti Maraden; Colm Feore at the Stratford Festival in 2009. I was too young to see Christopher Plummer play the role at Stratford in 1962 (remounted the following season with John Colicos), but I practically memorized the recording of Plummer's Tony award-winning performance in the 1973 musical adaptation. There's the 1990 film version starring Gerard Depardieu; and Steve Martin's *Roxanne* from 1987. Placido Domingo sang the title role at The Met in a 2005 production of Franco Alfano's adaption as an opera. There has been a "Bollywood" *Cyrano*, performed in English, Hindi and Urdu, at the National Theatre in London; and an adaptation with an all-female cast at the Southwark Playhouse in London in 2016.

For Frank Langella's 1997 production at The Roundabout, I imagined a moment in the play that happens offstage (which is to say, in our imagination). Cyrano is alone in his tent in the middle of the night, writing Christian's final, fateful letter to Roxane. He's "choosing his rhymes" (his expression from Act 1 as he prepares to fight Valvert) — I should think that the whole charade is very difficult for him by this point.

The Shaw Festival's wonderful 2019 production, starring Tom Rooney and Deborah Hay, was scheduled to tour in the winter of 2021. One of the venues was the Grand Theatre in London, Ontario, so I was thrilled to have the opportunity to create a new poster for it in The Grand's signature scratchboard style. I started working on a swashbuckling portrait of Rooney in the title role. I love a poster concept that allows the play title to be integrated into the illustration; here, the calligraphic title letters make a visual reference to the trophy hats, "skewered" on a sword after Cyrano defeats a hundred opponents at the Porte de Nesle (again, offstage).

The Grand's 2020–21 season was derailed by COVID-19, unfortunately, so this poster has not been widely seen.

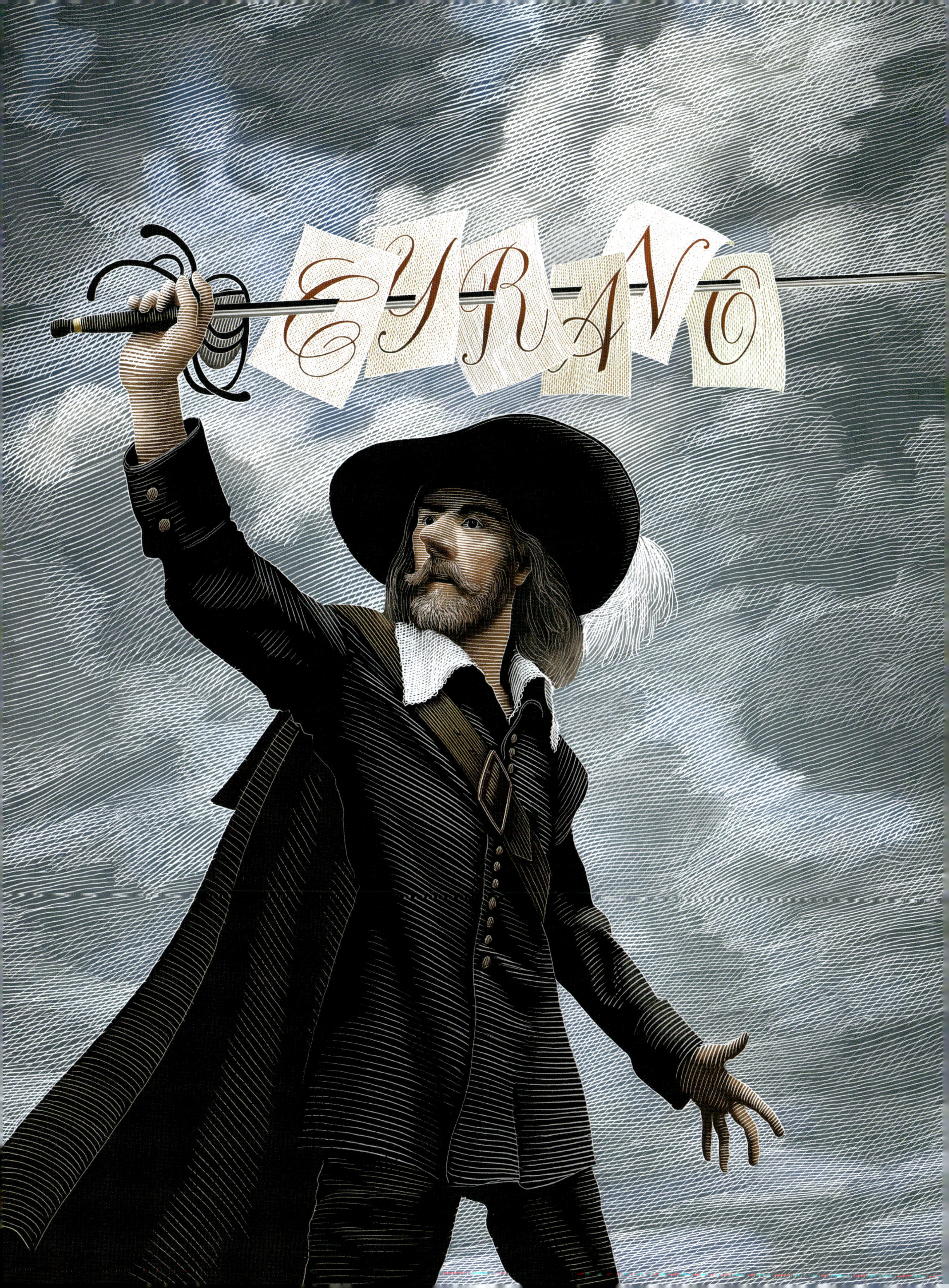
CYRANO

Bernard Shaw's *Misalliance* is such fun. Afternoon tea at the country estate of underwear tycoon John Tarleton is interrupted when an airplane crash-lands in the conservatory. The handsome young pilot runs off with Tarleton's daughter, Hypatia. His passenger turns out to be a dazzling Polish acrobat with an unpronounceable last name (Lina Szczepanowska), for whom all the men fall head-over-heels in love. The play is loaded with sexual tension. Shaw's witty dialogue covers a range of topics from relations between parents and children to the future of the British aristocracy, to the role of women in a modern society.

I'm sure it never occurred to him but the airplane was a gift from Shaw to future generations of poster designers. It provides a perfect metaphor for this play, conveying the exhilaration of flight, speed and risk — it must have taken some nerve to climb into one of these machines in 1908!

I included two posters for *Misalliance* in *A Fine Line* but I have revisited the play twice over the past decade, so here are new ones. For the Pearl Theatre Company's 2009 revival in New York, we are looking up at some fancy acrobatic skywriting. The Shakespeare Theatre of New Jersey's 2015 poster is from the opposite perspective — a bird's-eye view of Hypatia and the pilot chasing each other through a hedge maze.

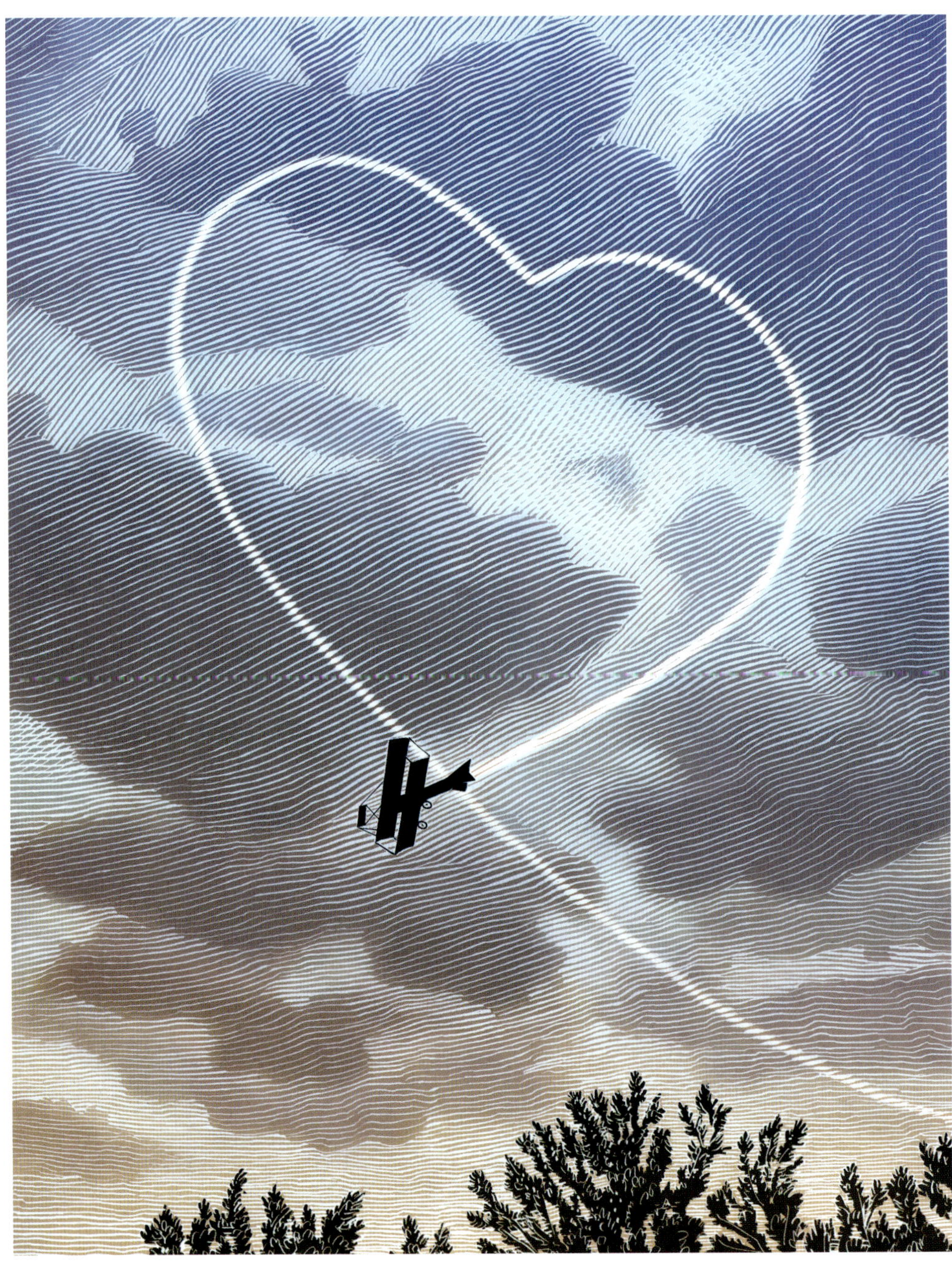

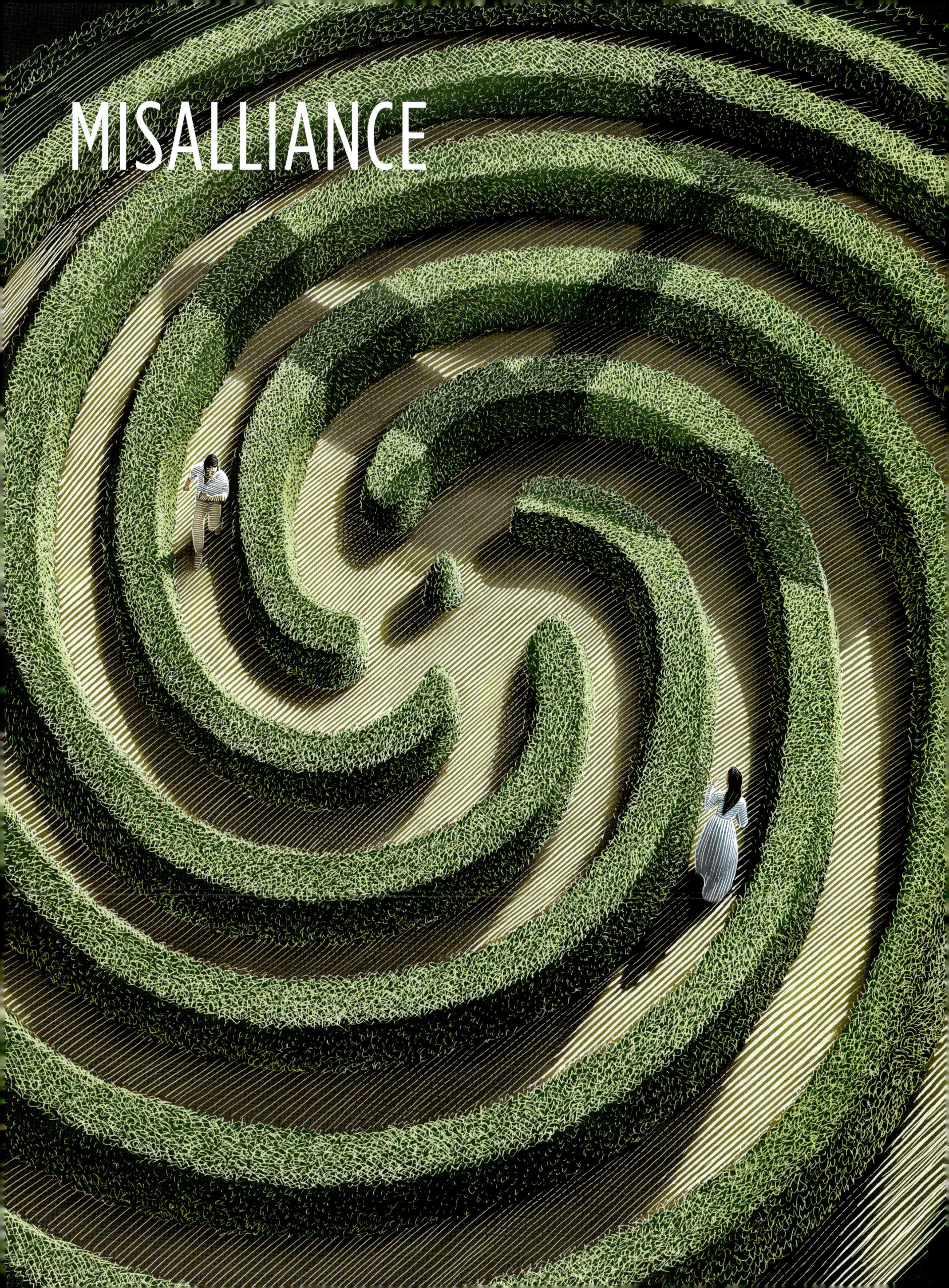
MISALLIANCE

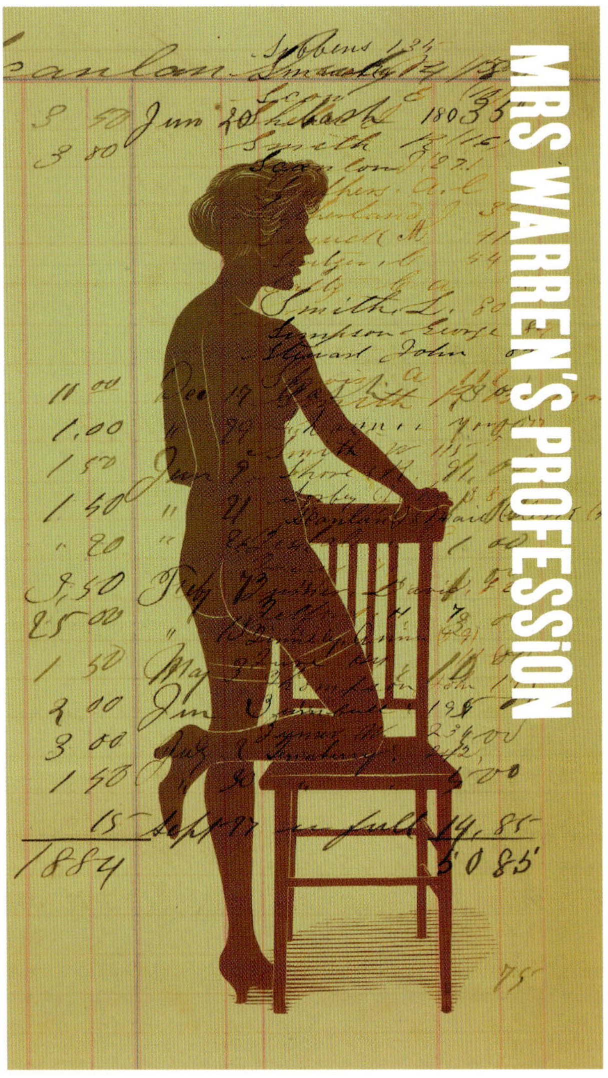

Mrs. Warren's profession is the oldest one: she runs a string of brothels across Europe, and she is very good at her job. She had good looks and a good head for business, and Shaw points out this was about the only way a woman could employ herself in the 1890s and earn as much as a man.

Her daughter Vivie has won a mathematics prize at Cambridge University and aspires to a career as an actuary. But Vivie is appalled to discover the source of the money that financed her education and opportunities.

A poster image for *Mrs. Warren's Profession* somehow needs to make reference to these two contrasting worlds. The common denominator between mother and daughter turns out to be — accounting! Vivie is a math whiz, and Mama, obviously, would have kept excellent records of all her clients. For the Denver Center Theatre Company's 2005 poster, I superimposed the silhouette of a young woman over a page from a Victorian ledger book, which I found in the collection of our local Stratford Archives. It came from a clothing store — the dates and prices written beside men's names were just what I was looking for. My scratchboard silhouette figure is adapted from one of E.J. Bellocq's 1912 portrait photographs of prostitutes in Storyville, the red-light district of New Orleans.

Mrs. Warren's Profession was written in 1894 but banned from public performance in England until 1925. The first American production in 1905 was shut down and the cast arrested for "offending public decency."

Shaw's *Candida* feels more modern than you might expect for a play written in 1895. There's a romantic triangle. The Reverend James Mavor Morell preaches in church on Sunday morning, but his true calling seems to be political lecturing and social reform. The play is set in the living room of the parsonage in North London that he shares with his wife, the title character. The Morells have befriended an idealistic young poet, Eugene Marchbanks. Both men adore Candida, in different ways, for quite different reasons — and she is attracted to them both for their very different qualities.

Marchbanks' infatuation is evident throughout the story, but I was taken with a scene in which he declares to Candida that his only desire is to say her name over and over again. The illustration conveys the young poet's obsession with an older woman; the calligraphy stands in for her spoken name. This poster was for the 1993 Broadway revival, starring Mary Steenburgen, Robert Foxworth and Robert Sean Leonard — one of my first assignments for the Roundabout Theatre Company.

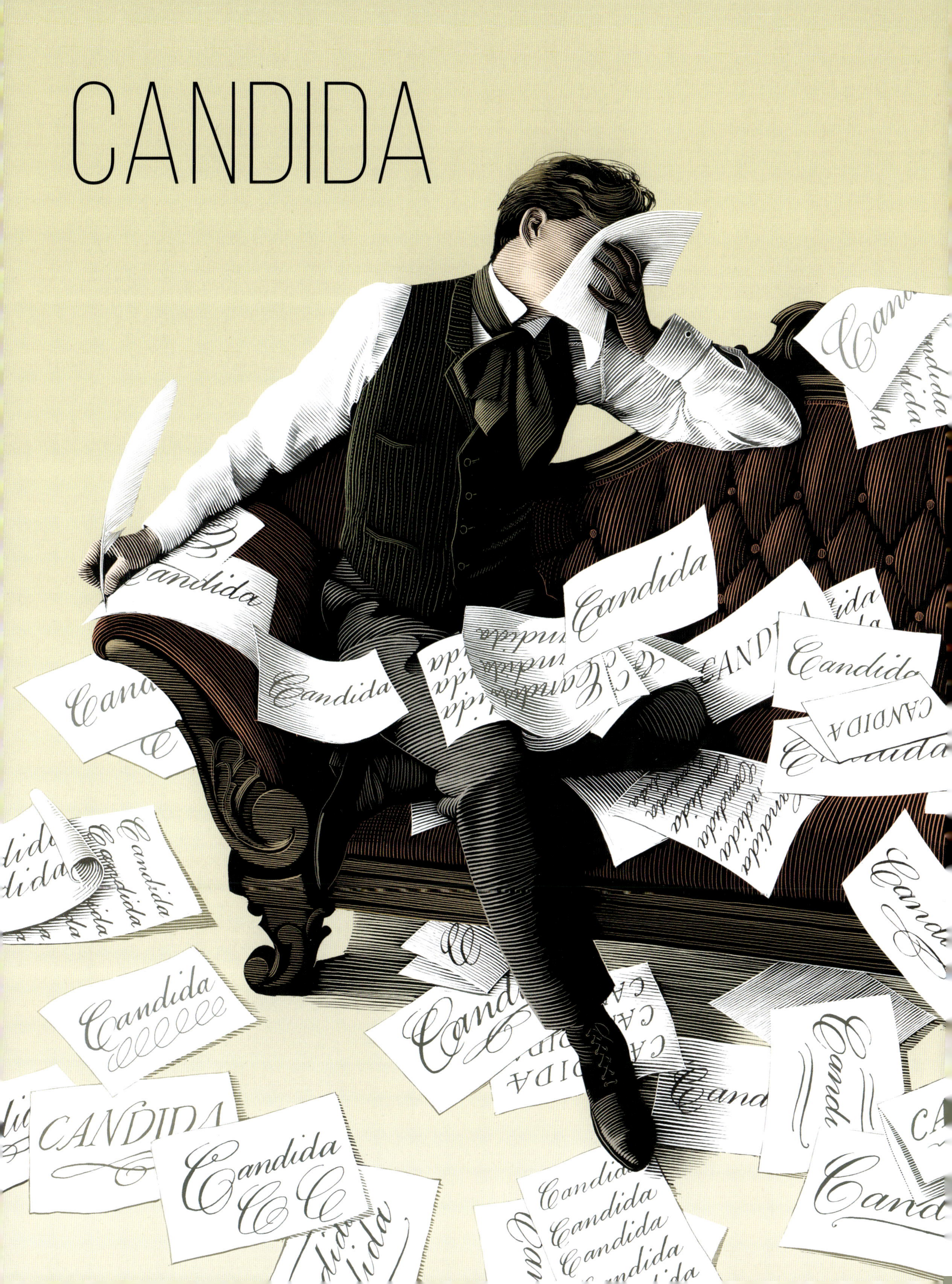
CANDIDA

The Devil's Disciple, written in 1897, was a huge hit and became Shaw's first financial success. Set in New Hampshire during the Revolutionary War, this action-packed melodrama is full of surprising role reversals. The plot constantly turns our expectations upside-down. "Bad lot" Dick Dudgeon, the social outcast, turns out to be the hero. The humble village minister becomes a man of action, rescuing Dick from the gallows at the last possible moment. British officers, initially the villains of the story, end up its merriest fools. For The Shakespeare Theatre of New Jersey's 2014 production, I put Dick Dudgeon on a "wanted" poster. The Queen Anne red ensign was the British flag during the U.S. War of Independence. Stephen Gartner was the model.

Arms and The Man premiered in 1894. Shaw plays here with love and war — naïve young Raina has her romantic ideas about soldiers shattered when Captain Bluntschli, running for his life in a panic retreat over the Dragoman Pass during the Serbo-Bulgarian war, takes refuge in her bedroom. The play was an instant success. Audiences roared with laughter on opening night, but Shaw was chagrined (he claimed) because the comedy had overshadowed his serious arguments and the play's anti-war message. The play still resonates today because humans are still going to war — 125 years after its premiere, nothing seems to have changed except the uniforms. This poster was for a production in 2000 at the Roundabout Theatre Company starring Henry Czerny and Katie Finneran, directed by Roger Rees. Shauna Black was the model.

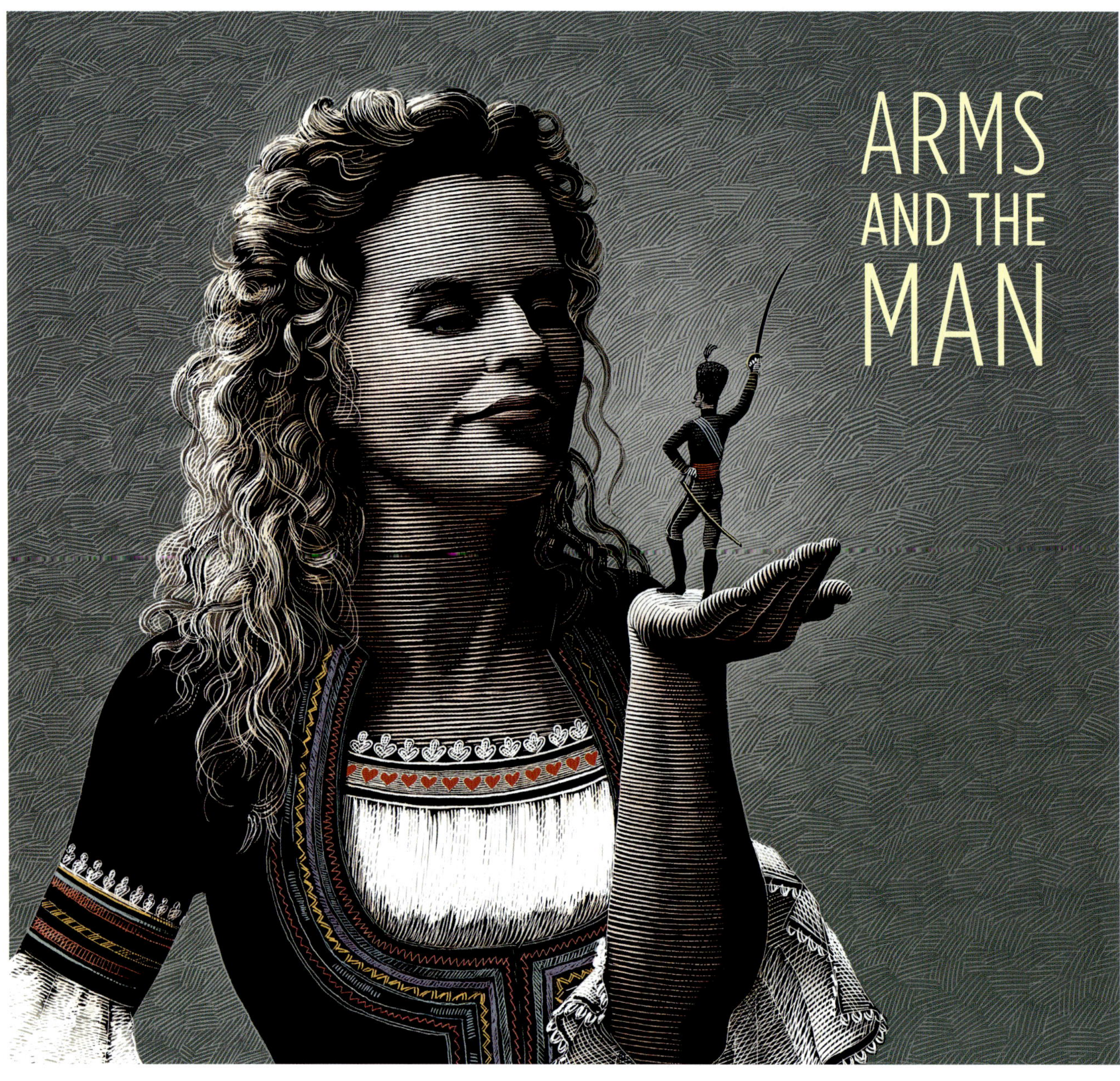

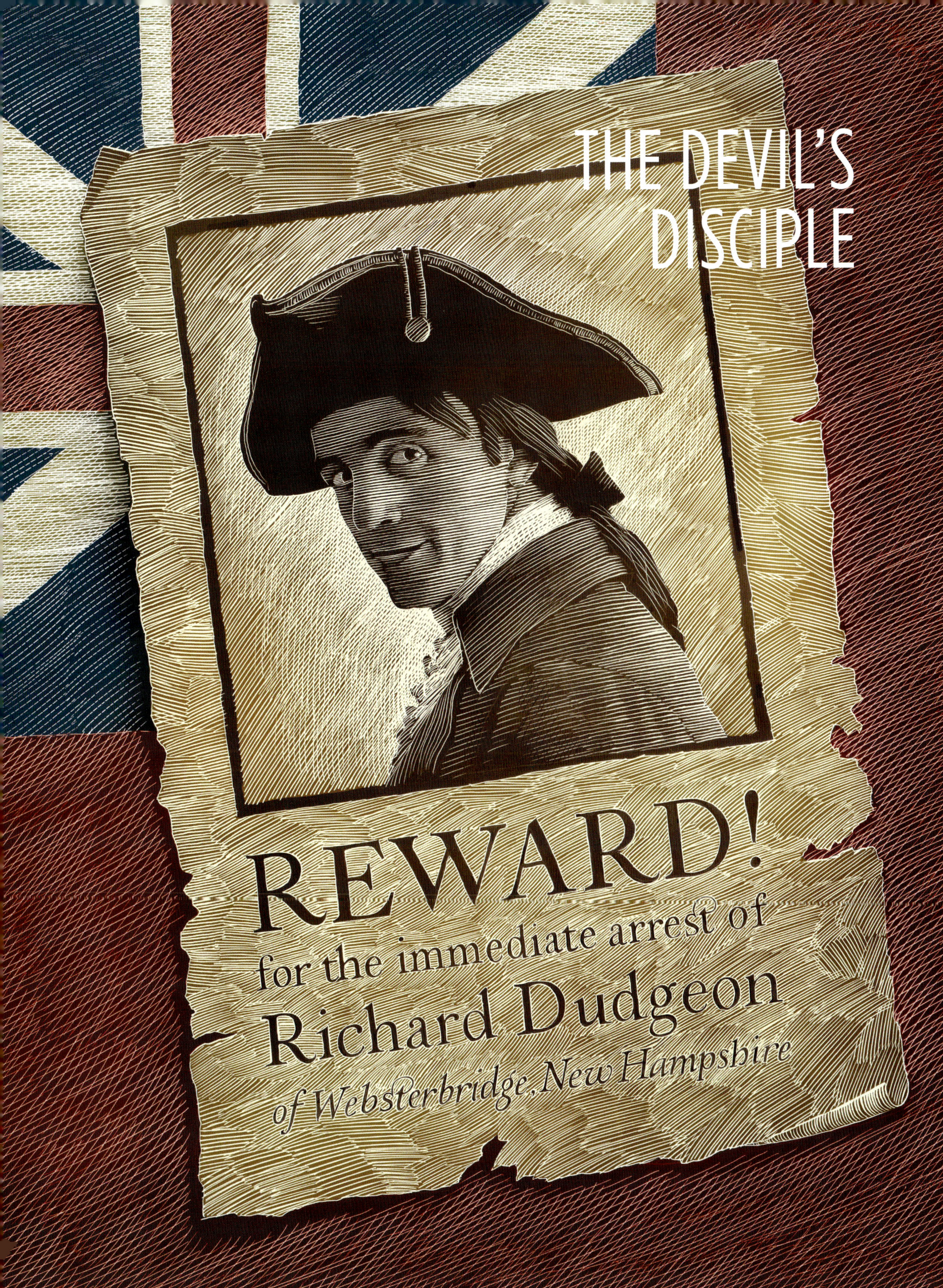
THE DEVIL'S DISCIPLE
REWARD!
for the immediate arrest of
Richard Dudgeon
of Websterbridge, New Hampshire

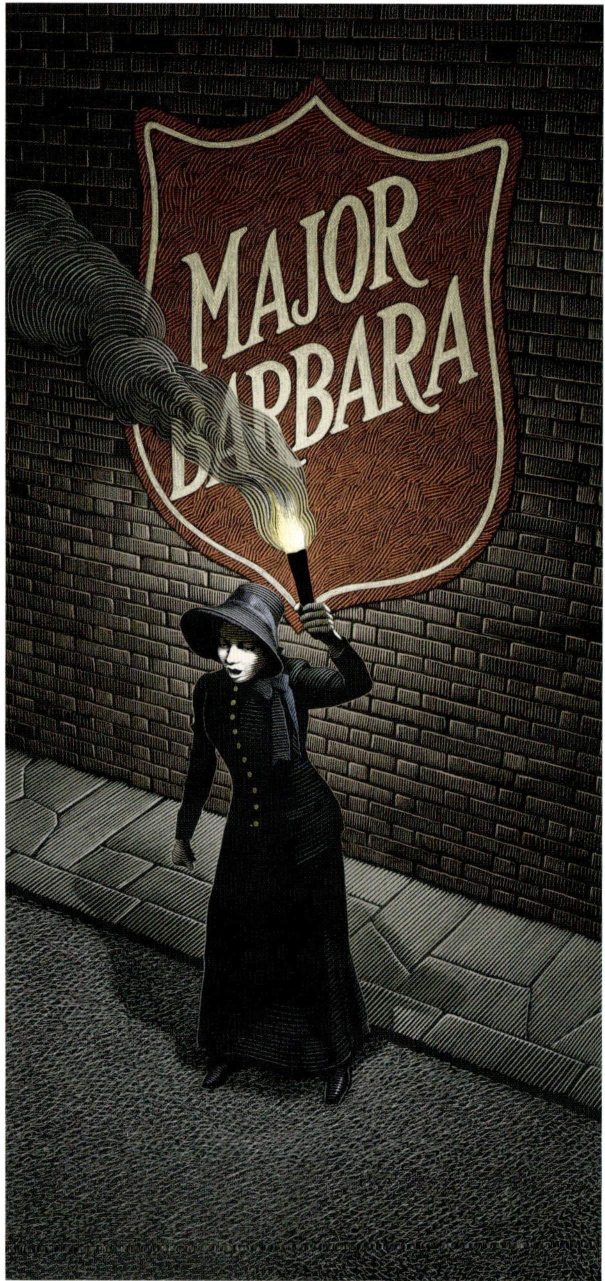

Bernard Shaw wrote *Major Barbara* in 1905 but the play's debates feel more topical and more provocative than ever. Millionaire arms manufacturer Andrew Undershaft and his daughter Barbara, who runs an East End London Salvation Army shelter, seem to be on opposite sides of every moral, political and religious divide. The play asks tough questions: Which is the greater human atrocity — poverty or war? Can money and power buy spiritual salvation?

My poster for Daniel Sullivan's fine 2001 production at the Roundabout Theatre, starring Cherry Jones, is an image of urgent, angry protest. The Salvation Army's motto is "Blood and Fire" — but the blazing torch in the dark night refers equally to Undershaft's cannons and gunpowder. Taking a few typographic liberties, I was able to combine the play title with the Salvation Army's familiar shield logo in my illustration.

Heartbreak House is Shaw's apocalyptic "dream play." Captain Shotover, the central character, is an ancient mariner embodying Prospero, Lear and Leonardo da Vinci all rolled into one. Two superb productions are still in my head. Both were mounted at the Shaw Festival and both starred Douglas Rain: Christopher Newton's unforgettable staging in 1985; and Tadeusz Bradecki's in 1999 (with costumes designed by Christina Poddubiuk). I also saw Paul Scofield play Shotover in Trevor Nunn's 1992 production in London. So I was thrilled (and a little terrified) to get the poster assignment for the Roundabout's 2006 Broadway production, starring Philip Bosco.

The architectural metaphor of the title refers to England itself. Shaw's detailed stage directions specify that the interior of Captain Shotover's house "resemble the afterpart of an old-fashioned, high-pooped ship with a stern gallery." I combined the ship metaphor and the house metaphor and came up with a stately British mansion adrift on an inky ocean, smoke from its chimneys swirling in the dusky twilight.

Shaw wrote *Heartbreak House* during the darkest days of the World War One. I think of the play as a bookend to *Major Barbara* — Undershaft's challenge "dare you make war on war?" was still a message of hope in 1905. But Shotover's warning to "learn navigation" is aimed squarely at a society that had failed to do so.

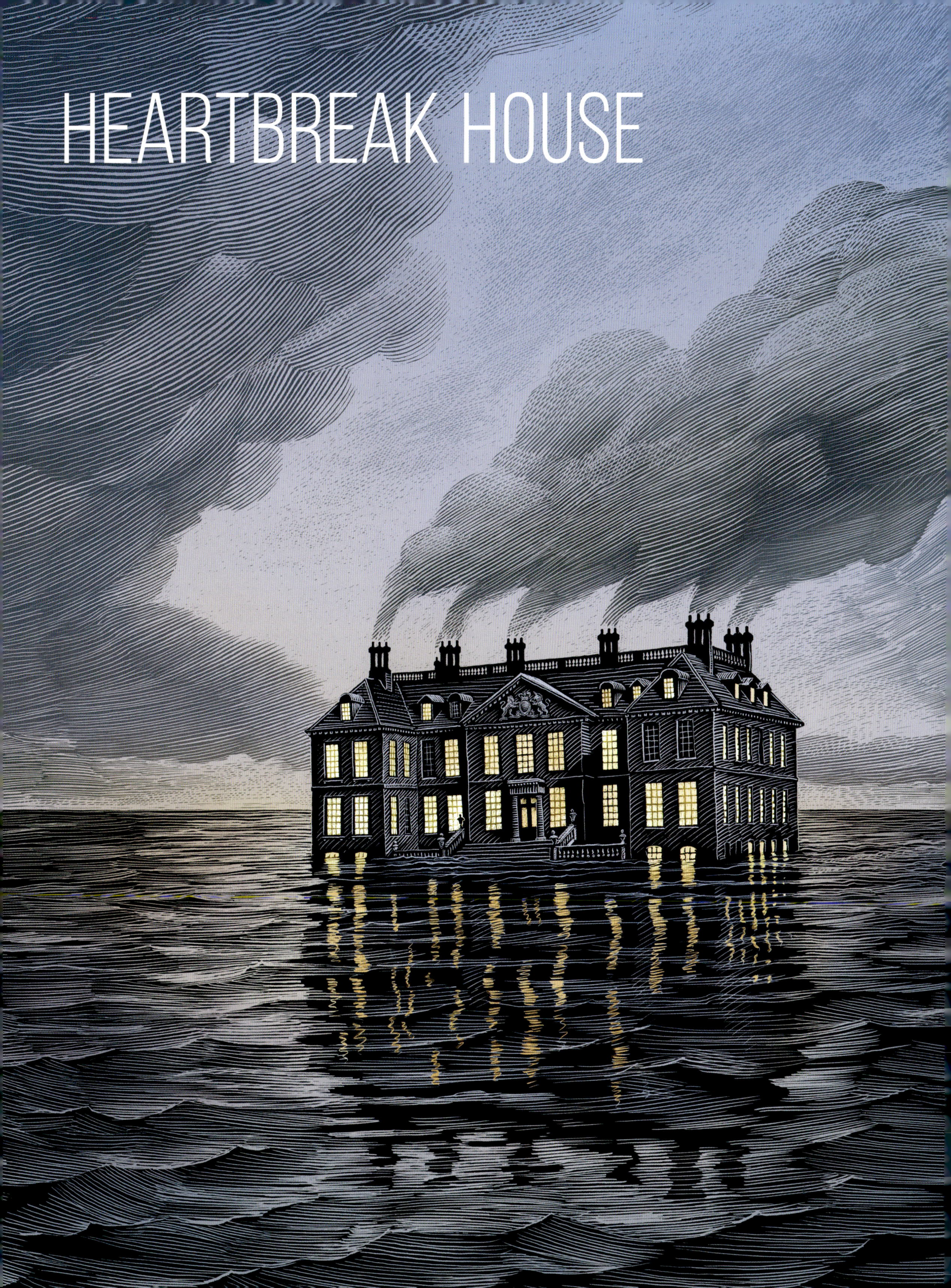
HEARTBREAK HOUSE

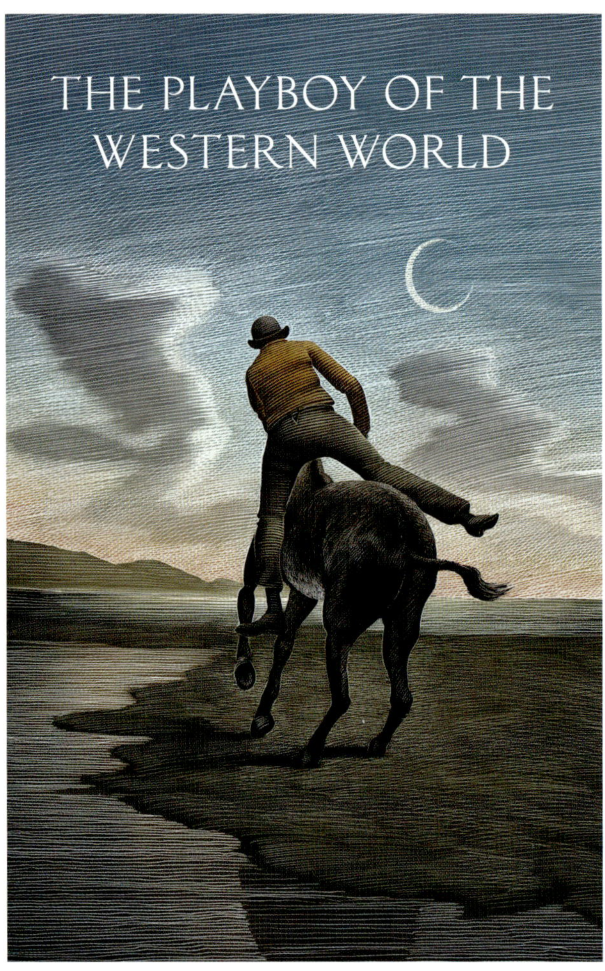

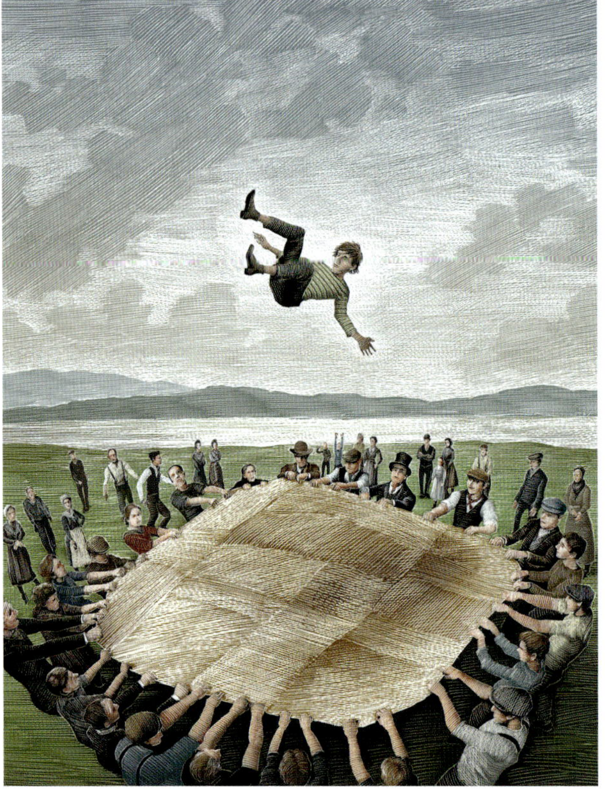

I love working with theatre directors who have a strong vision for a project. This poster for Sean O'Casey's *Juno and the Paycock*, for the Roundabout Theatre Company in 2000, reflects John Crowley's strong feelings about the Irish Civil War, "the archetypal Irish tragedy" and the criteria behind his powerful production.

Crowley had staged the play earlier that same year at the Donmar Warehouse in London, where he was associate director. In a phone chat several weeks before starting rehearsals in New York, he told me that it was essential to get the world of 1924 Dublin "exactly right," but warned that the poster image should avoid any parochial "shamrockery" and go for the larger universal themes, which are timeless.

If there was going to be a human figure, Crowley thought it should probably be female. "The men fire the bullets; the women have to pick up the pieces" was how he summarized "the troubles" in Ireland throughout the 20th century. (Jez Butterworth's stunning new play *The Ferryman* demonstrates how Crowley's statement still resonates.)

Religious iconography, especially statues (specifically the *Pietà*), came up repeatedly. Crowley had seen a photograph of a statue of the Virgin Mary defaced with bullet holes, which created a tension between the violent and the eternal. He suggested that a rich area of the play to mine for images was in Act II, when old Mrs. Tancred interrupts the mirth of the Boyles' party as she leaves for her son's funeral. She berates the guests for their unfeeling behaviour and prays aloud, "Sacred Heart of Jesus, take away our hearts of stone and give us hearts of flesh." Her words are echoed precisely by Juno at the end of the play as she leaves to identify the body of her own son.

From half a dozen different pencil sketch concepts, Mr. Crowley picked a weeping classical statue wearing a crown of stars (both Juno and the Virgin Mary are "the Queen of Heaven"). The play title started out in Roman type with formal serifs, but ended up as a hand-drawn graffiti-like scrawl, scratchy and violent.

A masterpiece of Irish comedy is J.M. Synge's *The Playboy of the Western World*. A young man stumbles into a pub in rural County Mayo, scared out of his wits, blurting out that he has killed his father. Instead of being shunned as a murderer, he finds himself lionized as a folk-hero. The village girls go crazy for him — he's the centre of attention — until his father shows up very much alive. I created posters for The Pearl Theatre Company in 2009 and The Shakespeare Theatre of New Jersey in 2013.

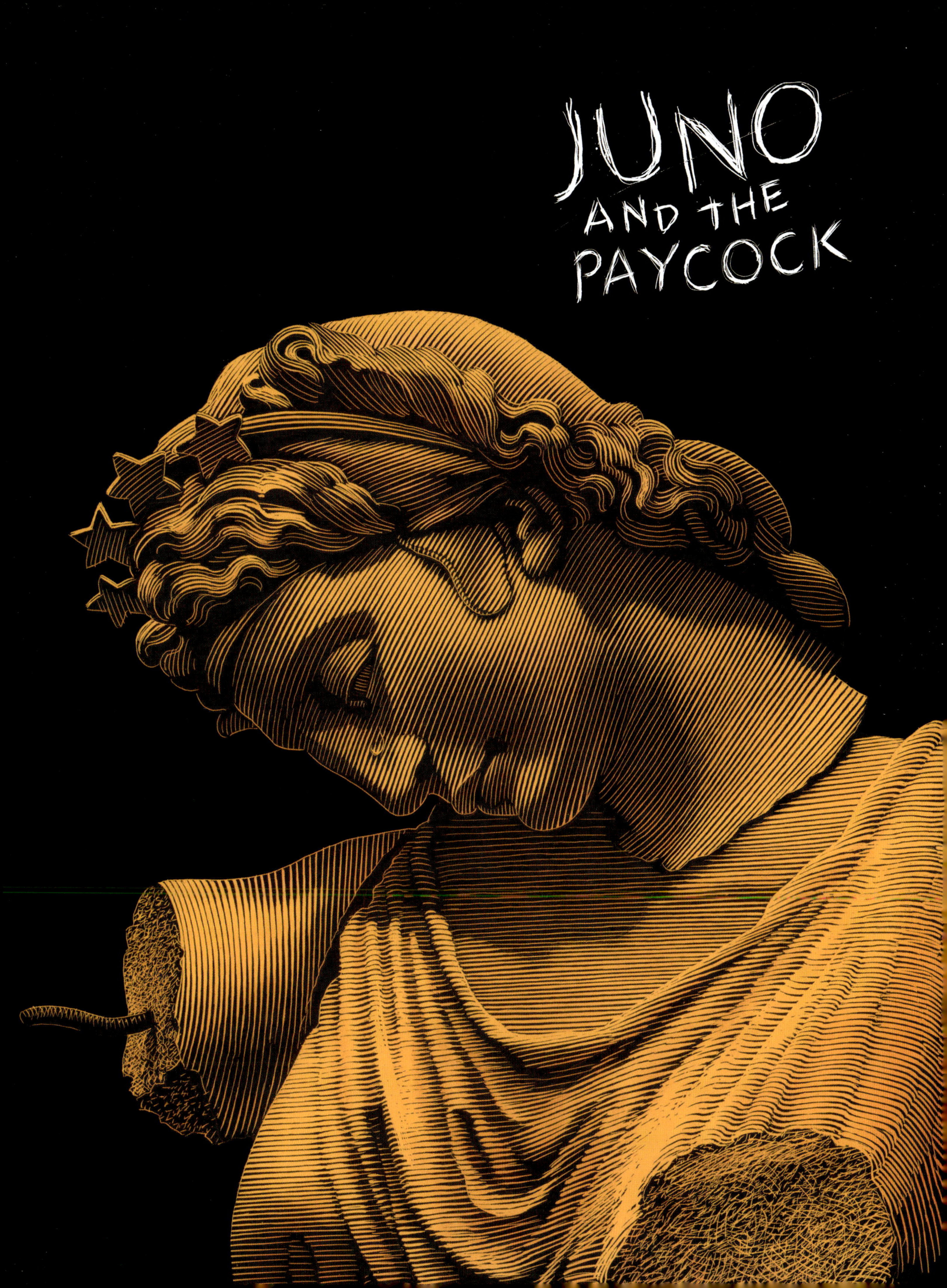

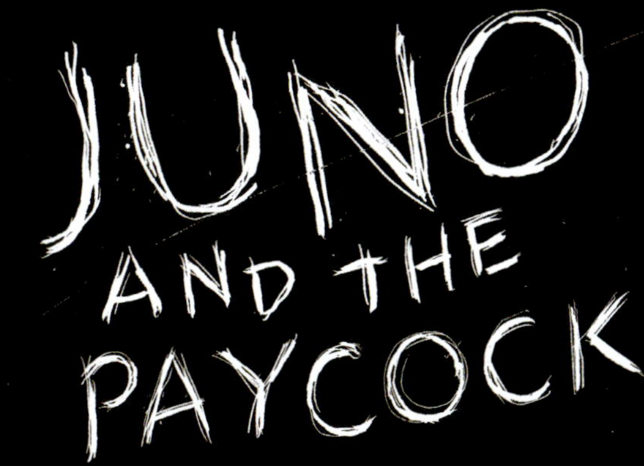
JUNO
AND THE
PAYCOCK

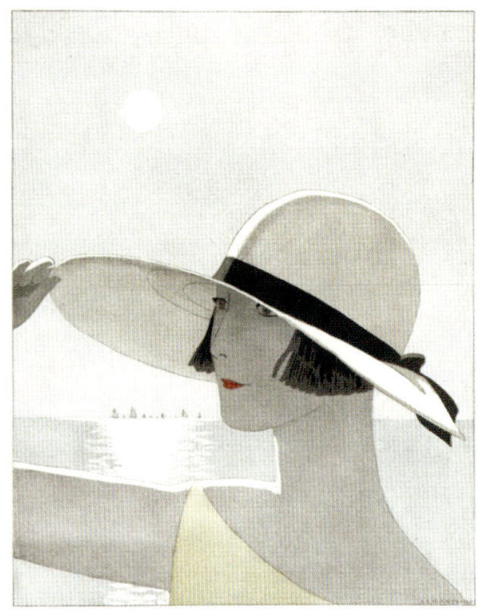

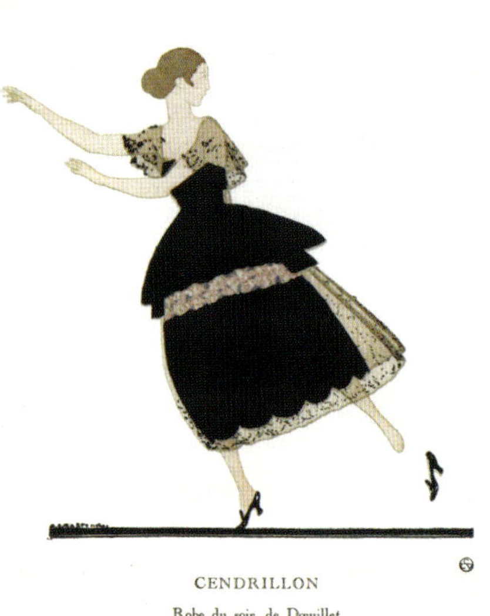

CENDRILLON
Robe du soir, de Dœuillet

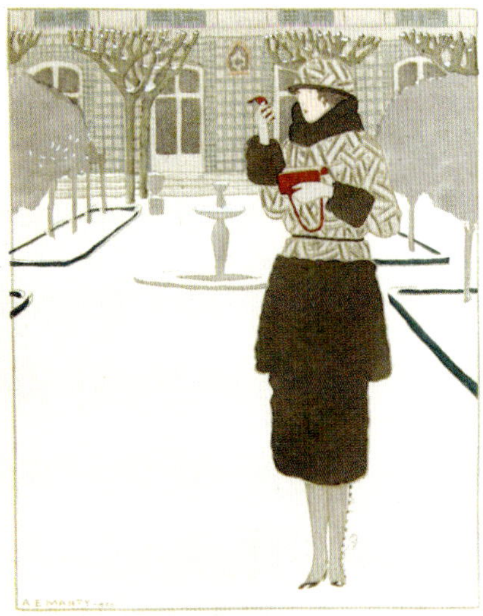

The two main characters in Hungarian playwright Ferenc Molnár's *The Guardsman* are named only The Actor and The Actress. She has had affairs with dozens of men — but none has ever lasted longer than six months. The Actor has won her love and they have been married — for five and a half months.

The Actor suspects that his wife may preparing to leave him for someone new — and from hints he has picked up, thinks that she is interested in an exotic Cossack Guardsman at the Imperial Palace. He is the best actor in Budapest, so he decides to impersonate his rival — and seduce his own wife. Knocking on his own front door wearing an elaborate disguise, he introduces himself as Count Victor de Latour-Schonichen of the Imperial Royal Arciere Guards.

The play is part Strindberg, part Pirandello and part Feydeau. It can be played as a bourgeois, boulevard comedy (Alfred Lunt and Lynne Fontanne made it a Broadway hit in 1924) — or as a sad, dark, lonely play about a troubled marriage. Playwright Richard Nelson created an adaptation for the Kennedy Center in 2013 and points out that the key is how The Actor's ruse is perceived by The Actress. "If the wife knows that the husband is dressing up as the Guardsman, then it's a one-joke show. If the wife doesn't, and she falls in love with him — someone she thinks is someone else — then it's a dark, dark problem." I first discovered the play in the Stratford Festival's 1977 production starring Maggie Smith and Brian Bedford, directed by Robin Phillips.

I have a collection of *pochoir* prints — beautifully drawn fashion plates from the early 20th century with hand-stenciled colour — by French illustrator A.E. Marty. These lovely little compositions with costumed figures against clean, flat backgrounds provided the inspiration for my 2015 poster for *The Guardsman* at The Shakespeare Theatre of New Jersey. Our Cossack Prince Charming is leaning in from the edge of frame; The Actress is turned away but letting him kiss her hand. I put lots of space between them to signal the ambiguity of their relationship. My fabulous models were actors Stephen Gartner and Robin Evan Willis.

For this production in New Jersey, Bonnie Monte directed her own adaptation. She worked from a literal English translation by Gábor Lukin, a great-grandson of Molnár himself. *The New York Times* noted that Bonnie had "fashioned a fresh version of the play to reveal a thorny edge that can prick the heart while tickling you to laughter." Bonnie's script was published in 2019 by Joseph Weinberger Ltd. and Music Theatre International (Europe), with my illustration wrapping around the front and back cover.

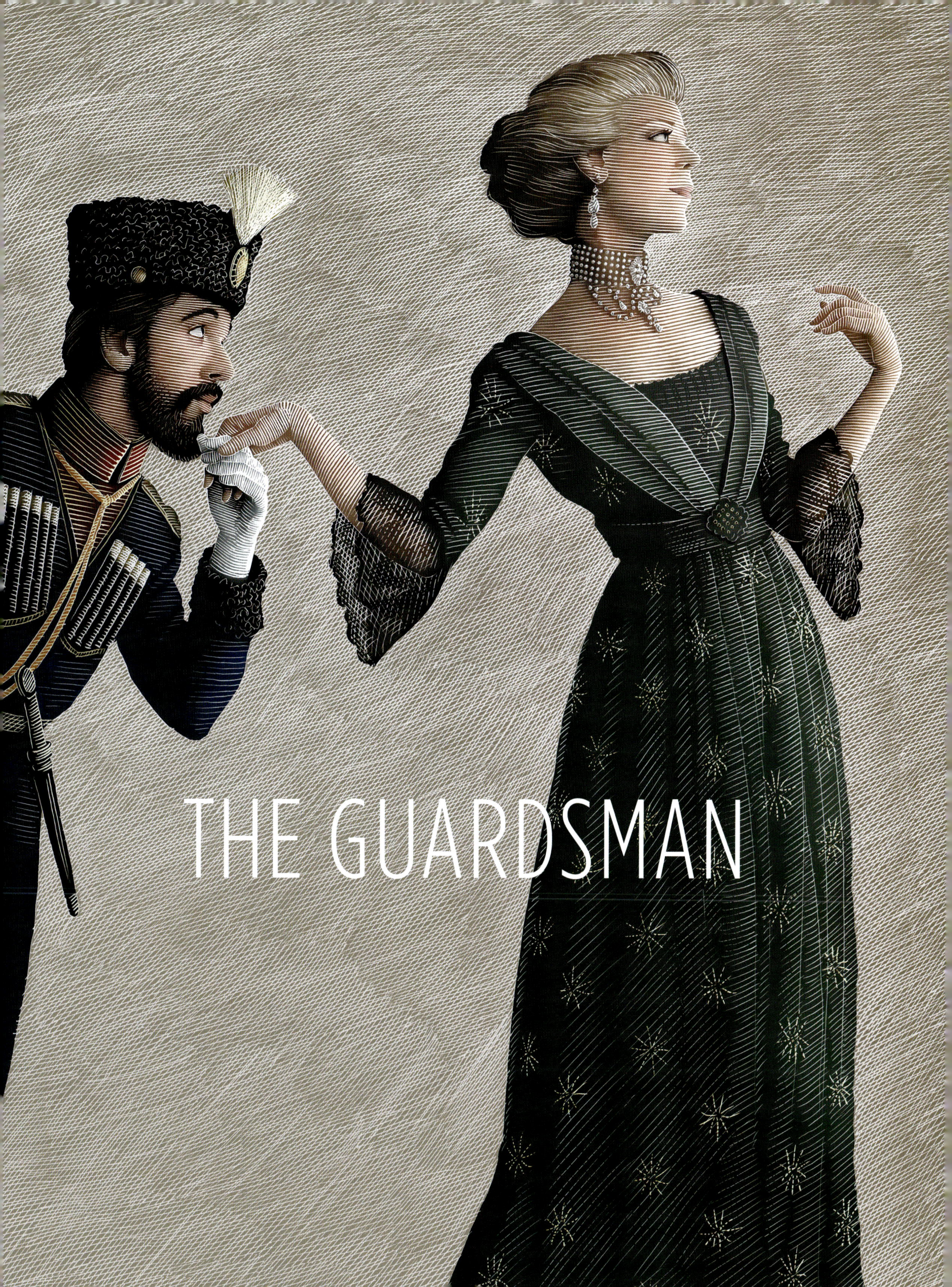

THE GUARDSMAN

Noël Coward called *Blithe Spirit* "a light comedy about death." It was written in 1941 at the height of the Blitz, as Londoners lived under the nightly threat of bombs crashing through their roofs. London theatregoers desperately needed something to lift their spirits, and Coward's play became an instant hit. The central character is Charles Condomine, a writer. In order to get background material for his next novel, he has invited Madame Arcati, a dubious and eccentric local spiritualist, to give a séance. Charles is a skeptic — he doesn't take any of this seriously — until the ghost of his glamorous first wife Elvira wafts in, conjured from the great beyond.

The title of this play comes from the first line of Percy Bysshe Shelley's poem "To a Skylark" (1820) — but Coward's title spirit is anything but blithe. Elvira has been finding eternity rather boring, and her scheme is to steal Charles away from his second wife, Ruth.

Staging the play requires some special effects — a real challenge for a set designer's ingenuity and a production department's budget. Several scenes call for objects on the set to be moved by ghosts unseen by the audience. Happily, it's much easier to generate paranormal activity in an illustration. I suggested a comic "haunting" by animating the living room furniture for a 1996 production at Arena Stage in Washington, D.C. The illustration was colourized and reused for The Shakespeare Theatre of New Jersey's production in 2018.

The same theatre staged Coward's *Fallen Angels* in 2013. The play about two wives admitting to premarital sex and contemplating adultery was provocative in 1925 — it was almost banned because the Lord Chamberlain's office felt that the loose morals of the main characters would create a scandal. Christina's idea of footsie under the table, slightly naughty in a gentle 1920s way, underscored the period through the shoes.

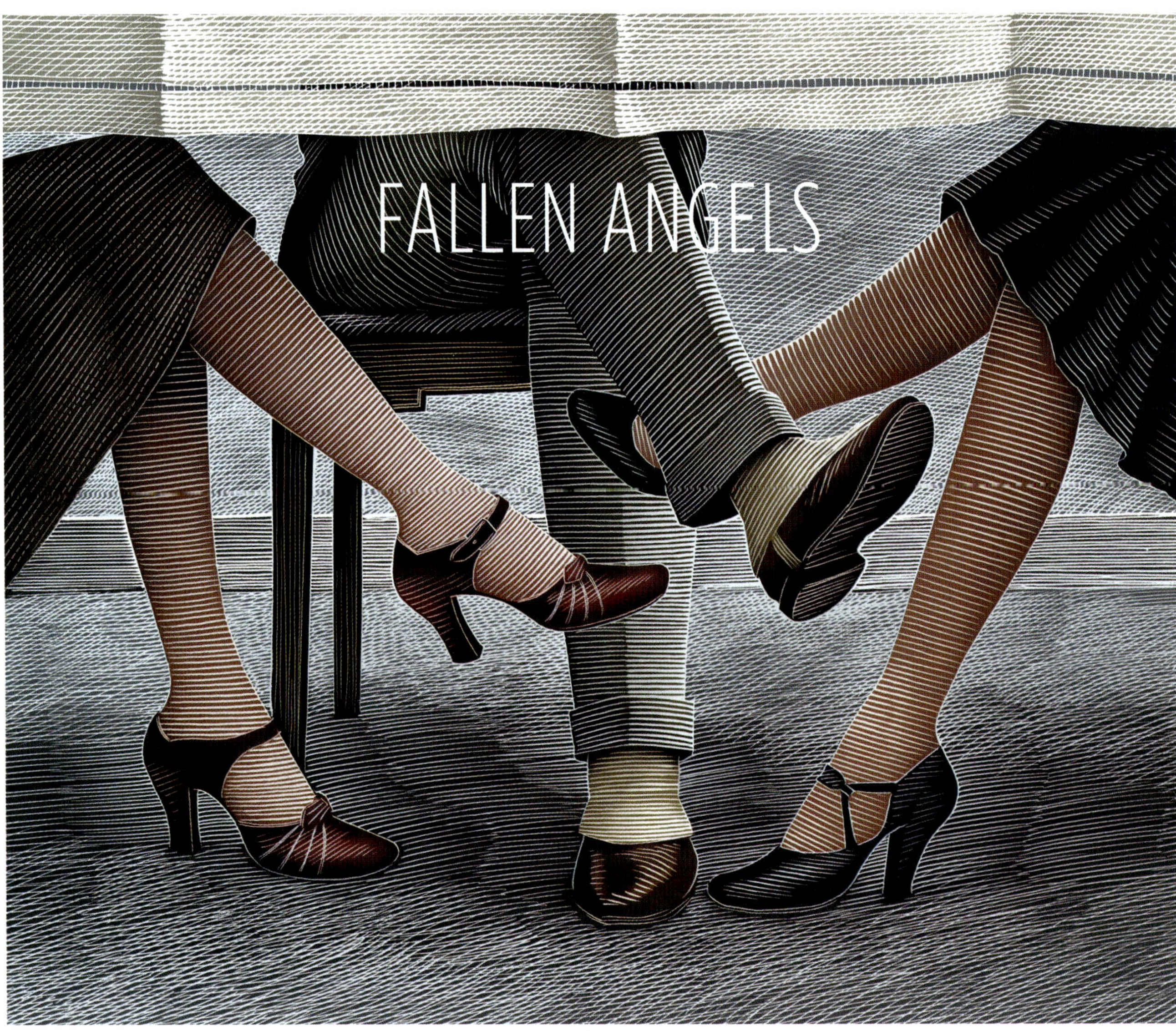

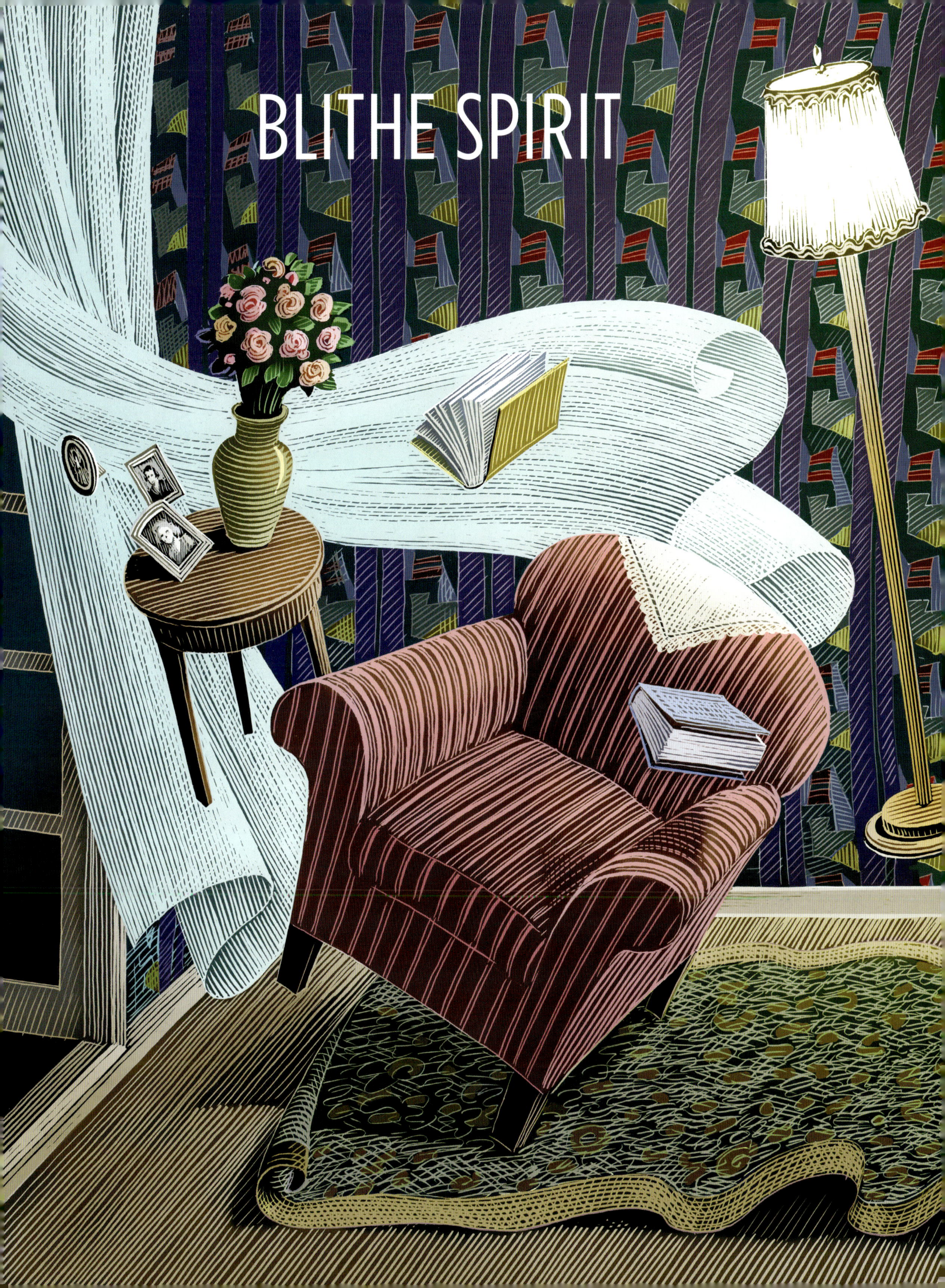
BLITHE SPIRIT

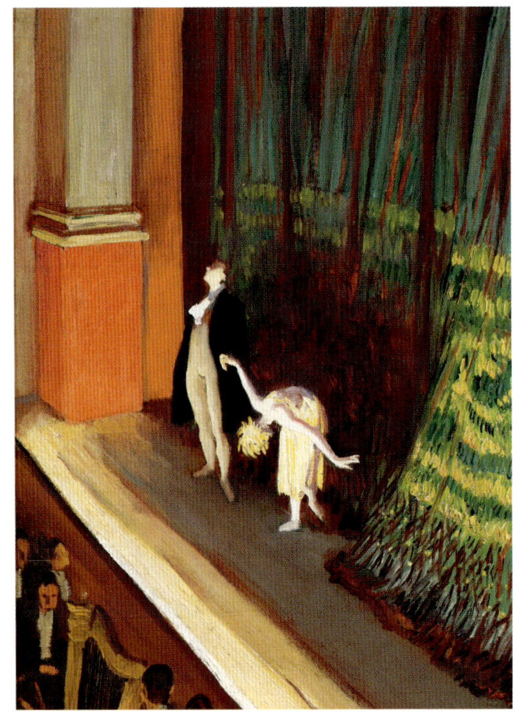

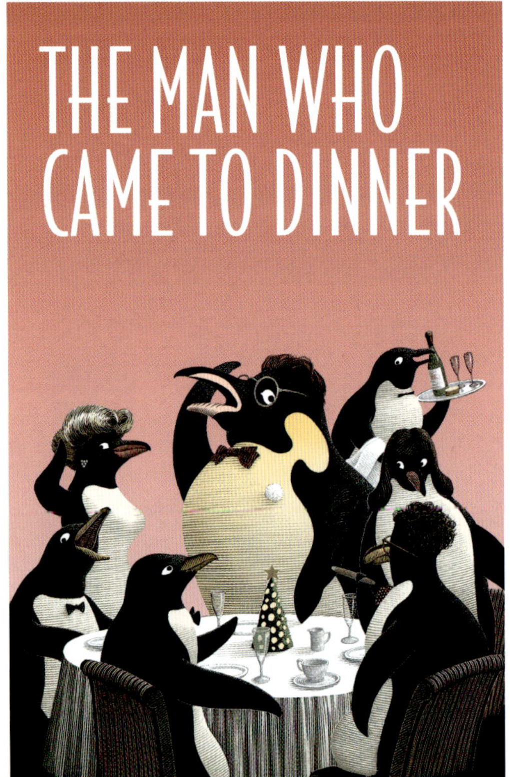

Top: *Pavlova Taking a Bow*, 1920, by Laura Knight (Atkinson Art Museum, Southport, UK). The prima ballerina is shown here with Alexander Volinine, a member of Diaghilev's Ballets Russes and Pavlova's frequent partner on international tours.

When George S. Kaufman and Edna Ferber's play *The Royal Family* opened at the Selwyn Theatre in December 1927, everyone in New York knew that it was based on the Barrymores — America's most famous family of actors. The glamorous Cavendish family in the play are thinly disguised versions of Ethel Barrymore, her brother John Barrymore, their lovers, parents, children and entourage.

The entire play takes place in their swanky New York apartment — from production photos you would never know it's a story about the theatre. But all they talk about is their lives on stage. This was my clue that the poster illustration should take us to the theatre, showing our matinée idol main characters basking in the ovation of their adoring fans.

I have always loved the work of British artist Dame Laura Knight (1877–1970). She loved the world of the theatre and painted actors and dancers onstage, backstage and in their dressing rooms. I based my illustration loosely on *Pavlova Taking a Bow*. Knight captured a wonderful sense of grand gesture here — a declamatory theatrical style that belongs to an earlier era. My poster was for a fine production that opened The Shakespeare Theatre of New Jersey's 2015 season.

Another famous Kaufman comedy is *The Man Who Came to Dinner*, written this time with Moss Hart, in 1939. Sheridan Whiteside, the star of a national radio show, is visiting a private home in a small town in Ohio. Whiteside slips on some ice and breaks his hip. He becomes an unwilling houseguest for six weeks of convalescence — the obnoxious, insulting Whiteside takes over the house and turns everyone's lives upside down. It's a nightmare for the hosts but hilarious for the audience.

Kaufman and Hart based Whiteside on Alexander Woollcott, the famous and feared drama critic for *The New York Times* and one of the first radio stars in America. Woollcott had a vast circle of celebrity pals — so does Whiteside. Noël Coward, Harpo Marx and others drop by to cheer up the invalid. Whiteside receives phone calls, telegrams and Christmas presents from an absurdly wide range of celebrities including Alfred Lunt and Lynn Fontanne, Gertrude Stein, Somerset Maugham, Salvador Dali, Mahatma Gandhi and Shirley Temple. Admiral Richard E. Byrd, the first man to fly over the South Pole, sends Whiteside a crate of live penguins as a Christmas present in Act III.

Woollcott, known for his acid wit, was a member of the celebrated Algonquin Round Table — an influential group of New York writers, actors and critics (including George S. Kaufman and Harpo Marx) who gathered for lunch every day at the Algonquin Hotel on West 44th Street. They dubbed themselves "The Vicious Circle." I combined the Algonquin Round Table with Admiral Byrd's penguins in my poster for the Roundabout Theatre Company's Broadway revival in 2000, starring Nathan Lane.

The innumerable text references to celebrities who were household names 80 years ago may mean that the play has become difficult to stage nowadays. The Stratford Festival considered a production for their 2019 season but dropped the idea because they worried that modern audiences would have no idea who most of these people were.

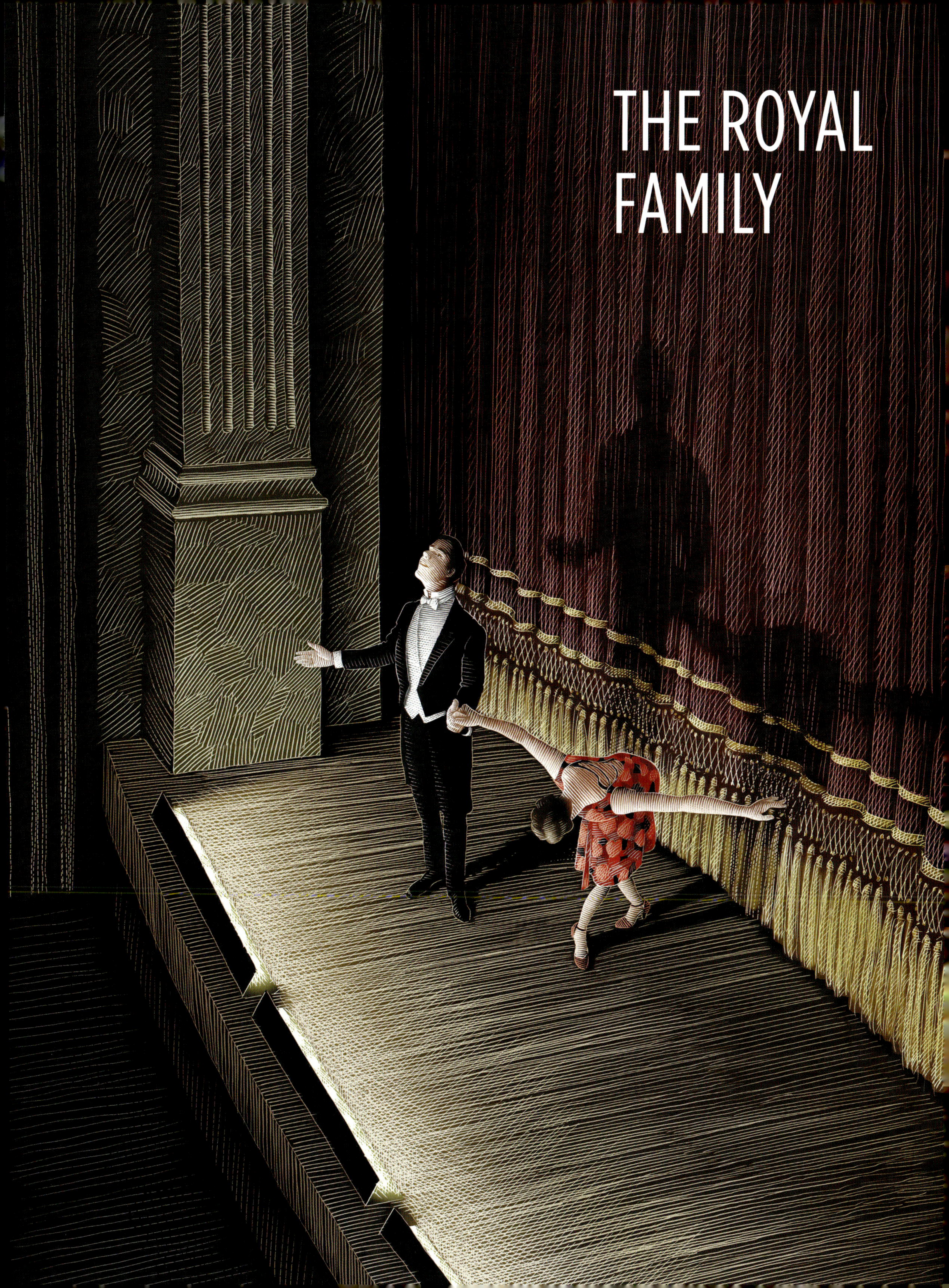
THE ROYAL
FAMILY

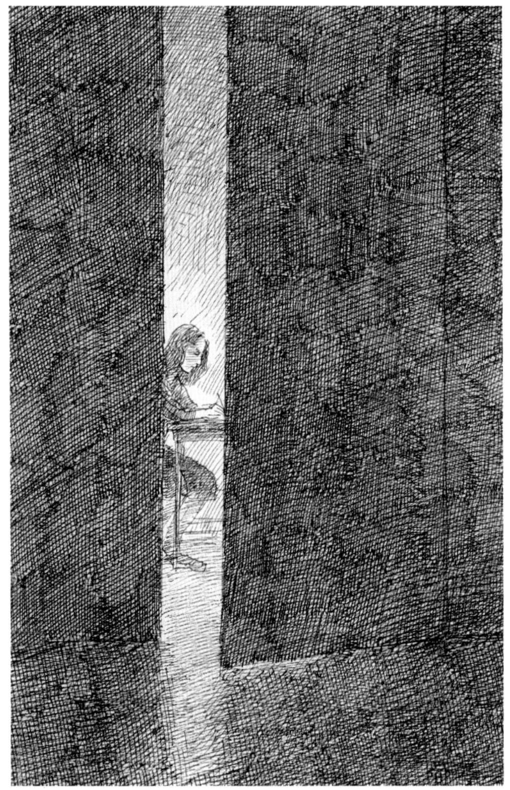

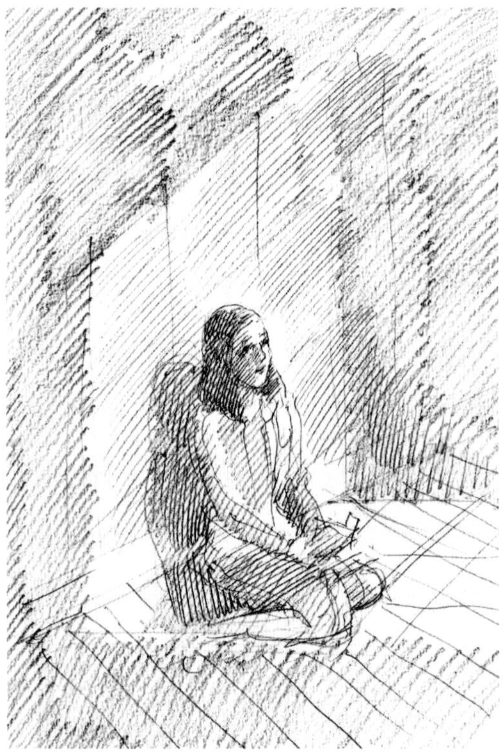

When The Shakespeare Theatre of New Jersey assigned *The Diary of Anne Frank* on their 2015 playbill, I immediately recalled my visit to the Anne Frank House Museum on the Prinsengracht Canal in central Amsterdam. You climb the steep stairs hidden behind a bookcase and you're standing in the secret apartment in the attic — the very rooms in which the play takes place.

Picturing those empty rooms, I started with sketches of the title character — visible through a doorway in a darkened room, sitting at a table writing in her diary. Too dreary. Maybe Anne looking out through a window at the sky would feel more hopeful. Then it struck me that everyone knows what Anne looks like — could we do this without the poster being a portrait?

By complete coincidence, the Stratford Festival had programmed the play that same season, and their poster image influenced my thinking about this question. Stratford is the largest classical theatre company in North America — any comparison to Shakespeare New Jersey is like David and Goliath. Stratford's image was a smiling sepia-toned portrait of the actress in the title role. My client was concerned that the image should not be too dark — but Stratford's went too far in the opposite direction.

The action of the play takes the audience inside the secret apartment. The convention of the play is that the characters can never leave the apartment, so the actors never leave the stage, even at intermission. I had purchased a postcard on my visit to the museum, which was pinned up in my studio for many years — a sombre black-and-white view of the back of the house, with that attic window where the family was hidden.

That photograph became my reference for the illustration. It's twilight and the architecture is silhouetted against a glowing sky with a sense of life and hope. Every window is dark except a faint light on in the attic. It seemed much more evocative to imagine Anne looking out through that window at the sky than to show her doing so.

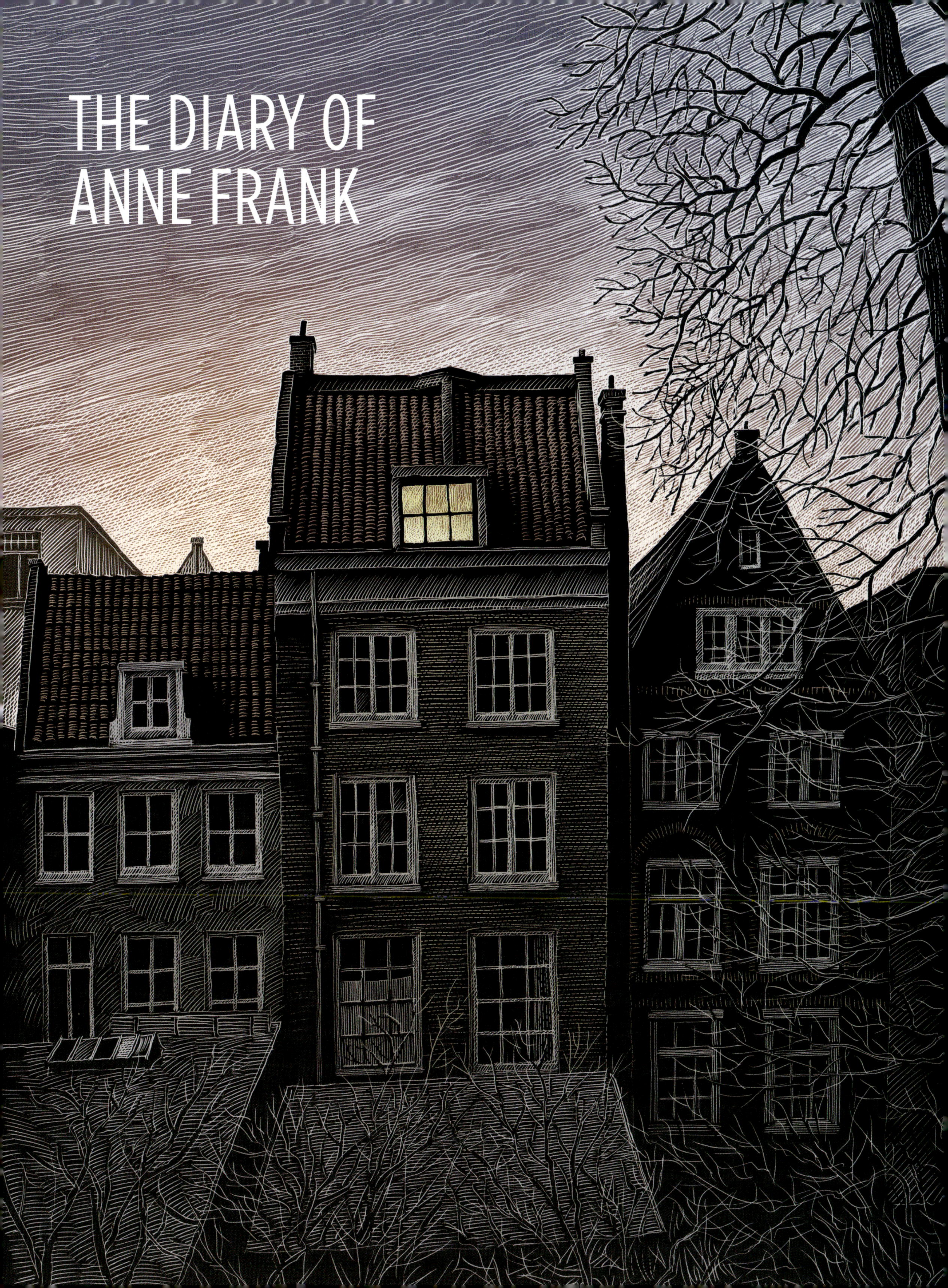
THE DIARY OF
ANNE FRANK

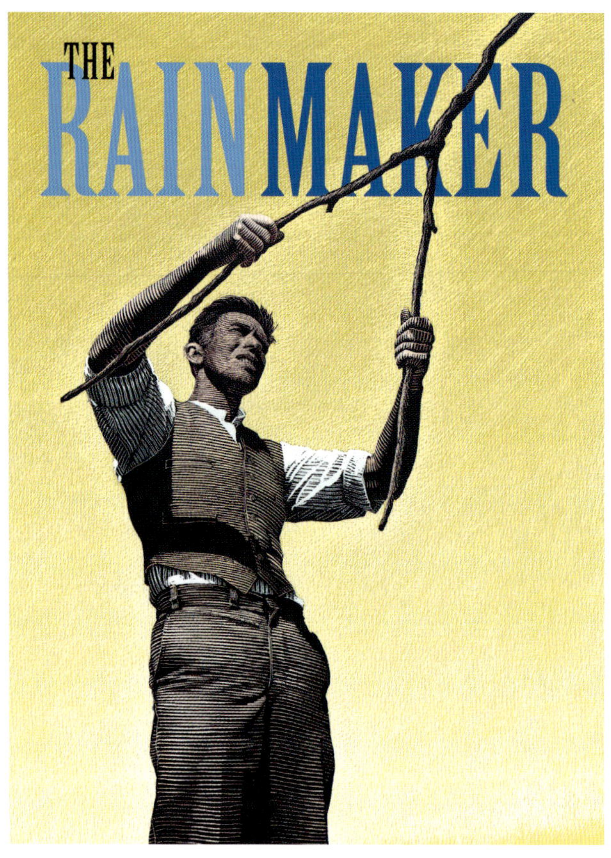

The Rainmaker is a Cinderella story set in the Dust Bowl of the 1930s. The play was written in the early '50s by N. Richard Nash. Lizzie Curry, a spinsterish farm girl, hopes and dreams of finding a man who will "stand up straight" — but her hopes and dreams are drying up as rapidly as the watering hole for the cattle on their struggling ranch. Bill Starbuck, a con man and lost soul at the end of his own road, promises to conjure up rain if the Curry family will part with $100, which they can ill afford. Two droughts end during the last scene of the play — the real one that threatens the livelihood of the farm and the spiritual one that envelops these two characters.

The original 1954 production starred Geraldine Page as Lizzie and Darren McGavin as Starbuck. The Broadway revival by the Roundabout Theatre Company in 2000 starred Woody Harrelson and Jayne Atkinson and was directed by Scott Ellis. My poster featured Starbuck, not with the "magic" staff he carries in the script but with a v-shaped twig to signify dowsing — or divining — the mysterious ability to find water or hidden treasures buried in the earth. My friend Antony John modeled for this poster (he loved the idea of standing in for Woody Harrelson!). Antony runs an organic farm near Stratford and once hired a water dowser who actually pinpointed an underground water source on the farm using two brass rods. But a 2017 article in *The Guardian* asks "Water divining is bunk — so why do myths continue to trump science?" and referred to the practice as "medieval witchcraft." A little "who to believe" controversy feels perfect for this play.

The Rainmaker was assigned again for The Shakespeare Theatre of New Jersey's 2019 season. While Starbuck is the catalyst of the story, Lizzie is the main protagonist. Christina suggested the play is not about rain at all — it's about quenching thirst. She imagined a hot, dry, parched Lizzie, pouring a glass of water over herself.

Bonnie Monte loved the pencil sketch, but felt strongly that the glass should be empty. If water is splashing over her face, it would indicate that Lizzie is "quenched" — satisfied physically, spiritually, emotionally or sexually. Bonnie wanted the poster to convey that she's still thirsty. Bonnie chose the play because it's about hope. I argued that an empty glass seems pretty hopeless, and that we should include water as a metaphor for the fulfillment that Lizze eventually, unexpectedly finds. But it's Bonnie's production, and I was happy to defer. I was actually a little nervous about rendering water running down Lizzie's face, neck and dress using only engraving lines — it was certainly easier to draw "dry." We did reference photos both ways, in a shower enclosure, just in case — Caitlin Luxford, my very patient model, was completely soaked by the time we finished shooting.

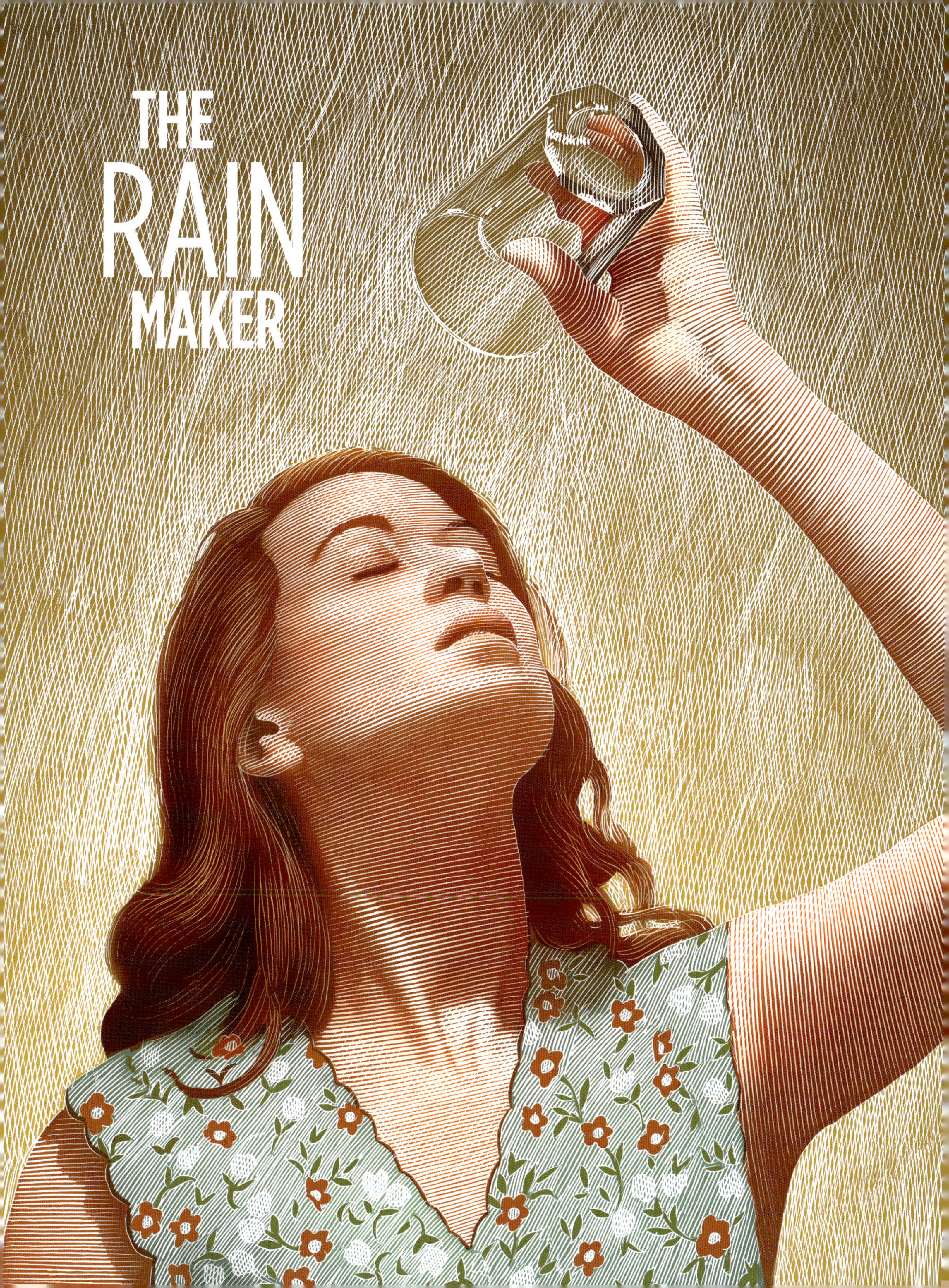
THE
RAIN
MAKER

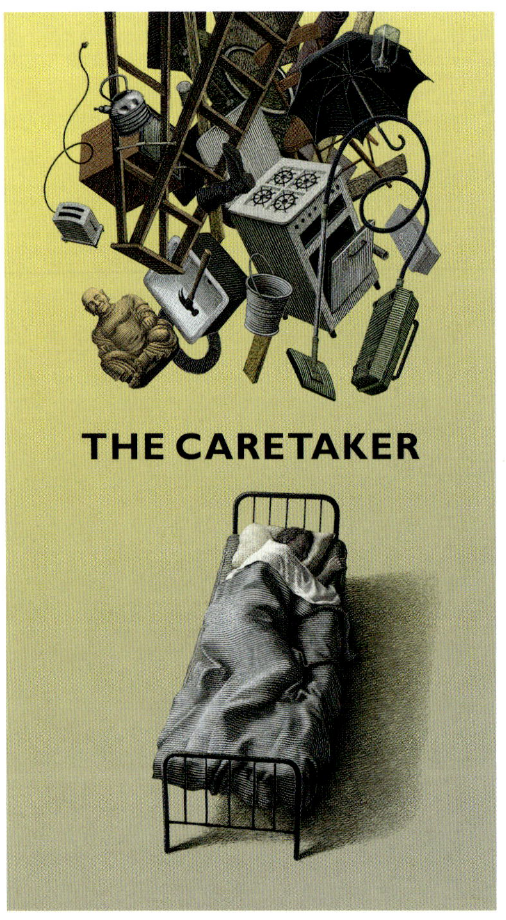

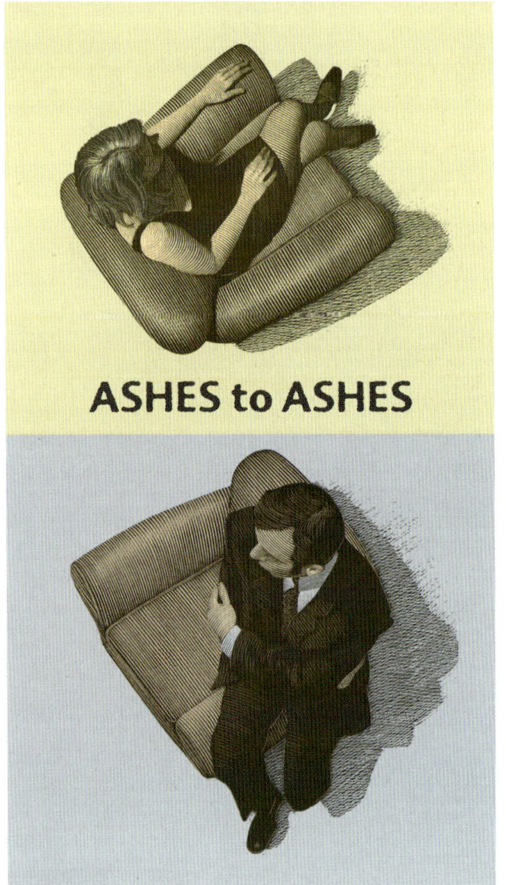

Betrayal, written in 1978, is Harold Pinter's deconstruction of a romantic triangle. The scenes unfold in reverse chronological order — as the play progresses, we are more and more aware of what lies ahead for the characters. We also realize that none of the three characters sees the whole picture. I worked up sketches for the Roundabout Theatre Company's production in 2000, directed by David Leveaux and starring Liev Schreiber, John Slattery and Juliette Binoche. Everyone liked this silhouette of a nude woman peering through Venetian blinds — it was elegant and sexy, and also somehow about hiding dark secrets. I love the work of the British sculptor and wood engraver Eric Gill (1882–1940). I drew this figure from a model using the louvered blinds in my bathroom, but the style was inspired by Gill's confident woodcuts.

The Caretaker was Harold Pinter's breakthrough success in 1960. Reading the text, it's easy to see how the description "Pinteresque" has come to mean something ambiguous and disturbing. On the surface, *The Caretaker* is the story of two brothers, Aston and Mick, and a homeless derelict named Davies. The setting is Mick's junk-filled London apartment. The power struggles between the three characters have been interpreted as an allegory for the shifting demographics of British society in the early '60s. For the Roundabout's production in 2005, starring Patrick Stewart, Kyle MacLachlan and Aidan Gillen, I illustrated the contents of Mick's junk shop of a bedroom (almost all of these objects are specified in the text) floating menacingly above a man asleep in bed. This nightmare might belong to any of the three characters in the play, so I was careful to leave the identity of the figure ambiguous; Don Spiers was my model, standing in for those illustrious actors.

Pinter's cryptic *Ashes to Ashes* is a dense, poetic, challenging 45-minute one-act play. It was written in 1996; the Roundabout produced it in 1999. Karl Reisz, the director, gave me a synopsis of the action when we first spoke by phone: "It's about a couple, who has been married. He tries to get through to her, but is unable. They say unforgivable things to each other — then it's over." It was indeed baffling on first reading, but on further study it began to unfold, and it seemed like this compact text was addressing huge universal themes: the Holocaust, ethnic cleansing in Eastern Europe, dominance and submission, victims and victimizers on a larger social scale as well as within the intimate scale of a marriage. I faxed off several pencil sketch concepts to Mr. Reisz in London. He showed the sketches to Mr. Pinter over dinner and replied to me with a disarmingly simple suggestion from the playwright himself: "Two figures sitting in chairs — they should be sophisticated, literate, elegant people — together in the same room but looking away from each other. And she should be 'within herself.'" My personal moment of Pinter clarity. This production starred Lindsay Duncan and David Strathairn, and I knew it would not be possible for these actors to pose for the illustration themselves. The overhead angle made it easier to substitute models (thank you, Susan Dunfield and Bill Aitchison).

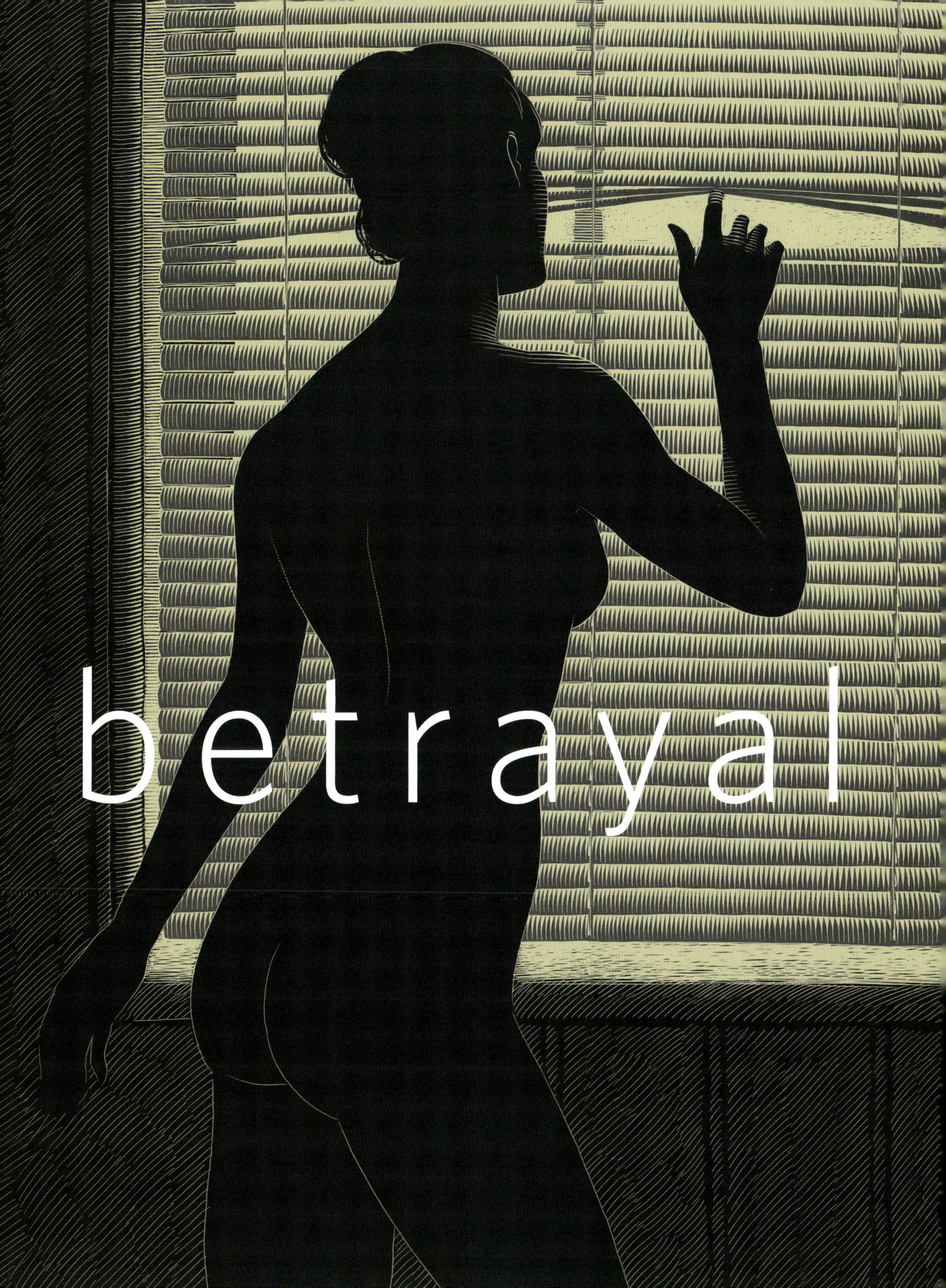
betrayal

It's no exaggeration to think of Sebastian Barry's 1995 play *The Steward of Christendom* as a sort of Irish *King Lear*. Thomas Dunne, the central character, has long monologues of Shakespearean proportion; he has three daughters and his mental faculties are less than stable. The play is set in 1932 in a psychiatric facility, but the time period shifts earlier, to the troubled years of the Irish Civil War, as Dunne is haunted by recollections of his mistakes in both public and personal life. I was asked to create the poster for a 2014 production at the Mark Taper Forum in Los Angeles, starring Brian Dennehy.

The play is not so well known, at least in North America, but a star of this magnitude provides marketing compensations. The only prerequisite for the art was that it would be a portrait of Mr. Dennehy. Coincidentally, he was part of the 2013 Stratford Festival acting company so I was able to meet with him over coffee to discuss the project. At age 75, Brian admitted that this would probably be one of his last "big" starring roles — it's just hard to memorize this much text.

My first sketches showed Dunne curled up on his bed as if in the storm scene in *King Lear*. The client was concerned that, in this pose, Brian might not be instantly recognizable; but also that the portrait not feel so spent, so collapsed — so beaten as to present an aura of hopelessness. Dunne has not yet given up. The director suggested that the image should have an edge of Dylan Thomas:

> Do not go gentle into that good night,
> Old age should burn and rave at close of day,
> Rage, rage against the dying of the light.

I mentioned to Brian that the haunted, humanistic portraits of the British painter Lucian Freud seemed like a useful reference point. Brian laughed and told a story about having lunch one day at the Wolseley — the grand café on Piccadilly next door to the Ritz, in London — and Lucian Freud was sitting a few tables away. Freud asked Brian to join him and asked if he would consider sitting for a portrait! The project actually got as far as doing reference photos, but the painting never happened.

I had better luck than Mr. Freud — after working through preliminary pencil sketch ideas, Brian visited my studio and graciously posed for this illustration.

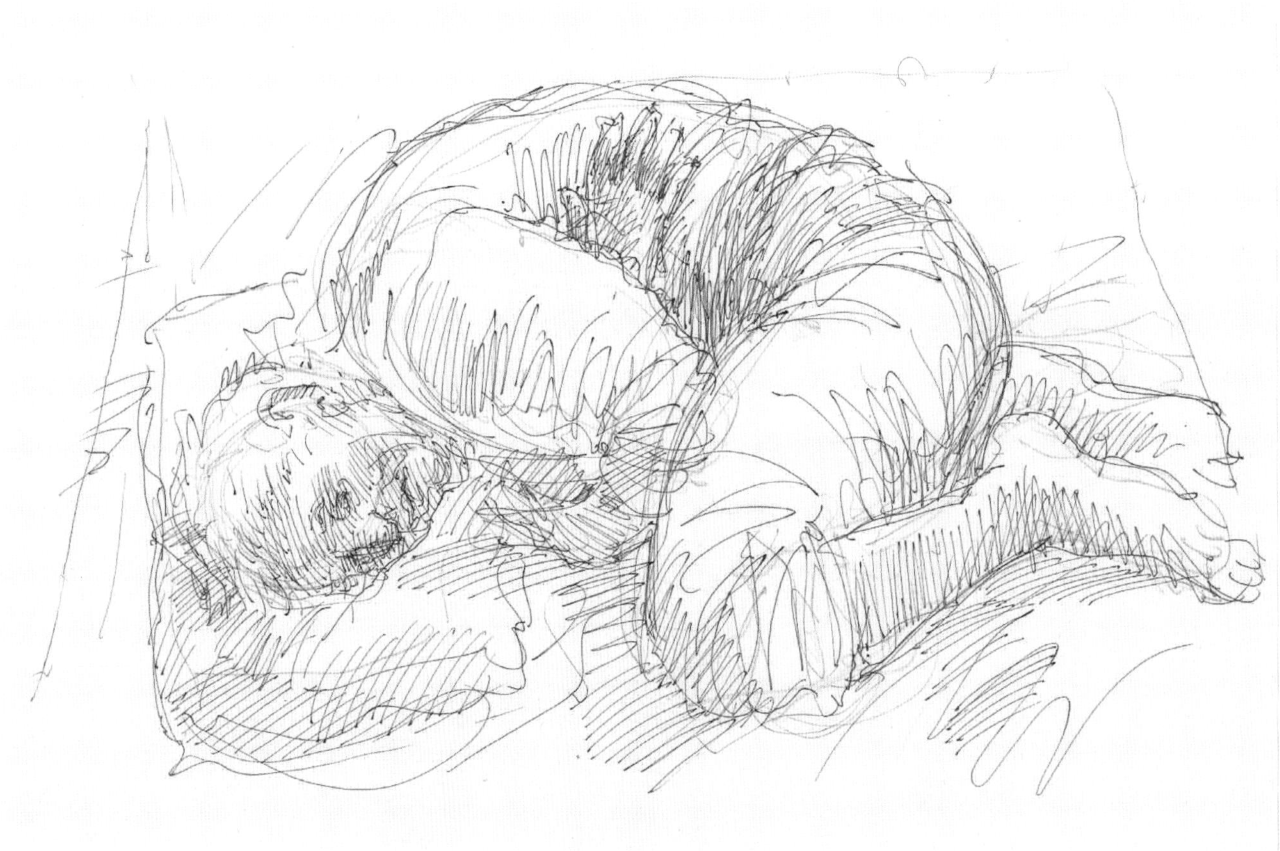

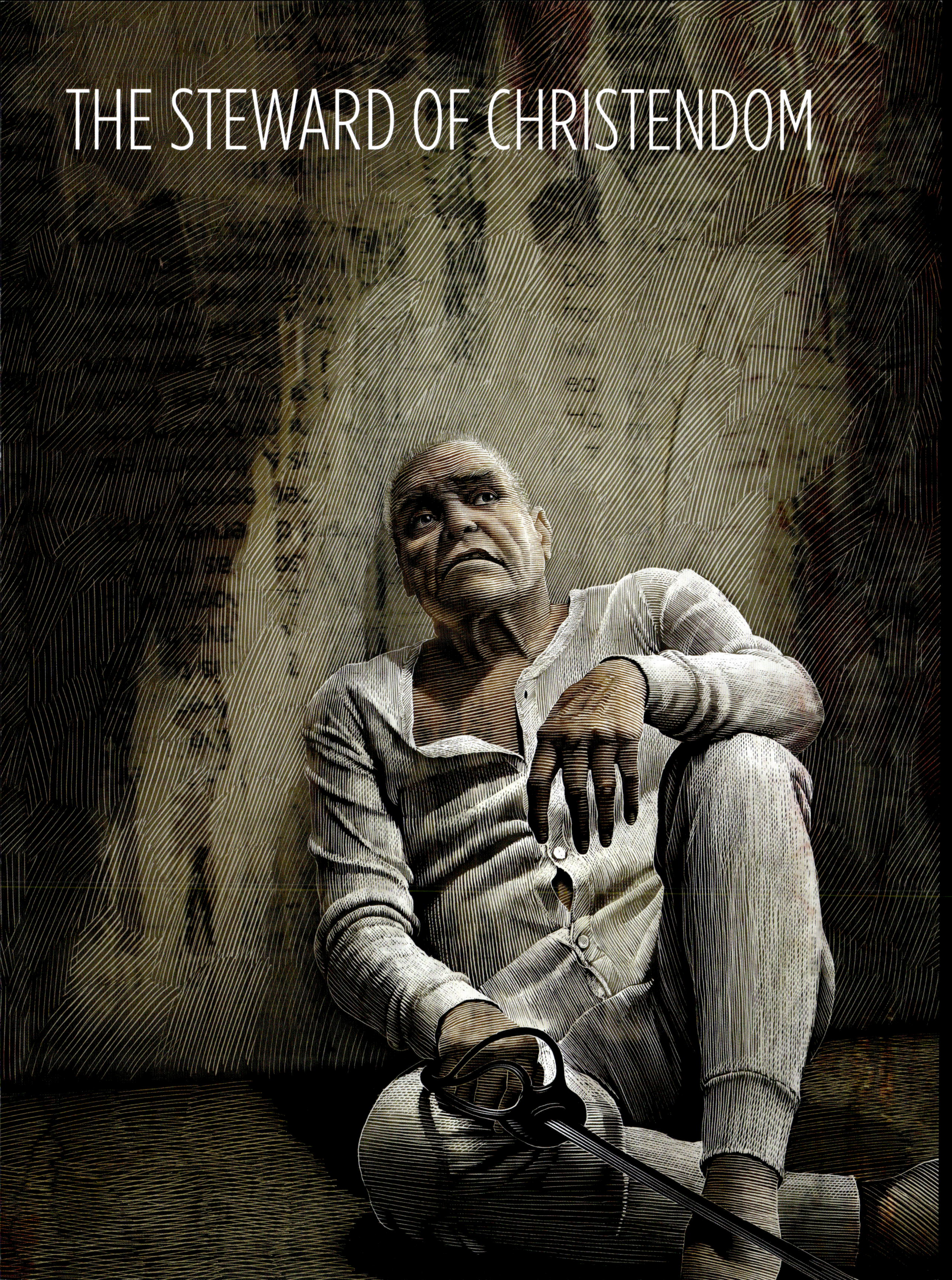
THE STEWARD OF CHRISTENDOM

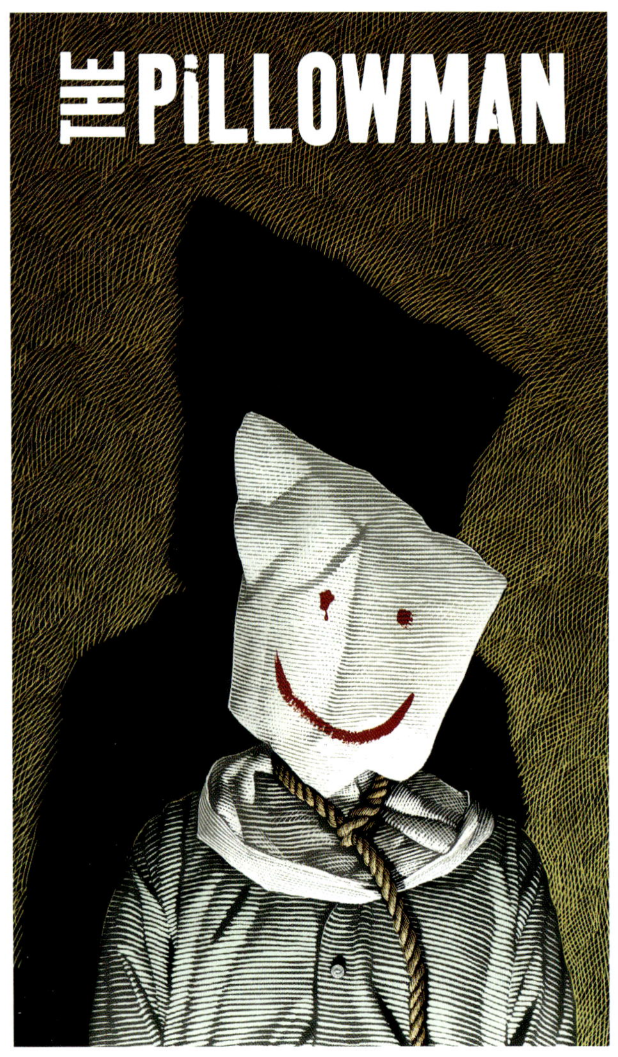

Bonnie Monte put Joe Orton's 1969 witty and profane *What the Butler Saw* on her 2017 season playbill at The Shakespeare Theatre of New Jersey. The setting is an examination room in a private psychiatric clinic where Dr. Prentice is attempting to seduce an attractive prospective secretary. She is persuaded to undress as part of her job interview but — surprise! — the doctor's wife arrives unexpectedly. Mrs. Prentice is being seduced by a bellboy at the Station Hotel, who tries to blackmail her with pornographic photos. A government inspector comes in, sent by Dr. Prentice's "immediate superiors in madness." And a bobby arrives, looking for a missing "part" of a statue of Sir Winston Churchill that was destroyed in a gas main explosion. Half the cast disrobes down to their underwear, often trading clothes as Mrs. Prentice drunkenly notes, "the world is full of naked men running in all directions!"

This play must have scandalized its original London audiences — but then the Labour Party had swept into power in 1964 following the Profumo affair, and legalized homosexuality and the death penalty were topics of public debate. The times, they were a changin'.

Martin McDonagh's 2003 play *The Pillowman* is a stunning black comedy about crime and punishment, and childhood fears we never really outgrow. The protagonist writes Brothers Grimm–like fantasy stories about young children being killed in a variety of gruesome ways. In the opening scene, two police detectives are interrogating him about a string of child murders that seem to mirror his stories. The synopsis includes sexual abuse, torture, severed fingers and heads and premature burial. Not a play for the faint of heart.

Which brings up a marketing challenge. A theatre poster needs to convey accurately what the play is about — if the play is disturbing, the poster should convey that. But the point of the exercise is to sell tickets, not to frighten people away!

One of these nightmare stories is about a nine-foot-tall man made of pillows "with two button eyes and a big smiley face." The Pillowman's sad job is to visit adults who have had a terrible life and who are about to commit suicide. He comforts them, then takes them back in time and convinces them to avoid the years of pain ahead by taking their own lives as children. I wanted to use this perversely compassionate fantasy creature — but my first sketches looked like the Michelin Man or the giant marshmallow man from *Ghostbusters*.

Christina solved it — a innocuous smiley face painted on a pillowcase. But the shape of the hood over a man's head evokes those shocking 2003 photographs from Abu Ghraib prison in Iraq. The rope around his neck and the cast shadow on the wall suggest the claustrophobia and terror of a prison interrogation. A tear on the smiley face seemed like the right finishing touch.

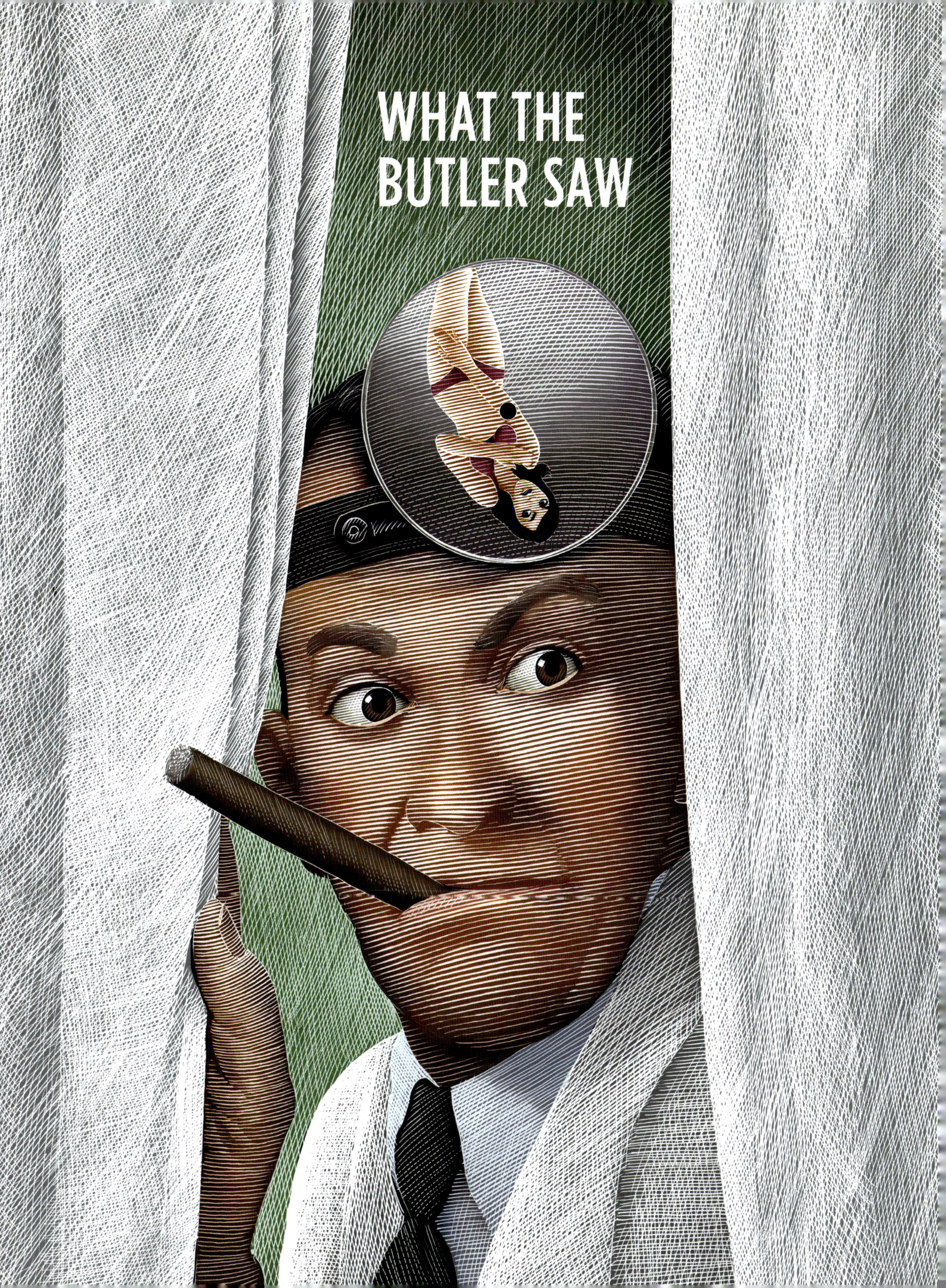
WHAT THE
BUTLER SAW

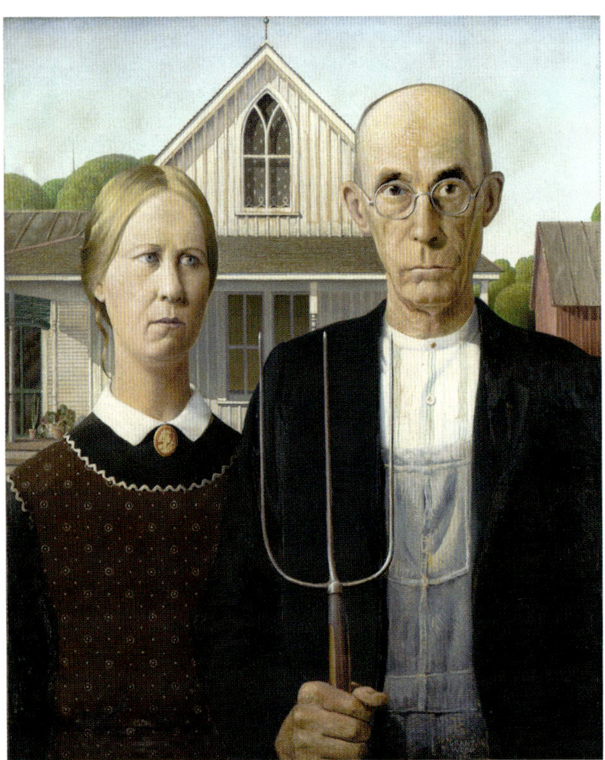

Buried Child is classic Sam Shephard — a darkly funny and disturbing allegory of the American Dream gone wrong. The play premiered in 1978 and won the 1979 Pulitzer Prize for Drama — and it seems more timely than ever today.

Vince brings his girlfriend, Shelly, home to the family farm in Illinois. She is at first charmed by rural setting, comparing the farm house to a "Norman Rockwell cover or something." Then she meets his crazy family — his ranting, alcoholic grandparents, Dodge and Halie, and their two sons: Tilden, a hulking semi-idiot, and Bradley, who has lost one leg in an accident with a chainsaw.

Gradually, the family's dark secrets begins to emerge. Years ago Dodge, the grandfather, buried an unwanted newborn in some undisclosed location in the backyard (there are hints about an incestual relationship between Tilden and his mother). For years the family has lived under a cloud of guilt that is finally dispelled when Tilden unearths the baby's mummified remains and carries it upstairs to his mother in the final scene. This act seems to purge the family of its curse.

Maybe it was the Norman Rockwell reference in the script that put Grant Wood's iconic *American Gothic* into my head as a perfect visual metaphor for the mythology the play so sharply contrasts. With the possible exception of the Statue of Liberty, Wood's 1930 painting has been adapted more than any other American icon I can think of for editorial cartoons and political satire.

I changed the pitchfork in the original to a rusty old shovel as a reference to the play title, and made the serene blue sky more threatening. If the old farmer is Dodge, he would be wearing a baseball cap; the international signal for distress is a flag flying upside down. I added a cornfield almost obscuring the house — a reference to a specific scene in the play but used more for a sense of nature out of balance.

The Shakespeare Theatre of New Jersey's 2018 production commemorated the playwright's death in 2017.

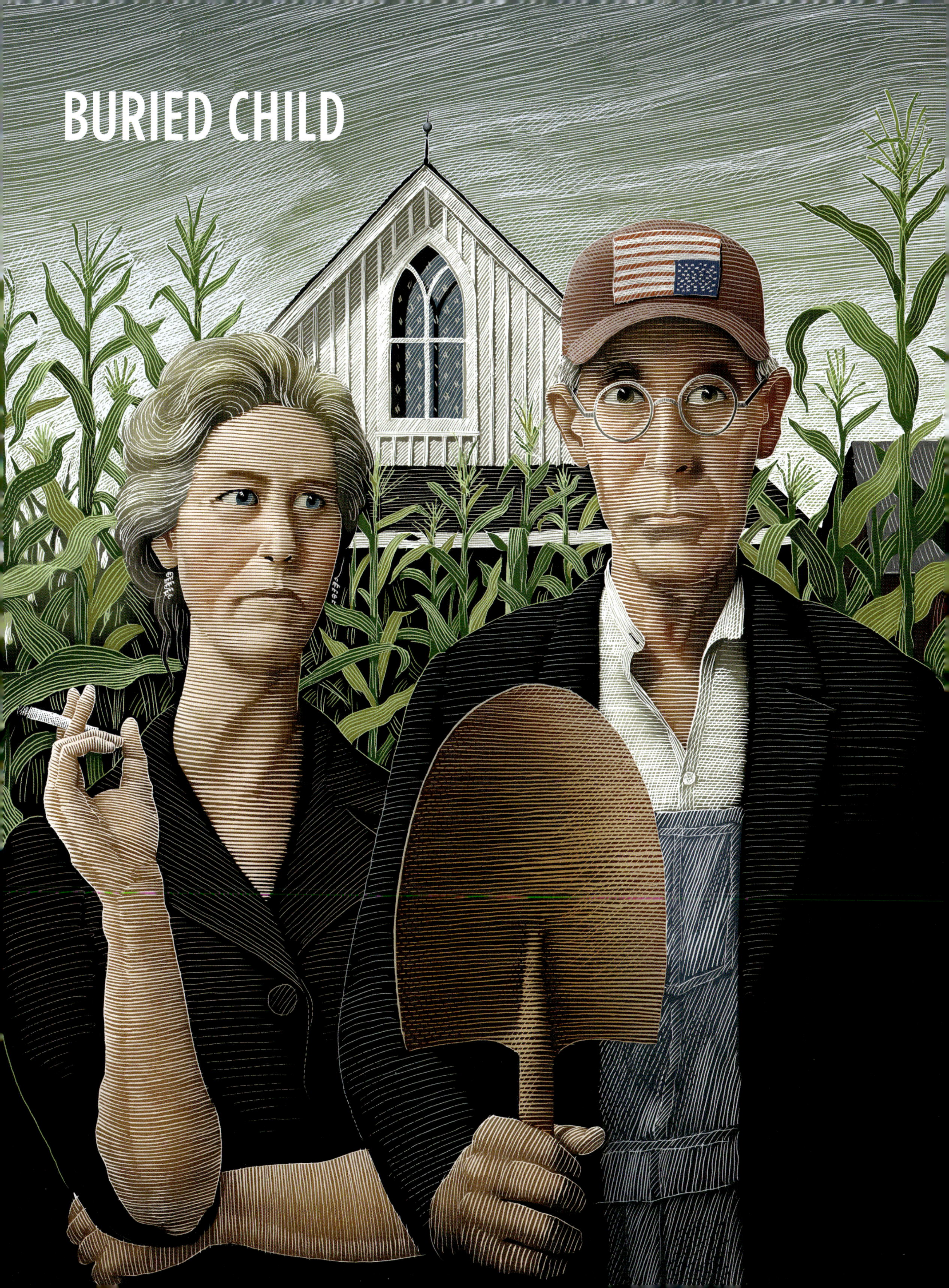
BURIED CHILD

The Complete Works of William Shakespeare (Abridged) is one of those titles that I had quietly hoped I might avoid over the course of my career — but there it was on The Shakespeare Theatre of New Jersey's 2016 season. Billed as "an irreverent, madcap romp," three actors perform highlights of the 37 plays in 97 minutes, at breakneck speed, with a lot of audience participation. Not my cup of tea, personally, but it does have a daredevil energy — and bravo if it can introduce younger audiences to the Bard. To that end, tickets to this production were free for ages 18 and younger. I live near a skateboard park, and I'm always astounded at the tricks these kids can do — that seemed like a great metaphor for fearlessly exploring the Canon. My giant book from the illustration found its way into the set design of the production.

The holiday show that same year was a stage adaptation of Dylan Thomas' *A Child's Christmas in Wales*. Christina proposed this beautiful, simple idea of a boy catching snowflakes on his tongue.

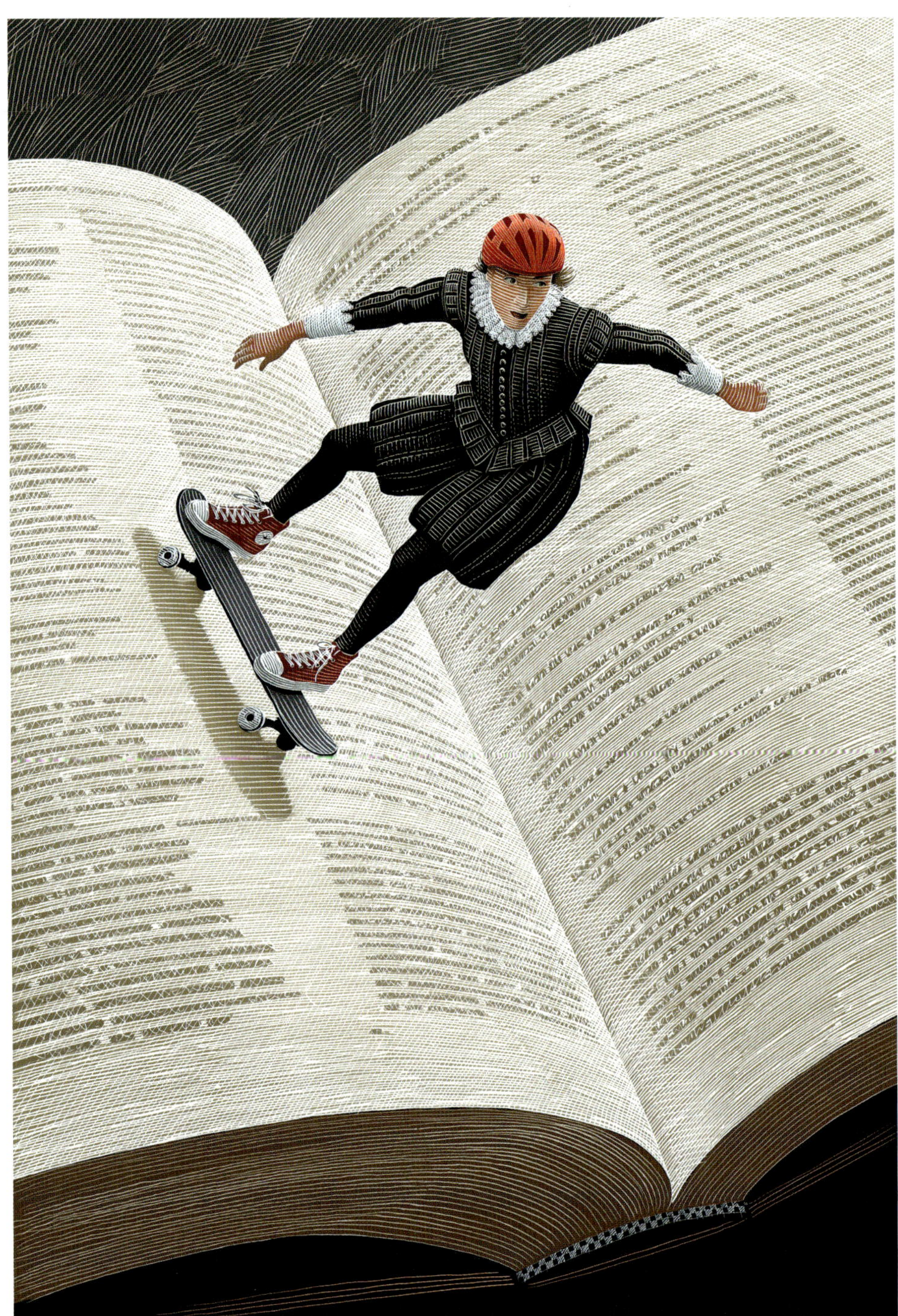

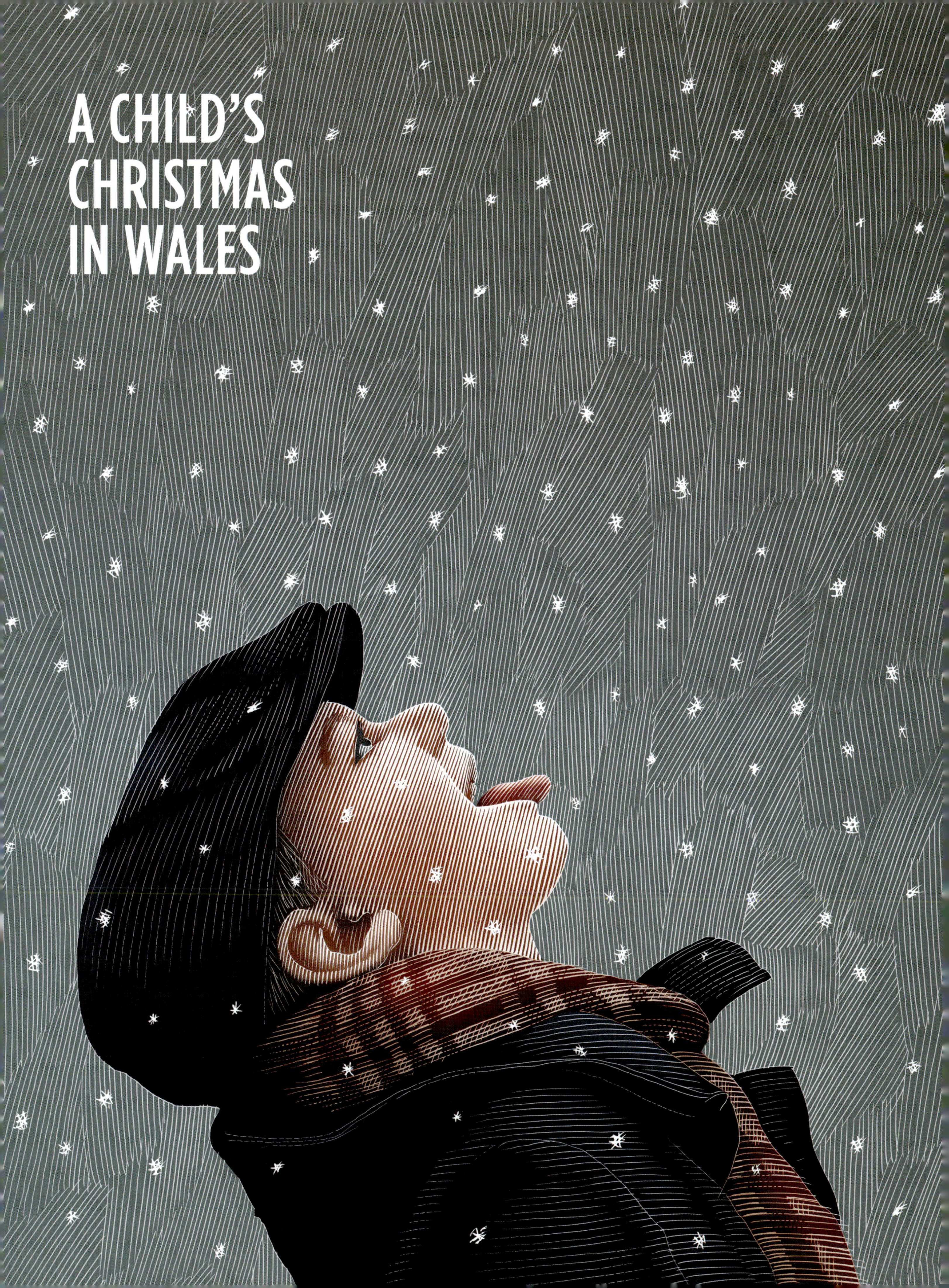
A CHILD'S
CHRISTMAS
IN WALES

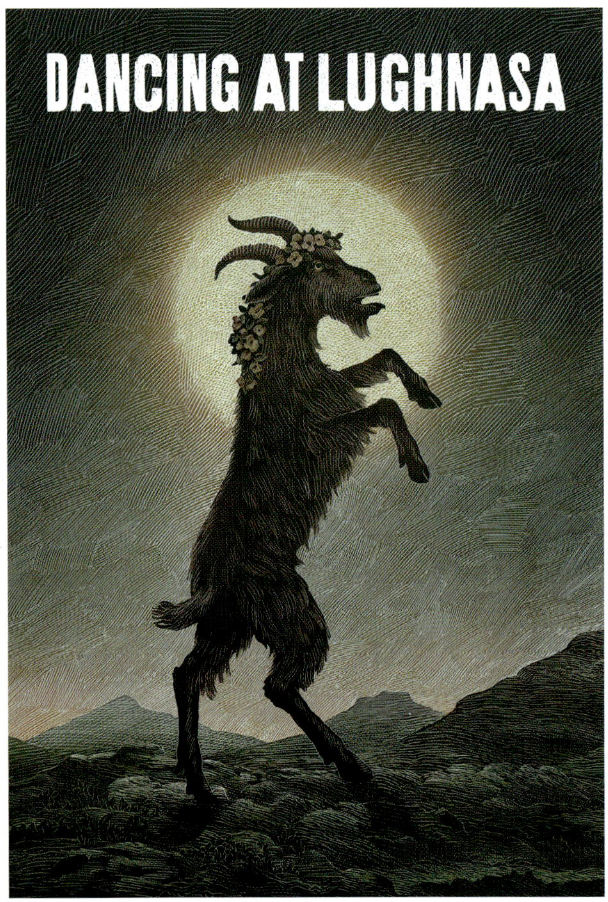

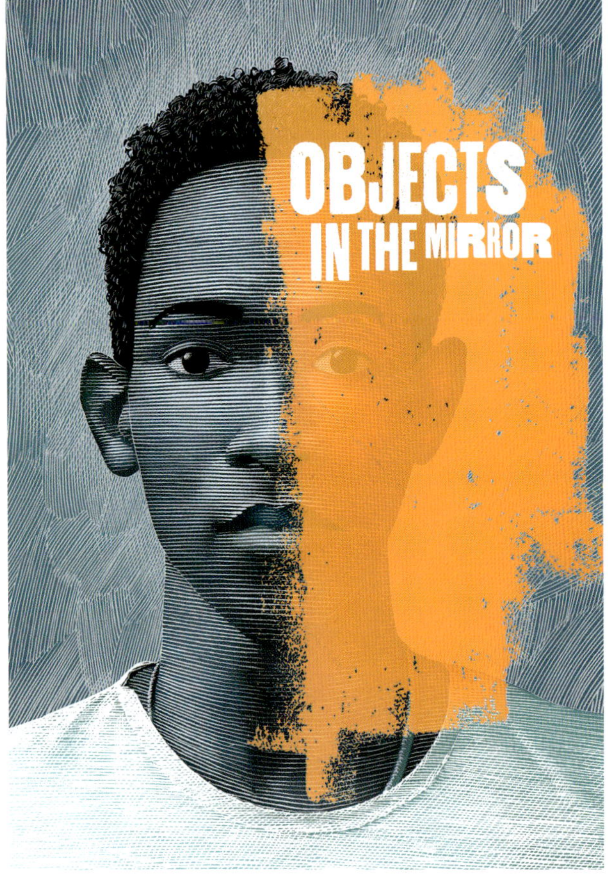

Most of the theatre companies I work for have been established for many years, but in 2015 I was asked to create a graphic identity for a brand new professional company in Dublin, Ohio. Tantrum Theatre was founded by the University of Ohio's College of Fine Arts as a training and performing opportunity for its theatre students. The name has a witty association with the university — their mascot is a bobcat; the collective noun for a group of these large felines is a tantrum of bobcats.

Tantrum's first season included *Little Shop of Horrors*, the horror/comedy/rock musical by Howard Ashman and Alan Menken about a hapless florist shop worker who raises a plant named Audrey that feeds on human flesh. I saw the original Off-Broadway back in 1983. Prop tendrils were rigged to drop onto the audience from the ceiling of the auditorium at the end of the show, as if the now gargantuan-size Audrey was reaching out to grab audience members. I based my Audrey on the Venus flytrap. As a child, I was fascinated with this carnivorous species. Seymour's nerd glasses with tape around the bridge and broken lenses are all that's left of him — spit back out as indigestible.

Brian Friel's *Dancing at Lughnasa* was also on the playbill that first season. The title comes from *Lughnasadh*, the Celtic harvest festival, during which the story takes place. This is an autobiographical play — the five central characters are based on Friel's mother and her four sisters in rural Donegal. The play is set in 1936 when Michael, his narrator character, is seven years old (Friel was born in 1929 so he was seven that year as well). The Church is central in the characters' lives but there are strong pagan undercurrents, including Michael's uncle Jack, a priest "gone native" and shipped home from Africa in disgrace. Picking up on those undercurrents, I suggested a huge goat, decked with flowers, silhouetted against the moon.

In 2019, Tantrum produced *Objects in the Mirror*, Charles Smith's play about how the developed world treats refugees. Shedrick, a young Liberian man, has managed to escape the horrors of civil war and African refugee camps and begin a new life in Australia. Shedrick and his family have reinvented themselves to get across checkpoints and borders, changing their stories to suit circumstances. At first the concocted stories bend the truth only slightly; but eventually they become complex layers of deception. Shedrick is "hired" by an Australian diplomat to do odd jobs including house painting. Over the course of the play, Shedrick paints a foyer over and over again because he can still see the old color coming through — it always needs another coat. This provided a metaphor for the poster. The portrait looks like a passport photograph with half the face "painted out" — but the engraving lines are still faintly visible. You can never completely cover up the real person underneath.

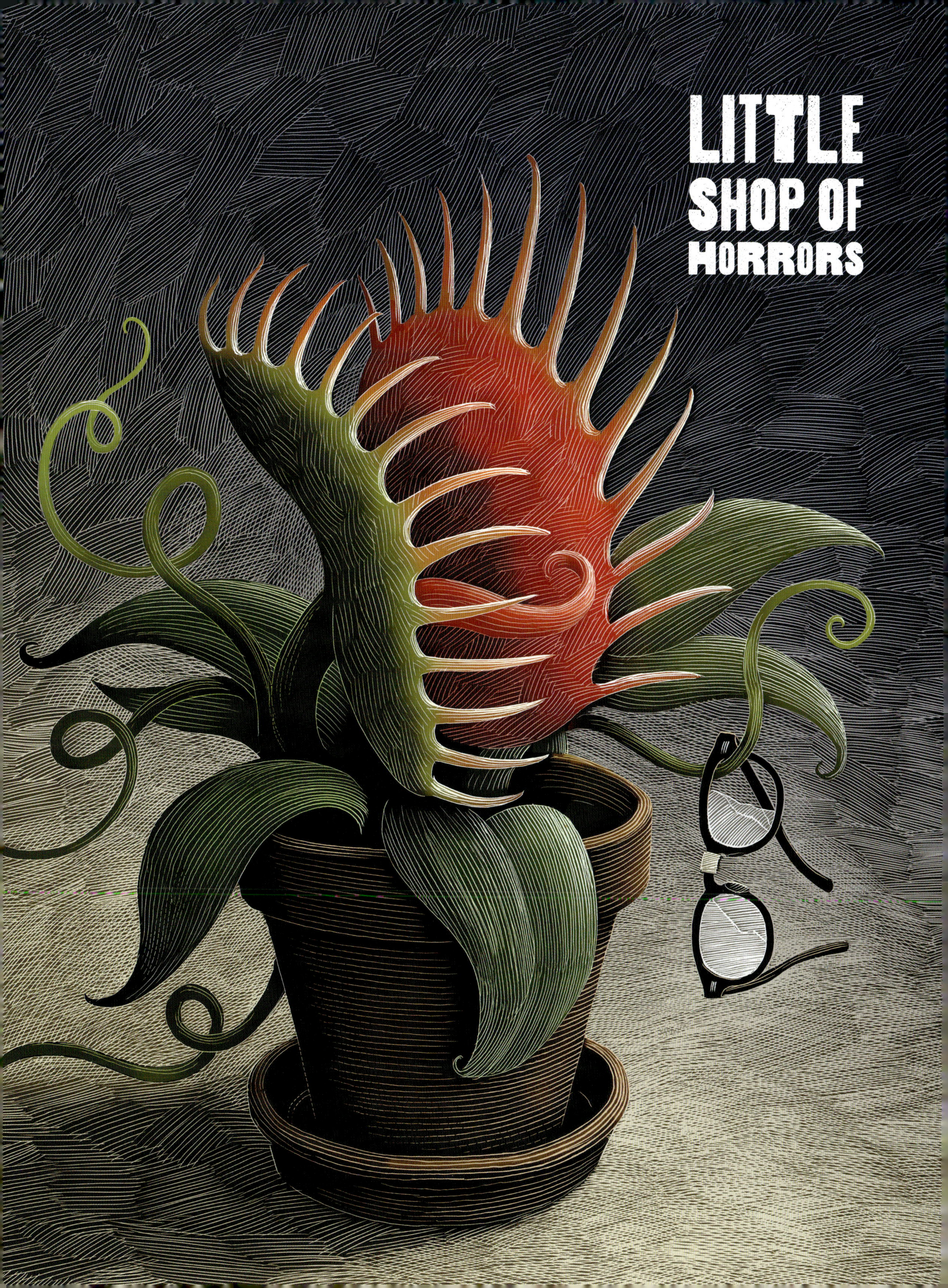
LITTLE
SHOP OF
HORRORS

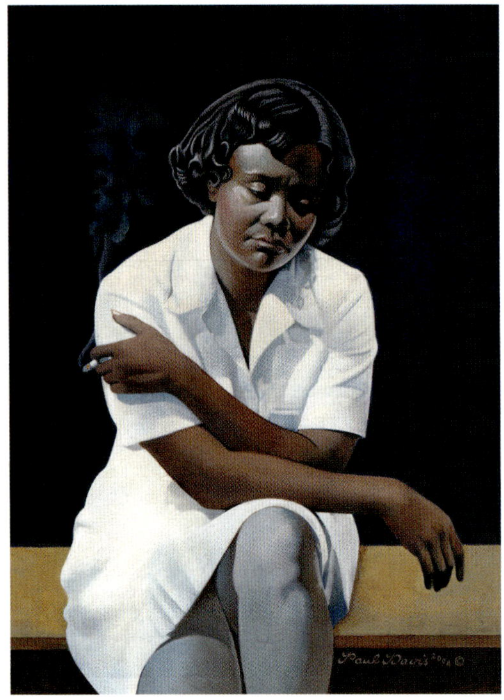

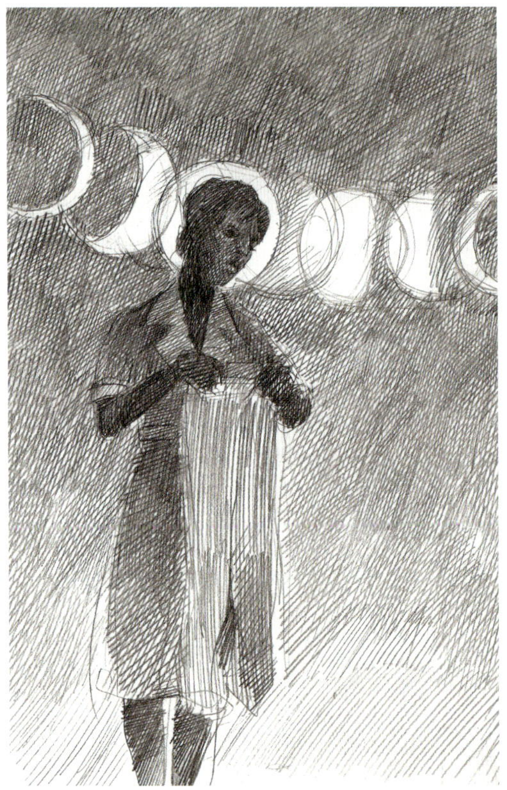

I have always loved the theatre posters of Paul Davis; I finally got to meet him in person and tell him so at the opening of a recent exhibition in New York in which we both had work. Davis was first hired by Joe Papp in 1975 to create posters for the Public Theater, and his bold, iconic portraits became this theatre's signature graphic identity for decades.

Caroline, or Change, the musical by Tony Kushner and Jeanne Tessori, originated at the Public Theater in 2003. It was directed by George C. Wolfe. Paul Davis created the poster — a pensive portrait of Tonya Pinkins in the title role of a black maid who works for a Jewish family in 1963 Louisiana. Davis tells a wonderful story about this image — when he showed it to the theatre's advertising agency, they said they wanted her "to be more cheerful." Tony Kushner had the clout to step in and say "absolutely not," which saved the art from rejection.

I was asked by Tantrum Theatre in Dublin, Ohio, to create a poster for their 2017 production of *Caroline*. I had seen the original production in New York — the Davis poster seemed perfect and it was a challenge to find a new approach. (An insurmountable challenge for some theatres, evidently — in doing picture research for this assignment I came across a poster for another production, done as a photograph, with a different actor, posed and lit exactly like the Davis painting.)

The central relationship in the story is between the illiterate Caroline and Noah, the eight-year-old son of her Jewish employer. The "change" in the title has several meanings — the huge changes in society brought about by the Civil Rights movement, but also the pocket change from Noah's allowance that he absentmindedly leaves in his pockets, which Caroline finds each time she does the family's laundry. In addition to the African-American and Jewish characters, Kushner includes a gallery of fantastical characters who act as a kind of chorus — a sympathetic washing machine, a radio (a trio of Motown singers) and an opera-singing moon.

The moon is also a perfect metaphor for change, with its phases and cycles and gravitational pull. I liked the idea that the full moon in the sky behind Caroline forms a subtle halo around her head — a kind of blessing or benediction that she's not even aware of.

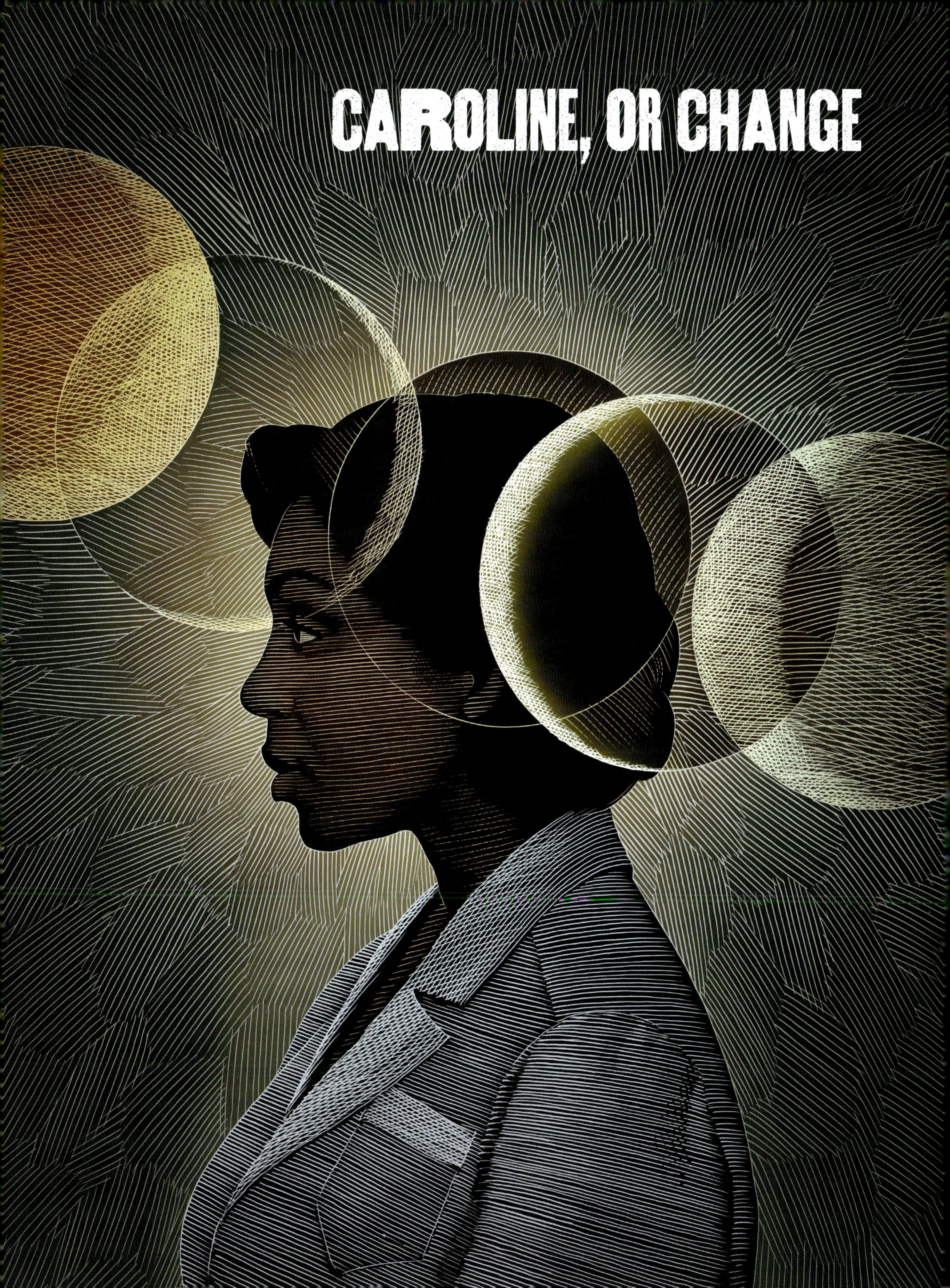
CAROLINE, OR CHANGE

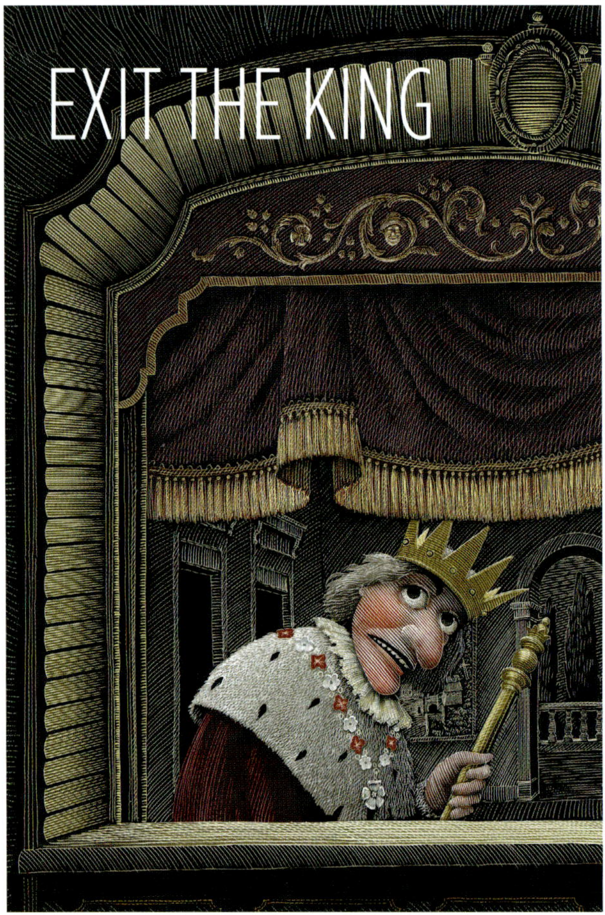

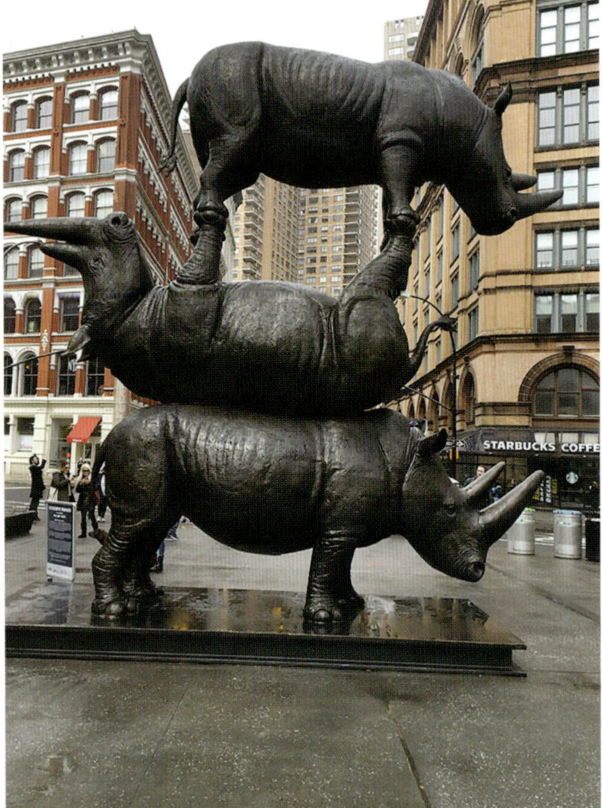

Romanian-French playwright Eugene Ionesco (1909–1994) was one of the most important figures of the French avant-garde theatre. Early in his career in Paris he rubbed shoulders with Hemingway, Picasso, Sartre and Henry Miller. He has been called a "tragic clown," the "Shakespeare of the Absurd," the "*enfant terrible* of the avant-garde" and the "inventor of the Metaphysical Farce." There is much grist here for an illustrator's mill.

In 2019, Tantrum Theatre programmed *Rhinoceros*, one of Ionecso's most famous plays, written in 1959. Monsieur Bérenger lives in an ordinary provincial French town. He works in the local newspaper office and flirts with Daisy, the typist. He drinks a bit too much, and he's often late for work. In Act 1, Bérenger is sitting in a café with his friend, Jean. They debate with a logician about syllogisms ("All cats die. Socrates is dead. Therefore Socrates is a cat"). They are interrupted when a rhinoceros rampages across the town square, trampling a woman's cat. It turns out that townspeople are turning into rhinoceroses. Jean turns into a rhinoceros. By the end of the play, Bérenger is the only human left.

Laurence Olivier played Bérenger in the original production, directed by Orson Welles at the Royal Court Theatre in 1960. Benedict Cumberbatch played the role in a 2007 revival at the same theatre. Zero Mostel and Gene Wilder starred in a 1973 film version.

I love these ungainly beasts. I have visited them in zoos from Toronto and Detroit to Budapest. They have a noble pedigree in art history, from Albrecht Dürer's engraving in 1515 to Gillie and Marc Schattner's life-size sculpture *The Last Three*, commemorating the demise of the Northern White Rhino, installed in Astor Place in New York in March 2018.

For the Tantrum assignment (is there a better-named theatre to produce this play?), I was looking for the right balance of comedy, absurdity and nobility. I sketched a portrait idea but Christina upped the game with a concept that felt edgier and a lot more fun: a rhino falling from the sky, about to squash that poor cat. I underscored the surrealism with clouds and a bowler hat borrowed from Rene Magritte (an article of human clothing made reference to the human-to-animal transformations).

Bonnie Monte directed Ionesco's *Exit the King* at The Shakespeare Theatre of New Jersey in 2016. The main character here is King Bérenger, struggling to come to terms with his own death (Bérenger is the main character's name in many of Ionesco's plays — his own semi-autobiographic everyman). King Bérenger made me think of George Cruikshank's Mr. Punch. Maybe because of those deer-in-the-headlights wild eyes. Maybe because the little theatre in the Cruikshank illustrations feels like the murky throne room in the play.

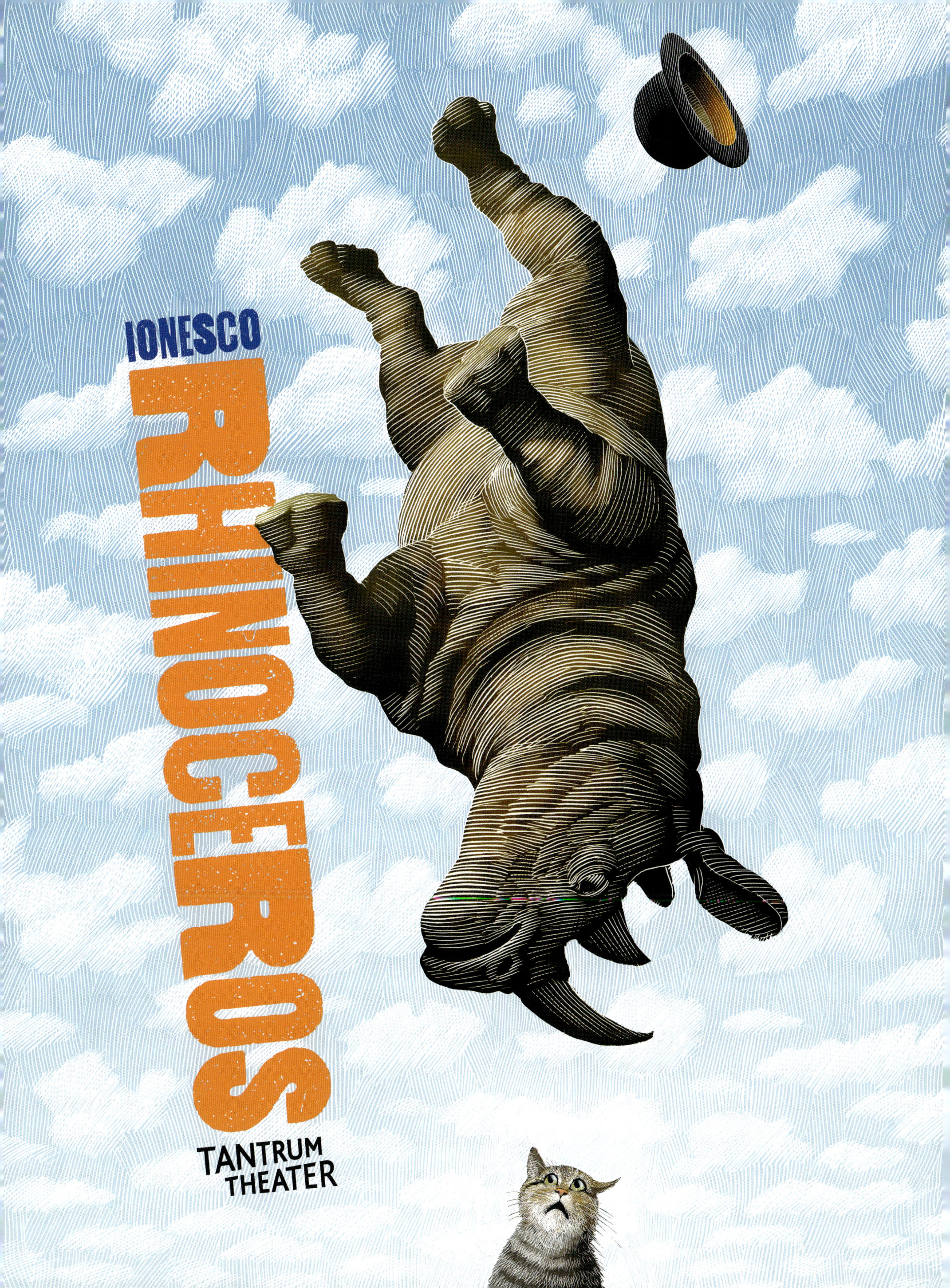
IONESCO
RHINOCEROS
TANTRUM
THEATER

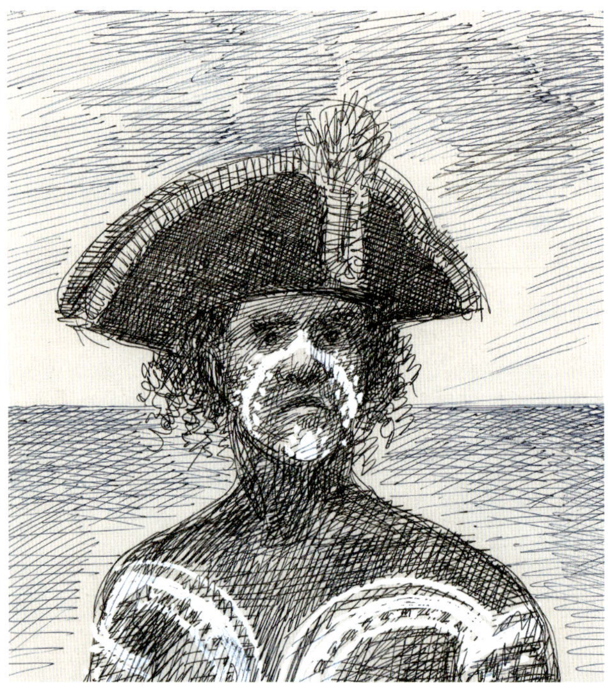

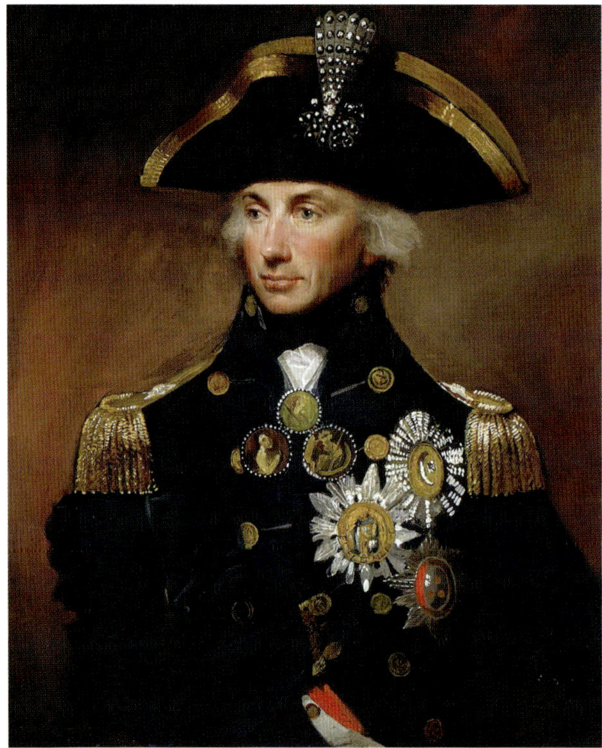

Admiral Horatio Nelson, 1799, by Lemuel Francis Abbott (National Maritime Museum, Greenwich, UK).

Tantrum Theatre announced a new production of Timberlake Wertenbaker's *Our Country's Good* in 2020. I recall a very fine production of the play in Toronto, not long after it was written in 1988. It's an interesting choice for a revival this particular year because it deals head-on with colonialism and racism.

Our Country's Good is set in the 1780s — a British convict ship arrives in Australia to set up the first penal colony there. The ship's captain and his contingent of Royal Marines allow the prisoners to rehearse and stage a makeshift production of George Farquhar's *The Recruiting Officer*, in which a young woman disguises herself as an officer in order to be near the man she loves. This play-within-the-play, in the hands of the convicts, is highly entertaining — but it's also a social experiment about the value of art. The captain and his officers debate whether theatre can be a humanizing force in this new world.

Wertenbaker's play is intentionally double-cast so each actor plays contrasting characters — an actor might play a convict from the lowest level of society, and also one of the privileged British officers. Director Ameenah Kaplan cast the production interracially and intersexually — she felt that this would challenge the audience to empathize with the plight of a character by seeing their argument from another's point of view. She observed "this production reflects our desire to see if we can know each other a little better by walking a mile in another person's shoes, if only on the boards."

Wertenbaker includes an Aboriginal character who watches the British ship arrive, and prophesizes that nothing will ever be the same. I made a rough sketch of this Aboriginal character, wearing the tricorn hat of a British naval uniform from the period — a symbol of white privilege and power in the context of the story. I wanted to show the colonizer and the colonized simultaneously — a surprising, even shocking juxtaposition of clashing cultures.

Ameenah loved the concept, but in her production the character was to be played by a female actor. Changing the sex didn't seem to make the image any less powerful. The Aborigines of Australia share a good deal of their genetics with other Polynesian and Asian peoples—if you go back 40,000 years, you'll find genetic similarities with Papuans. My friend Alia Hussey is a striking woman of Jamaican and South-Asian Indian heritage, and she graciously agreed to pose for this Black Lives Matter image.

Unfortunately, Tantrum's plans were upended by COVID-19. Public health regulations prevented face-to-face rehearsal (to say nothing of performance), so the project is waiting to be rescheduled sometime in the future.

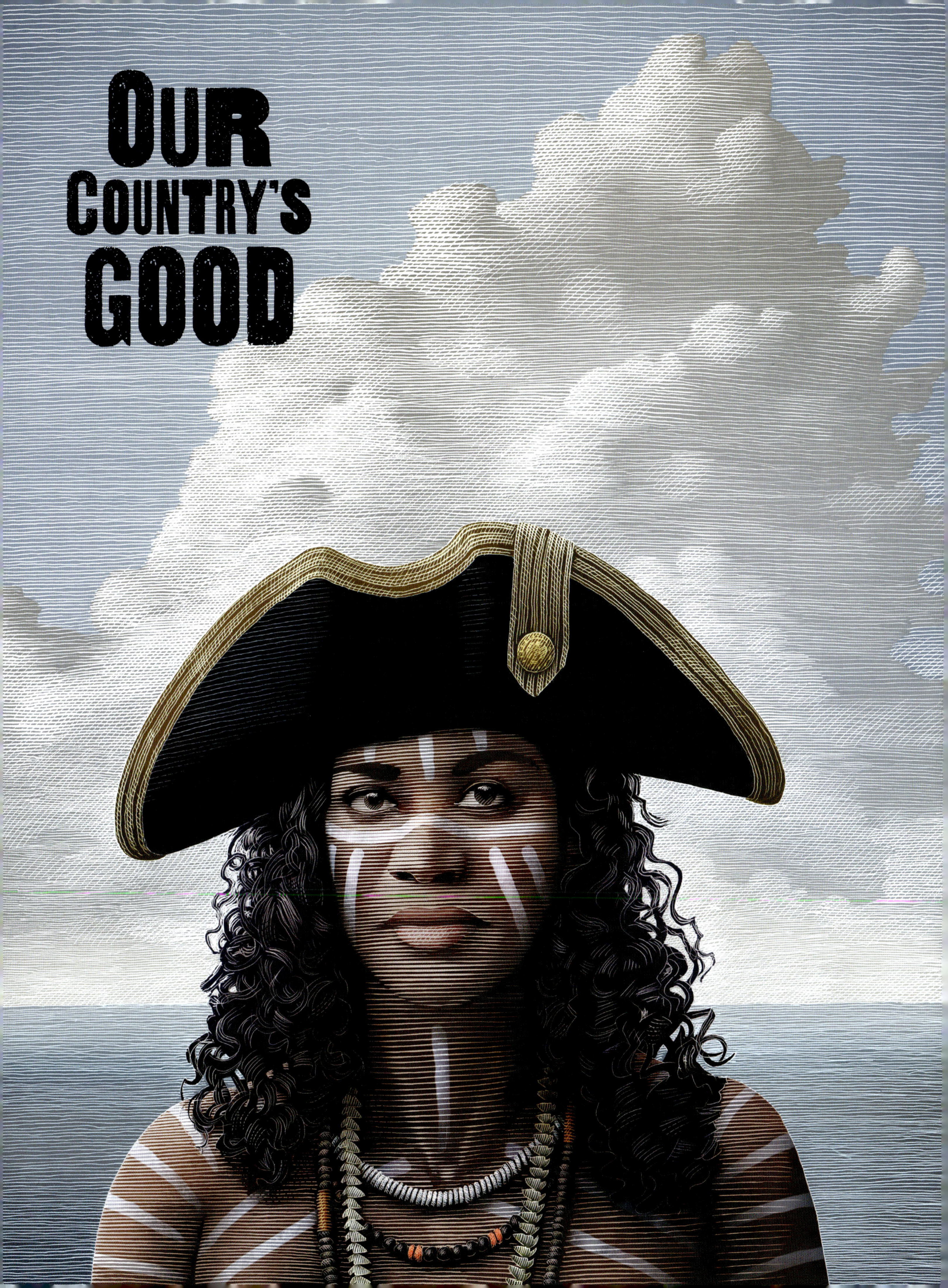
OUR
COUNTRY'S
GOOD

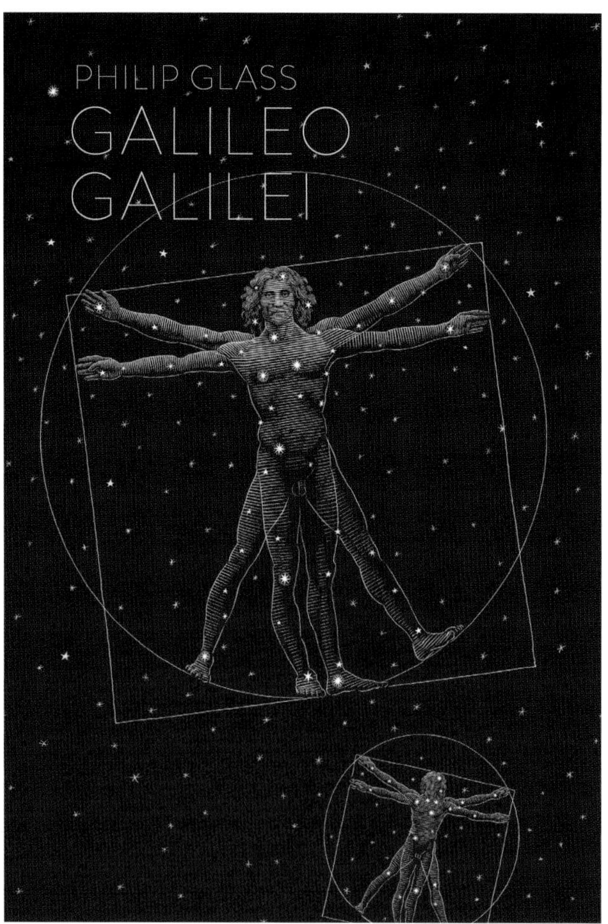

Tantrum Theatre's brave poster assignments in the summer of 2020 provided welcome focus during the ongoing uncertainty of COVID-19. *Natasha, Pierre & the Great Comet of 1812* is based on a single, thin paragraph from *War and Peace*. People make jokes about starting Tolstoy's monumental novel and never finishing it; I started an audio book version, with an excellent narrator, and only made it to Chapter 16 (the entire reading takes 55 hours). So it's no surprise that an electro-pop musical version is not going to delve very deeply into its source material. *Great Comet* was a Broadway hit in 2017 (I didn't see it) — I gather that the theatre was configured with café tables, and the audience could order vodka and perogies during the show.

I found my concept right there in the title — I have always loved comets (you will see a couple of other examples in this book), so I turned the characters into constellations on a Napoleonic period map of the heavens. Star charts are drawn with flat, two-dimensional figures because it's the clearest way to show how the stars connect together to form mythological heros or the creatures of the zodiac. But my comet is a surreal light source, illuminating Natasha — she magically becomes a three-dimensional figure in its glow. (My model was Evie O'Toole.) The stars themselves are a riot of colour, like rock concert lighting; I snuck in a Fender Stratocaster constellation, so that the firmament would not look exclusively historical.

I had just finished this scratchboard comet when we got a visit from a real one! We had spectacular views of Comet Neowise through binoculars in late July (visible to the naked eye near the Big Dipper). A wonderful coincidence.

I had used a constellation metaphor several years earlier for a very different musical subject. I was asked by Cincinnati Opera to create a poster for their 2013 production of *Galileo Galilei* by Philip Glass. Like Harold Pinter's *Betrayal*, Glass's story unfolds in reverse chronological order. It opens with Galileo's trial and inquisition for heresy when he is old and blind — his "crime" being the hypothesis that the Earth revolves around the Sun, which was considered blasphemous by scholars and clergy alike. The opera explores Galileo's life and work, his break with the Church, and expands into the greater oscillating relationship of science to both religion and art. In the last scene, Galileo is a young boy watching an opera composed by his father, Vincenzo Galilei, about the motions of the celestial bodies. I turned Leonardo da Vinci's iconic "Vitruvian Man" drawing into a 17th-century constellation map. Leonardo intended his anatomical proportions of the human body to be an analogy for the workings of the universe — which seemed the perfect metaphor for Galileo.

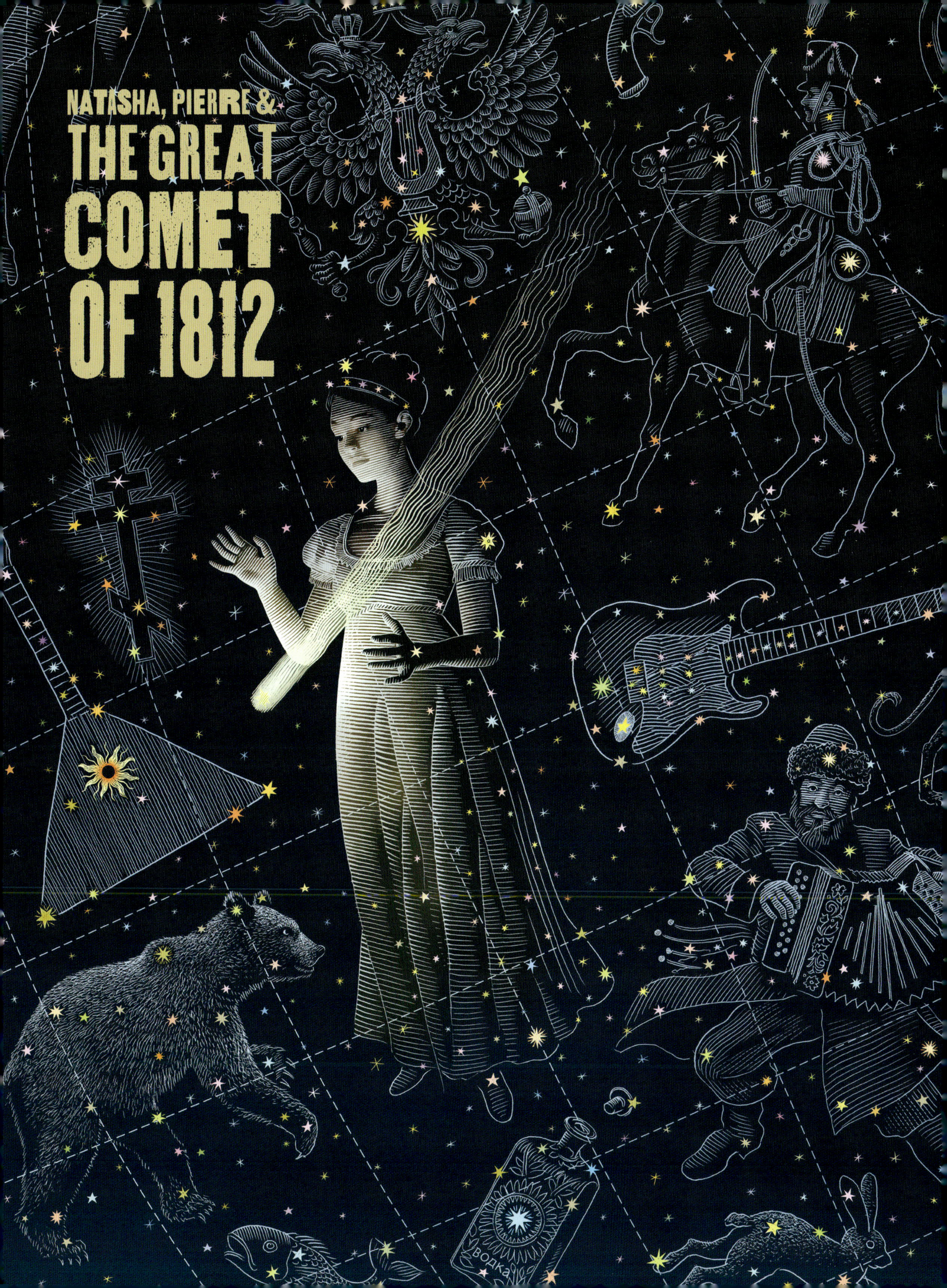
NATASHA, PIERRE &
THE GREAT
COMET
OF 1812
водка

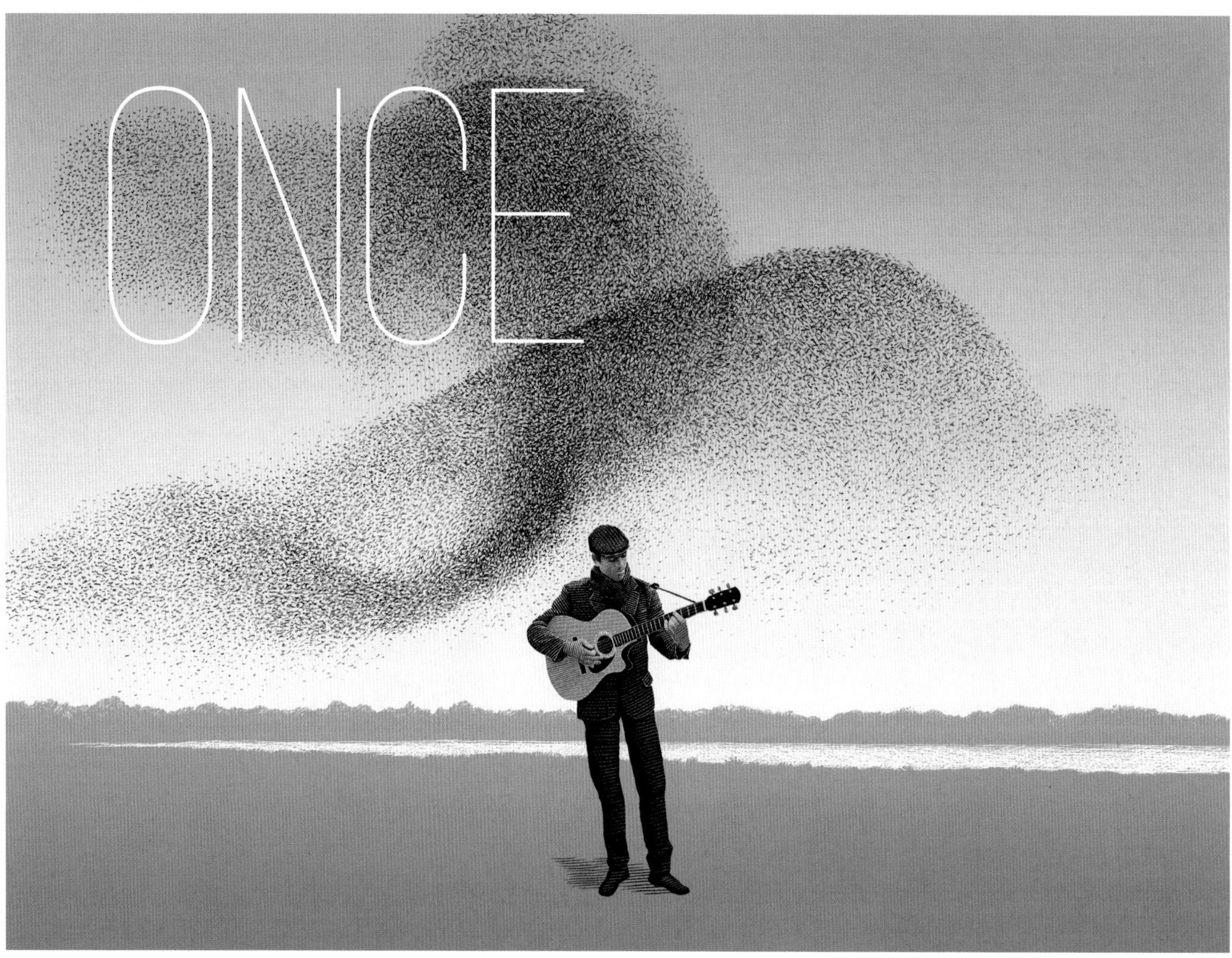

I never saw the Irish film upon which the stage musical *Once* is based. I first became aware of the show in New York in 2012 when I noticed the Broadway logo with the fabulous calligraphic guitar strings. Paul Nolan starred in that Broadway production in 2014 and I finally had a reason to put the show at the top of my list. "Guy" was a perfect role for Paul — we were thrilled to see his very fine performance, along with his handsome mug on the giant billboards in Times Square.

Dennis Garnhum kicked off his first season at the Grand Theatre in 2017 with *Once*, so I had to come up with a fresh approach for a poster. I did not have casting in time for the brochure deadlines, so naturally I thought of Paul for the illustration. The title suggests a moment in time of heightened significance. I was trying to think of a lyrical visual metaphor — and came up with a murmuration of starlings. We've all seen these large, undulating flocks on Facebook and, if we're lucky, in nature. Thousands of birds moving as one — there one moment and gone the next.

Canada legalized the cultivation, possession, acquisition and consumption of cannabis for recreational use in 2018 — the first G7 and/or G20 country to do so — and it didn't take long for someone to write a musical comedy on the subject!

Grow, by Matt Murray, Colleen Dauncey and Akiva Romer-Segal is initially about the Amish tradition of *Rumspringa* — the coming-of-age ritual during which Amish adolescents leave the comfort of their sheltered communities to explore the outside world. They must then decide whether to commit to the Amish faith forever — or to start a new life on their own.

Nineteen-year-old twins Hannah and Ruth leave their rural home and head to Toronto. Hannah is the more ambitious of the sisters, but Ruth has a more useful skill — she's a genius at growing crops. Her green thumb saves the day when they start working at an illegal marijuana grow-op in a Parkdale basement. The plants are barely alive but Ruth quickly turns the small-time operation into a booming success. The twins eventually realize they are fish out of water in the big city and return home to their family and their farm. Alice Wilson was my model for both twins. This world premiere production was postponed by COVID-19, but the plan is to produce it in 2022.

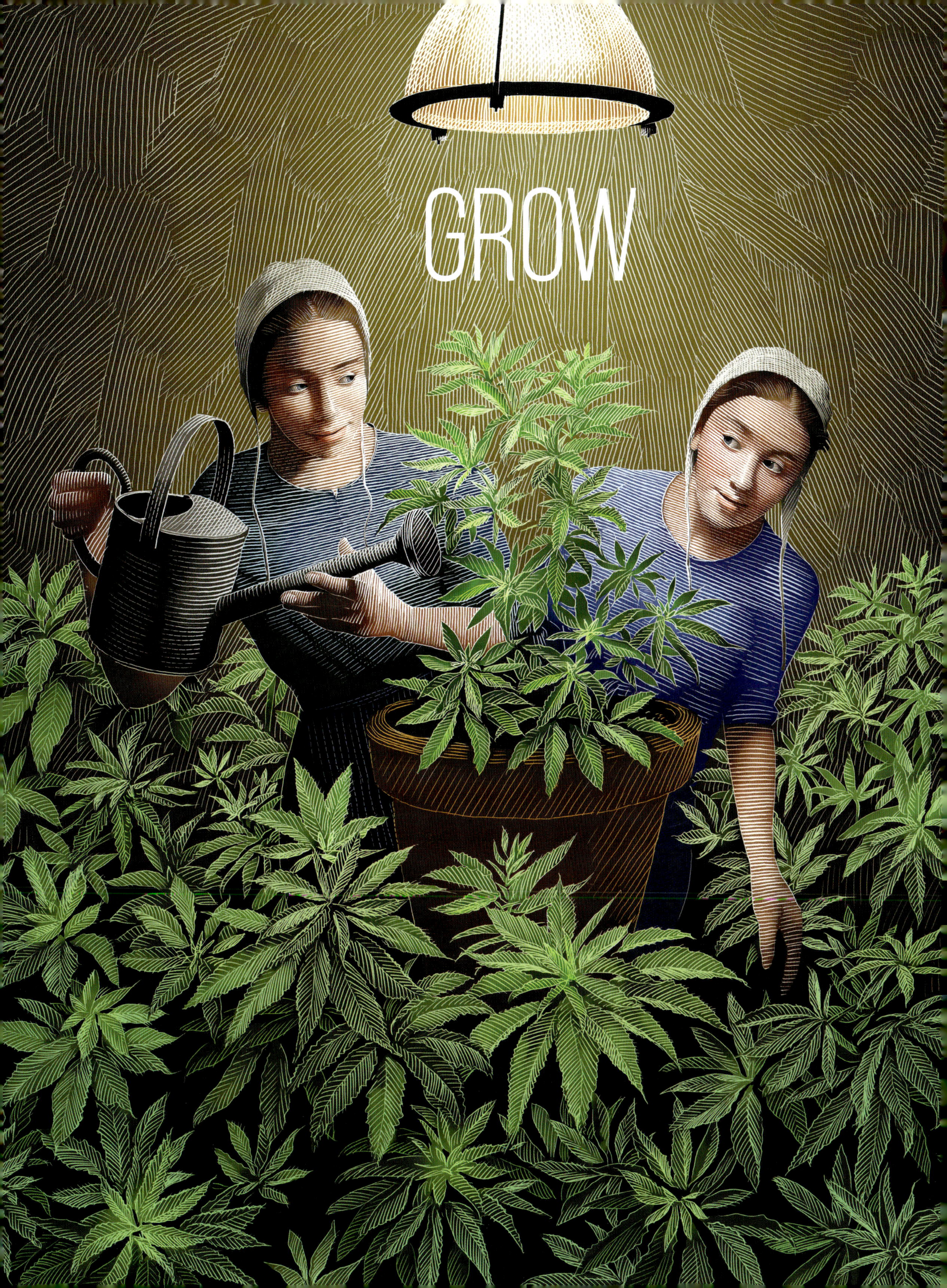
GROW

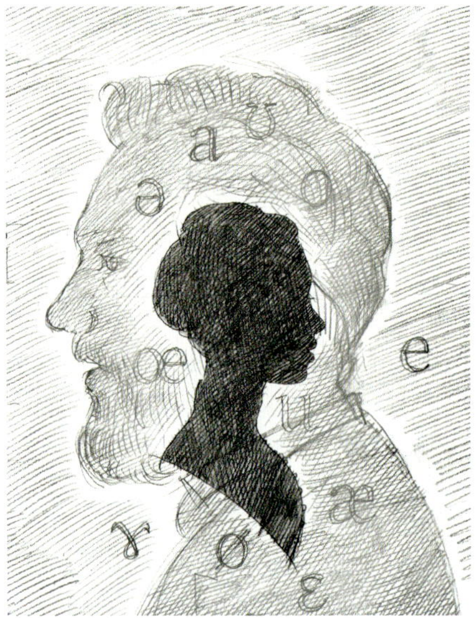

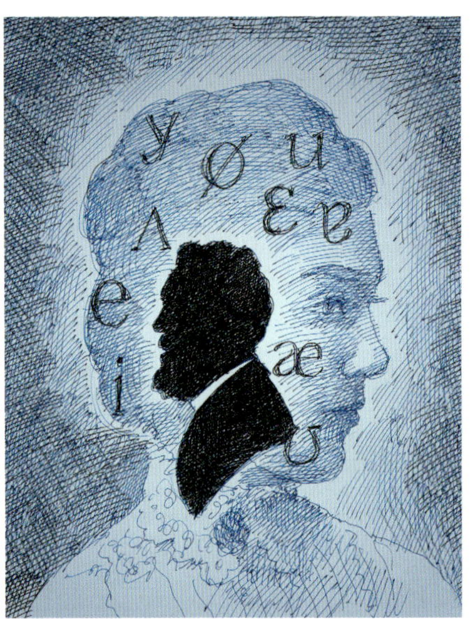

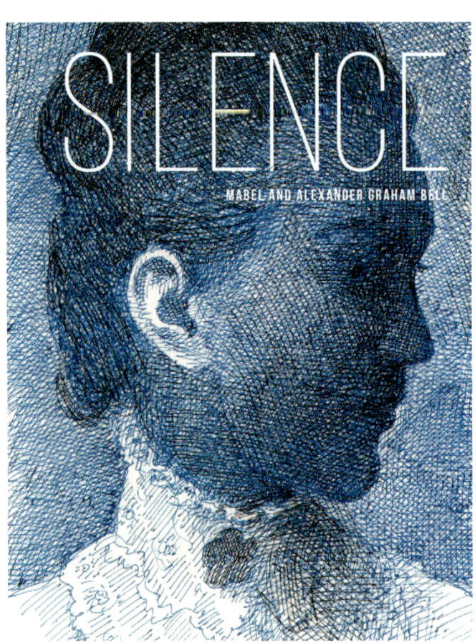

In January 2018, the Grand Theatre presented the world premiere of Trina Davies' *Silence: Mabel and Alexander Graham Bell*, directed by Peter Hinton and starring Tara Rosling. The production toured to the National Arts Centre in Ottawa the following September.

Bell is famous for inventing and patenting the first practical telephone — but his new device was of little use to his wife, Mabel Gardiner Hubbard, who was profoundly deaf. Bell's mother gradually lost her hearing when he was a boy growing up in Scotland, and he had developed techniques for helping deaf people communicate. His helped his father with the development of a system of Visible Speech and taught at a private school for the deaf in London. Bell moved with his family to Canada, and then he established himself at a School for the Deaf in Boston where Mabel was one of his students.

The play is written from Mabel's point of view. She can lip-read, so the audience hears the other characters' dialogue when she can see them. But if they are out of her line of vision, we can no longer hear them either. Light is used as a visual equivalent for sound — darkness on stage is silence.

My initial sketches were based on Victorian portrait silhouettes — they instantly convey the period setting and seem a perfect metaphor for the contrast of light and shadow in the play. The "black hole" created by the silhouette is like a window into Mabel's deaf world. Depicting her in silhouette gave her a sense of mystery, which I really liked. I looked at images by the South African artist William Kentridge — I love his silhouetted figures holding megaphones, often layered over collages of typography.

The sketch the client picked was a solo portrait of Mabel — her ear highlighted but her eye and mouth falling into deep shadow. Over the illustration I added a layer of vowel sounds from a phonetic alphabet chart.

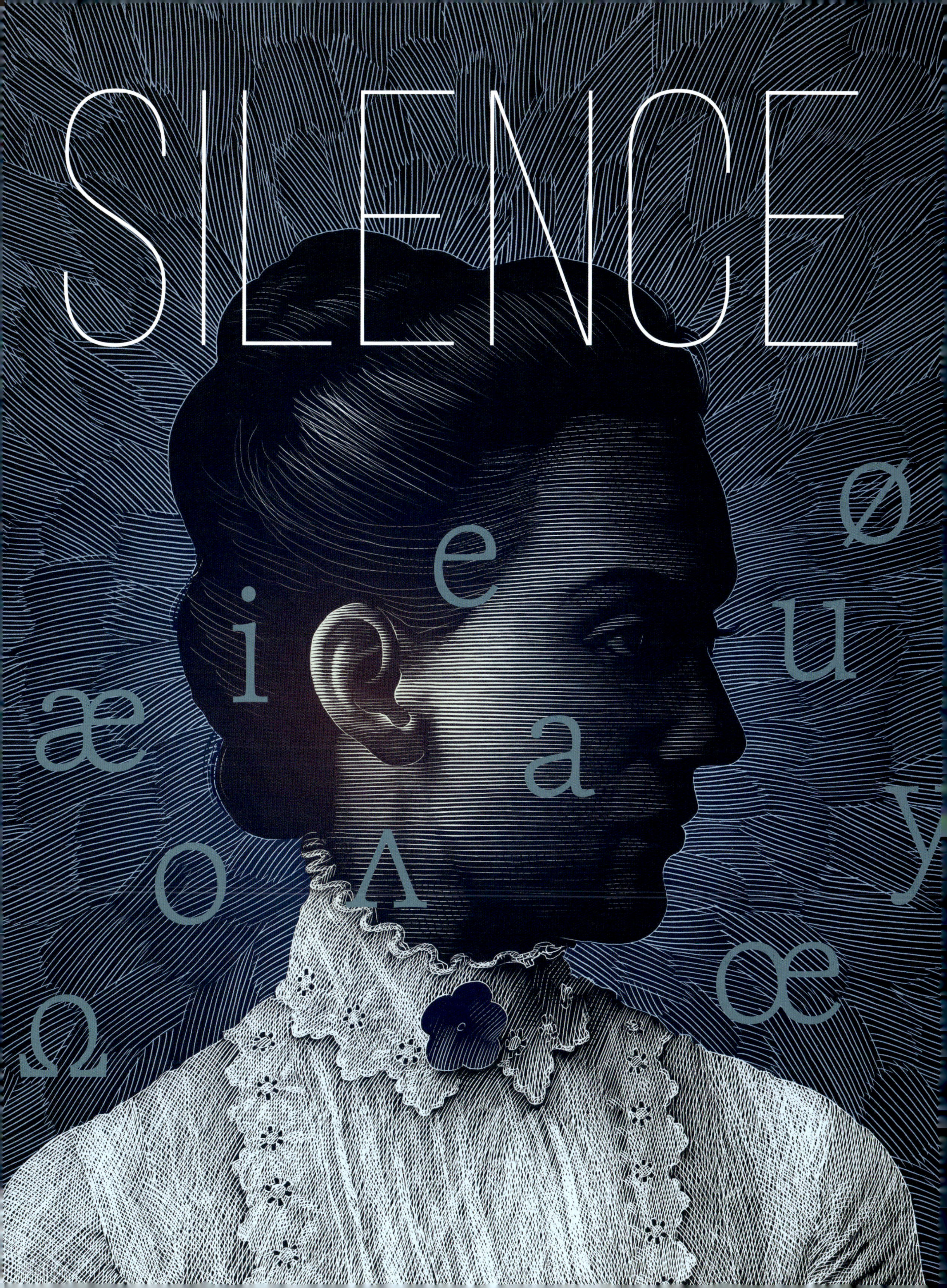
SILENCE
ø
e
i
u
æ
a
y
o
ʌ
œ
Ω

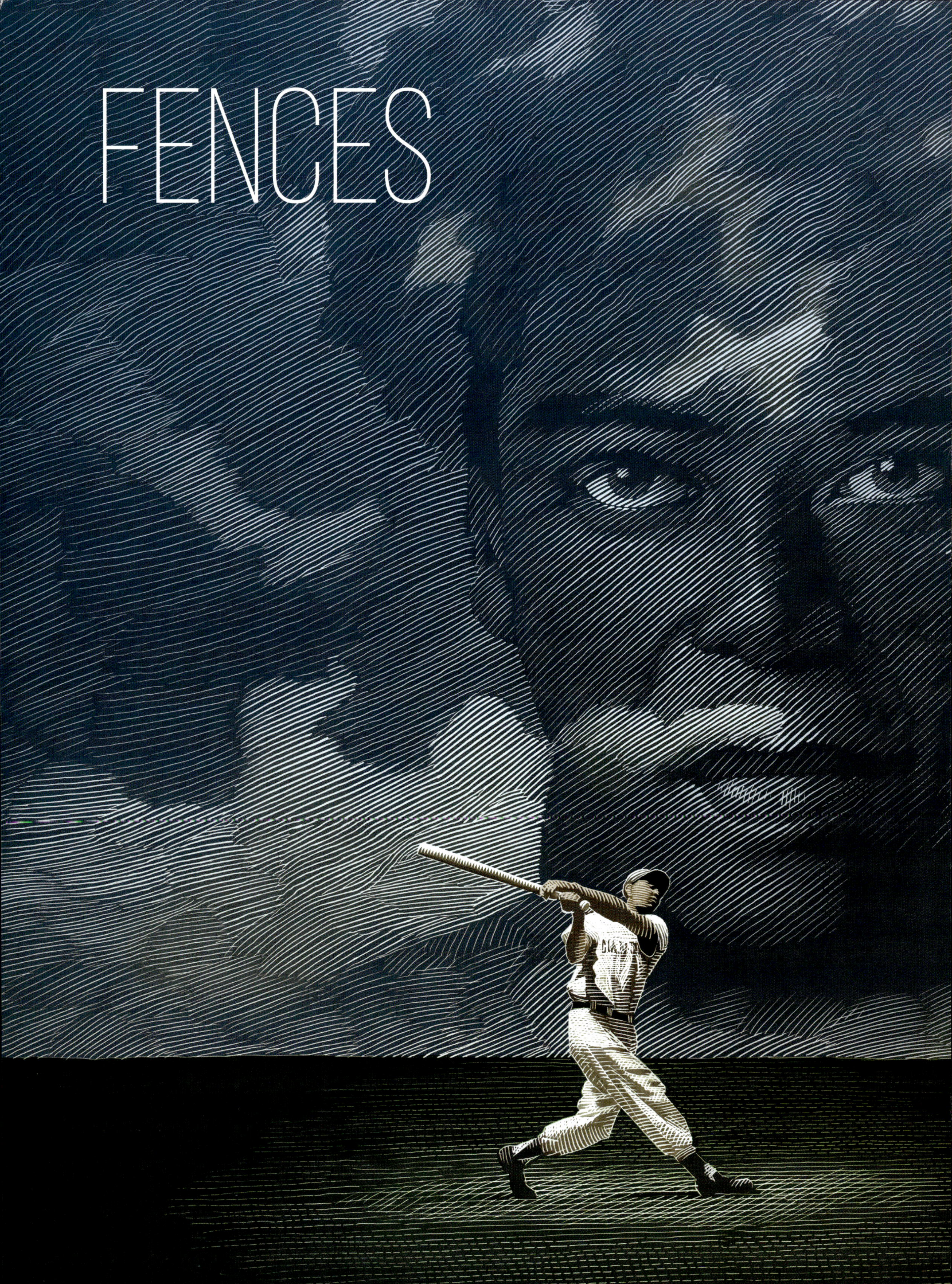
FENCES

Fences occupies the 1950s decade in August Wilson's 10-play cycle about the black experience in 20th-century America. It premiered at Yale Repertory Theatre in 1985. A Broadway production starring James Earl Jones followed in 1987 and won just about every Tony Award possible. The play won the 1987 Pulitzer Prize for Drama. I saw the extraordinary 2010 Broadway revival with Denzel Washington and Viola Davis and hoped that the play would come along as a poster assignment one day. I got my wish when the Grand Theatre planned a 2019 production starring Nigel Shawn Williams.

In his youth, Troy Maxson was a talented star in Negro League baseball. But the colour barrier was still in place so he was not allowed into the major leagues, and he now supports his family working as a trash collector. He admits to his wife Rose that he has been having an affair and that his mistress is pregnant. His son Cory has an opportunity for a college football scholarship, but Troy stubbornly refuses to allow him to accept it — and the father/son relationship falls apart. Seven years pass; Troy has died, and Rose and Cory struggle with feelings of resentment, respect and forgiveness.

I juxtaposed the young, handsome Troy in his crisp white uniform with a ghost-like portrait of Williams in the clouds.

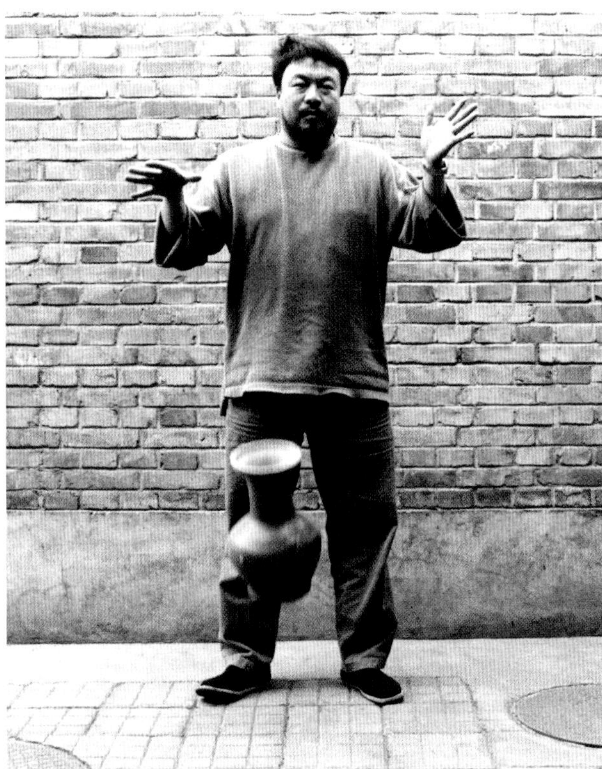

Margaret Atwood wrote *The Penelopiad* as a novella in 2005 — a retelling of the events in *The Odyssey* from Penelope's point of view, with half of her title borrowed from *The Iliad*. Atwood then adapted it for the stage with an all-female cast in 2007 — it premiered in a co-production between the National Arts Centre in Ottawa and the Royal Shakespeare Company in Stratford-upon-Avon. Both the book and the stage version begin with Penelope, in Hades, speaking the extraordinary line "Now that I'm dead, I know everything."

I knew the story of Odysseus returning home to Ithaca after 20 years of wandering to find a hundred opportunistic suitors pressuring Penelope to choose one of them as her new husband. I knew the dramatic scene where Odysseus, disguised as a beggar, strings his old bow and, with the help of his son Telemachus, massacres all the suitors. But Atwood focuses on Penelope's 12 maids — her loyal servants who were hanged by Odysseus in the bloody melee. I had not remembered that sad and shocking scene in this mythology.

The Grand Theatre announced a new production for January 2019. Artistic Director Dennis Garnhum's only criteria was that the poster image feel "contemporary." He wanted to avoid a poster looking like something for an ancient Greek play — Atwood is telling a story with a classical setting, but it's very much from a modern perspective.

So I knew not to put a model in ancient Greek costume — but I still needed a visual anchor from the world of the story to give context and perspective. I was looking for a concept that would reflect the boldly theatrical script and staging. I sketched a modern Penelope holding a priceless ancient Greek vase painted with the 12 maids — and she's dropping it. It's a dangerous image: two seconds later and the maids are shattered into a thousand pieces on the floor. But maybe the vase magically floats there in mid-air if you let go of it — our laws of physics and gravity may not apply in the ancient Greek underworld or afterlife.

My illustration makes incidental reference to a famous 1995 performance art piece by the Chinese artist and activist Ai Weiwei entitled *Dropping a Han Dynasty Urn*. The model for this illustration was actor Jessica B. Hill.

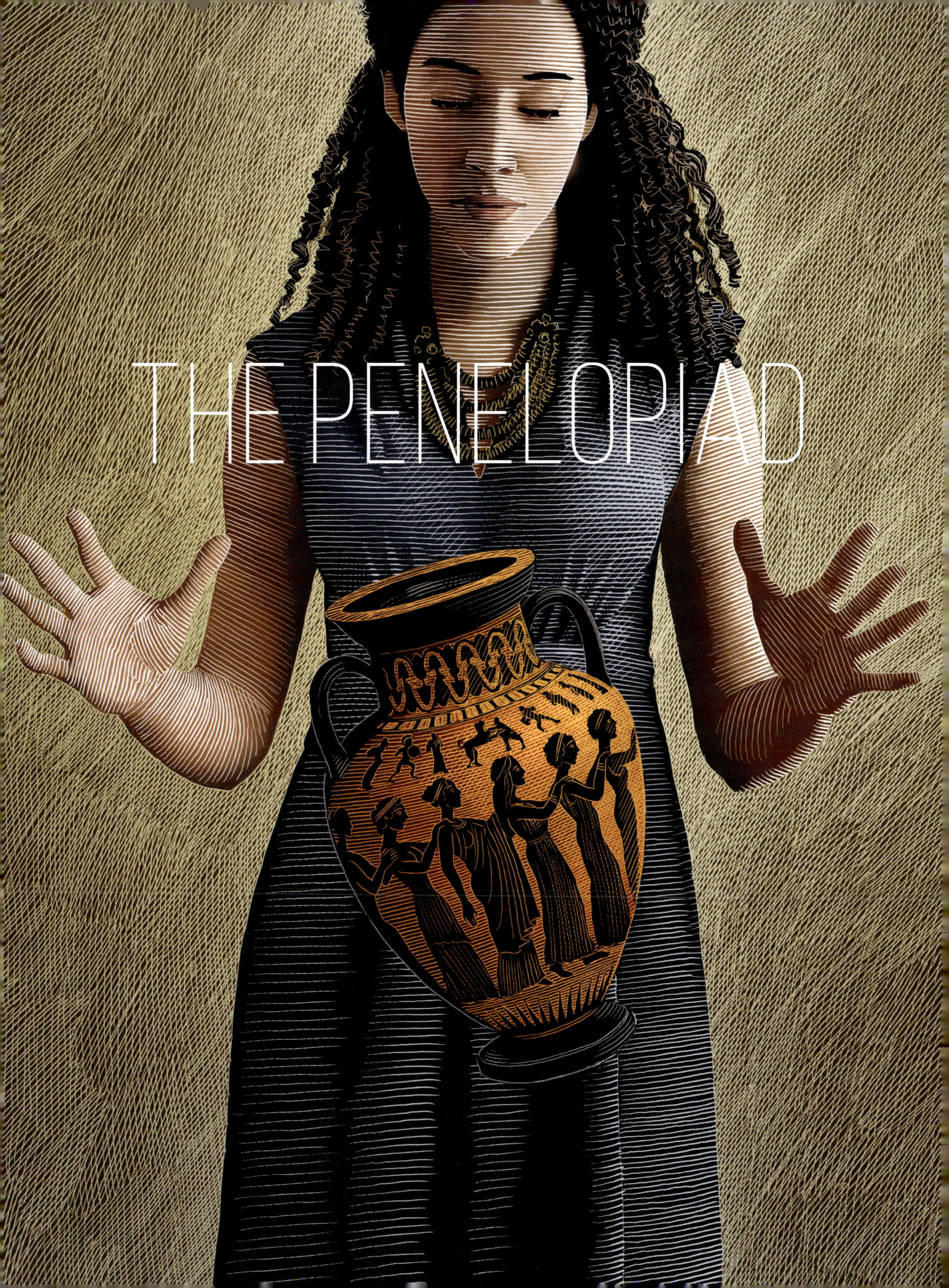
THE PENELOPIAD

Dennis Garhnum directed a stage adaptation of the famous movie *Chariots of Fire* at the Grand Theatre in 2017. Action filled the entire theatre as the auditorium was reconfigured to accommodate a running track through the audience. The story revolves around the friendship (and rivalry) between Harold Abrahams and Eric Liddell and their gold medal performances at the 1924 Paris Olympics. My poster illustration is based loosely on a photograph of Liddell, "the Flying Scotsman," in the classic starting block position.

To commemorate the centennial of the end of World War One in November 2018, Garnhum directed his own stage adaptation of Timothy Findley's 1977 novel *The Wars* at The Grand. We are in the same trenches here as in R.C. Sherriff's *Journey's End*. A mother watching her son go off to war made me think of Noël Coward's *Cavalcade*. Robert Ross, the troubled young officer at the centre of Findley's story, always seems to be moving against a cataclysmic tide of events. I have rejected concepts that involve crowd scenes (they take forever to engrave), but this play is about the terrible human cost of war so it seemed right to show Robert with his platoon. Lambs to the slaughter. The biggest rendering challenge was getting the shapes of the helmets consistent.

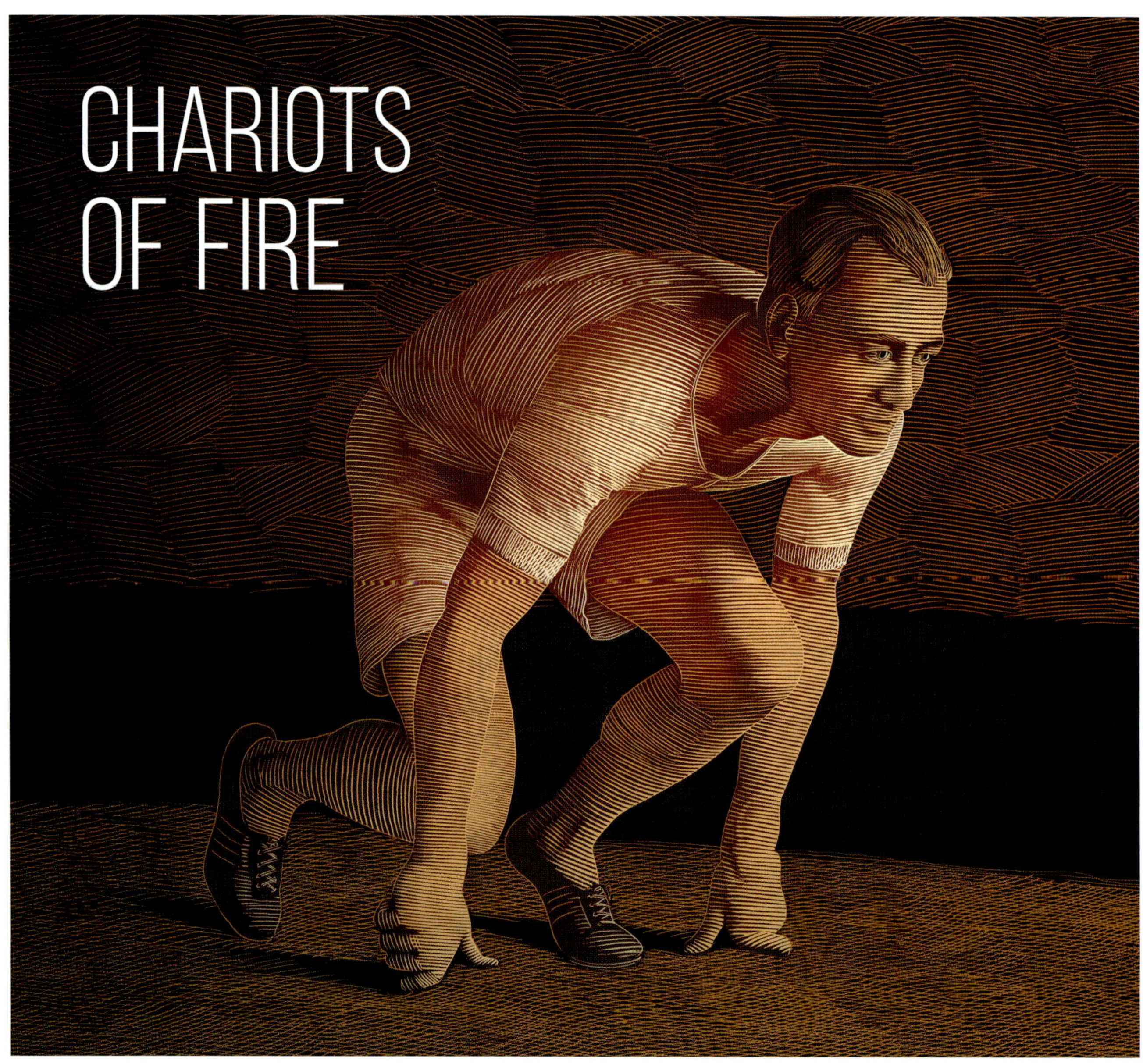

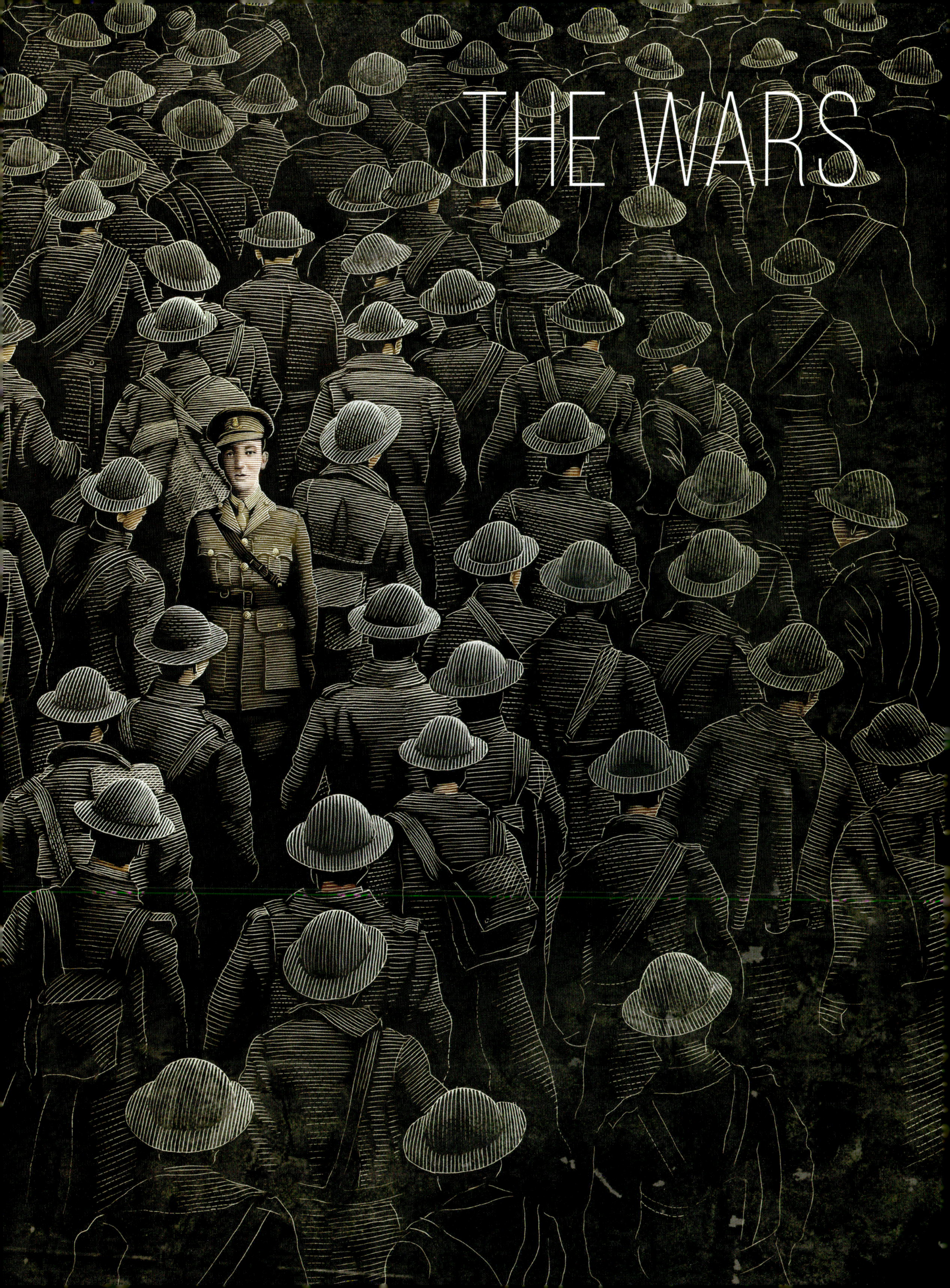
THE WARS

Rebecca Northan is an actor, director and comedian with a extraordinary gift for improvisation. The Grand presented her show *Blind Date* in 2018. Northan picks her co-star "date" for each performance from the audience — a different gentleman every night. Rebecca transforms herself into Mimi, a sexy, single French girl in a hot red dress — with a clown nose to remind everyone involved not to get too carried away. Mimi makes a big impression — she visited my studio to pose for this illustration. Northan has been doing the show for 10 years in New York, Toronto and across North America, and recently supervised a new production in Oslo, Norway.

Prom Queen is a musical based on the 2002 true story of Marc Hall, a Catholic high school student. Hall is gay, and when the school board denied him permission to bring his boyfriend to the prom, Hall took them to court — and won. Dennis Garnhum picked *Prom Queen* for the Grand Theatre's 2018 High School Project because it allows students to play characters their own age in a story of empowerment and triumph. A huge controversy broke out (generating amazing publicity for the show nine months before it opened) when the local school board pulled funding because of the subject matter — then changed its mind and restored it. Christina nailed the clear, simple concept for the poster — two boys pinning corsages on each other.

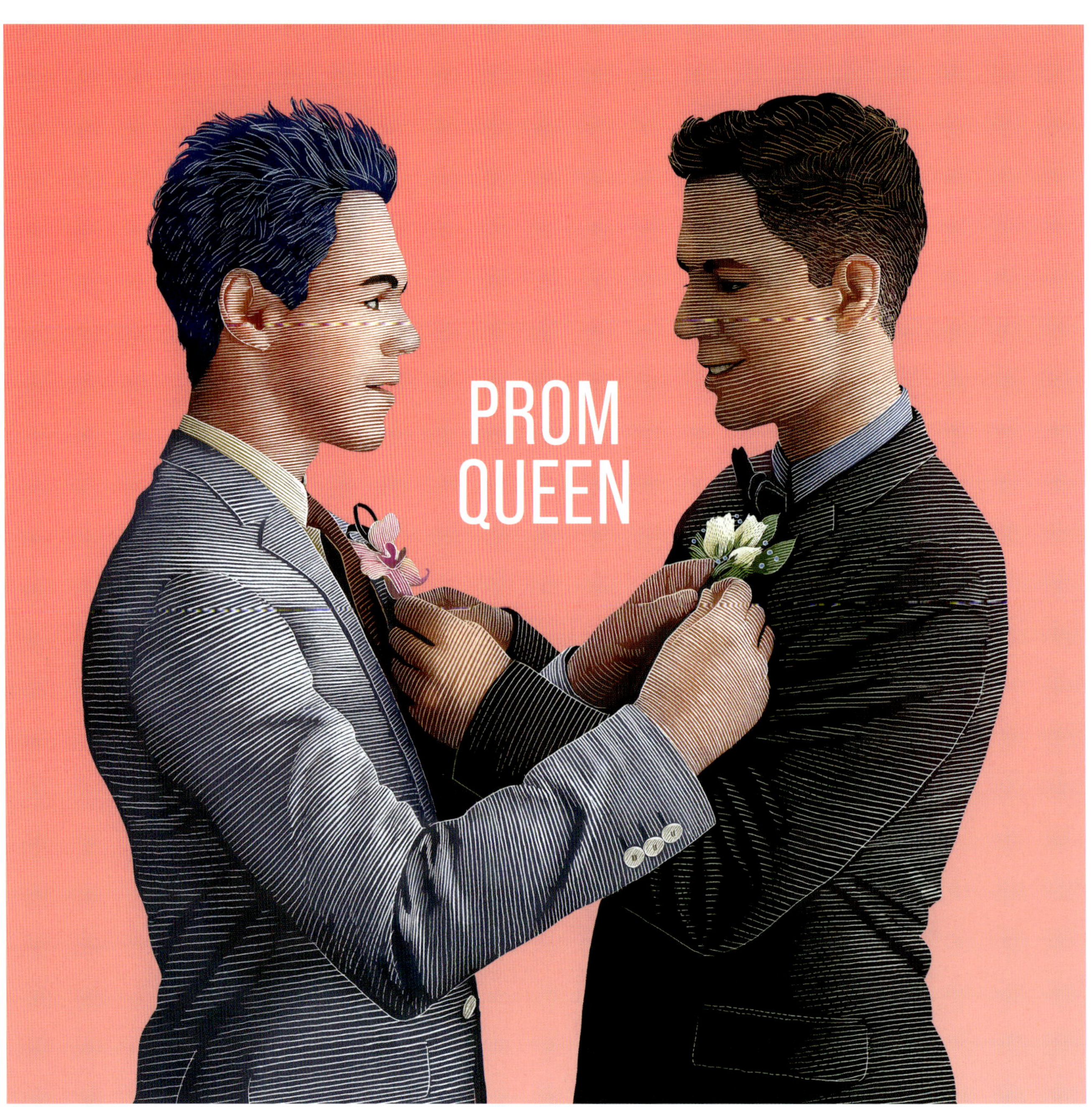

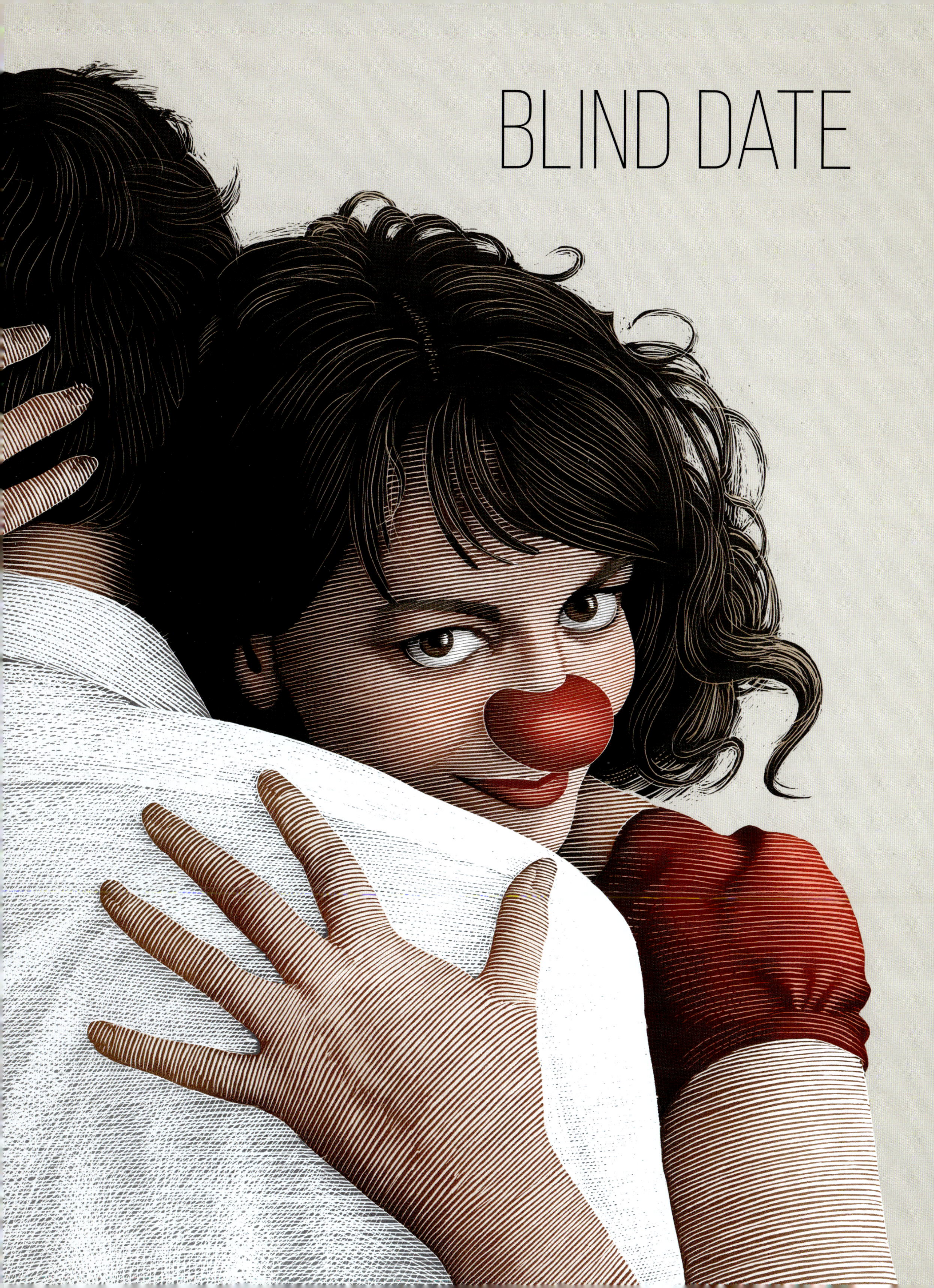
BLIND DATE

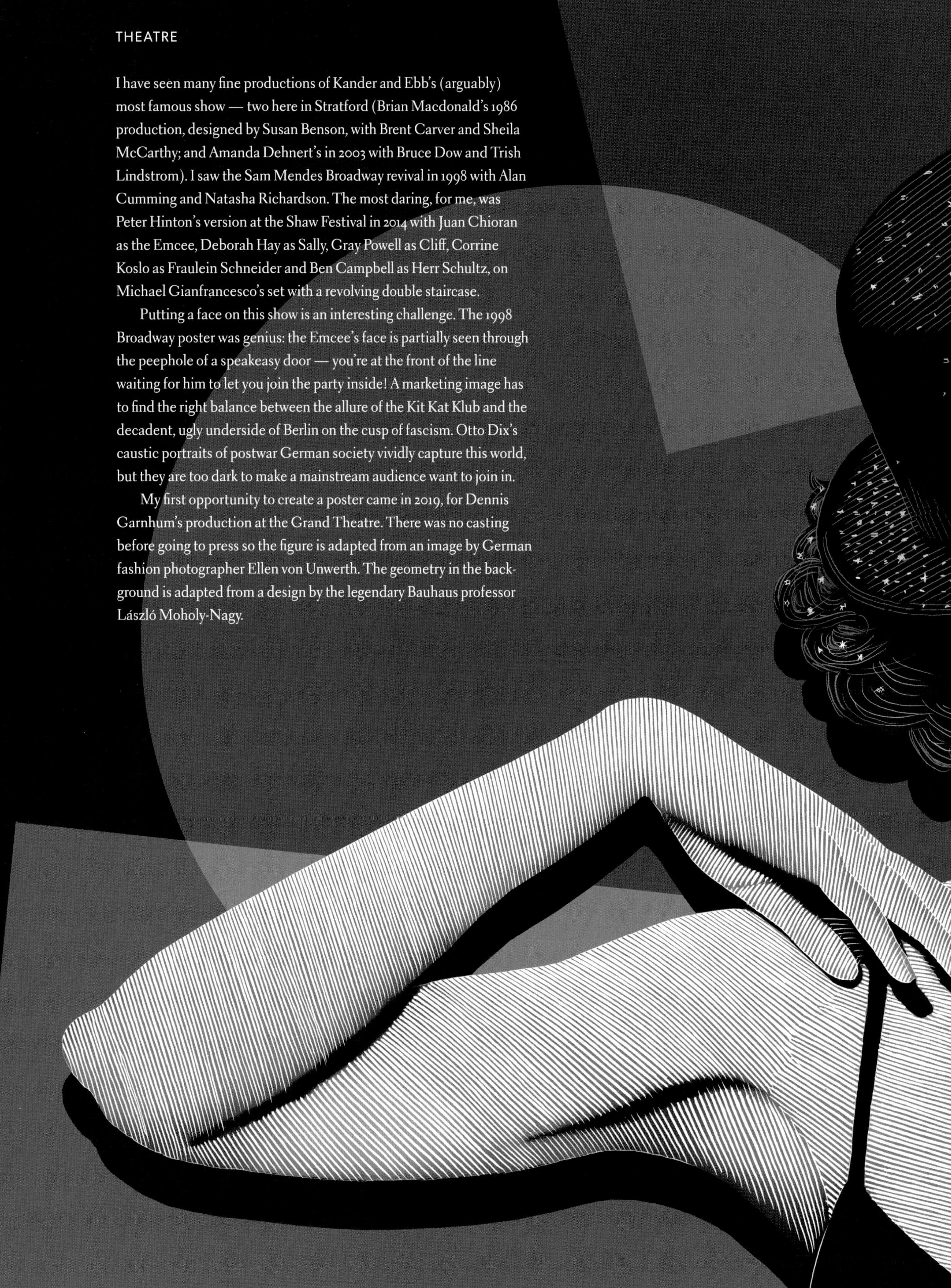

I have seen many fine productions of Kander and Ebb's (arguably) most famous show — two here in Stratford (Brian Macdonald's 1986 production, designed by Susan Benson, with Brent Carver and Sheila McCarthy; and Amanda Dehnert's in 2003 with Bruce Dow and Trish Lindstrom). I saw the Sam Mendes Broadway revival in 1998 with Alan Cumming and Natasha Richardson. The most daring, for me, was Peter Hinton's version at the Shaw Festival in 2014 with Juan Chioran as the Emcee, Deborah Hay as Sally, Gray Powell as Cliff, Corrine Koslo as Fraulein Schneider and Ben Campbell as Herr Schultz, on Michael Gianfrancesco's set with a revolving double staircase.

Putting a face on this show is an interesting challenge. The 1998 Broadway poster was genius: the Emcee's face is partially seen through the peephole of a speakeasy door — you're at the front of the line waiting for him to let you join the party inside! A marketing image has to find the right balance between the allure of the Kit Kat Klub and the decadent, ugly underside of Berlin on the cusp of fascism. Otto Dix's caustic portraits of postwar German society vividly capture this world, but they are too dark to make a mainstream audience want to join in.

My first opportunity to create a poster came in 2019, for Dennis Garnhum's production at the Grand Theatre. There was no casting before going to press so the figure is adapted from an image by German fashion photographer Ellen von Unwerth. The geometry in the background is adapted from a design by the legendary Bauhaus professor László Moholy-Nagy.

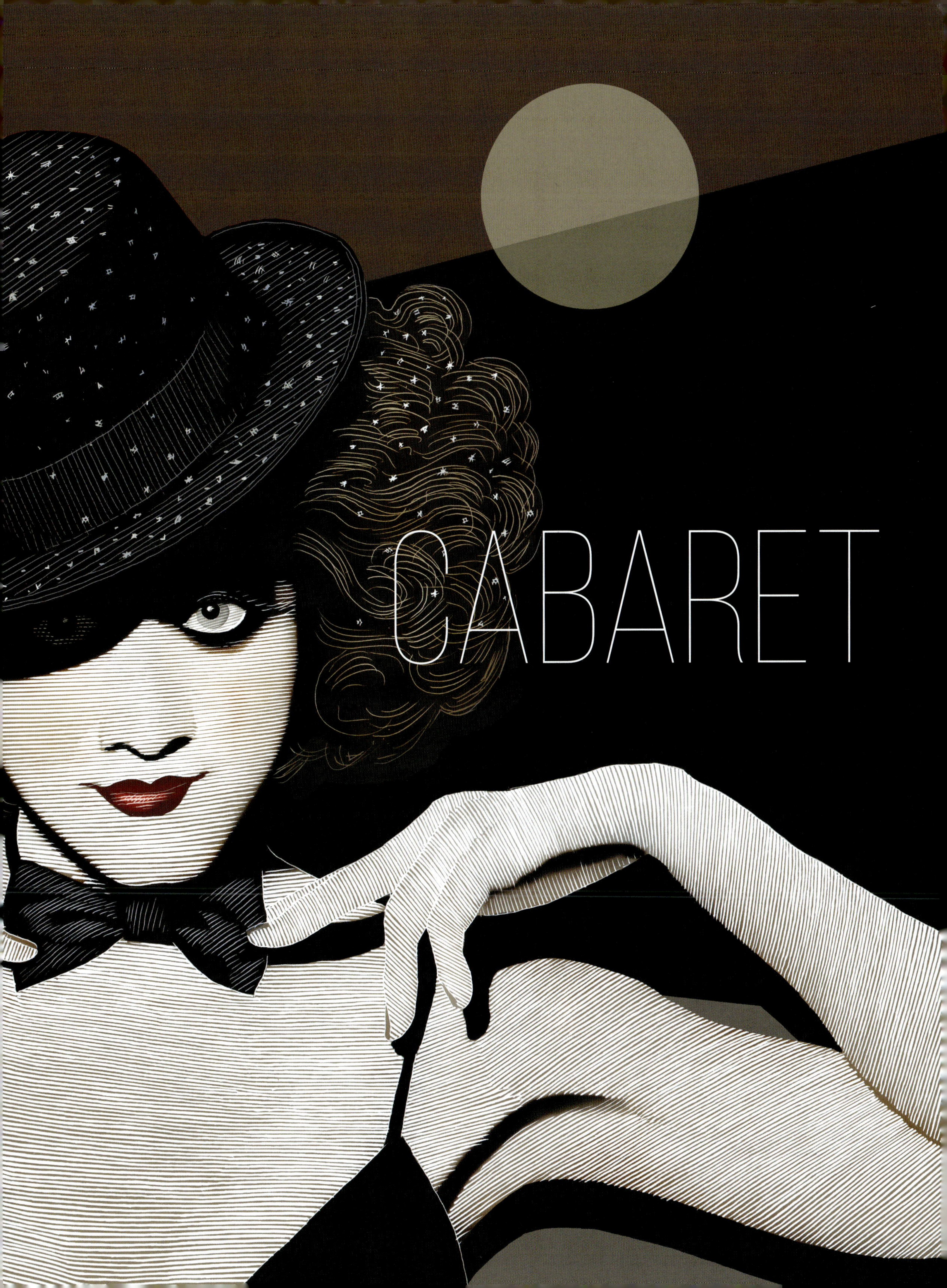
CABARET

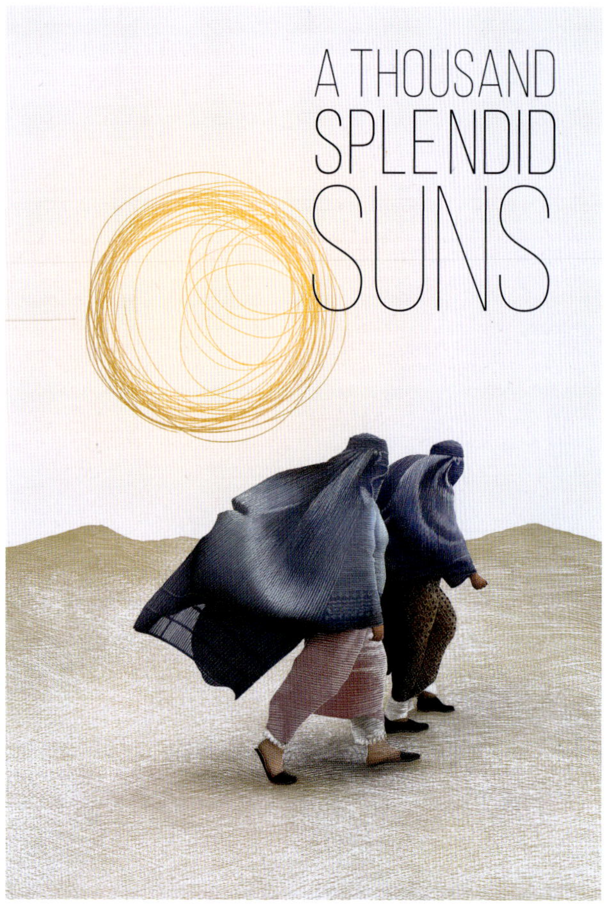

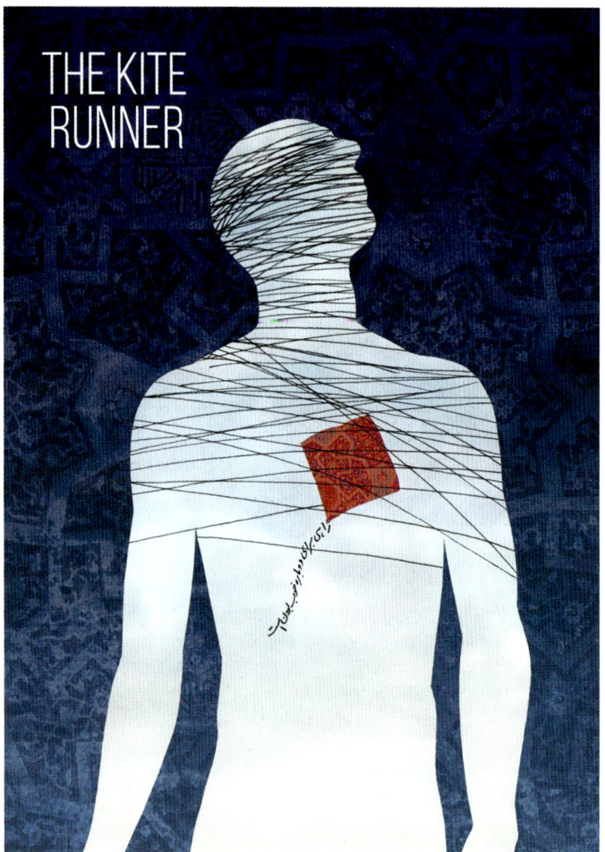

Most of my theatre assignments are for plays from my own cultural background — I'm a middle-aged white guy familiar with the standard North American, British and European repertoire. So I look forward to plays from outside my own tradition as learning opportunities that expand my horizons.

Tara Beagan's 2017 play *Honour Beat* explores the complexities of family relationships from a First Nations perspective. The play is set in the palliative care ward of a hospital where two sisters, in their 50s, are saying goodbye to their 80-year-old mother. Their shared past includes good times and bad (like everyone's), and the memories of their younger years take the audience on a spiritual journey with great humour and honesty. The play also explores thorny questions around medical assistance in dying — legal in Canada since 2016.

At the very end of the play, the sisters dress their mother in ceremonial clothing for her final journey. We suggested a simple poster idea — a pair of moccasins floating in the sky (like Georgia O'Keeffe's deer skulls), with a sliver of moon. Everyone loved the concept, but here's where it's so easy for someone unfamiliar with the culture to make a mistake. I had included decorative beadwork on my first rough sketch in the form of leaves and flowers. It turns out that floral decoration is associated with Cree, Anishinaabe and Métis — but the family in the story is Lakota Sioux, and their typical decoration style is geometric (the pyramid-style shapes represent mountains). I corresponded with the playwright who made sure that these details were correct. Tara made the suggestion that, out of respect for the unnamed artisans, my illustration should reflect a synthesis of the sources I was looking at, rather than being a direct copy of the beadwork on any specific pair of moccasins.

Carey Perloff's world premiere production of Khaled Hosseini's *A Thousand Splendid Suns*, set in Kabul, was on the Grand Theatre's playbill in 2018. The sun was represented on stage by set designer Ken MacDonald by a huge, tangled coil of wire suspended against the sky. My poster image of two Afghan women — Miriam and Laila, whose lives are thrown together through tragedy — included a scribbled sun based on Ken's design. I used Photoshop filters to achieve the glow, and kept the sun on a layer so it could be moved to suit the composition of vertical or horizontal ad shapes.

Theatre Calgary presented a stage adaptation of *The Kite Runner*, Hosseini's other famous novel set in Kabul, in 2013. Christina proposed this simple, eloquent concept — a man's silhouette bound up with a tangle of strings and a kite representing his heart. Emily Cooper added the subtle sky and Islamic patterns in the background.

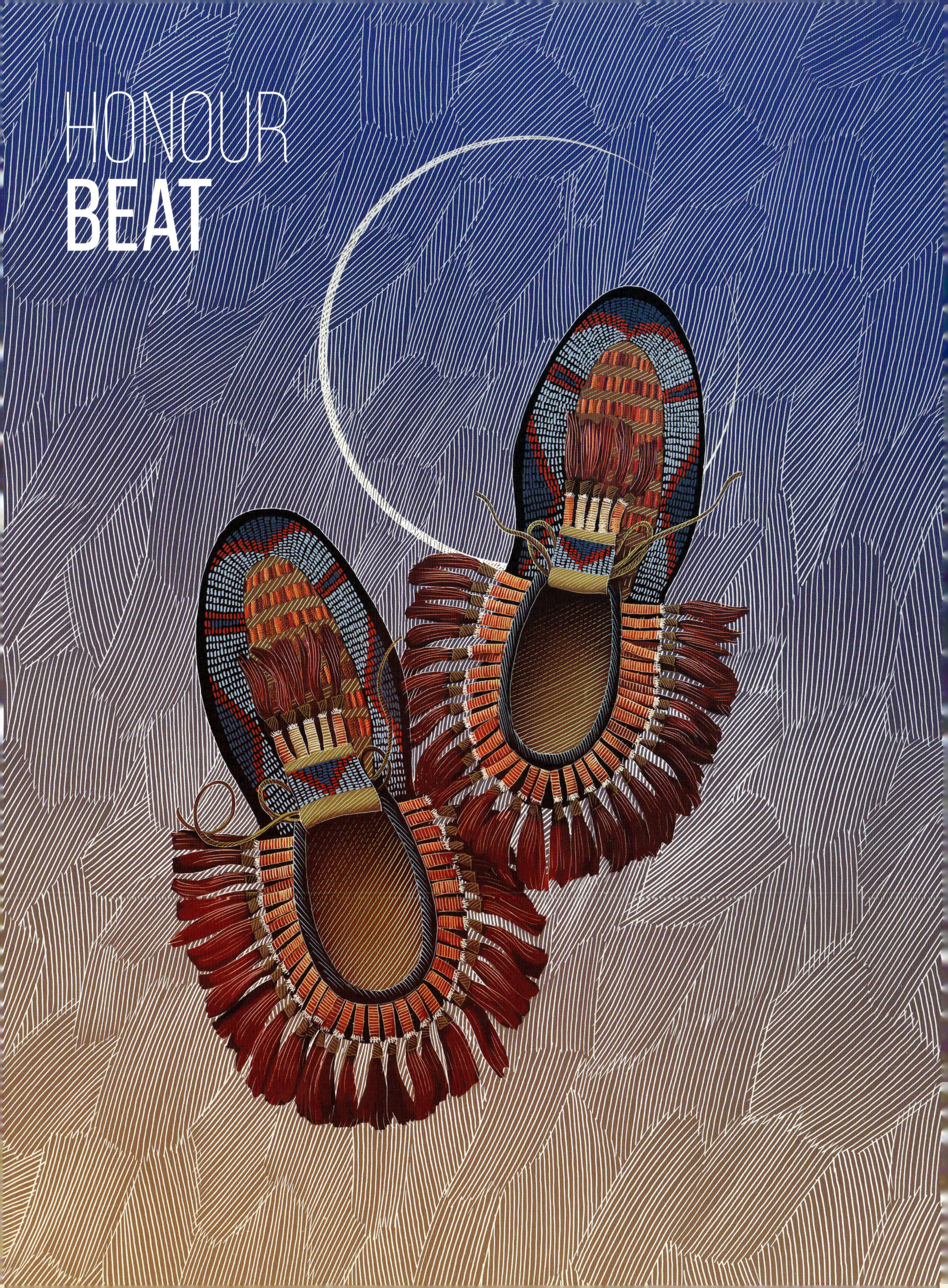
HONOUR
BEAT

The Grand Theatre announced Hannah Moscovitch's edgy, engrossing new play *Sexual Misconduct of the Middle Classes* as part of the 2020 season. It's a two-hander: John is an attractive, forty-something-year-old successful novelist and university English professor. He's a literary star but his personal life is falling apart. He catches himself admiring a student — a girl in a red coat. Nineteen-year-old Annie is an aspiring writer and a huge fan of John's work. She lives just down the street from him and gets locked out of her apartment one day... We have seen stories of teacher-student affairs many times, but a female playwright's perspective on abuse of authority is more nuanced than most. Moscovitch turns our expectations upside-down, re-envisioning the scenario for our #MeToo era. The poster is about the power dynamics — John's expression is aloof, tinged with arrogance and sexual suggestion; Annie is completely confident.

Emma Donoghue's novel *Room* appeared in 2010 — it was an international bestseller. Donoghue adapted it for a 2015 film, then wrote a stage version which premiered in London, UK, in 2017. But Emma Donoghue lives in the *other* London — the one in Ontario, Canada — so when Dennis Garnhum proposed that The Grand would love to present the North American premiere, the author was immediately on board.

The story is narrated by five-year-old Jack, who lives with his mother in a tiny single-room "cell." Because it's the only environment he has ever known — his Ma loves him and keeps him happy and healthy — Jack thinks his life is perfectly normal. The only other person that Jack has ever seen is Old Nick, who visits the room at night and brings them food and supplies. What Jack doesn't know is that Old Nick kidnapped Ma when she was 19 years old and has kept her imprisoned for the past seven years. Old Nick rapes Ma when he visits the room — Jack is the product of one such sexual assault. Ma devises an escape plan that involves pretending that Jack has died (the first half of the play takes place in Room; the second half in the real world after their rescue). Ma is reunited with her family and tries to reclaim her life. Jack finds himself overwhelmed by this brave new world and wants only to return to the safety of Room.

Like all theatre companies, The Grand had to shut down operations when the COVID-19 pandemic hit. That painful announcement was made on the afternoon of March 13 — cancelling *Room*'s opening night. Hopefully, both these productions can be presented in a future season.

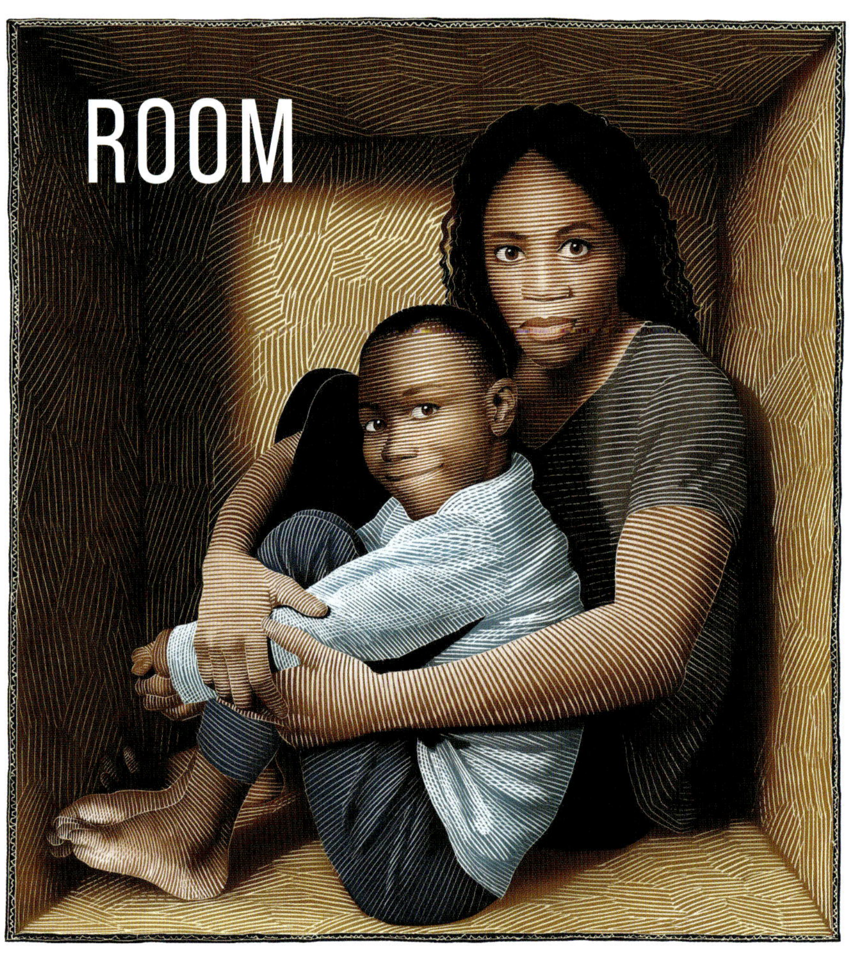

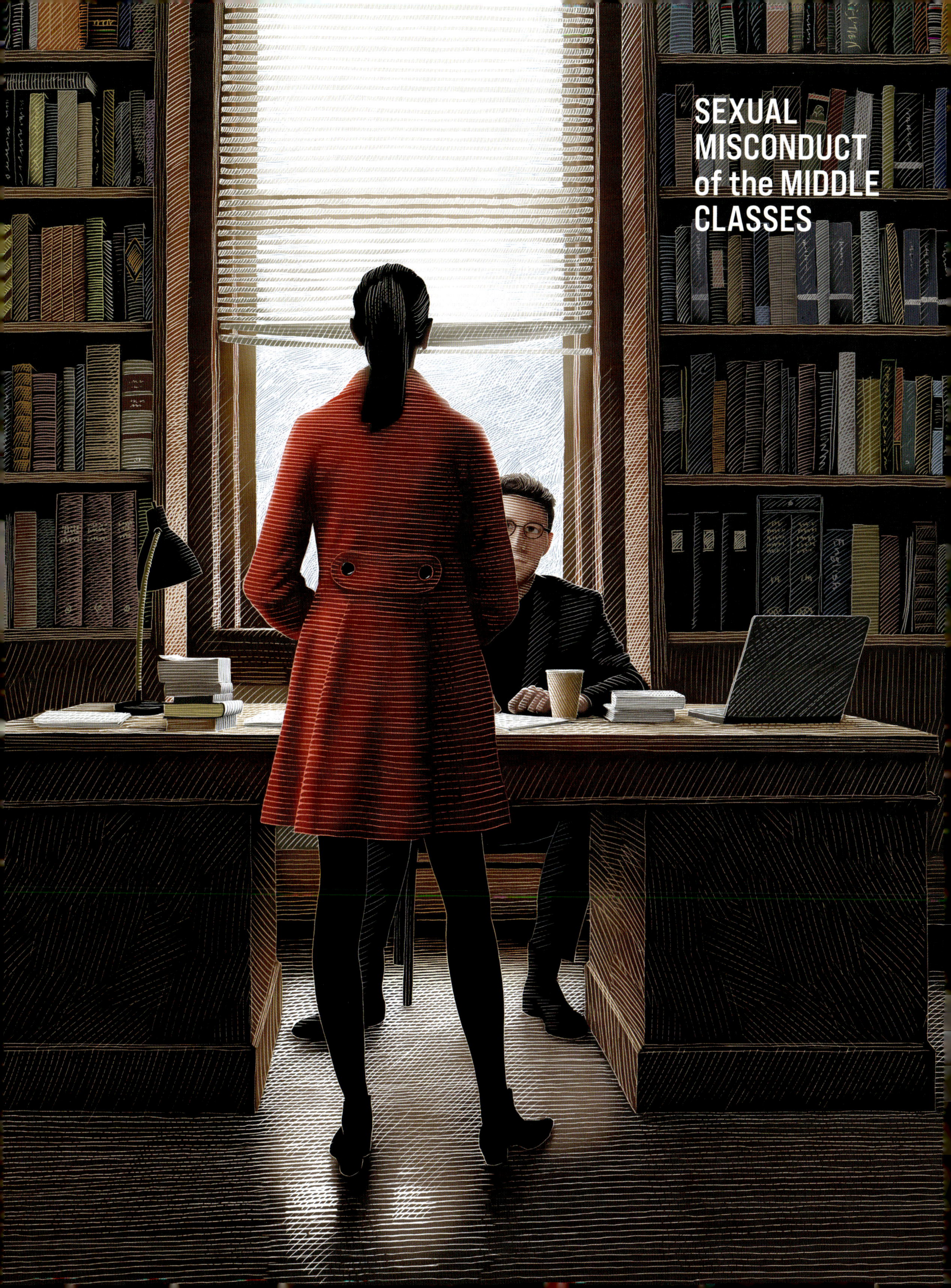
SEXUAL
MISCONDUCT
of the MIDDLE
CLASSES

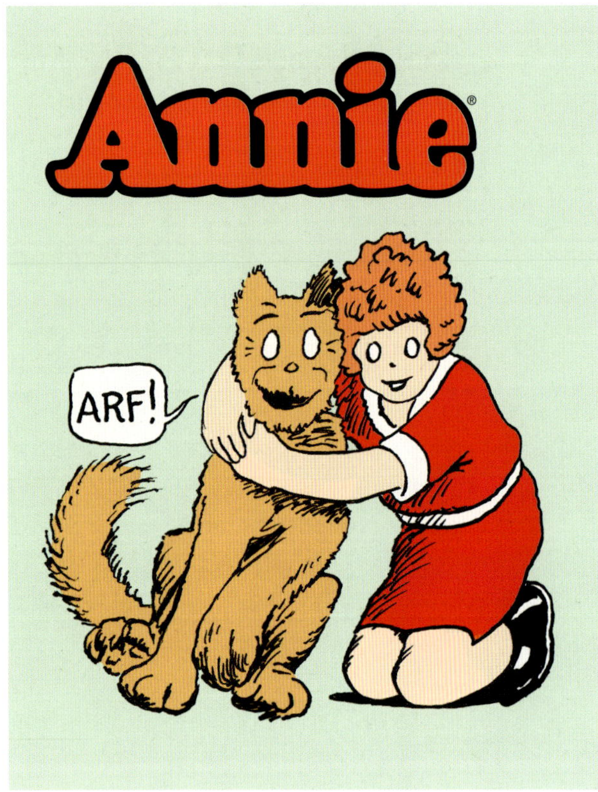

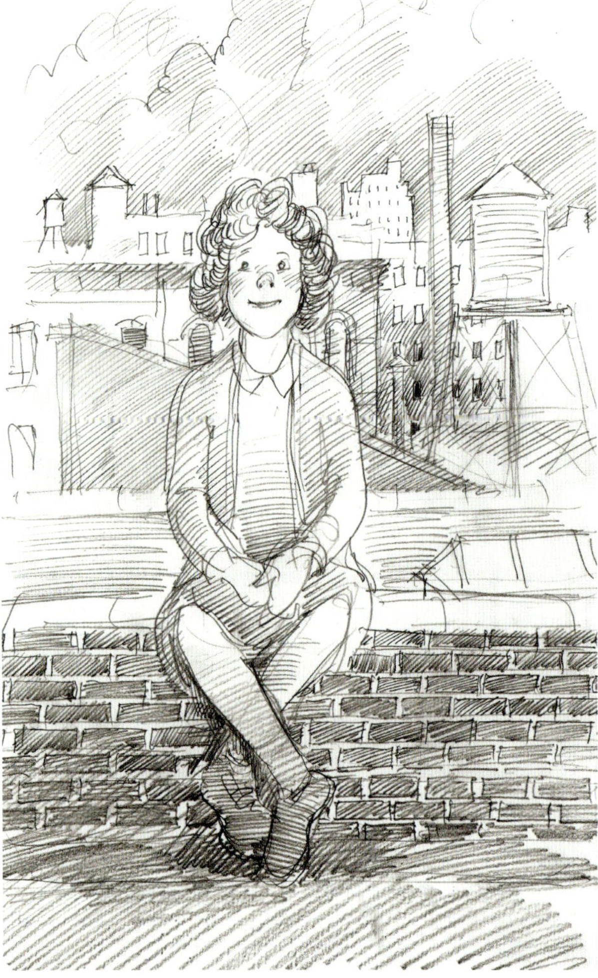

The Grand Theatre announced a new production of the popular Broadway musical *Annie* for November 2020. I will confess that this is a show I had hoped to get through my career without ever having to work on. I love Harold Gray's comic strip drawings from the 1920s — the best way to channel Gray's ever-chipper little heroine, it seemed to me, was to use his original art for the poster illustration. There was no reason to re-render her in scratchboard.

But then along came COVID-19 and theatre companies around the world were knocked sideways. The Grand's entire 2020–21 season was cancelled. They carefully avoided that word, calling it a postponement — a "Grand Intermission" — but that made it no less traumatic for theatre artists, administrators and audiences. Our Punch & Judy studio had specialized for decades in graphic design for performing arts clients, and suddenly we had no work at all.

As we were thinking about how The Grand might put any kind of a good face on the lockdown, Christina realized that *Annie*'s most famous song, "The Sun'll Come Out Tomorrow," makes the best tagline imaginable for these uncertain times — a reassuring message of optimism and hope. This was exactly what the theatre needed to say to its community in London, so I started working on sketches for a new illustration.

Director Dennis Garnhum was already thinking about staging the show. Annie's life in the orphanage is grim; Dennis felt that the only way she is able to keep her chin up is by climbing up onto the roof early every morning — if the sun rises, bringing light and warmth, Annie knows that she can face the day, too. So we knew we wanted to see the rooftops of lower Manhattan at dawn. I tried every pose I could think of — sitting, standing, facing towards us, facing away from us. A three-quarter view from the back worked best — this angle allows us to see what she's seeing, and it makes the illustration more about the sun than about the little girl.

I made my nine-year-old model, Adelia Wilson (and therefore her mom), get up at 6 AM to get sunrise lighting. She has straight, blonde hair (dyed pink at the time), so I had to invent Annie's curls. Two years before, at age seven, Adelia had modeled for my cover for Gregory Maguire's *After Alice*, which also appears in this book.

Our plan, eventually, is to use the Harold Gray artwork as the poster for the show, and this illustration as the season brochure cover. Whenever the sun eventually comes out.

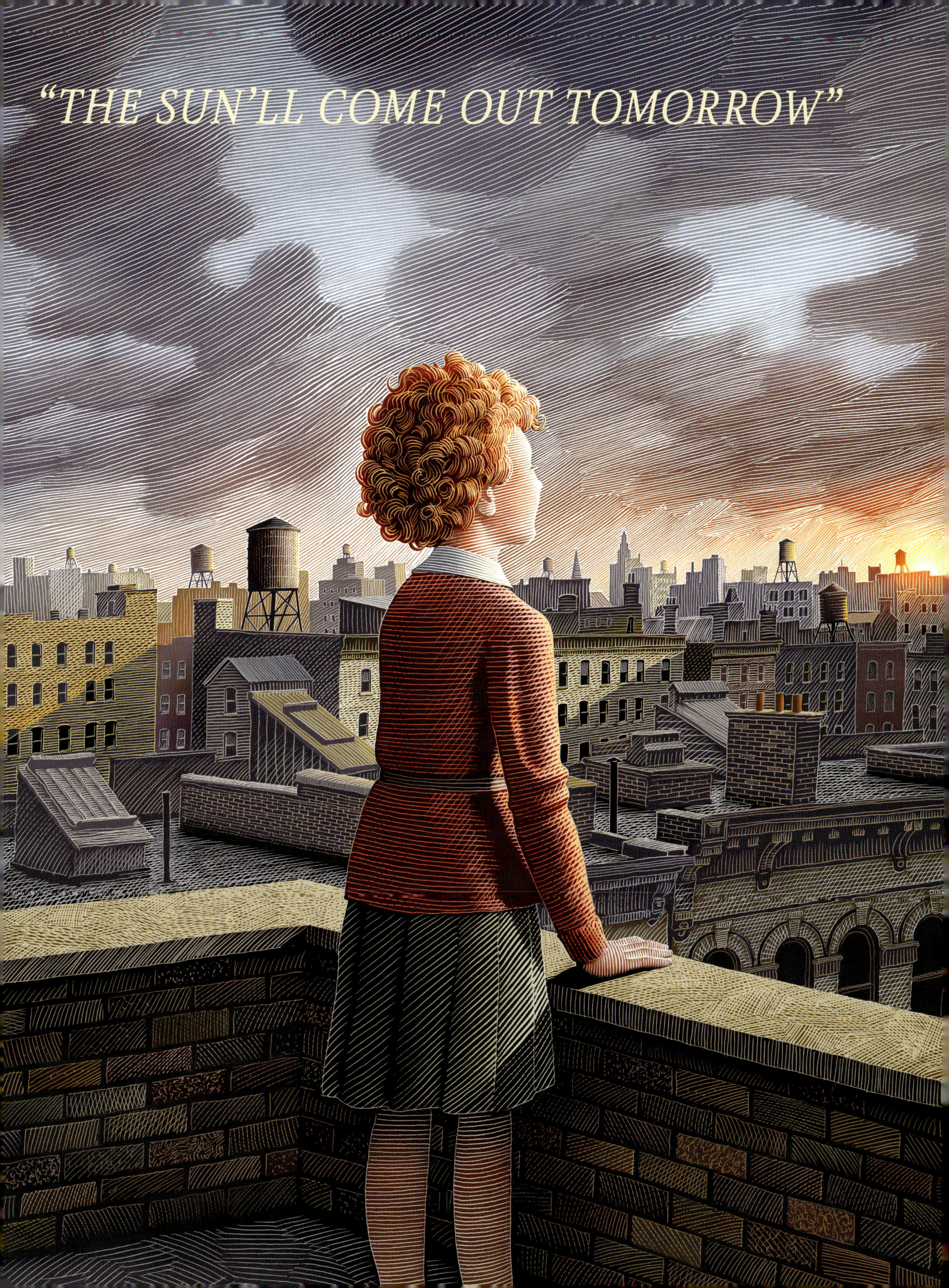
"THE SUN'LL COME OUT TOMORROW"

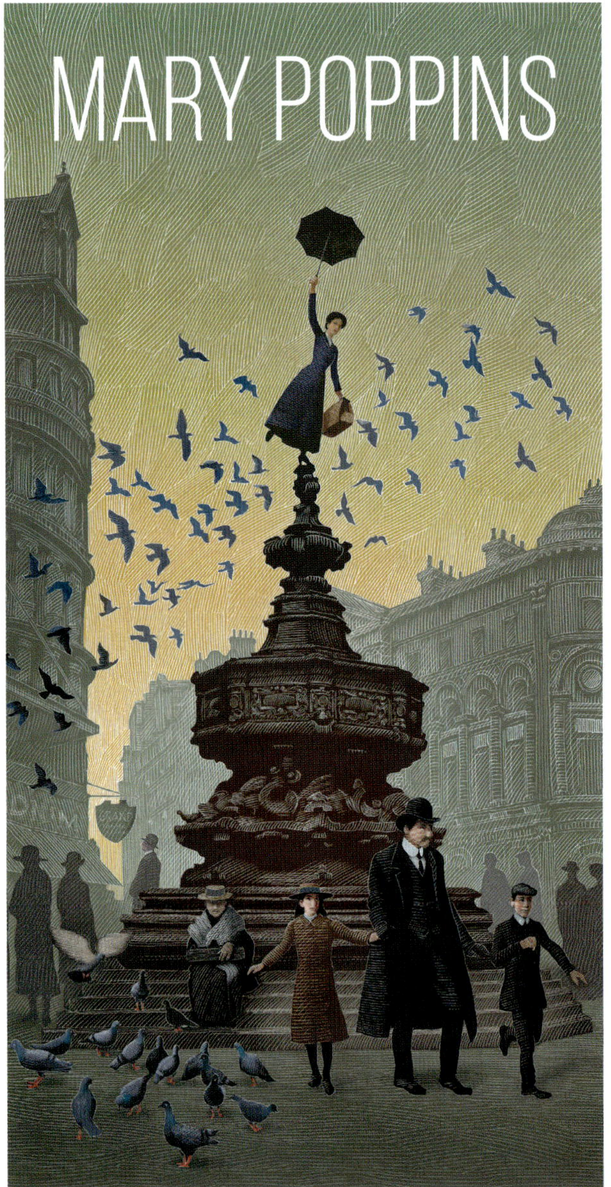

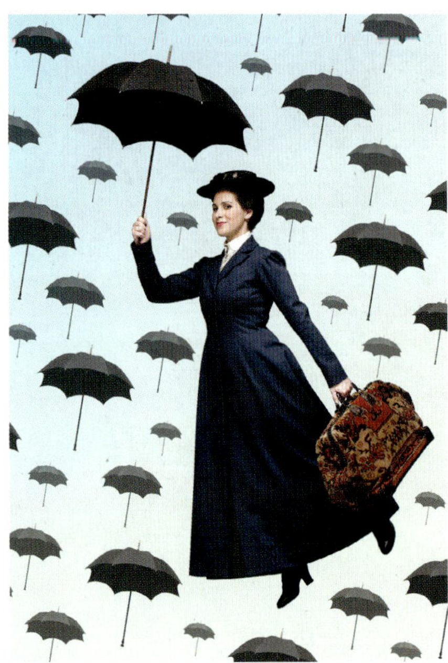

The most famous marine disaster of all time might sound like an unlikely subject for a Broadway musical, but *Titanic* won all five Tony Awards for which it was nominated in 1997, including Best Musical and Best Score. The *New Yorker*'s review observed, "It seemed a foregone conclusion that the show would be a failure; a musical about history's most tragic maiden voyage, in which 1500 people lost their lives, was obviously preposterous... Astonishingly, *Titanic* manages to be grave and entertaining, somber and joyful; little by little you realize that you are in the presence of a genuine addition to American musical theatre."

Titanic's composer Maury Yeston has explained that he was drawn to the project by the archetypal aspirations that the ship represented. The designers and builders were striving for great artistic and technological feats. Immigrant passengers in Third Class dreamed of a better life in America; middle-class passengers in Second Class aspired to live a leisured lifestyle in imitation of the wealthy and privileged passengers in First Class. The collision with the iceberg dashed all of these dreams simultaneously, and Yeston felt that the stories of both passengers and crew had the potential for great emotional and musical expression onstage.

The Grand Theatre in London, Ontario, announced a production of *Titanic* in 2020. I didn't want to use an image of the ship itself for the poster — everyone can picture photographs of the majestic vessel, or those lurid illustrations visualizing the ship's last terrifying moments (the accident occurred at 11:40 PM on April 14, 1912). I turned the grand ship into a grand piano sinking beneath the waves, with sheet music tumbling into the water representing the lifeboats.

The Cameron Mackintosh/Disney stage version of *Mary Poppins* first hit the stage in 2004, and it's still going strong — probably because it makes pots of money. I loved the 1964 film (or maybe I only loved Julie Andrews). I enjoyed Emma Thompson playing P.L. Travers in *Saving Mr. Banks*, and I thought Emily Blunt was wonderful in *Mary Poppins Returns*. I've never seen the stage musical, although I have designed posters for it twice. I worked with Christina and David Cooper on a photographic illustration for Theatre Calgary in 2014 — Julie Martell was our model. Then the show came up again as a scratchboard assignment for the Grand Theatre in 2019. I wanted an unexpected flash of Mary Poppins magic — something surprising but familiar in the centre of London. I wondered if she might replace Admiral Nelson atop his column in Trafalgar Square. That idea was too vertical for most of our applications, and she was too far above the street to connect with people — so I moved a few blocks over and substituted her for the famous statue of Eros in Piccadilly Circus.

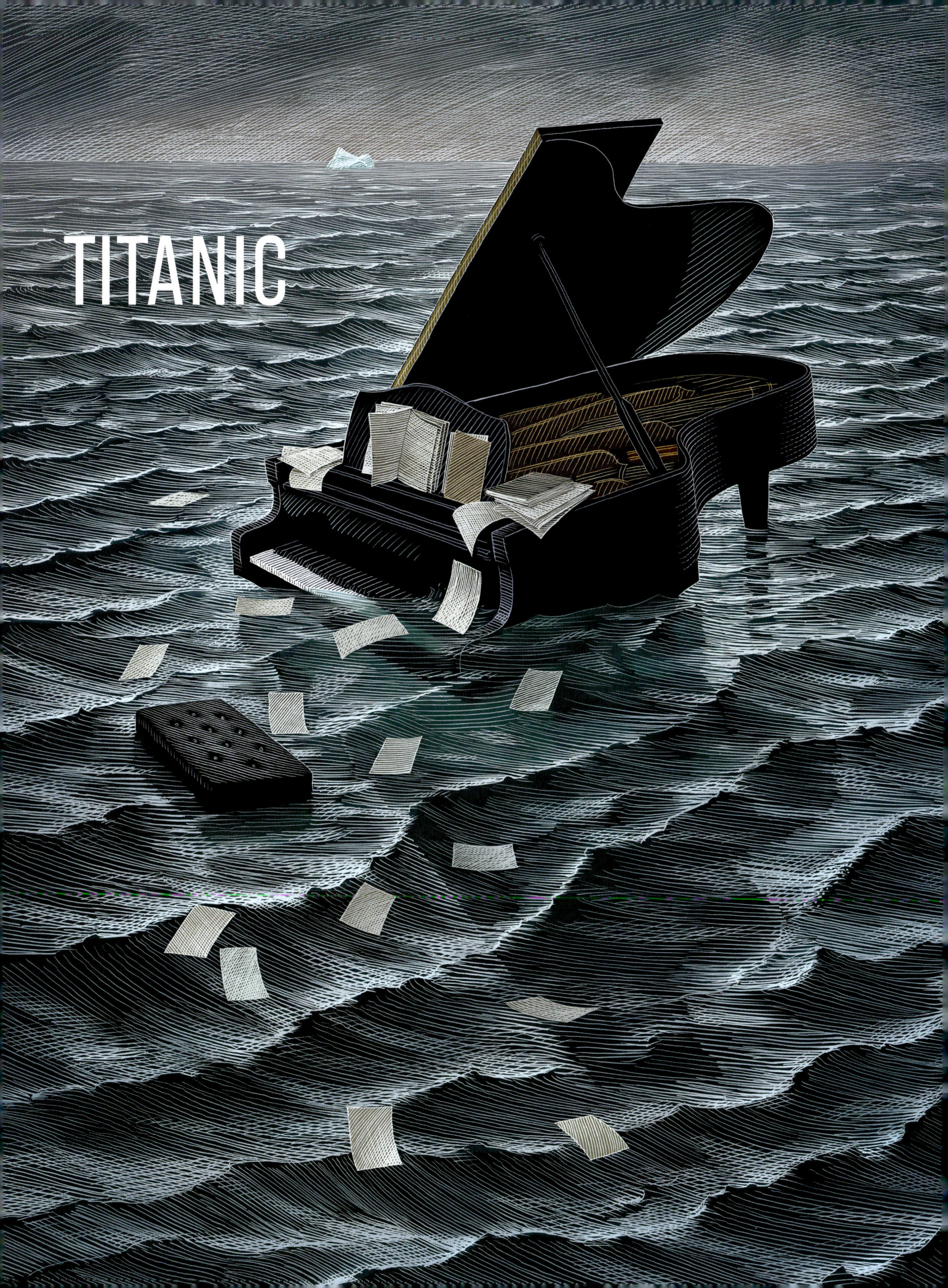
TITANIC

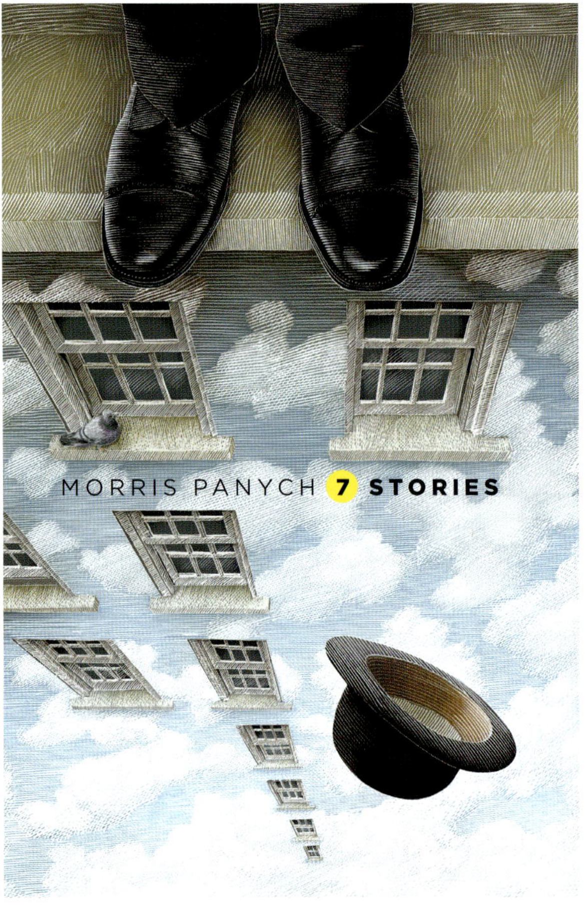

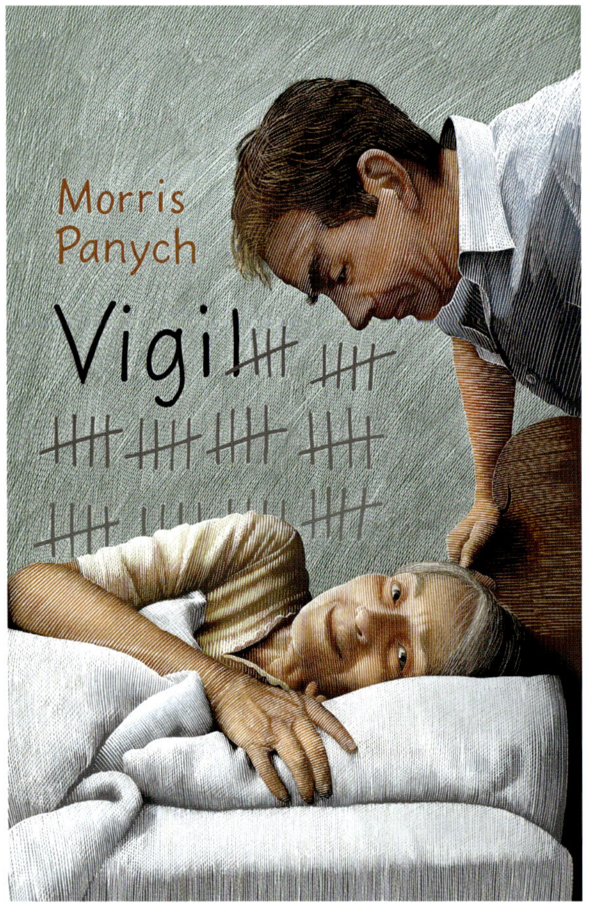

Playwright, actor and director Morris Panych is "a man for all seasons in Canadian Theatre." He has written 30 plays that have been produced around the world in a dozen languages. He has directed over 90 productions including most of his own works. I loved his Shaw Festival productions of *Nothing Sacred* (2004), *The Doctor's Dilemma* (2010) and *Arms and The Man* (2014, one of the best productions of the play I have seen). *The Overcoat*, co-created/directed with Wendy Gorling in 1998, was a brilliant non-verbal adaptation of a short story by Nikolai Gogol — a physical theatre piece with stunning choreography, set to the music of Shostakovich.

But it is Panych's dark, funny, absurdist plays that have established his lasting reputation. *7 Stories* is an absurdist comedy about a man contemplating suicide. In *The Shoplifters*, two women are apprehended for stealing by two security guards in a grocery store, and the reasons for and nature of theft come under hilarious philosophical scrutiny. These plays are all published by Talon Books in Vancouver, who commissioned a series of cover illustrations.

In *Sextet* (2014), two violinists, two violists and two cellists are stranded in a blizzard on the last night of a winter tour. They are forced to check into a motel — where there are only four available rooms. Tired of the Brahms and Schubert they have been performing, and quickly tiring of one another, the six sexually entangled musicians confront their harmonies and dysfunctions. Richard Ouzounian, reviewing for the *Toronto Star*, felt that this was perhaps the best script Panych had ever written. Damien Atkins played Harry, a cellist, in the original production at Tarragon Theatre in Toronto and Morris suggested him as the model for my illustration.

Vigil (1995) is perhaps Panych's most widely produced play across North America (and a West End production in 2002). A solitary bank employee named Kemp impatiently awaits the death of his Aunt Grace, a silent, bedridden old woman. Kemp has 98% of the lines — ruminations and recollections and one-line zingers on mortality: "I'm concerned about your health these past few days. It seems to be improving." Morris suggested his "ideal casting" for my illustration — actors Tom Rooney and Joyce Campion (who lived, at the time, in a retirement centre a block away from our studio in Stratford).

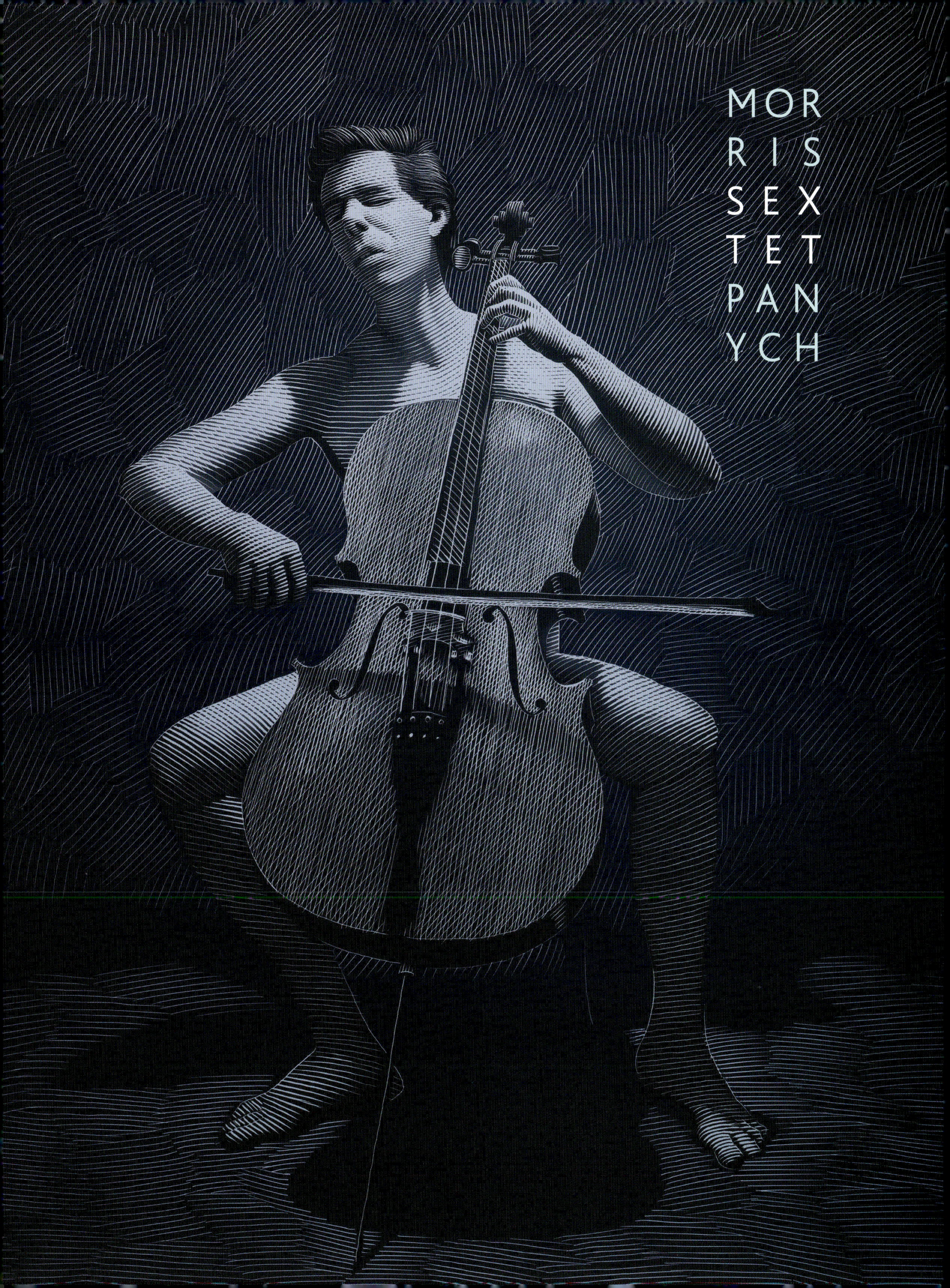
MOR
RIS
SEX
TET
PAN
YCH

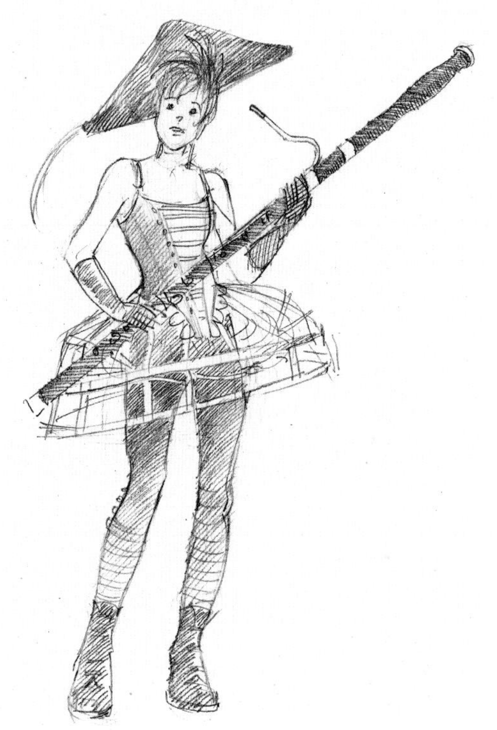

In 2012, the bassoonist Nadina Mackie Jackson embarked on an ambitious recording project: all 39 bassoon concerti by Antonio Vivaldi. Volume One was made with an elite ensemble including several musicians from the Tafelmusik Baroque Orchestra, led from the harpsichord by Nicholas McGegan.

Nadina is a brilliant and flamboyant performer — her bright blue hair is as distinctive as her musical virtuosity. She's a very busy performer and teacher. The licence plate on her pickup truck reads NADIVA. Keeping in mind the orphan girls at the Ospedale della Pietà in Venice for whom Vivaldi wrote this music, we created an 18th-century "avatar" for Nadina for this project. We imagined that, when all the other students are dutifully practising, Nadina would likely be cutting class, busking in the piazza.

For Volume One I turned Nadina into a gondolier, her bassoon reminiscent of the rowing oar. It seemed a fair metaphor — the skill and strength required to propel one of these beautiful vessels around the sharp turns of the Venetian canals might be compared to the expertise required of a bassoonist to navigate Vivaldi's scores. The rapid-fire runs sound effortless in Nadina's thrilling performance; the noble simplicity of the slow movements is haunting.

The projected series will eventually extend to five volumes to accommodate all 39 concerti — each cover will feature our Nadina avatar in a different location around Venice. With so many bridges, vestibules and spooky corners in the ancient labyrinth of the city, it will be hard to narrow down to a final list of locations. The next recording will be an excellent excuse for another trip there, to do location scouting in person!

Nadina commissioned Christina to design and build an actual garment based on the illustration, which she wears on stage when performing these wonderful concerti.

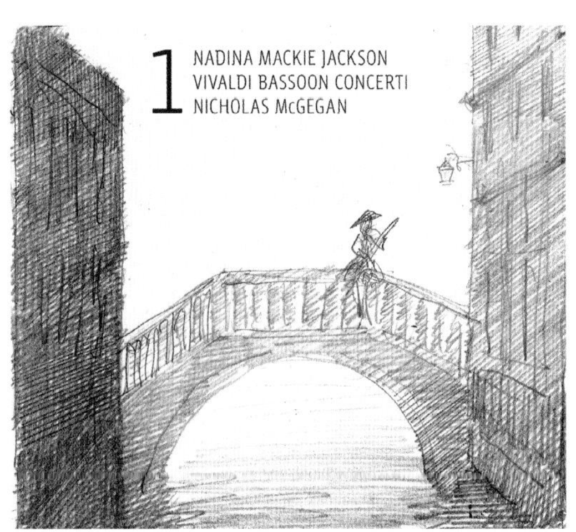

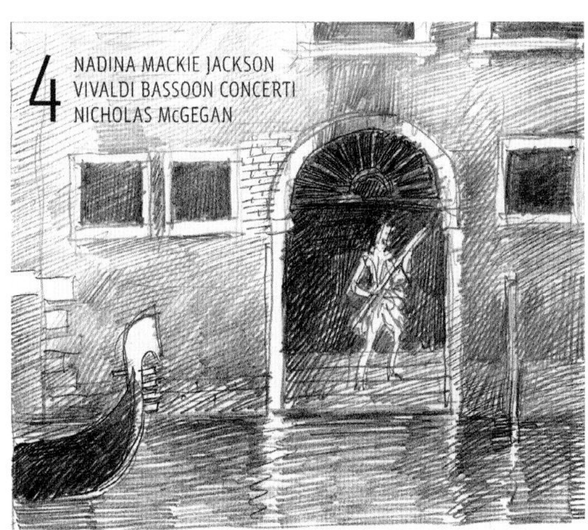

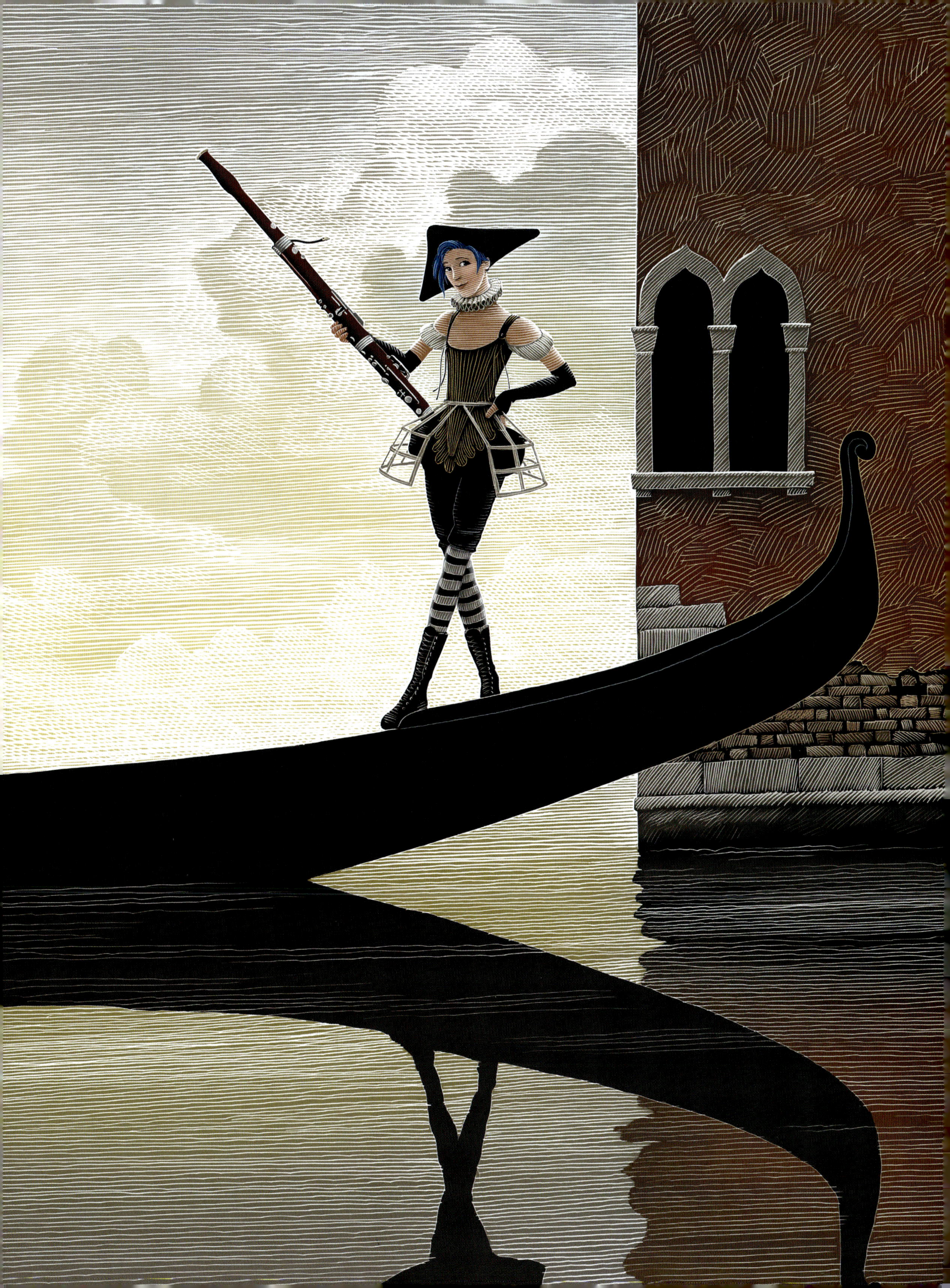

Stratford Summer Music asked for a poster to promote and commemorate their 15th anniversary season in 2015. We suggested the idea of a comet — an exceptional event, filled with wonder and magic, that appears or occurs only briefly, but periodically. Halley's Comet won't return to Earth until 2061, so we named this *Miller's Comet* after the Festival's Director John A. Miller. I made reference photos during daylight hours, but it was fairly easy to do a "day for night" change of contrast and depict a dawn sky over the Avon River evoking "the music of the spheres." The musical score visible in the comet's tail is from Berthold Carrière's *Music for a Midsummer's Night*, the Festival's signature opening night theme music (the clarinet line, if you're humming along).

In 2017, everyone was celebrating Canada's sesquicentennial, and graphic designers from coast to coast were faced with the challenge of coming up with imagery that would stand out from an overload of maple leaves, Mounties and beavers. Christina outdid herself on this one — the concept was inspired by Pierre Berton's famous aphorism about how you can identify a True Canadian: someone who knows how to have sex in a canoe. The swan immediately makes it a local Stratford scene. I tried to get the angle of his head to suggest a sense of curiosity — we can't quite see what's happening in the canoe, but he certainly can. The music on the floor of the canoe is a score by Canadian composer R. Murray Schafer, whose work was being performed during the season.

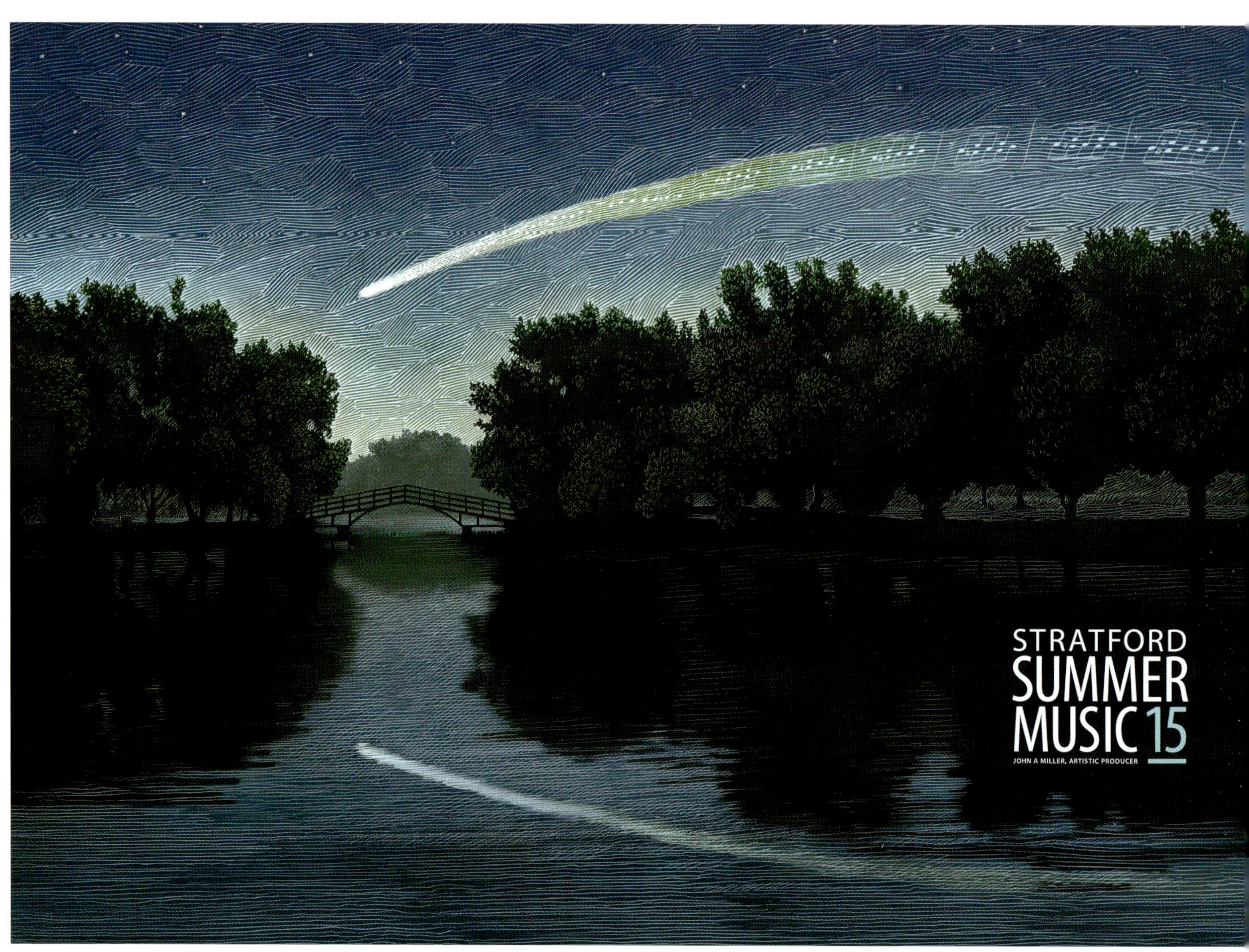

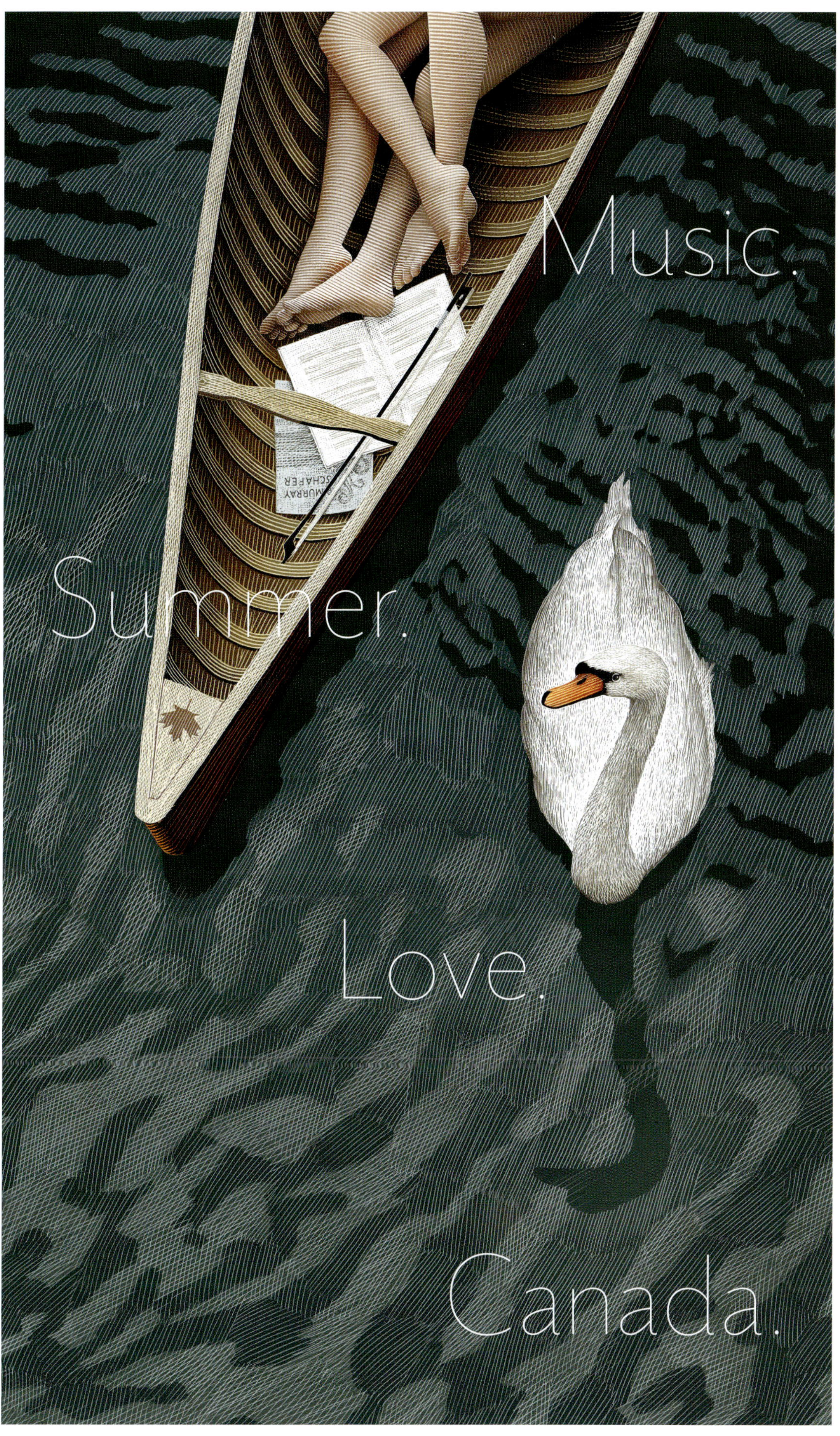
Music.
Summer.
Love.
Canada.

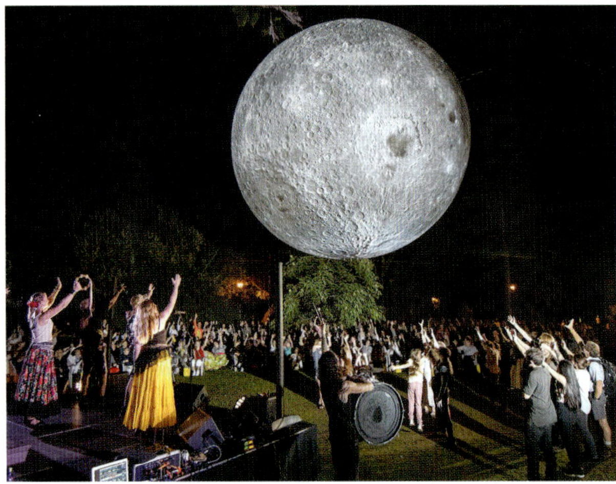

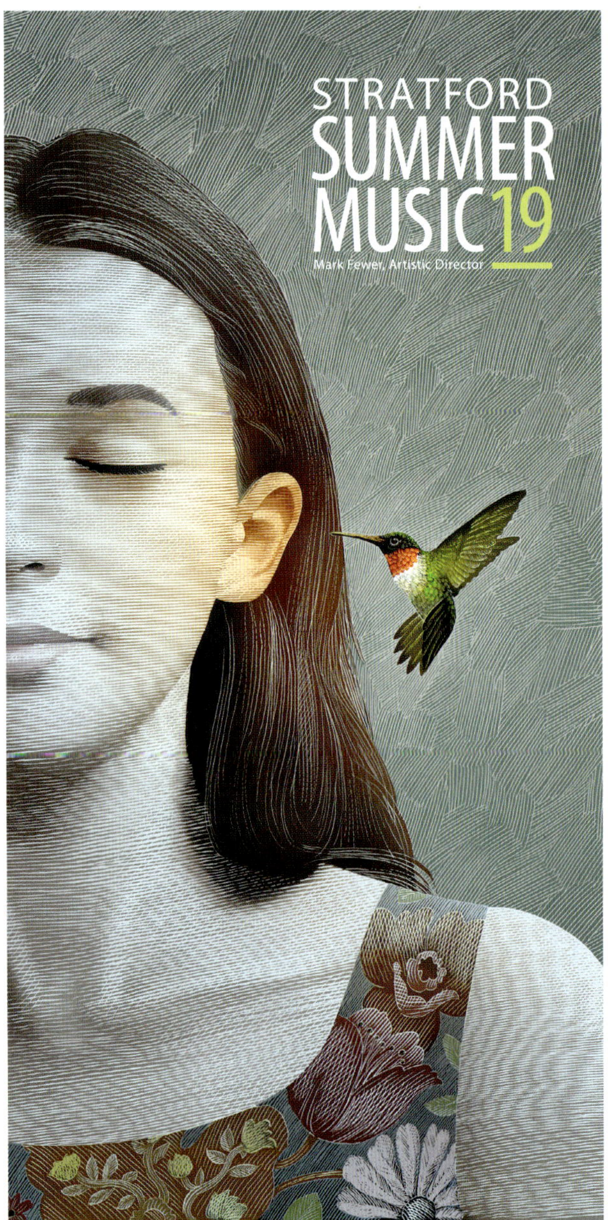

Top: 20,000 people visited Stratford Summer Music's presentation of the *Museum of the Moon* on Tom Patterson Island in Stratford, August 2018 (photo by Scott Wishart).

John Miller's prerequisite for the 2018 Stratford Summer Music poster was that the image should include a full moon. He had arranged for British futurist/inventor Luke Jerram to bring his *Museum of the Moon* to Stratford for 10 days in August. This sculpture installation reproduces the lunar surface, assembled from NASA photographs, on a 23-foot diameter inflatable sphere (a giant balloon), illuminated from within.

John had announced that he would retire from Stratford Summer Music at the end of 2018, after 18 seasons at the helm. So I suggested a portrait concept for the poster — Miller as Pan, the ancient Greek god of nature, always associated with music by his famous pipes — silhouetted against a huge full moon. The idea was that you would recognize John only from his distinctive black-framed glasses — I think he enjoyed being mythologized as part of his final season at the Festival.

Mark Fewer, a busy professional violinist, was named artistic director of Stratford Summer Music starting in 2019. Mark wanted the poster for his first season to focus on youth. He was fascinated by children (even babies) encountering the world of music for the first time — "sounds and sweet airs that give delight" to quote from *The Tempest*. Miranda's "O, brave new world" seemed a perfect description of Mark's artistic vision for his first season.

I had done some rough sketches a few years earlier of a girl, eyes closed, with a bird perched on her finger and singing into her ear. It felt like a half-baked idea and I had discarded it — but here was an opportunity to revisit. I got rid of her hand, which never felt right, and turned the bird into a ruby-throated hummingbird (the only one we get here in Ontario). Hummingbirds are the only avians that hover — and there is no bird with a more musical name! Seeing a hummingbird in my garden, or feeling one zoom past my ear, always lifts my spirits — a magical close encounter with nature. The challange was how to translate that magic into a visual representation of music. The solution was using colour to show what she's hearing. It's important to have the right face for a portrait illustration; I was casting about for a model when the marketing director in the Summer Music office suggested her 13-year-old niece. Evie O'Toole, appropriately enough a talented singer, dancer and actor, turned out to be perfect for the project. She has modeled for a couple of subsequent illustrations featured in this book.

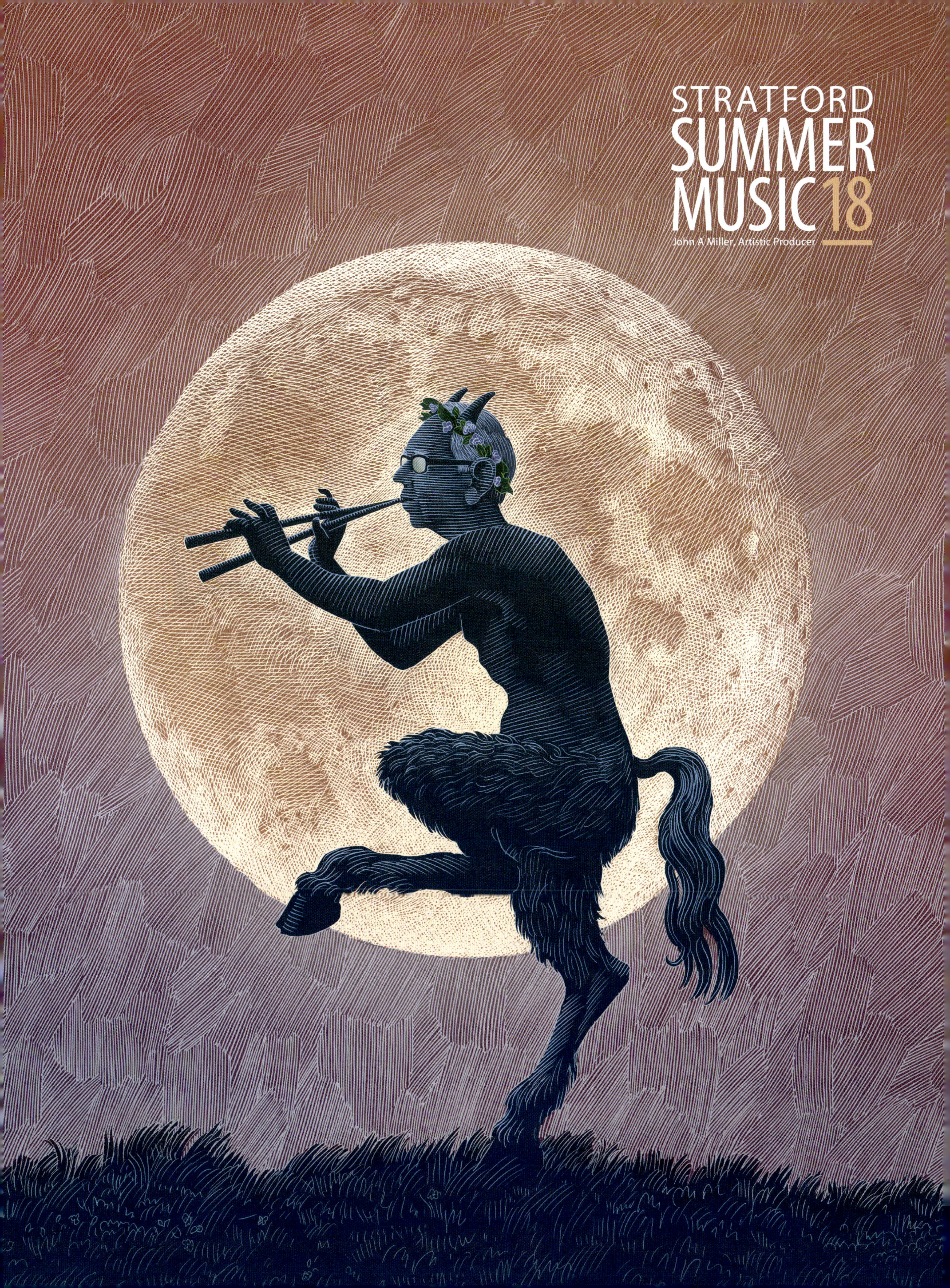
STRATFORD
SUMMER
MUSIC 18
John A Miller, Artistic Producer

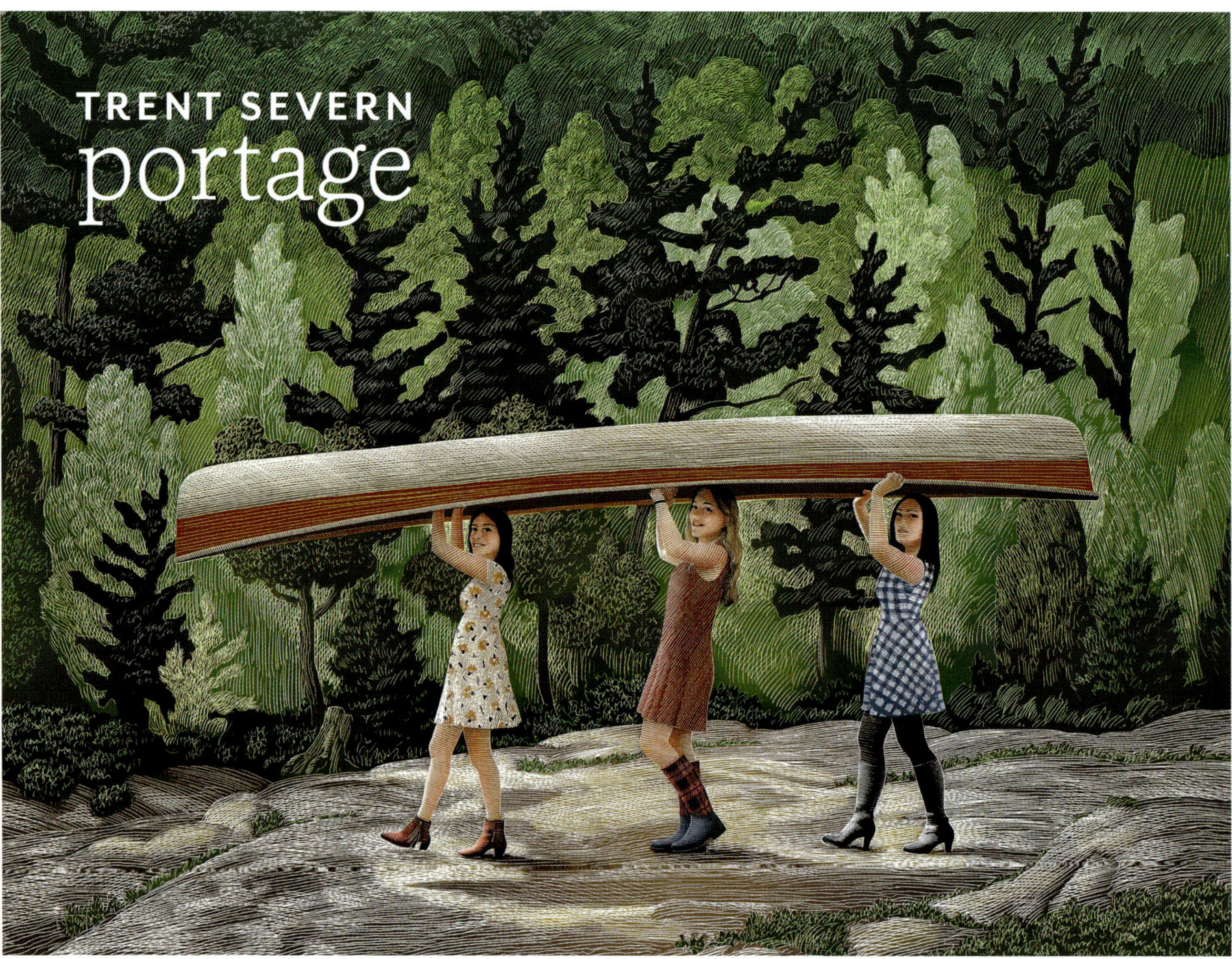

Music Niagara is a summer festival in Niagara-on-the-Lake, Ontario, founded by violinist Atis Bankas. When the initial focus on chamber music was expanded to include a wider range of music, I was asked to create a graphic identity for their new name. I designed a logo with staff lines reminiscent of a gentle "wave," reflecting the idyllic setting on the shore of Lake Ontario. It's always tempting to use the poster image to make reference to the many excellent wines produced in the Niagara region. Grape vines growing in the shape of a treble clef for the 2011 season poster is also a little *homage* to Milton Glaser's 1968 poster for a music festival at Temple University in Philadelphia.

Trent Severn is a Canadian folk trio based in Stratford. Dayna Manning (guitar/banjo), Emm Gryner (bass) and Lindsay Schindler (fiddle) write and sing contemporary songs about our nation's people and places with humour, humanity and heart. I was familiar with their songs through hearing them on CBC radio — then I met Dayna in person, and after establishing that we loved each other's work, she asked me to think about creating a poster for the group's upcoming tour.

After a little brainstorming, I did a quick sketch of the three bandmates portaging a canoe through a northern Canadian landscape — a "travel" image seemed appropriate for taking their show on the road. They loved the idea — so much that they quickly decided to call their upcoming third album *Portage* and use the poster illustration as the cover art.

We set up a reference photo session with a canoe. The landscape was invented from photos, my own sketchbook from a canoe trip years ago to Killarney and from Group of Seven paintings — I tried to capture the rugged shapes of those weathered pine trees in scratchboard. We worked closely with Emm and Dayna on the design of the CD package and booklet, which is illustrated with maps of the Canadian wilderness.

It was while we were working on *Portage* that Gallery Stratford invited me to exhibit the original engravings for Jane Urquhart's book of Canadian essays, *A Number of Things*. The show opened in March 2017 and Trent Severn played a couple of sets of songs from the new album at the opening.

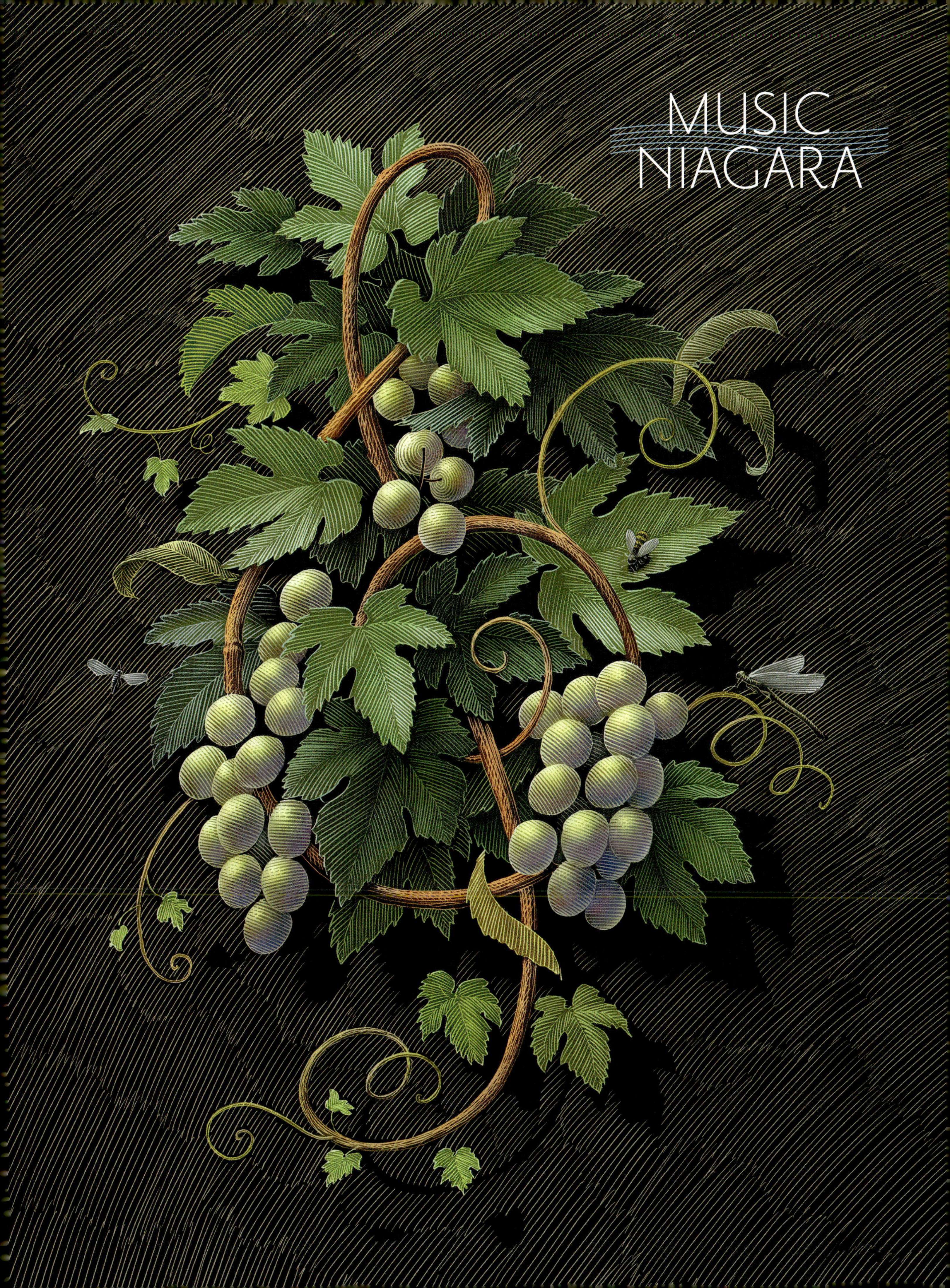
MUSIC
NIAGARA

Music Niagara's 2016 season poster stretched the region's fruit-growing metaphor to its limit. Music Niagara was first founded as a chamber music festival — so imagery based on string instruments always seems like a natural fit. Traditional botanical prints of the 18th and early 19th century connect with the history of Niagara-on-the-Lake and the region's bountiful fruit orchards. Botanical prints are always labelled with the Latin name of the plant so we called this the "Strad Pear" — a brand new species!

We adopted Sir John A. Macdonald, Father of Confederation and Canada's first Prime Minister, to help celebrate the sesquicentennial in 2017. He was evidently a dour old Scotsman, but here we've turned him into a music lover — sleeves rolled up and playing fiddle tunes in a Niagara backyard. He certainly visited the area — I found a record of a visit to St. Catharines, so the local history connection is completely genuine. I hoped this would give people a smile, and I like to think that it side-stepped the usual "Canadiana" clichés.

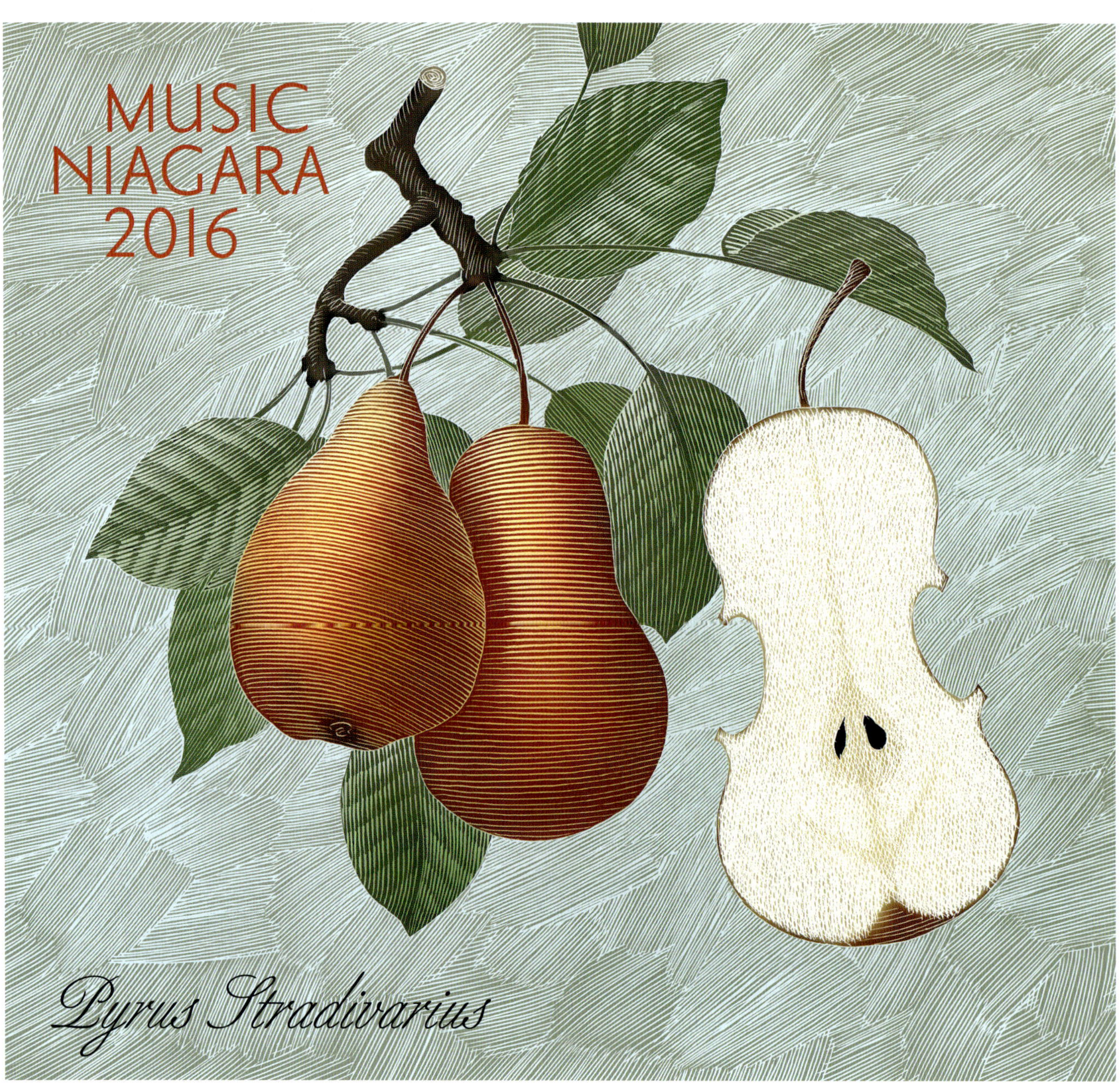

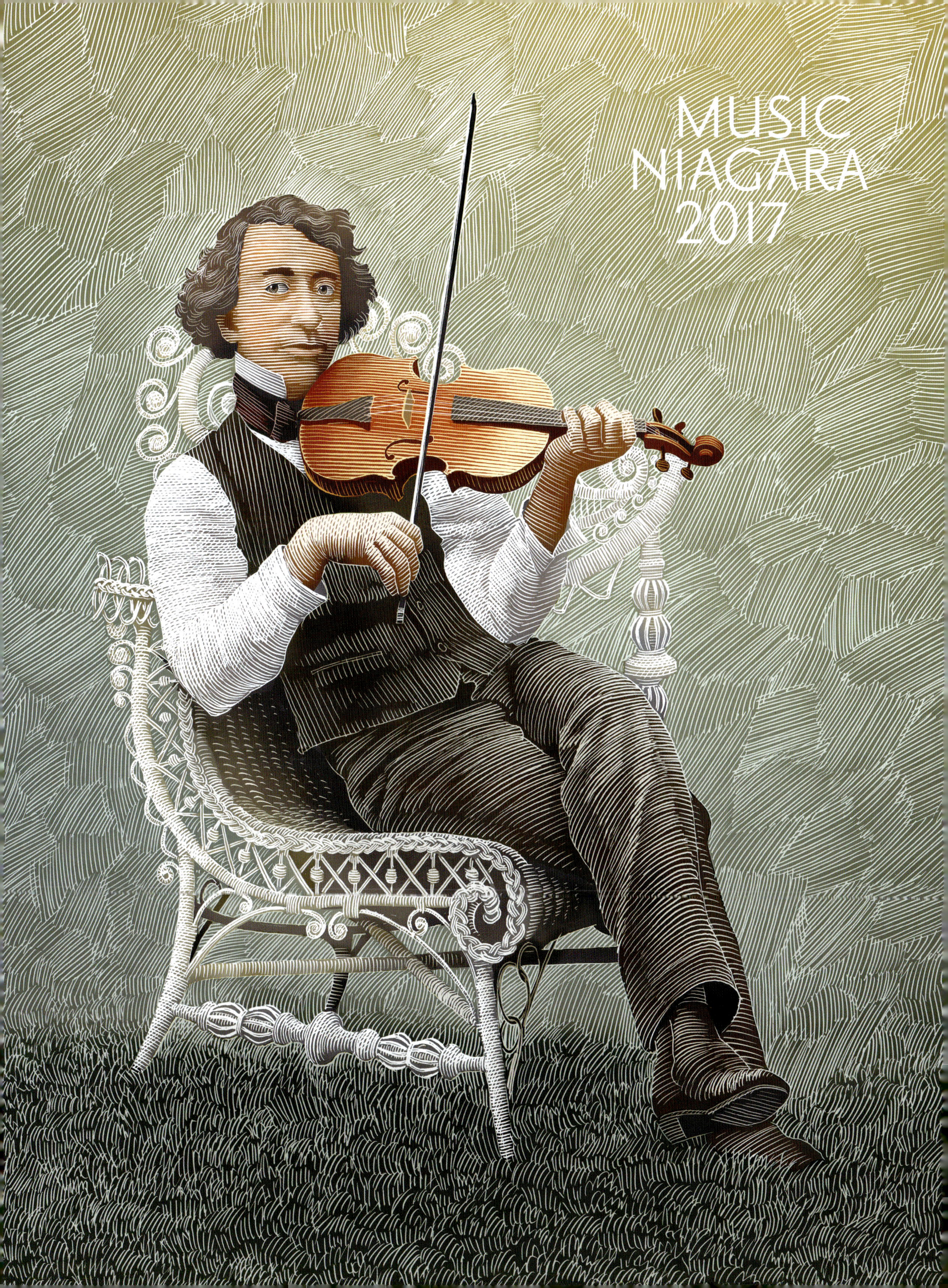
MUSIC
NIAGARA
2017

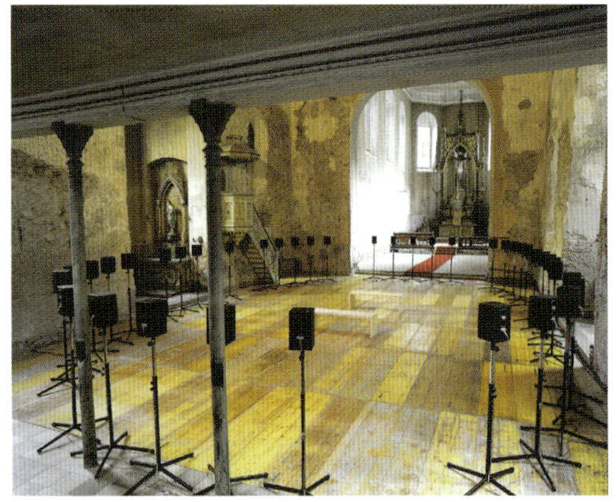

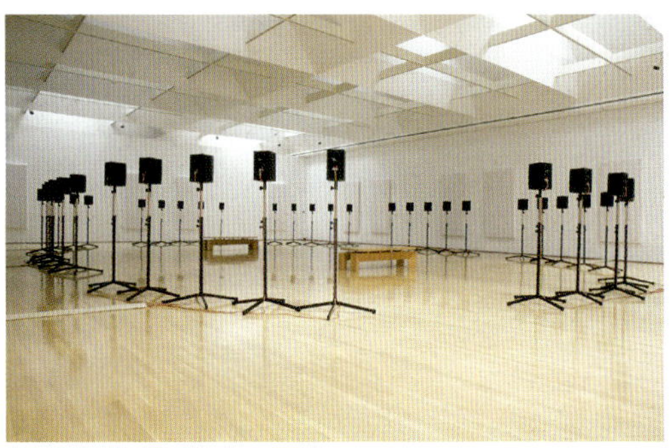

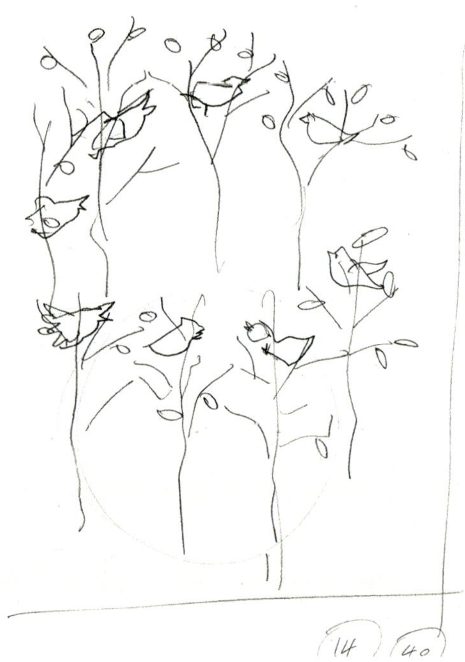

Janet Cardiff's audio installation *Forty Part Motet* has been exhibited around the world in spaces ranging from ancient churches to modern art museums; Christina's first rough concept sketch for Scott's poster illustration.

Forty Part Motet, Janet Cardiff's magical sound sculpture from 2001, is based on the Thomas Tallis motet *Spem in Alium*, composed around 1570. Cardiff recorded a British choir singing this famous work using one microphone per singer. The work consists of 40 speakers, arranged at "ear level" in a large circle, and a computer that plays back the music on a 14-minute loop. A listener can stand in the middle of this circle and hear a beautifully balanced "virtual choir" — or move close to individual speakers to hear the line of each single voice. I had encountered the work at the National Gallery of Canada, and again at the Museum of Modern Art in New York and loved the juxtaposition of ancient music and cutting-edge technology.

Stratford Summer Music presented *Forty Part Motet* as the centrepiece of its 2008 season. I was asked to create a poster illustration and began thinking about a visual representation of Cardiff's deconstruction of Tallis.

Christina came up with a simple concept that maps the structure of Cardiff's installation: a circle of trees and in each tree, a singing bird.

I started looking at imagery contemporary with the music. The richly decorated scenes in Renaissance tapestries are woven from single threads of various colours. This seemed a great metaphor for Tallis' intricate polyphony made up of individual vocal lines.

The famous Unicorn Tapestries at the Metropolitan Museum of Art in New York came to mind because of their natural woodland settings with birds and animals. The unforgettable Unicorn Tapestries at the Musée de Cluny in Paris depict allegories themed around the five senses — taste, sight, touch, smell and hearing.

The tapestries and the Tallis motet have a powerful sense of mystery in common. I tried to evoke this in the illustration by borrowing the flattened, vertical perspective of Renaissance forms — balanced by a contemporary aesthetic in the drawing.

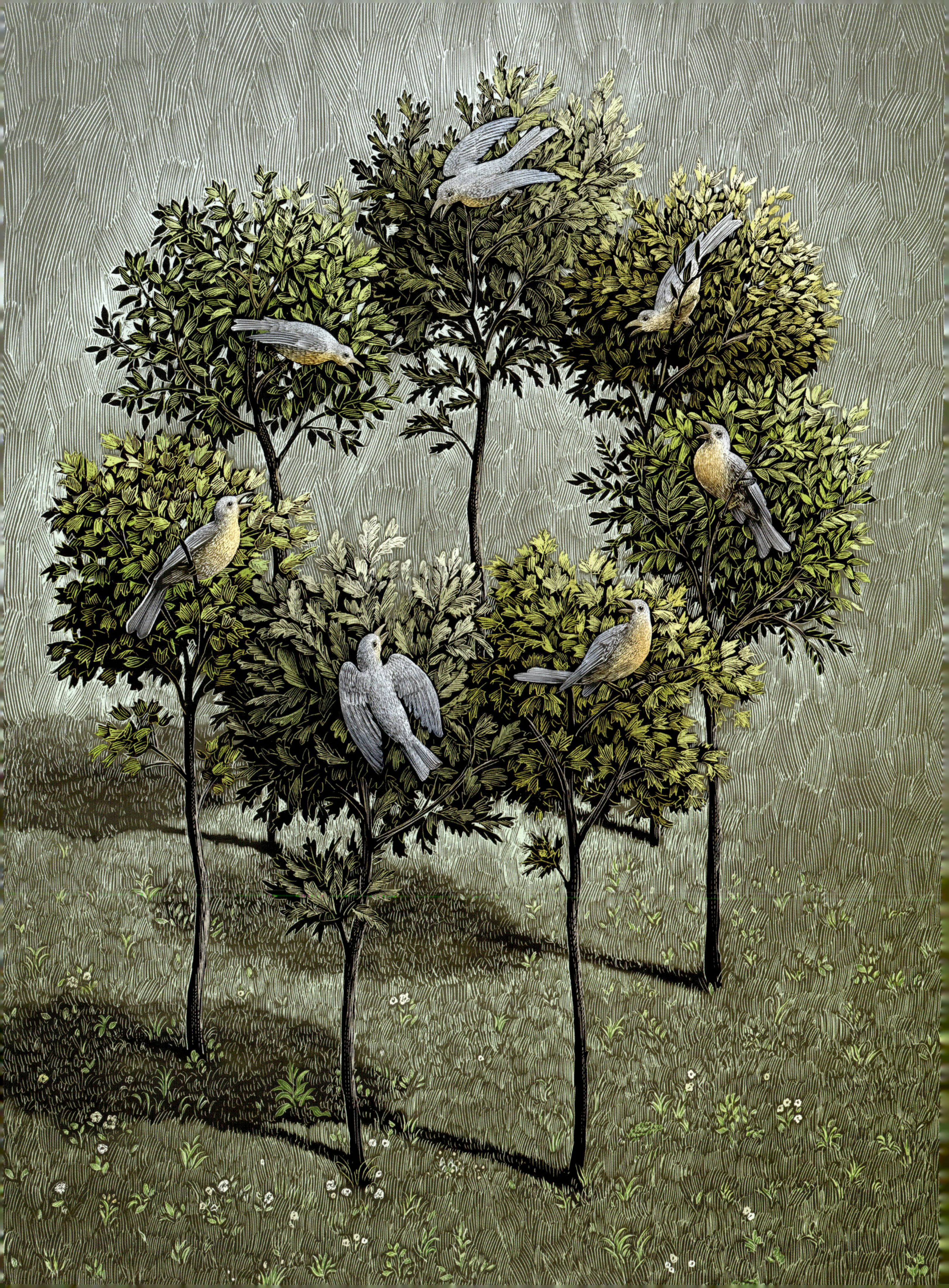

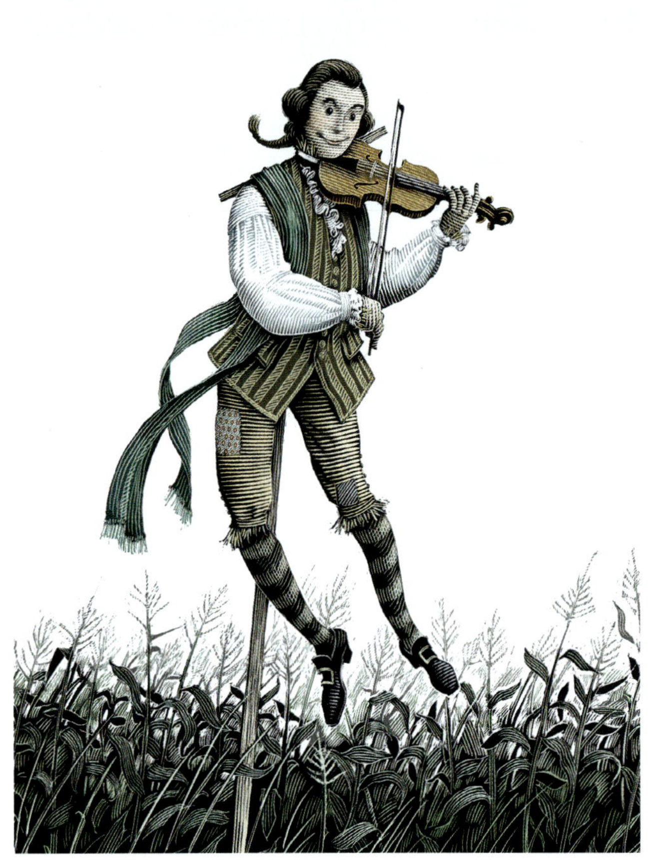

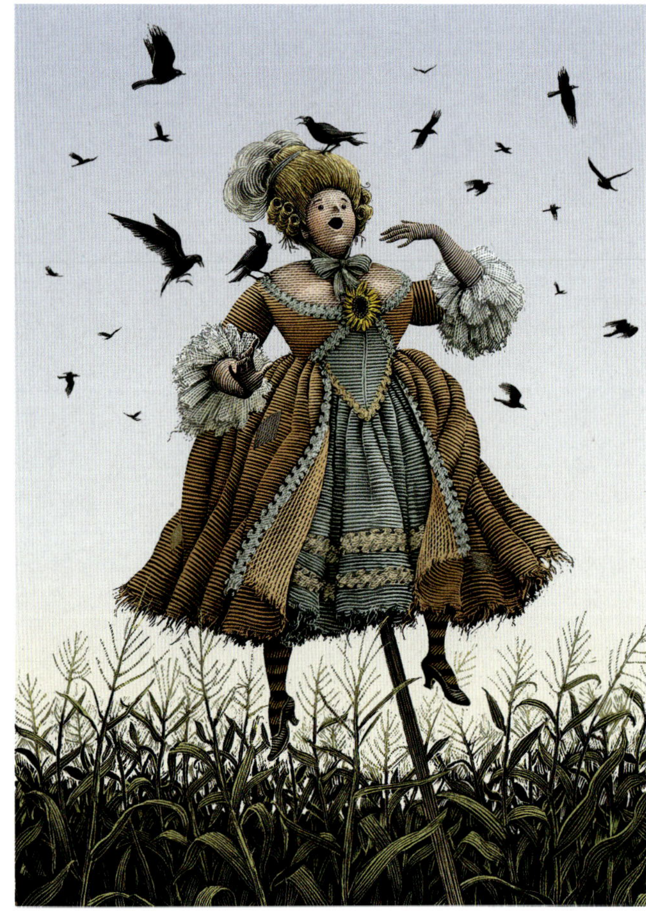

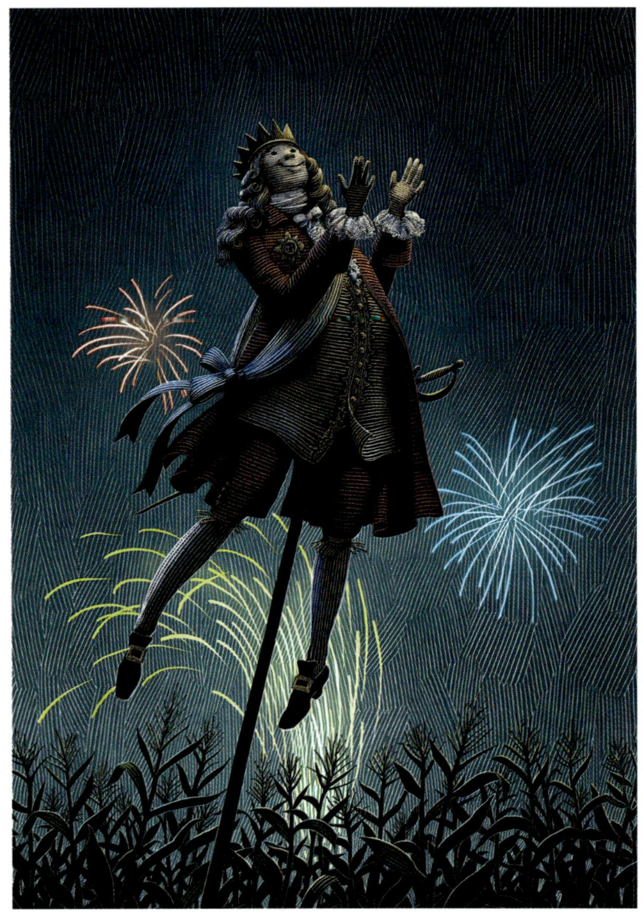

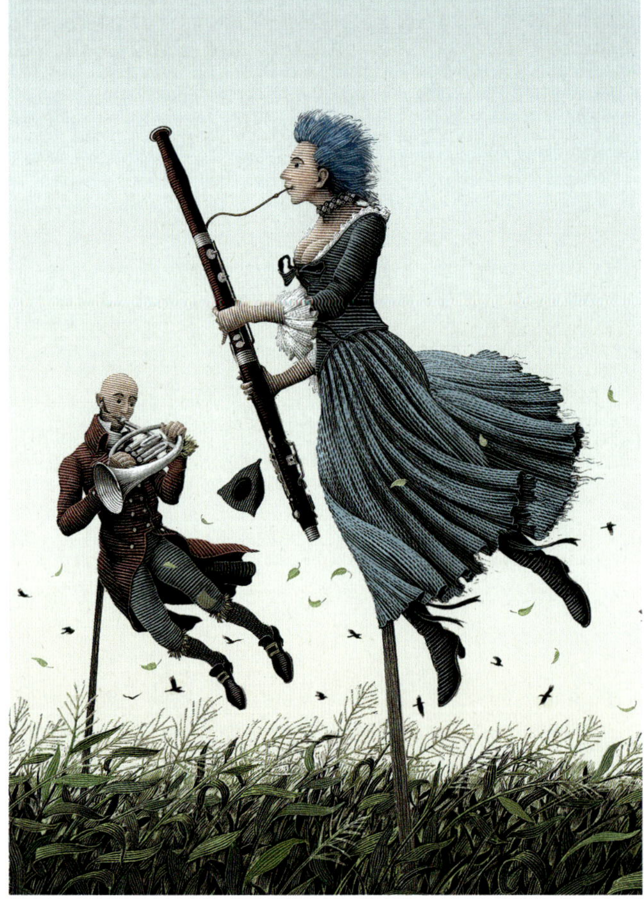

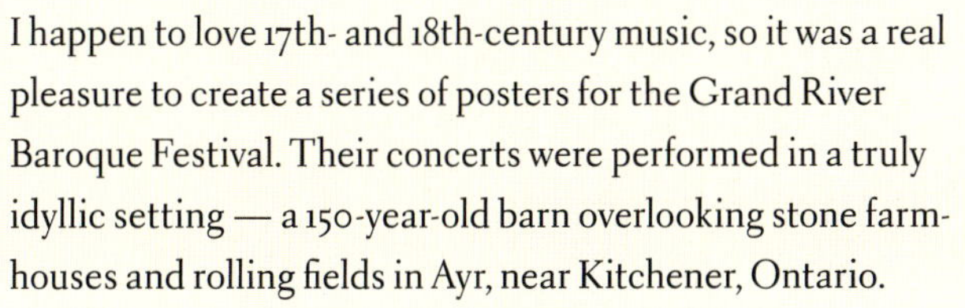

I happen to love 17th- and 18th-century music, so it was a real pleasure to create a series of posters for the Grand River Baroque Festival. Their concerts were performed in a truly idyllic setting — a 150-year-old barn overlooking stone farmhouses and rolling fields in Ayr, near Kitchener, Ontario.

For the initial assignment in 2006, I was looking for a concept that would connect with the rural agricultural traditions of the region. Christina suggested the idea of a scarecrow, dressed in tattered 18th-century clothing, playing a violin for an audience of birds perched on the letters of wordmark.

In 2007, I drew a female scarecrow playing a baroque flute and for 2008, an operatic soprano. Nadina Mackie Jackson and Guy Few took over as artistic directors in 2009 so we featured scarecrow portraits of them. The opening performance for 2010 was Handel's *Music for the Royal Fireworks* — so the scarecrow was King George II for whom it was written.

Milton Glaser's ongoing series of posters for the Cooperstown Chamber Music Festival (in the town famous for baseball) was very much an inspiration for my scarecrows. His delightful musical cows — playing string quartets in white tie and tails — provide a great example of how classical music can be marketed with a sense of freshness and wit.

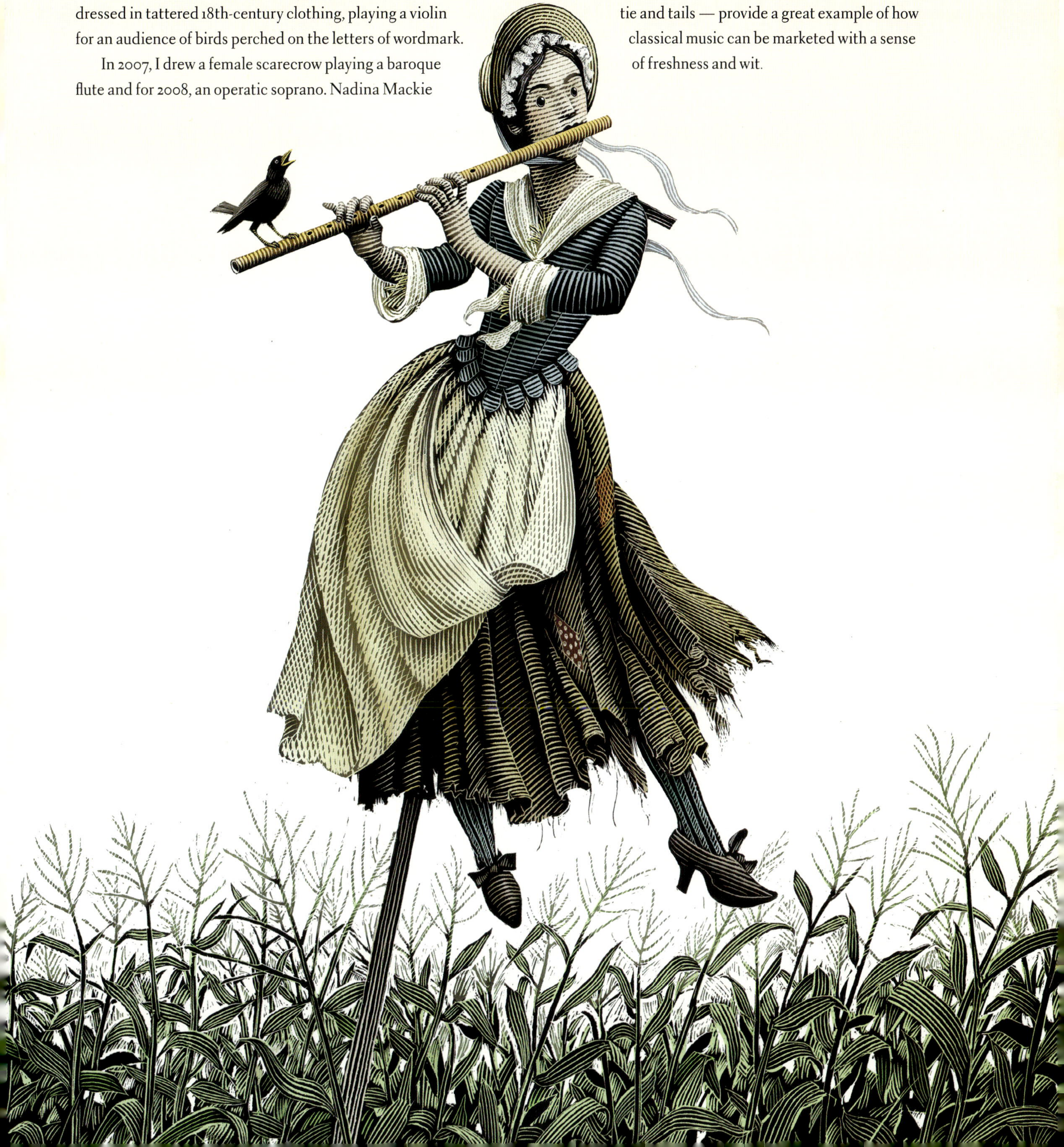

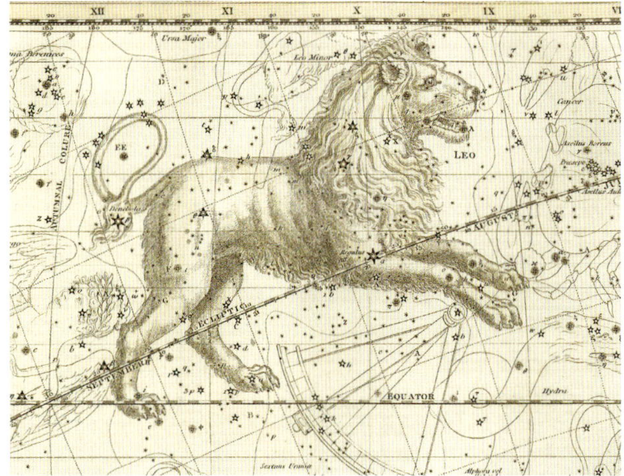

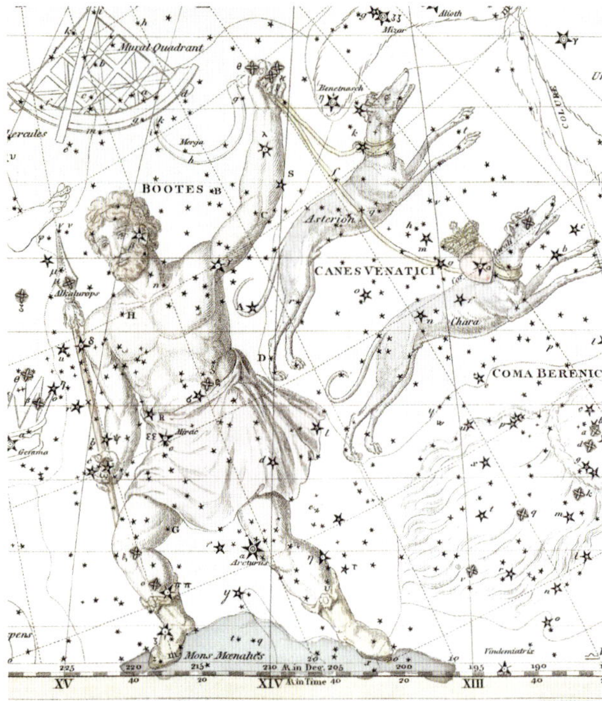

Source material for this project included a range of 17th-century maps of the heavens — shown here are Leo and Bootes.

It's great to get occasional illustration assignments outside of our usual performing arts "orbit." I was asked to create a poster to commemorate the 75th anniversary of the venerable McDonald Observatory, which is operated by the University of Texas at Austin. When the observatory opened in 1939 in the Davis Mountains of West Texas, it boasted the second-largest telescope in the world. Technology has moved on, of course, but the facility still does important work in optical and infrared spectroscopy, extragalactic and theoretical astronomy.

The observatory is popular for its star parties under some of the clearest and darkest night skies in North America, and the poster was intended to boost public awareness and graphic identity. "The stars at night are big and bright, deep in the heart of Texas," goes the old song.

I quickly realized that a concept relating to stellar spectroscopy, meaningful for the scientists who work there, would be over the heads of the general public (not to mention that of the illustrator). On the other hand, an image generic enough to be appreciated by non-scientists might be too simplistic for the astrophysicists. As I worried about this, it occurred to me that the dome of a classic Texas cowboy hat is the same shape as the observatory dome.

I had a great assignment back in 1994 from *The New York Times* — illustrating five stylish cowboy hats for a fashion article in the Sunday Magazine (under the cheeky headline THE BUCKAROO STOPS HERE). They arranged to send me the actual hats to work from — five huge boxes arrived by overnight courier from the Man's Hat Shop in Albuquerque. They were spectacular, and I suspect very expensive; we all took turns wearing them around the house. Unfortunately, we had to return them when the drawings were finished.

But those hats gave me the idea that this poster could make a nice visual pun. Hoping the McDonald astronomers would go for a little surrealism and have a sense of humour, I sent off pencil concept sketches — and they loved the idea.

I loved astronomy as a kid; I learned the constellations from the rather pathetic stick-figure star charts in my Boy Scout Handbook. But if you lived in the 17th century and you were lucky enough to have access to the richly illustrated maps of the heavens published by astronomers of the day, you might easily imagine heroes and monsters from classical mythology coming vividly to life in the sky. Two or three centuries is insignificant in the astronomical perspective of time, but these historical engravings remind us that looking up in wonder at the night sky is a universal human experience.

The poster appeared on shirts and mugs and was even recreated in three dimensions as a parade float.

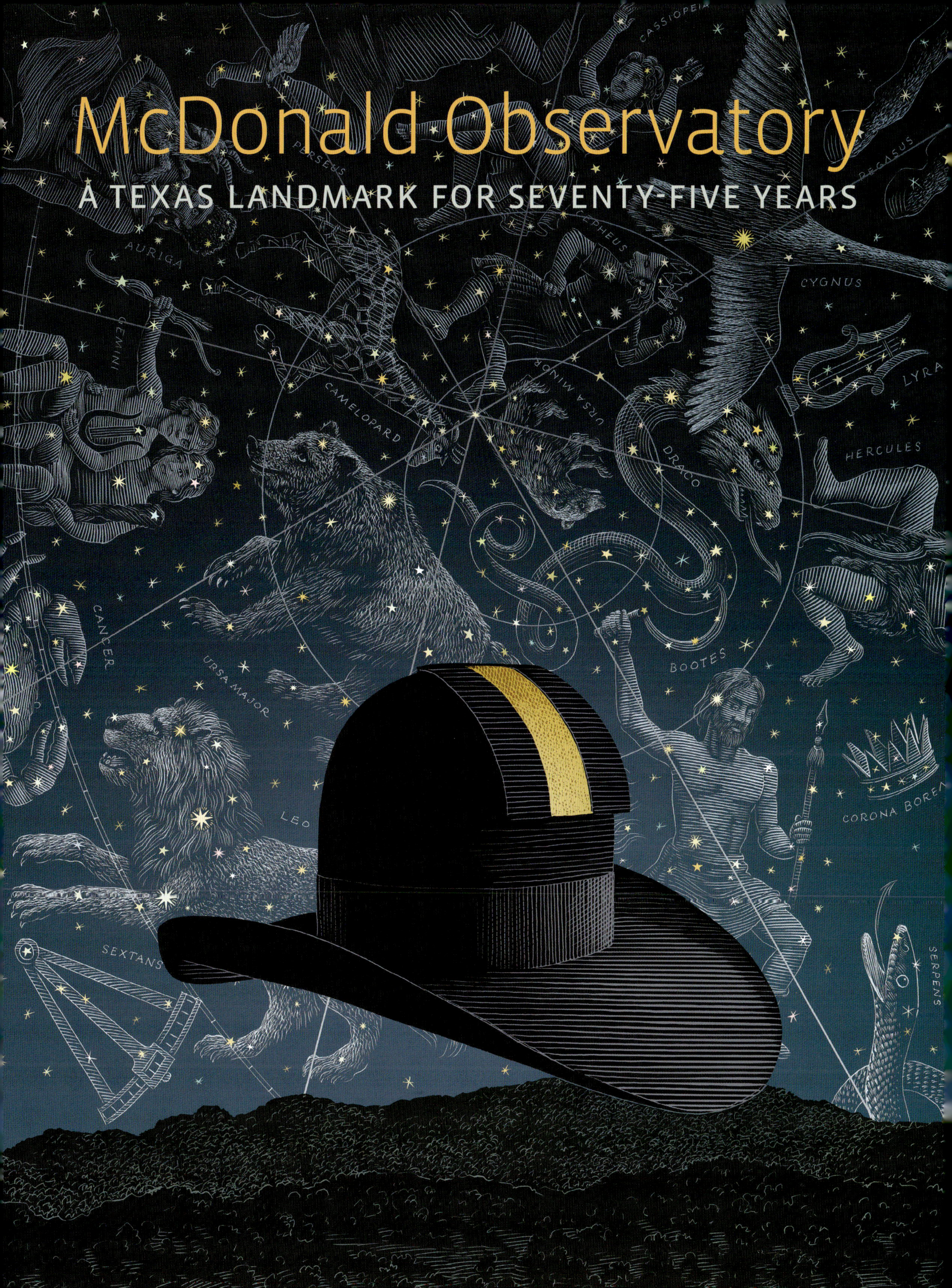
McDonald Observatory
A TEXAS LANDMARK FOR SEVENTY-FIVE YEARS
CASSIOPEIA
PERSEUS
PEGASUS
CEPHEUS
AURIGA
CYGNUS
GEMINI
CAMELOPARD
URSA MINOR
LYRA
DRACO
HERCULES
CANCER
BOOTES
URSA MAJOR
LEO
CORONA BOREA
SEXTANS
SERPENS

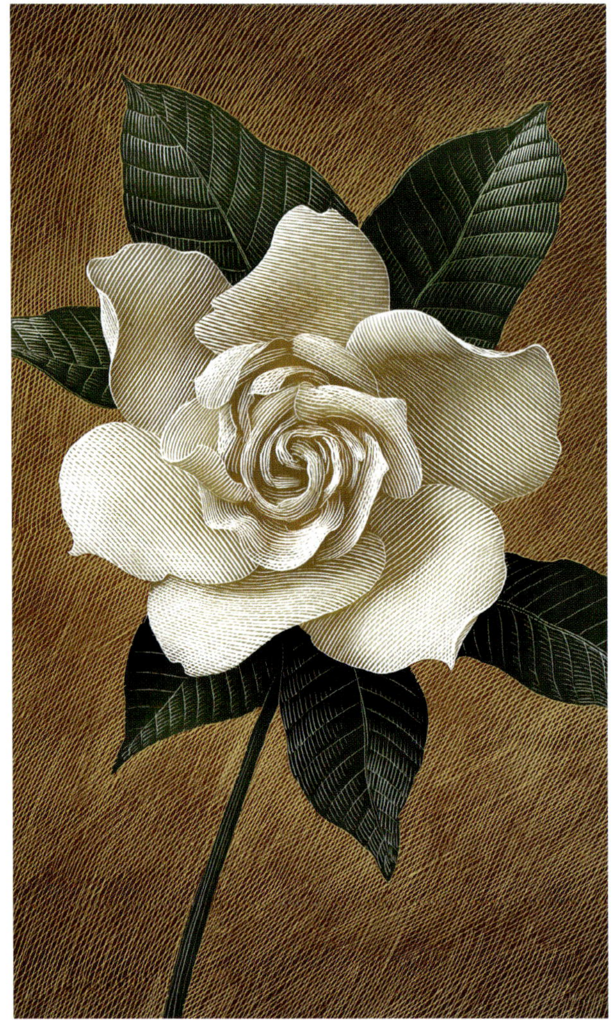

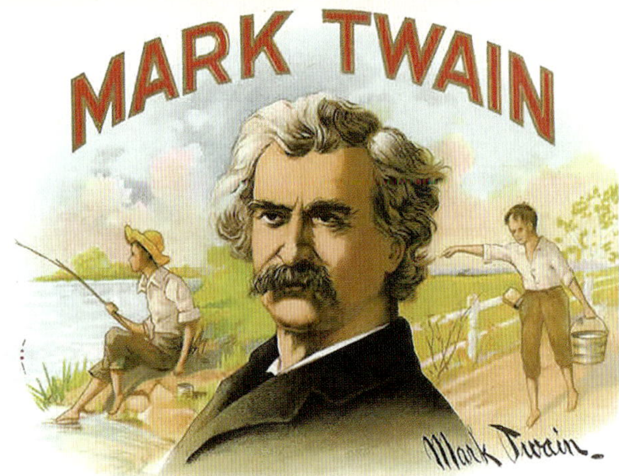

Anne Twomey, art director at Hachette Book Group, asked me to create cover illustrations for *Twain & Stanley Enter Paradise*, the final novel by the Cuban-American author Oscar Hijuelos. His novel *The Mambo Kings Play Songs of Love* won the Pulitzer Prize for Fiction in 1990. Hijuelos had just finished the manuscript for *Twain & Stanley* before he died from a heart attack in 2013, and the book was published posthumously.

Twain & Stanley Enter Paradise is based on the real lifelong friendship between two of the most famous men of the 19th century. Samuel Clemens was working as a steamboat pilot on the Mississippi River years before he began publishing stories under the pen name Mark Twain. Henry Morton Stanley immigrated from Wales to New Orleans as a teenager; he would fight in the Civil War, and later become famous exploring Central Africa. The young men shared a passion for books and an ambition to become authors. The third main character is Stanley's wife Dorothy Tennant, a Victorian painter who was a friend of Twain.

Hijuelos embellishes the historical record with fictional episodes, letters and stories. A central section of the novel follows Twain and Stanley on a trip to Cuba — the paradise of the title. I read the manuscript and found it completely engrossing. I get a lot of "historical pastiche" assignments — authors trying to write in the style of an earlier century — but they rarely get it right. Modern idioms always stick out like a sore thumb. So I was impressed that Hijuelos pulls this off so convincingly — it felt like reading Dickens.

We considered a number of different directions for the cover art. I sketched portraits of Twain and Stanley in the style of Cuban cigar box art. Then we received an email from Hijuelos' widow, Professor Lori Marie Carlson, who had been involved with the project from the start. She had a flash of inspiration that the cover should be a steamboat, simple and powerful against an apricot-coloured sunset. She felt strongly that it was "almost as if Oscar was telling me this." She also suggested that the back cover illustration should be a painter's palette (representing Dorothy Tennant); that evolved into a gigantic, voluptuous gardenia blossom.

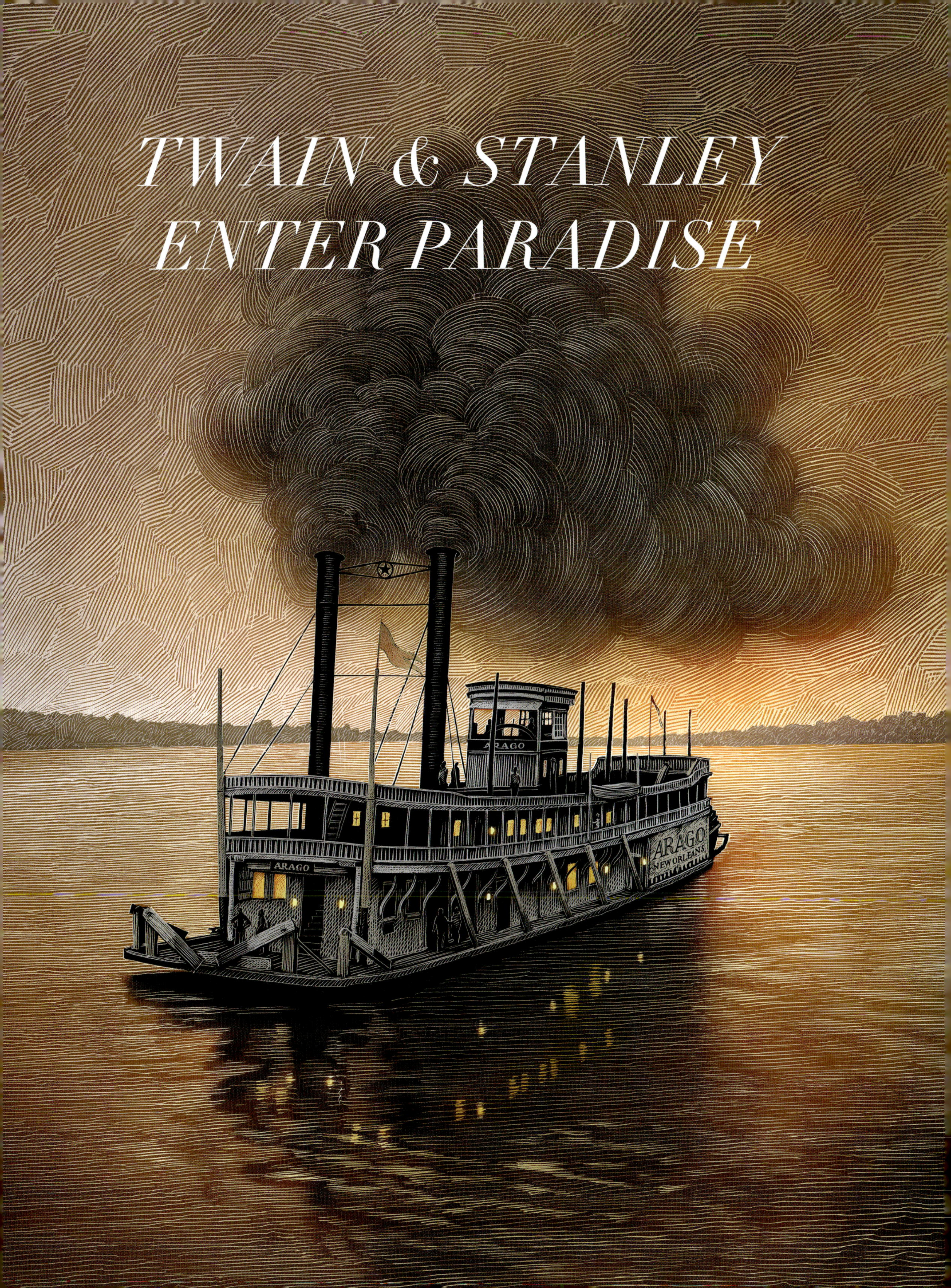
TWAIN & STANLEY
ENTER PARADISE
ARAGO
ARAGO
ARAGO
NEW ORLEANS

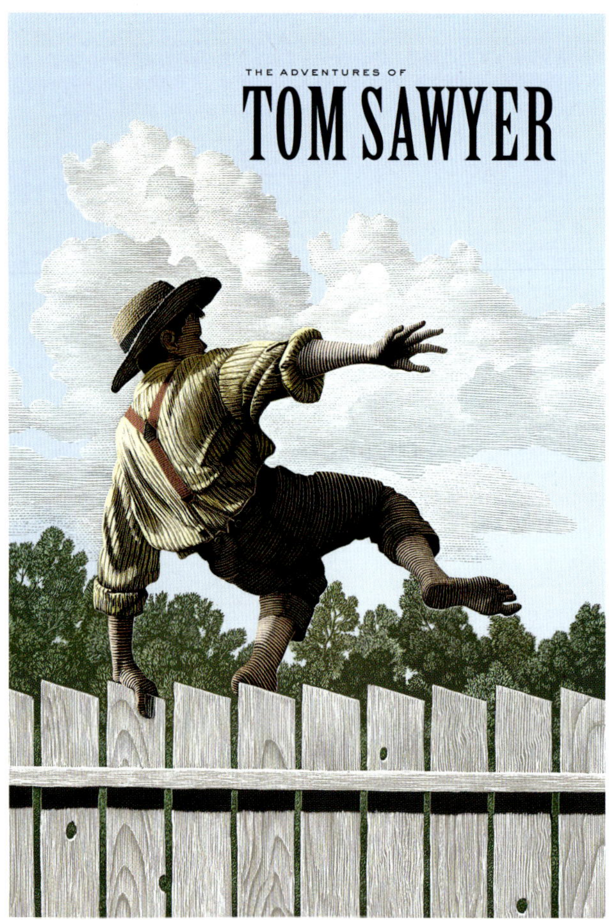

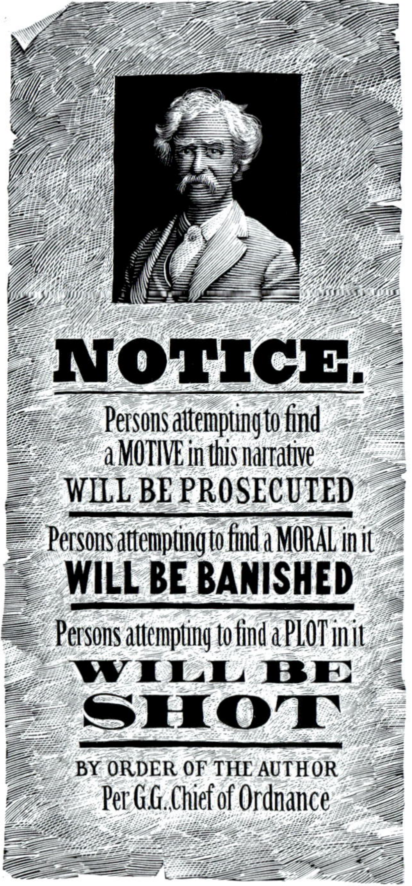

I received a fortuitous phone call in 2003 from Karen Nelson, an art director at Sterling Publishing in New York, asking if I might be interested in working on a series of children's classics they were about to publish. I could never have imagined, at the time, that I would end up illustrating 36 titles over a 15-year period — it was a very happy collaboration.

On the list that first year was Mark Twain's *Tom Sawyer*, published in 1876. Every chapter in the book takes us off on some new exploit with Tom and his cohorts along the Mississippi River. The idea of vaulting a fence had a nice energy — it seems just what Tom would do (well-brought-up boys would walk around to the gate). I liked the idea of making reference to the most famous scene in the book (whitewashing the fence) without actually showing it. More importantly for a cover, it invites young readers to follow Tom off on his next adventure. My model was an 11-year-old in our Stratford neighbourhood with a sly grin and exactly the right spirit for the character.

Twain's *Adventures of Huckleberry Finn* is widely acknowledged as the great American novel of the 19th century. Throughout the story, Huck is in moral conflict with the received values of society in the post–Civil War South. Twain said, "a sound heart is a surer guide than an ill-trained conscience." Huck makes his choices based on his own valuation of Jim's friendship and human worth — usually in direct opposition to the things he has been taught.

The cover had to be a "journey" idea reflecting the scale of the novel. The central image of the raft was almost obligatory — the white boy and the black man drifting down the river together — but they had to feel dwarfed by the vast landscape. George Caleb Bingham (1811–1879) was my principal reference for the river scene on the cover. Bingham painted scenes of everyday life along America's western frontier (which in those days was Missouri).

Huckleberry Finn opens with a formal "Notice" from the author — a tongue-in-cheek statement about his intentions for the story, written in the style of a poster from the period. This gave me the idea for my black-and-white interior illustrations. I drew up the (fictional) handbills and printed ephemera mentioned in the text. Several came with specified wording — the posters printed for the king and the duke's theatrical performances, for example: "For 3 nights only! The World-Renowned Tragedians David Garrick the Younger and Edmund Kean the Elder! In the Thrilling Tragedy of THE KING'S CAMELOPARD. Admission 50 cents. Ladies and Children not admitted." I augmented these with likely examples such as a runaway slave poster offering a reward for Jim.

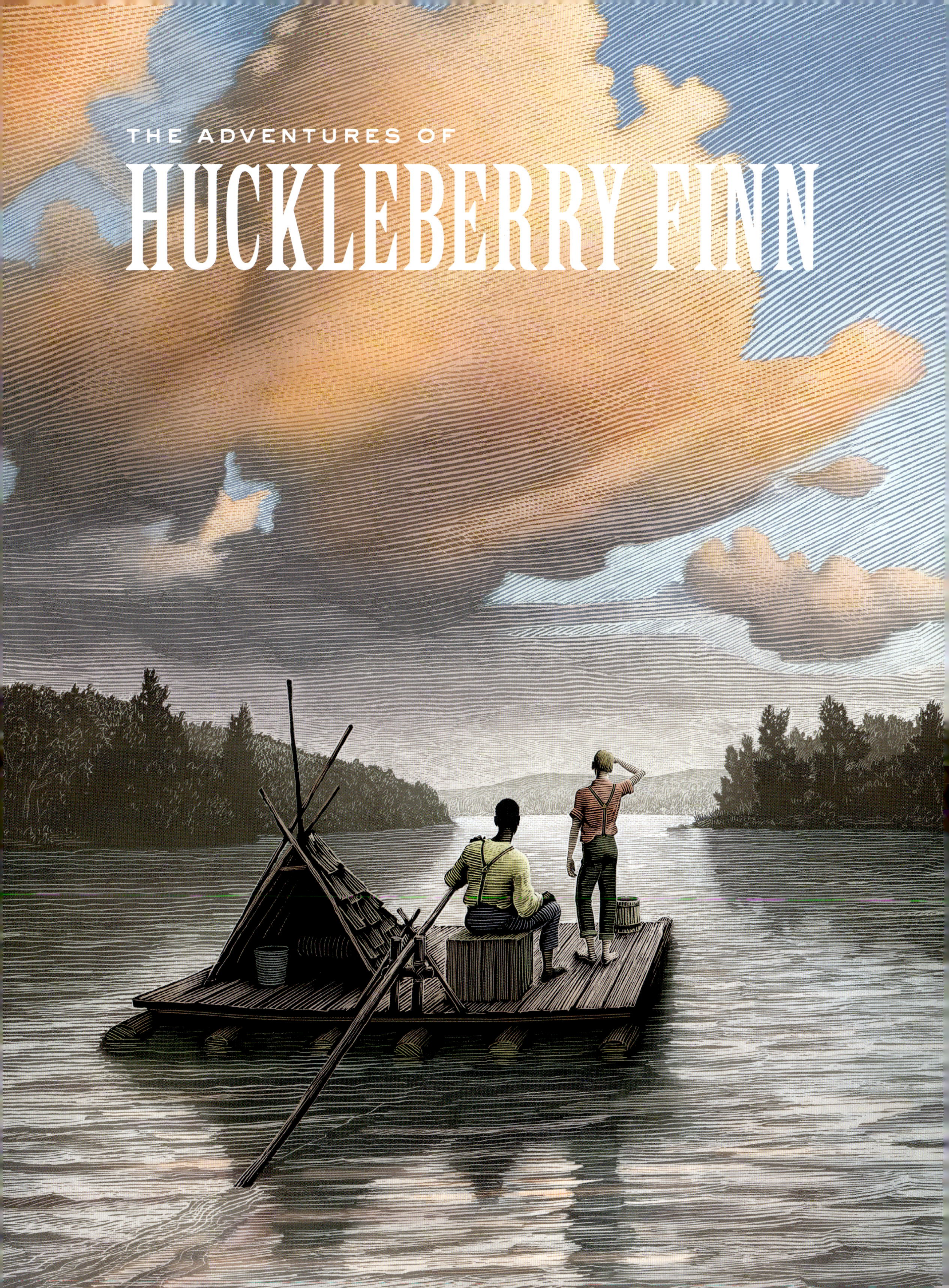
THE ADVENTURES OF
HUCKLEBERRY FINN

I have created covers for four novels by Gregory Maguire, the *New York Times* best-selling author of *Wicked*. Maguire's novels are imaginative "backstories" to classic fairy tales — part of their charm is that Maguire's narrative blends so seamlessly with the details that we distantly remember about these stories from when we first encountered them.

He explores neglected minor characters and misrepresented villains. *Confessions of an Ugly Stepsister* is a Cinderella spinoff, from Charles Perrault and the Brothers Grimm. *Wicked: The Life and Times of the Wicked Witch of the West* is a riff on L. Frank Baum's *The Wonderful Wizard of Oz*. My first Maguire assignment was *Hiddensee* in 2016 would — a fantastical biography of Drosselmeier, Klara's godfather in E.T.A. Hoffmann's *The Nutcracker*. I illustrated the cover for *A Wild Winter Swan* in 2020, in which Maguire transposed Hans Christian Anderson's "The Wild Swans" from it usual medieval European storybook setting to the Upper East Side of New York City at Christmastime in 1962.

Then, in 2021, Gregory returned to his Oz canon with *The Brides of Maracoor* — Volume One of a new trilogy. These brides are priestesses-for-life in a cloistered religious order on a remote island. Their rituals include the twisting of seaweed into nets, thereby segmenting time into its daily allotments. The brides believe that they control the destiny of the universe in some mysterious way — you can't help but think of the Norns, who spin the thread of human life, measure it out, and cut it to the length they have preordained, in Norse mythology.

A strange girl with green skin washes ashore after a terrifying storm. This is Rain, the main character of the saga — Elphaba's granddaughter from the iconic *Wicked* novels. My 15-year-old model, Evie O'Toole, had never heard of Maguire's novels, so had no connection to the story at all. But her mom loved them — she had read them in a book club, before Evie was born, so *she* was more excited about the project than her daughter. I sent the colourized illustration to Evie when it was finished, and her charming reply was "my favorite colour is green."

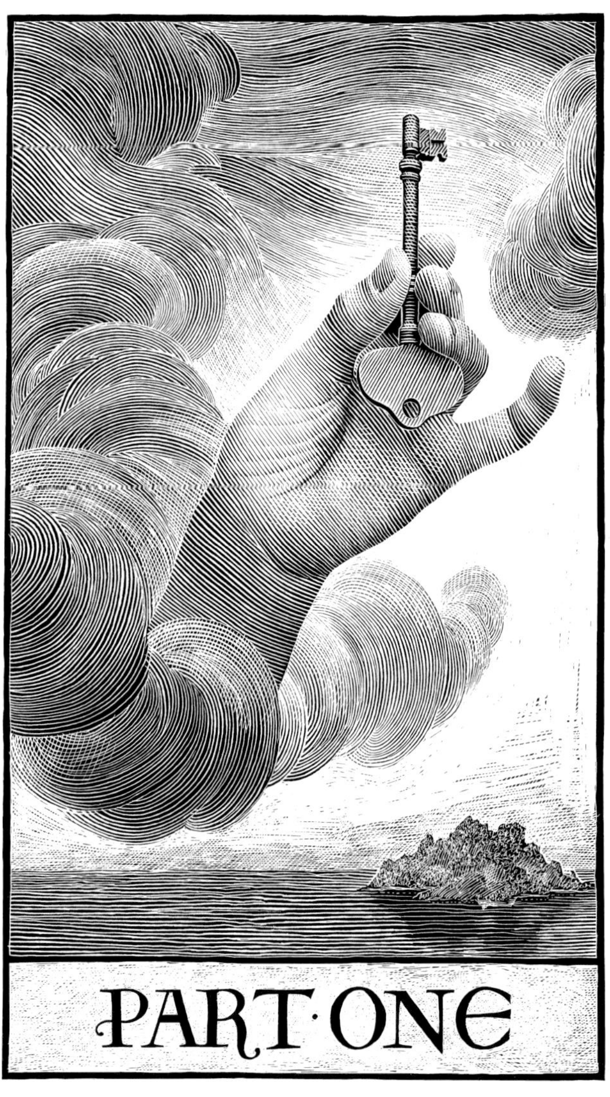

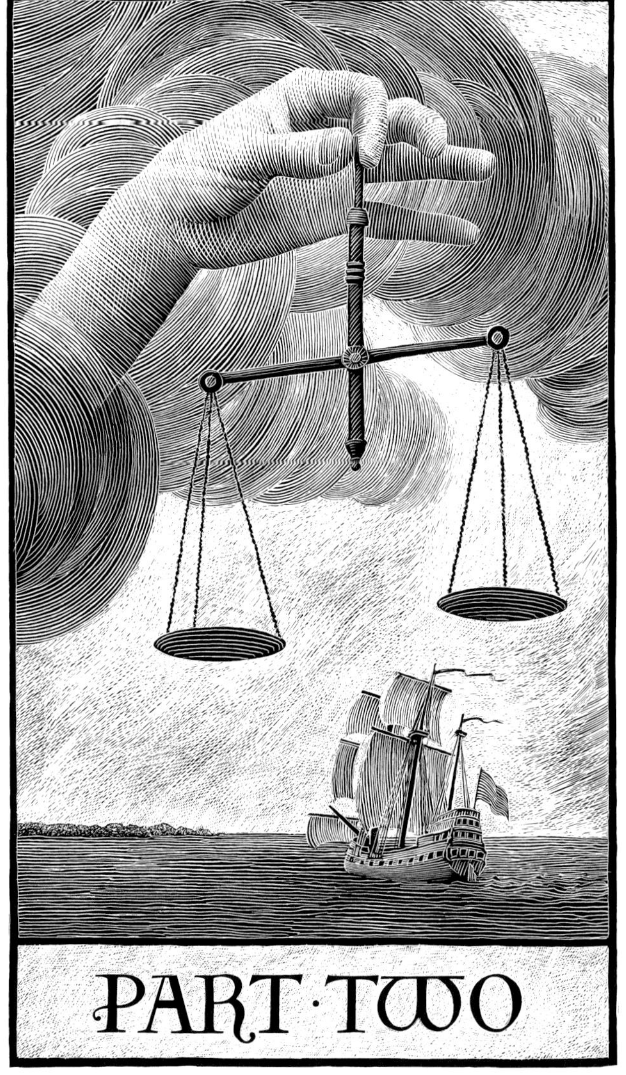

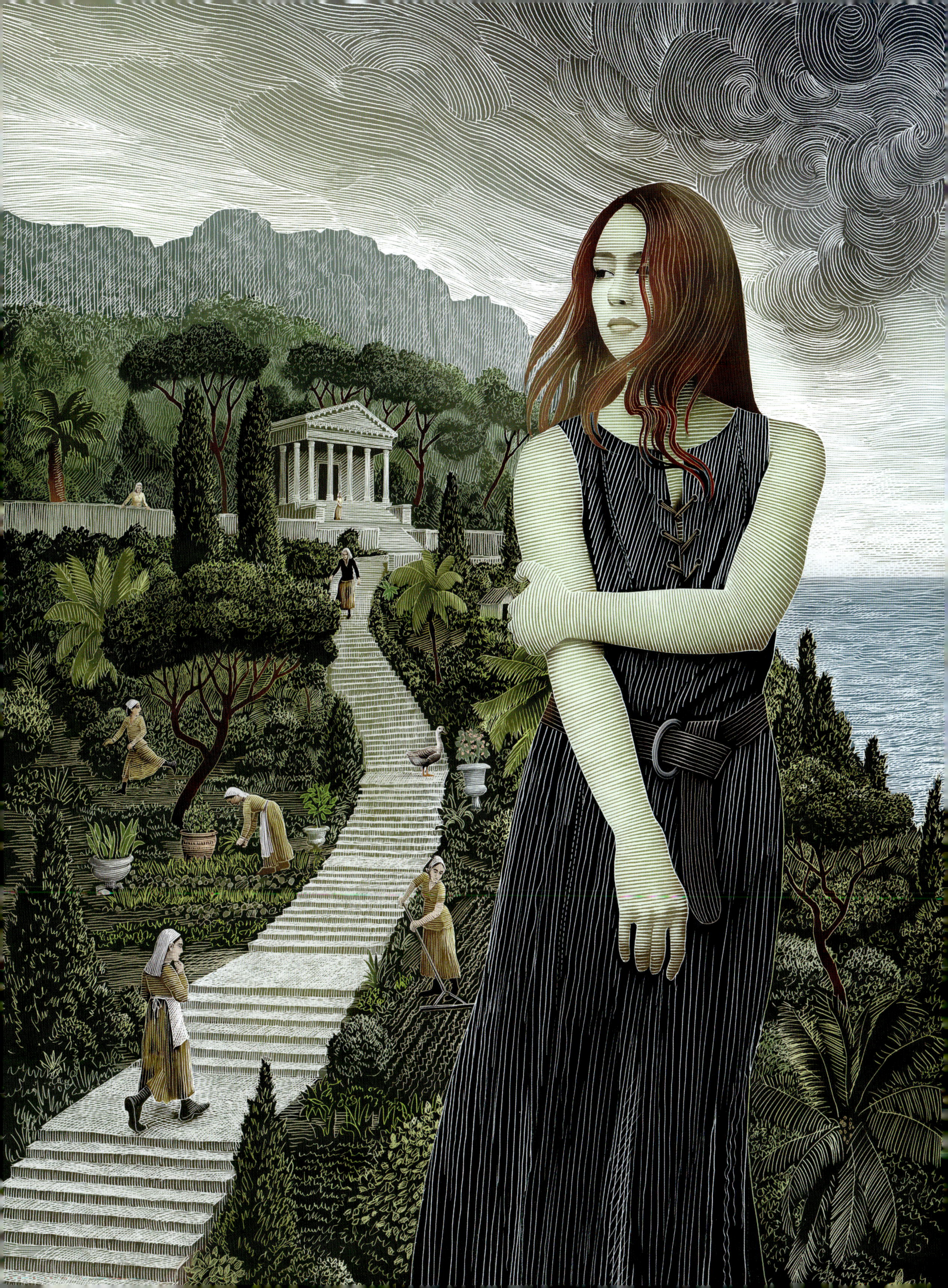

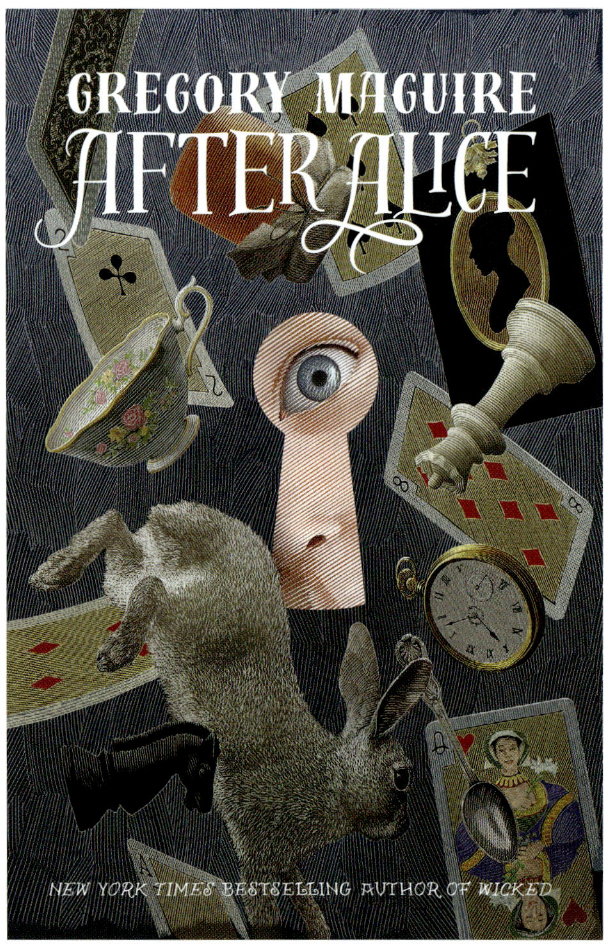

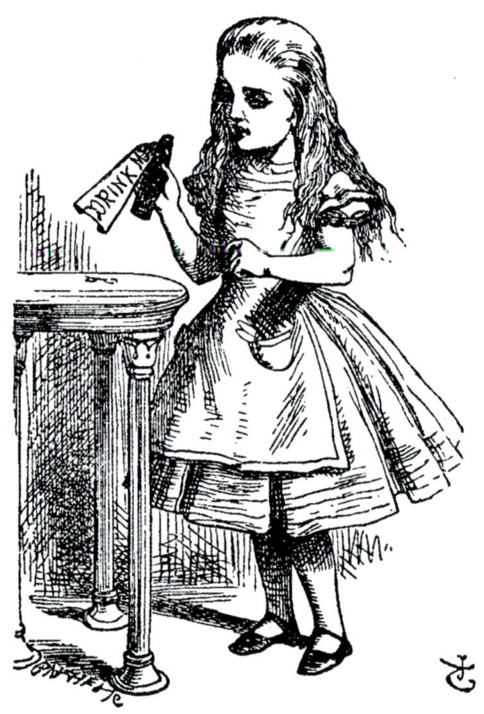

HarperCollins assigned a second Gregory Maguire cover in 2018 — for *After Alice*, his journey into Lewis Carroll territory. This novel was published in 2015 (the 150th anniversary of the publication of Carroll's original) but it had never received the "double cover" treatment, so they wanted to make this novel part of the series, visually.

Maguire's main character is Ada Boyce, neighbour and best friend of Alice. Thanks to Sir John Tenniel (and countless illustrators of subsequent editions of *Alice*), we think of Carroll's heroine as a beautiful Victorian child. Ada is the opposite — she's unlovely and bent-backed, confined to an agonizing iron corset meant to correct her posture. On a sunny midsummer morning, Ada slips away from home and her adult guardians to hunt down Alice, plants a foot wrong and tumbles down Carroll's rabbit hole — half an hour after Alice's adventure has already begun. As Maguire's title suggests, Ada spends much of the book trying to catch up with Alice in Wonderland. She encounters the White Rabbit, the Mad Hatter, the Caterpillar and the Cheshire Cat — all of whom reply to Ada's inquiries that, yes, Alice was just here 10 minutes ago.

The story unfolds with scenes in dreamlike underground Wonderland and in the real world above ground. Maguire weaves in the social and historical tensions of Victorian Oxford, as well as real-life characters (Alice's father entertains a visiting celebrity, Charles Darwin).

My very first sketches had Ada in the above-ground world on the outer cover, and Alice in the underground world, peeking out from the hidden cover below. But that seemed too complicated — readers won't know who they are, or why there are two girls, until they have read the book. Ada is Gregory's stand-in for Alice, so I merged them into one girl who could be either character. Most readers will assume she's Alice, but since Alice does not actually appear until the very end of the book, I like to think of her as Ada.

I wanted to play with scale (as both Carroll and Maguire do) — Alice/Ada too large to fit through a door, or too small. And she encounters many doors. Opening the cover of the book is like the reader opening the door to the story. So the idea is very simply — Alice/Ada looking out at us from inside the story, through a keyhole. Falling through space on the jacket (down the rabbit hole) are playing cards, a tea cup, chess piece, and the back end of a white rabbit — all tropes in the world of this story. Adelia Wilson was my model for this illustration.

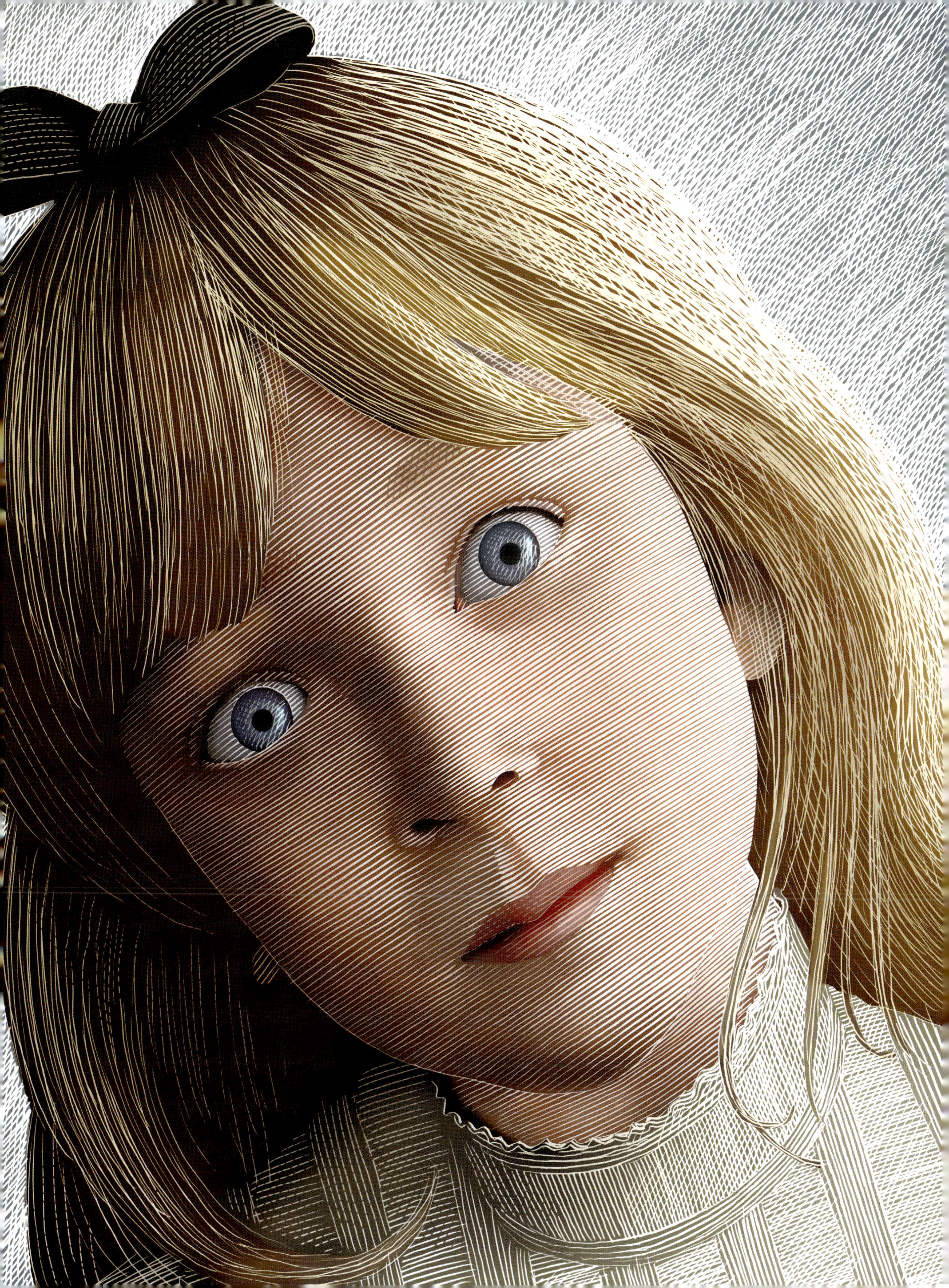

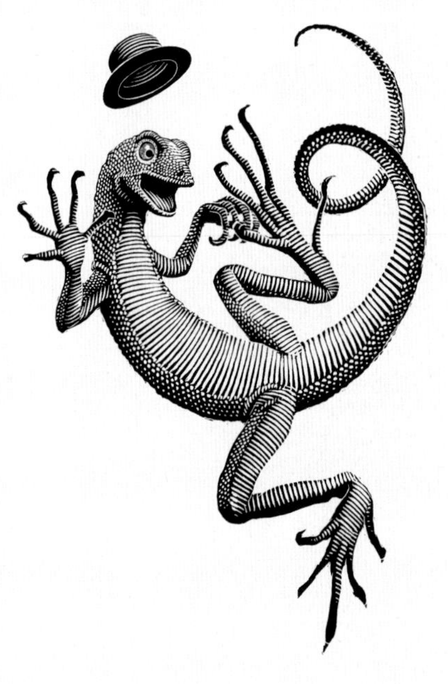

Gregory Maguire's *After Alice* was not my first trip to Wonderland. A visit to Deyrolle, the extraordinary 19th-century taxidermy shop on Rue du Bac in Paris, inspired my cover of the Sterling Classics edition of the Lewis Carroll original. The atmosphere of a dusty old museum of natural history recalled Alice's fall down the rabbit hole, past cupboards and bookshelves. Instead of empty jars of orange marmalade, the shelves at Deyrolle were crowded with a surreal menagerie of stuffed birds, butterflies, fossils and skeletons. I explored each room, coming face to face with lions, polar bears, pelicans, flamingos, zebras, a moose and a giraffe peeking around the upper corner of a 10-foot doorway. I swear I saw a white rabbit disappearing down the corridor.

I sent a rough concept sketch to Karen Nelson, my art director at Sterling Publishing in New York, afraid that they would find my approach too dark for the Children's Classics section at Borders or Barnes & Noble. I was happily surprised to be mistaken on this one — they gave me a green light to go full-speed ahead.

I needed detailed costume reference for this complex pose. Christina designed Alice's dress and we hired a cutter from the Stratford Festival wardrobe shop to build it for Michaela Bekenn, our 11-year-old model.

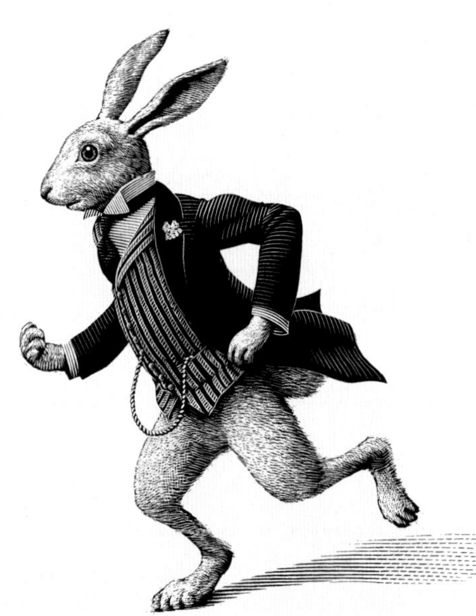

Perched on top of a tall A-frame ladder in a darkened rehearsal hall, I made reference photos looking straight down at Michaela, who was lying on her back on an exercise mat. I had positioned floodlights at floor level at one end of the room — when I rotated this horizontal composition by 90 degrees into a vertical, it gave me the illusion of a light source overhead as Alice is falling through space.

I drew a dozen black-and-white interior illustrations for this edition including Bill the Lizard, the White Rabbit and the Cheshire Cat (disappearing from its tail).

Of the 36 titles I illustrated for Sterling over 15 years, *Alice* was certainly one of the most rewarding, and most humbling. It's an honour to be one small link in the chain of the book's illustrious 154-year published history. Everyone knows the iconic illustrations by Sir John Tenniel, created for the original edition in 1865. (I could empathize with the story that Tenniel was unhappy with the print quality of the very first edition and insisted on a reprint.) I have a copy of the Peter Newell edition published in 1901. I love Arthur Rackham's superlative illustrations, published in 1907 — Carroll's text had just entered the public domain in Britain, catalyzing several new editions including Rackham's. My single favourite edition, for its astonishing ingenuity and freshness, is Lisbeth Zwerger's, published in 1999 — her watercolour illustrations take my breath away.

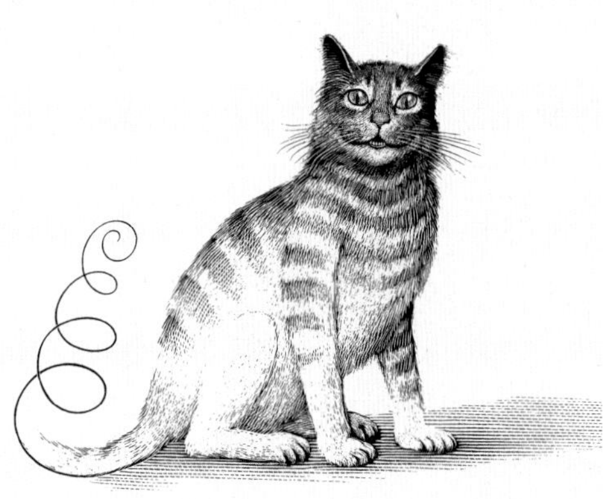

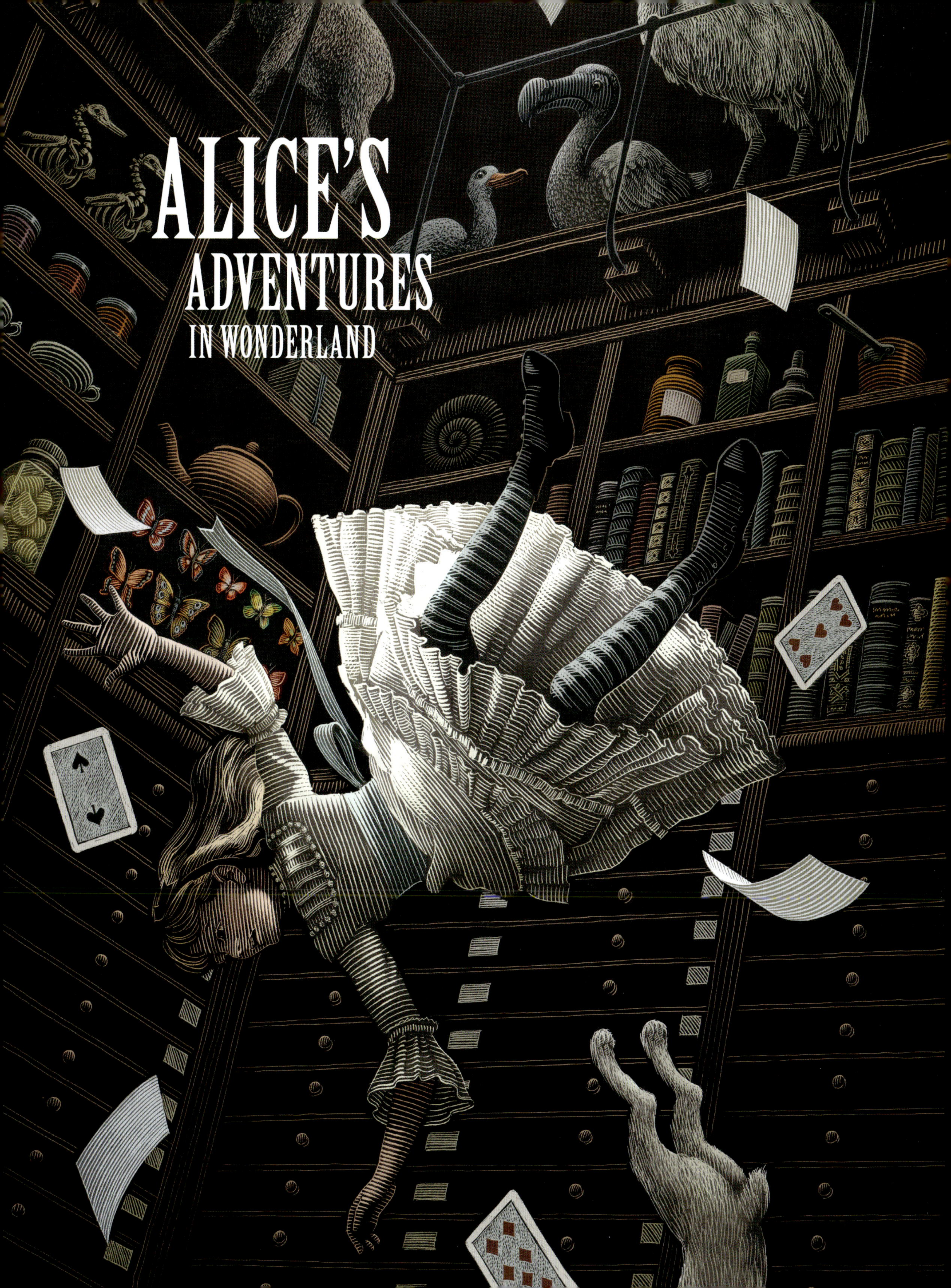
ALICE'S
ADVENTURES
IN WONDERLAND

"Believe me, my young friend, there is nothing — absolutely nothing — half so much worth doing as simply messing about in boats." Ratty's credo in the opening chapter of *The Wind in the Willows* set the theme and tone for my cover illustration. I grew up messing about in sailboats on Lake Michigan and Lake Huron — it wasn't exactly the Thames, but I can certainly identify with Ratty's point of view.

I realized that I had great reference material for this illustration at my fingertips. For the Shaw Festival's 2003 season brochure, I had art-directed a series of photo illustrations showing members of the acting ensemble enjoying various recreational pursuits in and around Niagara-on-the-Lake. One shot featured two actors in a vintage wooden rowboat. We found an idyllic location on Martindale Pond, famous for the annual Royal Canadian Henley Regatta, in St. Catharines. Photographer David Cooper perched on a small bridge to get the high-angle shot looking down into the boat.

The handsomely produced Sterling Classics volumes sell for $10 each — an amazing bargain — but this does impose limitations on the illustration budget. The main emphasis is on the cover, but several black-and-white interior spot illustrations are also part of each assignment.

For *The Wind in the Willows*, the obvious choice was to portray Mole, Ratty, Badger and Toad of Toad Hall. But how to approach them in a fresh way? It's impossible to think of these characters without picturing Ernest H. Shepard's famous illustrations, first published in 1931, which he developed in consultation with Kenneth Grahame. And I adore the Arthur Rackham illustrations of these characters, published in 1940.

I remembered a book in Christina's costume reference library — *Jocks and Nerds: Men's Style in the Twentieth Century* by Harold Koda and Richard Martin. The authors approached men's fashion thematically, through archetypes such as The Rebel, The Cowboy, The Military Man, Joe College and The Businessman. I borrowed this whimsical system of organization to give Mole, Ratty, Badger and Toad their own distinct character through what they were wearing. Mole is the perfect Nerd; Ratty falls somewhere between The Worker and The Sportsman; Badger is The Man About Town; Toad is surely The Dandy.

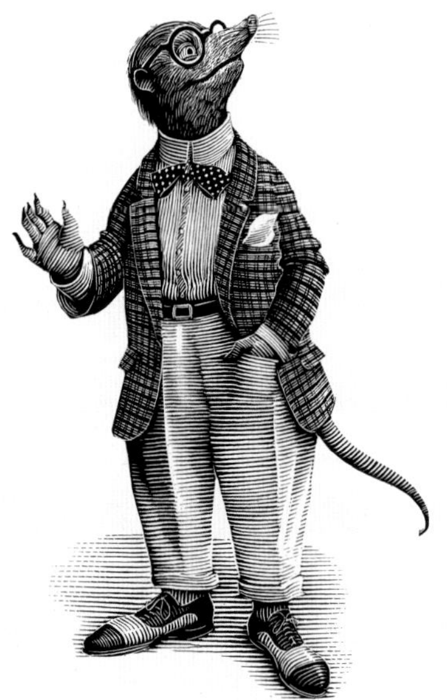

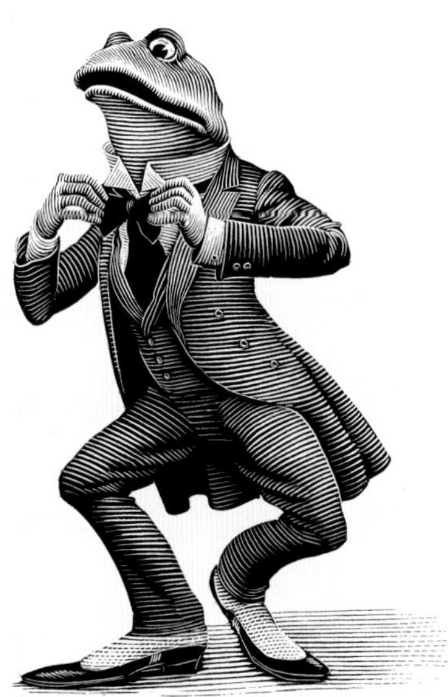

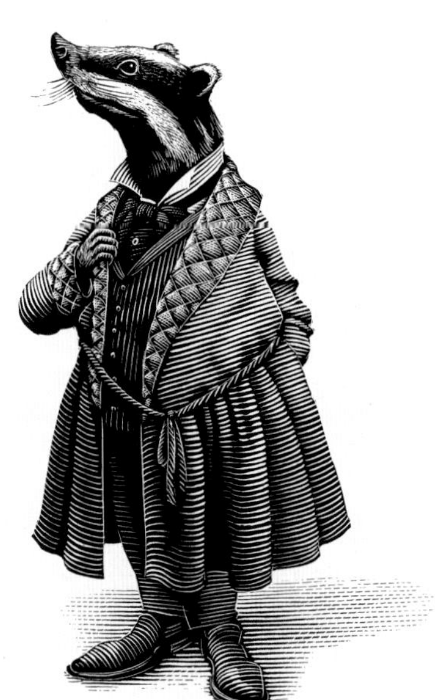

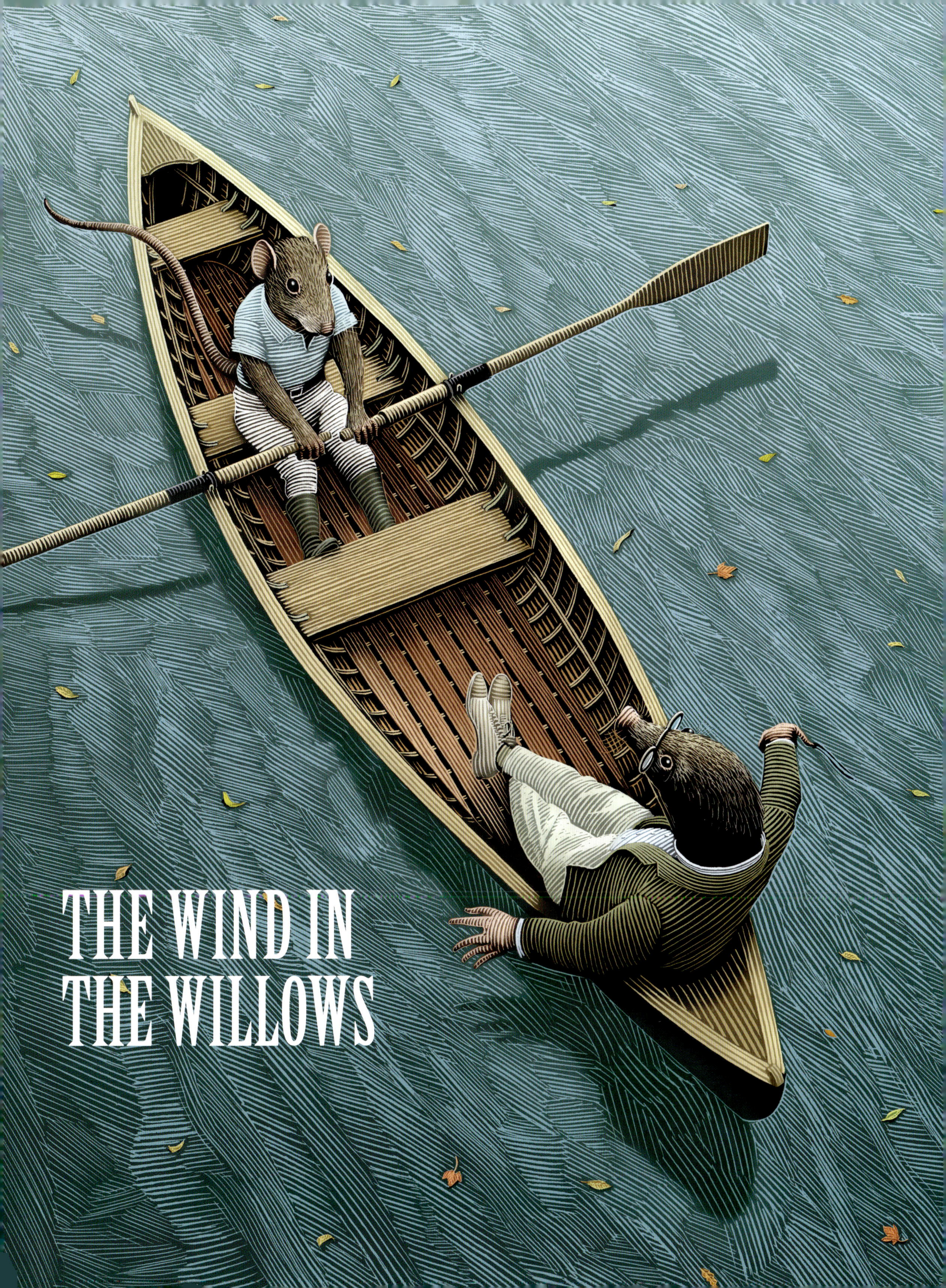
THE WIND IN
THE WILLOWS

Everyone has his or her own idea of what the world's greatest detective looks like. Arthur Conan Doyle described him very much as he appeared in *The Strand* magazine, illustrated by Sidney Paget. You can take your pick from many film and television incarnations — John Barrymore, Basil Rathbone, Peter Cushing, Christopher Plummer, Robert Downey Jr., or Benedict Cumberbatch. My personal favourite is Jeremy Brett.

My instinct was to avoid portraiture altogether because, inevitably, some readers would disagree with my choices — and elect *not* to buy the book because of its cover. An atmosphere of mystery was essential.

I often design publications that require historical picture research, and when this assignment came along I remembered a haunting series of Edwardian lantern slides I had seen on a visit to the Mary Evans Picture Library in Blackheath Village, in Southeast London. I adapted one of these twilight scenes along the Thames Embankment, the familiar dolphin-standard lanterns reflected on the wet paving stones. The figure silhouetted in the fog might be Holmes or it might be one of the criminals he is pursuing.

Robert Louis Stevenson's *The Strange Case of Dr. Jeykll and Mr. Hyde* was assigned in 2011. Here again, a portrait idea seemed wrong for the cover (although it would have to be a double portrait, as Stevenson's premise is that Hyde is an inextricable, integral part of Jekyll). I did a street scene with Jekyll as the picture of an elegantly dressed Victorian gentleman; Hyde is represented by a big, ominous cast shadow. A shadow contrasting the person or object casting the shadow is an old cliché, but it gave the requisite spooky atmosphere. I added some tattered Victorian posters on the wall to suggest a seedy part of the city.

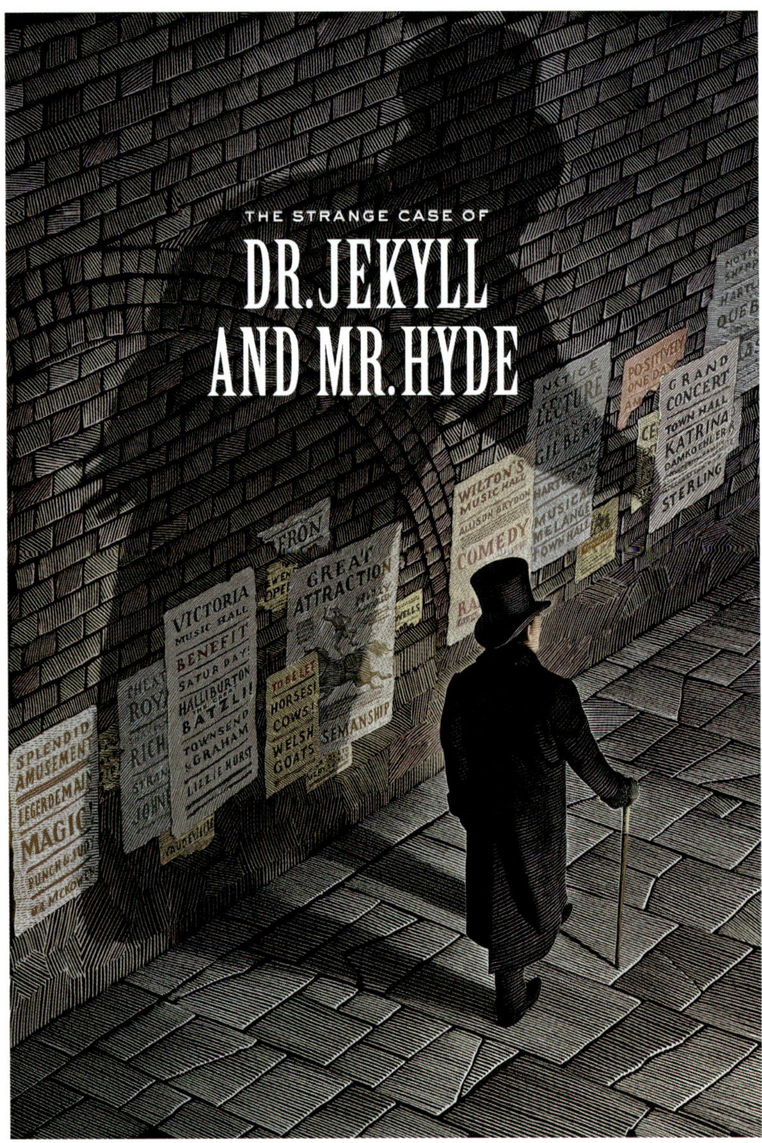

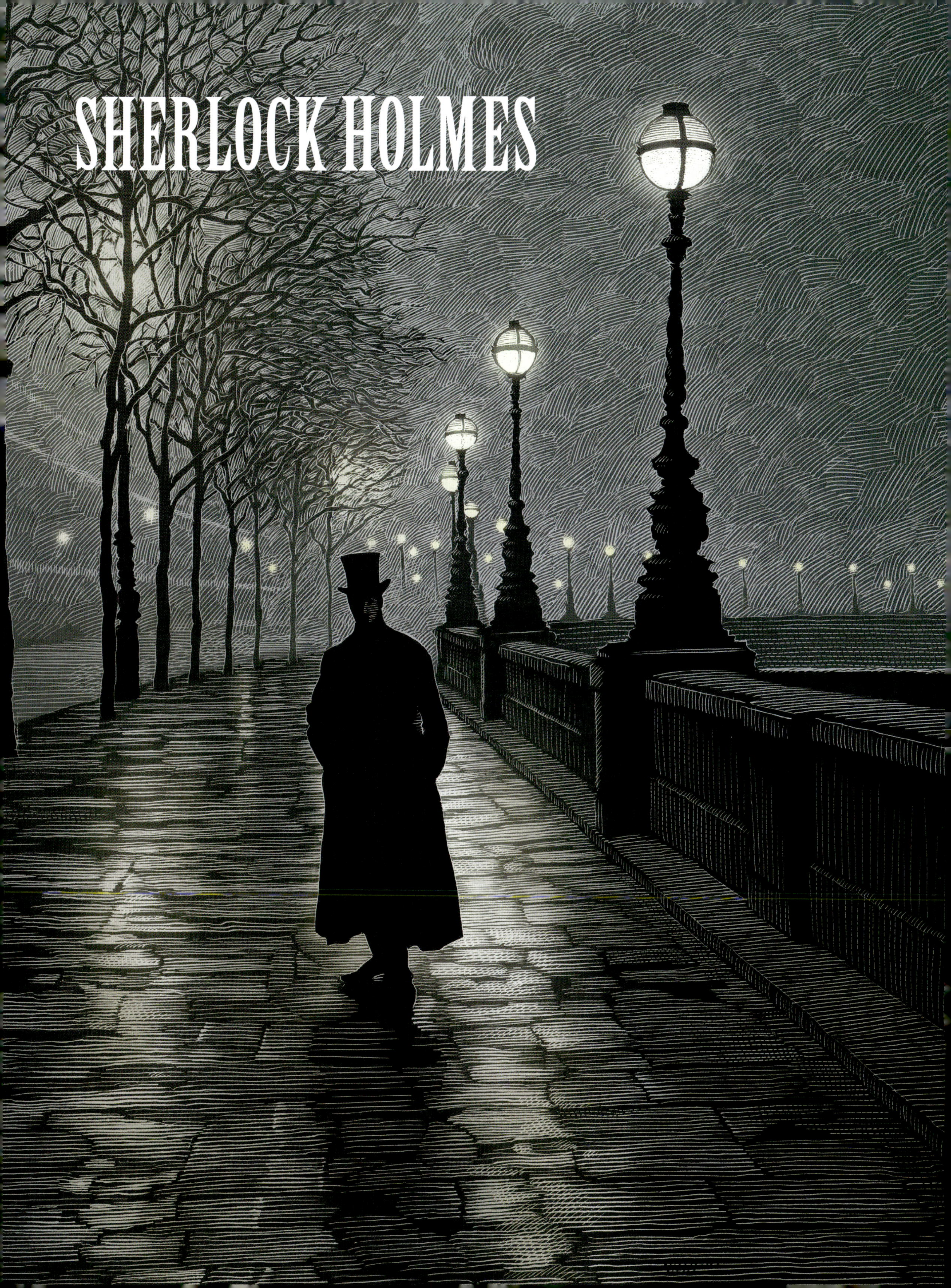
SHERLOCK HOLMES

Sometime in 2006, a friend asked what I was working on. I mentioned this assignment, and his immediate and genuine response was "Oh, I love *The Jungle Book*!" Then my friend slipped into a creditable Louis Prima imitation, singing "I Wanna Be Like You" — and I realized that it's the animated Disney film that most people connect with this title. I remember it fondly, too, but it has nothing to do with Rudyard Kipling. King Louie, Disney's swinging orangutan, does not even exist in Kipling's original version.

Kipling wrote *The Jungle Book* in 1894 — a series of seven fables, each paired with a song relating to the action or characters: "Hunting Song of the Seeonee Pack," "Road Song of the Bandar-Log" and "Parade Song of the Camp Animals." John Lockwood Kipling, Rudyard's father, illustrated the first edition. *The Second Jungle Book* followed in 1895; the Sterling Classics edition combines both books — 15 stories in total.

Kipling uses the animal kingdom of the Indian jungle to teach moral lessons. The Law of the Jungle is a set of rules for the survival of individual, family and community. "Nature, red in tooth and claw" is the deadly serious tone throughout — the animals greet each other not with "good morning," but with "good hunting."

Eight of the chapters tell the story of Mowgli (although not in chronological order) from infant "man cub" to manhood. In the final chapter, "The Spring Running," Mowgli, now 17, leaves the jungle forever, deeply torn between the family of animals he knows and loves and feelings for the outside world, which he doesn't fully understand. I was tempted to put Mowgli on the cover — but that would exclude half of the stories in the book in which he doesn't appear. Nature itself is the common denominator. I decided on Hathi, the wise old elephant who appears in several of the stories, representing order, dignity and obedience to the Law of the Jungle.

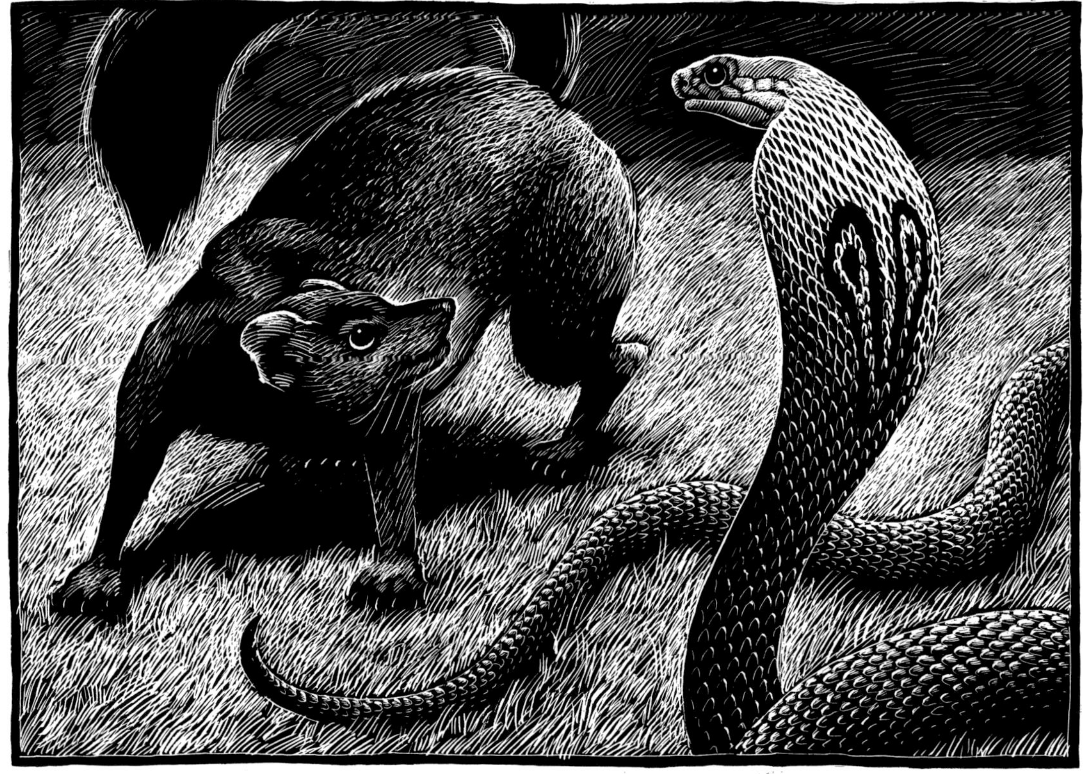

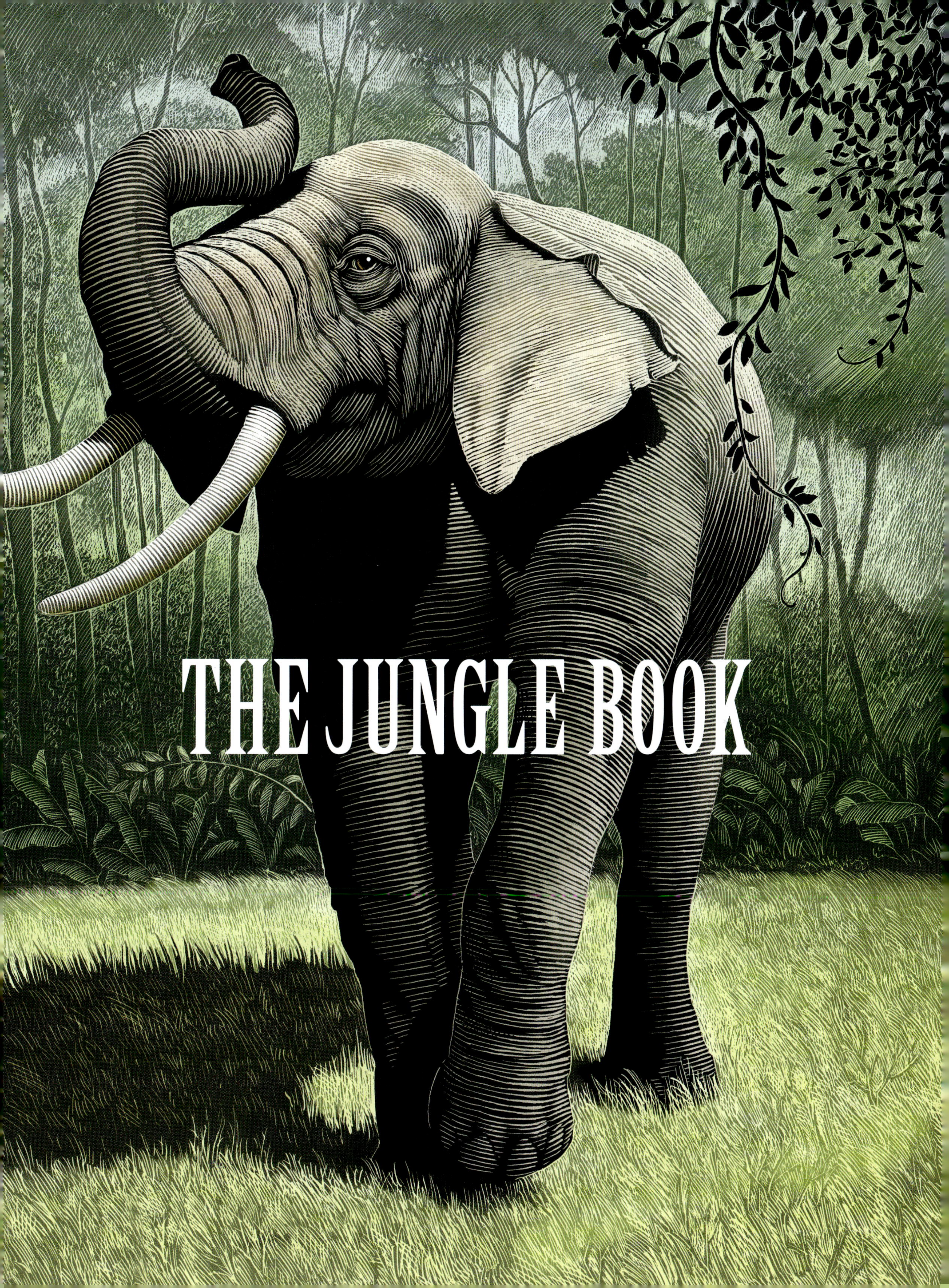
THE JUNGLE BOOK

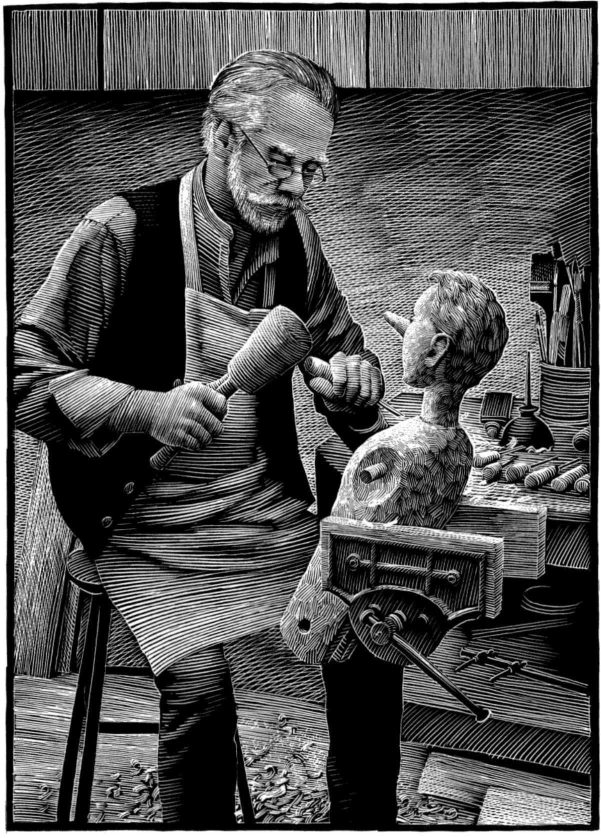

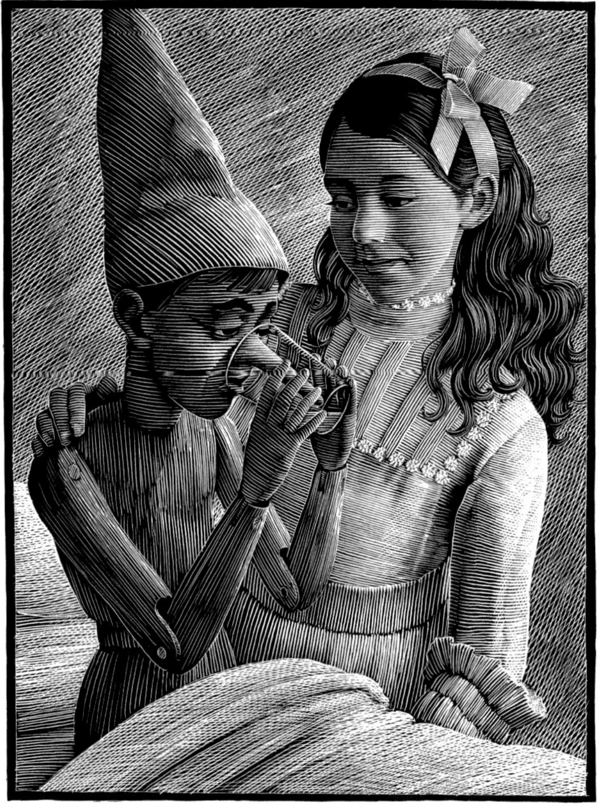

No book made a bigger impression on me as a child than *Pinocchio*. I grew up with an oversize Grosset & Dunlap edition from 1955, with illustrations by the great Libico Maraja (1912–1983). His leering Puppet Master had a long black beard and a whip made of snakes — he occupied a full page so he towered over Pinocchio and the other puppets. Equally vivid were the muscular, shaggy and oddly scaly Green Fisherman; four black rabbit Pallbearers with Pinocchio's coffin; the gaping mouth of sea monster about to swallow Pinocchio as he swims for his life; and the rather gruesome hanging scene. I loved it!

So I was truly delighted in 2013 when *Pinocchio* was assigned in the Sterling Classics series. This is a story with archetypal themes of good and evil, naiveté and maturity, truth and dishonesty (when Pinocchio lies, he literally wears his guilt on his face). He is a puppet — by definition controlled by someone else — the perfect metaphor for an inexperienced and overtrusting kid, trying to be good, but so easily manipulated by the shady characters he meets along the way. The story provides tools to navigate one's way through life and become a better person.

I love puppets (guess where that started), and I used a wonderful 19th-century marionette from our own collection as my cover model — I altered the face to give him boyish features and a long nose, but his costume was perfect as found, including the hat, the ruff and the buttons. He still occupies a place of honour on my studio wall.

I have been less than complimentary in these pages about the Disney versions of many of these classics. Their 1940 film version of *Pinocchio* is admirable in many ways (it's the darkest of all the Disney films), but still the Maraja book illustrations feel more truthful than animated films. As always, Disney takes too many liberties — the talking cricket is a minor character in Collodi's original text, but he has been elevated to co-star status in the film (and looks more like an English gentleman than an insect). "When You Wish Upon a Star" and "Hi-Diddle-Dee-Dee, an Actor's Life for Me" are wonderful songs, but turning the story into a musical adds a veneer of entertainment that obscures the intentions of the original.

I included a flip-book — a small drawing placed at the bottom of every page. If you fan through the Sterling edition with your thumb, you can watch Pinocchio's nose grow to a ridiculous length. Ken Dubblestyne, one of the Stratford Festival's master prop builders, was my model for Gepetto. Madison Van Der Straeten was the Blue Fairy.

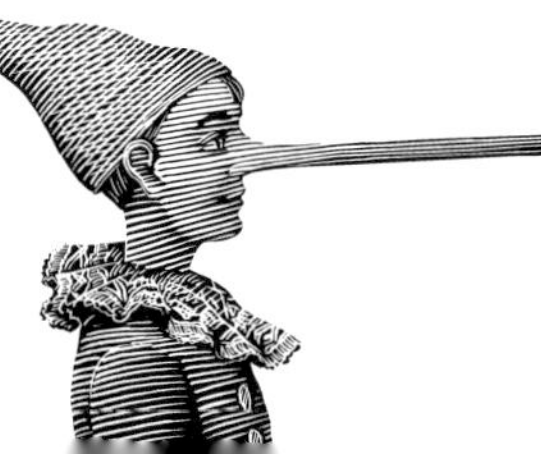

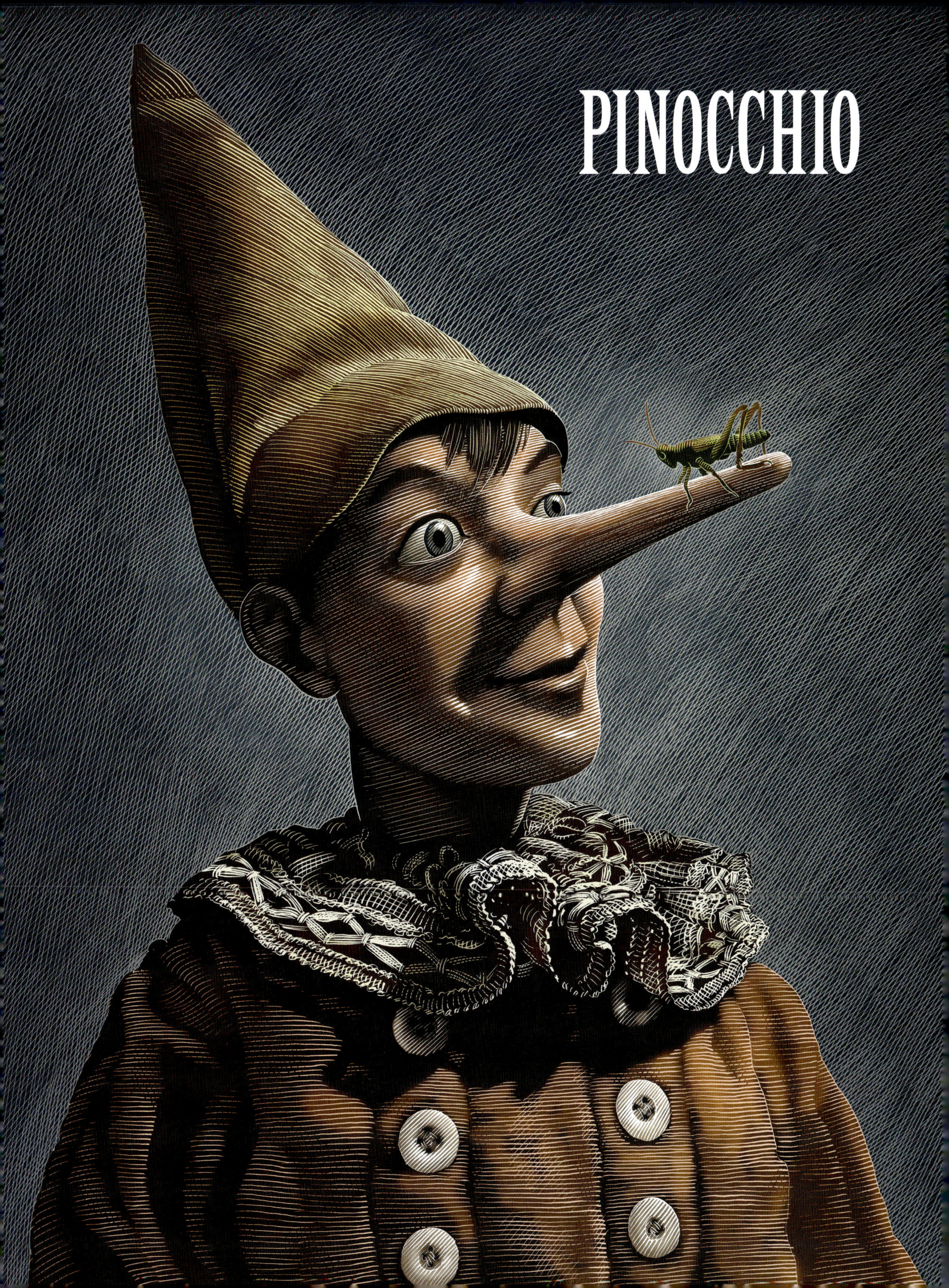
PINOCCHIO

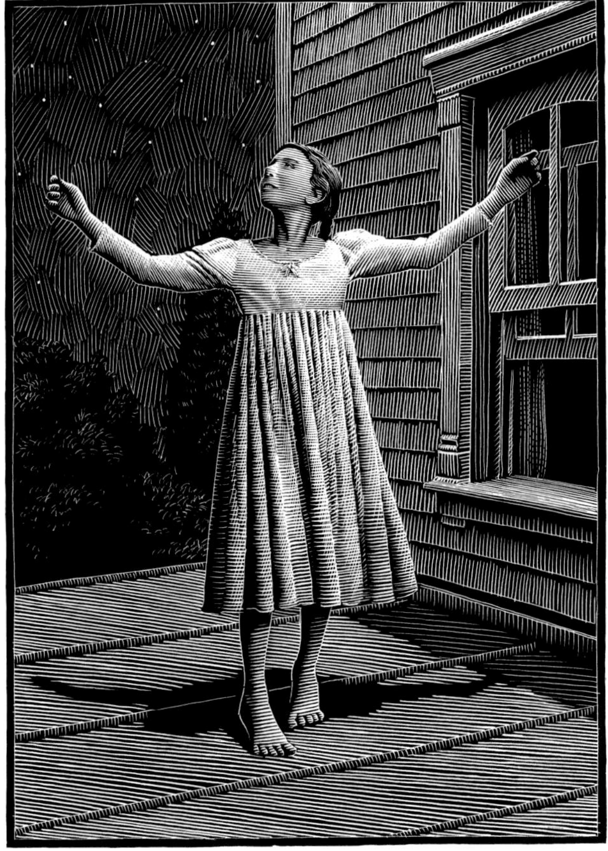

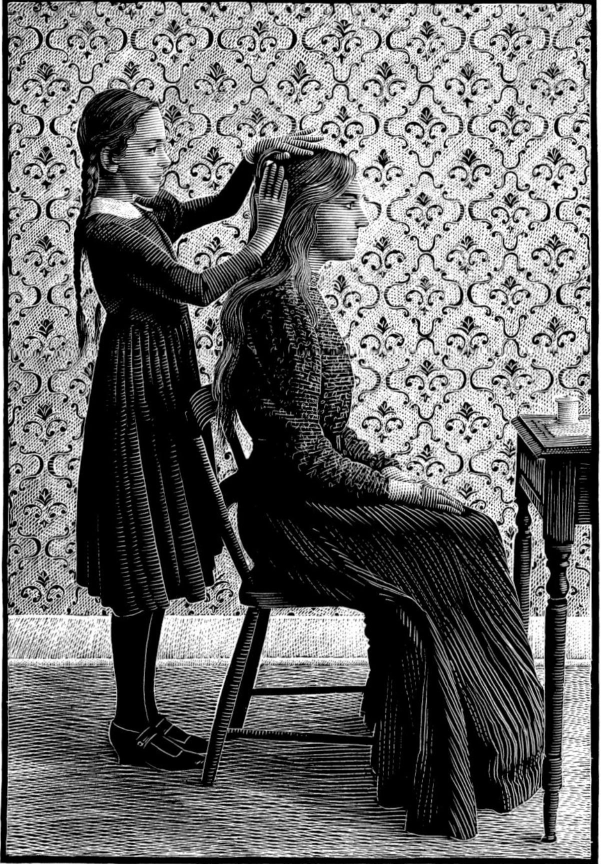

The art directors at Sterling assigned Eleanor H. Porter's *Pollyanna* in 2011. This was a worrisome assignment because of the saccharine stereotype around this 11-year-old orphan and her irrepressible optimism. To me, she's just completely implausible. Pollyanna tackles every situation she encounters with her "glad game" — finding something to be glad about in every set of circumstances, no matter how bleak it might be. Her very name has come to mean an excessively cheerful person — even to pejorative connotations. I love this lyric from the introduction to the song "But Not For Me" from George and Ira Gershwin's *Girl Crazy*, written in 1930:

> I never want to hear from any cheerful pollyannas
> who tell me fate supplies a mate / that's all bananas.

Pollyanna is taken in by her stern, cold spinster aunt who lives in a dour town in Vermont. With her sunny personality and a gift for bringing happiness and light into people's lives, she gradually transforms everyone she meets.

For my cover, I put our young heroine on a hillside with the town in the background. Pollyanna is like a little ray of sunshine, and I liked the idea that a rainbow follows her around, without her being aware of it, like a location pin on a Google map of the town. Glass prisms, which reflect light into little rainbows, appear in several scenes in the story so the cover concept makes a connection with the text.

A rainbow is a real challenge to render in scratchboard. It's a soft-focus atmospheric phenomenon — the antithesis of hard-edged engraving lines. I modulated the texture of the sky, but the finished effect relies mostly on the masks I use to add colour, in Photoshop channels.

The success of many of these Sterling illustrations seems to depend on casting the right models. That's a complex equation of intangible factors beyond age and physical description in the text — it has to be someone with a plausible demeanour for the character. Casting child models obviously depends on the co-operation and support of their parents, and we've been very lucky this regard in our little town. Alice Wilson was the perfect model for Pollyanna.

It did occur to me, having illustrated all of them, that Pollyanna Whittier's story is basically the same as Anne Shirley's and also Heidi's. Johanna Spyri published *Heidi* in 1881 — there's a central plot line with Heidi's friend Klara who can't walk. Pollyanna's blind optimism is tested towards the end of the book when she is struck by a car and loses the use of her legs. Lucy Maude Montgomery published *Anne of Green Gables* in 1908; Eleanor Porter's book wasn't published until 1913. I'll bet there's a thesis paper about this somewhere.

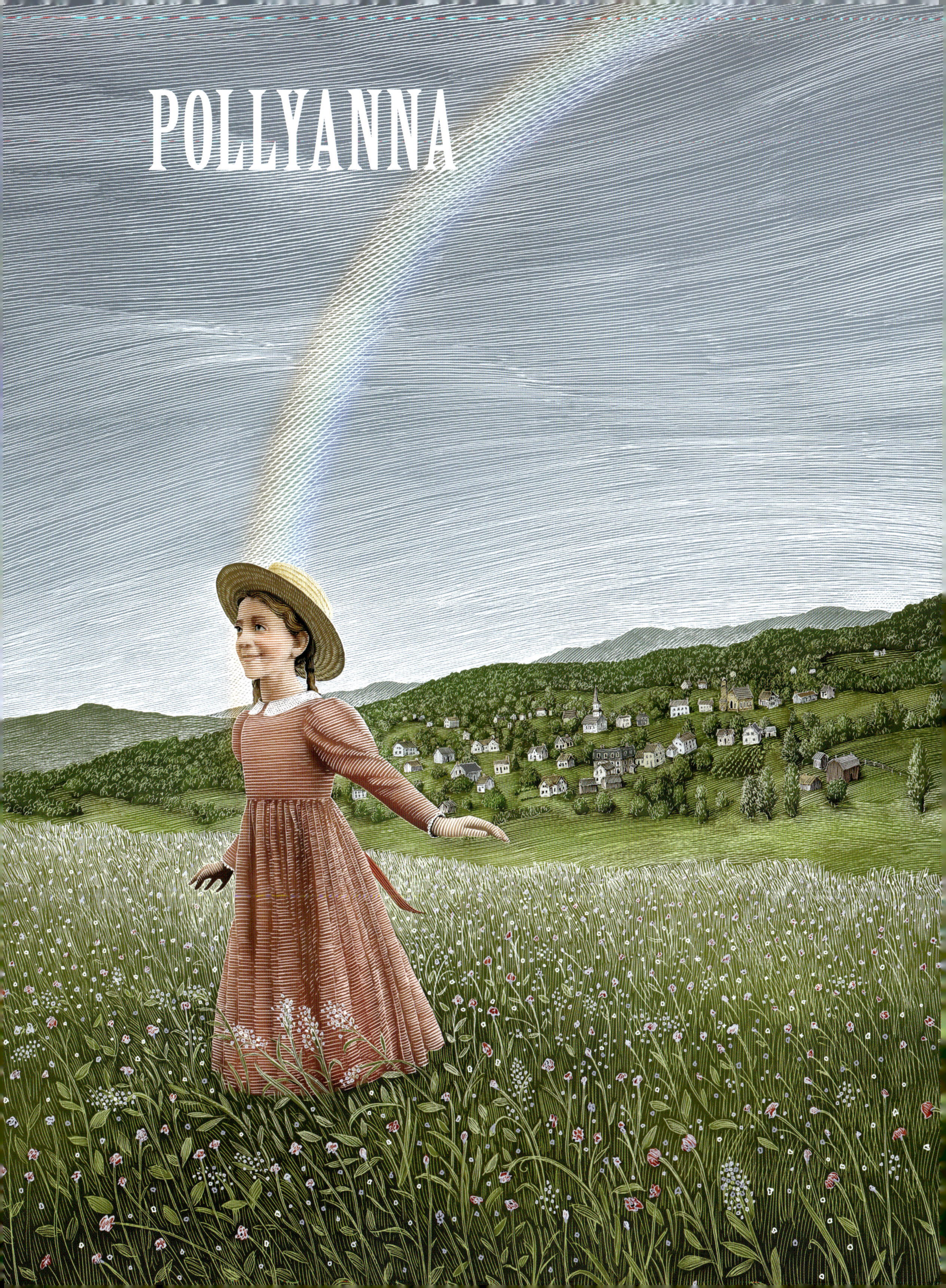
POLLYANNA

Like everyone, I love *A Christmas Carol* for its humanism, its social conscience and the hope it inspires of redressing the mistakes of your life. I marvel that these themes are still as potent today as they were in 1843 when Dickens first published it (at his own expense — his publisher didn't think it would sell).

When I first encountered the book as a child, however, it was simply as a terrific ghost story. Dickens' descriptions of the spirits are vividly cinematic — one thinks immediately of the many film versions of the story, but Dickens was writing 50 years before the earliest movie camera existed. My favourite comes when Marley's ghost walks through the bedroom door: "His body was transparent, so that Scrooge, observing him, and looking through his waistcoat, could see the two buttons on his coat behind."

Scrooge relives his entire life in one night, including a frightening vision of his own death, miserable and alone, if he does not mend his evil ways. I wanted the cover to be as spooky as possible.

Scrooge is haunted in bed — the one place that he should feel most secure and safe. The bed (and the bed curtains) are mentioned dozens of times in the text — the final terrifying vision in the graveyard ends as the Phantom's hood "shrank, collapsed, and dwindled down into a bedpost."

I expanded on my earlier theatre poster idea of showing Scrooge's reaction to seeing a ghost (rather than the ghost itself) — only this time we see the entire bed. The walls of the room have dissolved away to reveal a moonlit sky, suggesting the breadth of Scrooge's supernatural journeys through time and space.

I used Cecil Beaton's 1927 photo of Edith Sitwell in her great four-poster as my reference for the bed and the atmospheric paintings of Yorkshire artist Atkinson Grimshaw (1836–1893) for the cloudy, glowing sky.

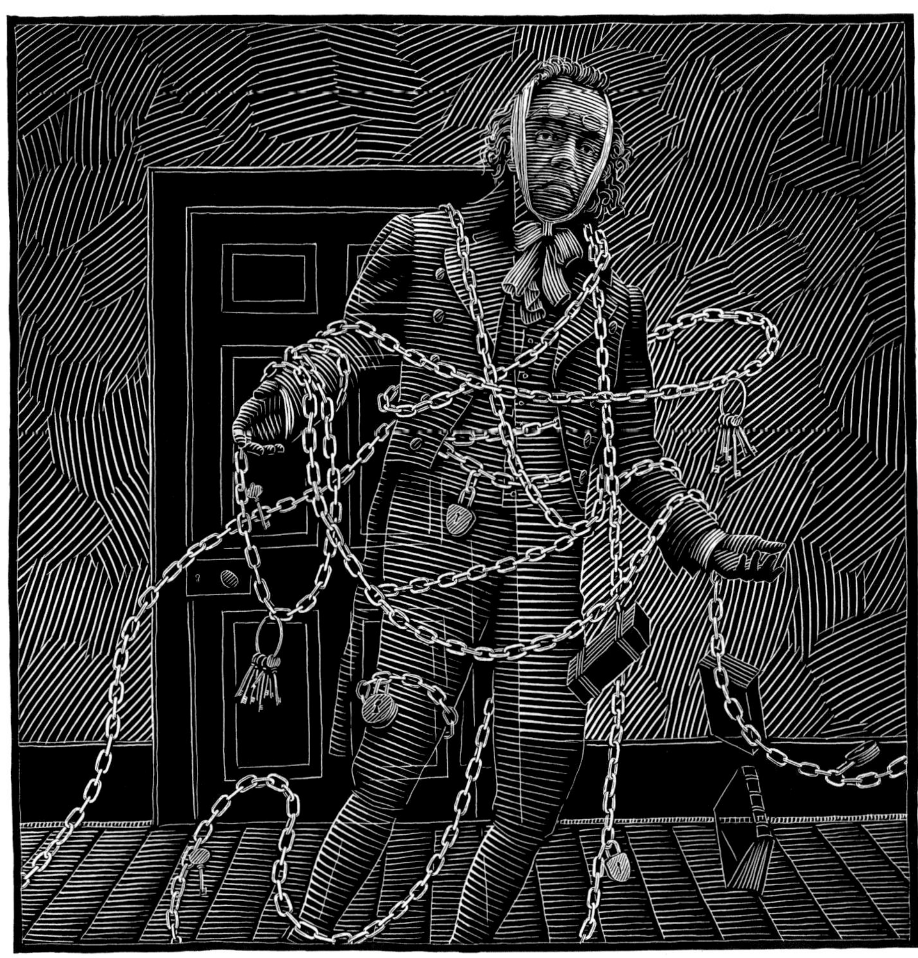

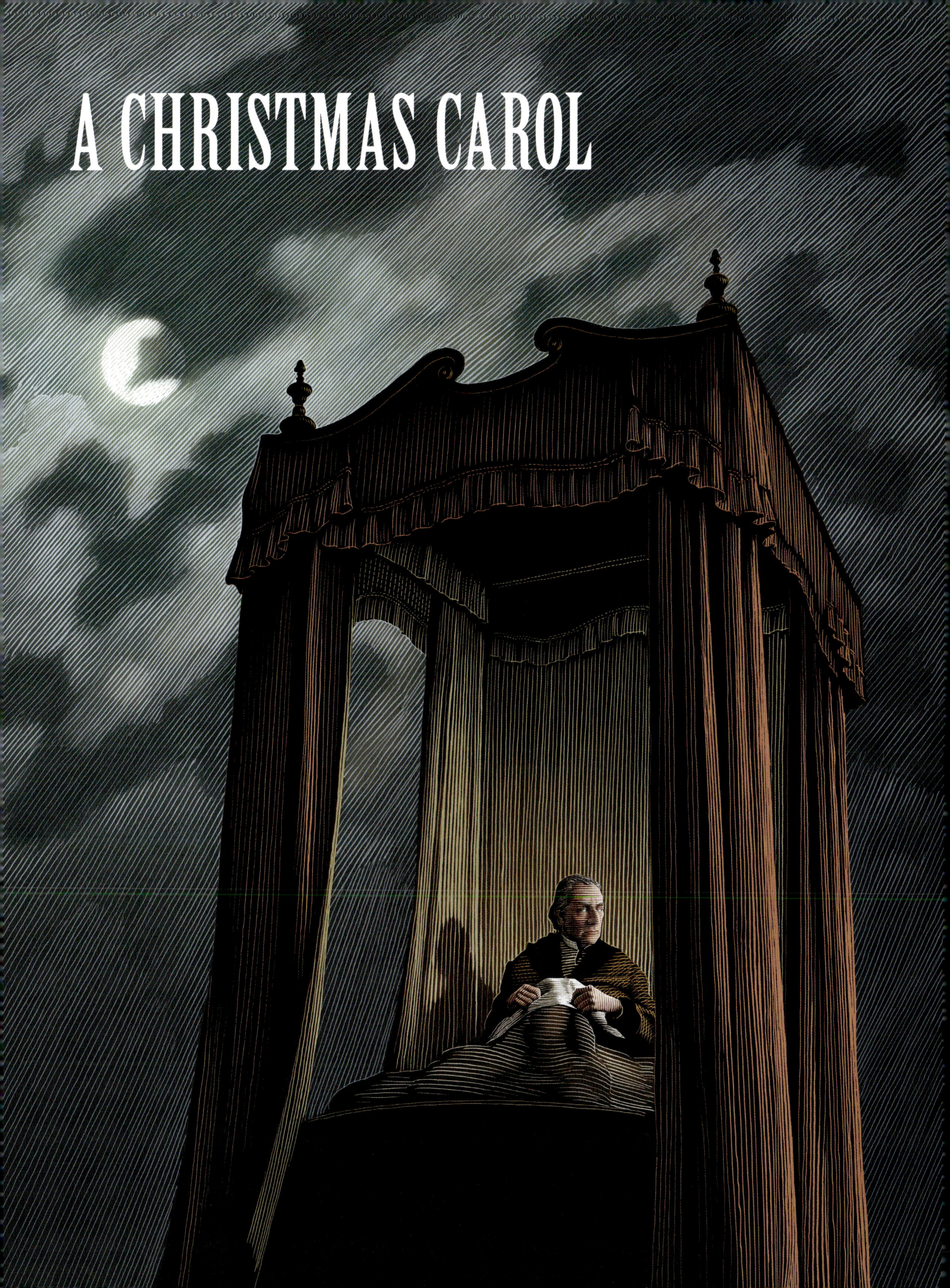
A CHRISTMAS CAROL

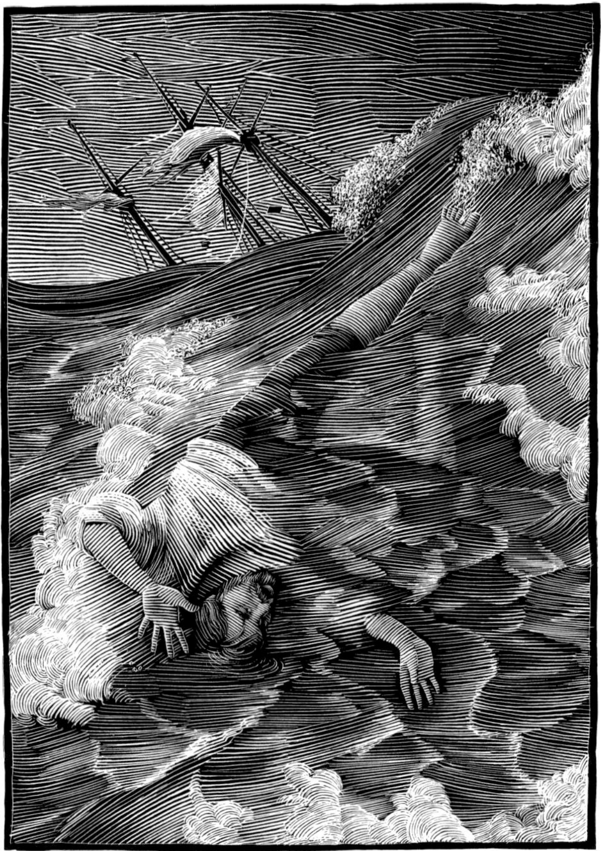

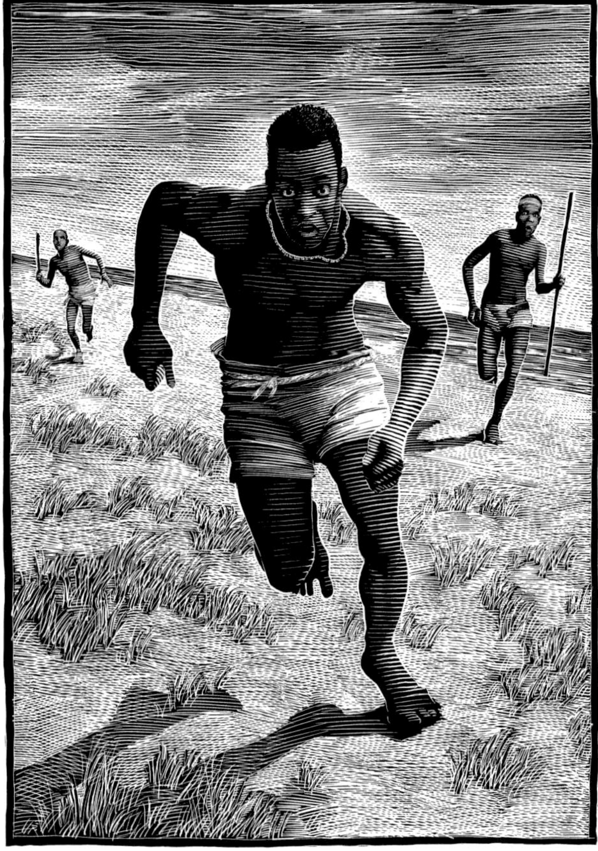

I had never read *Robinson Crusoe* before this assignment. Daniel Defoe published his novel in 1719 so it's the earliest of the 36 titles in the Sterling Classics series. This is a famous adventure story but it also has a deeply introspective side — 27 years of solitude gives Crusoe plenty of opportunity to contemplate life, philosophy, theology and what he believes in. He often thinks back to how his father tried desperately to discourage his inclination to go to sea in search of adventure. The book is beautifully nuanced in these areas — it feels quite modern at times, notwithstanding its 18th-century prose.

Crusoe is the only survivor of a shipwreck and spends these 27 years alone on an island. The only "voice" he hears during this entire time is Poll, a parrot, whom he teaches to speak. In one scene, Crusoe is asleep, having been very ill, when he is awakened by a voice calling his name — "Poor Robin Crusoe — where are you Robin?" He thinks he's dreaming and is "dreadfully frightened" in his dazed state, until he realizes that it's the parrot talking to him.

Crusoe takes Poll with him when he finally leaves the island, so the parrot is the centrepiece of my cover — its brilliant feathers contrasted against the dark figure of the title character in shadowy silhouette. An ocean horizon in the background conveys the setting (with a sand beach visible in the foreground so it's clear he's on land, not on a ship) and fabulous clouds in the sky.

This edition includes five interior illustrations in black and white. I wanted to illustrate the vivid storm scene that maroons Crusoe on the island — it was an interesting challenge to draw a figure overpowered by huge waves. Stratford actor Michael Spencer Davis was my model for the cover and the interior illustrations.

In his 25th year on the island, Crusoe observes a tribe of cannibals on the beach, about to kill a man. The sacrificial victim escapes and outruns his pursuers (Crusoe ambushes them, saving the man's life, and the rest of the tribe departs, never knowing what happened to their companions). Crusoe names his new companion "Man Friday," commemorating the day on which the events occurred; Friday becomes a main character in the last section of the story. Three centuries later his name is still used to describe an indispensable assistant — *His Girl Friday* is a 1940 screwball comedy film starring Rosalind Russell as an ace reporter and Cary Grant as her cynical editor and ex-husband (a adaptation of the play *The Front Page*).

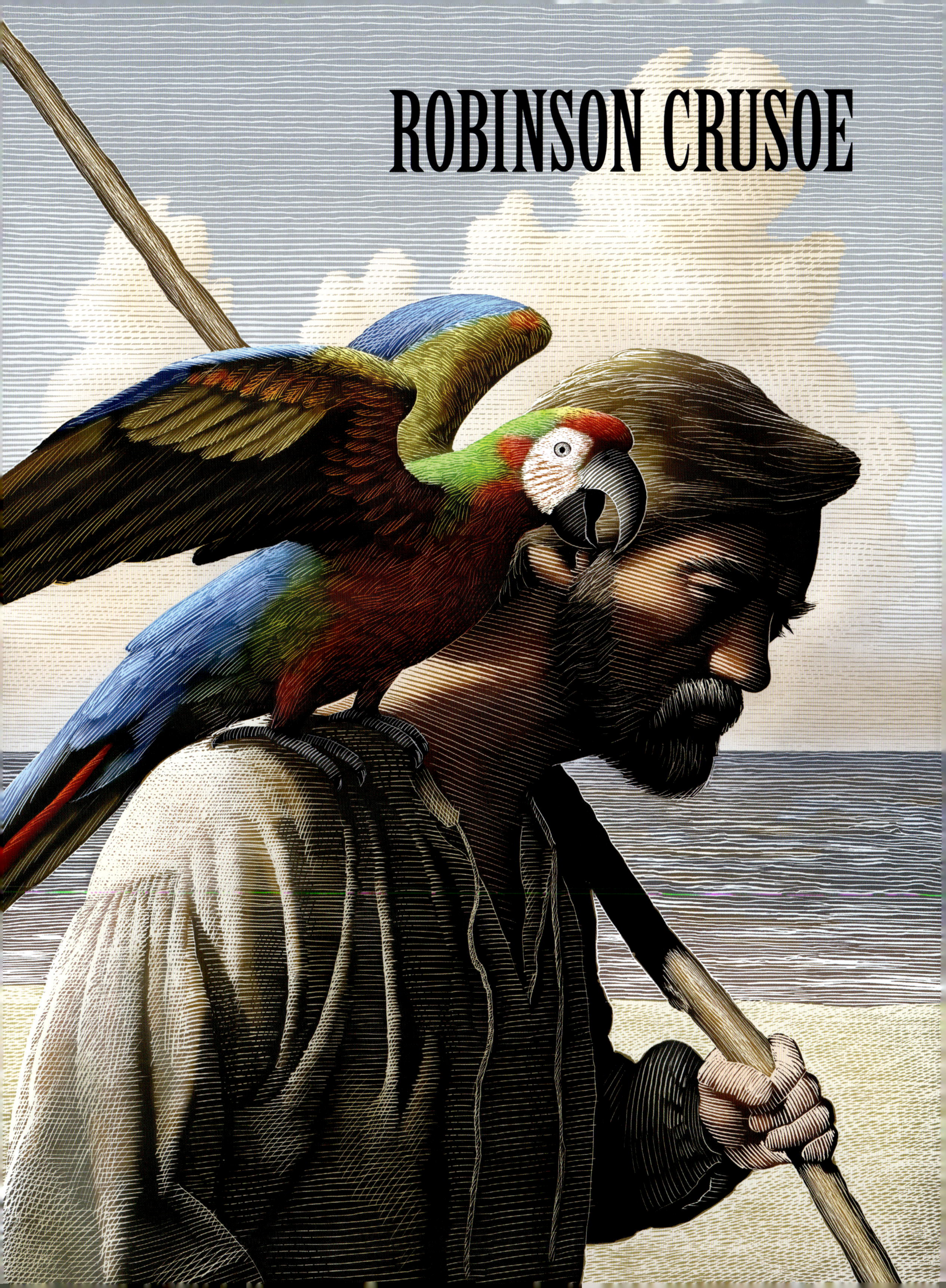
ROBINSON CRUSOE

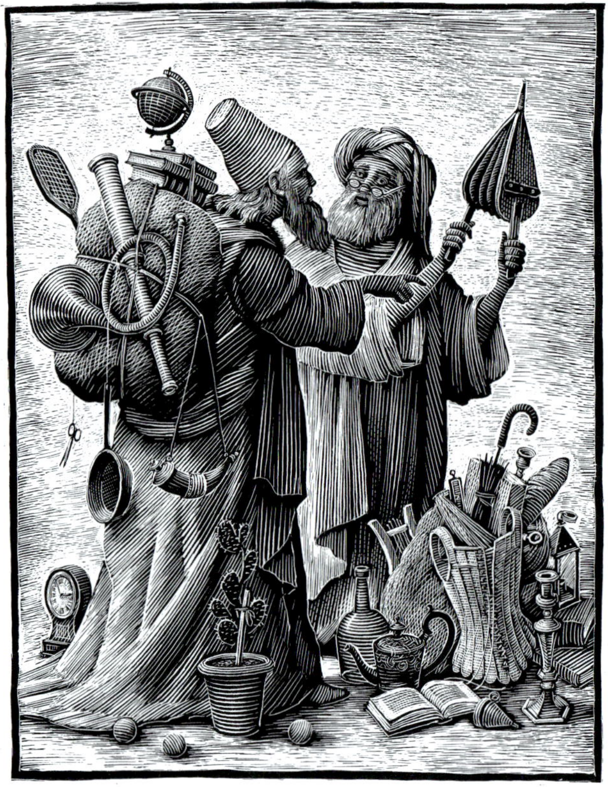

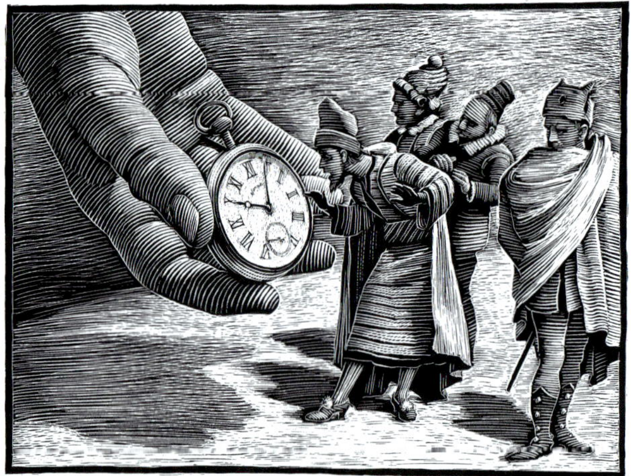

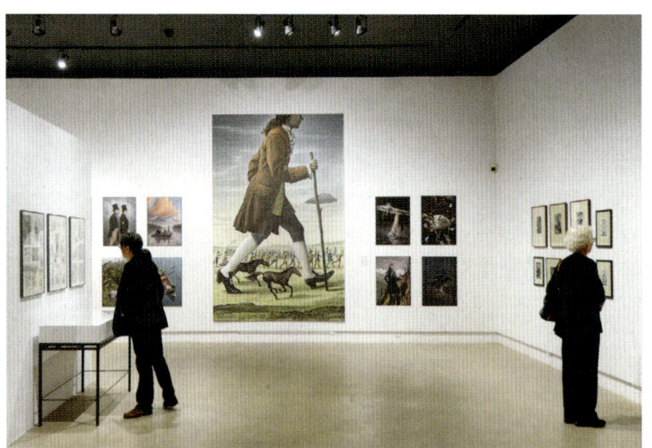

Gulliver's Travels follows Jonathan Swift's title character through four fantastic "voyages" to parts of the Earth that were highly exotic in the 18th-century imagination. The title page of the 1726 first edition reads: *Travels into Several Remote Nations of the World, In Four Parts, By Lemuel Gulliver, First a Surgeon, and then a Captain of Several Ships.*

Everyone knows the first voyage — to Lilliput, where the inhabitants measure no higher than Gulliver's ankles. The illustration possibilities with this contrast of scale are endless. And irresistible — almost all the cover illustrations for the various editions throughout the book's history focus on a scene from Lilliput.

Looking for a road less travelled, I decided that I didn't want a Lilliput scene for my cover. But which of the other voyages to use? In Brobdingnag the scale device is reversed — Gulliver is six inches tall in a world of giants. The flying island of Laputa is inhabited by magicians devoted to mathematics and music, but utterly unable to apply their learning to any practical use. In the country of the Houyhnhnms, Gulliver encounters a utopian civilization of horses (they have no word in their language for lying) — and a race of humans in their basest form, called "Yahoos," who are kept as servants and livestock.

My little moment of epiphany came when I gave up trying to choose between them. I realized that I could combine elements from all four voyages on the cover. The idea for this came from the text: Swift gives us an introduction in the form of letters from Captain Gulliver. The premise is that they were written by the elderly Gulliver years after the four voyages — a reminiscence, like the structure of Coleridge's *The Rime of the Ancient Mariner*.

I went for the fantastical — a towering figure too large to fit on the page. In a 2013 exhibition of my work at Gallery Stratford, I included this image as a blowup that pushed the scale of the figure taller than the 12-foot ceiling of the room.

The black-and-white interior illustrations focussed on the individual voyages. I also included maps of the far-flung locations of each voyage, drawn to look like ship's charts from the 18th-century, as chapter openers. *Gulliver* is a complex work that gets darker and bleaker as it progresses. Young readers will certainly enjoy their visit to Lilliput; the satire of the third and fourth voyages will be waiting for them when they're a little older.

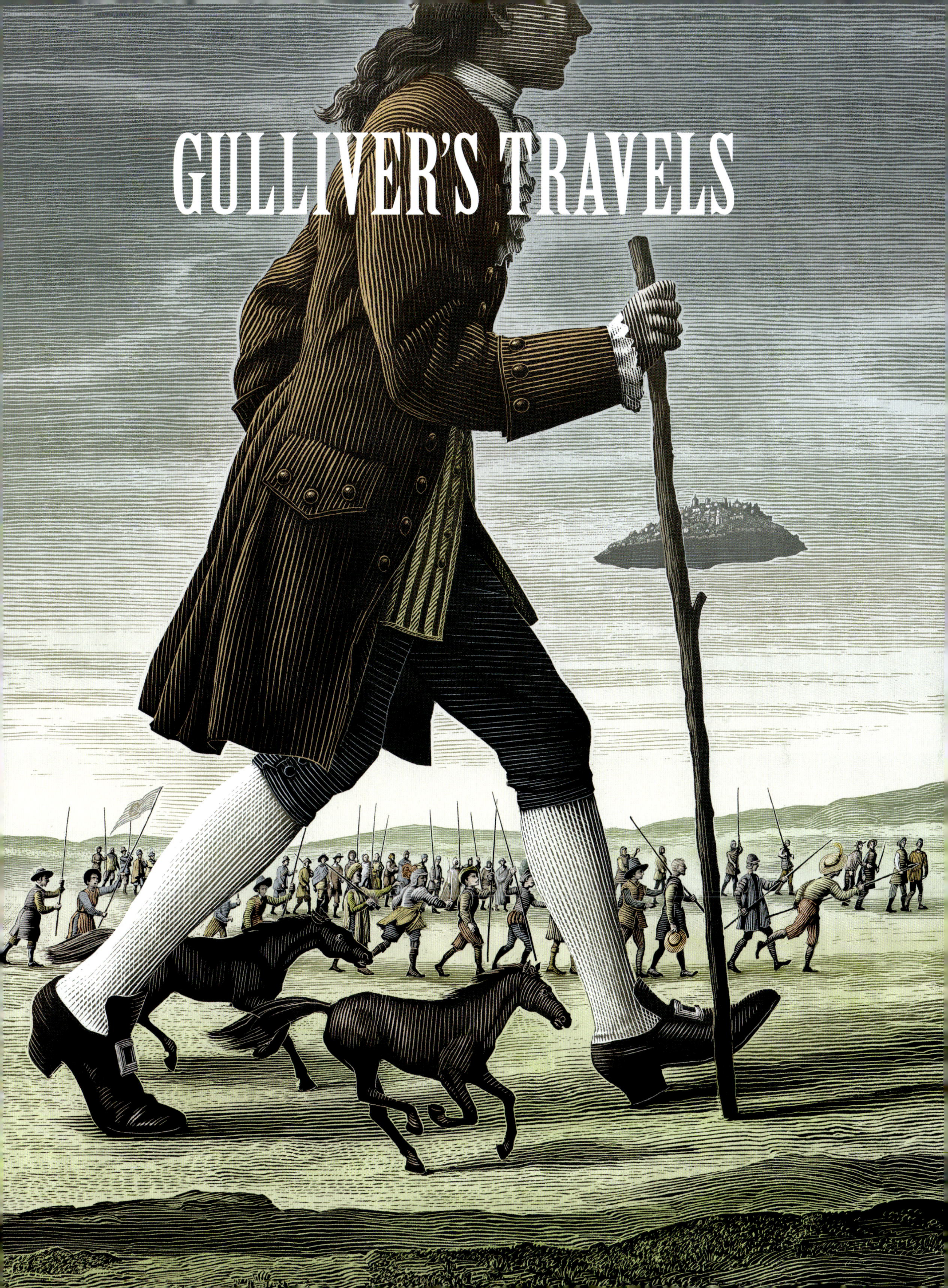
GULLIVER'S TRAVELS

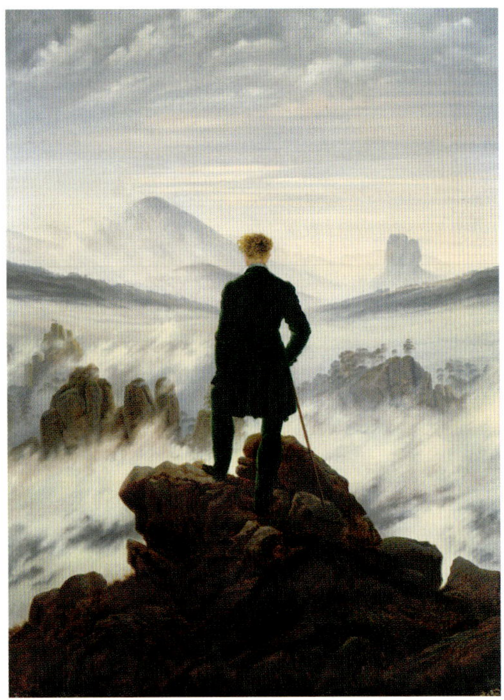

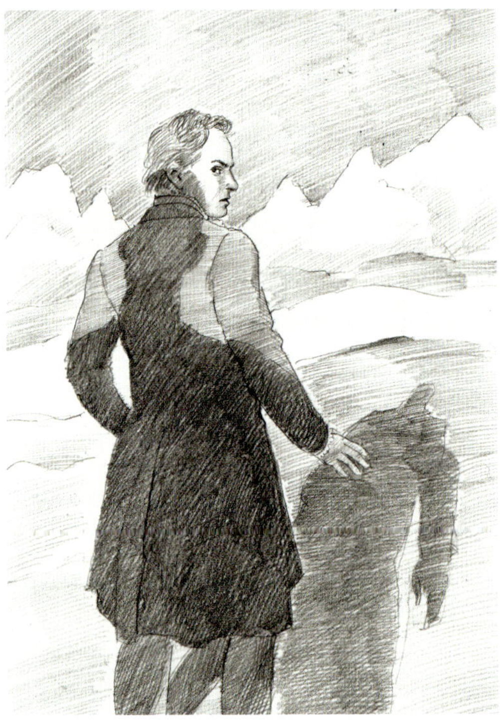

The Wanderer Above the Sea of Fog, 1818, by Caspar David Friedrich; Scott's pencil sketch for the *Frankenstein* cover.

The 19-year-old Mary Shelley and her husband Percy spent the cold, rainy summer of 1816 on Lake Geneva with their pal Lord Byron. They amused themselves by reading German ghost stories, then challenged each other to write their own tales of the supernatural. Mary's entry in this cozy Gothic contest was *Frankenstein*.

Her subtitle, *The Modern Prometheus*, refers to the Greek myth of the ambitious and rebellious Titan who plays with fire and gets burned when Zeus catches up with him. Written in the early years of the Industrial Revolution, Shelley's story is a cautionary tale of modern man's "over-reaching" his place in nature.

Victor Frankenstein is the gifted young scientist who discovers the secret of galvanism — returning a corpse (in this case, an assemblage of body parts) to life. From the moment Victor successfully imbues his Creature with life, he realizes that he has gone too far. I wanted the cover to suggest Victor's horror at what he has done.

I also wanted to show troubled relationship between Victor and his creation — so the Creature had to be present as well. They spend much of the book playing cat-and-mouse — the Creature seems to be lurking around every corner as Victor travels across Europe — hence the idea of "shadowing" or stalking. I wanted to avoid giving away what "the monster" actually looks like, so we see Victor from the Creature's point of view. I played with overlapping their two shadows on the ground to suggest a deformed figure — in one early sketch Victor's arm and the shadow arm on the ground are intentionally mismatched.

The novel begins and ends on a ship frozen in Arctic ice fields, and the big confrontation scene takes place in a dramatic Alpine landscape. When I think of mysterious, atmospheric, Romantic vistas, Caspar David Friedrich comes immediately to mind — he was my reference for the landscape, including the bare trees and crows.

In 2017, the Art Gallery of Ontario presented a fascinating exhibition of the film director Guillermo del Toro's eclectic career, entitled *At Home with Monsters*. The last room was devoted to *Frankenstein* on the occasion of the bicentennial of the first publication of the novel on January 1, 1818. One enormous wall was wallpapered with the covers from over 600 different editions, modern and historical, from all over the world. I smiled when I spotted mine, and thought, to myself, "I finally made it into the AGO."

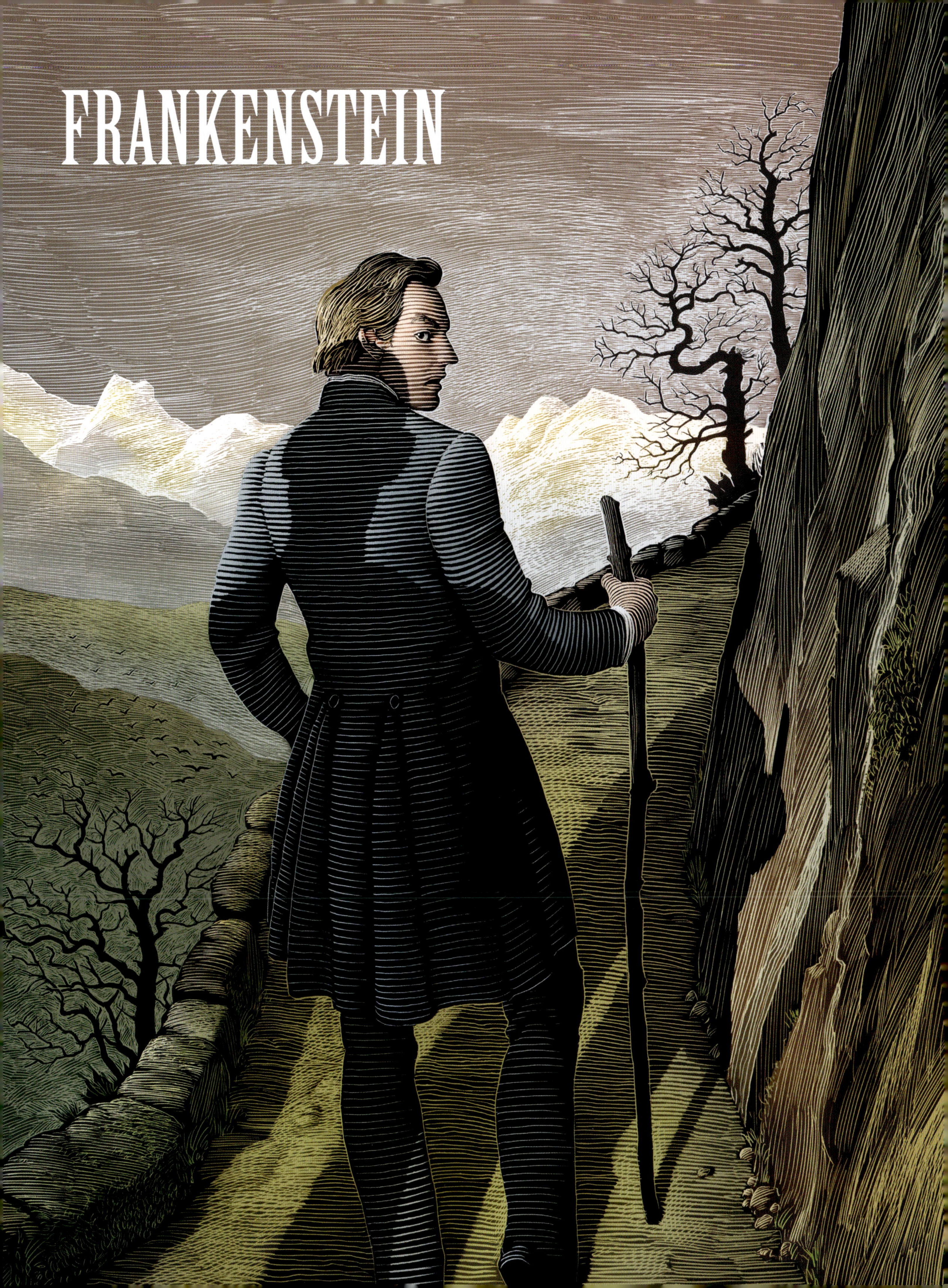
FRANKENSTEIN

Bram Stoker's immortal novel is unique in its format. It unfolds entirely in epistolary format — the story is told through a long series of letters and diary entries written by the novel's main characters, with detail filled in by various newspaper clippings, and ship's logbook entries. We know it's fake news but the documentary format is vividly effective at making supernatural phenomena seem very real.

The story opens with Jonathan Harker's visit to Castle Dracula in Transylvania, to complete the formalities of the Count's purchase of a property in England called Carfax Abbey. Carfax Abbey is fictional, but it was inspired by a visit Bram Stoker made to Whitby Abbey in North Yorkshire. Stoker sets an entire sequence of scenes in and around Whitby, although he doesn't mention the Abbey specifically. (St. Mary's Church and its graveyard, which are immediately beside the Abbey, are mentioned by name in the story.) Dracula arrives in England at Whitby, on a ship that lands during a violent storm, laden with dozens of boxes of earth from home which allow him to sleep during daylight hours.

I love Stoker's idea that the Count's "lair" is a ruined church, so I based my illustration of Carfax Abbey on the real Whitby Abbey. The ruined Gothic window in the west facade is a gaping hole that resembles a huge mouth frozen into a scream. It's not hard to imagine the broken tracery mullions as fangs.

Dracula was published in 1897. The west facade of Whitby Abbey sustained major damage during a German naval attack in December 1914. It took some digging to find a pre–World War One photo of the Abbey to confirm that the window I drew looked exactly the same as when Stoker saw it.

Dracula can change his shape at will — he turns into a bat, a wolf, a dog, even a mist. I pictured him (in human form) standing on one of the Abbey's turrets — where no mere mortal could ever climb, let alone keep their balance. He's half Batman, half Wim Wenders' angel perched on edge of the skyscraper, looking down at the city in *Wings of Desire*.

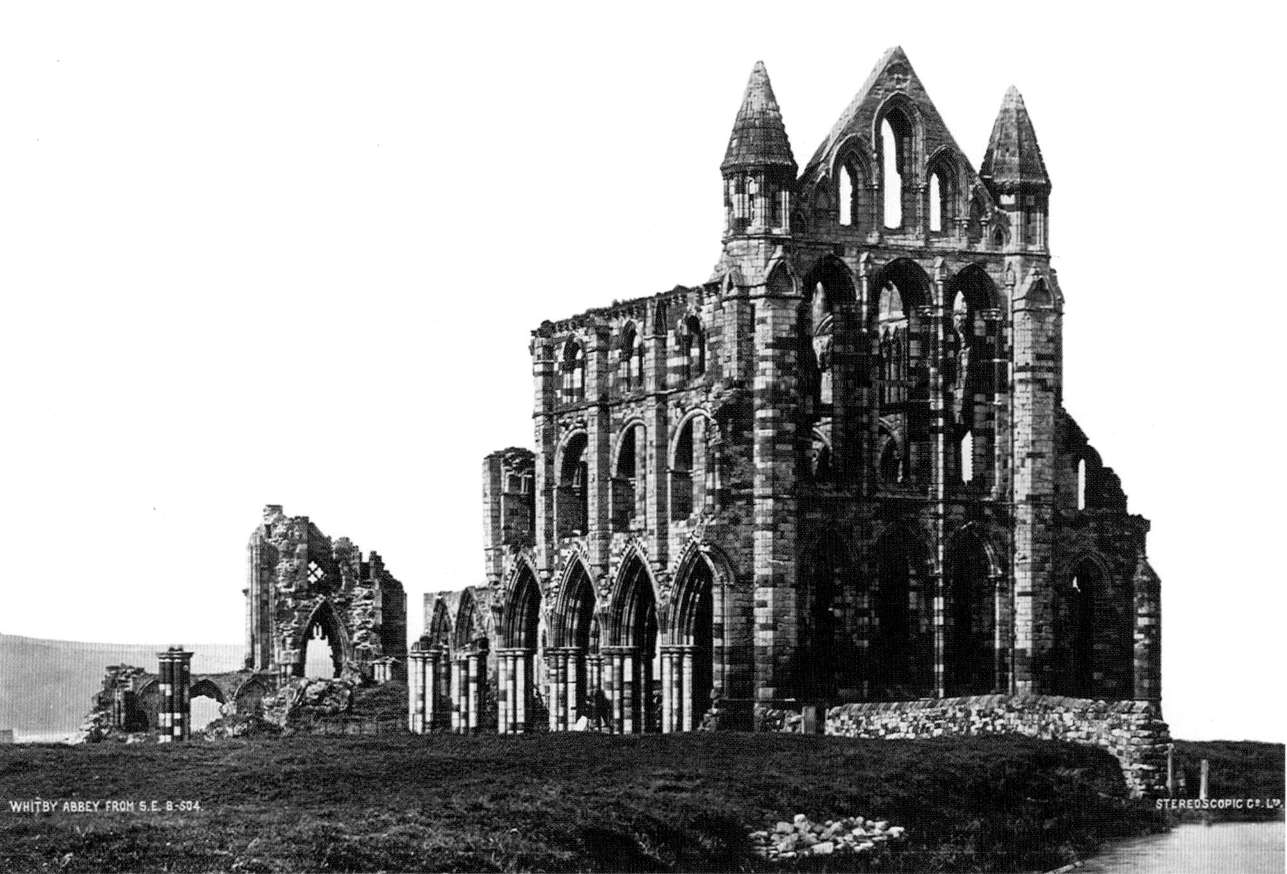

The west facade of Whitby abbey (viewed from the opposite direction as the cover illustration) in a 19th-century photograph by the London Stereoscopic Company Ltd.

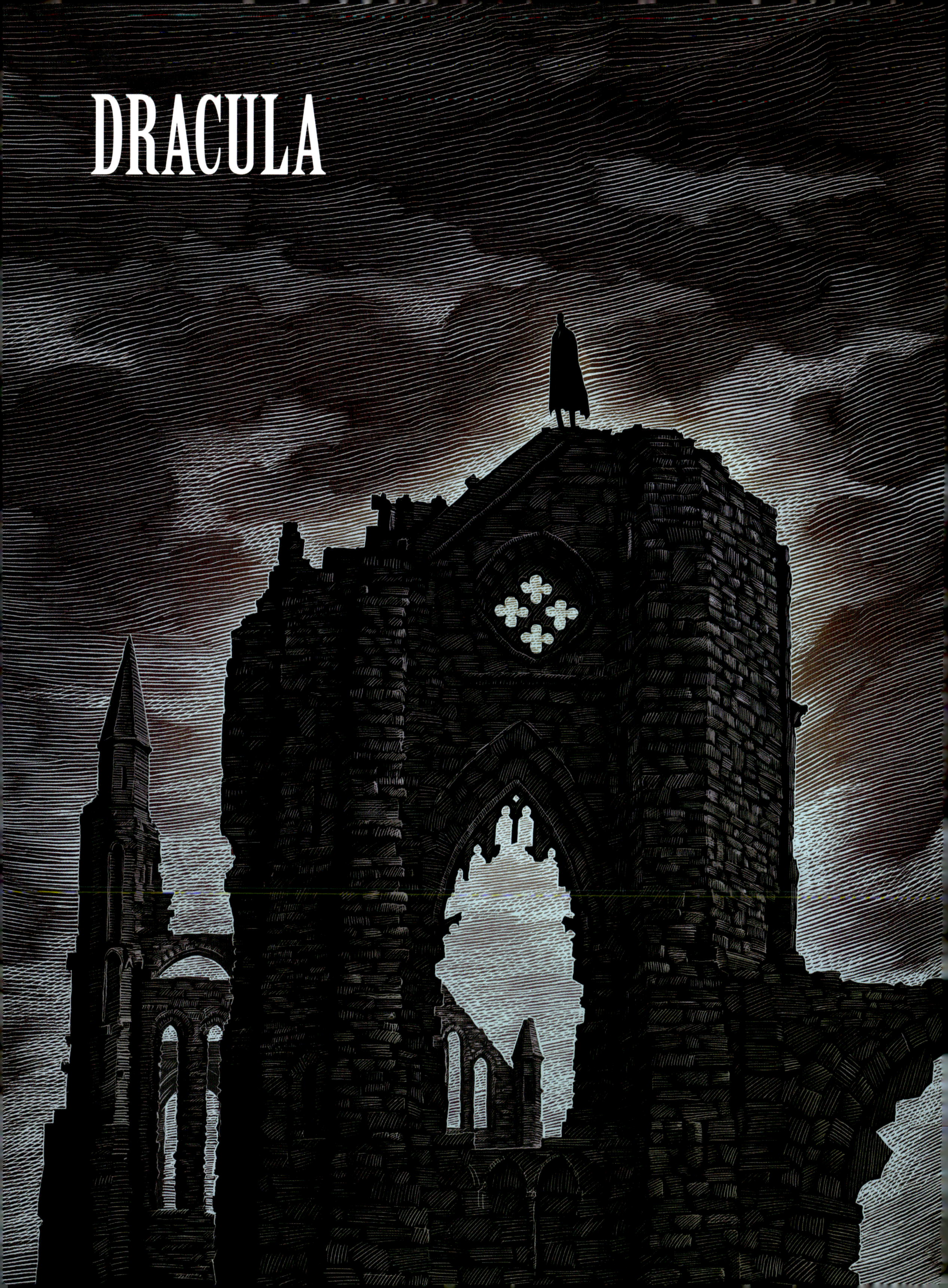

DRACULA

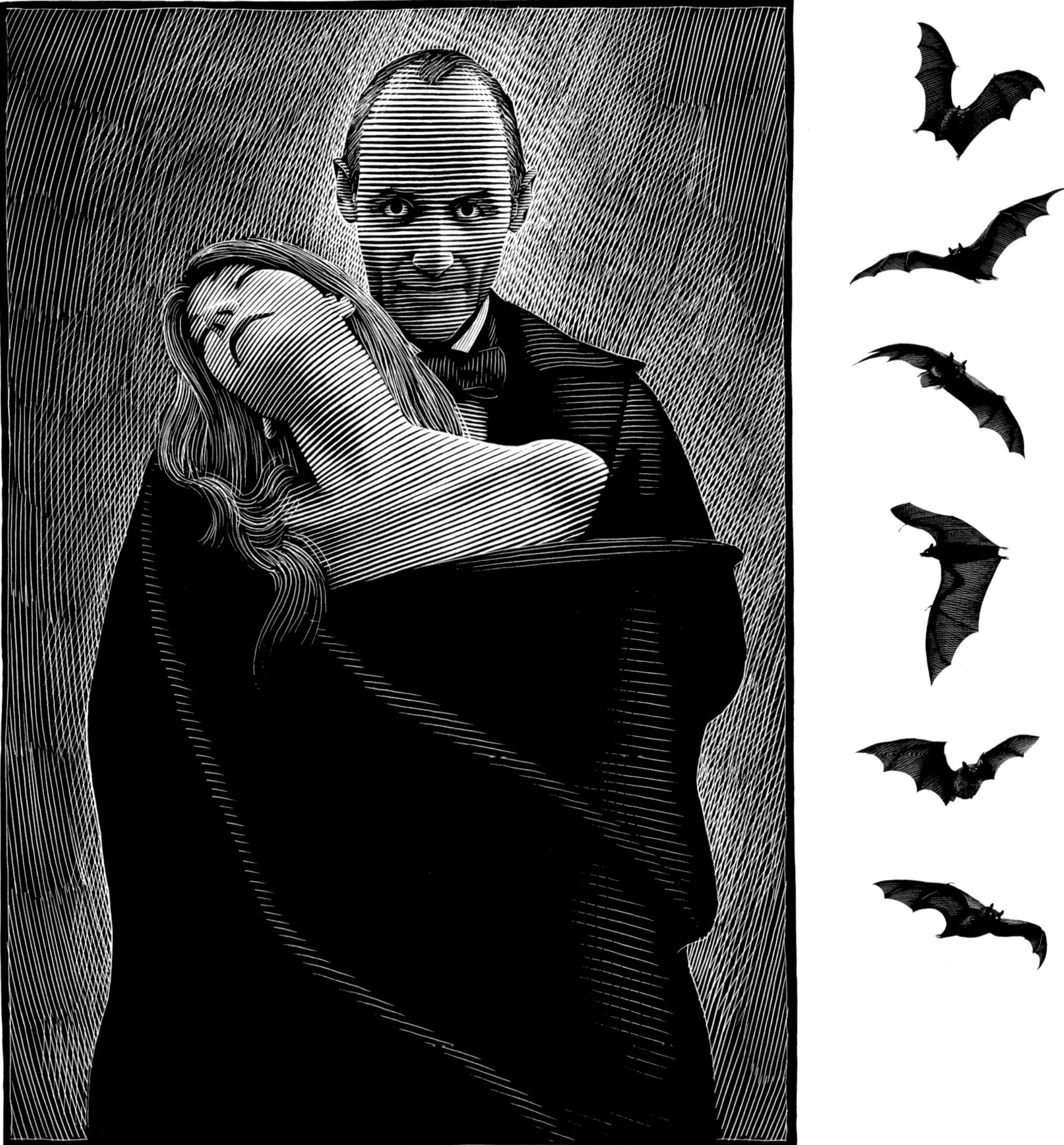

Bram Stoker's physical description of Count Dracula perfectly fits Stratford actor Colm Feore, who very graciously agreed to model for this project with his wife Donna Feore as Mina. My portrait illustration of Renfield, who eats flies hoping to obtain their life force for himself, is based on an photograph by Nadar, part of a series in 1854 documenting physiological experiments in which the facial muscles were stimulated by electrical current. My model for Professor Van Helsing was Manfred Meurer, who runs a wonderful antiquarian book shop in Stratford. Paul Nolan was my model for Jonathan Harker, reflected in his shaving mirror (the Count is standing behind him — this scene originated the legend that vampires cast no reflection in a mirror). The bats in various flying poses were used as chapter heads throughout the book.

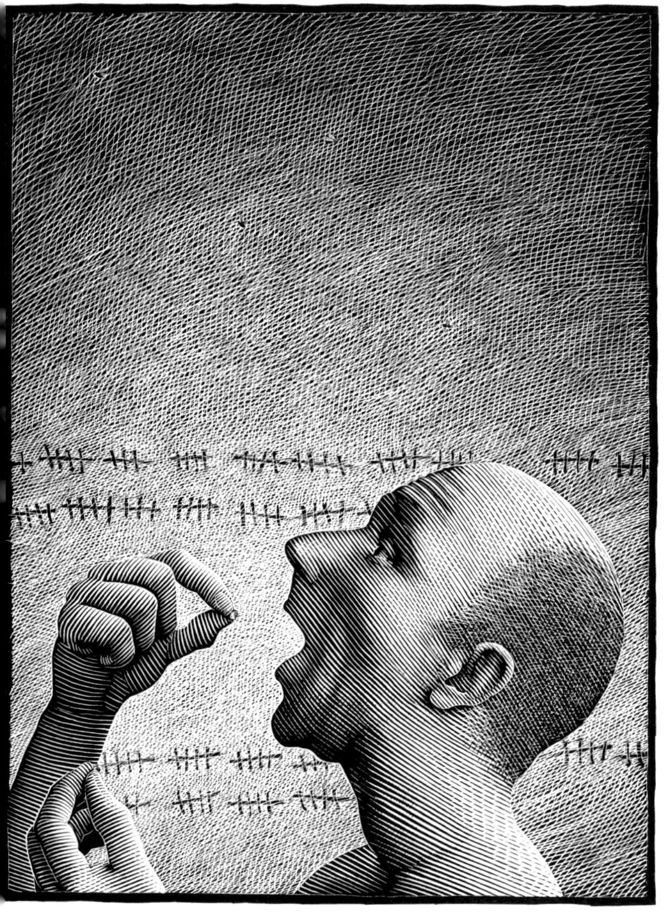

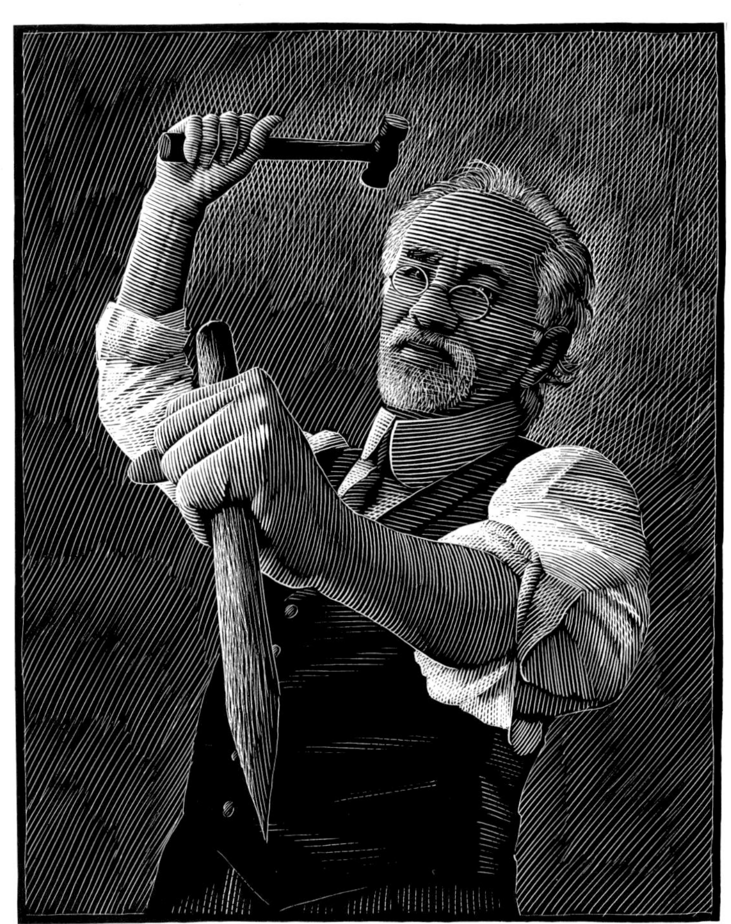

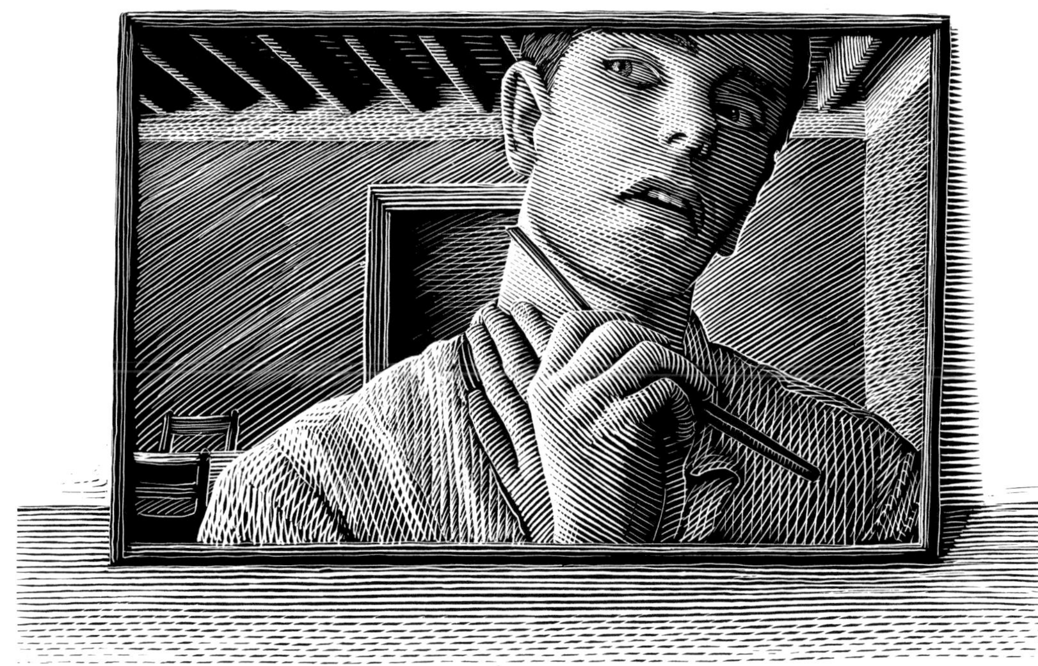

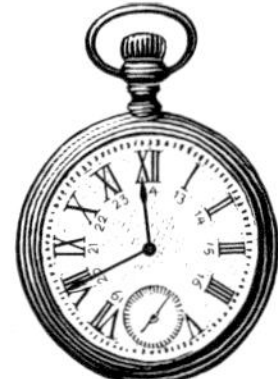
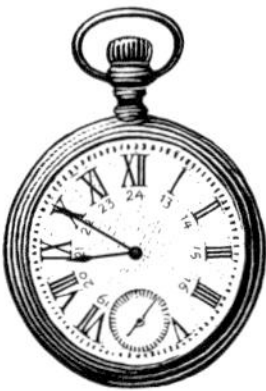
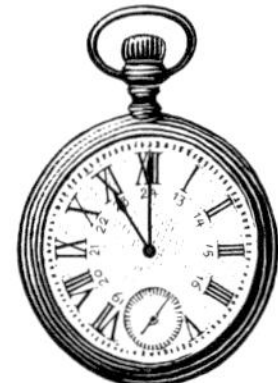
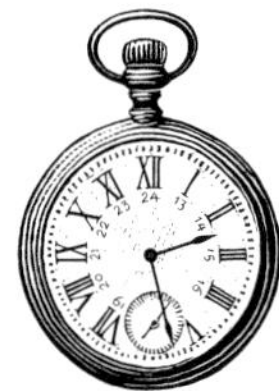
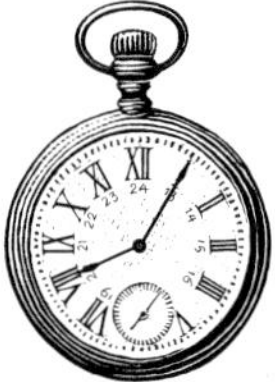
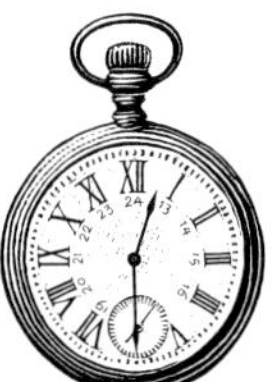
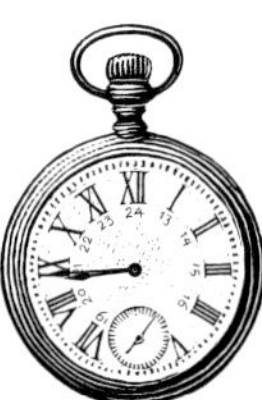

When the assignment came in for *Around the World in Eighty Days*, my first thought for a great cover was the scene in which Phileas Fogg crosses Europe in a hot-air balloon. When I read the Jules Verne novel, however, I was taken aback to discover that scene does not exist! Fogg travels from London to Paris and across Europe by rail in a single, uneventful paragraph. The hot-air balloon was an invention of the popular 1956 film starring David Niven, the young Shirley MacLaine and a host of celebrities in cameo roles. Back to the drawing board.

A trip around the world in 80 days would have seemed an impossibility in 1872, but Phileas Fogg accepts this challenge on a £20,000 wager (equivalent to £2,500,000 in today's currency). His race against the clock is crowded with obstacles. The rail line across India turns out to be unfinished, so Fogg purchases an elephant and sets off through the jungle. A sledge rigged with a sail saves the day when a train connection is missed in snowy Nebraska. The steamer crossing the Atlantic runs out of coal, so the masts, decks and cabins are dismantled and burned to keep pressure in the boilers. But none of these episodes is longer than a couple of pages — so putting any one scene on the cover seemed to miss the arc of the whole story.

I took this cover in a more playful direction than others in the Sterling series — Fogg is literally dashing around the world, pocket watch in hand, on a gigantic Victorian library globe. (I picture a globe like this one in the corner of the reading room at the Reform Club, where the wager begins and ends.) Fogg is circling the globe from west to east — a little clue to the ingenious happy ending that Jules Verne springs on the reader (and Fogg himself) in the final chapter of the story.

The text is peppered with reference to schedules, departures and arrivals — specific times of day and night. I used Fogg's watch for the chapter heads, but each one is different: I changed the hands to reflect a specific time reference in each chapter.

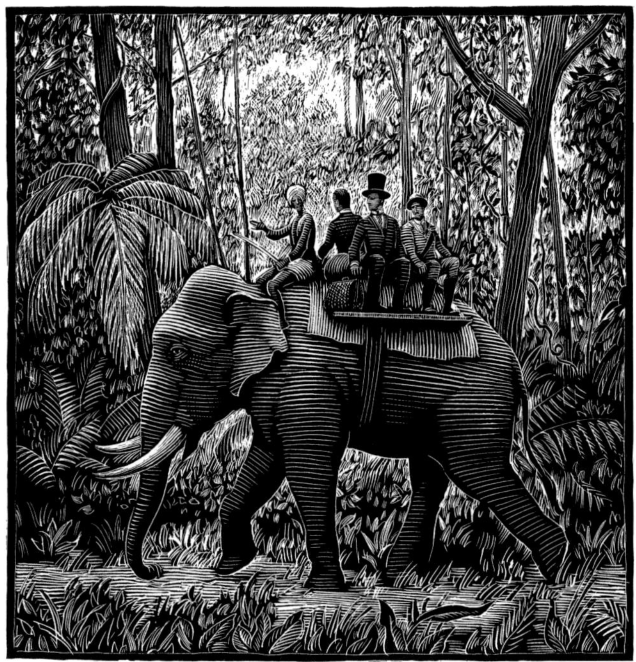

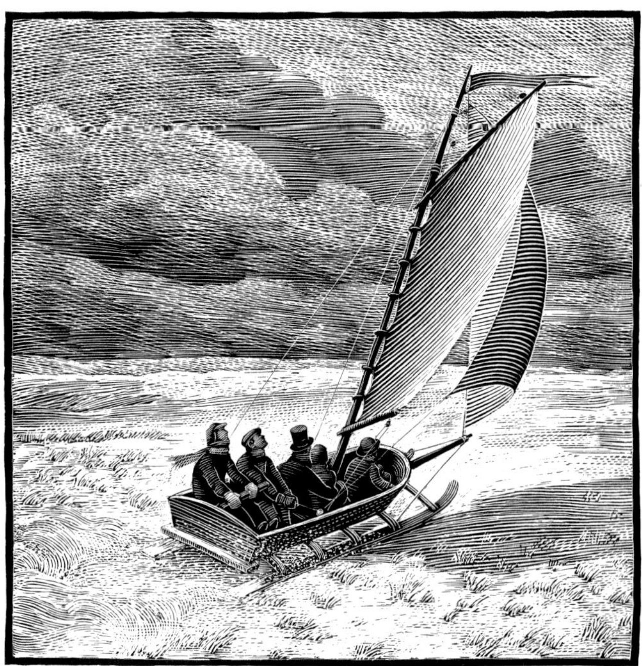

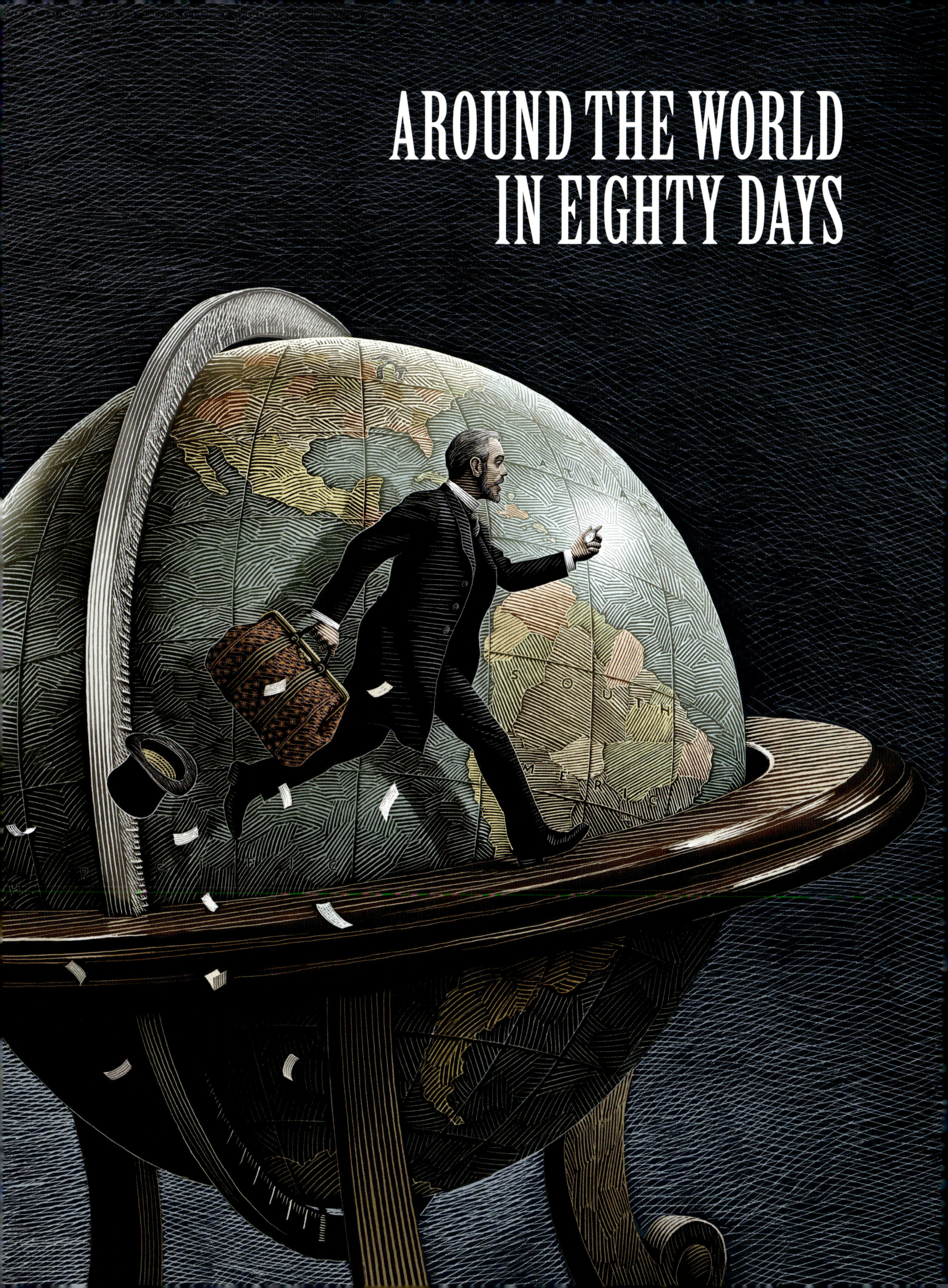
AROUND THE WORLD
IN EIGHTY DAYS

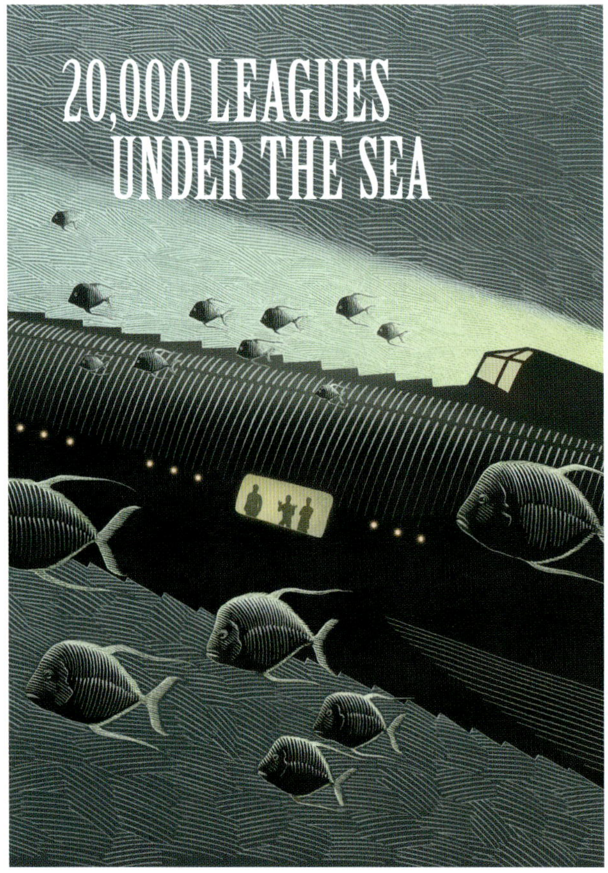

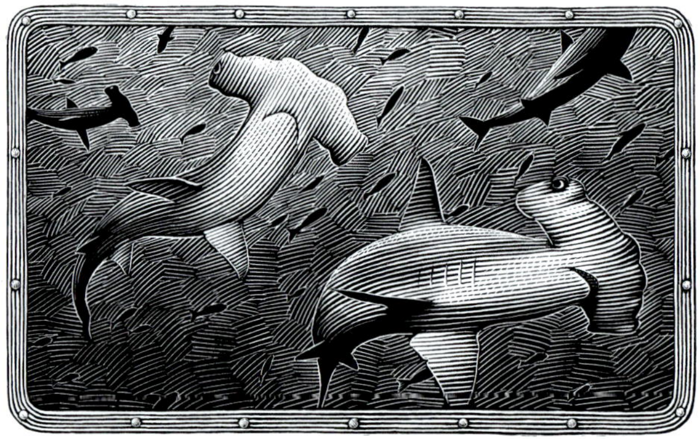

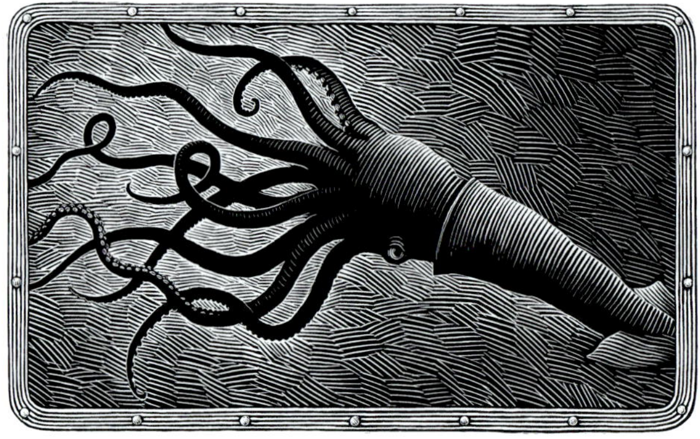

The Sterling Classics series includes Jules Verne's famous subterranean and submarine adventure stories. *Voyage au centre de la Terre* was published in 1864, inspired by a scientific publication the previous year entitled *Geological Evidences of the Antiquity of Man*. Verne's story concerns a professor and his nephew who decipher an ancient coded message written by a legendary Icelandic alchemist who claims to have discovered a passage to the centre of the Earth. Following these instructions, they descend into the crater of an extinct volcano in Iceland, with a resourceful local hunter as their guide. They encounter strange and wonderful phenomena, become separated and reunited, run out of water but tap into an underground river. They discover a vast subterranean sea, build a raft and set sail, and observe prehistoric plants and animals (sometimes too close for comfort) — before finally being shot out of a live volcano in southern Italy.

I wanted my cover to convey the dramatic scale of the underground landscape and a sense of adventure and danger. The three explorers use Ruhmkorff induction coils as their underground light source — an early form of portable electric lamp invented only a few years before the story was written. Verne tells us that they are extraordinarily bright — scratchboard is great for lighting effects so I imagined three silhouetted figures at the top of the page, descending into darkness.

This underground light source is similar to descriptions of the brilliant searchlight of Captain Nemo's famous, fantastic submarine *Nautilus* in *20,000 Leagues Under the Sea*, which was assigned by Sterling a year before *Journey*. Here again the protagonists are a trio of Europeans. The narrator is Professor Arronax, a famous marine biologist; his faithful assistant Conseil and a hot-tempered Canadian master harpooner accompany him on the adventure. These three figures are visible in silhouette through the rectangular window on the cover.

For the black-and-white interior illustrations, I picked a range of marine creatures mentioned in the text — vast schools of fish, sea turtles, stingrays, sharks and giant squid. They are all framed in that same rectangular window, now from the inside looking out. This takes readers inside the submarine where they can join our protagonists in observing the marvels of the oceans.

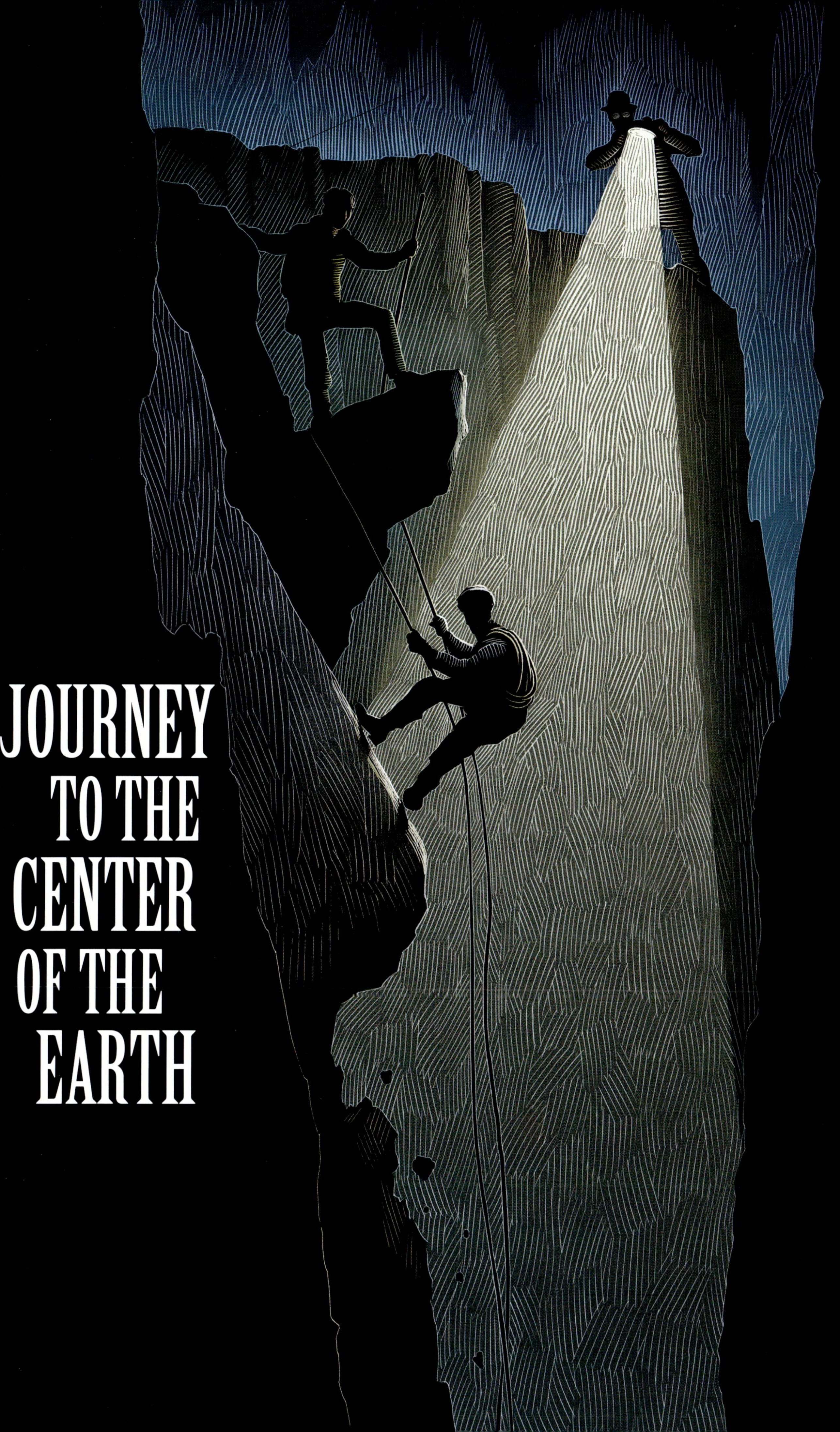

JOURNEY TO THE CENTER OF THE EARTH

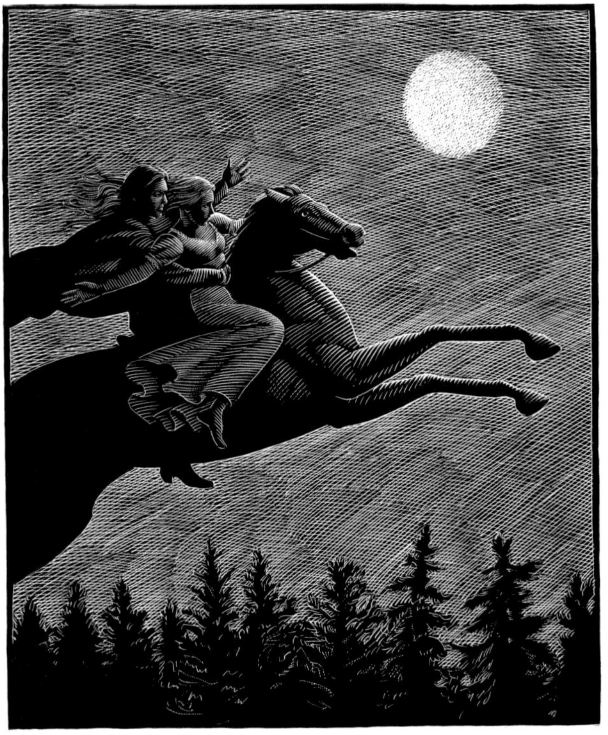

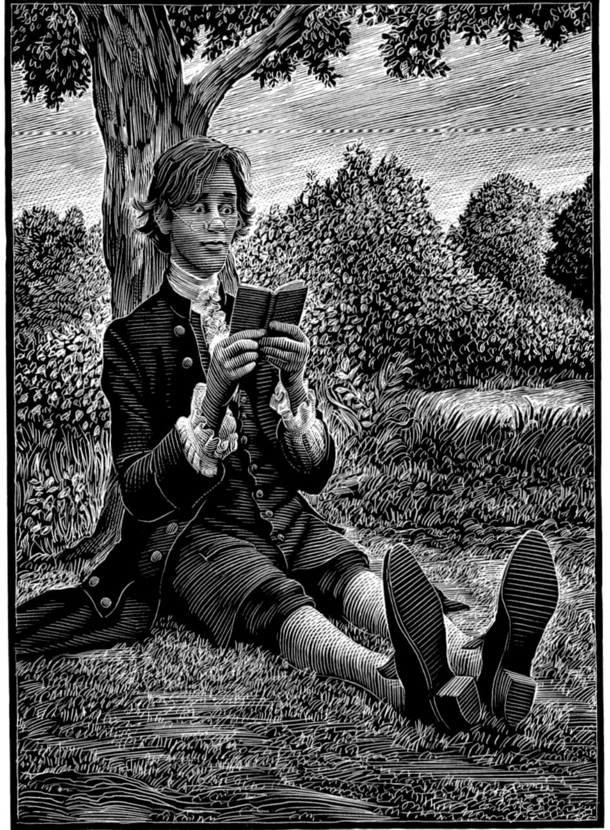

Sterling assigned an edition of four Washington Irving stories in 2012 — each with "local legends" of the supernatural woven through them. The best known is "The Legend of Sleepy Hollow" (written in 1820), so it went on the cover. Ichabod Crane is the village schoolteacher and choir director; Irving describes him as a scarecrow who has escaped the cornfield. Crane has spent the evening at a house party where the other guests have been telling ghost stories, including the local legend of a Headless Horseman. The party breaks up late at night, and Crane rides home through the woods on a "broken-down plow-horse" named Gunpowder. Crane's worst fears are realized when he meets the Horseman, and a terrifying pursuit ensues — the Horseman matching Gunpowder's stride precisely. It's the literary equivalent of Wagner's "The Ride of the Valkyries."

Irving implies in an epilogue that the Horseman was only a figment of Crane's overly suggestible imagination (or perhaps the prank of a romantic rival) — so I drew the Horseman as if he is Crane's own cast shadow. I tried to make the Horseman look completely real as Crane sees him — but from the reader's perspective this provides a less paranormal explanation.

"The Spectre Bridegroom" (1819) is a lovely sleight-of-hand trick. It's a great yarn about a princess who is wooed by a handsome but evidently not-of-this-world suitor. He has been observed late at night hanging out under her bedroom window and, to the deep concern of her family, she seems to fancy him. The story reaches its climax when she is discovered missing from her chamber one morning. My illustration shows the princess being abducted, just as her family has imagined — but Irving has crafted a delightful surprise ending that upsets all expectations.

Also included are "Rip Van Winkle" (1819) — I got to draw the title character both before and after his 20-year nap! — and a Faustian tale called (1824).

I worked with some great models on this project — playwright and director Amiel Gladstone was my Ichabod Crane. Stephen Gartner played young Rip Van Winkle. J. Todd Adams was Tom Walker and Scott Wentworth, Old Scratch.

I devised a series of pumpkins as chapter heads, including horns for the Devil and a toothless grin for old Rip Van Winkle — comic versions of the much scarier jack-o-lantern on the cover.

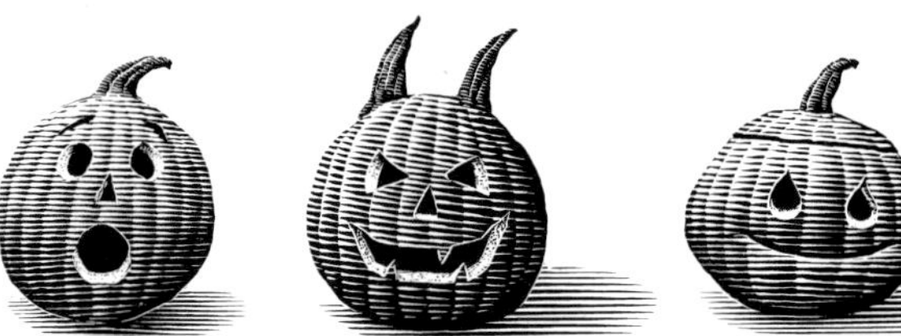

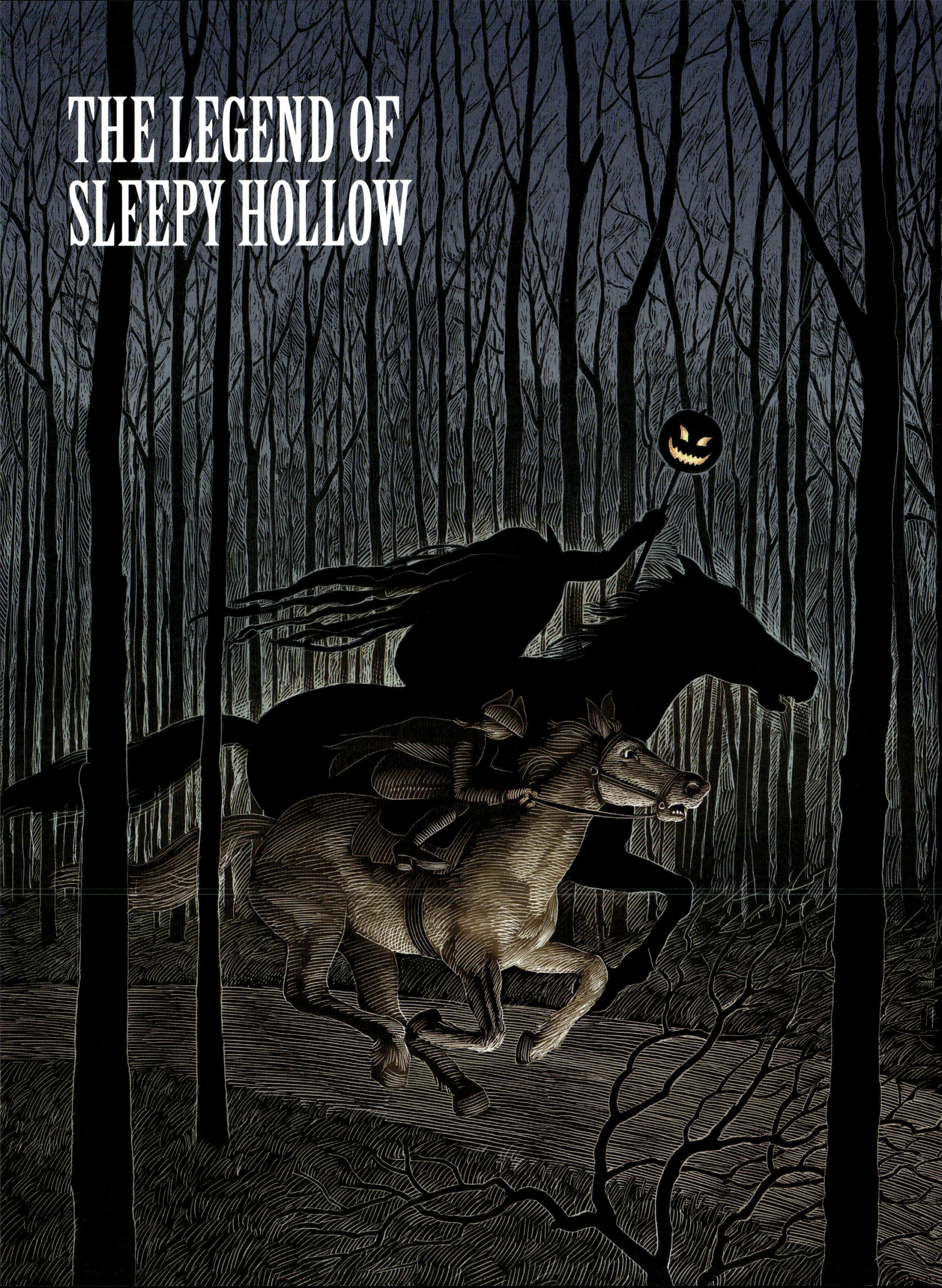
THE LEGEND OF
SLEEPY HOLLOW

Sterling assigned a volume of 25 stories by Edgar Allen Poe in 2010. Death is never far away in Poe, so a graveyard seemed like an obvious cover idea — a grouping of monuments and headstones of different shapes and sizes, loosely representing the variety of stories in the collection. I was in London with Christina earlier that year, and we visited Highgate Cemetery. I had made both sketches and photographs, not knowing that the Poe assignment was lurking around the corner. When it came in, I realized that I already had my picture research.

"The Raven" is not included in this collection (it's a poem, not a story) but this overgrown graveyard scene was a little too *nature morte* and needed a focal point, so I added a big crow alighting on a funeral monument.

"The Oval Portrait" is a story of an artist who asks his beautiful young wife to pose for him. Jealous that her husband's art distracts him from her, she agrees and sits for him. Day after day, week after week, he becomes more obsessed by capturing her likeness perfectly. He spends all his time looking at the painting and not at her. When he finally finishes the painting and looks up, he realizes that she is dead. I have a small collection of portrait miniatures and used them to set up a *trompe l'oeil* composition with the shadow of the story's narrator falling across the portrait in the oval frame that he has become obsessed by.

The violence in "Berenice" is not revealed until the end of the story when we learn that the object of the narrator's obsessive "monomania" is his beloved's teeth. In my first pencil sketch I had arranged Berenice's 32 teeth like an expensive pearl necklace in a jewellery box. The editor felt that I had moved too far away from Poe's text about the teeth falling out of a box along with some dentistry tools and scattering across the floor. I acquiesced and changed the composition.

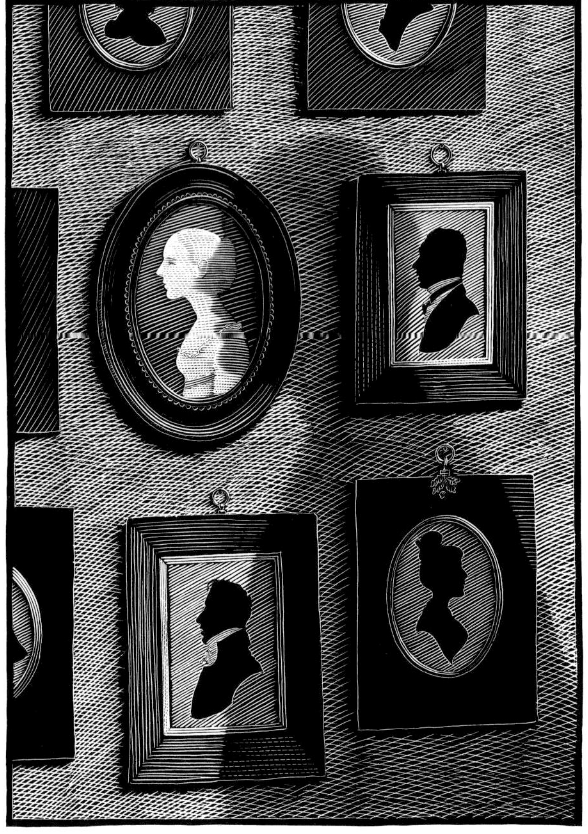

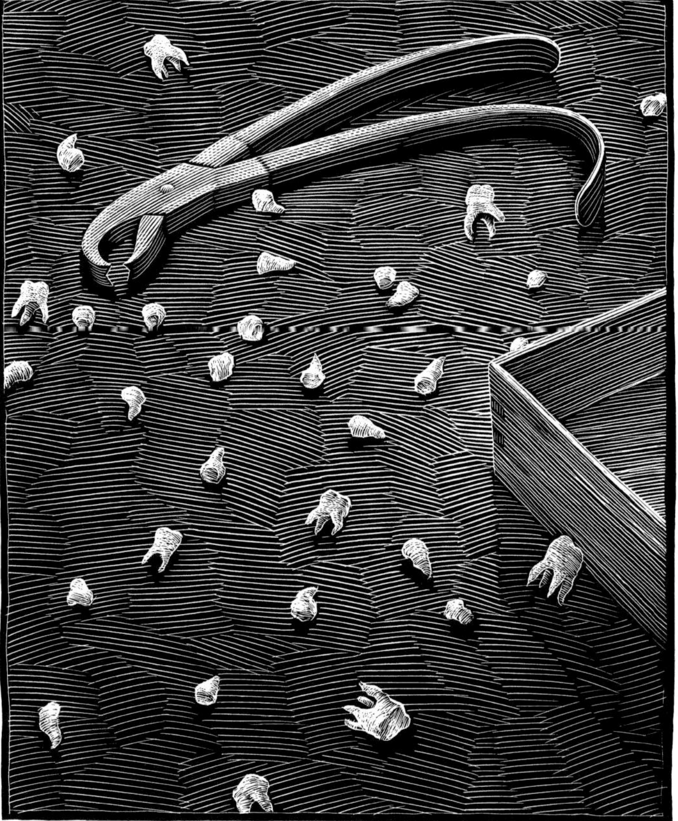

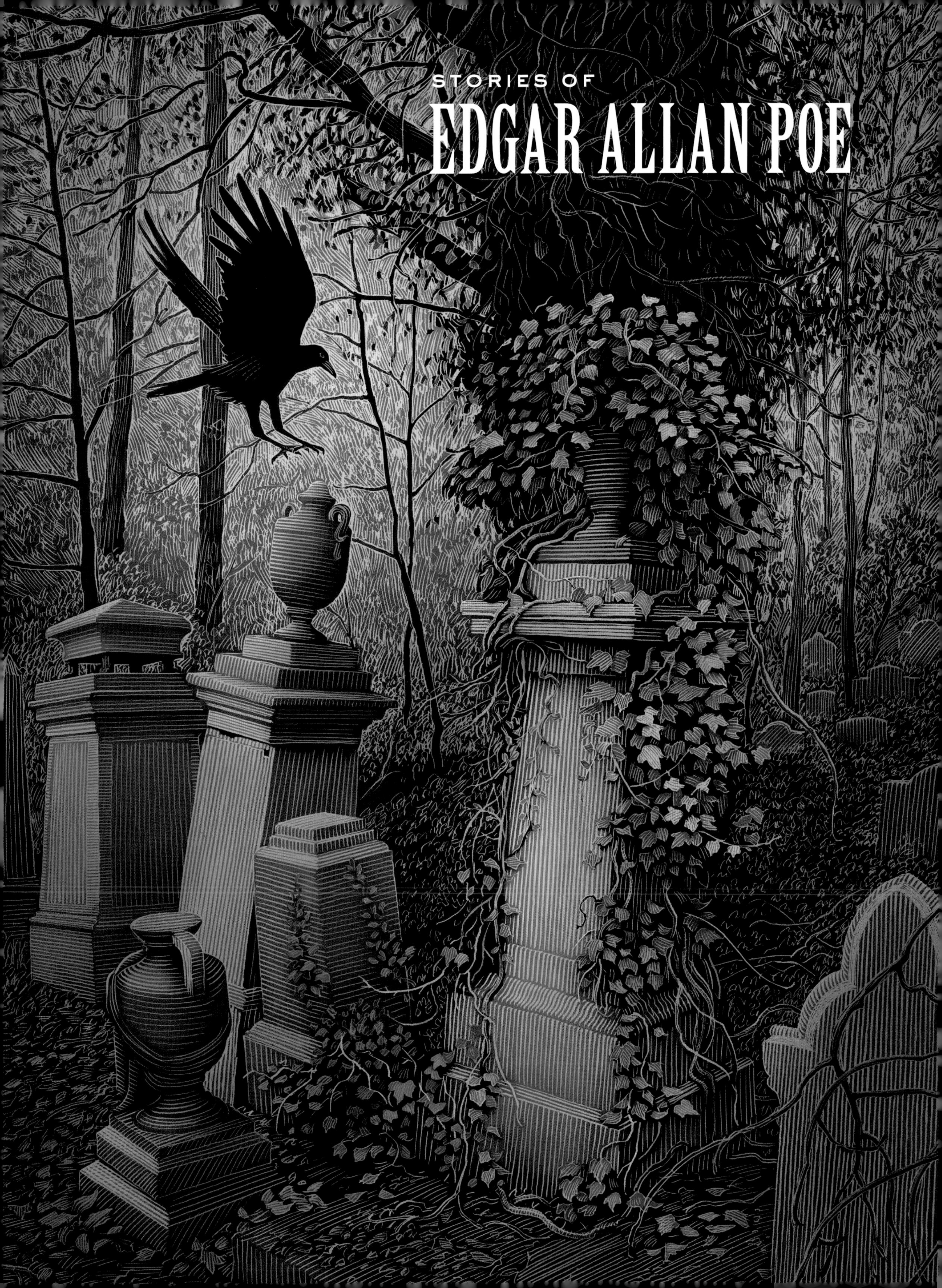
STORIES OF
EDGAR ALLAN POE

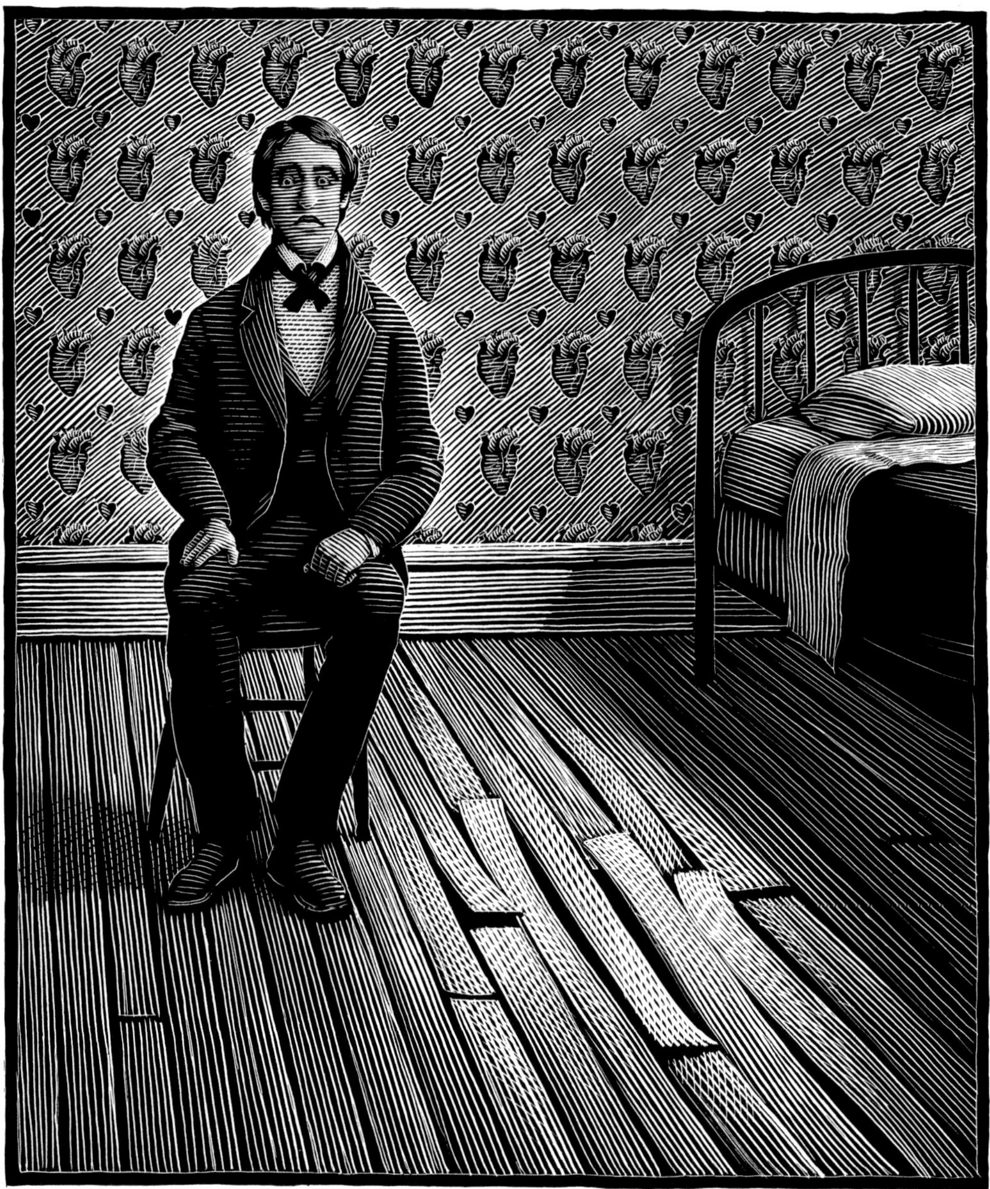

"The Tell-Tale Heart" was my favourite illustration for this book but it never appeared in print because of a (rare) disagreement with the editors over interpretation. The narrator has murdered an old man with a pale, filmy "vulture eye" and disposed of body under the floorboards of the victim's bedroom. He almost pulls off a perfect crime, but as he chats up the police officers investigating the old man's disappearance, he imagines that he hears his victim's heart beating from under the floor. The sound grows louder and louder until, in a panic, he blurts out a confession.

I wanted to find a visual equivalent for the sound of the old man's heart thumping away inside the narrator's head. I showed the floorboards coming alive, twisting and buckling with each heartbeat over the spot where the body is buried.

In Poe's text, the floorboards look normal and the police hear nothing unusual. I felt that readers are sophisticated enough to appreciate surrealism and metaphor (and hoped they would notice my wallpaper made of anatomical hearts). But the editors were uncomfortable with anything other than a literal depiction of the scene and the illustration was cut from the book.

Sterling invited me to pick the individual stories in the book for interior black-and-white illustrations. At the top of my list was "The Pit and the Pendulum." Rather than showing the narrator tied down, as many illustrators have done, my perspective is looking up towards the machinery in the ceiling — putting the reader in the narrator's (extremely uncomfortable) position. It's a Spanish Inquisition story so my razor-sharp pendulum is reminiscent of a censer, incense wafting behind it on each heavy swing back and forth.

Not many of Poe's stories have a sense of humour, but "Some Words with a Mummy" is a delight — you can sense his tongue placed firmly in his cheek. My illustration shows the moment that the mummy is brought back to life by the application of electrical current from a galvanic battery.

A *memento mori* — a symbolic reminder of mortality — was used as the spine icon and chapter heads.

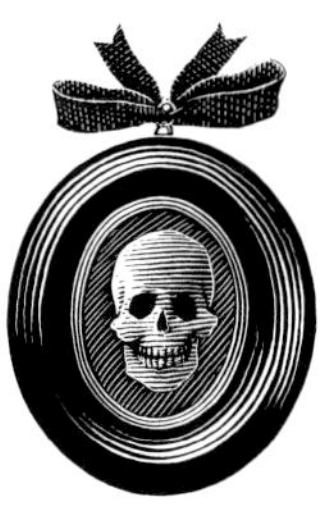

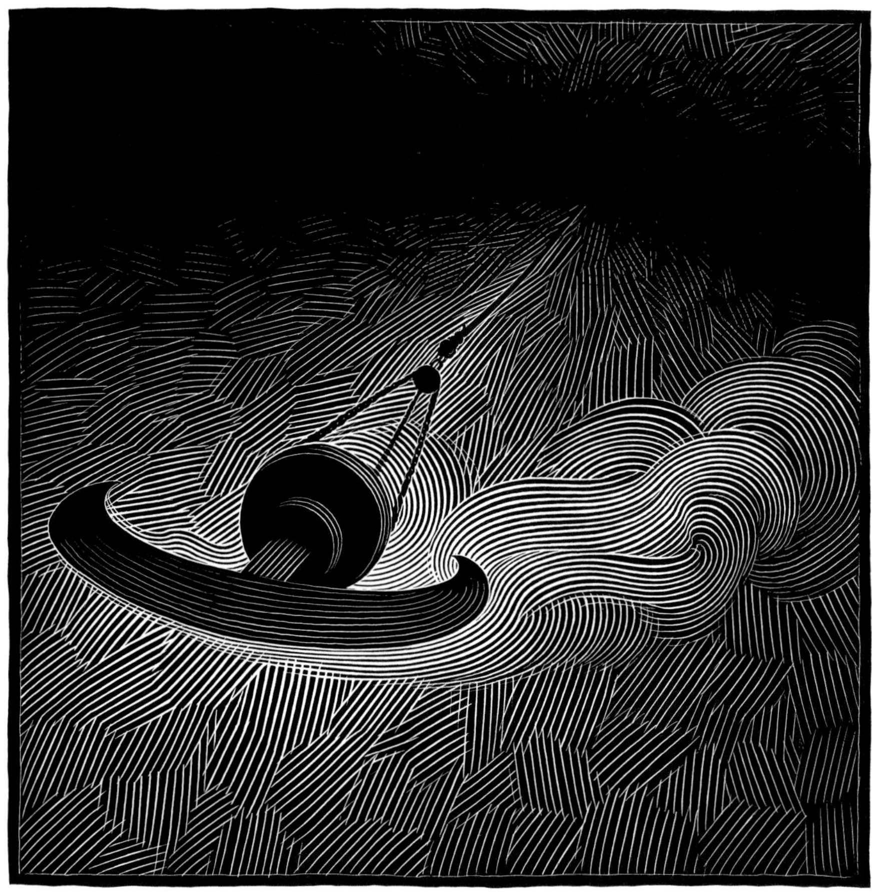

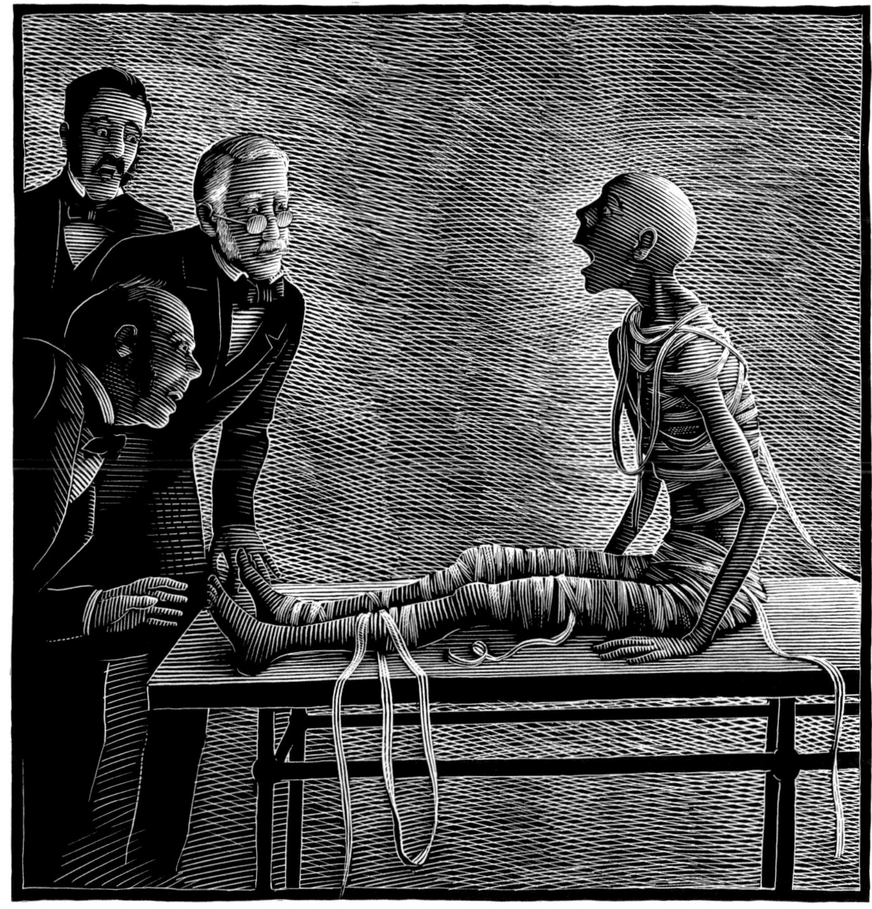

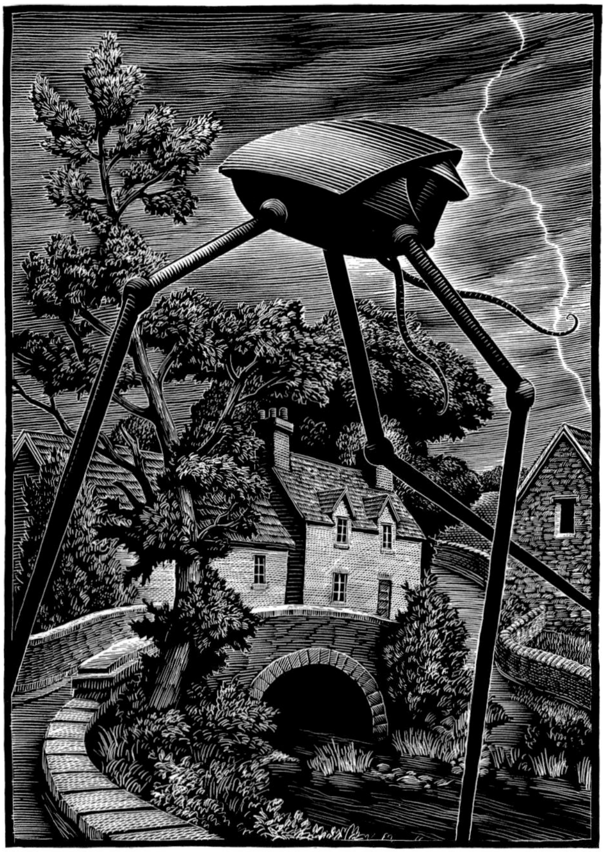

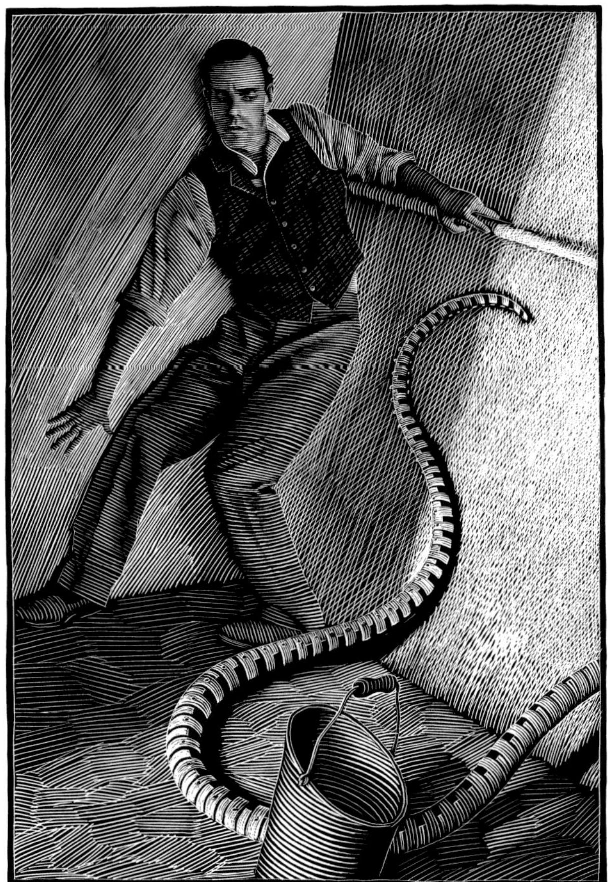

I'm embarrassed to admit that I was more familiar with *The War of the Worlds* from the famous 1938 Orson Welles radio broadcast, set in New Jersey and New York City, than with the original H.G. Wells novel, set in England in 1898. I can blame only my suburban American upbringing.

Wells was one of the first authors to imagine a conflict between man and an extraterrestrial race. I had tackled one antecedent in the Sterling Classics series — the Laputa section of Jonathan Swift's 1727 *Gulliver's Travels*. My Jules Verne covers had verged into sci-fi territory, but *War of the Worlds* was the first time we had tackled a story with full-scale death and destruction.

It seemed to me that the front cover needed a dynamic battle scene. In Chapter x, the narrator finds himself caught in the path of a one of the Martian fighting machines — he narrowly escapes being stepped on — and gives us a vivid description:

> And this Thing I saw! ... A monstrous tripod, higher than many houses, striding over the young pine trees, and smashing them aside in its career; a walking engine of glittering metal, striding now across the heather; articulate ropes of steel dangling from it, and the clattering tumult of its passage mingling with the riot of the thunder.

This scene gave me the idea of putting the reader in the narrator's position, looking straight up at a Martian fighter against a firey sky on the front cover.

The unnamed narrator is a philosophically inclined writer, so it's easy to think of him as Wells himself — who was 32 in 1898. I asked Paul Nolan to be my model for a couple of the interior illustrations. In one scene, the narrator is holed up in a ruined house, hiding from the Martians. He's in the company of a deranged curate, who ends up as a Martian's lunch. A tentacle from one of the Martian machines comes poking around the room — at one point it touches the terrified narrator's boot, but moves on — so I saw him backed into a corner trying to keep out of its way.

Wells lived in Woking, Surrey — the initial Martian landing takes place on Horsell Common, near Wells' house. While working on the story, he evidently enjoyed shocking his friends with details of destroying his neighbourhood with the Martian heat ray. A large public sculpture of a tripod fighting machine, entitled *The Martian*, was designed and built in downtown Woking by artist Michael Condron in 1998, the centennial of the novel. Photos of Condron's sculpture provided helpful reference photos for my illustrations.

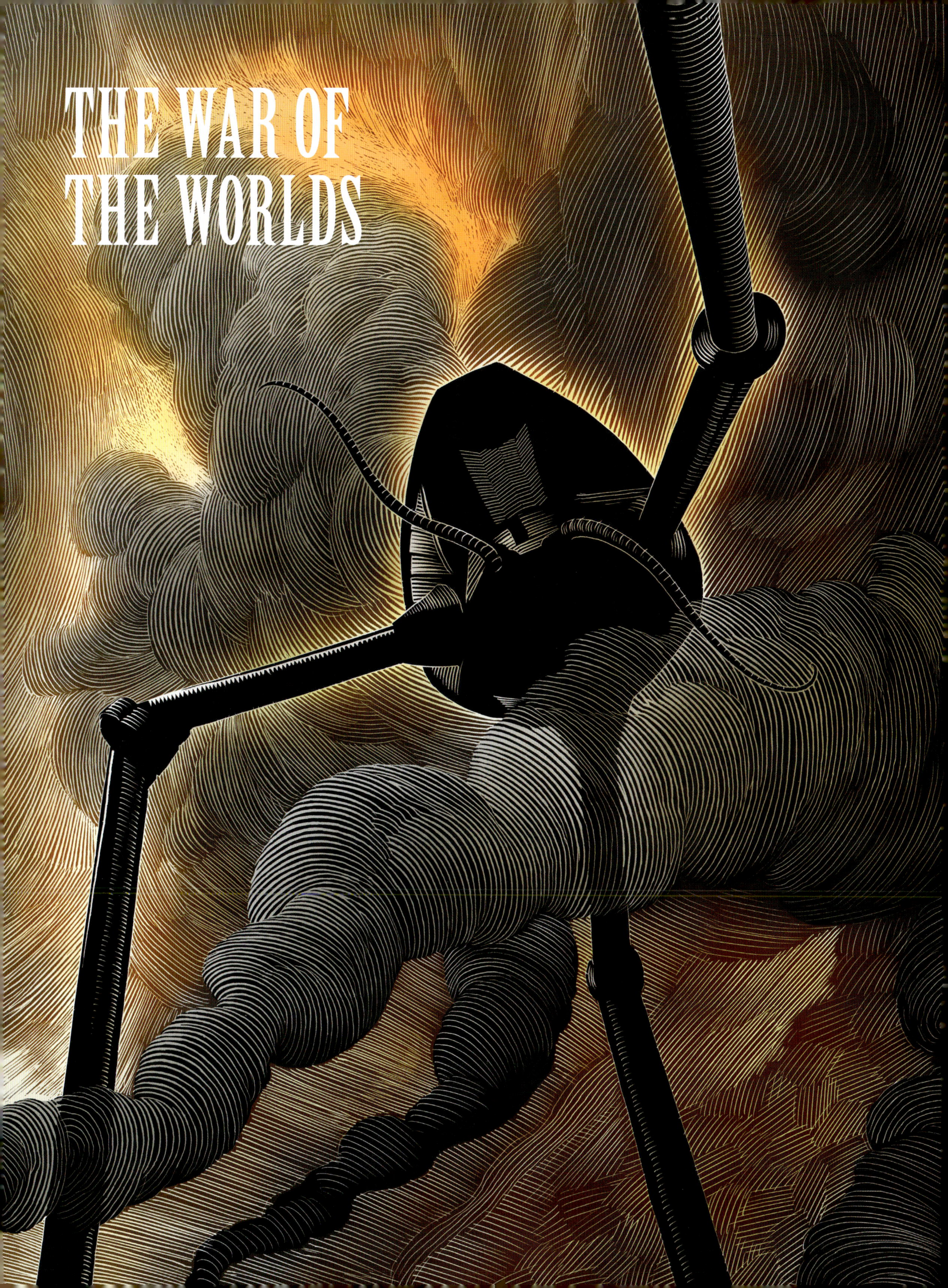
THE WAR OF
THE WORLDS

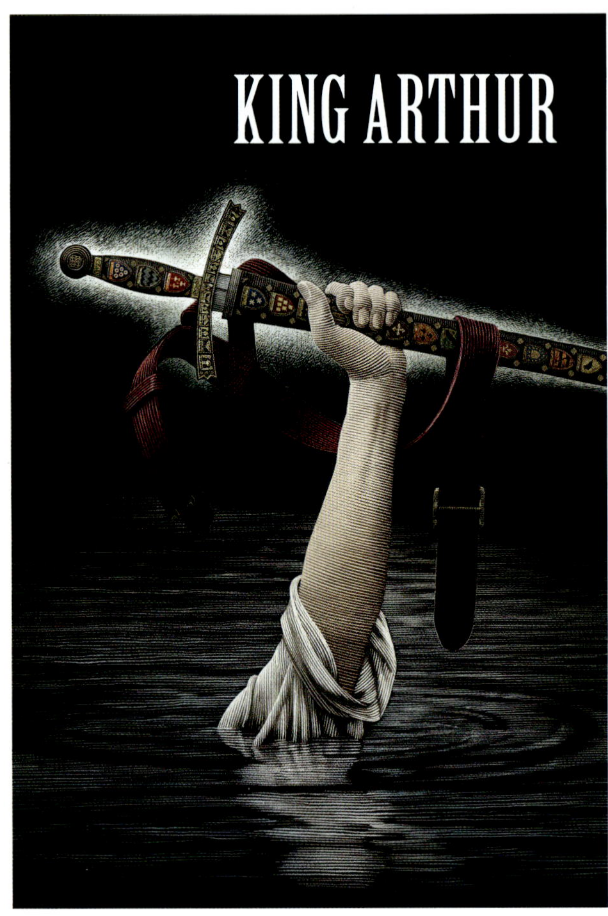

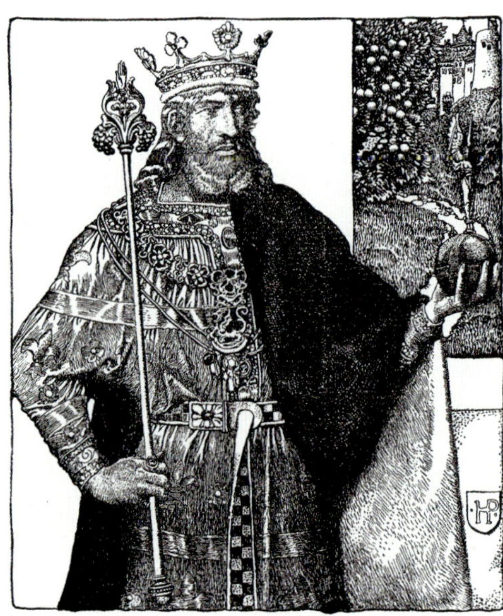

Illustration by Howard Pyle for *The Story of King Arthur and His Knights*, 1903.

Chris Curry, an art director at *The New Yorker*, called in 2013 to commission an illustration to accompany a review by Adam Gopnik of a newly published epic poem by J.R.R. Tolkien entitled *The Fall of Arthur*. Tolkien had written this in the 1930s but set it aside to work on *The Hobbit*. I proposed an underwater view of a crown, sinking into the dark depths of the sea. Everyone loved it, and the art was finalized (and paid for) — but unfortunately it was never published. As it was explained to me, Mr. Gopnik simply had too much on his plate with other assignments and the review never got written. So this is the first time the drawing has appeared in print.

I loved everything Arthurian as a kid — I remember a grade-school knight costume for Halloween with a breastplate hammered out of an industrial-size tin can (I soaked off the cherry pie filling label), a football helmet covered with aluminum foil, finished off with an ostrich plume. I memorized the original cast recording of *Camelot*. So I was thrilled when Sterling assigned *King Arthur* in 2005. But there was a hitch. The text selected by the Sterling editors (probably because it was public domain) was written by Howard Pyle.

If anyone could be considered the Father of American Illustration, it would be Howard Pyle (1853–1911). In a letter to his brother Theo, Vincent van Gogh mentioned that Pyle's work "struck me dumb with admiration." An Anglophile, Pyle wrote and illustrated four volumes of Arthurian stories, plus *The Merry Adventures of Robin Hood*, and a story of knighthood under Henry VI called *Men of Iron*. Pyle's text has a certain charming staginess — "Know, thou unkind knight, that I have come hither for no other purpose than to do battle with thee" — but feels concordant with his brilliant, stylish drawings. To me, the Victorian text and pictures are inseparable; being asked to "re-illustrate" Pyle seemed a dubious task.

That being said, I wasn't about to turn down the assignment. *The Story of King Arthur and His Knights* is a lengthy book (Sterling shortened the title for this edition, but not the text). Pyle includes the memorable scene in which Arthur receives his legendary sword, *Excalibur*, from the mystical Lady of the Lake, and this seemed ideal for the cover. Pyle details the heraldry on the shields of the knights from the many fiefdoms and minor kingdoms, which are unified for the first time under Arthur's reign. Pyle describes *Excalibur* as beautifully and elaborately decorated with gold and precious stones. I imagined the mythical sword blazoned with "the arms of the realm."

To draw convincing water reflections, I needed very specific reference. I called my photographer friend David Cooper in Vancouver, and he shot his daughter in a swimming pool, her arm raised out of the water holding a broom handle!

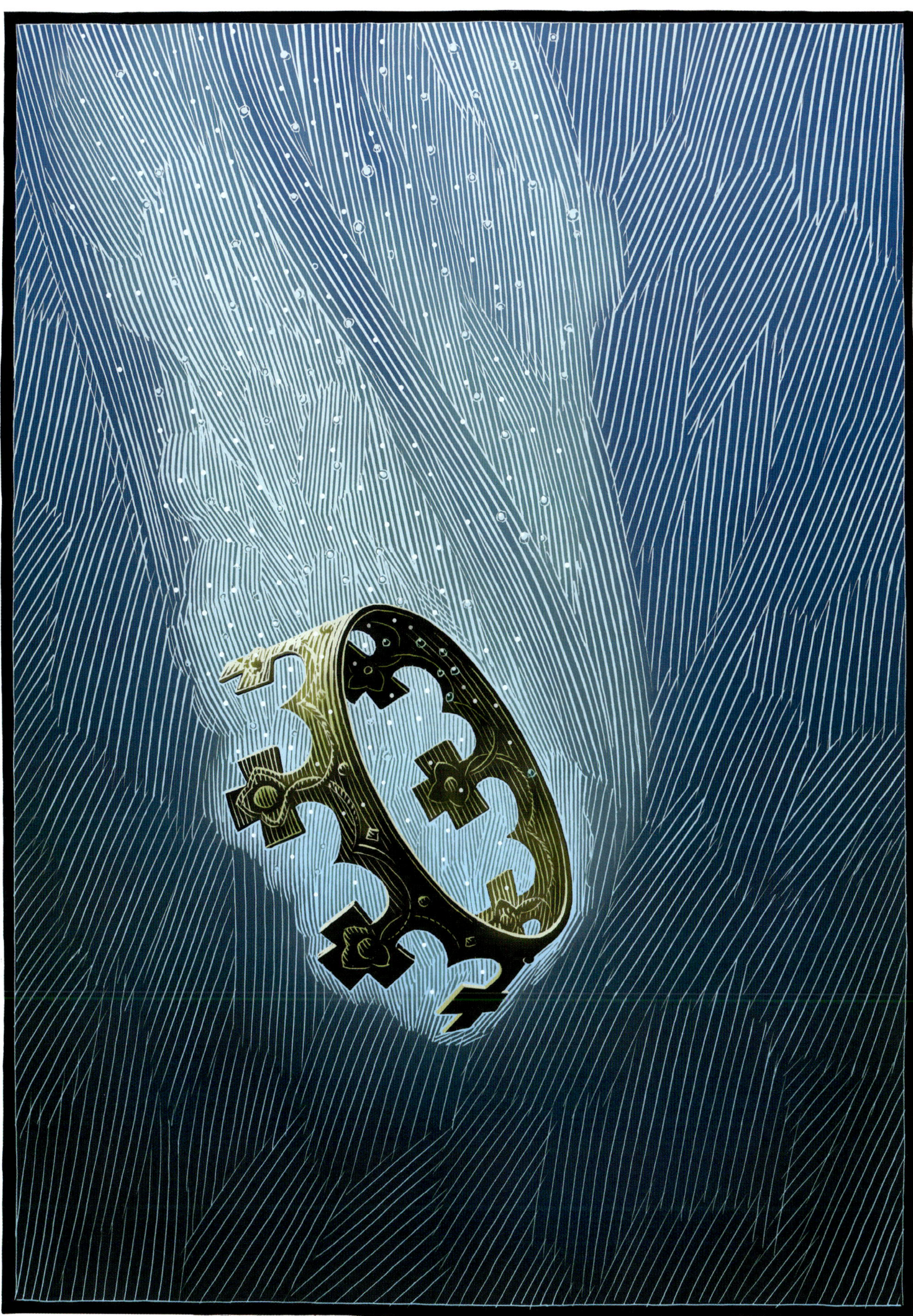

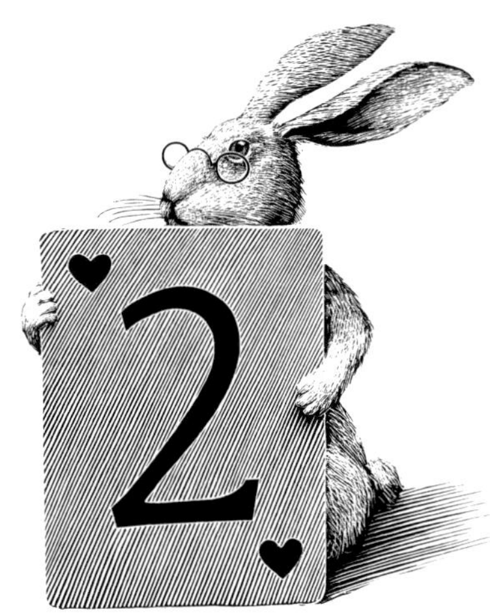

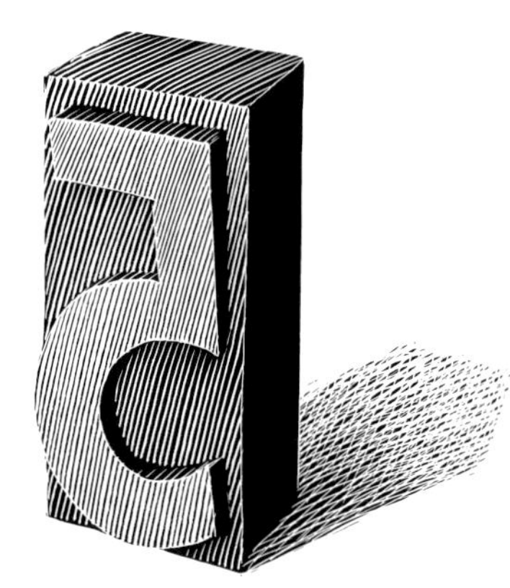

Bedford/St. Martin's in Boston is a publisher of college textbooks for humanities subjects. Their art director Anna Palchik called in 2012 to commission a cover and 12 chapter numeral illustrations for a new book entitled *Reading Children's Literature: A Critical Introduction* by Carrie Hintz and Eric Tribunella. I was invited to design the book as well as illustrate it. I was even able to make suggestions for many of the illustration examples used throughout the text.

The chapter numerals reflect the topics under discussion. Chapter 2 covers the Early History of Children's Literature, so I used the White Rabbit from *Alice* holding a playing card. Poetry is the subject of Chapter 3 so I drew a *trompe l'oeil* set of rearrangeable fridge magnets words. Chapter 4 is about Fairy Tales — my little "entomology fantasy" came from Victorian painting and illustration where butterflies were a common visual metaphor for fairies.

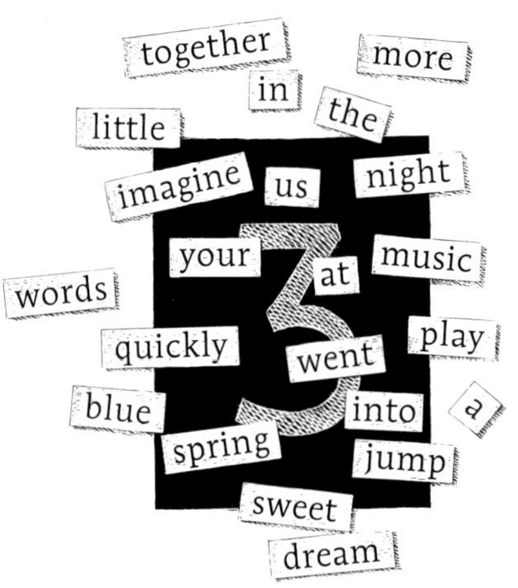

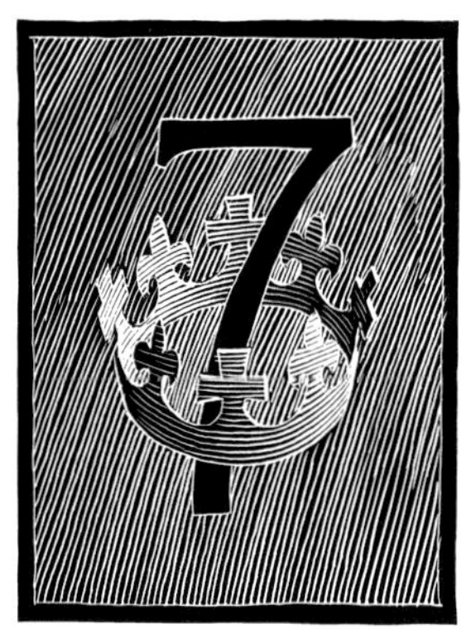

Some of these were easy — the crown for Chapter 7 on Historical Fiction; a diagram of a spacecraft orbiting the Earth and the moon traces the numeral 8 for a chapter on Science and Discovery. Some were challenging — such as chapters on race and ethnicity, and gender and sexuality.

I wanted the cover to convey the magical way in which books can capture a child's imagination. I liked the idea of showing a child reading, since that's the universal experience here. Every student who purchases this textbook for their class will draw on his or her own memories of the subject. I started sketching a boy reading where the light source would be the pages of the book — a way to represent the inspiration and illumination that comes from these books.

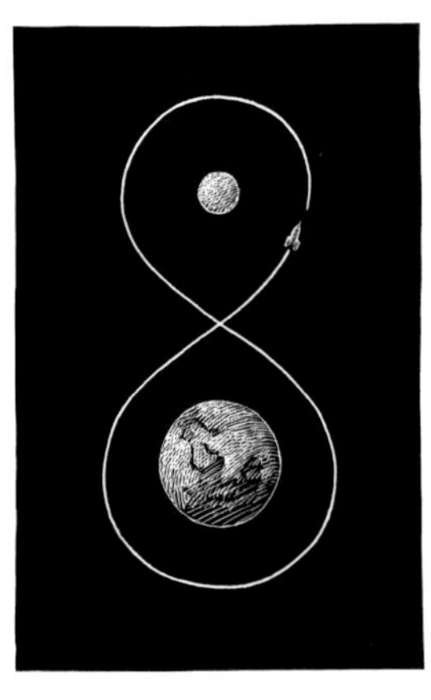

It seemed like a way to push this idea a little further might be to add some surreal objects flying up from the pages, representing the "content" that he's absorbing. The chapter numerals were fresh in my head (indeed, still on my drawing table), and they already represented the wide range of children's literature discussed in the text. Adding these objects to the cover seemed like a whimsical touch to balance a serious academic discussion of the subject.

Reading Children's Literature had established itself as the leading textbook in the field, so I was surprised to learn that Bedford/St. Martin's had sold the rights to Broadview Press in Canada, who published a second edition in 2019.

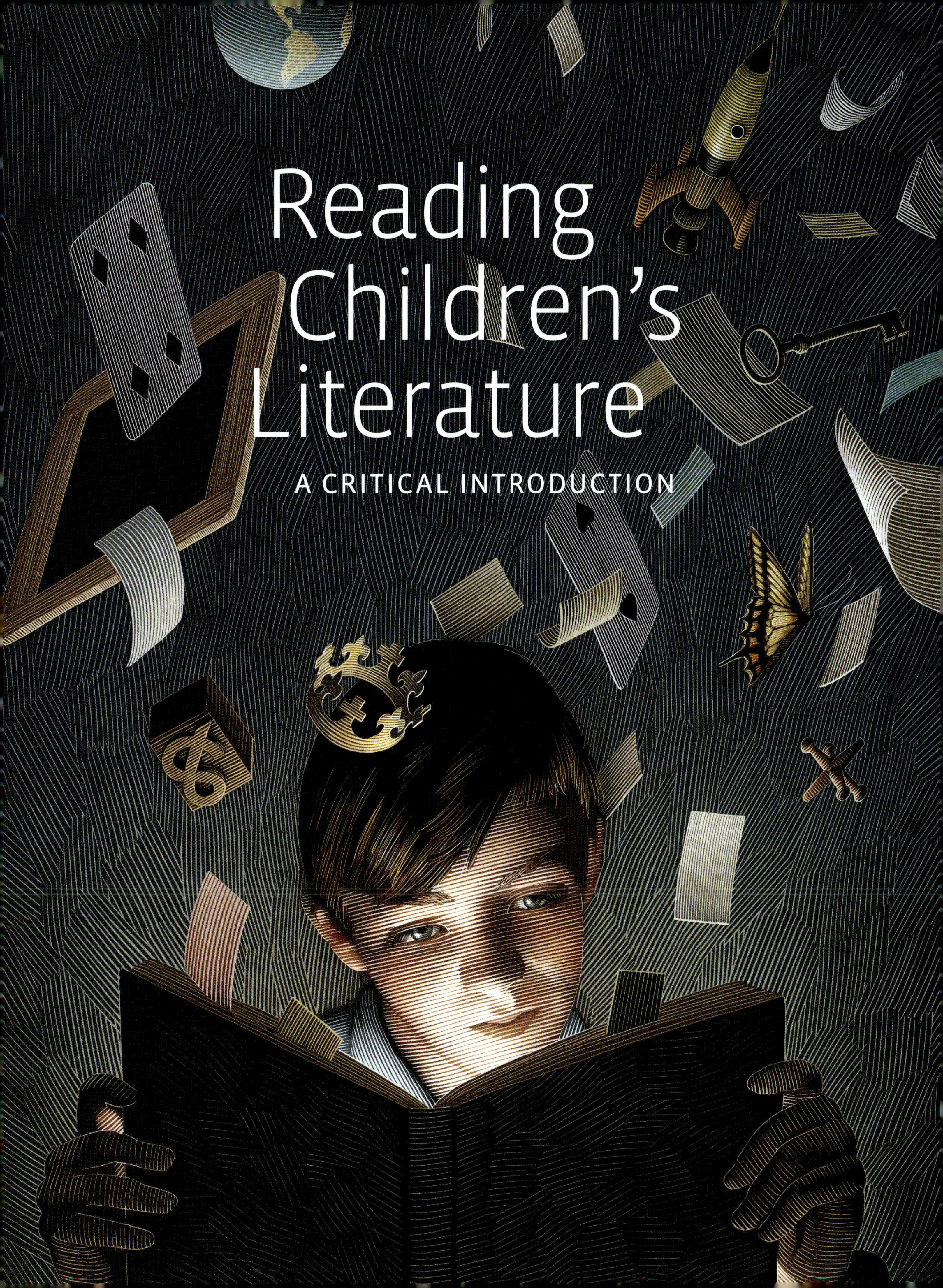
Reading
Children's
Literature
A CRITICAL INTRODUCTION

Ursula Marlow, the heroine of Clare Langley-Hawthorne's trilogy of Edwardian mystery novels, is an Oxford graduate, an aspiring journalist and a devoted suffragette. Somehow I was not surprised that she's a headstrong Belgravian heiress and stunningly beautiful, to boot.

Consequences of Sin is set in 1910, but the plot revolves around an ill-fated expedition to Venezuela years earlier. Ursula discovers a lost diary full of dark family secrets; there's a text about dreams and nightmares, which suggested a surreal collage of fragments from Ursula's past — the cover illustration became a visual puzzle containing clues to the mystery. As an experiment, I drew some of these components separately and overlapped them in Photoshop, allowing the layers to interact with each other in ways I could never achieve in a single drawing.

The Serpent and the Scorpion begins in Egypt in 1912, so I decided to use the Sphinx as my focal point — a symbol of mystery and riddles, wisdom, vigilance and strength. Its human head and animal body represent the union of intellectual and physical powers — perfect for a mystery set in the Edwardian period.

The trilogy was completed with the publication in 2014 of *Unlikely Traitors*. Now it's the winter of 1913. Ursula's fiancé, Lord Wrotham, is arrested on charges of espionage, and she is drawn into the shadowy world of the Fenians in Ireland as she tries to clear his name.

For continuity, it was important to use the same model for all three illustrations. Fortuitously, I picked a model who was willing to return twice to the "role" of Ursula. Sophie Jones was a high school student when I asked her to pose for the first cover; we set up costumed reference photo sessions for the second and third covers in Toronto backyards over the next several years.

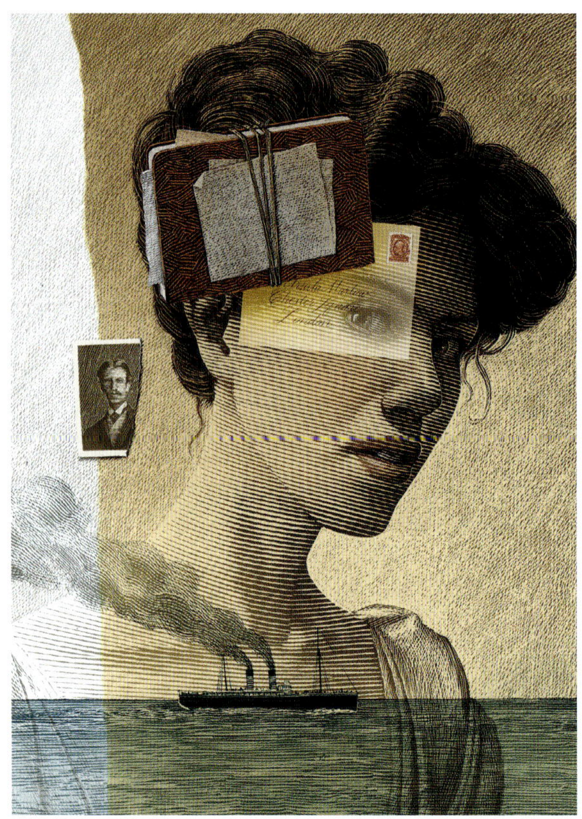

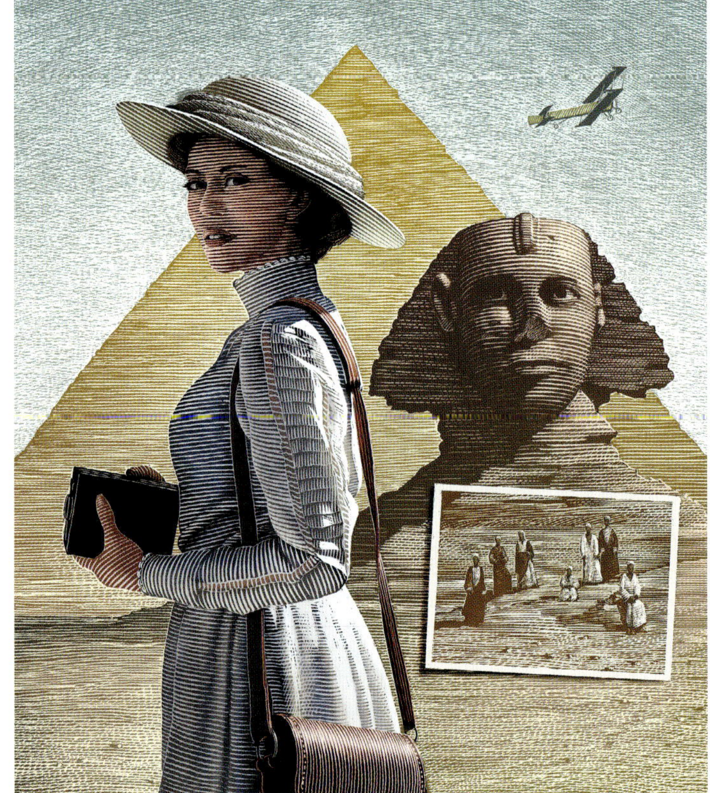

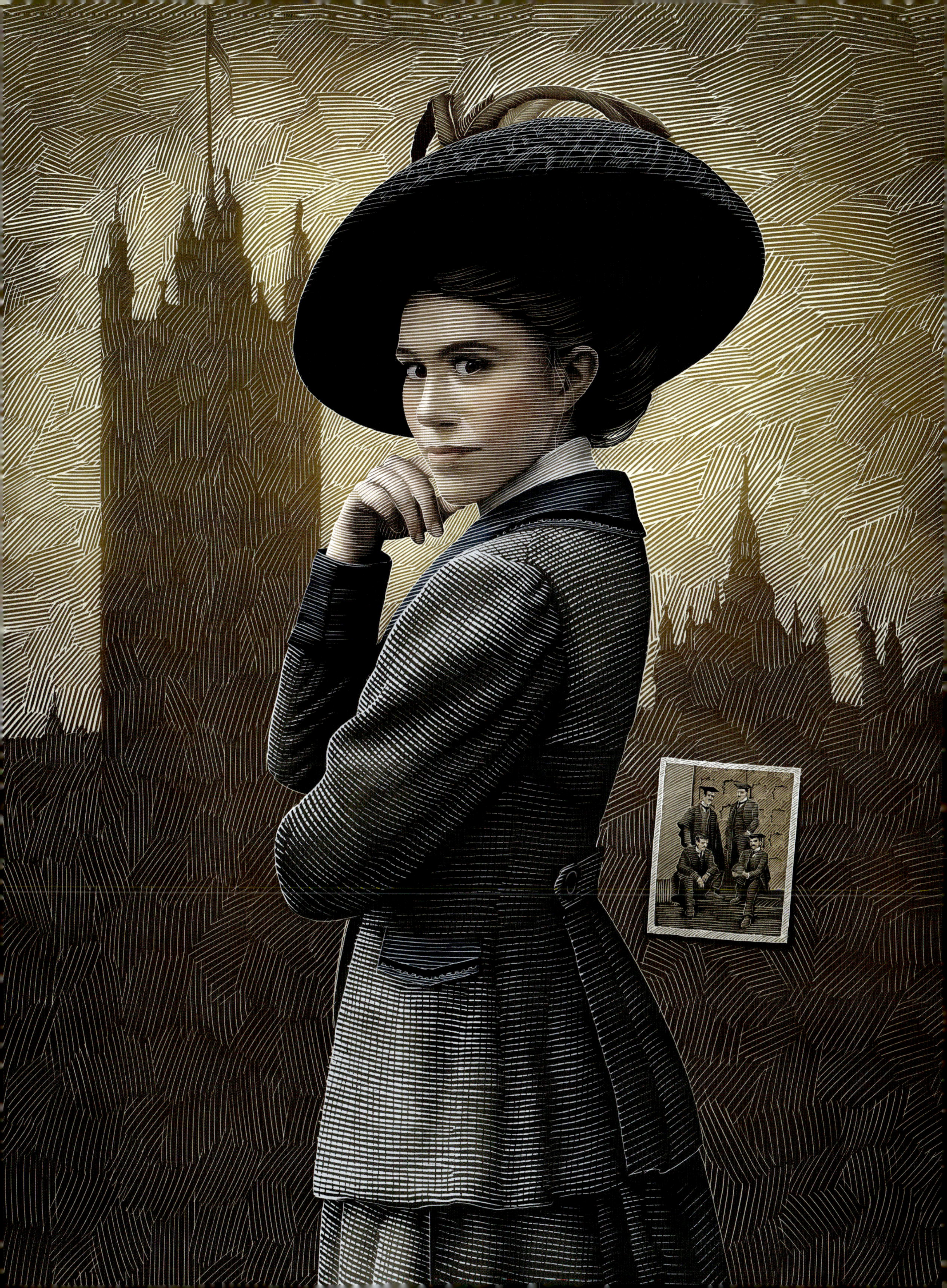

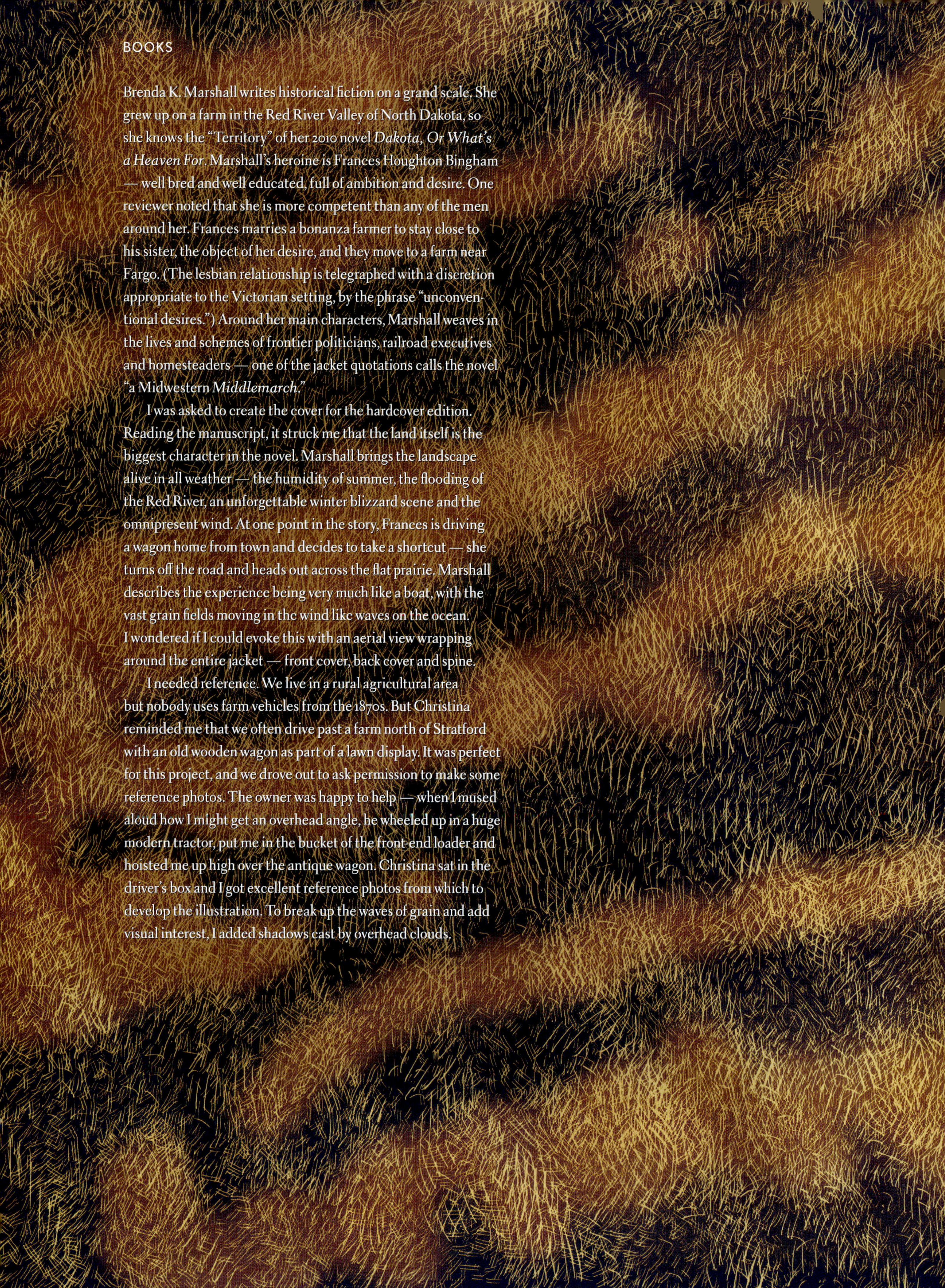

Brenda K. Marshall writes historical fiction on a grand scale. She grew up on a farm in the Red River Valley of North Dakota, so she knows the "Territory" of her 2010 novel *Dakota, Or What's a Heaven For*. Marshall's heroine is Frances Houghton Bingham — well bred and well educated, full of ambition and desire. One reviewer noted that she is more competent than any of the men around her. Frances marries a bonanza farmer to stay close to his sister, the object of her desire, and they move to a farm near Fargo. (The lesbian relationship is telegraphed with a discretion appropriate to the Victorian setting, by the phrase "unconventional desires.") Around her main characters, Marshall weaves in the lives and schemes of frontier politicians, railroad executives and homesteaders — one of the jacket quotations calls the novel "a Midwestern *Middlemarch*."

I was asked to create the cover for the hardcover edition. Reading the manuscript, it struck me that the land itself is the biggest character in the novel. Marshall brings the landscape alive in all weather — the humidity of summer, the flooding of the Red River, an unforgettable winter blizzard scene and the omnipresent wind. At one point in the story, Frances is driving a wagon home from town and decides to take a shortcut — she turns off the road and heads out across the flat prairie. Marshall describes the experience being very much like a boat, with the vast grain fields moving in the wind like waves on the ocean. I wondered if I could evoke this with an aerial view wrapping around the entire jacket — front cover, back cover and spine.

I needed reference. We live in a rural agricultural area but nobody uses farm vehicles from the 1870s. But Christina reminded me that we often drive past a farm north of Stratford with an old wooden wagon as part of a lawn display. It was perfect for this project, and we drove out to ask permission to make some reference photos. The owner was happy to help — when I mused aloud how I might get an overhead angle, he wheeled up in a huge modern tractor, put me in the bucket of the front-end loader and hoisted me up high over the antique wagon. Christina sat in the driver's box and I got excellent reference photos from which to develop the illustration. To break up the waves of grain and add visual interest, I added shadows cast by overhead clouds.

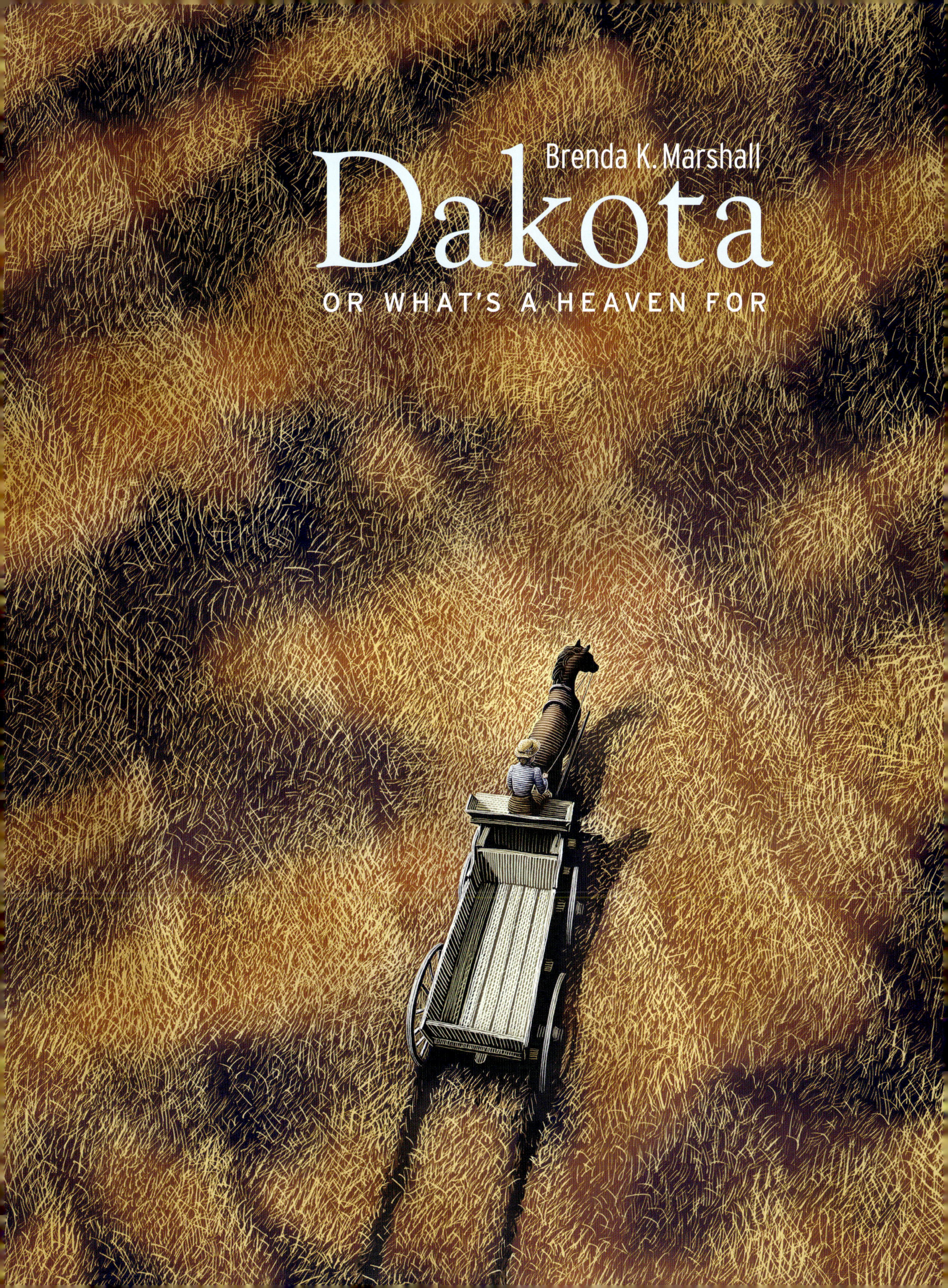
Brenda K. Marshall
Dakota
OR WHAT'S A HEAVEN FOR

I received a call from Mary Opper, creative director at Penguin Canada, in late 2009. They were publishing a collection of 20 biographies under the series title *Extraordinary Canadians*. The biographers in the series qualify for this distinction as much as their subjects — series editor John Ralston Saul had matched up contemporary authors with historical subjects based on personal and professional connections across generations. So former Governor General of Canada Adrienne Clarkson wrote the biography of Dr. Norman Bethune, who effectively brought modern medicine to rural China. Jane Urquhart wrote about Lucy Maude Montgomery. Margaret MacMillan wrote the Stephen Leacock biography. Writer and artist Douglas Coupland interpreted the life and work of communications guru Marshall McLuhan. Canadian illustrators were then hired to create cover art for the series (my favourite is Anita Kunz's portrait of Lucy Maude Montgomery with a miniature Green Gables cottage on her Edwardian hat).

John Ralston Saul had saved one book for himself to write. Louis-Hippolyte LaFontaine and Robert Baldwin were pre-Confederation politicians, visionary leaders from Lower and Upper Canada. Saul argues that Canada did not begin in 1867; rather its foundations were laid years earlier by LaFontaine and Baldwin. They created a reformist movement for responsible government run by elected citizens instead of a colonial governor. From 1848 to 1851, they revamped judicial institutions, established official bilingualism and a public education system, and designed a network of public roads. Opper invited me to create the cover for LaFontaine and Baldwin.

The faces of the other subjects in the series are mostly familiar to readers, but LaFontaine and Baldwin's political careers predate the advent of photography so we don't really know what they looked like. I love having licence to improvise.

Christina has an extensive costume history reference library right here in our studio. I found wonderful portrait reference from LaFontaine and Baldwin's heyday — nothing telegraphs the early Victorian period like the tall top hats fashionable during the 1830s and '40s. I came across a number of English caricatures, beautifully rendered in watercolour by Richard Dighton (1795–1880) with the stylistic convention of depicting the subjects walking in profile from left to right.

I proposed a double portrait of our dynamic duo, walking arm-in-arm to suggest a physical closeness to their partnership. I sketched in a stormy sky behind them to represent the political climate they had to weather. JRS (as Penguin referred to Saul) liked the concept so I set up reference photos with models who fit the physical descriptions and felt right temperamentally (thank you to Stratford actors Michael Spencer Davis and Mike Nadajewski).

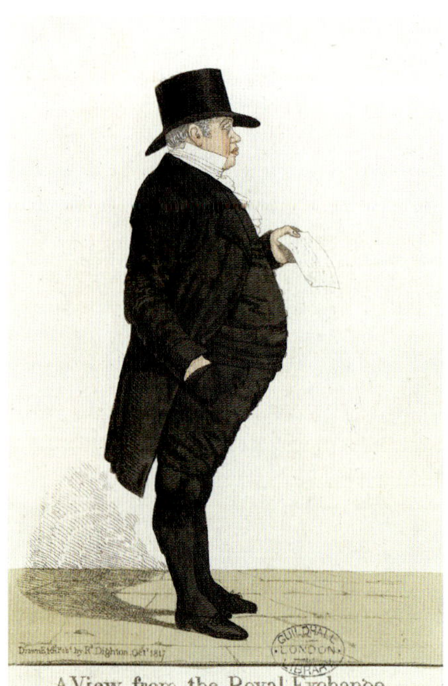

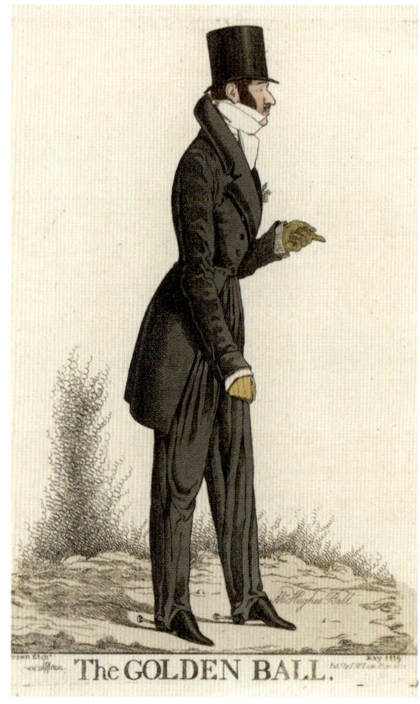

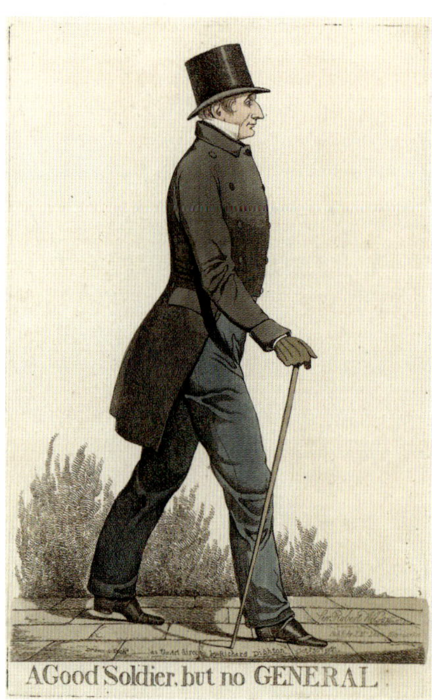

Caricatures by Richard Dighton: "A View from the Royal Exchange" is an 1817 portrait of Mr. Nathan Rothschild; "Golden Ball Hughes" was the nickname acquired by Edward Hughes Ball when he inherited an enormous fortune in 1819 (which he promptly spent on aristocratic indulgences); an 1821 portrait of Sir Robert Thomas Wilson captioned "A Good Soldier but no General" (all Bridgeman Images).

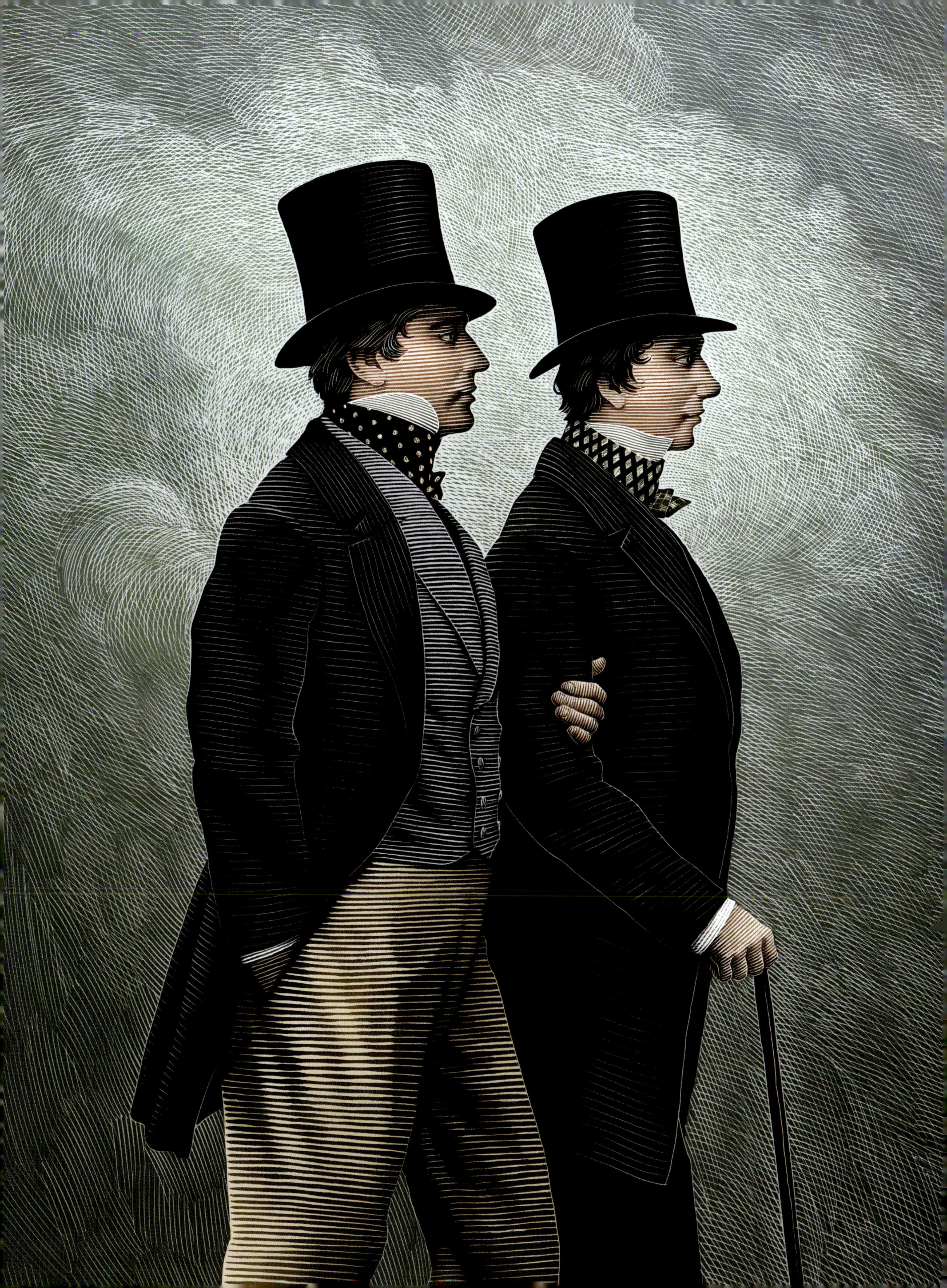

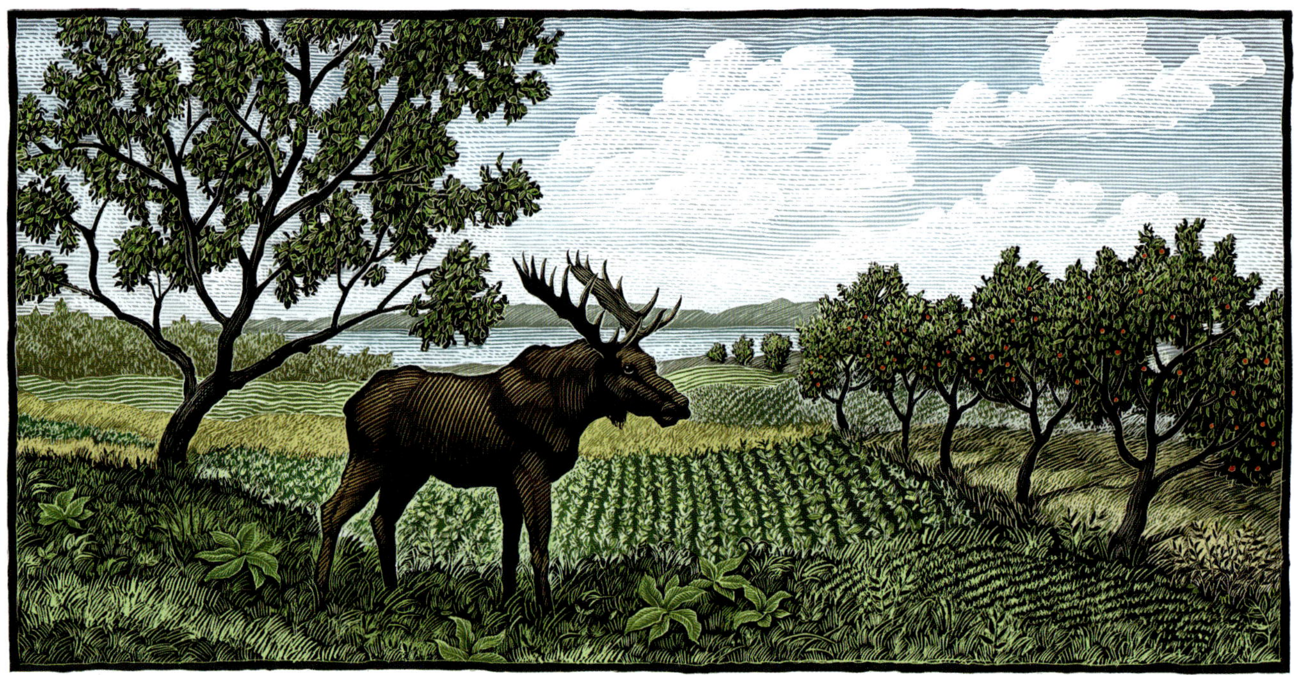

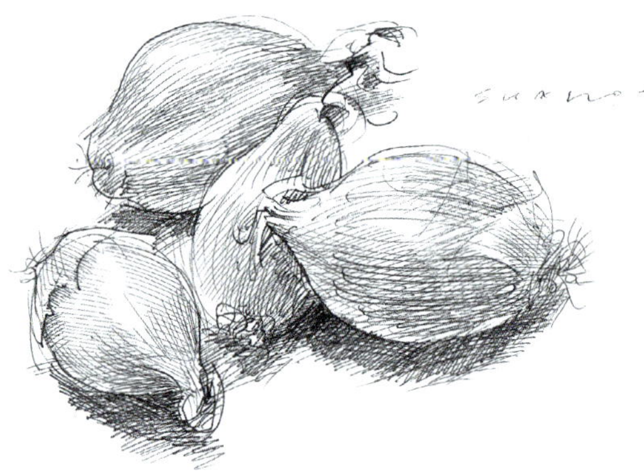

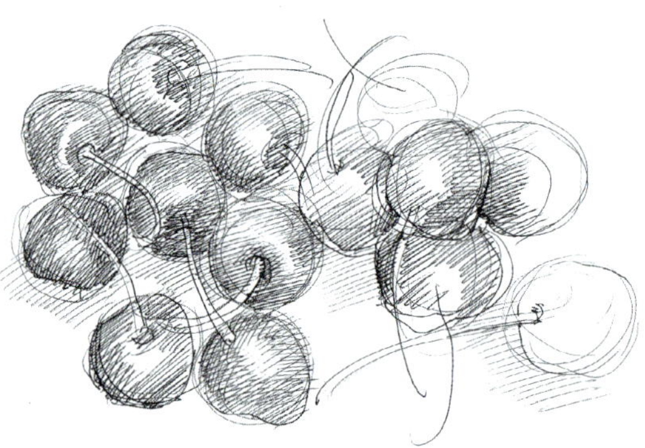

I enjoy cooking — we have shelves of cookbooks, and Christina regularly clips new recipes from *The New York Times* and *The Globe and Mail* to try. We also love eating in restaurants and working with chefs. The Punch & Judy studio has a portfolio of graphic identity and menu design for many restaurants over the years. So I was happy to get an assignment in 2009 to illustrate a cookbook for Moosewood Restaurant. The Moosewood Collective, as it is officially called, opened their celebrated vegetarian and vegan restaurant in Ithaca, New York, in 1973. They had produced a dozen cookbooks in the ensuing 35 years, and a few more since mine.

The cover concept was assigned by an art director at Simon & Schuster, their publisher. I never quite understood how a moose in a vegetable garden reflected the particular focus of the book, titled *Moosewood Restaurant Cooking for Health*. The restaurant's logo consists of a moose standing under a tree — that seemed to be the extent of the rationale, so I did not question it too deeply.

For the interior, they requested a series of spot illustrations of raw ingredients — produce from the garden on the cover (anything that moose didn't eat, presumably). I made a series of pencil sketches of fruits and vegetables — twice as long a list as we had room or budget for. Simon & Schuster put me directly in touch with the people at Moosewood, which was a more efficient way of working through approvals. Susan Harville and Ned Asta were delightful to work with. Christina and I were travelling through New York State later that summer and they invited us to visit them in Ithaca. We were treated like visiting royalty at the restaurant; they put us up overnight in a beautiful cottage on Cayuga Lake and spent a day showing us their town and the Finger Lakes region.

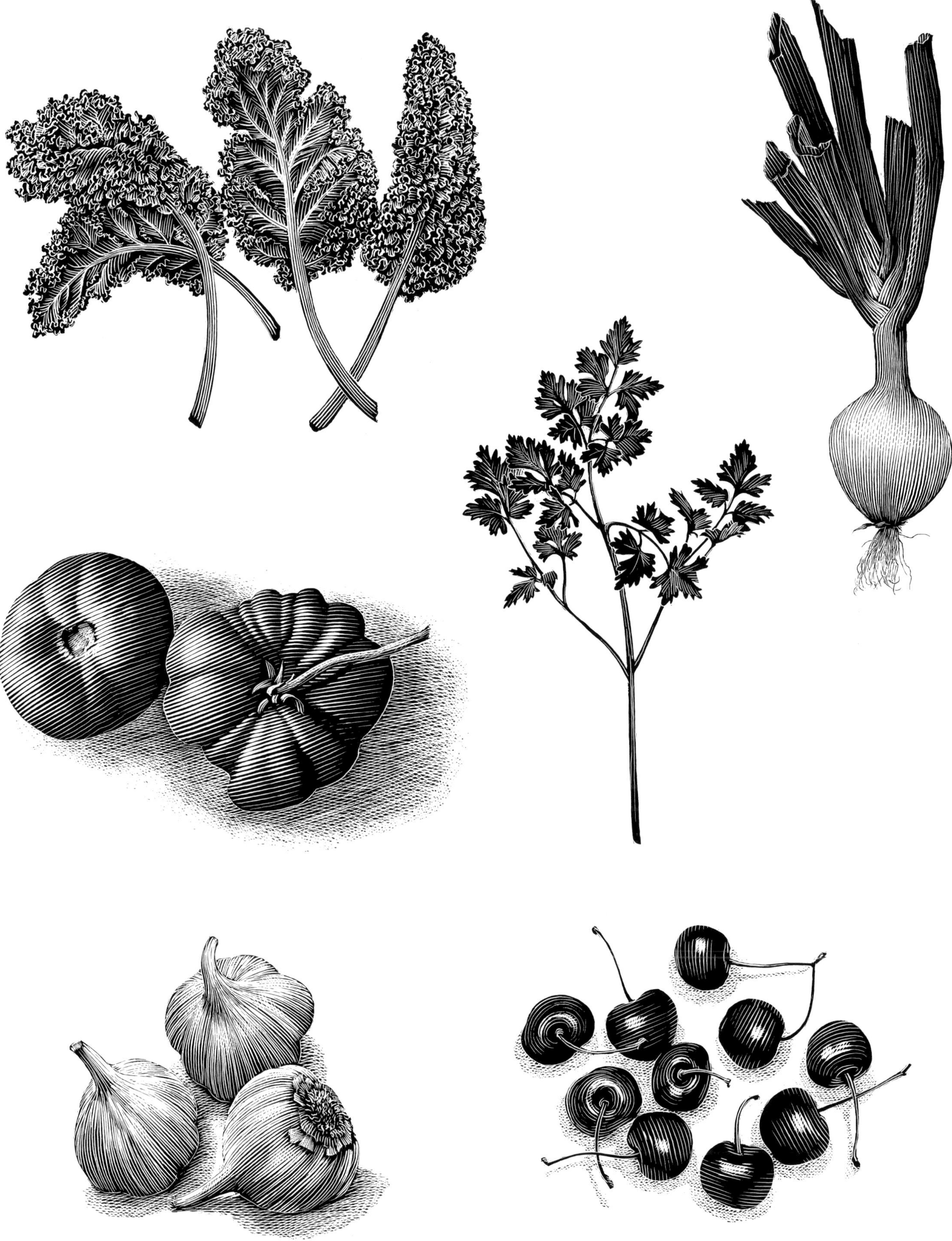

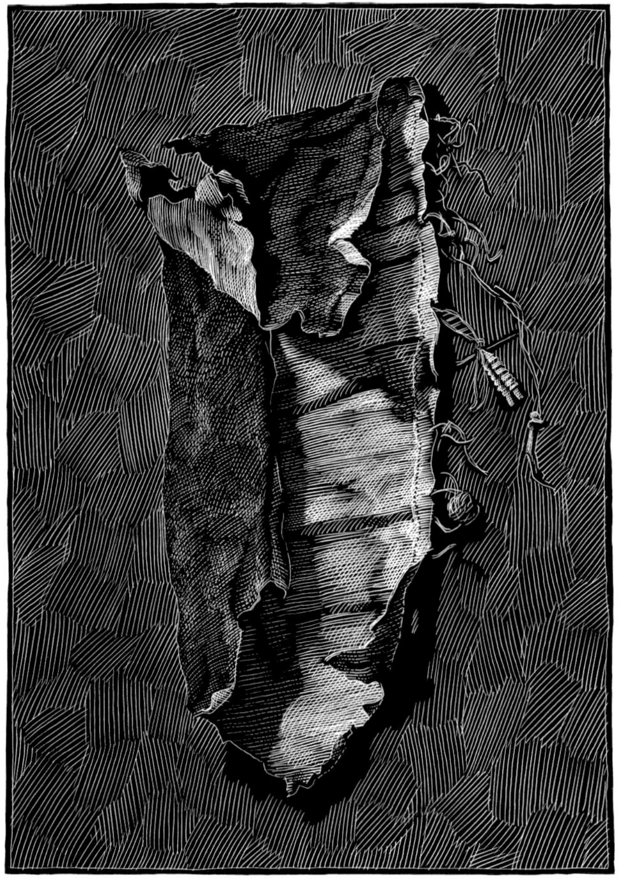

In December 2013, I received an invitation from Jane Urquhart to work together with her on a book project. HarperCollins had commissioned her to write a book for Canada's sesquicentennial in 2017, which would include a collection of essays and stories inspired by 50 objects or artifacts of her choice. It was to be a "literary" book bringing together Urquhart's skills as both a novelist and poet. Jane wanted an image to accompany each essay, but wanted to avoid the kind of colour photography often used in commemorative coffee-table books. She asked if I would be interested in creating scratchboard engravings for each of the objects. I signed on immediately.

The project represented a wonderful journey of artistic collaboration and discovery. Often my drawings were created simultaneously while Jane wrote, both of us interpreting the same subject, each through our own lens. Many of Jane's objects are symbolic of the memories that make up our history. I tracked down as many as possible in person, in order to make sketches or reference photos from life.

The illustrations for *A Number of Things: Stories of Canada Told through Fifty Objects* are all black and white except for the Canada goose on the facing page, featured on the cover.

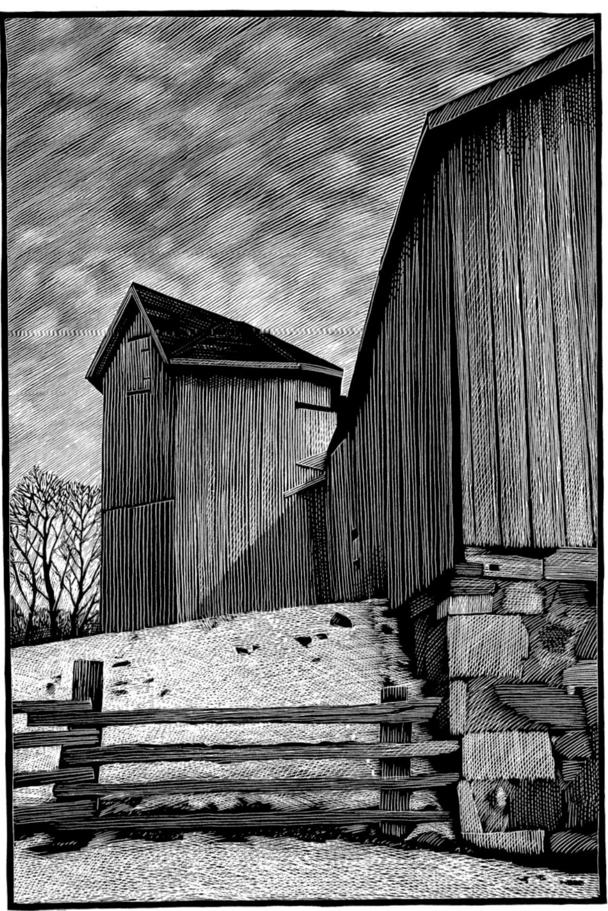

THIS PAGE:
The book opens with poignant essay about colonialism. The Beothuk were an indigenous hunter-gatherer people in Newfoundland before European contact; and because of that contact, now extinct for 200 years. This beaver hide legging, decorated with bird claws and bone pendants, was discovered in 1827 in a Beothuk burial site, wrapped around the body of a small child, presumably by its mother.

An essay on barns traces changes in Canadian agriculture over the decades and the impact of these traditional structures on our rural landscape and occupations. Jane allowed me to pick any barn I liked for the illustration. The real challenge was the vertical format of this series — barns seem to fit more naturally into a horizontal composition. I found this wonderful example, with its unique six-sided silo, on a farm near St. Marys, Ontario, in early spring.

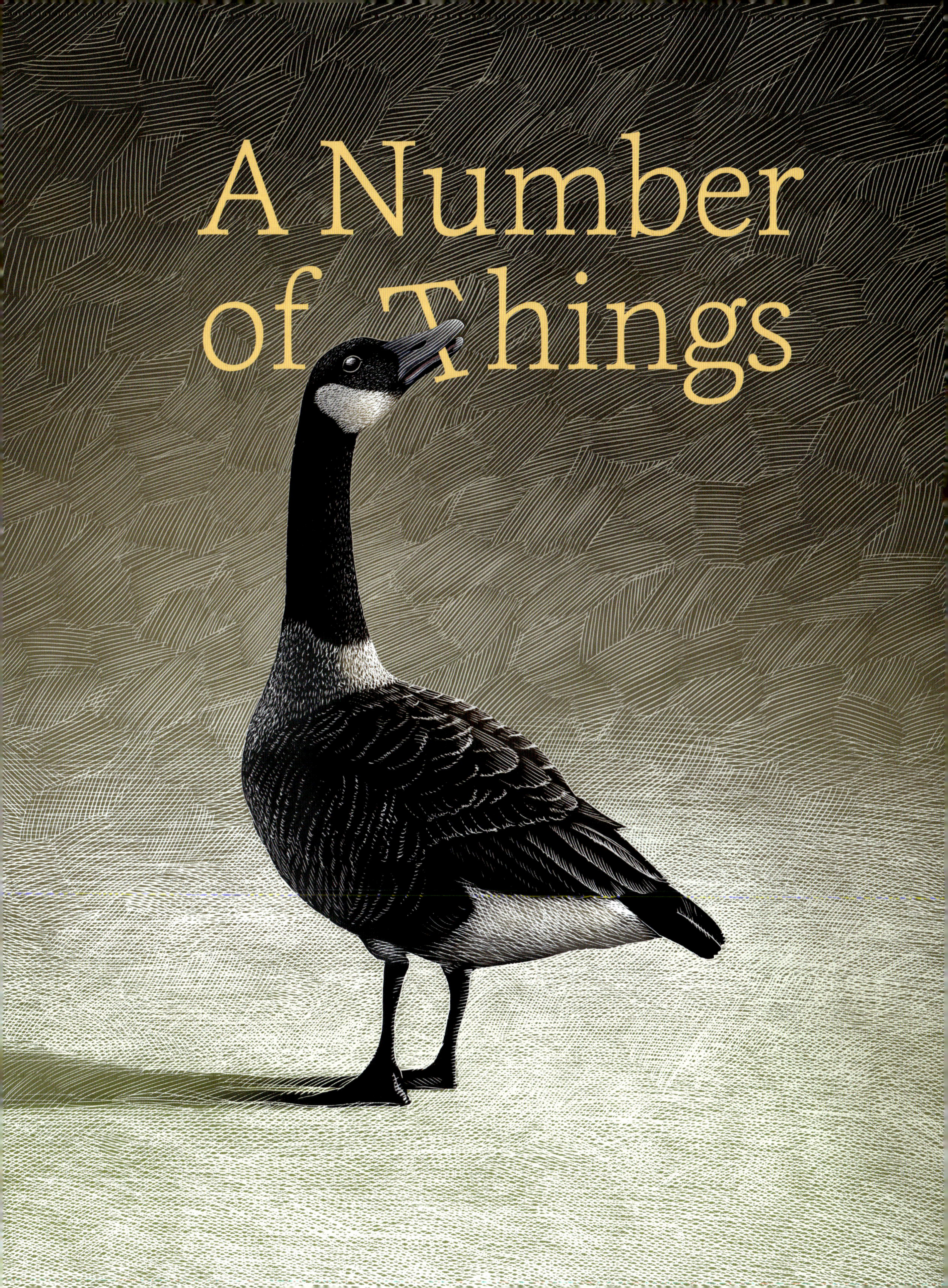
A Number
of Things

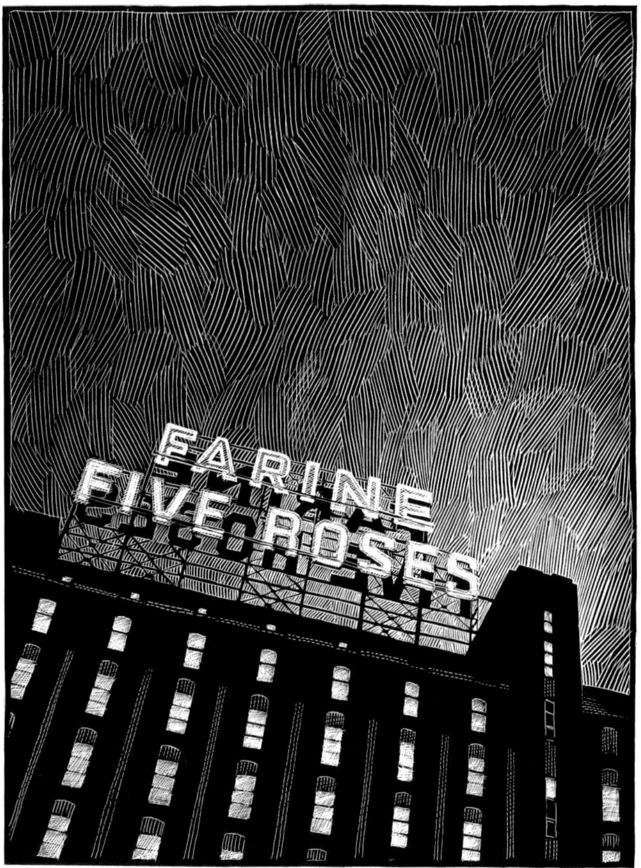

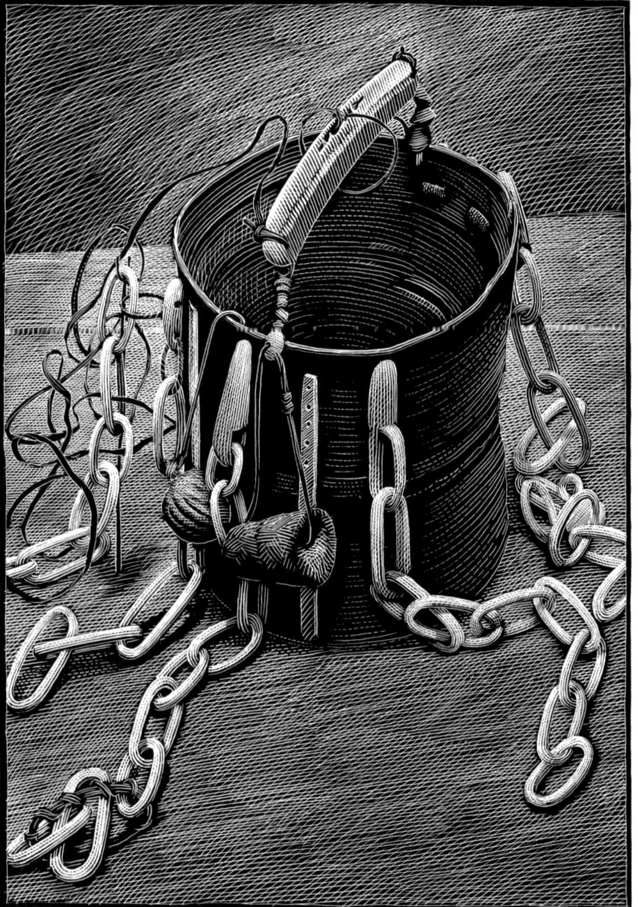

THIS PAGE:
Jane's essay on the Five Roses Flour sign in Montreal is really about the history of language in Quebec —from Ojibwa to French to English. The iconic neon sign dates back to the 1940s, but the Quiet Revolution in the 1960s and '70s led to language laws requiring that the word flour appear in French. The words "Five Roses" were allowed to remain in English because it was part of a corporate identity. I noted with irony that the French and English words are in two different typefaces.

An absorbing essay about this ceremonial Inuit whaling bucket describes the fundamental importance of the bowhead whale to Inuit culture and spirituality. Richly decorated with carved whalebone, this artifact is part of an exhibit at the Canadian Museum of History in Gatineau, where I stood for an hour with my sketchbook, trying to block out the chattering student tour groups.

OPPOSITE, CLOCKWISE FROM TOP LEFT:
Jane grew up in Ontario's far north and vividly recalls the de Havilland Beaver bush plane as the only means of transportation between the far-flung settlements. My challenge as an illustrator was how to capture an accurate, interesting perspective. I was able to borrow a beautifully detailed scale model of this iconic aircraft — on a sunny day, I placed the model on a sheet of clear plexiglass, making it easy to adjust the height and angle of the plane and its cast shadow.

Jane suggests in an essay entitled "Mountain Spirits" that the totem poles, painted longhouses and vivid, powerful masks of the Nuu-chah-nulth peoples on the west coast of Vancouver Island are among the most important works of art in the world. These masks, now in the collection of the Royal British Columbia Museum in Victoria, have open mouths — as if singing or breathing the mountain wind. Jane observes "they seem themselves to be germinating, turning into landscape."

For an essay called "Tar Sands," Jane asked me to find the biggest, ugliest piece of heavy equipment used in the controversial process of extracting bitumen from the ground in Northern Alberta. This dumptruck is the size of a house.

Jane acquired this Cree basket in 1993 on a visit to Wanuskewin, an ancient spiritual site of the First Nations Plains peoples north of Saskatoon. It's only nine inches in diameter, but daunting in the complexity of its woven reeds. The key to the drawing was to zoom in on a small area — which allowed the engraving lines to convey a sense of the various textures.

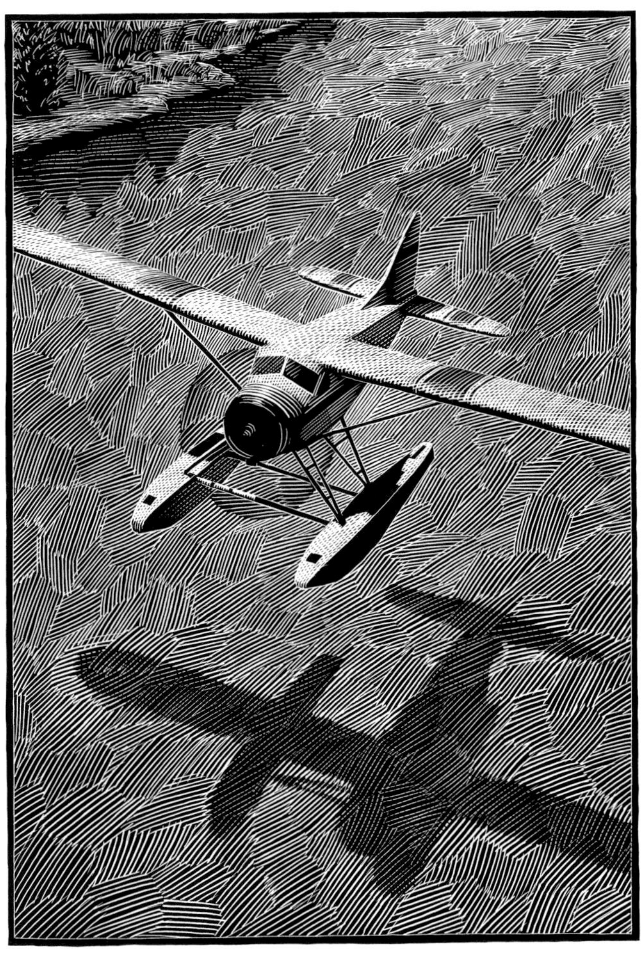

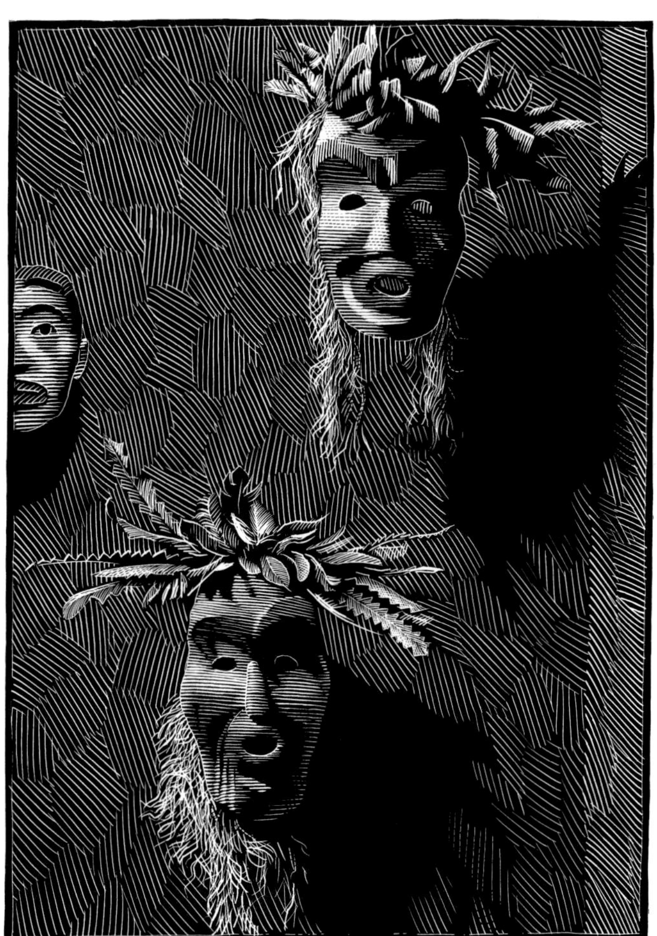

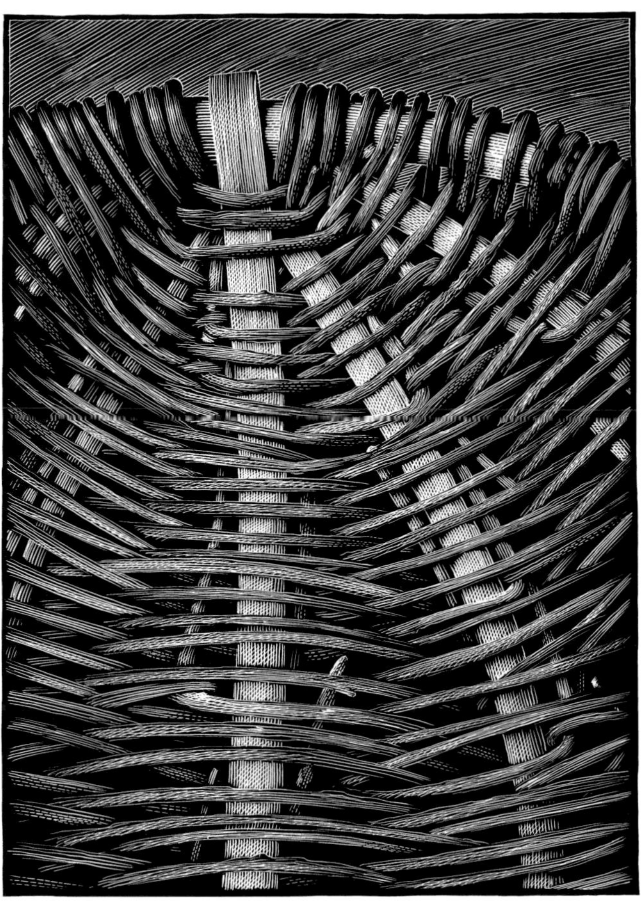

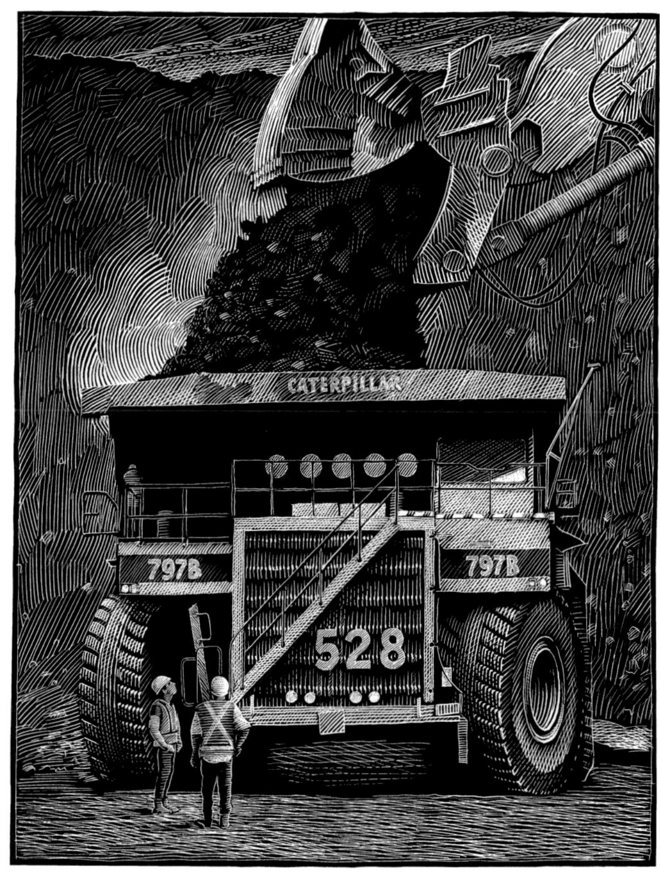
CATERPILLAR
797B
797B
528

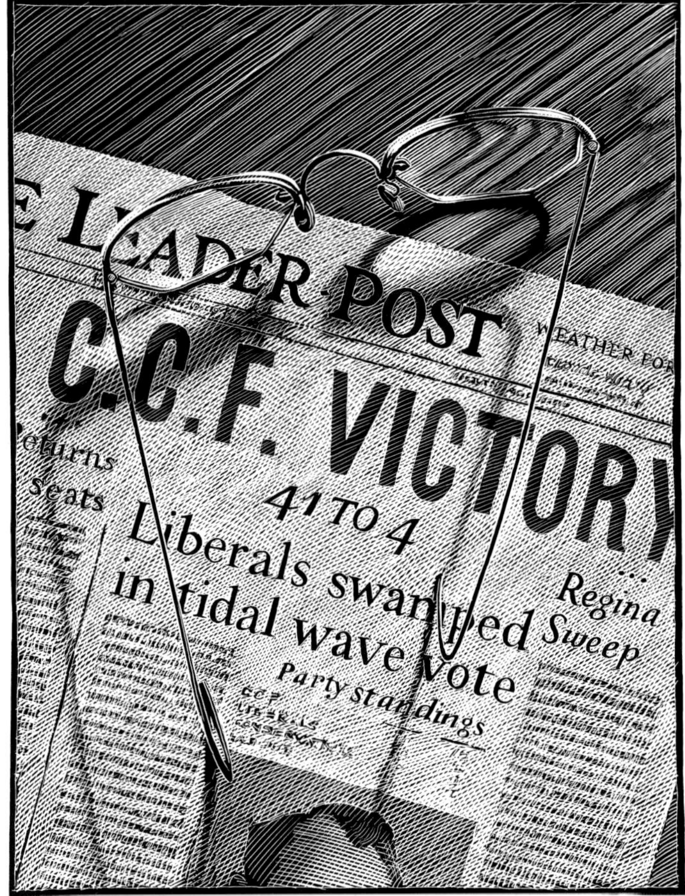
LEADER POST
C.C.F. VICTORY
41 TO 4
Liberals swamped
in tidal wave vote
Party standings
Regina
Sweep

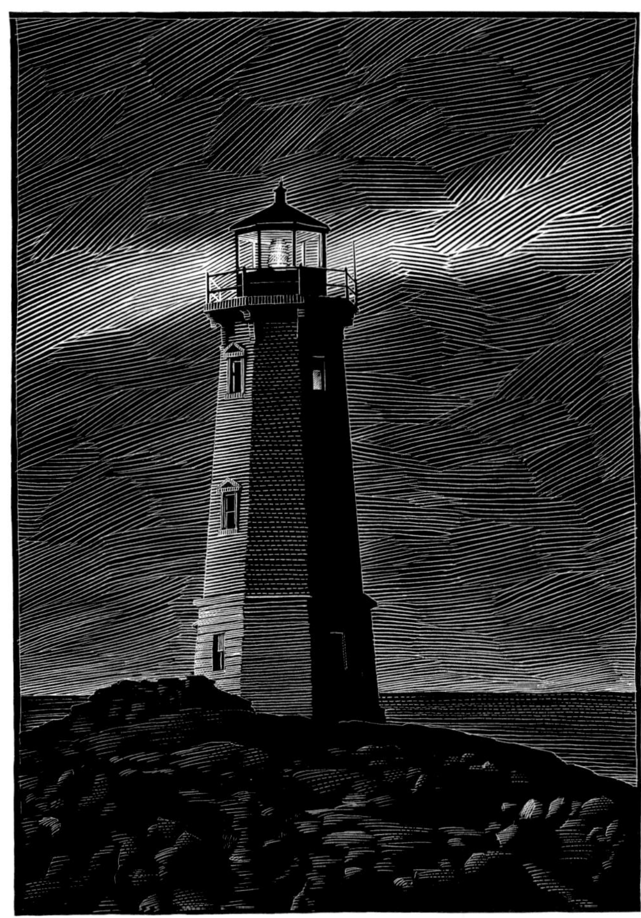

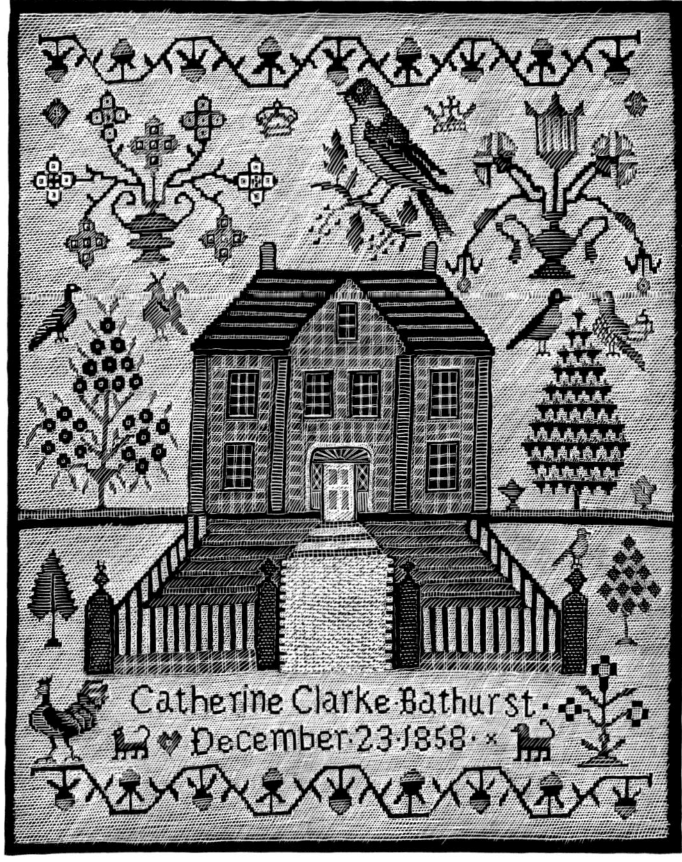
Catherine Clarke Bathurst
December 23 1858

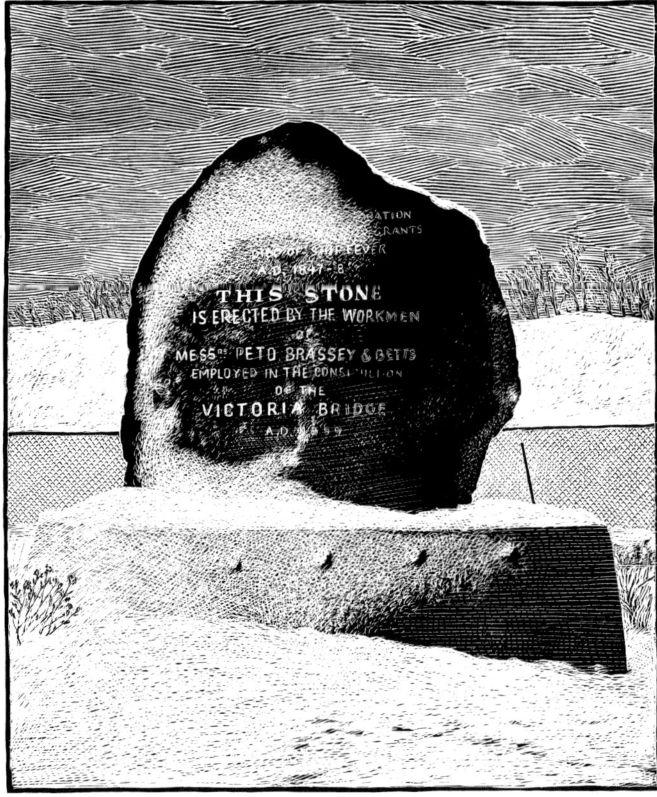
THIS STONE
IS ERECTED BY THE WORKMEN
VICTORIA BRIDGE

OPPOSITE, CLOCKWISE FROM TOP LEFT:

As premier of Saskatchewan, Tommy Douglas established a province-wide universal healthcare system, which became the template for the national Medicare program. Urquhart specified Tommy's distinctive wire-frame glasses as one of her objects — a lovely metaphor for a man of such vision. Goo Goo Goggles, a marvellous optician in Victoria, B.C., features an extensive inventory of vintage frames. I sent reference photos of Douglas, and they had the exact style in stock, so I was able to set up this illustration as a still life in my studio.

Jane included an essay about lighthouses because she wanted to underscore that the federal government was shutting them down at an alarming rate. This is the lighthouse at Louisbourg, Nova Scotia, built in 1923 on the site of Canada's very first lighthouse in 1734.

Montreal's "Big Black Rock" monument marks a mass grave of 6000 Irish immigrants, victims of a typhus epidemic in 1847. I visited the monument at the foot of the Victoria Bridge and found that a dusting of snow had traced the contours of the stone — some parts of the typographic inscription were highlighted and other areas completely hidden. I made detailed sketches on site, from which I developed the illustration.

At the end of an essay about needlepoint samplers, Jane reveals that this example was stitched by Alice Munro's great-grandmother (in 1858). In order to draw it, I had to borrow it from Munro's living room wall in Clinton, Ontario. It was a thrill to have the Nobel Prize–winning author drop it off in person and visit our studio.

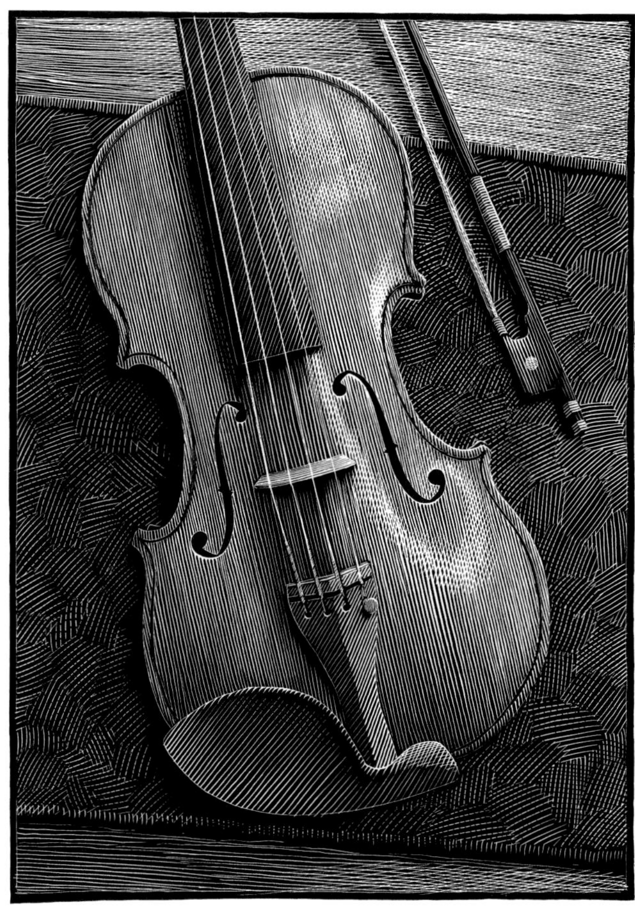

THIS PAGE:

Jane paid tribute to her friend Jacques Israelievitch, concertmaster of the Toronto Symphony Orchestra for almost 30 years, in an essay about his violin made by G.B. Guadagnini in 1782. Sadly, Israelievitch passed away in 2015; I spent an afternoon drawing his violin at the legendary George Heinl & Company in Toronto.

There's no more evocative symbol of winter in Canada than a pair of skates. Jane's essay touches on hockey, but is more about the pleasures of skating on the village pond or the Rideau Canal in Ottawa. Old leather skates have more character than modern hockey skates for the purpose of a drawing — I found this battered pair on eBay for $10.

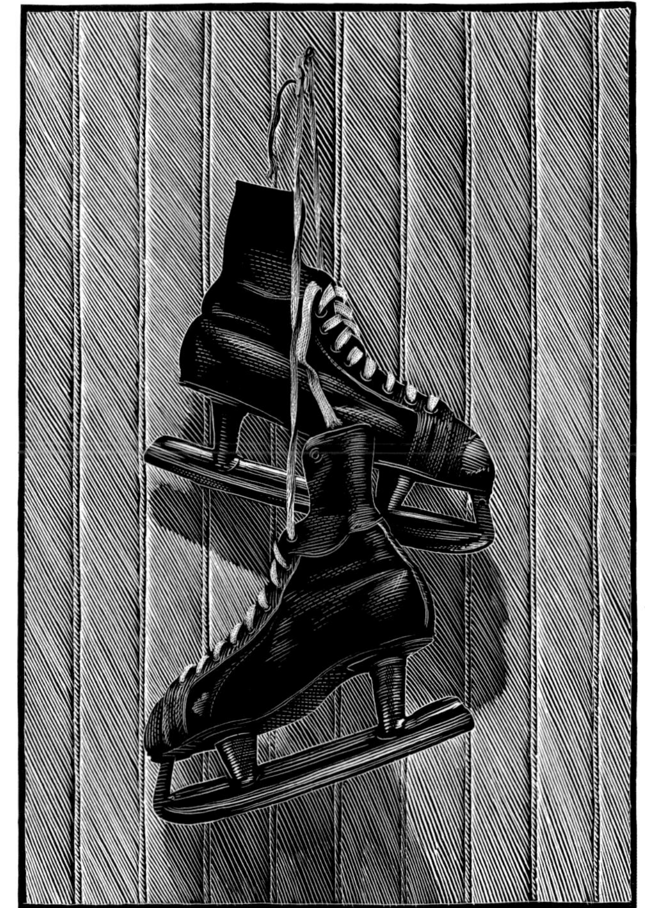

THIS PAGE:
A Number of Things: Stories of Canada Told through Fifty Objects was published in October 2016. Gallery Stratford invited me to show the original engravings in an exhibition, which we titled *The Facing Page*, in March 2017. Jane was at the opening and read from the book.

OPPOSITE, CLOCKWISE FROM TOP LEFT:
Jane's essay on the Acadian oyster evokes all the sensory delights of the bivalve molluscs, but also employs them as a symbol of the *Grand Dérangement* — the deportation of 11,500 Acadians from their homeland by the British during the French and Indian War (1755–1764). A fishmonger in Toronto had Beausoleil oysters from Miramichi Bay — which both looked and tasted fabulous.

Lester B. Pearson's Nobel Peace Prize medal, awarded in 1957 for his diplomatic genius, is now part of the Visual Art Collection of the Canadian Department of Foreign Affairs. I was allowed to hold the original solid gold medal in my own hand for reference for this illustration. The medal was designed by the Norwegian sculptor Gustav Vigeland in 1902.

Jane wanted to include a Stratford Festival object and invited me to make the choice. I requested the velvet coronation robe worn by Alec Guinness in the Festival's inaugural production of *Richard III* in 1953. Festival Archivist Liza Giffen set up the massive garment on a mannequin stand for me to draw — no small request as it takes three people to carry it from storage!

Baltej Singh Dhillon was at the centre of the RCMP turban controversy in 1988–89 — the symbol of his Sikh religion was not allowed to be worn as part the Mountie uniform. After heated debate, the rule was finally changed in 1990 to reflect the federal government's "strong commitment to a multicultural society." Dhillon very graciously posed for this portrait illustration.

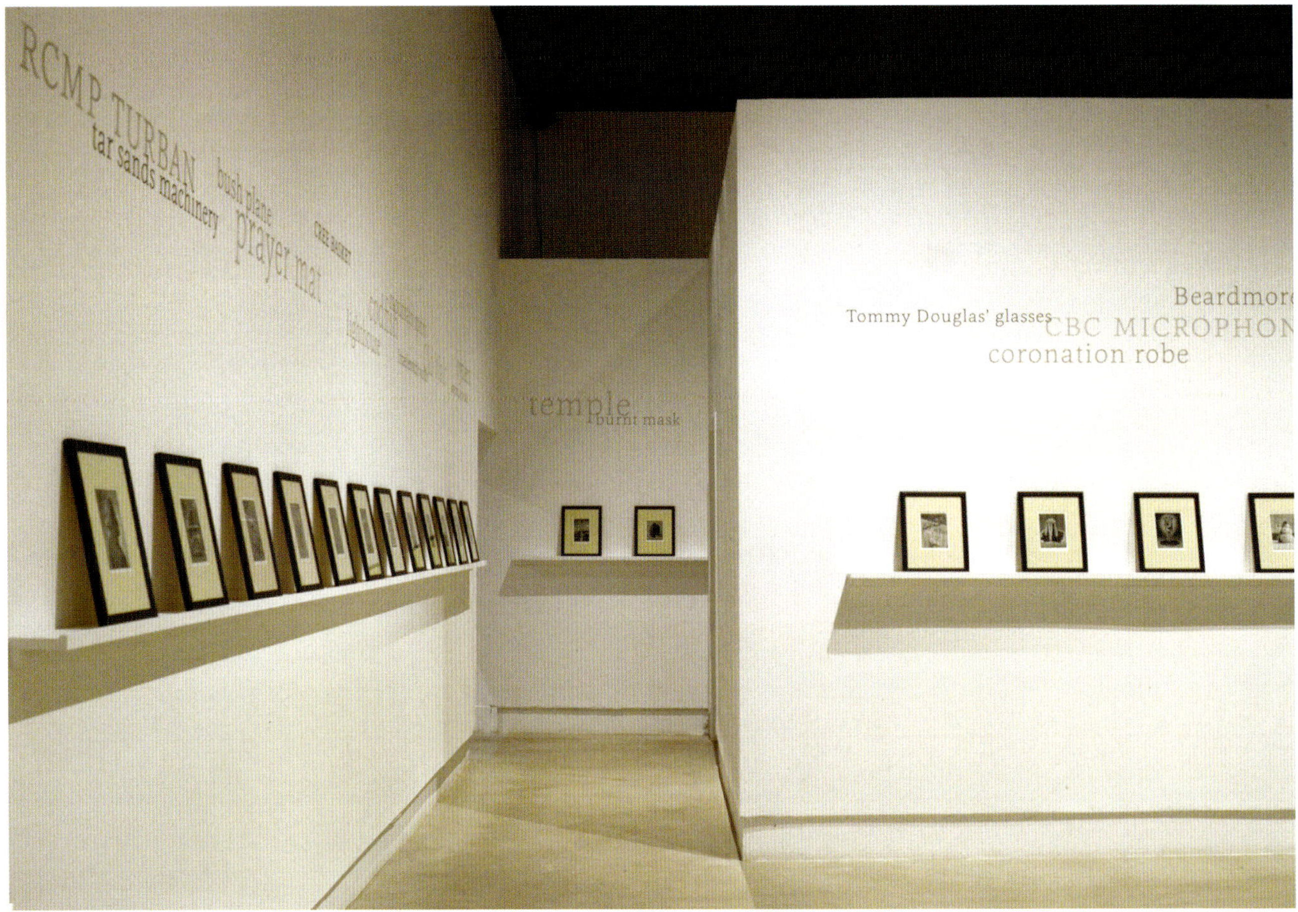

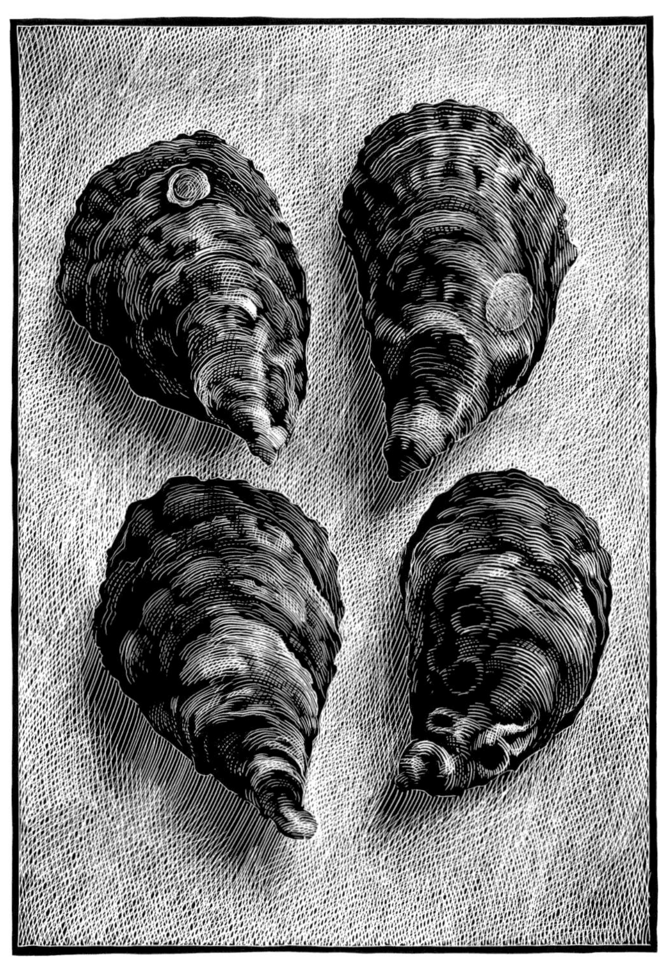

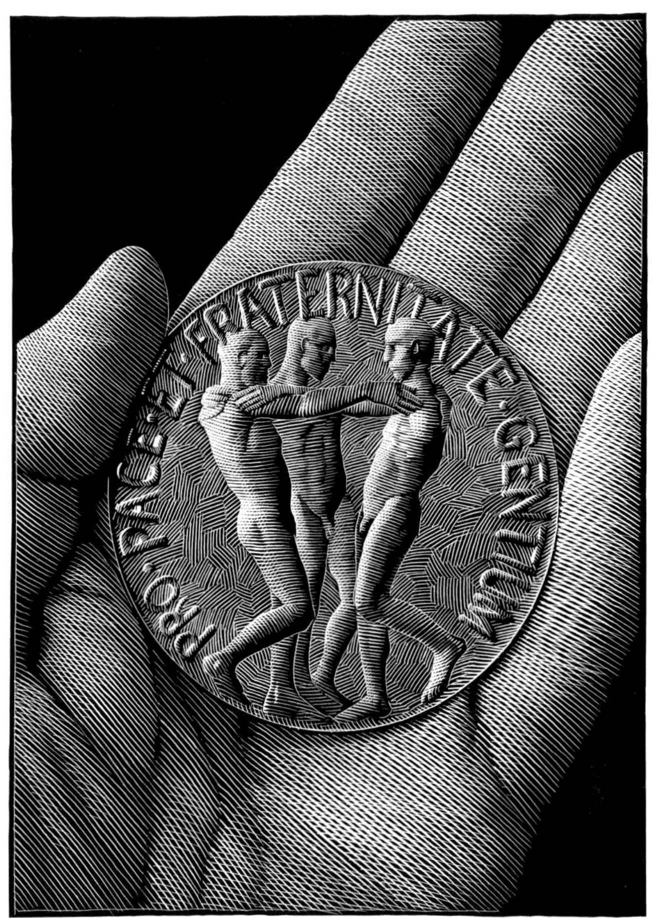
PRO·PACE·ET·FRATERNITATE·GENTIUM

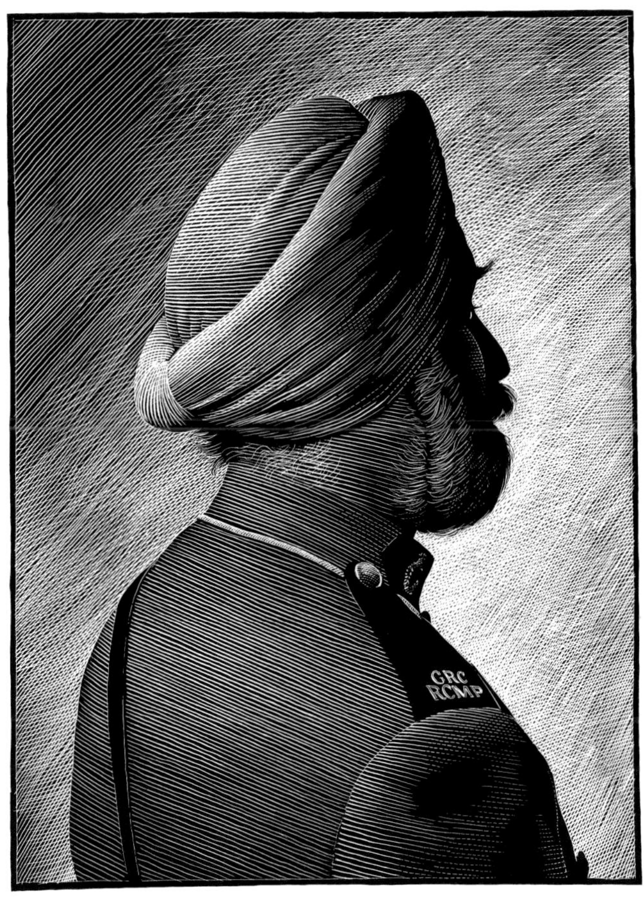
GRC
RCMP

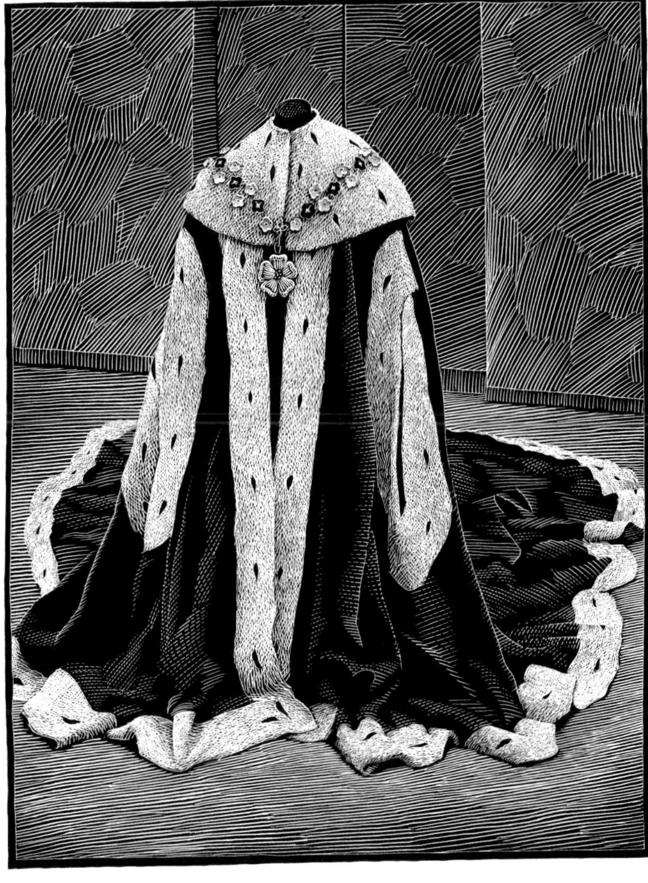

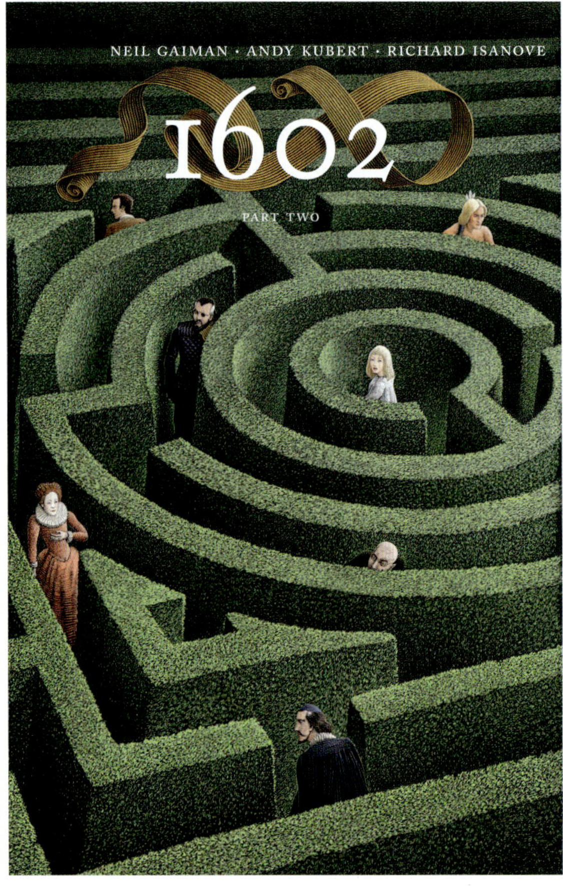

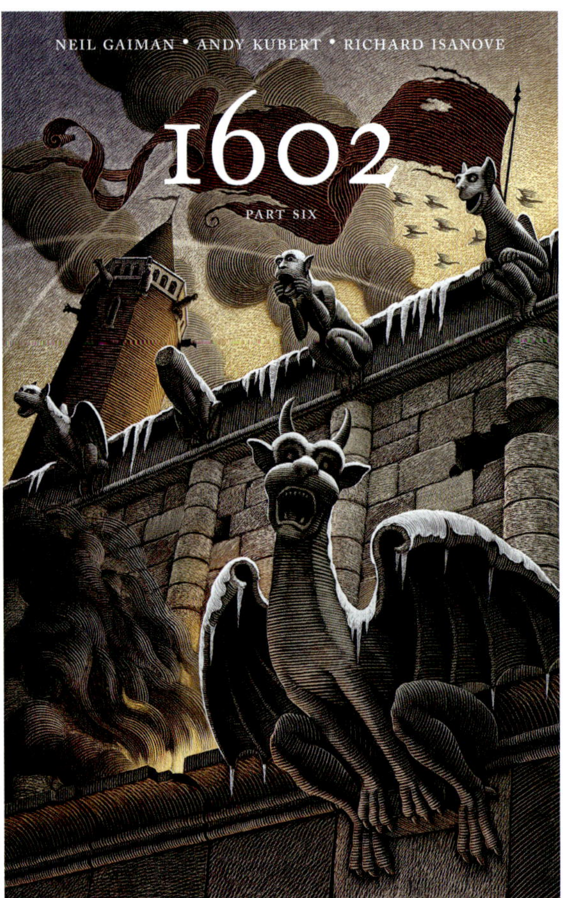

In early 2003, I received an out-of-the-blue phone call from Nick Lowe, an editor at Marvel Comics, asking if I might be interested in illustrating eight covers for a graphic novel by Neil Gaiman. I had not read a comic book since I was 10 years old, and I had to ask — why on Earth would he want me for a project like this?

Nick said that he had noticed my posters for the Roundabout Theatre Company in New York, and he thought that my engravings would evoke the historical setting of this story. Also, scratchboard is a medium rarely employed in the comic book world, and he wanted this high-profile series to have a distinctive look. I loved those answers, and I said yes immediately.

Gaiman's saga is set in the year 1602. The characters are 17th-century versions of familiar Marvel superheroes — Spider-Man, the Fantastic Four, the X-Men, Daredevil, Captain America. Sir Nicholas Fury and Dr. Strange are courtiers in the service of Queen Elizabeth I (who died in 1603). I looked at a lot of period engravings in preparation for this project — Jacques Callot and Stefano della Bella were especially useful for their flamboyant storm scenes and threatening skies.

Renaissance paintings and graphics sometimes include images of scrolls or banners floating in mid-air, with commentary about the scene or words a character might be speaking. (Historical precedent for comic book dialogue balloons, perhaps?) I suggested a floating scroll on each cover as a logo device for the series. Because *1602* is a short title, I treated the type as a juxtaposition — clean, reverse letterforms placed over the scroll, rather than a *trompe l'oeil* rendering of the numerals on the scroll.

The scroll became a different element in each cover — sometimes a flag, sometimes a banner. For *Part Three* it's the ribbon attached to a portrait miniature of Elizabeth — in the clutches of the story's principal villain, Otto von Doom.

1602 received mixed reviews when it came out. *Time* magazine rated it as the worst comic of 2003. But *Entertainment Weekly* loved the combination of writing and moody artwork and said, "the Marvel Universe hasn't been this engrossing in ages." The series won several awards, including the Quill Book Award for Graphic Novels; I was personally chuffed to receive a nomination for the 2004 Will Eisner Award for Best Cover Artist. Not surprisingly, there were several *1602* sequels and I was invited to continue working on covers — but Gaiman had moved on from the project, and I found that the new scripts lacked the audacious novelty of the initial eight-part saga, so I politely declined.

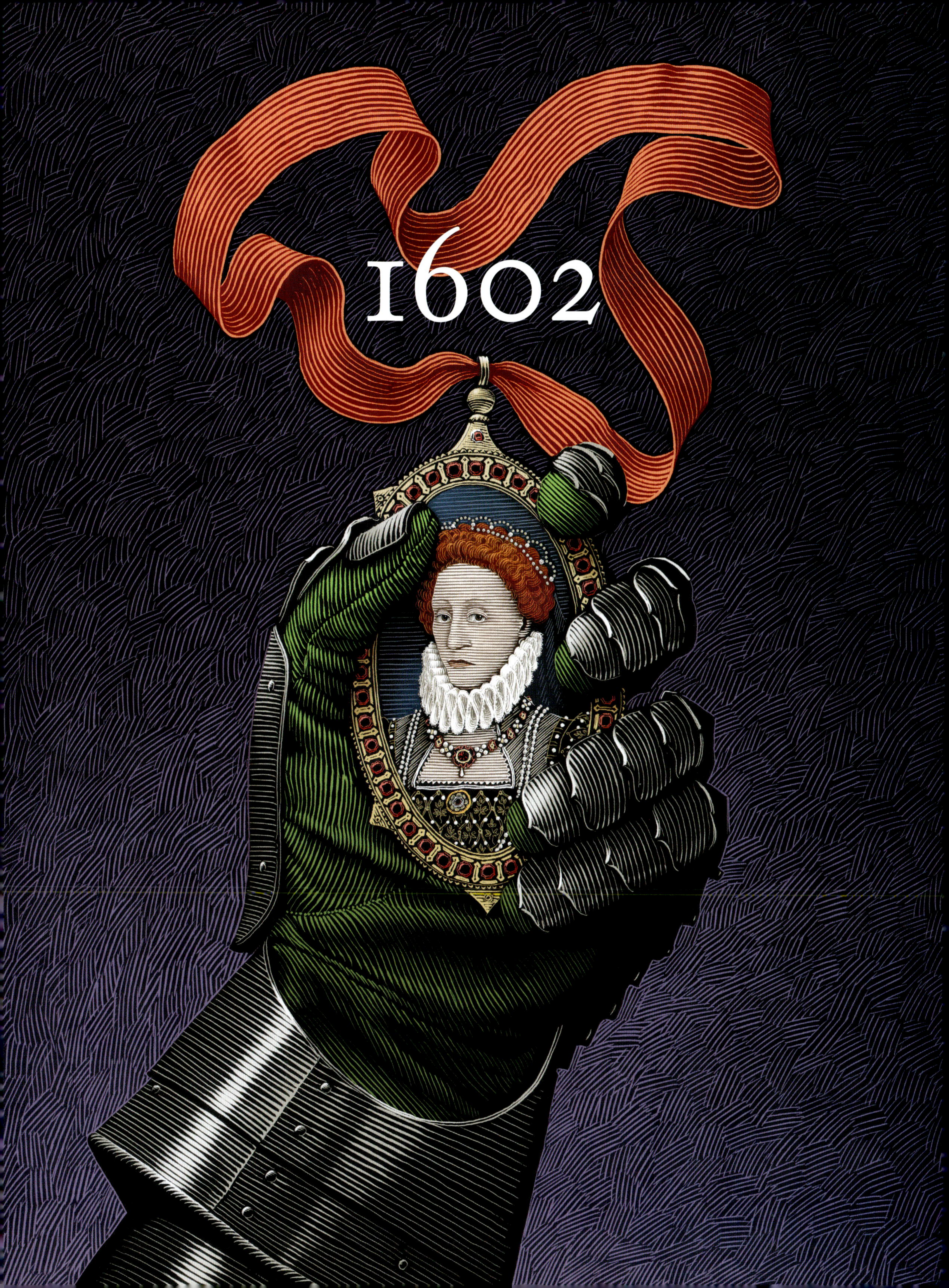
1602

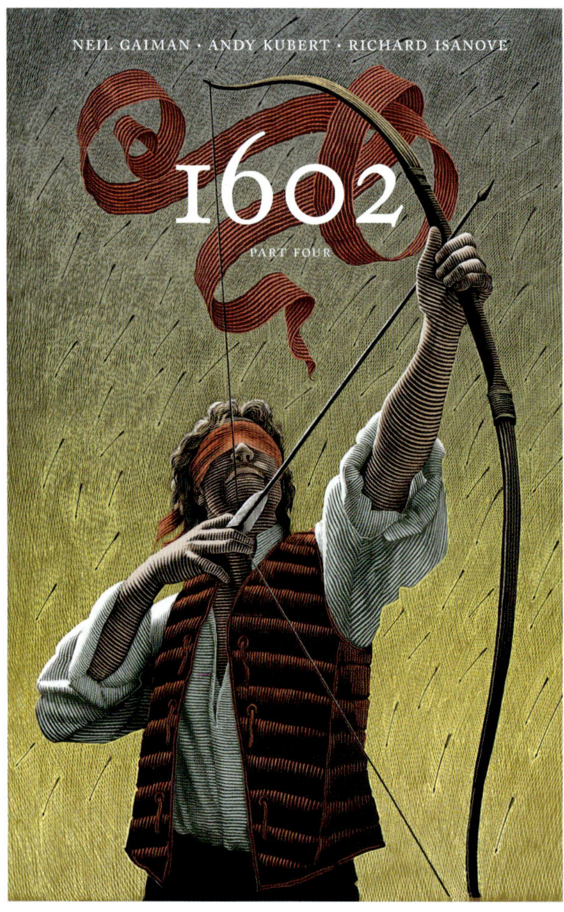

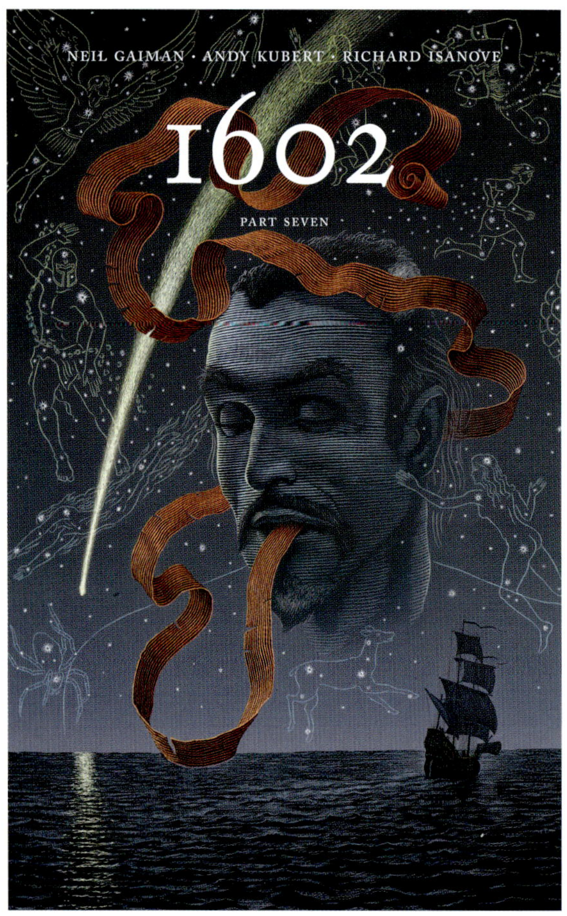

Neil Gaiman wanted the cover of the final chapter to signal that the story shifts from Europe to the New World. I researched 17th-century maps of Virginia and decided to incorporate their delightfully naive topographic decoration — hills, trees, animals and sailing ships, all completely out of realistic proportion — into my illustration.

I was fascinated by the place names: a crazy mix of Latin, Dutch, French and English, reflecting the colonial demographics of the time and place. All the names and spellings on this cover come from period sources — including the names of the Native American nations used to describe regions and territories.

The focal points of period maps are elaborate, decorative compass roses with lines radiating out to the far corners of the Earth. I thought it would be very cool to use a compass rose to make reference to the rip in time at the centre of the story — a glittering point of light that Neil calls "the singularity." I wanted to transform a compass rose into a mysterious light source shining on the three principal characters. A surreal "glow," created with a feathered brush in Photoshop, enhanced the effect. I usually try to avoid subjecting scratchboard lines to electronic special effects, but if ever there was a project to throw caution to the wind, this was it. I made pencil studies of the figures with separate light sources, then composited them to look as if they were standing on the map.

I found models based on who might have the right look for a certain character. Stratford Festival actor and director Scott Wentworth seemed ideal for this Elizabethan incarnation of Nick Fury — but I was a little nervous about asking a leading actor in North America's most important classical theatre company to model for a comic book project. I got my nerve up and called him — and I couldn't believe my luck: Scott is a long-time comic collector and fan, and was thrilled to play one of his all-time favourite Marvel characters!

We met for dinner when the Part Eight appeared in print; I framed the final pencil sketch for the illustration on the facing page as a thank-you gift. Completely unexpected was the thank-you gift I received in return — a first edition copy of *Nick Fury, Agent of* S.H.I.E.L.D., the first appearance of the character in print on June 1, 1968, from Scott's own collection. It was published by Marvel Comics Group, cover price 12¢. I cried with delight.

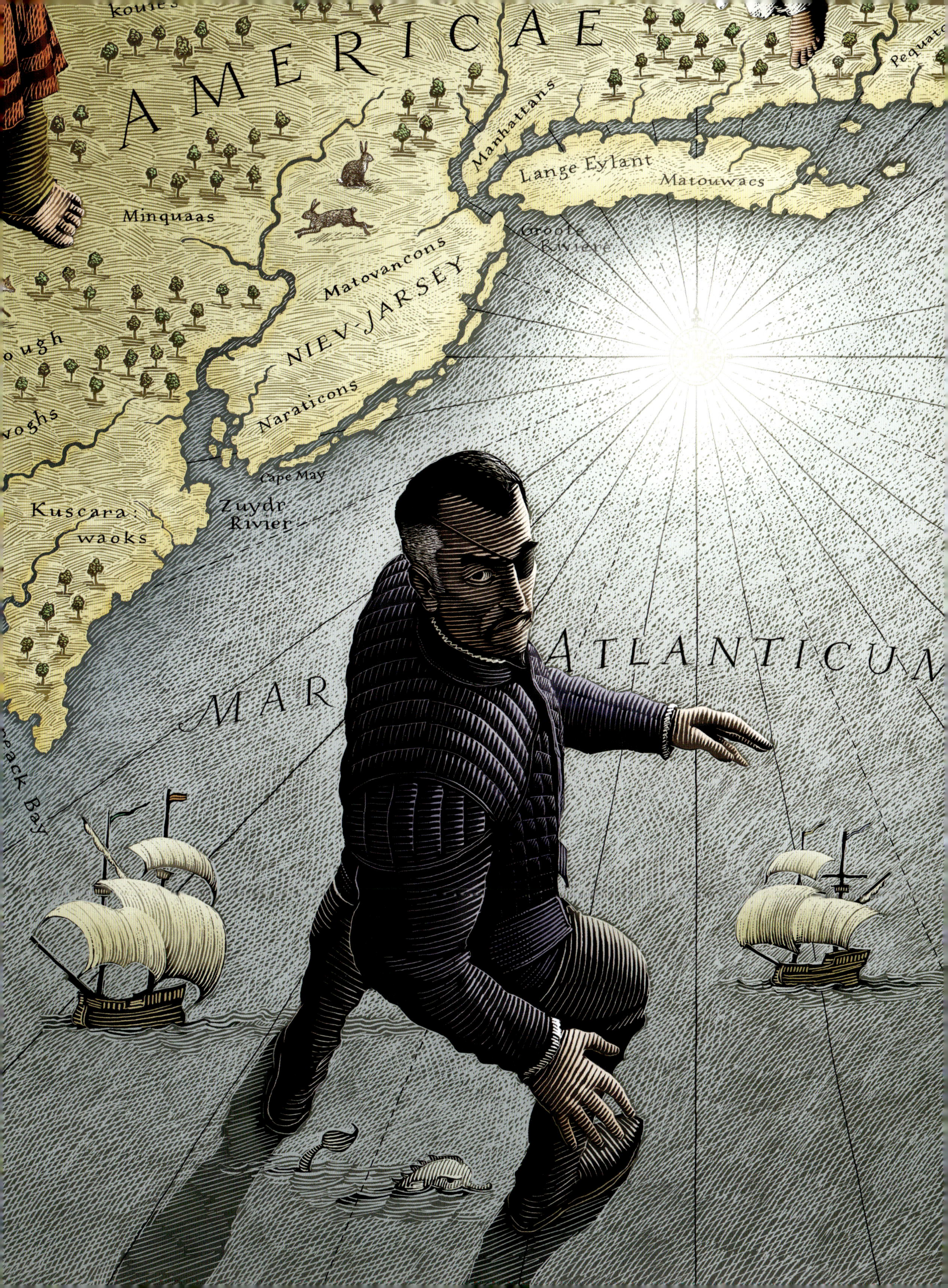

AMERICAE
Manhattans
Lange Eylant
Matouwacs
Minquaas
Matovancons
NIEV-JARSEY
Naraticons
Cape May
Zuydr Rivier
Kuscara: waoks
MAR
ATLANTICUM

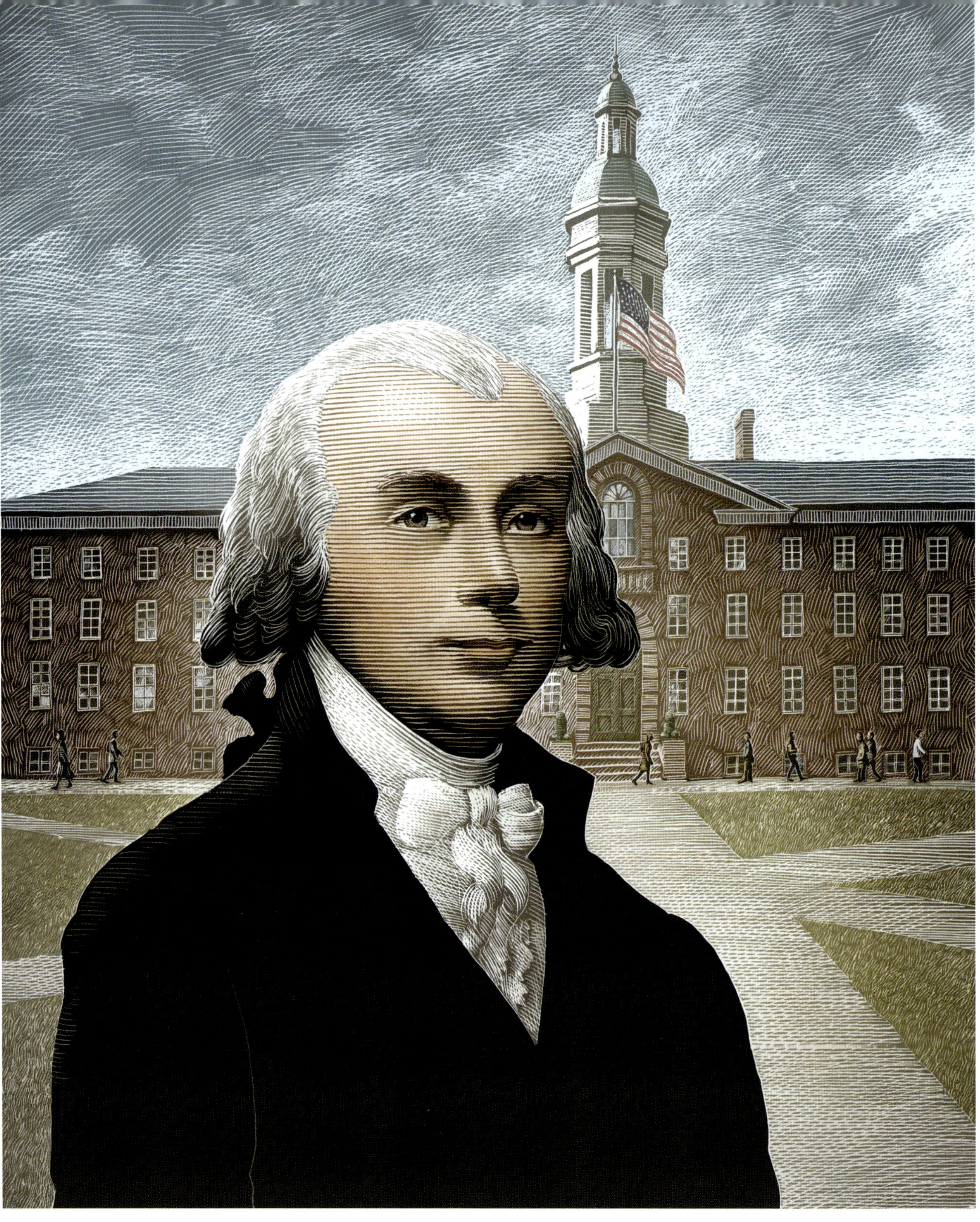

In 2008, a special issue of *Princeton Alumni Weekly* ranked the 25 most influential alumni from the University's 261-year history. The "winner" was James Madison — class of 1771. Fourth President of the United States, Madison was a principal author of the U.S. Constitution and the "Father of the Bill of Rights." He was Thomas Jefferson's Secretary of State from 1801 to 1809 and supervised the Louisiana Purchase, which doubled the size of the country.

I was asked to supply a cover portrait for the magazine. For reference, I looked at a number of primary sources — Gilbert Stuart painted several portraits that captured a consistent likeness. These images from the period have generic "statesman" backgrounds — a bit of drapery or the base of a classical column. I wanted to include an architectural landmark so the cover would be specific to Princeton, and the obvious choice was Nassau Hall.

In 2014, I was asked to create a cover portrait of Miguel de Cervantes for *The College*, the alumni magazine of St. John's College in Annapolis, Maryland. Cervantes was a contemporary of Shakespeare (both died in April 1616), but we have no idea what he actually looked like so I was free to pick a model who I would like Cervantes to look like (in this case, a meltingly handsome Spanish dancer in Toronto).

Christina proposed making his ruff into a book fantasy — leave it to a theatre designer to turn a 17th-century costume detail into a literary reference. *Don Quixote* is often called the first modern novel so the metaphor fits perfectly. Alonso Quixano, Cervantes' protagonist, is a country gentleman who reads too many books on chivalry — which leads to the distortion of his mental faculties and his "transformation" into Don Quixote. Gustave Doré established the archetype for the character in 1863 with his unparalleled engravings — an older man, tall and gaunt with soulful eyes. This is a portrait of the author, not the character, but a touch of the fantastical Quixano/Quixote certainly seemed appropriate for his author.

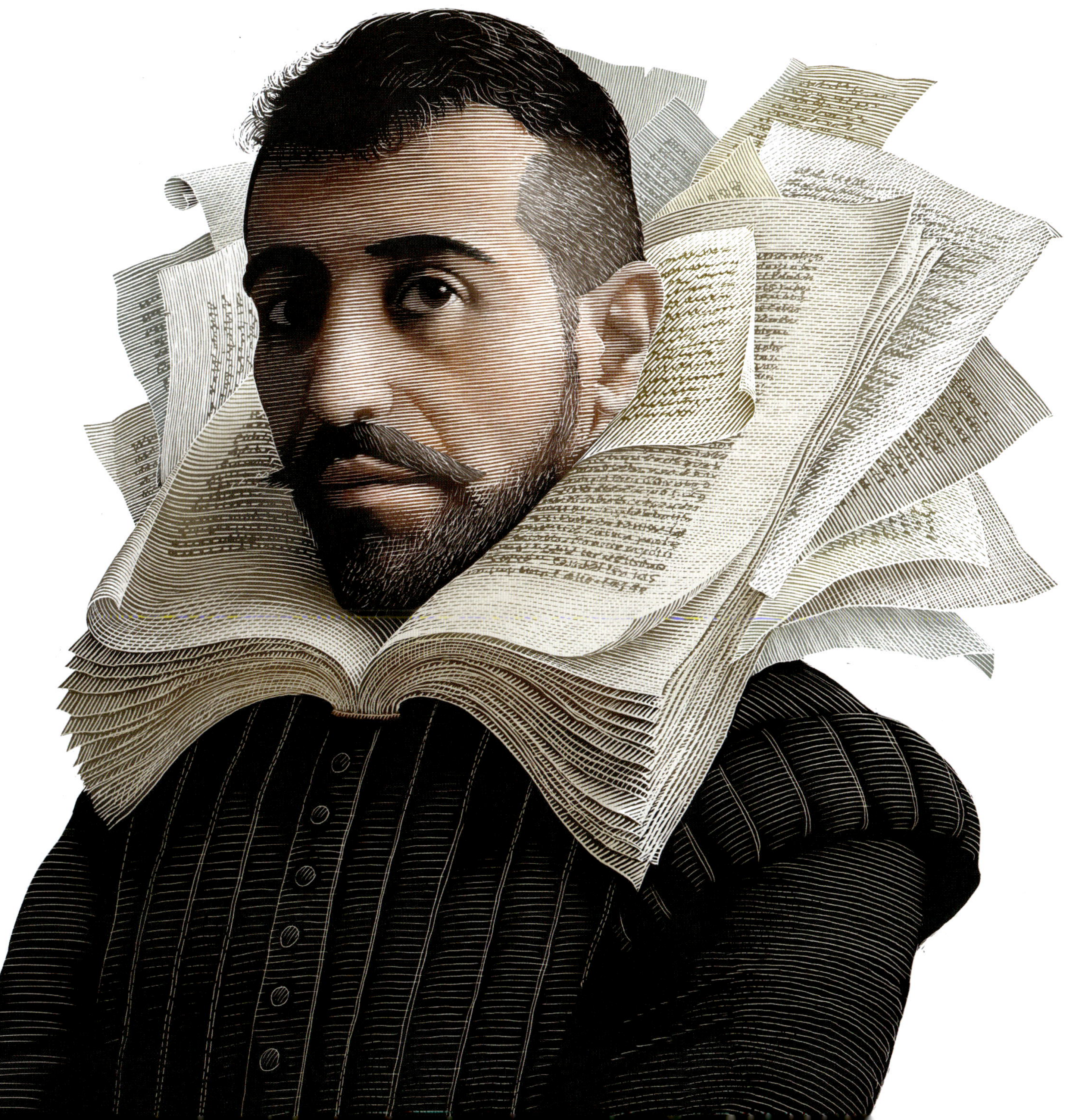

American costume designer Irene Sharaff (1910–1993) designed over 70 films including *Hello, Dolly!, Funny Girl, Flower Drum Song, Porgy and Bess, Guys and Dolls, A Star is Born* (the 1954 original), and *Meet Me in St. Louis.* She won five Academy Awards — for *West Side Story* in 1961, *Cleopatra* in 1963, *Who's Afraid of Virginia Woolf?* in 1966, *The King And I* in 1956, and *An American in Paris* in 1951 — and a Tony Award for the original Broadway production of *The King and I* in 1952.

Sharaff's memory and legacy are kept alive by an award, bestowed annually to a costume designer who has achieved great distinction in theatre, film, opera or dance. The award is administered by TDF (Theatre Development Fund) in New York. Our Punch & Judy studio had been doing a lot of graphic design work for TDF, and we were asked to upgrade the invitation package for the 25th Anniversary edition of the awards in 2019. Irene Sharaff needed a new graphic identity.

For many years, TDF had used a wonderfully dramatic portrait photograph of Sharaff in profile — but the black and white image was of poor contrast and quality. She's wearing a black sweater in front of a black background, so her pale skin ends abruptly, creating the disconcerting impression of a decapitated head.

I proposed that a new scratchboard illustration — against a clean white background — would make for a fresh take on the familiar brand. Stephen Cabral, my client at TDF, had pointed out that Sharaff was famous for her "Egyptian eye." After her design for Elizabeth Taylor in *Cleopatra*, Irene adopted this eye makeup and wore it for the rest of her life. It struck me that Sharaff's profile portrait was a '60s version of the famous portrait bust of ancient Egyptian Queen Nefertiti (c.1370–c.1330 BC). Sharaff's fabulous hairdo is the same proportion as Nefertiti's headdress, and they have the same long, elegant neck and regal bearing. So I gave myself the license to fill in the fine detail missing from Sharaff's photo from Nefertiti's features, modeled over three thousand years ago.

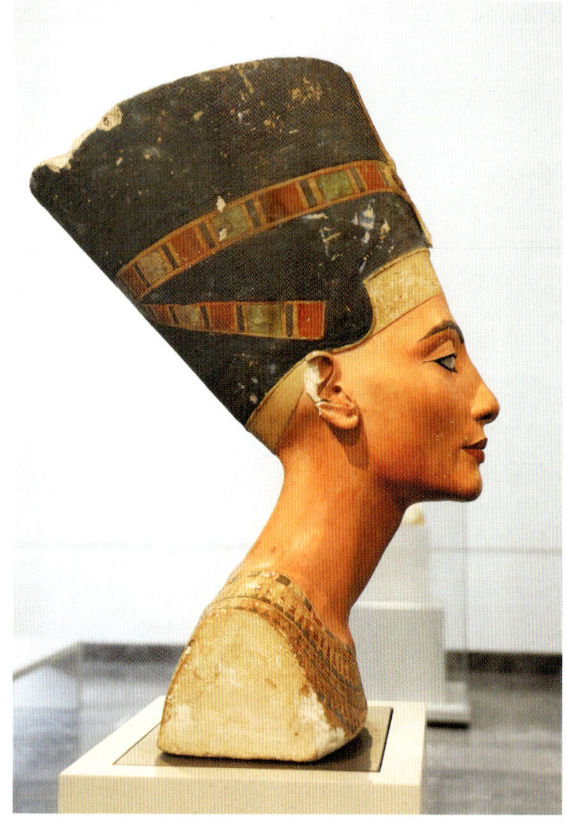

Bust of Nefertiti, Altes Museum, Berlin.

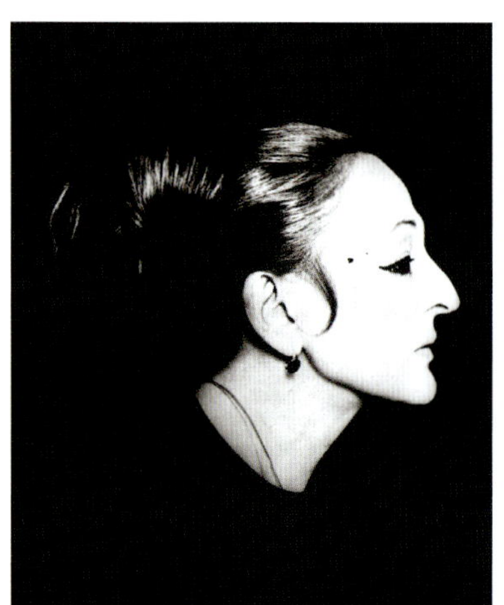

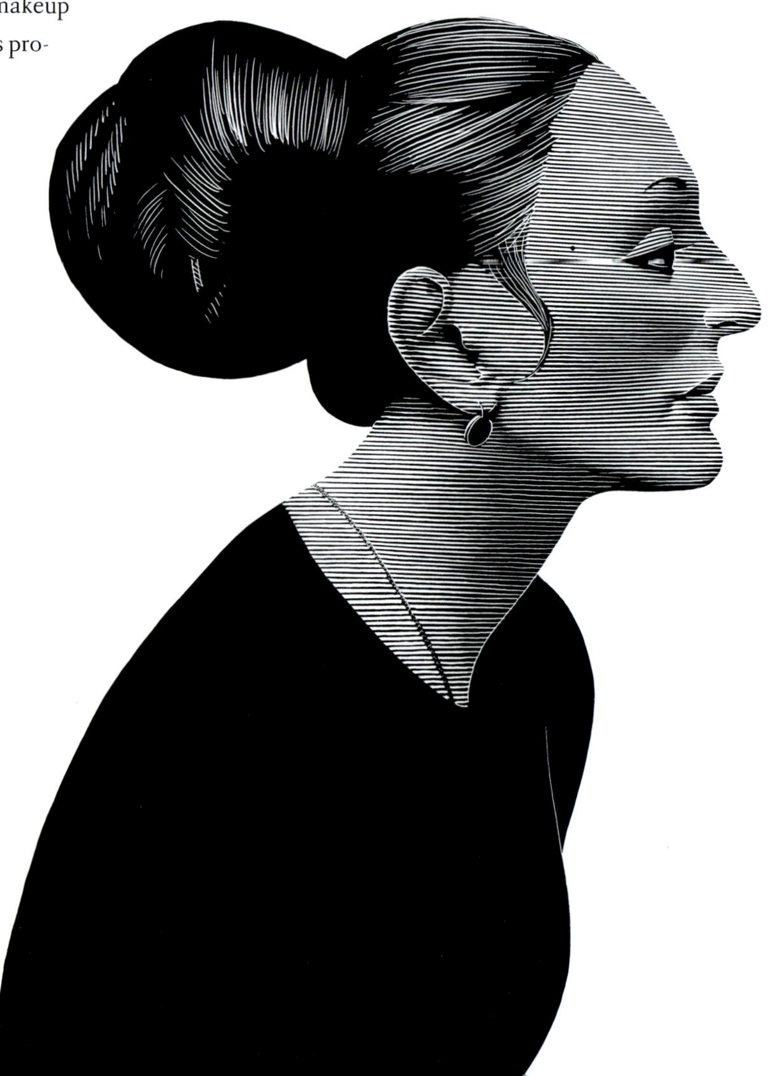

Langdon Hall, the grand and gracious country house hotel in Cambridge, Ontario, is set among gardens designed by the Olmsted Brothers (sons of Frederick Law Olmsted, designer of Central Park). Wilks Bar, the casual dining room on the property, required a graphic identity for menu covers. The handsome panelled room is named for Eugene Langdon Wilks, great-grandson of John Jacob Astor and the original builder of the house in 1902. A portrait of Wilks seemed obvious — but oil paintings and photographs felt old-fashioned and overly reverential. I suggested that a silhouette portrait of Mr. Wilks would acknowledge the history of the house, and at the same time serve as a sophisticated contemporary logo. Unfortunately no such portrait exists — so I created one in scratchboard. I placed the elegant Edwardian figure against strong colours on the covers of the bar's food menu and drink menu (the orange colour gradation was inspired by a glass of fine cognac).

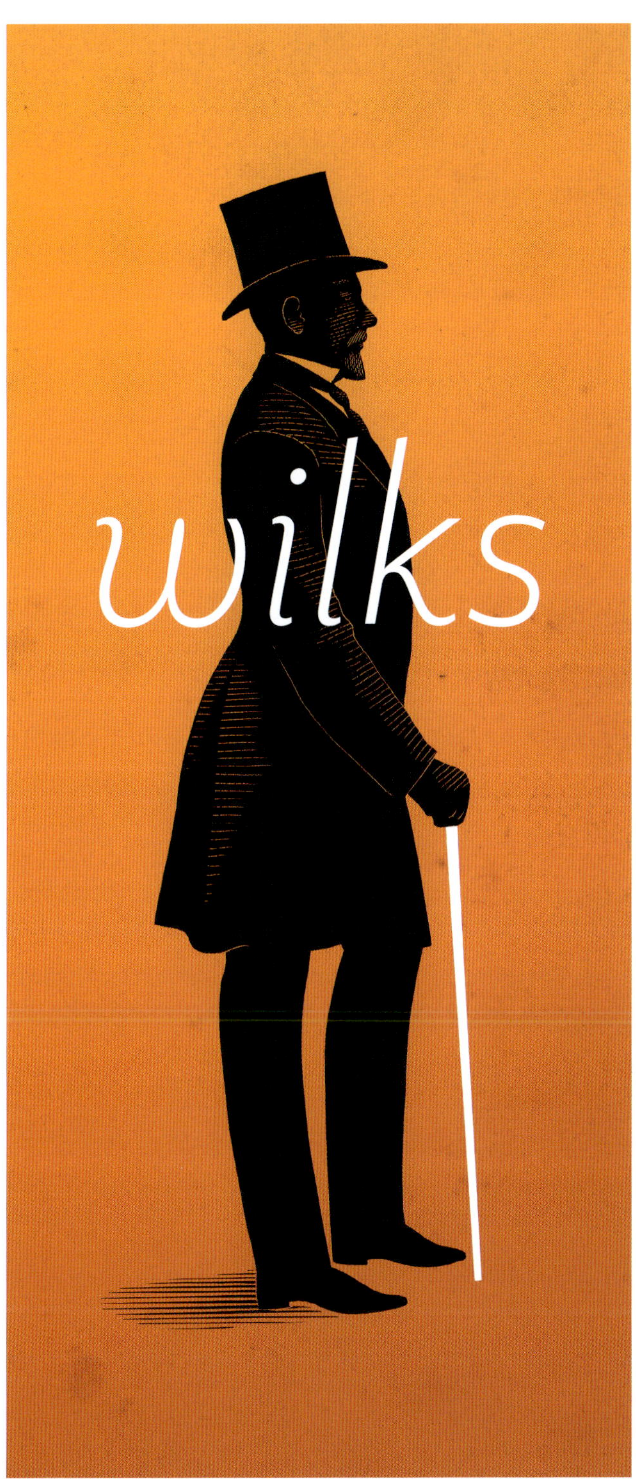

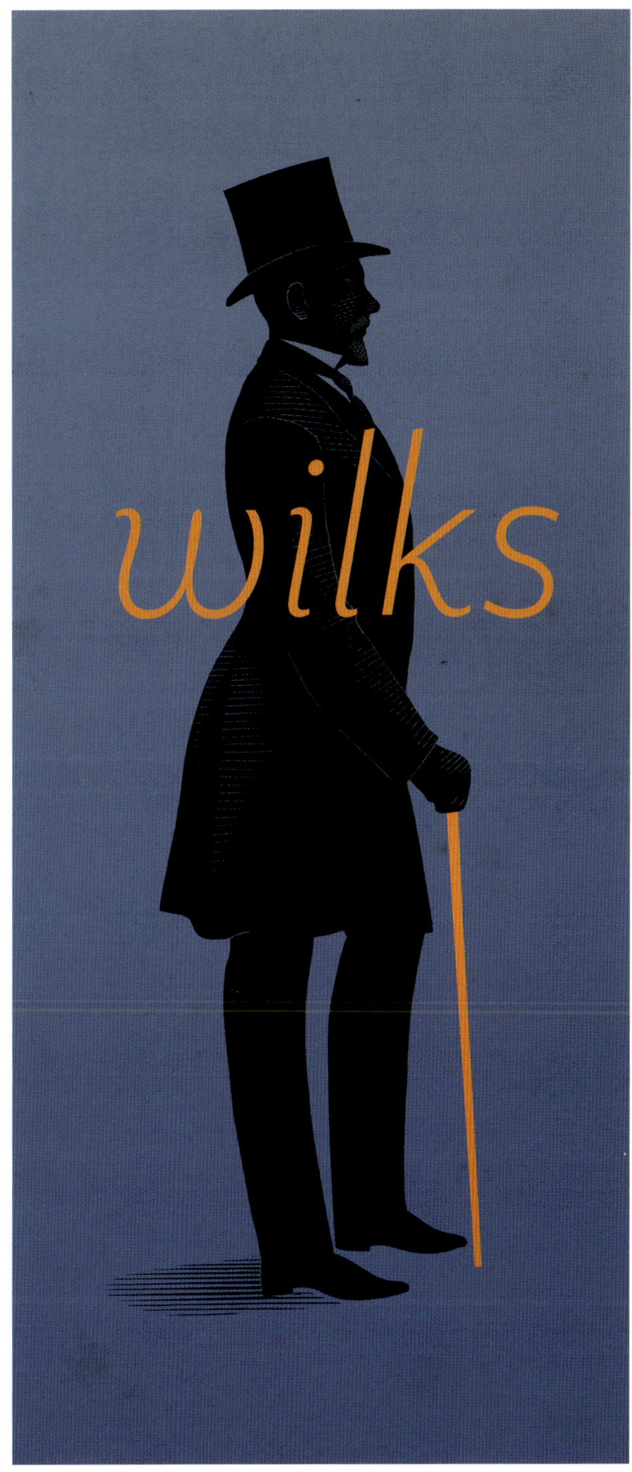

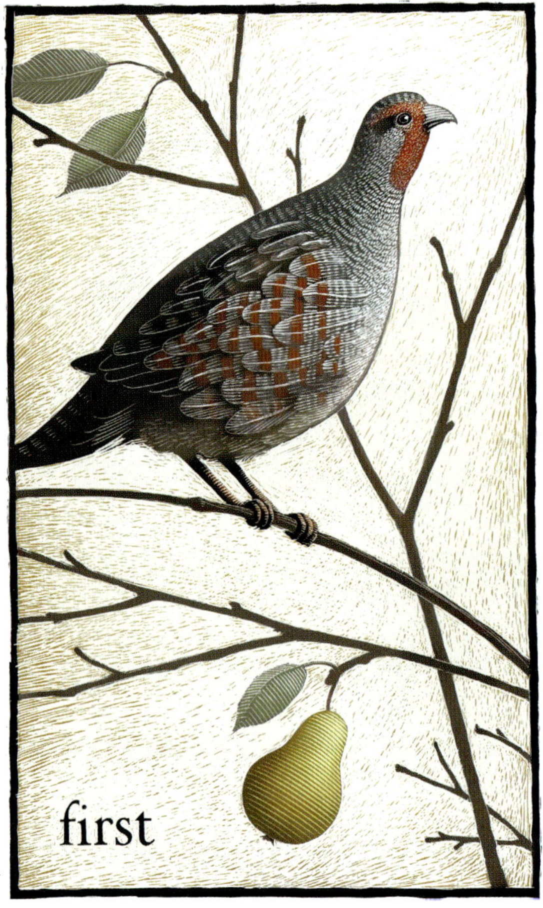

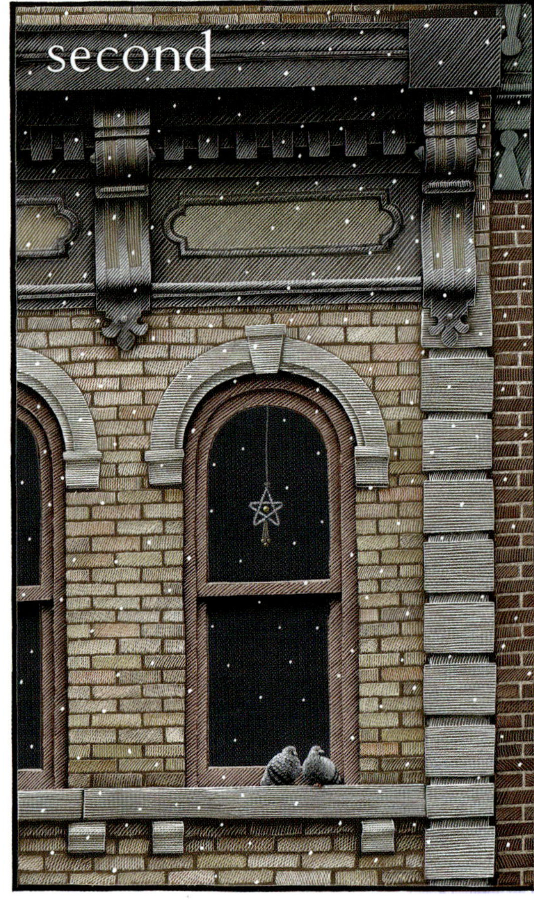

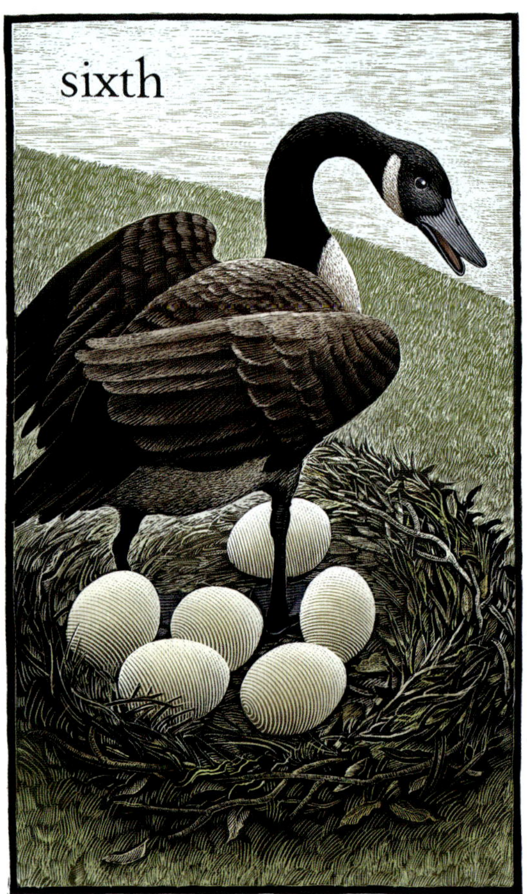

Christina and I started a "Perth County Twelve Days of Christmas" series in 2001 — one numeral per year. Instead of storybook settings from medieval Europe, we wanted to feature the birds, farms and rural traditions in and around our home in Stratford, Ontario. Our Four Calling Birds were chickadees at the suet feeder in our backyard. Swans are Stratford's famous civic symbol. Our Eight Maids work on a local dairy farm. Our Ladies Dancing is a scene from a fiddle-and-step-dance competition. Ten Lords a-Leaping is a pickup hockey game on the frozen Avon River. Our Twelve Drummers are woodpeckers hard at work on a weathered tree trunk in the Old Grove.

We finished the project in 2012, and Firefly Books published it as a little holiday gift book. Forgive the pop-up ad here, but it's entitled *My True Love Gave to Me* and it makes a lovely stocking-stuffer.

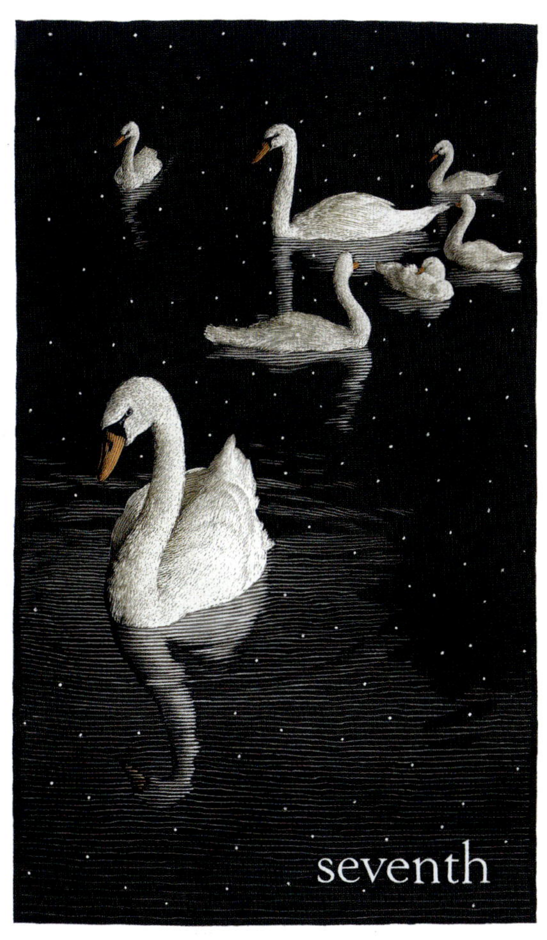
seventh

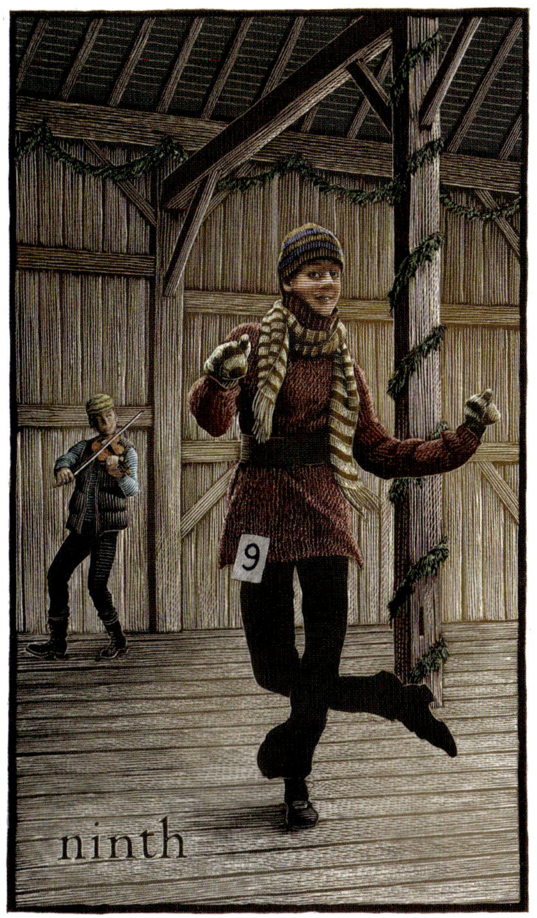
9
ninth

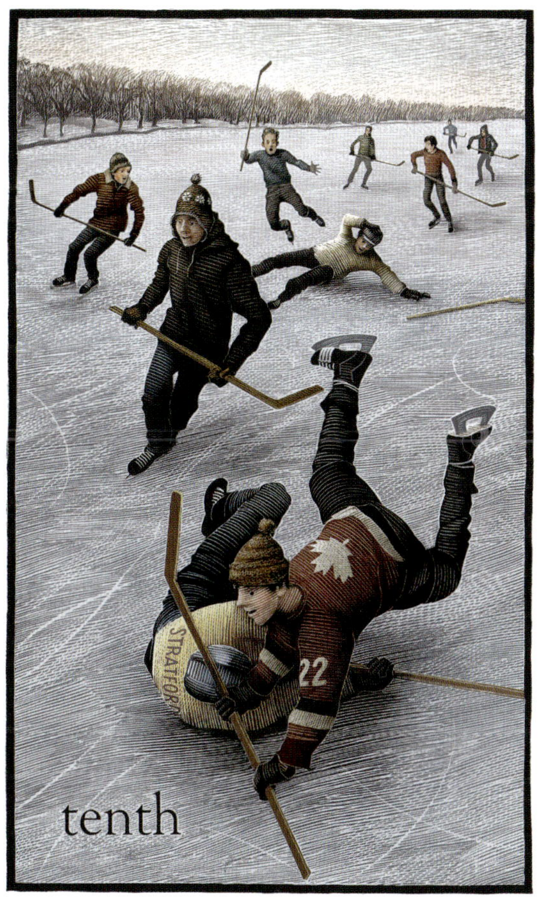
STRATFORD
22
tenth

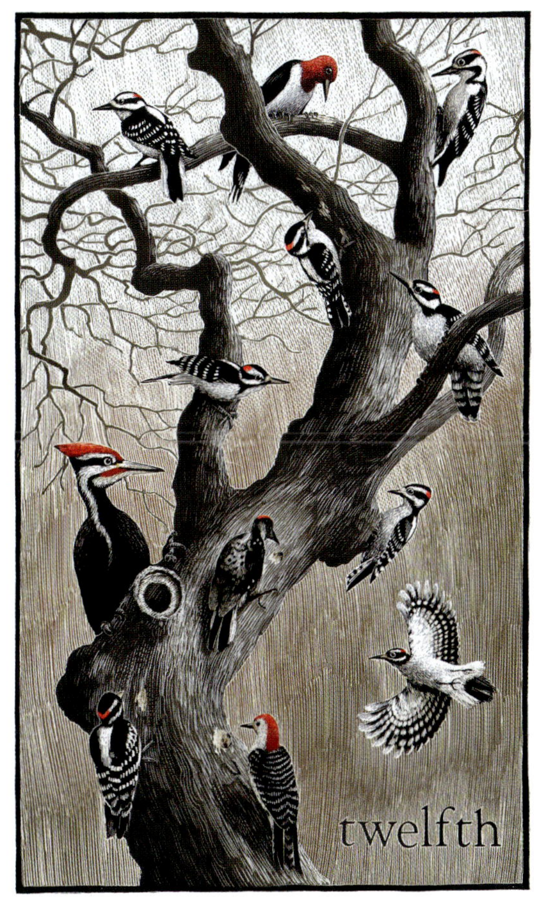
twelfth

We finished our *Twelve Days of Christmas* series in 2012 and realized that our cards for many years have reflected only the secular side of the holiday season. On a visit to Quebec City a few years ago, we came upon an extraordinary folk art *crèche* in an old town antique shop — hundreds of hand-carved wooden figures in a naive style including angels, shepherds, wise men and animals. We were struck by the simplicity and eloquence of the work.

This was our inspiration to try a *crèche* series of our own. We wanted to portray the characters in the Nativity story in contemporary dress — as if they were everyday people you might run into on the street.

First installment was the Annunciation. We imagined the angel Gabriel as a 12-year-old girl holding a lily and floating a few inches off the floor. Then Mary as a pregnant waif, and Joseph travelling with cheap suitcases and backpacks.

The Herald Angel that makes such an impression on the Shepherds is wearing a gold-sequined minidress, cowboy boots and a white fur hat, and she's playing an accordion. We've done three shepherds in a range of age groups. We have started in on the Magi — our Balthazar has attributes of Athena, the Greek goddess associated with wisdom, including her owl (a Snowy Owl, because they migrate from their usual habitat in the Arctic as far south as Stratford, in search of food — we love spotting them here during the winter months).

We plotted out the Nativity characters leaving one wild card spot open — a stable boy or girl? That donkey? A camel? The pandemic of 2020 suggested a front-line nurse "Angel."

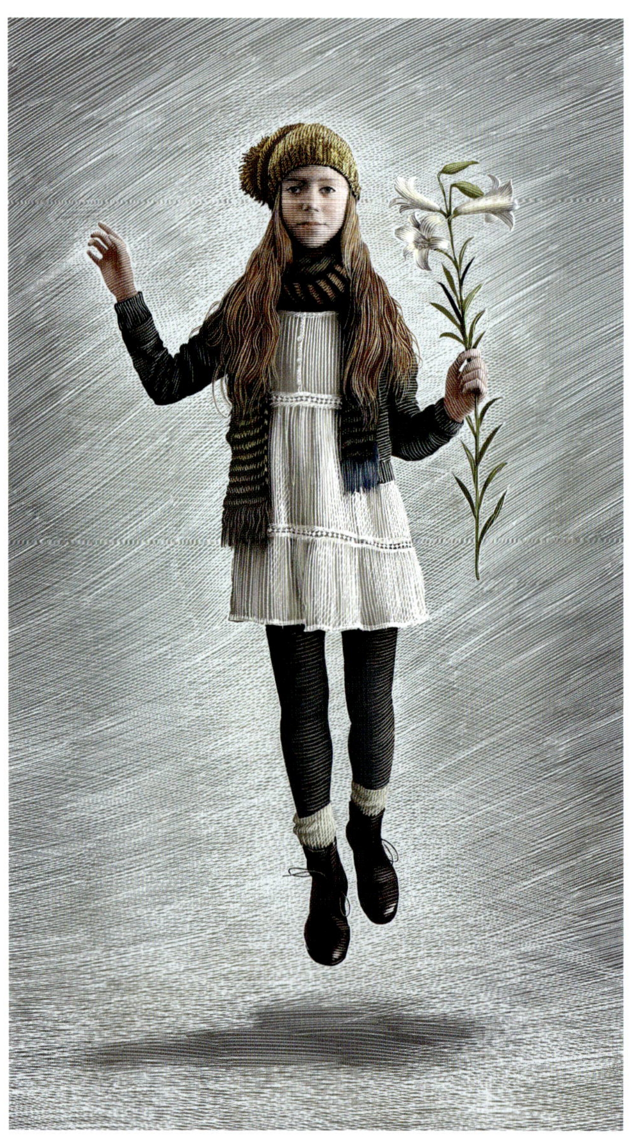

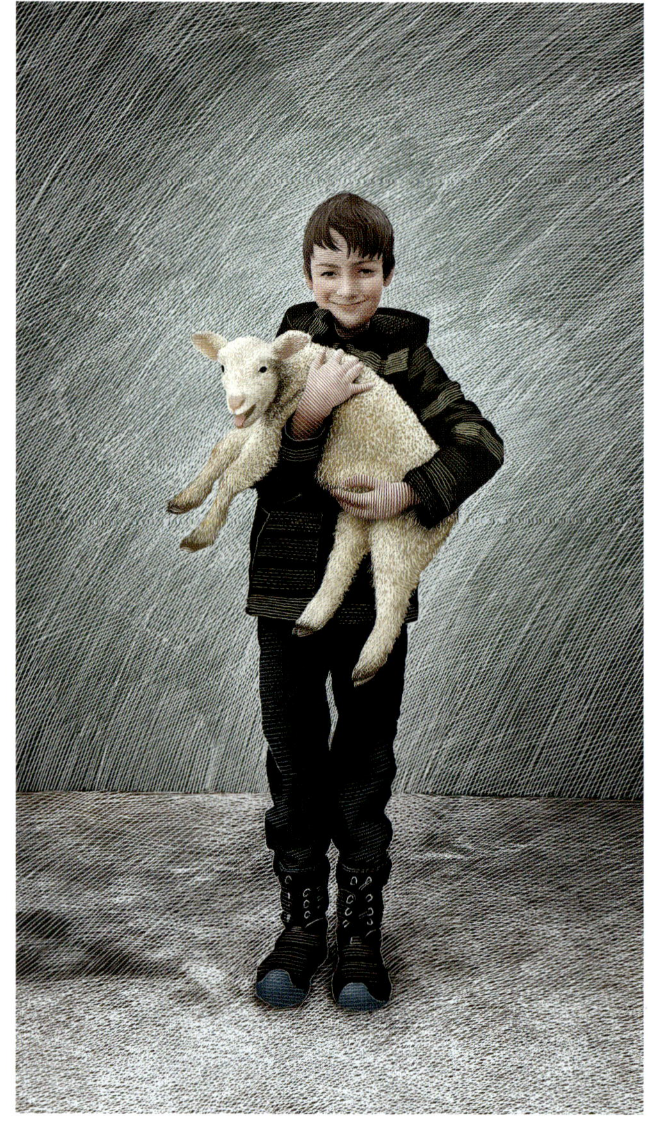

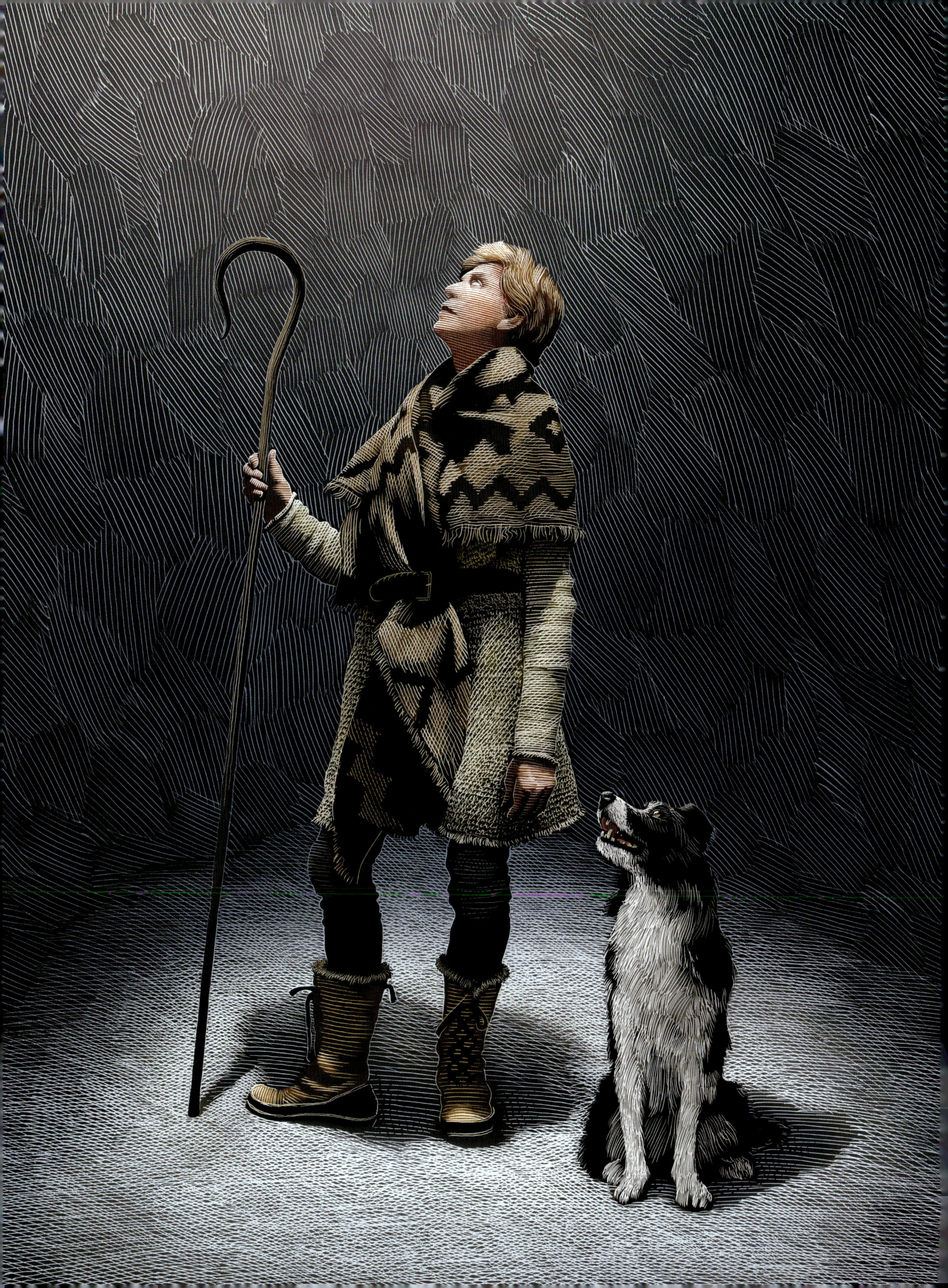

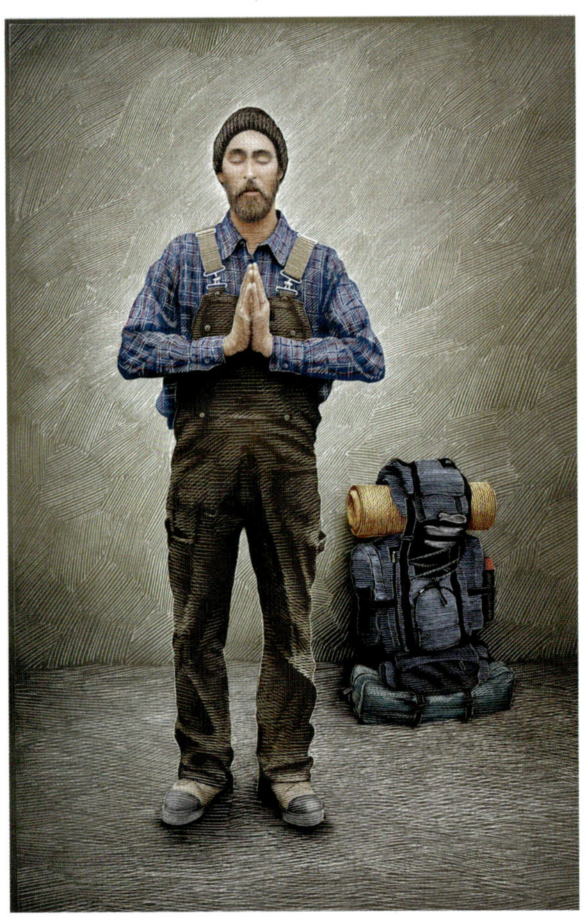

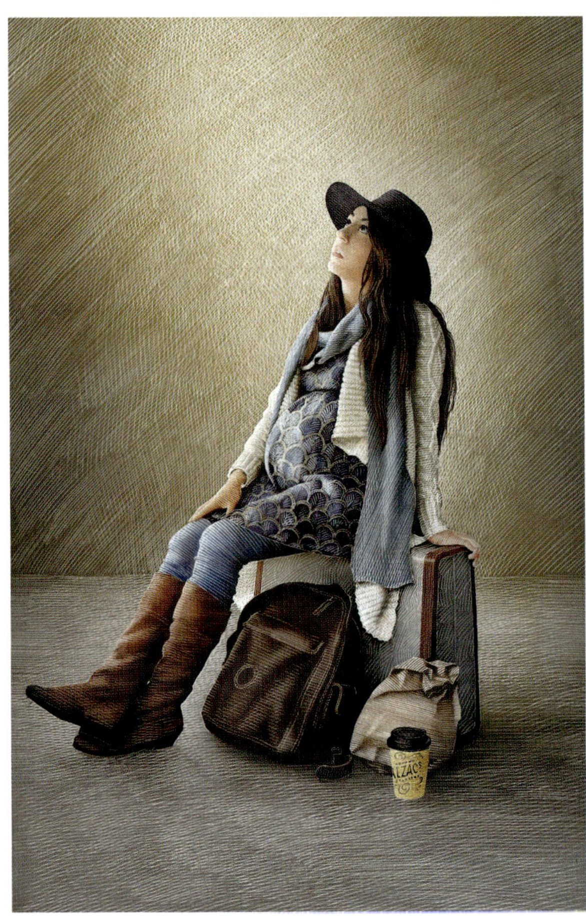

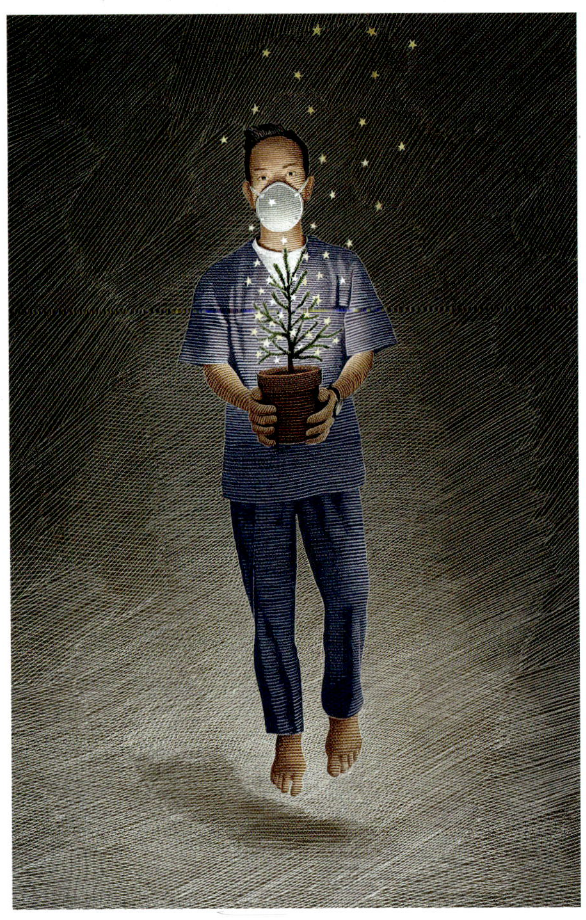

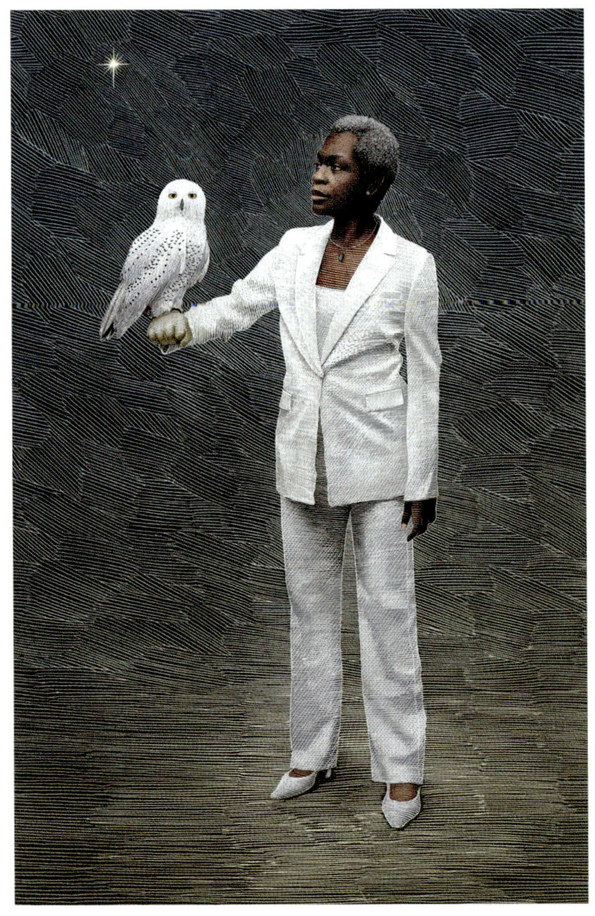

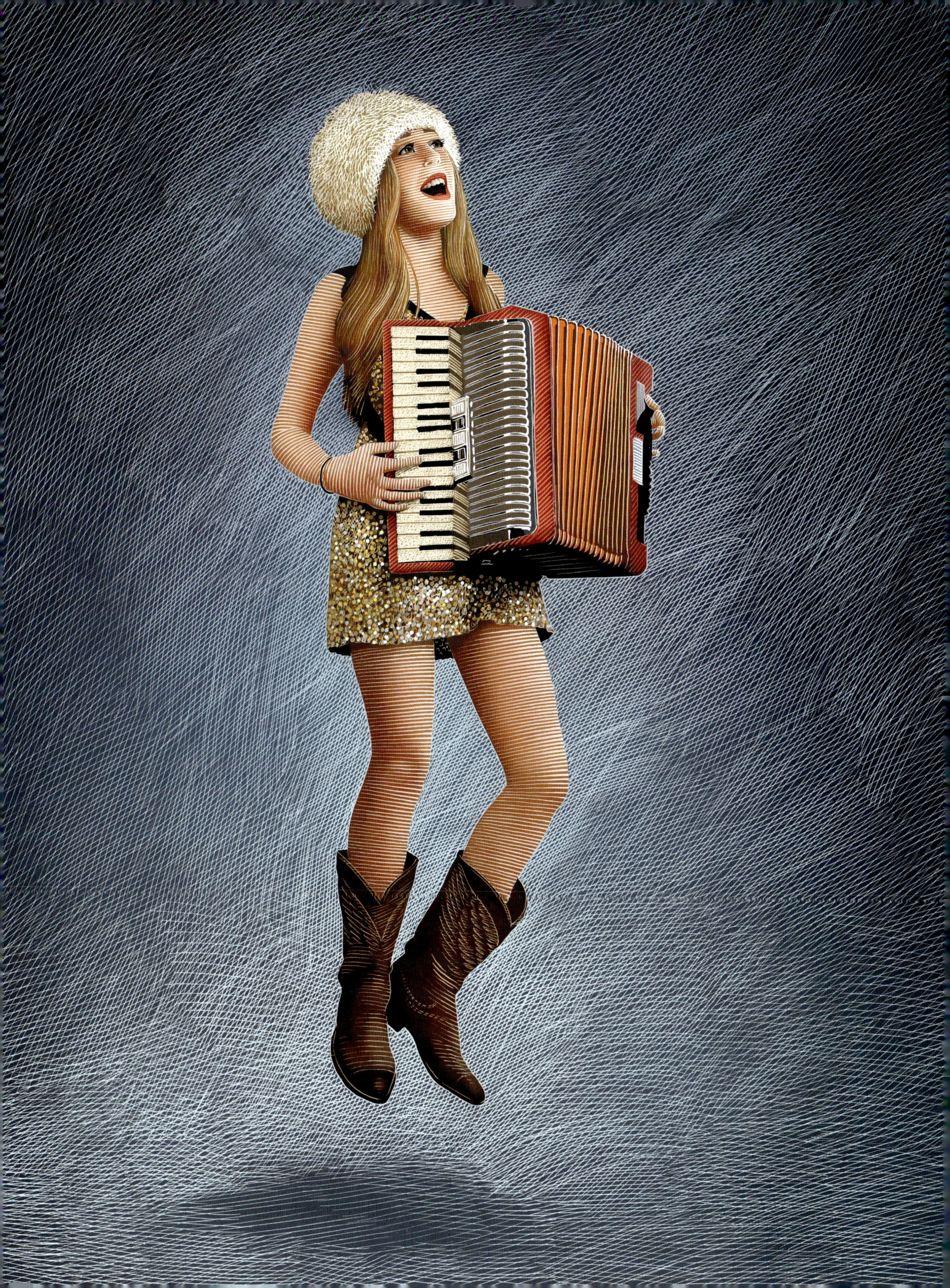

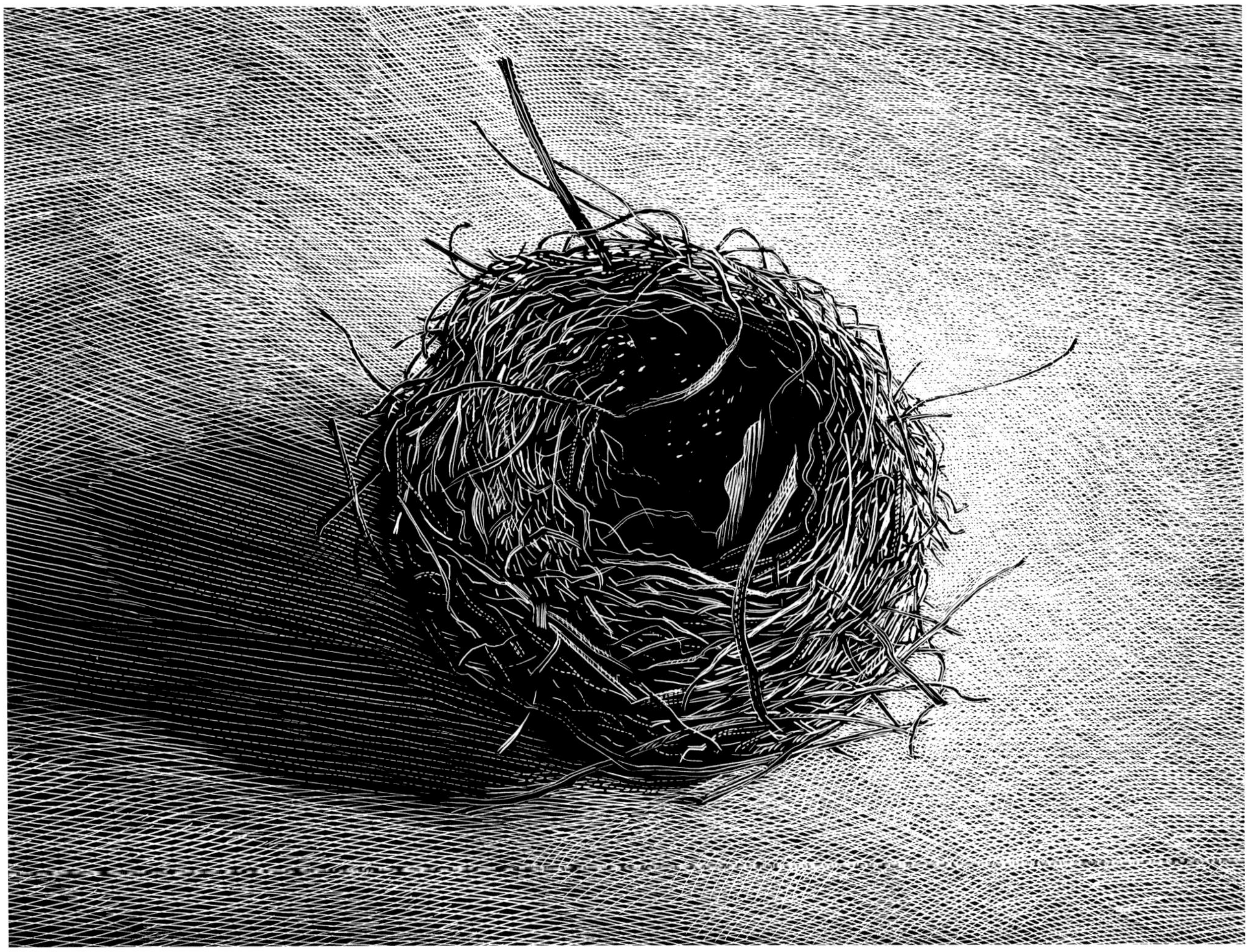

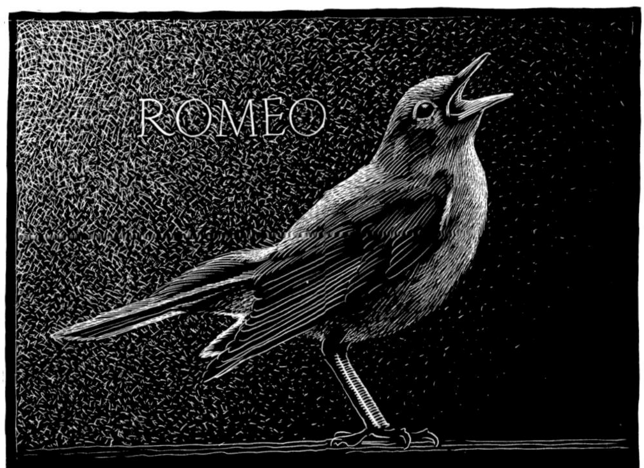

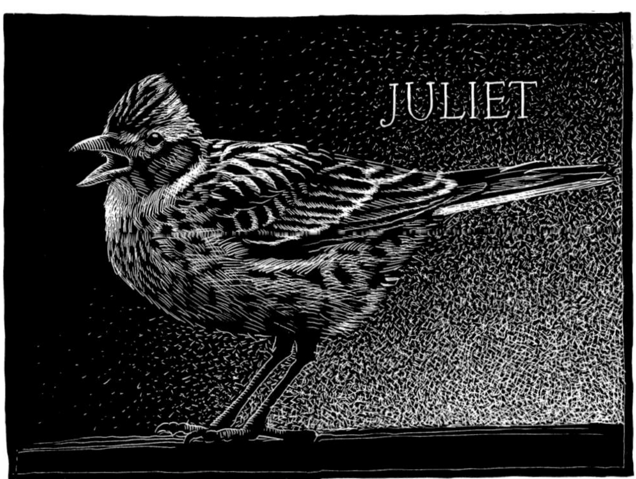

Christina has a wonderful collection of birds' nests — she added one recently with particularly fine detail, and I made a drawing of it for her. It was a good exercise in texture and shading. She designed sets and costumes for the Stratford Festival's 2017 production of *Romeo and Juliet*. My opening night "card" was a scratchboard drawing of the nightingale and the lark heard outside Juliet's bedroom window as the young couple's night together comes to an end.

Opposite: Tommy Stubbins, with Polynesia the parrot, from the Sterling Classics edition of *The Voyages of Doctor Dolittle* by Hugh Lofting, published in 2012.

Communication Arts invited me to participate in "Insights," their ongoing column of interviews, in 2012. I love this series because they send the same list of questions to each illustrator, and it's interesting to see the wide variety of different experiences reflected in the responses.

If you have a degree in what field is it? BFA, magna cum laude, from the University of Michigan School of Art in Ann Arbor. This is the first time I've been asked that question in more than a decade.

Have you always been able to draw or was it a skill you learned in college? Learning to draw is a lifetime study. I'm 56 and maybe, hopefully, finally starting to get the hang of it. I'm pretty religious about doing life drawing once a week and I've recently taken a couple of anatomy courses. It's all cumulative.

What was your first paid assignment? A theater poster for a high school production of the musical *Once Upon a Mattress.* I misspelled the hand-drawn title with only one "t" and had to reprint at my own expense — an excellent lesson for a beginner.

Which illustrator (or fine artist) do you most admire? Milton Glaser.

What would you be doing if you weren't an illustrator? There are many wonderful teachers in my family, but I don't think I have the patience for that (although having summers off would be brilliant). I love type and letterforms carved in wood and stone; an assistant and graphic designer who worked with me for fifteen years shared this enthusiasm and we made a pact that one day we would withdraw from society and go off to live in the woods and learn stone carving. I'm looking forward to that.

From where do your best ideas originate? They're often stolen (in the sense that we all take acquired information and reconfigure it). But received information is not the same as inspiration. Inspiration is a mystery; the spark comes from an ability to associate or juxtapose visual ideas in witty, unexpected ways. My wife, Christina Poddubiuk, is a theater set and costume designer with an honors English degree and she's particularly adept at the exercise of distilling a play or novel into a visual metaphor — many of my best ideas are her inspirations, bless her.

How do you overcome a creative block? I'll do something else for awhile, to reboot my brain, then approach it fresh. Problem-solving requires enough time for patterns to form and associations to be made. Your imagination is still working on problems

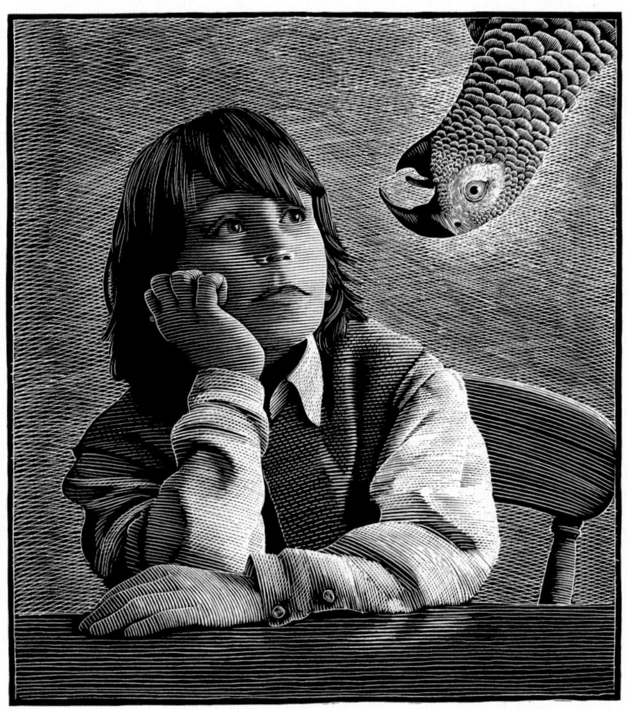

subconsciously, even when focused on other things. Highway driving works nicely — your immediate focus is on the car in the next lane, but another part of the brain is still working away on the back burner, trying to connect the dots.

In one word describe how you feel when beginning a new assignment. Solvent.

Do you have a personal philosophy? Whatever it is that each of us is given to do in our little span of time, we need to do it with passion, rigor and commitment to excellence. My disclaimer here is that I don't have children, so my work/life balance is a bit skewed, but I think that spending one's time working to create beautiful things makes for a pretty interesting life.

Do you have creative pursuits other than illustration? Theater, music and opera. I do a lot of cooking. I love to travel and always carry a sketchbook. I played piano and classical guitar many years ago and would love to pick those up again.

What music are you listening to right now? J.S. Bach, Six Suites for Unaccompanied Cello.

What's your favorite quote? "If it were easy, anyone could do it." —Unknown

Do you have any advice for people just entering the profession? It gets harder.

What's one thing you wish you knew when you started your career? It gets harder.

The exercise of drawing generally involves making black lines (using pencil, ink, charcoal or crayon) on white paper. The tone of the paper establishes the value of the highlights — so all the marks made on the page automatically describe shadows. The more lines you add to a drawing with hatching to build up areas of tone, the further you render the shadow areas.

Scratchboard (or scraperboard, as the British call it) is exactly the opposite — white lines are drawn onto an all-black background — so the lines describe highlights. A similar experience would be drawing with a piece of chalk on a blackboard. Drawing in reverse is a little tricky. When I first tried scratchboard, I quickly realized that the free-form cross-hatch lines I used with pen-and-ink did not translate well into this new medium. I taught myself how to use evenly spaced parallel lines to create areas of tone. The eye registers areas of closely spaced lines as grey tone, the same way that halftone dots create the grey tones in a photograph printed in a newspaper.

The board itself is a machine-prepared surface of hard white chalk on a cardboard or Masonite baseboard. A thin layer of black ink covers the chalk surface, and lines are created by scratching through the black ink into the white chalk underneath with a sharp blade. There are knives intended as scratchboard tools, but I usually work with X-ACTO knife blades — no.11 for fine lines, and no.2 or no.24 for heavier lines. You can vary the line width to an extent by pressing harder on the blade (cutting deeper into the surface). This variation in line width creates the dynamics of tone, from stark contrasts to subtle shadings of light falling across a surface.

Scratchboard often looks like engraving — the lines are, literally, engraved — but this is not a printmaking medium. In traditional engraving, lines are cut into a surface (a block of wood or a metal plate), which is then inked and printed onto sheets of paper, creating an edition of multiple prints. A finished scratchboard drawing is a single original, reproduced like any drawing or photograph by scanning or other photo-mechanical process. It's a black-and-white medium — I add colour, if required, once the line drawing is finished.

Preliminary pencil sketches are used to work out every detail of the drawing before starting on final art. Indeed, the protocol of the illustration business requires the client's approval of the sketch before proceeding to the final art. The approved pencil sketch is also used to transfer the structure of the drawing onto the surface of the board — so I have a roadmap in place when I start "scratching."

Scratchboard is not the speediest medium with which to work. Precision and discipline are essential. I'm often asked, "How long did it take you to do that?" For the record, most of the full-page illustrations in this book took two solid days of engraving; and that long again to add colour. An alternate meaning of the word discipline is punishment — but I actually enjoy the engraving process. Within the structure transferred from the pencil sketch, there's plenty of room for spontaneity, invention and variation of line quality. The direction and spacing of lines are completely improvised. There's also lots of opportunity to mess up if you're not concentrating — minor corrections are possible but if a drawing goes off the rails, there's nothing to do but start over again. Therefore I always start with the hardest part of the drawing (faces, for example).

My illustrations are almost always commissioned for print reproduction. Once the drawing itself is finished, the process shifts gears into preparing the finished art for a printer.

The key characteristic of scratchboard is sharp, crisp, clean line quality. "Line art" is the graphic term for sharp-edged, solid black art with no gradation of tone. In the pre-digital days of offset lithography, line art was printed by placing the original under a graphic arts camera and making a film negative at the size you wanted to reproduce the art. The camera was actually a light-proof room with the lens mounted in the wall. Outside the room, a large copy stand was positioned precisely in line with the lens; banks of bright lamps were set at 45-degree angles to eliminate glare. The operator stepped through a light-lock and worked, literally, inside the camera. The film negative was used to burn a printing plate, and the resulting line art reproduction looked precisely like the line art original. That was in the good old days.

In the space of 15 years, the printing industry has undergone a fundamental shift towards digital technology. The changes have been revolutionary. Files are now output electronically, directly onto the printing plate, eliminating film negatives from the process entirely. Very few printers even operate cameras any more — soon the film and chemicals required to run them won't even be manufactured.

Line art is now reproduced through a "bitmap" pattern of digital pixels, which renders curved edges as tiny "stairsteps." The sharp, crisp line quality is lost — a difficult and frustrating compromise for a scratchboard illustrator to have to make.

To counteract this bitmap effect, I scan scratchboard originals at 600 pixels-per-inch, at 400%. Then I reduce the scan to 25% (back to its original size), which boosts the resolution to 2400 pixels-per-inch. This makes the pixel stairsteps finer and closer together, and less obvious to the eye, but you can never eliminate them entirely.

Image quality suffers even more when we move from the

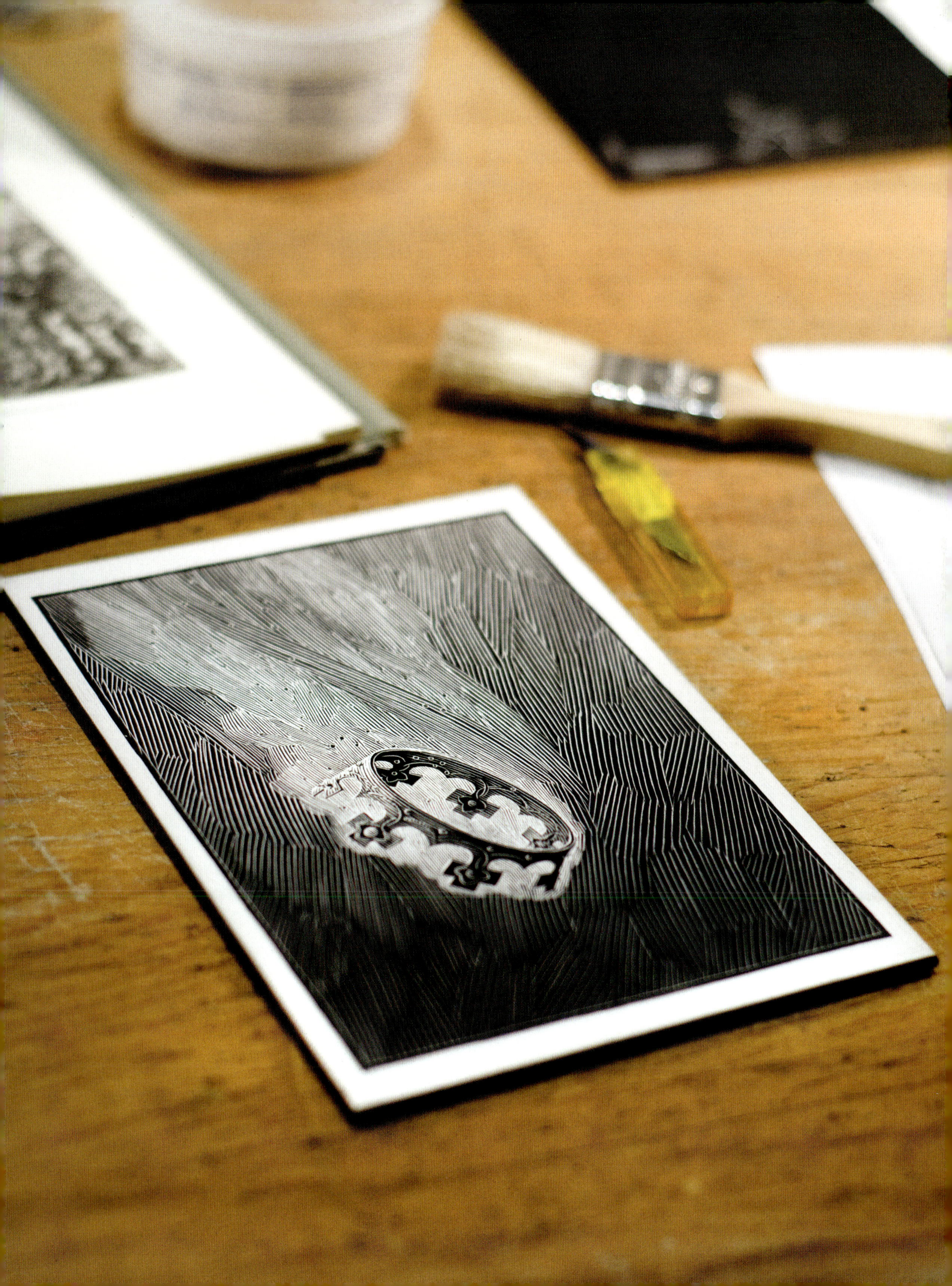

world of print into the online universe. When my illustrations appear on websites at standard 72 pixels-per-inch monitor resolution, the engraving lines can become blurred and distorted. There's not enough resolution to render the images accurately. On a tiny iPhone screen, scratchboard is often unrecognizable.

Challenges can come from old technology as well as new. For many years I used a product called Essdee scraperboard, manufactured by a small art supply company in Kidderminster, in the British Midlands, not far from Stratford-upon-Avon. I travelled to London every year on a picture research trip for the Shaw Festival's theatre programmes. To save shipping costs, I purchased my board in England and brought it home with me on the plane. In 2008, I found that I was down to my last carton of board, and I called to order fresh supplies as usual. My heart skipped a beat when the girl on the desk said, "I'm afraid we don't make that anymore."

I spoke with the company's director, hoping there might be some last stock — somewhere — that I could get my hands on. I nervously explained that my entire career depended on his product. There was a pause, and he responded, "Well, I guess you had better think about a new career."

They had been forced by new health and safety regulations to stop using an animal-based glue in manufacturing the board. They had come up with a synthetic equivalent that worked well to adhere the chalk to the baseboard, but over a number of years, the new glue actually began to erode the metal parts of the machinery. The day finally came that the surface quality of the board was compromised — and the relatively small quantity of the product they sold every year would not begin to cover the costs of refurbishing the aging equipment. *C'est la vie.*

Over the past decade I have adjusted to working with

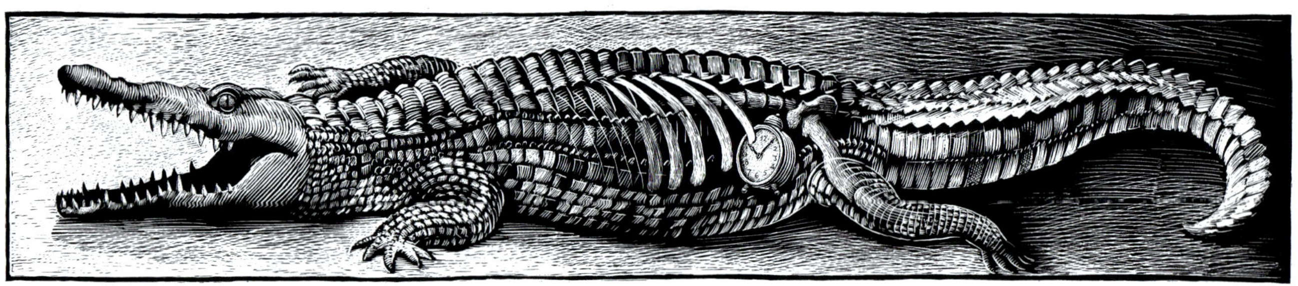

This page: the Crocodile from the Sterling Classics edition of *Peter Pan*, published in 2008. Scott based this illustration on his own sketch, made from life in the reptile house at the Jardin des Plantes in Paris. Opposite: 2018 Christmas card illustration for Langdon Hall in Cambridge, Ontario.

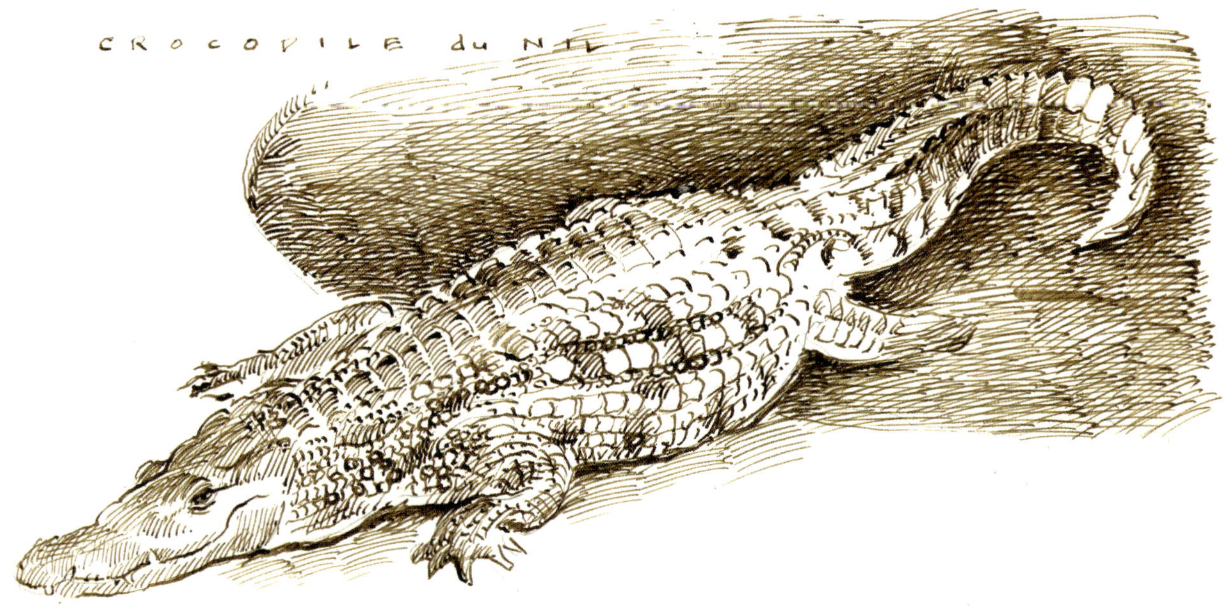

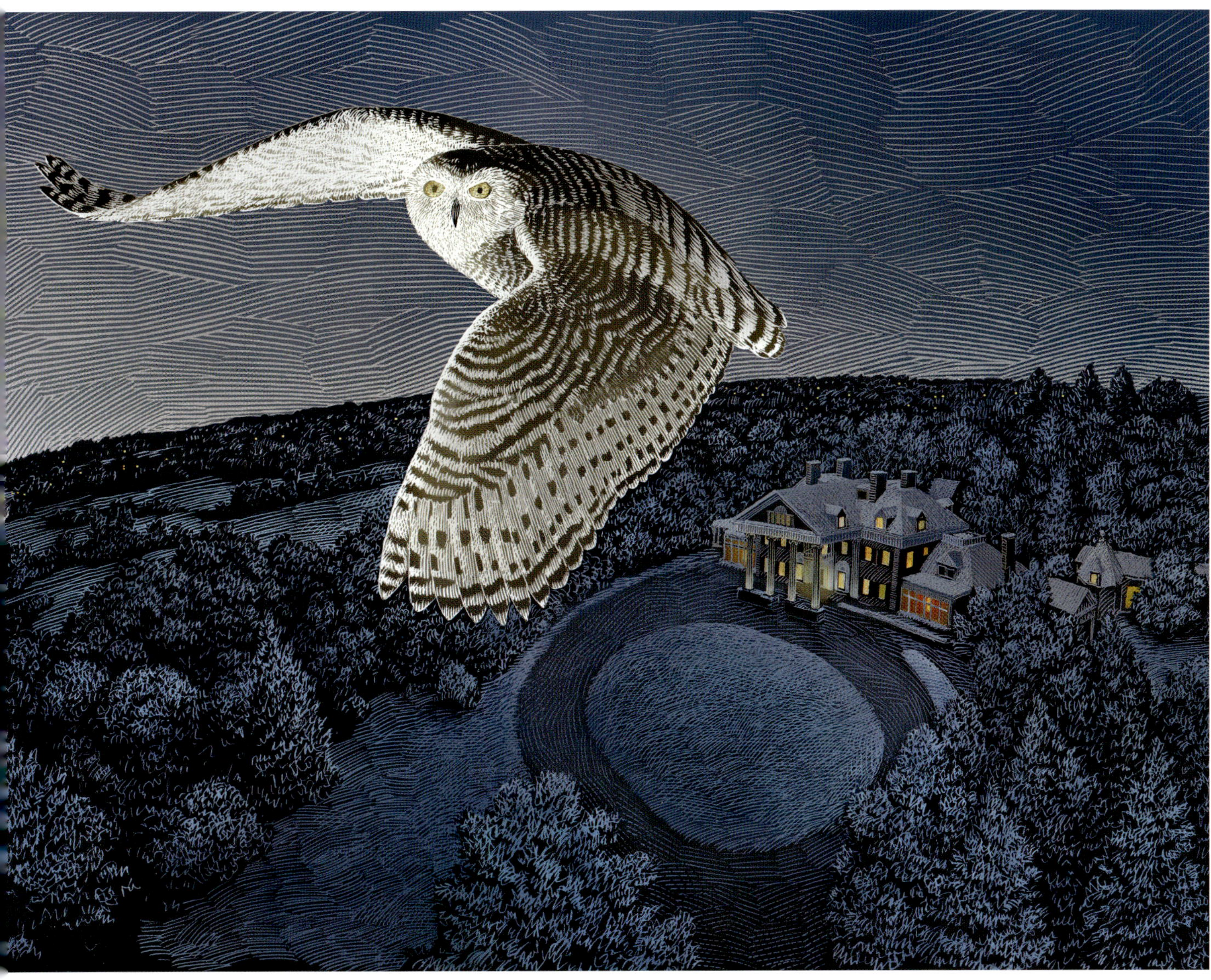

"Claybord," made by Ampersand in the U.S. — it's on Masonite, not cardboard, and I find that it holds an even sharper edge than the Essdee board. But it's always worrying when a product or service that's not a big seller is first in line for cutbacks.

ADDING COLOUR

The glory of scratchboard is the dramatic rendering of lights and darks. The key to adding colour to scratchboard, it seems to me, is to avoid competing with the linework. I find the best approach is to build up layers of flat colour on top of the black lines — as in a colouring book.

There are two types of colour printing in offset lithography — "flat colour" and "full colour." Flat colour means that if you want a particular shade of orange, you mix that exact shade of ink (using the Pantone ink matching system). In full colour (or process colour), tiny halftone dots in the three primary colours — cyan, magenta, yellow — plus black, reproduce the full range of colours in the image. Where yellow dots overlay magenta dots, the eye perceives orange. I have used both printing methods for my posters, but full colour CMYK reproduction is now almost ubiquitous.

Before digital printing, I frequently printed multiple colour posters using many layers of flat Pantone inks. I cut masks for each different area of colour using rubylith, a transparent red acetate material that photographs as black under the camera. A local printing company here in Stratford allowed me to work closely with the pressmen in their shop. Press approvals became part of the creative process. We experimented with a "split-fountain" technique to achieve gradations of colour

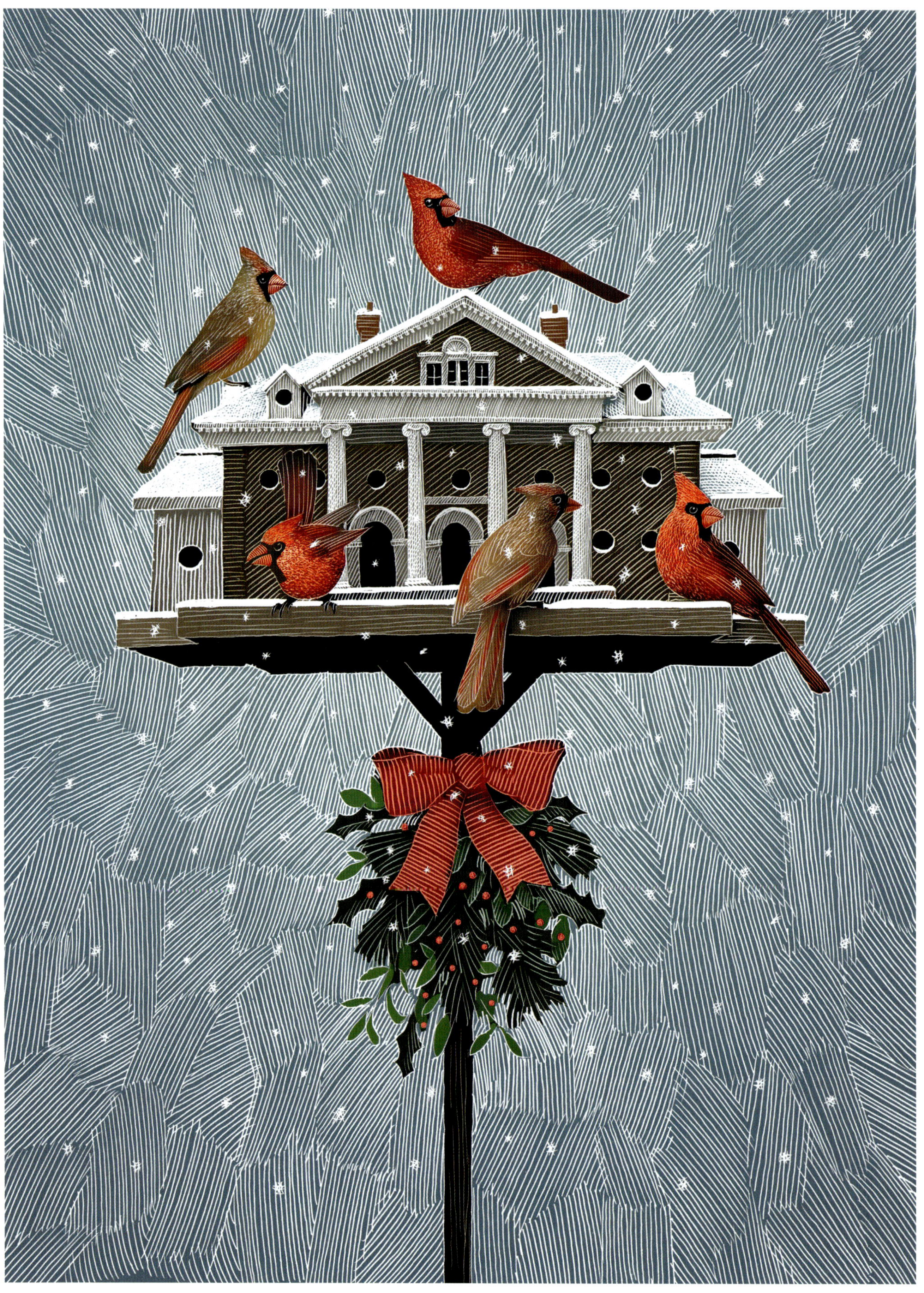

2017 Christmas card illustration for Langdon Hall in Cambridge, Ontario.

along a single ink roller. If a colour was slightly off, we would climb up on top of the press and alter it.

I know that other scratchboard artists add colour to the original board itself. I have never tried that — still so much to learn. In pre-digital days, I sometimes made photostats of the scratchboard originals and tinted them by hand using Marshall's photo oils. Photostats are probably extinct now but they reproduced only pure blacks and whites as line art — no grey tones. Marshall's are little tubes of intense but transparent pigment intended to tint black-and-white photographic prints. I liked the greyed-out quality of the Marshall's colours; the tinted photostat was then scanned as a colour original.

Now, colour is almost always added digitally. I still make masks for the different areas of colour, but now these are drawn in Photoshop, using channels. The mask isolates all the pixels in one area of the drawing — a background, for example. I can use the mask to lighten the black lines in that background area (lightening the pixels), or flood colour over the lines (darkening the pixels). Two colours can be overlapped, creating a third colour. Working electronically, I can see these colour effects on a monitor and experiment with them until I get an effect that I like. The history palette in Photoshop provides a wonderful safety net — if I don't like a colour effect, I can "undo" as many steps as I need to. I can just go back and try something else. I can save a copy of the file, try another effect, then compare different versions side by side. You can't do that with a brushstroke or a pen line on a piece of paper.

Another advantage of working digitally is the ease of making proofs and sending them electronically to clients for approval. When a project is finished, I can send huge files to the designer or directly to the printer using an FTP (File Transfer Protocol) server, or one of the many file transfer services such as WeTransfer.

DESIGN

Great illustration relies on strong composition — the arrangement of visual elements that provides structure for the page and controls where the viewer's eye should look. Brainstorming sessions with Christina often yield big ideas which then need to be tested on paper — often I have made a rough sketch of my impression of what we talked about, and her "that's not how I saw it at all" reaction reminds me of how subjective the development process can be. Variations on proportion, perspective, symmetry and balance (or their opposites), and point-of-view are all carefully worked out in pencil sketches before sitting down to start the final engraving art. I constantly work at improving my drawing skills which is, happily, a lifetime study.

A successful poster or book cover is a synthesis of typography and illustration working together on the page. I'm a graphic designer as well as an illustrator and, for me, the words and the pictures have equal importance. Whenever I start a new poster project, I find myself thinking about the style and character of the type design at the same time as the illustration.

This can be really annoying for art directors who might want to hire me only as an illustrator. For me, nothing ruins an illustration assignment like an insensitive, inappropriate type layout — which I might only see for the first time when the printed samples arrive. I now ask art directors to allow me to design the type, or to allow me to participate in the process — and this usually works out very happily. On the other hand, I hasten to add, it's truly exhilarating to collaborate with a designer who brings a fresh perspective to the project. I love it when an art director takes a design further than I ever would have or could have — which happens frequently.

Everyone has heard the term "Digital Native," used to describe someone who has grown up with digital technology and is completely comfortable with it — and "Digital Immigrant," to describe someone like me, who has had to learn the technology as a second language. I began my graphic design career in the pre-Macintosh era, and as much as I enjoy working with the powerful digital tools in Adobe Photoshop and InDesign, I would not want to be without the hand skills I acquired back in the dark ages. I have a pet theory that the digital revolution has actually made hand skills more valuable.

A great illustration always starts with a great concept. The process of distilling a script down to a poster image — or a novel down to a cover — is a mysterious. Christina refers to the problem-solving process as "connecting the dots." She looks first at the world of the play — the historical setting, social attitudes of the time and place, contemporary literature or art history references, as well as the specifics of plot and character. Once a set of reference points is established, she looks for a solution that touches on as many of them as possible. With luck, the result is a concept that resonates on several levels at once, making the image more memorable. The process never ceases to be interesting.

We thrive on creative collaboration with clients, directors and other designers who challenge us to do our best work. Art and design is our vocation and avocation. We cross paths daily with painters, poets, playwrights, chefs, actors and musicians. Their disciplines inform ours — which always keeps us looking forward to the next assignment.

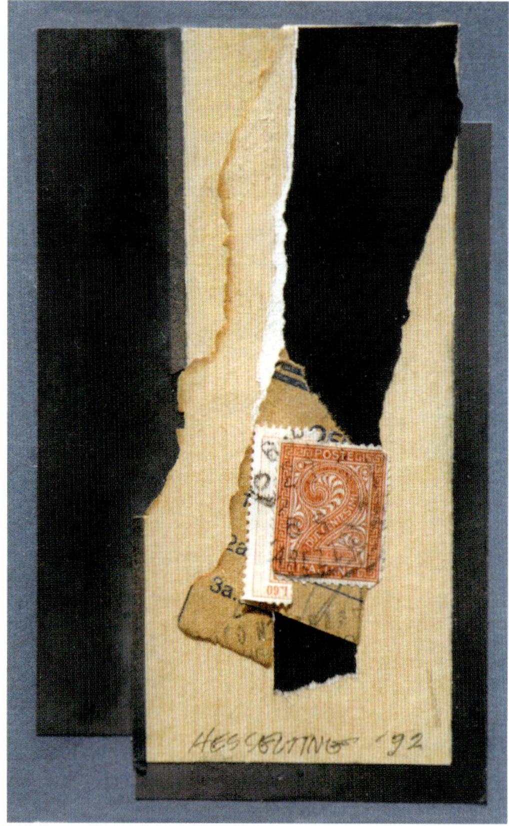

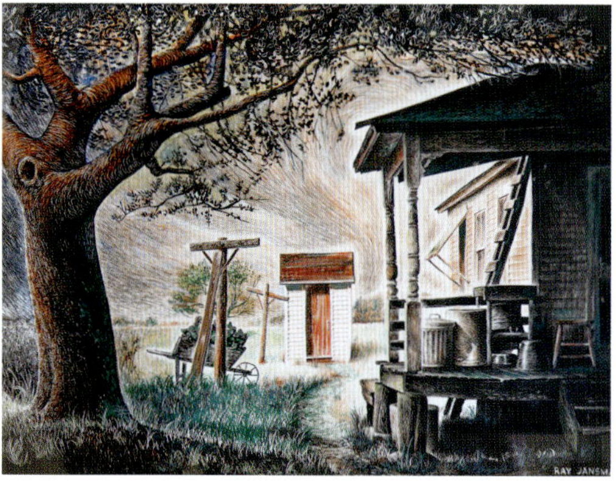

A 1992 collage by Doug Hesseltine, reproduced slightly smaller than actual size. Doug's abstract compositions are often made from ripped paper with a variety of contrasting textures. He collected paper ephemera — old stamps, calling cards and *biglietti* with interesting typography or calligraphy — in order to introduce visual focal points with a sense of history.

The Outhouse on the Johnson Farm, a scratchboard drawing of the family farm in Fremont, Michigan, 1950, by Ray Jansma (11.5" x 16"). Jansma evidently considered this an important work — it was hanging over the artist's bed during the last years of his life. Scott acquired it from his estate and is still trying to figure out how Jansma achieved the delicate layers of colour.

Our childhood experiences have profound influences on our adult lives. Marge, my mother, trained as a signpainter, so I knew that rounded letters properly extend slightly above and below the guidelines almost before I could put them together into words. My dad, Frank, was a high school music teacher — I grew up as he was directing productions of *Camelot*, *Carnival* and *Brigadoon*, which meant that I got to hang out backstage, climb around on the catwalks of J.W. Sexton High School's auditorium and work the mysterious levers and wheels of the enormous 1940s-vintage lighting board. Early artistic inspiration and encouragement came as well from Ray and Phyllis Jansma, who demonstrated by their wonderful example that making art and music in a home studio environment is a perfectly normal career choice. Phyllis and Marge were best friends since the third grade in Detroit.

My path towards a career in design and illustration really began in Doug Hesseltine's classroom at the University of Michigan School of Art. Immensely articulate about the creative process, Doug fostered in his students a superior standard for visual and verbal communication skills. He instilled a rigorous problem-solving methodology as the key to successful design solutions, and I came away feeling well-equipped to tackle any design assignment. Hesseltine's individualistic graphic designs are informed by his expertise as a painter and collage artist; not surprisingly, the visual language of his paintings and collages is distilled from his sensibilities as a graphic designer.

Marge, Frank, Ray, Phyllis and Doug have all passed away since I wrote about them 10 years ago in *A Fine Line*. Original Hesseltines and Jansmas hang on the walls of my home so, in a sense, Doug and Ray continue to inspire me every day.

I moved from Ann Arbor to Stratford, Ontario, in 1980 into a welcoming and supportive community of artists. Ken Nutt continues to share his expansive knowledge of art and illustration. Ken runs an open studio life drawing class every Wednesday evening at Gallery Stratford (for almost four decades now!) which continues to sharpen my drawing skills.

Huge appreciation to graphic designer Allysha Witt, my collaborator and accomplice in the studio for four years ("assistant" is an inadequate job description), for her support on many of the projects in this book. While I was in my drawing studio sweating over the illustrations, Allysha was managing the design studio, handling deadlines for countless season brochures, posters and ads with aplomb. Thanks also to Grace Stallard, our newest Punch & Judy designer.

Special gratitude goes to Peter Hinton for his wonderful introduction to this book, to the excellent copy editor Ashley Rayner for honing my texts, and to Lionel Koffler and Michael Worek at Firefly Books for undertaking this project (again).

As I've noted throughout this book, the creative collaboration with my wife, theatre designer Christina Poddubiuk, amounts to more of a shared authorship. My best posters are informed by her conceptual insights, and this book would not exist without her patience, generosity and love.

INDEX

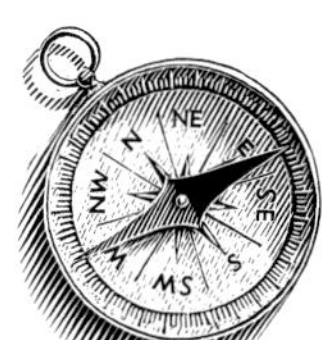

Chapter head from the Sterling Classics edition of *The Voyages of Doctor Dolittle*.

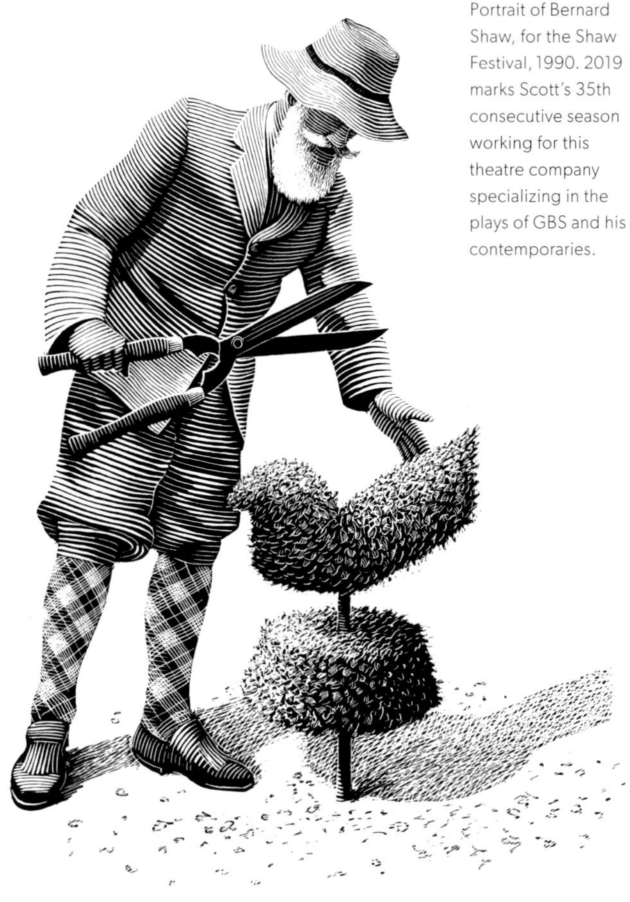

Portrait of Bernard Shaw, for the Shaw Festival, 1990. 2019 marks Scott's 35th consecutive season working for this theatre company specializing in the plays of GBS and his contemporaries.

Chapter head from the Sterling edition of *Great Expectations*. The sealing wax initials are for Philip Pirrip, the main character — better known as Pip.